1943
China at the Crossroads

This page is intentionally left blank.

1943
China at the Crossroads

Joseph W. Esherick
Matthew T. Combs

EDITORS

East Asia Program
Cornell University
Ithaca, New York 14853

The Cornell East Asia Series is published by the Cornell University East Asia Program (distinct from Cornell University Press). We publish books on a variety of scholarly topics relating to East Asia as a service to the academic community and the general public. Address submission inquiries to CEAS Editorial Board, East Asia Program, Cornell University, 140 Uris Hall, Ithaca, New York 14853-7601.

Cover photos
(front)
  Generalissimo Chiang Kai-shek, U.S. President Franklin D. Roosevelt, and British Prime Minister Winston Churchill, Cairo Conference, Egypt, November 25, 1943.
  Henan Province, people in famine-struck region, 1943.
(back)
  Mao Zedong and Kang Sheng in Yan'an. Date unknown.
  Mme. Chiang Kai-shek addresses the House of Representatives, February 18, 1943.

Number 180 in the Cornell East Asia Series
Copyright © 2015 Cornell East Asia Program. All rights reserved.
ISSN: 1050-2955
ISBN: 978-1-939161-60-4 hardcover
ISBN: 978-1-939161-80-2 paperback
ISBN: 978-1-942242-80-2 e-book
Library of Congress Control Number: 2015945076

Contents

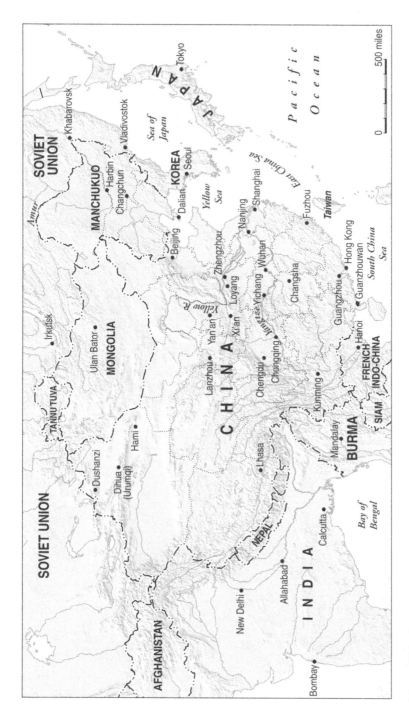

Map 1: China in 1943.

Map 2: Eastern China in 1943.

Preface

Joseph W. Esherick and Matthew T. Combs

In the master narrative of modern Chinese history, the year 1943 is usually passed over with little notice. Great attention is paid to critical
watersheds in Chinese history—to the end of the empire in 1911, the
triumph of the Nationalist Party in 1927, the outbreak of full-scale war
with Japan in 1937, the victory of the Chinese Communist revolution in
1949, and the death of Mao Zedong and the initiation of the period of
"reform and opening" in 1976–1978. When this book was first conceived,
the reaction of most colleagues was, "Why 1943?" Few could think of
anything significant that happened in 1943. What can we learn if we focus
our attention on such a forgotten year? Can the investigation and analysis
of a variety of separate incidents, trends, and controversies in a single year
help us understand deeper underlying changes in Chinese politics and
society? Is it not likely that the dramatic moments of regime change listed
above had their origins in subtler developments in politics and society
during the intervening years? These are the questions addressed in this
volume on China in 1943.

The book is founded on the premise that China underwent fundamental changes during the War of Resistance against Japan. Most importantly, the war undermined support for Chiang Kai-shek's Nationalist
Party and allowed a dramatic increase in the size, strength, and following
of the Chinese Communists. At the beginning of the war in 1937, Chiang
Kai-shek was the indispensable leader of China. The nation rallied behind
his determined resistance to Japanese aggression. Internationally, he was
featured as Man of the Year on the cover of *Time* magazine, and the Soviet

Union rushed massive assistance to his cause in the form of guns, ammunition, artillery, tanks, and warplanes. The Chinese Communists, by contrast, were a ragtag band of hearty survivors of the militarily disastrous Long March, holed up in the caves of Yan'an in the barren and impoverished hills of northern Shaanxi. By the end of the war, the Communists led an army of a million men and held a number of relatively stable bases behind Japanese lines, while Chiang Kai-shek's National Government (Guomin zhengfu) was increasingly viewed as an inept, corrupt, self-serving authoritarian regime whose claim to represent the nation was challenged not only by Communist revolutionaries but also by pro-Japanese collaborators, liberal intellectuals, and a growing number of foreign journalists and diplomats.

During the course of the war with Japan, something fundamental happened to shift the tides of history away from Chiang Kai-shek and his Nationalist Party and in the direction of the Chinese Communist Party under Mao Zedong. Sometime during the war, China reached a "tipping point." Most accounts have focused on 1944, when Chiang's forces crumbled before Japan's Ichigo offensive, the Stilwell crisis provoked American disillusionment with Chiang's regime, liberal intellectuals came together in a revived Democratic League, and the Communists prepared for the Seventh Party Congress that would solidify Mao Zedong's commanding position. For many years, the conventional narrative of wartime China was shaped by such American journalists as Theodore White, Graham Peck, and Edgar Snow. *Thunder out of China*, which White coauthored with Annalee Jacoby, was particularly influential. It presented the war as "the story of the tragedy of Chiang K'ai-shek," the personally incorruptible but authoritarian leader of a Guomindang dictatorship that was "feudal-minded," faction-ridden, and increasingly corrupt.[1] U.S. Foreign Service officers like John S. Service and John P. Davies authored a wealth of similarly critical reporting on the Nationalist regime.[2] These sources were im-

---

[1] Theodore H. White and Annalee Jacoby, *Thunder out of China* (New York: William Sloane, 1946), quotes on xv, 310; Graham Peck, *Two Kinds of Time* (1950; reprint, Seattle: University of Washington Press, 2008); Edgar Snow, *The Battle for Asia* (New York: World, 1942).

[2] Service's dispatches have been collected in Joseph W. Esherick, ed., *Lost Chance in*

portant in shaping academic writing on the wartime period, from John K. Fairbank (himself an Office of War Information officer in wartime China) to the influential writings of Lloyd Eastman.[3] The apotheosis of this view was Barbara Tuchman's Pulitzer prize–winning *Stilwell and the American Experience in China.*[4] Written at the height of the Vietnam War, it constructed a powerful narrative around a courageous, straight-talking American general's doomed attempt to rescue a corrupt and conservative Asian regime confronted by foreign enemies and a popular Communist insurgency.

More recently these views of a stubborn and authoritarian Chiang Kai-shek leading a corrupt and ineffective Nationalist Party have been challenged on a number of fronts. Jay Taylor's biography of Chiang Kai-shek makes extensive use of Chiang's diaries and presents a decidedly sympathetic portrait of the Generalissimo as a "modernizing neo-Confucian" and a "national leader with a strategic vision." Significantly, Taylor is highly critical of Stilwell, properly condemning his "insolent manner," but also treating the campaign to reopen the Burma Road as largely a product of Stilwell's obsession with avenging his 1942 defeat there.[5] In Chinese, Qi Xisheng has explored the Sino-American wartime alliance in exhaustive detail, presenting a picture far more sympathetic to Chiang Kai-shek and highly critical of Stilwell's role and George Marshall's overall strategy.[6] Most importantly, a UK-based body of scholarship

---

China: The World War II Dispatches of John S. Service (New York: Random House, 1974); on Davies, see John Paton Davies, Jr., *China Hand: An Autobiography* (Philadelphia: University of Pennsylvania Press, 2012). Many of their and other officers' reports were published in the volumes of *Foreign Relations of the United States.*

[3] John K. Fairbank, *The United States and China*, 3rd ed. (Cambridge, MA: Harvard University Press, 1971), 240–58; Lloyd Eastman, *Seeds of Destruction: Nationalist China in War and Revolution, 1937–1949* (Stanford, CA: Stanford University Press, 1984); and Eastman's essays in Lloyd E. Eastman, Jerome Ch'en, Suzanne Pepper, and Lyman P. Van Slyke, eds., *The Nationalist Era in China, 1912–1949* (Cambridge: Cambridge University Press, 1991).

[4] Barbara W. Tuchman, *Stilwell and the American Experience in China, 1911–1945* (New York: Macmillan, 1970).

[5] Jay Taylor, *The Generalissimo: Chiang Kai-shek and the Struggle for Modern China* (Cambridge, MA: Harvard University Press, 2009), 141–335, quotes on 2, 11, 227–28.

[6] Qi Xisheng (Hsi-sheng Ch'i), *Jianba nuzhang de mengyou: Taipingyang zhanzheng qijian de Zhong-Mei junshi hezuo guanxi (1941–1945)* [Allies with swords drawn and bows

has emerged to challenge the "Stilwell-White paradigm ... of military incompetence, corruption, a debilitating obsession with the Communists, authoritarianism, and a blind refusal to fight Japan" and bring the focus decisively back to 1944.[7] Cambridge University's Hans van de Ven has concentrated on the military history of Nationalist China. His *War and Nationalism in China, 1925–1945* opens with a chapter, "Stilwell Revisited," that presents a powerful argument that the American "ideology of the offensive" combined with journalists' and military leaders' "Orientalist discourse about Chinese civilization" to produce an overly negative assessment of Chiang's prosecution of the war. He dismisses authoritarianism and corruption as useful concepts to analyze Nationalist politics.[8] In his account, Chiang Kai-shek was doing reasonably well in the resistance to Japan until 1944, when Stilwell diverted all resources to the Burma campaign, opening the central China front to Japan's Ichigo offensive.[9] Oxford's Rana Mitter similarly criticizes "Stilwell's failed strategy"; notes that in the Allies' global war strategy, China "was a secondary, or indeed tertiary priority"; and suggests that more attention be given to "the extent to which Western and particularly American action and inaction were responsible for the decayed and flawed state of Chiang's regime."[10]

Taylor, Qi, van de Ven, and Mitter have certainly destroyed the myth of Stilwell's heroic struggle on China's behalf. But was the fatal weakening of Chiang Kai-shek's regime all due to Stilwell and the Burma campaign? It seems to us that Stilwell's faults cannot demonstrate Chiang's strength. The thesis of American responsibility for Nationalist China's failure removes all agency from Chiang's regime and diverts attention from both conscious choices and systemic weaknesses. We would also dispute the dismissal of critical views of the Nationalist Party as the product of American journalists', diplomats', and military officers' "Orientalist" bias. That

---

taut: Sino-American military cooperation during the Pacific War], 2 vols. (Beijing: Shehui kexue wenxian chubanshe, 2012).

[7] Hans van de Ven, *War and Nationalism in China, 1925–1945* (London: RoutledgeCurzon, 2003), 7.

[8] Ibid., 12.

[9] Ibid., 1–63, quotes on 8, 10.

[10] Rana Mitter, *Forgotten Ally: China's World War II, 1937–1945* (Boston: Houghton Mifflin Harcourt, 2013), 260, 330.

bias was certainly there—and it is particularly evident in Stilwell's diary. But the same criticisms of corruption, low morale, evasion of responsibility, bureaucratic infighting, and ineffective governance can be found in contemporary Chinese sources, and indeed in the speeches and writings of Chiang Kai-shek himself.

Most importantly, the premise of this book is that the crises of 1944 had deeper roots, and to understand them we ought to look closely at the previous year. This does not mean that the collapse of the Nationalists and the victory of the Communists became inevitable in 1943. Had events developed differently, it is entirely possible that history might have tipped again in a different direction. The chapters of this book argue for a new sense of contingency, not a relocation of the inevitable. By exploring in detail the events that shaped the national narrative, one discovers a host of individuals making a variety of choices that, if made differently, could well have altered the course of history. These chapters also show that once we focus on a particular year, we realize that much more happened than we usually remember. In 1943, the "unequal treaties" were revoked; Chiang Kai-shek wrote *China's Destiny* and met with Roosevelt and Churchill in the Cairo Conference; Mme. Chiang made her historic speeches to the U.S. Congress; Xinjiang was recovered from a decade of Soviet domination; Henan suffered a devastating famine; and the Communists endured the final phase of their Rectification Campaign in the leftist excesses of the "Rescue Campaign." By exploring these and other incidents, this volume seeks to re-create the historicity of a particular moment in time, viewing a single year from a variety of different perspectives. This seems to us the best way to get beyond the excessive focus on Chinese-American relations that has characterized both the Stilwell-White paradigm and the van de Ven–Mitter challenge to it, and to understand the vast range of social, political, economic, military, and diplomatic developments that determined China's fate.

The book begins with an overview of the era by Joseph W. Esherick, which sketches the domestic and international context for the events of 1943 and relies heavily on Chiang Kai-shek's diaries and activities to analyze the Generalissimo's strategy for the war against Japan and his competition with the Communists. It focuses in particular on the nature of

Chiang's regime and the critical decisions he made in 1943 to reverse earlier intentions to remove Stilwell and launch a military campaign against the Communists. From there we turn to several chapters devoted to clear achievements of the Nationalist regime, to capture some of the optimism that prevailed in the early months of 1943. Grace Huang analyzes Mme. Chiang Kai-shek's tour of the United States, noting the glowing press reception and her special appeal to American audiences (chapter 2). Mme. Chiang was a compelling figure as a beautiful, strong, and articulate woman, and a cosmopolitan representative of the Chinese people; yet her aristocratic lifestyle caused problems in less public dealings with Americans. Judd Kinzley and Jianfei Jia describe China's recovery of sovereignty over the western province of Xinjiang (chapter 3). In a move that Chiang Kai-shek called the "greatest achievement" of the republican era, the National Government gained control of this resource-rich region that in the previous decade had become a virtual colony of the Soviet Union and began energetic planning for its development.

On National Day, October 10, 1942, the United States and Great Britain announced their intention to abrogate the "unequal treaties" they had imposed on China since the Opium War. New treaties were signed in January 1943, the same month that Japan renounced its privileges (while continuing its occupation) in a treaty with the collaborationist regime in Nanjing. The abrogation of the "unequal treaties" was greeted with great celebrations in China, and the next two chapters relate to the new treaties. First, Thomas Worger explores the central feature of the new treaties: the renunciation of extraterritoriality, the legal provision whereby foreign citizens were immune from Chinese prosecution and tried for any offense in consular courts (chapter 4). The foreign powers had previously insisted that immunity from Chinese justice was necessary until China established a legal system that was not subject to political interference and corruption. In the end, however, the renunciation of extraterritoriality came not from any renewed confidence in China's courts, but from the Allies' political decision to boost Chinese morale during the war. Ironically, the move co-incided with a Nationalist Party initiative to increase party influence over the judiciary—a policy that continues to this day under the Communist Party. Dawn Maleenont explores one of the greatest Chinese disappointments with the new treaties, the British refusal to return Hong Kong or even to renounce control over the New Territories (chapter 5). Hong Kong had been ceded to Britain in the first "unequal treaty" following the Opium War, and its recovery had been a staple of Chinese nationalist ambitions throughout the twentieth century. When the new treaties returned Shanghai and other treaty port concessions to China, most Chinese expected that Hong Kong, or at a minimum the leased portion in the New Territories, would also be returned. Maleenont analyzes the multiple domestic factors and strategic considerations that fatally weakened the Chinese bargaining position in negotiations with Britain for the new treaty.

Daniel Knorr analyzes *China's Destiny*, the book that Chiang Kai-shek wrote to catalogue the ills that the "unequal treaties" had wrought and celebrate the future that he imagined for a fully sovereign China under the Nationalist Party (chapter 6). Chiang spent a great deal of time working on the text and was pleased with his accomplishment, but in the end the book aroused withering critiques from the Communists, the collaborationist regime in Nanjing, liberal intellectuals, and wartime allies. The competition among these groups formed the deep structure of Chinese politics in this era, but the areas of agreement in the Communist, liberal, and collaborationist critiques of *China's Destiny* were particularly notable. Yidi Wu examines the Chinese Communist Party in 1943, in particular the Rescue Campaign directed by the security chief Kang Sheng with the alleged purpose of rescuing people who had been misled by the enemy to serve as secret agents spying on the Communist regime (chapter 7). Through a careful examination of the Nationalist Party's efforts to infiltrate agents into the Communists' northern Shaanxi base and Chiang Kai-shek's threats to launch a military assault, she concludes that the Communists were justifiably sensitive to Nationalist threats, but they knowingly exaggerated the civil war crisis, and their search for potential spies developed into a witch hunt fueled by hundreds of forced confessions.

When, in the fall of 1943, Chiang Kai-shek abandoned his plans to resolve the Communist problem by force, he opted for a political solution, one key component of which was to be the transition to constitutional rule. Xiao Chen examines the constitutional struggles of 1943–1944 and the way in which a government initiative helped animate a movement of liberal intellectuals with different priorities, especially demands for political freedom and economic democracy (chapter 8). In the end, liberal disillusionment with the Nationalist regime led them to support the Communists' call for coalition government.

In the next two chapters, our concern shifts from elite politics to daily life in wartime China. Matthew Combs's chapter on inflation in Chongqing demonstrates that rampant inflation affected everything from food to housing to health care; and counterproductive price controls raised doubts about the competence of the government (chapter 9). The impact was lightest on workers whose wages were pegged to inflation and peasants who grew their own food, but devastating to the middle class. One group of peasants who most assuredly did suffer in 1943 lived in the drought-stricken province of Henan. Their tragic plight is graphically described by Kathryn Edgerton-Tarpley (chapter 10). Critical Chinese reporting on this famine led to the temporary shut-down of the respected *Dagongbao* newspaper, and foreign reporting was a considerable embarrassment to the Nationalist regime, whose prioritizing of rations for the army exacerbated famine conditions. Significantly, Edgerton-Tarpley finds, Communist base areas located behind Japanese lines in northern Henan seem to have implemented somewhat more effective relief measures, while the late and ineffective Nationalist response undermined the legitimacy of the regime. When Japan's Ichigo offensive began the next year, some peasants even turned on the Nationalist soldiers.

Amy O'Keefe's essay on the independent Chinese Christian pastor Wang Mingdao brings us to the Japanese-occupied areas of China (chapter 11). Most accounts of wartime China privilege the Nationalist and Communist resistance to the Japanese invasion. But by the end of the war, close to half of the Chinese population lived under Japanese occupation, and it is far too simple to dismiss this massive population as all puppets or collaborators. At the same time, the late war years left little doubt in the minds of any who read the newspapers that Japan would lose the war. They could see, even in the heavily censored press of occupied China, that both Japan and Germany were steadily losing ground to the Allies. With Japan's defeat only a matter of time, their concerns were not political. We see this in Wang Mingdao's determined efforts to stay independent of the Japanese Christian union, as he had of all other affiliations that conflicted with his fundamentalist beliefs. O'Keefe's account of this apolitical pastor and others who turned to religion in a time of war is an important reminder that politics and patriotism were not paramount concerns for all Chinese. Chuning Xie explores what happened when a former French colony on China's southern coast was transformed from a refuge from war and a smuggling gateway to Free China into a Japanese-occupied city (chapter 12). Here we get a real sense of what the war meant to ordinary Chinese far from the country's political centers. There is more smuggling than patriotic resistance; local elites and common gangsters engage in their own survival strategies; and Nationalist Party officials seem to live in a world of mutual suspicion, clique competition, and rampant corruption. Here, perhaps, we see the true underbelly of China at war.

Finally, Hsiao-ting Lin's discussion of Chiang Kai-shek and the Cairo Conference brings us back to elite politics in the final months of the year (chapter 13). Cairo in many ways encapsulated the disparate faces of China in 1943. On the one hand it represented China's initiation into the elite club of Great Power politics. It was Chiang's moment to sit as an equal with President Roosevelt and Prime Minister Churchill—an arrangement that would have been unthinkable just a few years earlier. The Allies decided that at the end of the war, China would regain sovereignty over its lost territories in Manchuria and Taiwan. Yet at this critical moment, Chiang and his aides made a poor impression: ill informed, indecisive, unwilling to commit to a common strategy of military action against Japan. By the end of the conference, the British were looking forward to working with Stalin, and Roosevelt was thinking about alternatives to the Generalissimo's leadership.

This project began when Esherick decided to focus his final research seminar at the University of California, San Diego, on China in 1943. Students from UCSD and UC Irvine participated, and we traveled together to use the library collections at UCLA, Berkeley, and Stanford, and the invaluable archives of the Hoover Institution with Chiang Kai-shek's diaries, the Stilwell and T.V. Soong papers, and a host of other wartime sources. The staff at all these collections were unusually helpful, and we offer our sincere thanks for their professional assistance. Travel and other costs of the seminar were generously supported by the Hwei-chih and Julia Hsiu Endowment at UCSD. Because the seminar papers left considerable gaps in our coverage of important events in 1943, additional chapters were solicited from specialists in the field to complete the volume. Most of the authors were able to gather again in the spring of 2013 for a workshop at UC Irvine, generously supported by Jeff Wasserstrom and the UC Irvine History Department and Center for Asian Studies. There the final themes and organization of this volume were worked out.

At the presentations for the seminar at UCSD and the workshop at UC Irvine, faculty of those institutions were unusually generous in offering comments and criticisms. The authors of this volume have benefited greatly from suggestions by Thomas Bernstein, Frank Biess, Suzanne Cahill, Tim Cheek, Paul Pickowicz, Ting Zhang, and especially Sarah Schneewind and Jeff Wasserstrom. Two readers for the Cornell University East Asia Series provided valuable suggestions and criticisms that have allowed all of us to strengthen our arguments. Karen M. Fisher did a thoroughly professional job of copy-editing the manuscript; Mai Shaikhanuar-Cota deftly shepherded the project through the entire editorial process; Philip Schwartzberg of Meridian Mapping drew most of the maps; Kyle David prepared the index; Paul Pickowicz and Karl Gerth at UCSD and Jeff Wasserstrom at UC Irvine provided subvention funding to support publication. To all of these we offer our heartfelt thanks.

I

Prologue

China and the World in 1943

Joseph W. Esherick

October 10, 1943: National Day in the wartime capital of "Free China." The weather was cloudy but comfortably cool; the stifling heat of Chongqing's summer had passed.[1] In the seventh year of the War of Resistance against Japan, the enemy air raids that had devastated the city were largely a thing of the past.[2] A great public celebration was now possible, and so, on this October morning, before a solemn crowd of over one thousand, Chiang Kai-shek was inaugurated as president of the Republic of China. Although he had ruled China since 1927, the presidency had been a ceremonial post held by the Nationalist Party elder statesman Lin Sen, who had passed away on August 1. Now Chiang could claim the title of chief of state, further cementing his hold on power as he prepared to meet with Franklin Roosevelt and Winston Churchill in a fall summit. The meticulously planned inauguration went off flawlessly, and Mme. Chiang (Soong Mayling/Song Meiling) assured her nervous husband that

---

[1] Huang Yanpei, *Huang Yanpei riji* [Huang Yanpei diary] (Beijing: Huawen chubanshe, 2008), vol. 8, 164.

[2] With the exception of one August 1943 attack on an arsenal, there had been no bombing since 1941. Acheson to Secretary of State, August 23, 1943, in *Foreign Relations of the United States: Diplomatic Papers, 1943, China* (Washington, DC: Government Printing Office, 1957), 102 (hereafter cited as *FRUS 1943*).

it was appropriately solemn and dignified. Chiang had now reached the pinnacle of his power, and yet he felt that the audience at the inauguration seemed embarrassed, even humiliated—perhaps because of the absence of the diplomatic corps and the cool international response to his big day.[3] Within a few days, the foreign ministers of Great Britain, the United States, and the Soviet Union would meet in Moscow. At the insistence of the United States and over the resistance of Britain and the USSR, the conference would formally include China as one of the postwar Great Powers—a decision that laid the foundation for China's eventual inclusion in the United Nations Security Council.[4] But on his inauguration day, Chiang felt slighted, and soon he was grumbling over the dispirited, foul, corrupt, and selfish members of his administration.[5]

In many ways, this inauguration day captured the spirit of China in 1943. On the one hand, it was a year of great triumphs. The "unequal treaties" that had shackled China since the Opium War a century earlier had been abolished, and the former "sick man of Asia" was now recognized as one of the Four Great Powers. Mme. Chiang Kai-shek made an impressive tour of the United States, including her historic addresses to both houses of Congress. Chiang himself joined Churchill and Roosevelt for a summit meeting in Cairo that produced the memorable photos of the Chinese leader sitting as an equal with the most powerful men in the world. The year also saw China regain full sovereignty over the resource-rich northwestern province of Xinjiang, which in the previous decade had been transformed into a virtual colony of the Soviet Union. Chiang Kai-

---

[3] Chiang Kai-shek, weekly reflection (October 1943), in Gao Sulan, ed., *Jiang Zhongzheng zongtong dang'an: Shilüe gaoben* [Archives of President Chiang Kai-shek: Draft chronology] (Taipei: Guoshiguan, 2011), vol. 55, 81 (hereafter cited as *SLGB*). This source, compiled in the 1950s, contains major sections of Chiang's diaries, as well as other official papers and a record of his activities for each day. I have used this source rather than the less accessible diary copies now held in the Hoover Institution Archives, unless the language of the original diary is significantly different. No foreign diplomats or newsmen were invited to the inauguration (Gauss to Secretary of State, October 19, 1943, in *FRUS 1943*, 361–62). Was the audience perhaps unaware of this, regarding their absence as a snub?

[4] Keith Sainsbury, *The Turning Point: Roosevelt, Stalin, Churchill, and Chiang Kai-shek, 1943. The Moscow, Cairo and Teheran Conferences* (Oxford: Oxford University Press, 1985), 61–62, 91, 105.

[5] *SLGB* 55:81 (weekly reflection, October 1943).

shek had celebrated these accomplishments in his book *China's Destiny*, where he proudly proclaimed his vision of China's past and future.

On the other hand, 1943 witnessed critical setbacks and disappointments for Chiang's Nationalist regime. There was the devastating famine in Henan Province, and the embarrassing fact that foreign journalists had spread the news to the world. In the capital and throughout China, inflation raged unchecked despite well-publicized government efforts to control prices. Local rebellions mobilized tens of thousands of disaffected peasants to resist military conscription and state grain requisitions in Gansu and Guizhou provinces. Most importantly, the Chinese Communist Party (CCP) was spreading its political and military infrastructure throughout north China, displacing local elites loosely linked to the Nationalist regime in the areas behind Japanese lines. Chiang Kai-shek contemplated using the opportunity presented by the Soviet Union's disbandment of the Communist International (Comintern) to launch a military assault on the Communist base and rid China of the Red menace once and for all. He abandoned the planned assault at the last minute, and Communist power continued to grow.

These and other developments are examined in the following chapters as we look at a single year in China's modern history from a variety of perspectives in an effort to uncover the determinants of the nation's trajectory. By focusing on a single year, we hope to capture some of the diversity and contingency of history, without losing sight of the larger forces working inexorably in the background.

THE WAR

In 1943, China was a nation at war. Japan's invasion of China began in 1931, when its army units in Manchuria sabotaged a Japanese-owned railroad and used the incident as an excuse to occupy northeast China, then set up the puppet state of Manchukuo headed by the last emperor of the deposed Qing dynasty. The loss of Manchuria deprived China of its key heavy industrial base, with major coal mines, steel mills, and its largest arsenal, whose output had surpassed that of all other Chinese arsenals combined.[6] From Manchuria, the Japanese slowly encroached on adjacent regions in Inner Mongolia and north China until a clash with Chinese forces near Beijing (then called Beiping) provoked sharp resistance and full-scale war in July 1937. Chiang Kai-shek's armies put up a determined fight for the nation's commercial and industrial center in Shanghai, but the Japanese responded with a devastating counterattack, which included an innovation in modern warfare: the sustained use of aerial bombing against civilian targets.[7] By the end of the year, the Japanese had broken through the Chinese lines and then wreaked their revenge on the nation's capital in the Nanjing Massacre.[8]

The Japanese strategy in China anticipated Hitler's blitzkrieg tactics in Europe. Overwhelming firepower from the air and land- and sea-based artillery were concentrated in an effort to break through Chinese defenses, allowing infantry to advance rapidly along rail and river transport lines to achieve a quick victory. After their initial valiant but costly attempt to blunt the Japanese assault in Shanghai, Chiang's armies resorted to the more conservative approach of "trading space for time," using China's over-whelming advantage in geographic size and human population to counter Japan's superior firepower in a protracted war.[9] The brutality of the Japanese assault, from the Rape of Nanjing to ritual executions of prisoners and the use of poison gas during their advance up the Yangzi (Yangtze) River,

---

[6] Joshua H. Howard, *Workers at War: Labor in China's Arsenals, 1937–1953* (Stanford, CA: Stanford University Press, 2004), 19.

[7] Peter Harmsen, *Shanghai 1937: Stalingrad on the Yangtze* (Philadelphia: Casemate, 2013); John W. Dower, *War without Mercy: Race and Power in the Pacific War* (New York: Pantheon, 1986), 38–41.

[8] Mark Peattie, Edward Drea, and Hans van de Ven, eds., *The Battle for China: Essays on the Military History of the Sino-Japanese War of 1937–1945* (Stanford, CA: Stanford University Press, 2011), provides the best military history of the war (pp. 139–80 on the early stages). Other useful studies are Rana Mitter, *Forgotten Ally: China's World War II, 1937–1945* (Boston: Houghton Mifflin, 2013); Hsi-sheng Ch'i, *Nationalist China at War, 1937–45* (Ann Arbor: University of Michigan Press, 1982); James Hsiung and Steven I. Levine, eds., *China's Bitter Victory: The War with Japan, 1937–1945* (Armonk, NY: M.E. Sharpe, 1992). On the Nanjing Massacre, Iris Chang's *The Rape of Nanking* (New York: Basic Books, 1997), ignited much useful debate. More dispassionate studies of the tragedy are found in Bob Tadashi Wakabayashi, *The Nanking Atrocity, 1937–38: Complicating the Picture* (New York: Berghahn, 2007); and Joshua Fogel, ed., *The Nanjing Massacre in History and Historiography* (Berkeley: University of California Press, 2000).

[9] Peattie, Drea, and van de Ven, *Battle for China*, 54, 86–87, 112–15, 183–84.

inspired a new sense of national purpose as Chinese rallied to resist the invaders. The government and patriotic businessmen cooperated in a massive effort to move industry and skilled manpower to the interior. Millions of workers, businessmen, technicians, civil servants, intellectuals, students, journalists, and ordinary citizens withdrew up the Yangtze to the new capital in Chongqing and other inland cities to continue the resistance. It was indeed "one of the greatest mass migrations in human history."[10]

In little more than a year, the Japanese had driven Chinese forces from all the major coastal cities and the central China metropolis of Wuhan, where the Chinese had hoped, but in the end failed, to hold the line.[11] Instead Chiang's forces hunkered down for a protracted war of attrition from the relative safety of their bastion in the fertile fields of Sichuan, above the treacherous gorges on the Yangtze River. In the spring of 1939, the Japanese launched murderous air raids that destroyed much of the wartime capital in Chongqing, but soon an effective network of air raid shelters and an efficient warning system relying on spotters near the Japanese airfields and along their flight paths cut Chinese casualties to a minimum.[12] As elsewhere in the history of modern warfare, the bombing of civilian targets served mainly to strengthen national resolve to resist.

December 1941 brought the Japanese attack on Pearl Harbor and a fundamental reshaping of the global strategic picture. After fighting pretty much on its own for four long years (ten years, if one counts from Japan's Manchurian incursion), China gained a crucial ally in the United States. Unfortunately, despite widespread American sentiment for immediate revenge on Japan, the Roosevelt administration gave priority to the rescue of Britain and the defeat of Hitler in a "Europe first" strategy. Even more sobering for the Chinese was the dismal showing of British forces in Hong Kong, Singapore, Malaya, and Burma and the quick defeat of the

---

[10] Theodore H. White and Annalee Jacoby, *Thunder out of China* (New York: William Sloane, 1946), 55. See also Liu Lu, "A Whole Nation Walking: The 'Great Retreat' in the War of Resistance, 1937–1945," PhD diss., University of California, San Diego, 2002; Mitter, *Forgotten Ally*, 109–23.

[11] Stephen R. MacKinnon, *Wuhan, 1938: War, Refugees, and the Making of Modern China* (Berkeley: University of California Press, 2008).

[12] Peattie, Drea, and van de Ven, *Battle for China*, 248–49, 256–82; White and Jacoby, *Thunder out of China*, 11–16.

Figure 1.1: Destruction from bombing of Chongqing. *Source:* "China at War" photo collection, Library of Congress.

Americans in the Philippines and the Dutch in Indonesia. In the battle for Shanghai, the Chinese had put up a much more determined fight and inflicted more Japanese casualties than the proud Europeans, but now China stood alone as the European colonial empires in Southeast Asia crumbled before the Japanese assault.[13] To add insult to injury, the British initially declined Chinese military assistance in the battle to keep open the supply line to China through their Burmese colony. In the words of the U.S. State Department, the British stance was motivated by their "reluctance to accept assistance from Orientals as derogatory to British prestige in Asia."[14] When Burma fell, China lost its last land link to the outside world, and soon despaired of receiving any substantial aid from the Allies.

Fortunately for the Chinese, the Japanese had also suffered chastening

---

[13] Gerhard L. Weinberg, *A World at Arms: A Global History of World War II*, 2nd ed. (Cambridge: Cambridge University Press, 2005), 310–22.

[14] Ballantine memorandum, January 21, 1942, in *FRUS 1942* (Washington, DC: Government Printing Office, 1956), 7.

losses in the fight for Wuhan; their forces were now fighting major battles in Southeast Asia; and soon much of their air force and many first-line army units were diverted to the campaign in the Pacific.[15] As a result, the bombing raids on Chongqing halted and the city was rebuilt; Japanese offensives were largely limited to local foraging operations; and the front lines hardened into a prolonged stalemate. Fighting alone, China became the "forgotten ally."[16] After suffering enormous casualties in the first years of the war, the Chinese now hunkered down, hoping to hold out until others could defeat Japan on their behalf.[17]

THE GENERALISSIMO

No individual was more central to the fate of wartime China than Chiang Kai-shek. The son of a Zhejiang salt merchant and favorite of a doting mother, he received a solid Confucian education in the final years of the Qing dynasty. Imbued with the nationalist fervor of an era that aroused revolutionary sentiments and military aspirations, Chiang enrolled in a Japanese military academy and then China's premier officers' training school in Baoding. When the 1911 Revolution toppled the Qing dynasty and established the Republic of China, Chiang became a loyal follower of Sun Yat-sen, leader of what would soon become the Nationalist Party (Guomindang/Kuomintang). In the 1920s, Sun appointed him head of the Whampoa Military Academy to train officers for the party's National Revolutionary Army. Sun also sent Chiang to the Soviet Union, then the chief financial and military backer of the Nationalist Party, to learn the secrets of the Red Army's success—but Chiang returned with an abiding suspicion of Soviet intentions in China. After Sun's death in 1925, Chiang led the Northern Expedition that unified the country, defeating or absorbing the warlord armies that had fractured the country since the early years of the republic. At a crucial juncture in 1927, Chiang turned on the Na-

---

[15] MacKinnon, *Wuhan*, 2; Peattie, Drea, and van de Ven, *Battle for China*, 250–51.

[16] Mitter, *Forgotten Ally*.

[17] White and Jacoby, *Thunder out of China*, 62–67; Graham Peck, *Two Kinds of Time* (1950; reprint, Seattle: University of Washington Press, 2008), 378 ff.

tionalists' Soviet sponsors, sending the Soviet advisers back to Russia and massacring thousands of their Communist Party and leftist protégées. The old capital in Beijing was abandoned, and Chiang presided over a relatively cohesive regime from a new capital in Nanjing.[18]

Chiang's National Government (Guomin zhengfu) in Nanjing was founded on a commitment to complete the national revolutionary mission of Sun Yat-sen. One of the government's first acts was to erect an immense mausoleum on the outskirts of the new capital and stage an elaborate procession in which Sun's body was brought by train from Beijing to be reburied in this new ceremonial center. Chiang himself played a central role in the ritual process and further cemented his ties to Sun's legacy by marrying Soong Mayling, the sister of Sun Yat-sen's widow.[19] The new Mme. Chiang was "cosmopolitan, articulate, intelligent, and wealthy,"[20] and as an American-educated Christian, she provided an attractive face for the regime's Western allies. As a condition for the marriage, Chiang had converted to Christianity and regularly read the Bible, said his prayers, and thanked God for his good fortune. But the ideological foundation of his regime was the commitment to Sun Yat-sen's legacy, and every Monday in schools, government institutions, factories, and military units, Chinese gathered to recite Sun Yat-sen's political testament and listen to inspirational appeals to dedicate themselves to completing his nation-building mission.[21] By portraying himself as Sun Yat-sen's most loyal disciple and linking Sun's Nationalist Party to the nation's modern rise, Chiang sought to link his own authority to the national destiny.

Throughout his adult life, Chiang Kai-shek kept a meticulous diary, whose daily entries provide greater insight into his private thoughts and

---

[18] The best biography of Chiang is Jay Taylor, *The Generalissimo: Chiang Kai-shek and the Struggle for Modern China* (Cambridge, MA: Harvard University Press, 2009); a more critical assessment is Jonathan Fenby, *Chiang Kai-shek: China's Generalissimo and the Nation He Lost* (New York: Carroll and Graf, 2004); a useful account of Chiang's early years is Pichon P.Y. Loh, *The Early Chiang Kai-shek: A Study of His Personality and Politics, 1887–1924* (New York: Columbia University Press, 1971).

[19] Liping Wang, "Creating a National Symbol: The Sun Yatsen Memorial in Nanjing," *Republican China* 21, no. 2 (April 1996): 23–64; Henrietta Harrison, *The Making of a Republican Citizen: Political Ceremonies and Symbols in China, 1911–1929* (Oxford: Oxford University Press, 2000), 207–39.

[20] Taylor, *Generalissimo*, 74.

[21] Henrietta Harrison, *China (Inventing the Nation)* (New York: Oxford University Press, 2001), 195–200.

psychology than we have for any other Chinese ruler past or present. In these entries we see a man of intense self-discipline, his tightly wrought manner often interpreted as a psychological overcorrection for an admittedly dissolute life as a young man in Shanghai.[22] But his rigid demeanor also came from his military training, and Chiang's genuine respect for the martial culture of both Japan and Germany was linked to the value he placed on discipline, order, and respect for authority.[23] By the wartime period, Chiang's discipline was less soldierly than Confucian and Christian, as he maintained a daily routine that began with morning prayers, silent meditation, and calisthenics, and ended with more prayers and meditation.[24] He summarized his accomplishments and failings in regular weekly, monthly, and annual self-reflections (*fanxing*). When his determined self-composure broke down in occasional explosions of anger, he would congratulate himself if he was able to conduct his next meeting with equanimity.[25] He admitted to being unsociable, disliking public ceremonies, and seemed happiest when alone with his family or silently meditating in some quiet pavilion.[26] As a "Bible-reading Confucian,"[27] he spent long hours in 1943 reading Confucian commentaries and Liang Qichao's writings on Chinese intellectual history.[28] During one air raid, he was forced to seek refuge in a roadside shelter and took out a book on Confucian philosophers, later commenting that "the profit from reading is greater than any riches or honor."[29] These studies were not just for pleasure or self-cultivation; he also sought to shape the nation's intellectual agenda, issuing orders to establish a Society for the Study of Tang Culture to combat the effete Confucianism of the Song and Ming dynasties.[30]

From these multiple sources—Japanese and German military culture,

---

[22] Loh, *Early Chiang Kai-shek*, esp. 64–65.

[23] Taylor, *Generalissimo*, 77, 101.

[24] *SLGB* 52:151 (1942 annual review). This entry notes that he had maintained his regime of daily meditation for over twenty years.

[25] *SLGB* 53:579 (June 7, 1943).

[26] *SLGB* 55:252 (October 31, 1943), 53:220–21 (April 12, 1943).

[27] Mitter, *Forgotten Ally*, 33.

[28] See, inter alia, *SLGB* 53:242–43 (April 16, 1943), 54:355–56 (August 22), 55:241 (October 30), 55:718 (1943 annual review).

[29] *SLGB* 54:361 (August 23, 1943).

[30] Gong'anbu dang'an guan, ed., *Zai Jiang Jieshi shenbian banian: Shicongshi gaoji muliao Tang Zong riji* [Eight years at Chiang Kai-shek's side: The diary of Confidential Secretary Tang Zong] (Beijing: Qunzhong chubanshe, 1991), 351, 367.

Figure 1.2: Generalissimo and Mme. Chiang Kai-shek in a Chongqing air raid shelter. *Source:* "China at War" photo collection, Library of Congress.

Christian faith, Confucian philosophy, and loyalty to Sun Yat-sen's legacy—came an increasingly authoritarian personality. Convinced of his own correctness, he railed against the stupidity, laxity, and selfishness of his subordinates. Surrounded by presumed incompetents, he was unable to delegate authority, once complaining, "I have to do everything myself."[31] This inability to delegate, plus his remarkable attention to detail, made him the ultimate micromanager, scolding a vice minister of foreign affairs for the poor quality of paper used for a diplomatic note,[32] complaining when he saw a copy of the national flag in which the points of the star were not precisely aligned in the vertical axis,[33] and stipulating appropriate

---

[31] *SLGB* 52:498 (February 16, 1943). Ray Huang makes the useful point that scarce resources made it difficult for subordinates to make crucial decisions on allocations. As a result, everything was referred to Chiang. Ray Huang, "Chiang Kai-shek and His Diary as a Historical Source," *Chinese Studies in History* 28, no. 1–2 (Fall–Winter 1995–1996), 45.

[32] Wu Guozhen, Huang Zhuoqun, and Liu Yongchang, *Wu Guozhen zhuan* [Biography of Wu Guozhen (K.C. Wu)] (Taipei: Ziyou shibao, 1995), vol. 1, 390.

[33] *SLGB* 53:80–81 (March 24, 1943).

dress for formal party meetings after observing with dismay a session in which the four people on the dais were all wearing different types of clothing.[34] Perhaps most difficult for those who sought to serve Chiang and interpret his intentions was his capacity, in the words of one U.S. Foreign Service officer, to be "alternately impassive and overwrought, obstinate and vacillating."[35] Mme. Chiang, who was presumably accustomed to this behavior, was to experience it when confronted with an invitation to visit Great Britain after her much-acclaimed visit to the United States. Her husband, angered and insulted by a Churchill speech that omitted China from the list of Great Powers, flip-flopped back and forth as he shot off one telegram after another advising on whether or not she should accept.[36]

Chiang's reaction to Churchill's speech was indicative of the guiding principle for his political behavior. Chiang was the supreme nationalist, committed to the same slogan—the revival of the Chinese nation (*Zhonghua minzu fuxing*)—proclaimed by the leaders of the People's Republic of China today.[37] Every challenge to China's interests was interpreted as a slight, an insult, a tendency of the Western powers to look down on the Chinese. The British and Churchill, the ultimate modern imperialist, were particular targets of Chiang's ire, and not without reason. In 1943, the British refusal to consider any concessions on the status of their Hong Kong colony during the negotiations to abolish the "unequal treaties" was particularly galling (see chapter 5). At times, British imperial meddling even provoked sympathy for the Axis Powers and Japan's anti-Western pan-Asian agenda. After receiving news of British interference in Tibetan affairs and Roosevelt's failure to end Churchill's waffling on the commitment to reopen the Burma Road, Chiang would write, "How did we get

[34] *SLGB* 54:552, 559–60 (September 18, 1943).

[35] John Paton Davies, Jr., *China Hand: An Autobiography* (Philadelphia: University of Pennsylvania Press, 2012), 43.

[36] *SLGB* 52:586 (February 26, 1943), 587 (February 27); *SLGB* 53:36–37 (March 14), 77–78 (March 24), 101–2 (March 26), 143 (April 1), 380–81 (May 7), 433 (May 15). On the Chinese reaction to Churchill's speech, see also Vincent to Secretary of State, April 8, 1943, *FRUS 1943*, 47.

[37] See Chiang's speech to the leaders of the New Life Movement in *SLGB* 52:528 (February 19, 1943).

stuck with this sort of dishonest and untrustworthy politician? You can see why Japan and Germany would wish to dispel their hatred and fearlessly embark on aggression."[38]

Chiang realized, in word if not in deed, that to gain real Great Power stature in the international community, China would have to strengthen itself. "Of the four countries in the United Nations, we are the weakest; and the treatment of the weak is like cripples or vagrants at the hands of local bullies. We must realize that if a person does not strengthen himself, no one can help. If a nation does not endeavor to strengthen itself, then friend and foe alike will treat it like meat on a chopping block. Beware!"[39] To Chiang and the Nationalist Party, the key to strengthening China was real national unity—overcoming the legacy of warlordism and political fragmentation that had plagued the Republic of China. This had been the purpose of Sun Yat-sen's revolution in the 1920s, and Chiang realized that his armies had achieved victory as much by absorbing rival warlord forces as by conquering them. The residual power of local warlords posed a constant challenge to the Nationalist regime, and on several occasions in the 1930s they rose in open revolt to Chiang's central government.

The War of Resistance against Japan rallied the country behind Chiang as never before, but it also seemed to increase his authoritarian tendencies. Theodore White and Annalee Jacoby compiled an incomplete list of the posts that Chiang held during the war. They included "chief executive of the Kuomintang; president of the National Government; chairman of the National Military Council, commander-in-chief of land, naval, and air forces; supreme commander, China theater; president of the State Council; chairman of the Supreme National Defense Council; director general of the Central Planning Board; chairman of the Party and Political Work Evaluation Committee; director of the New Life Movement Association; chairman of the Commission for Inauguration of Constitutional Government; president of the Central Training Corps; president of the School for Descendants of Revolutionary Martyrs; and president of the National

---

[38] Chiang Kai-shek diary, May 23, 1943, Hoover Institution Archives, Stanford, California. Cf. *SLGB* 53:487.

[39] *SLGB* 52:593 (February 28, 1943); cf. *SLGB* 54:622 (September 1943 monthly review).

Glider Association."[40] With so much power concentrated in his hands, Chiang had a distinct tendency to view himself as the embodiment of the nation's will. Signs of independence or resistance to his wishes were regarded as putting one's own selfish interests before those of the nation. Such behavior was most likely to provoke Chiang's ire, with the predictable result that he found himself surrounded largely by yes-men unwilling to bring unwelcome news.[41] Jiang Menglin, the loyal Nationalist intellectual who headed Peking University, reportedly complained, "No one tells him the truth, no one. I used to speak frankly to him, but I stopped doing so—it was no use. No one else would and he could not believe me. He will not listen to anything unpleasant, so nobody tells him anything but pleasant things. It is impossible to reason with him. ... He flies into a rage if anyone argues against with [*sic*] him."[42]

THE COMMUNIST CHALLENGE

Of all the challenges to Chiang Kai-shek's authority, none was more vexing than the CCP. Soon after its founding by a small group of intellectuals in Shanghai in 1921, the CCP, under strong pressure from the Communist International, had entered an alliance with Sun Yat-sen's Nationalist Party. While Sun was alive, the United Front worked relatively smoothly, for the Soviet Union provided critical support for both parties. After Chiang engineered the brutal massacre of Communist activists in 1927, however, the two parties became mortal enemies. The remnants of the CCP fled to the hills, built their own Red Army, and transformed their movement into a peasant-based revolution. In 1934–1935, Chiang Kai-shek's armies drove the Communists from their bases in the highlands of central China, and they embarked on the Long March that carried them

---

[40] White and Jacoby, *Thunder out of China*, 124. A footnote adds thirty-six additional posts, many of them president of various schools that Chiang periodically visited to exhort the students.

[41] *SLGB* 54:524 (September 13, 1943), 55:717 (1943 annual review); White and Jacoby, *Thunder out of China*, 126–31.

[42] "The Peanut. Thoughts by Ch.M.L.," Stilwell Papers, Box 41, Folder 2, Hoover Institution Archives, Stanford, California.

to the barren hills of northern Shaanxi. The Long March was both a heroic escape and a devastating military defeat in which the Red Army lost
90 percent of its forces, but in the end the movement survived with a
dedicated band of hardened revolutionaries under the leadership of Mao
Zedong.[43]

From the mid-1930s, as Japanese aggression posed a growing threat
to Chinese sovereignty, the Communists reoriented much of their propaganda to appeals for a unified national resistance to Japan. They were
encouraged in this by the Soviet Union—itself threatened by both Nazi
Germany and the virulently anti-Soviet Japanese army—which encouraged Communist parties around the world to enter antifascist united
fronts. From the press, liberal intellectuals, and campuses throughout
China came appeals and demonstrations urging Chiang Kai-shek to halt
his campaign against the Communists and enter into a united front
against Japan. The culmination of this process came in December 1936
when Chiang was kidnapped and held hostage by two of his own generals in Xi'an. With Stalin urging moderation from afar and the CCP
leader Zhou Enlai joining the negotiations in Xi'an, an agreement was
reached to end the long civil war and prepare to cooperate in resisting
Japan.[44]

When full-scale war broke out the following summer, Chiang's National Government became the focal point of national resistance. Communists, leftists, and progressive intellectuals joined the Nationalists in a
grand coalition to arouse their compatriots to resist the aggressors. As the
universities moved to the interior, students joined propaganda corps to
stage patriotic dramas, paint anti-Japanese slogans on walls, draw cartoons, print leaflets, and urge on the young soldiers at the front. During
the battle for Wuhan, there was a real sense of unified resistance, and in a

---

[43] For an excellent account of the early history of the party and the rise of Mao, see
Alexander V. Pantsov, with Steven I. Levine, *Mao: The Real Story* (New York: Simon and
Schuster, 2012), 1–288.

[44] Parks M. Coble, *Facing Japan: Chinese Politics and Japanese Imperialism, 1931–1937*
(Cambridge, MA: Harvard University Council on East Asian Studies, 1991); Yang Kuisong,
Xi'an shibian xintan: Zhang Xueliang yu Zhonggong guanxi zhi mi [New light on the Xi'an
incident: The mystery of Zhang Xueliang's relations with the Chinese Communists] (Nanjing: Jiangsu renmin chubanshe, 2006).

few key battles in the north, Communist and Nationalist troops fought together to confront the Japanese advance.[45]

In addition to the domestic pressure for Nationalist-Communist cooperation, there was a diplomatic incentive for Chiang to work with his erstwhile enemies. After his German military advisers withdrew at the beginning of the war, Chiang's principal source of foreign military aid was the Soviet Union. The Soviets were fully aware of Japan's hostility to their regime: Japan had occupied Vladivostok in the early years of the USSR; it had joined Germany and Italy in the Anti-Comintern Pact in 1936; and until the decision to attack Pearl Harbor and the European colonies of Southeast Asia, many in the Japanese Army command still preferred an attack on the Soviet Union.[46] Accordingly, from the first months of the conflict in China, the Soviet Union became the primary source of financial and military support for the Nationalist regime, supplying military advisers, arms, tanks, artillery, and volunteers to fly hundreds of combat aircraft.[47] This aid provided a key incentive for Chiang Kai-shek to maintain cordial relations with the Chinese Communists.

Under the terms of the United Front, the National Government recognized the Communist armies, the Eighth Route Army and the New Fourth Army, as integral parts of the nation's armed forces and provided them with arms and provisions, as well as a subsidy for the Communist regional government based in Yan'an. The presumption was that, although the Communist armies would keep their own commanders, those officers would be subject to the unified command of Chiang's general staff. But from the very beginning of Mao Zedong's rise to power, he had recognized that for his revolution to succeed, it would need its own army. Mao

---

[45] Chang-tai Hung, *War and Popular Culture: Resistance in Modern China, 1937–1945* (Berkeley: University of California Press, 1994); MacKinnon, *Wuhan*; Yang Kuisong, *Guomindang de "liangong" yu "fangong"* [The United Front and anti-Communist policies of the Guomindang] (Beijing: Shehui kexue wenxian chubanshe, 2008), 386–99.

[46] Herbert P. Bix, *Hirohito and the Making of Modern Japan* (New York: Harper Collins, 2001), 318–21; Edward J. Drea, *In the Service of the Emperor: Essays on the Imperial Japanese Army* (Lincoln: University of Nebraska Press, 1998), 26–32; Eri Hotta, *Japan 1941: Countdown to Infamy* (New York: Alfred A. Knopf, 2013), 119–35.

[47] Peattie, Drea, and van de Ven, *Battle for China*, 288–93; John W. Garver, *Chinese-Soviet Relations, 1937–1945: The Diplomacy of Chinese Nationalism* (New York: Oxford University Press, 1988), 37–52, 102–8.

was not about to surrender control of his armies to Chiang. So from the outset, the United Front was bedeviled by conflicts over the independence of the Eighth Route and New Fourth armies. In Chiang's eyes, these independent forces were a fundamental threat to national unity, and by the time he wrote *China's Destiny* he would refer to them as "disguised warlords and new feudalists."[48]

Any effective cooperation between Communist and Nationalist forces came to an end with the New Fourth Army incident of January 1941. Chiang had ordered the New Fourth Army to move north of the Yangtze River by the end of 1940, but the Communists feared a trap and hesitated. In the end, they moved by a circuitous route and were attacked by the Nationalist armies, which decimated the Communist headquarters battalion and took thousands of prisoners. It was a devastating military loss for the Communists, but an even greater propaganda defeat for the Nationalists, who were broadly accused of attacking a patriotic army in the midst of the struggle for national survival. From that time forward, the United Front existed in name only. The Nationalists cut off their subsidy to the Communist armies and regional government, and established a tight blockade of the area around Yan'an. The Communists expanded their bases behind Japanese lines, often displacing Nationalist forces, whom they accused of collaborating with the enemy. The Soviet Union, for its part, began preparing for the expected invasion from Nazi Germany, withdrew its pilots, terminated most of its aid for China, and secured its eastern front by signing a neutrality pact with Japan in April 1941.[49]

THE UNITED STATES AND CHINA

Few relationships were so fraught with tension and misperceptions as China's wartime relations with the United States. The Allies needed each

---

[48] Chiang Kai-shek, *China's Destiny and Chinese Economic Theory* (New York: Roy, 1947), 225. Chiang was particularly proud of this formulation, and regarded the angry Communist response as proof of their separatist intentions. *SLGB* 54:387 (Memo on Communist Policy, August 25, 1943).

[49] Gregor Benton, *New Fourth Army: Communist Resistance along the Yangtze and the Huai, 1938–41* (Berkeley: University of California Press, 1999), 511–616; Yang Kuisong, *Guomindang*, 424–59.

other. China needed U.S. military and financial assistance; the United States needed China to tie down Japanese troops and resources on the Asian mainland so that they were not diverted to confront the American advance across the Pacific. Neither side truly trusted or understood the other. Chiang and his regime were painfully aware of China's weakness and hypersensitive to any slight from their stronger ally; the United States was frustrated by China's passivity and defensive stance, giving little heed to the enormous losses China had suffered during the four long years that it had fought alone.[50]

Even before Pearl Harbor, there was considerable American sympathy for China's plight. Polls showed that among the public, 74 percent favored China, against only 2 percent for Japan. This sentiment was fueled by the strong pro-China stance of China-born Henry Luce and his influential chain of magazines: *Time* proclaimed Chiang Kai-shek and his wife "Man and Wife of the Year" in 1937.[51] The U.S. government, alarmed by Japan's expanding power in East Asia, also tilted toward China. In the summer of 1941, Roosevelt announced an oil embargo on Japan, which left the Japanese with only a few months' supply to fuel its aggression. In the negotiations with Japan that followed, the United States insisted that Japan abandon all territories seized from China as a condition for resumed trade. At that point, "confronted with military strangulation by oil embargoes and the choice of admitting defeat in China," the emperor gave final approval to the plan to knock out the U.S. Navy at Pearl Harbor and simultane-

---

[50] The list of books on U.S.-China relations during the war is as long as the problem is complex, the politics of the scholarship much colored by the postwar collapse of Chiang's regime and the triumph of the CCP. A brief list of key titles would include Herbert Feis, *The China Tangle: The American Effort in China from Pearl Harbor to the Marshall Mission* (Princeton, NJ: Princeton University Press, 1953); Tang Tsou, *America's Failure in China, 1941–50* (Chicago: University of Chicago Press, 1963); Barbara W. Tuchman, *Stilwell and the American Experience in China, 1911–1945* (New York: Macmillan, 1971); Joseph W. Esherick, ed., *Lost Chance in China: The World War II Despatches of John S. Service* (New York: Random House, 1974); Michael Schaller, *The U.S. Crusade in China, 1938–1945* (New York: Columbia University Press, 1979); Qi Xisheng (Hsi-sheng Ch'i), *Jianba nuzhang de mengyou: Taipingyang zhanzheng qijian de Zhong-Mei junshi hezuo guanxi (1941–1945)* [Allies with swords drawn and bows taut: Sino-American military cooperation during the Pacific War] (Beijing: Shehui kexue wenxian chubanshe, 2012); Hans van de Ven, *War and Nationalism in China, 1925–1945* (London: RoutledgeCurzon, 2003).

[51] T. Christopher Jespersen, *American Images of China, 1931–1949* (Stanford, CA: Stanford University Press, 1996), 24–58; Tuchman, *Stilwell and the American Experience*, 187–89.

ously attack southward to capture the European and American colonies in
Southeast Asia, including the Dutch oil fields in Indonesia.[52]

The Japanese attack and declaration of war against the United States
and Great Britain gave China two powerful allies, but, as noted above, the
initial results were discouraging. The British fought poorly to defend their
Asian colonies, and soon Burma was lost and with it China's last lifeline
to the outside world. For the next three years, the main route for military
supplies to China was the Hump, the air route from India over the Himalayan foothills to Kunming in southwest China. Described as "the most
dangerous, terrifying, barbarous aerial transport run in the world," the
route took planes well above their designed altitudes, in treacherous
weather, with only visual navigation, so that many planes and airmen were
lost. Tonnage was necessarily limited and further constrained by the poorly
maintained railway that served the Indian airfields in Assam.[53] As a result,
between 1941 and 1944, China received only a tiny fraction of the aid that
the United States offered to the Allied Powers: less than 1 percent of the
Lend-Lease total.[54]

Given the minimal aid China received from abroad, it mattered greatly
who was to be the recipient. Here, from the beginning, Chiang's regime
became embroiled in a conflict between two proud and determined American competitors. On one side was General Joseph W. Stilwell, an acerbic
infantry commander with considerable prior experience in China as a
military attaché, who was the choice of U.S. Chief of Staff George Marshall to command U.S. operations in China. His rival was Claire Lee
Chennault, an early advocate for air power in modern warfare, accomplished pilot, and brilliant aerial tactician who had left the Army Air
Corps to organize the American Volunteer Group (more commonly
known as the Flying Tigers) to assist China's war effort. After the United
States joined the war, Chennault was given command of the U.S. Army's
Fourteenth Air Force in China. The story of the conflict between Stilwell
and Chennault has been much told. Suffice to say, Stilwell's disdain for the

[52] Bix, *Hirohito*, 387–439 (quoted passage from p. 439); Weinberg, *World at Arms*, 245–63; Schaller, *U.S. Crusade in China*, 17–63.

[53] White and Jacoby, *Thunder out of China*, 154; cf. Weinberg, *World at Arms*, 639.

[54] Arthur N. Young, *China and the Helping Hand, 1937–1945* (Cambridge, MA: Harvard University Press, 1963), 350; cf. Qi Xisheng, *Jianba nuzhang*, 339–40, 369.

Generalissimo (whom he called "Peanut" in his diary) was widely known, and his brusque and intemperate manner made him a most inappropriate choice as the ranking U.S. officer in China. Chennault, by contrast, got on well with the Generalissimo, in part because he promised to defeat the Japanese from the air, a strategy that required little contribution from the Chinese side.[55]

When Stilwell was ordered to China in January 1942, he went as commanding general of U.S. forces in China and chief of staff to the supreme commander of the China Theater, who was Chiang Kai-shek. In the latter capacity, Stilwell was to discharge his primary duty: keeping open the Burma Road in "command [of] such Chinese forces as may be assigned to him."[56] The 1942 campaign in Burma was a disaster. The British defense was inept and feeble, and they scarcely disguised their disinterest in Chinese assistance. Stilwell urged more aggressive tactics, but in the process put Chinese troops in danger in ways that were repugnant to the Generalissimo. In the end, with his army in retreat to India (where they would be retrained and rearmed to reopen the Burma Road later in the war), Stilwell led a ragtag band of American officers, Chinese guards, and assorted British, Burmese, and Indians in a month-long retreat through the jungle. Chiang Kai-shek understandably thought the lonely trek a dereliction of Stilwell's command responsibilities, and by the summer of 1942 voices in both Chongqing and Washington were already calling for Stilwell's recall.[57]

THE WORLD AT WAR, 1943

In the global struggle against the Axis Powers, 1943 was unquestionably the year in which the tide of battle turned in the Allies' favor. The North

---

[55] Tuchman, *Stilwell and the American Experience*, 307–74; see also the protagonists' own accounts: Theodore White, ed., *The Stilwell Papers* (New York: Sloane, 1948); Claire Lee Chennault, *Way of a Fighter* (New York: Putnam, 1949).

[56] Tuchman, *Stilwell and the American Experience*, 246.

[57] Ibid., 266–325; Marshall to Roosevelt, October 6, 1942, *FRUS 1942*, 159; Taylor, *Generalissimo*, 194–216; Qi Xisheng, *Jianba nuzhang*, 101–296; memo of conversation with Stilwell, Chiang Kai-shek and Mme. Chiang, March 10, 1943, T.V. Soong papers, Box 60, Folio 1, Hoover Institution Archives, Stanford, California. For a searing critique of Stilwell in China, see van de Ven, *War and Nationalism*, 19–63.

African campaign ended with a convincing Anglo-American victory, which was quickly followed by the invasion of Sicily and then the Italian mainland, bringing the surrender of Italy and its fleet and Allied control of the Mediterranean. Though the Germans quickly occupied northern Italy and hard fighting remained on that front, as many as forty Axis divisions were diverted from the eastern front, considerably easing pressure on the Russians. By the summer of 1943, submarine warfare in the Atlantic was basically concluded in the Allies' favor, allowing the Americans to send ceaseless convoys of war material to Britain and the Soviet Union. The year also saw the development of the long-range B-29 bomber and the strategic bombing of German industry—an effort now known to have had limited impact but at the time a major boost to British and Russian morale after the pounding they had received early in the war.

Developments on the East European front were even more encouraging, as the relentless German advance was blunted and turned back. Hitler had publicly proclaimed Stalingrad a major objective, but in the bitter winter of 1942–1943 his forces were surrounded and besieged. In the end, after losing some 250,000 German soldiers in the effort, the last men surrendered in February. At the same time, the siege of Leningrad was broken, and during the course of 1943, the Germans were steadily driven back across the killing fields of Eastern Europe. By this time the Soviets were outproducing the Germans in both planes and tanks, and the outcome of the war was no longer in doubt.[58]

Meanwhile in the Pacific came progress of great import to the Chinese. The American-led offensive was beginning to show costly signs of progress in the Solomon Islands and New Guinea as MacArthur's forces moved north from Australia. American casualties in the bitter battles for Guadalcanal and Bougainville were greater than any other battles in the war, but they forced the Japanese to cancel a planned attack on Chongqing and to transfer several elite divisions and most of their aircraft to the war in the Pacific.[59] This naturally concerned the Americans, who pressed the Chinese to do more on their front. When Roosevelt made a speech stressing the importance of the China theater as well as the Pacific, Chiang

---

[58] Weinberg, *World at Arms*, 431–70, 586–609, 616–19.
[59] Peattie, Drea, and van de Ven, *Battle for China*, 43, 428.

Kai-shek was furious, complaining in his diary that FDR was "treating China like a sacrificial offering."[60] But gradually over the course of the year, the great air, sea, and land battles of the island-hopping campaign were turned by the overwhelming power of the American forces. By the end of the year, preparations were underway for the attack on the Gilberts and then the Marshall Islands, including Guam and Saipan, which would bring the Japanese homeland within range of the new American B-29s— the same long-range bombers that would eventually carry the atom bombs that brought the war to its conclusion.[61]

THE CHINA THEATER, 1943

In contrast to the major Allied victories elsewhere in the world, the China front was largely static. In January, when Chiang Kai-shek listed his priorities for the year, he stressed national unity and economic stabilization and made no mention of the war.[62] The consensus of foreign observers, even Chiang's supporters, was that Chiang's regime was not ready for any offensive but was instead "conserving its strength for ... postwar internal supremacy."[63] There were widespread reports of apathy and venality in the army,[64] and Chiang himself complained of the poor discipline, inept administration, and low morale of his forces.[65] With most Chinese forces uninterested in offensive action, the Japanese were able to deploy their

---

[60] *SLGB* 52:544 (February 21, 1943); cf. *SLGB* 52:445–46 (February 6), 52:491 (February 14). The offending words in Roosevelt's speech were the statement, "Great and decisive actions against the Japanese will be taken to drive the invader from the soil of China." Address to the White House Correspondents' Association, February 12, 1943, in Samuel I. Rosenman, ed., *The Public Papers and Addresses of Franklin D. Roosevelt*, vol. 12: *The Tide Turns* (New York: Russell and Russell, 1950), 79.

[61] Weinberg, *World at Arms*, 642–56.

[62] *SLGB* 52:204 (January 6, 1943).

[63] Patrick Hurley memorandum, November 20, 1943, *Foreign Relations of the United States: Diplomatic Papers. The Conferences at Cairo and Tehran, 1943* (Washington, DC: U.S. Government Printing Office, 1961), 265. (Hereafter cited as *FRUS Cairo.*) Cf. *FRUS 1943*, 26, 129–42, 166.

[64] Davies memoranda, March 9 and March 15, 1943, *FRUS 1943*, 27, 35. Corruption, war weariness, and official venality are major themes in Graham Peck's account of his experiences in these years, *Two Kinds of Time*, 357–550.

[65] *SLGB* 55:723 (1943 annual review).

Figure 1.3: Emaciated Chinese Army recruits. *Source:* U.S. Army Signal Corps photo, National Archives, College Park, MD.

elite units to the Pacific front, pulling their forces in China back to defend only major transport hubs, and leaving the task of peacekeeping in the occupied territories to Chinese, Manchukuo, and Korean puppet troops.[66]

By this stage of the war, Chiang was using his best troops to maintain the blockade against the Communists and prepare the offensive in Burma. The front lines were often held by the armies of former warlords. Some of these forces fought bravely and well, but the soldiers were ill fed, diseased, mistreated, and understandably prone to desertion. Among the officer corps, there was growing discontent over Chiang's preferential treatment of his own favorite commanders.[67] At the front, local commanders left to

[66] *SLGB* 53:209 (April 10, 1943), 228 (April 14), and 339 (May 3); Everett Drumright to Gauss, October 2, 1943, in *FRUS 1943*, 138–39; Peattie, Drea, and van de Ven, *Battle for China*, 43, 423–24.

[67] White and Jacoby, *Thunder out of China*, 129–44; Lloyd E. Eastman, "Nationalist China during the Sino-Japanese War, 1937–1945," in Lloyd E. Eastman, Jerome Ch'en, Su-

their own devices made opportunistic accommodations with the enemy—especially as the Japanese front lines were increasingly manned by Chinese puppet troops. Smuggling across the lines became common, as neglected advance units sought to support their own men. Some of this smuggling was certainly detrimental to the war effort, as the Chinese provided tungsten vital for Japanese munitions in exchange for gasoline or even luxury items.[68]

Through most of the early years of the war, the American press had been filled with stories of China's brave resistance to the Japanese invaders. But by 1943, more skeptical views were heard. At Mme. Chiang's February 19 press conference in Washington, one hesitant reporter asked about reports that "the Chinese were not utilizing their manpower to the full extent" in the war.[69] Pearl Buck published a widely read article in *Life*, which deftly balanced fervent praise of Mme. Chiang's visit with pointed warnings of stasis and corruption in the army and officers "going into business."[70] Most damningly, the *New York Times*' respected military correspondent Hanson Baldwin published a scathing article, calling any Chinese "victories" (his quotes) "Pyrrhic ones" and declaring bluntly that "Japan, not China, is winning."[71] The official Chinese reaction was intense and bitter, Chiang calling Baldwin's article "slanderous rumors" spread by the British and the Communists.[72] The U.S. Embassy noted that the various critiques had caused "some quiet satisfaction in the more liberal quarters,"[73] though "deeply ingrained slavishness to considerations of face" had

---

zanne Pepper, and Lyman P. van Slyke, *The Nationalist Era in China, 1927–1949* (Cambridge: Cambridge University Press, 1991), 134–48; Wu, Huang, and Liu, *Wu Guozhen zhuan*, 399–400.

[68] Davies to Gauss, March 9, 1943, *FRUS 1943*, 27–28; Acheson memorandum, April 7, 1943, *FRUS 1943*, 45; White and Jacoby, *Thunder out of China*, 72; John Hunter Boyle, *China and Japan at War, 1937–1945: The Politics of Collaboration* (Stanford, CA: Stanford University Press, 1972), 316–18; Peck, *Two Kinds of Time*, 572–75.

[69] "Joint Press Conference with Mme. Chiang Kai-shek," in Rosenman, *Public Papers and Addresses of Franklin D. Roosevelt*, vol. 12, 102–3.

[70] Pearl S. Buck, "A Warning about China," *Life*, May 10, 1943, 53–56.

[71] Hanson Baldwin, "Review of the Chinese Situation," *New York Times*, July 20, 1943. A fuller version was published in *Reader's Digest*, August 1943, under the title "Too Much Wishful Thinking about China."

[72] *SLGB* 54:186 (July 30, 1943).

[73] Acheson to Secretary of State, August 13, 1943, *FRUS 1943*, 87. One suspects that

caused "reactionary Chinese leaders" to reject all such criticism and respond with deep resentment.[74]

The most important fighting in 1943 was along the Yangtze River in western Hubei. The Japanese advance may have been a probe against the defenses of the capital, but more importantly it seems to have been a foraging expedition in the rich central China rice bowl. There were credible reports of looting and rape by Chinese troops after they ordered the residents to withdraw. Most disturbing, it seems that the invading army was composed largely of Chinese and Korean puppet troops under Japanese officers, yet still they inflicted over ten times the casualties that they themselves endured.[75] Chiang Kai-shek was clearly disheartened to learn that Chinese soldiers were fighting more effectively for Japan than for his cause, and he railed against the premature withdrawals, false reporting, and poor coordination of his own troops.[76] At the conclusion of the battle, Nationalist propaganda hailed the Japanese retreat to its prior positions as the "great victory of western Hubei" (*Exi dajie*), though Chiang privately attributed the enemy withdrawal to the protection afforded China by the Lord and Jesus Christ.[77]

The strong performance of the Chinese puppet soldiers in the west Hubei battles was a notable and worrisome development. Because Japan lost the war and history is written by the victors, those who collaborated with the Japanese have been demonized as traitors (*Hanjian* in Chinese). In recent years, several studies have explored the complex motives of those who chose collaboration.[78] In January 1943, disagreements with Great

---

the satisfaction was especially over the Buck article, which stressed the need to promote democracy in China.

[74] Acheson to Secretary of State, August 26, 1943, *FRUS 1943*, 106–7.

[75] White and Jacoby, *Thunder out of China*, 143–44; Peck, *Two Kinds of Time*, 532–34; Gauss to Secretary of State, November 5, 1943, *FRUS 1943*, 158–59 (reporting a *Dagongbao* special report that was apparently the source of Jacoby and White's account); Acheson to Secretary of State, June 19 and August 31, 1943, *FRUS 1943*, 67–68, 108–9.

[76] *SLGB* 53:511 (May 27, 1943), 54:21–24 (July 3, 1943).

[77] *SLGB* 53:525 (May 31, 1943), 563 (June 3). The "great victory of western Hubei" remains a staple of Chinese historiography of the war. See Wang Jianlang and Zeng Jingzhong, *Zhongguo jindai tongshi*, vol. 9: *Kang-Ri zhanzheng (1937–1945)* [History of modern China: vol. 9: The War of Resistance, 1937–45] (Nanjing: Jiangsu renmin chubanshe, 2007), 381–83. Thanks to Xiao Chen for this reference.

[78] Timothy Brook, *Collaboration: Japanese Agents and Local Elites in Wartime China*

Britain over the status of Hong Kong delayed the announcement of the new treaties with Britain and the United States. As a result, the Japanese renounced their extraterritorial privileges before the Allies, much to the annoyance of the Generalissimo.[79] In October, Japan signed an alliance with the Nanjing government of Wang Jingwei in which it promised complete withdrawal of all its forces within two years of the end of the war.[80] In November, Wang joined pro-Japanese leaders from India, Burma, and elsewhere in Asia for a grand conference to celebrate the Greater East Asia Co-prosperity Sphere.[81] Though the world war at large was certainly moving in the Allies' favor, in China, there was concrete evidence that "the process of 'conciliation' and 'pacification' in the occupied areas [was] proceeding steadily."[82] As Baldwin had warned, "Japan, not China, is winning."[83]

THE ECONOMY

In the summer of 1943, T.V. Soong met with Roosevelt's trusted White House aide, Harry Hopkins. Both Soong and Hopkins were keen supporters of Chennault's air-based strategy in China, and the Chinese foreign minister observed that with "growing American air strength in China, I am no longer much worried about our military situation. It is the economic outlook, inflation, which looks alarming."[84] The deteriorating economy and its effect on Chinese morale were a common refrain in reporting from China in 1943. In February, the State Department acknowledged that "the economic and psychological situation in China is

---

(Cambridge, MA: Harvard University Press, 2005); David P. Barrett and Larry N. Shyu, *Chinese Collaboration with Japan, 1932–1945: The Limits of Accommodation* (Stanford, CA: Stanford University Press, 2001). See also the earlier Boyle, *China and Japan at War*.

[79] *SLGB* 52:224 (January 9, 1943).

[80] Memo by Division of Far Eastern Affairs, November 3, 1943, *FRUS 1943*, 157–58.

[81] Mitter, *Forgotten Ally*, 304–6.

[82] Hornbeck memorandum, April 3, 1943, *FRUS 1943*, 43.

[83] In contrast to this contemporary assessment, Rana Mitter (*Forgotten Ally*, 6) writes that "Chiang won the war, but lost his country." This seems to me to perpetuate a dangerous myth. The defeat of Japan was accomplished by the United States and the Soviet Union. China was a vital ally, but Chiang did not "win the war."

[84] T.V. Soong memorandum, August 16, 1943, T.V. Soong Papers, Box 59, Folio 22.

already critical and is deteriorating."[85] In May the embassy in Chongqing reported that "economically the deterioration is rapid and is leading toward something that may eventually spell disaster."[86] Chiang Kai-shek would not have disagreed with this gloomy prognosis. Reviewing another week in the same month, he confessed, "My spirits are depressed. ... On the economic, diplomatic, party affairs and military fronts, there has been no progress. Dangers lurk everywhere in society, and the people's will is wavering."[87]

Given Free China's predominantly peasant economy, informed observers agreed that a full economic collapse was unlikely. Unless the harvest failed (as indeed it had in Henan: see chapter 10), most of the population would survive on what they could grow and produce locally. But by 1943, the Japanese blockade, persistent transport bottlenecks, and the lack of raw materials had brought an end to early wartime industrial growth, and manufacturing entered a period of decline. Factories closed, and labor unrest increased. By December, the Generalissimo judged that industry and the economy had registered "the most failures" of the year.[88]

As discussed in detail in chapter 9, the heart of wartime China's economic problem was its galloping inflation, which was in turn caused by government revenues lagging expenditures by about 75 percent. That gap was covered by printing money.[89] This inflation affected the population unevenly, with salaried employees in China's small middle class suffering the most and moneyed speculators profiting. Capital was diverted from investment to speculation and hoarding of scarce goods, with predictable effects on national morale and growing cynicism toward the war effort. Most critically, the utter failure of the government's much-advertised price controls was a major blow to the legitimacy of Chiang's regime. Needless to say, reports that price controls in the Japanese-occupied areas were more effective only further damaged popular morale.[90]

---

[85] Hamilton memorandum, February 11, 1943, *FRUS 1943*, 9.

[86] Atcheson to Secretary of State, May 28, 1943, *FRUS 1943*, 57.

[87] *SLGB* 53:392 (Weekly review, May 9, 1943).

[88] *SLGB* 55:718 (1943 annual review); cf. Eastman, "Nationalist China," 160–69; Peck, *Two Kinds of Time*, 518, 552–53.

[89] Eastman, "Nationalist China," 152.

[90] Memorandum of the British Foreign Office, July 5, 1943, in *FRUS 1943*, 71.

POLITICS

Domestic and international politics were intricately intertwined in war-time China, and 1943 provided several examples of this concatenation. The year began on an optimistic note, as the National Government's prestige was enhanced by the end of the "unequal treaties," a diplomatic achievement that Chiang Kai-shek hailed as the "greatest ever."[91] The recovery of Xinjiang was similarly greeted as "the greatest accomplishment since the founding of the National Government."[92] Both of these successes represented significant steps forward in China's quest to reclaim full national sovereignty—the first a concession of legal sovereignty by the Western allies, the second a reluctant relinquishment of economic and political influence in China's northwest periphery by the beleaguered Soviet Union. For a time, the recovery of Xinjiang even promised a new route for military assistance from the outside world, until the Soviets blocked the truck convoys that were to travel from Karachi to Tehran and then through the USSR to Xinjiang (see chapter 3).[93]

On purely domestic matters, the signs were less encouraging. In the poor provinces of Gansu in the northwest and Guizhou in the southwest, there were significant local rebellions provoked by state demands for taxes and conscripts. Resistance dragged on for several months and represented a notable challenge to central authority before a major deployment of troops restored order.[94] Meanwhile, students and intellectuals were becoming increasingly restive over the stifling censorship of news and information and the debilitating effects of inflation. On several occasions,

---

[91] *SLGB* 52:153 (1942 annual review).

[92] *SLGB* 52:157.

[93] On the proposed route to Xinjiang through the USSR, see *FRUS 1942*, 591–600; *FRUS 1943*, 590–613. When the Chinese request for supplies over this route included 1,100 tons of ammunition for Hu Zongnan, the American Lend-Lease administrator commented, "It is perhaps significant that in the eyes of the Chinese the most important item to be shipped in on the very first lot of supplies transported over this route was a consignment of over a thousand tons of ammunition to the general detailed by Chungking to hem in and watch the Chinese Communists." Stanton memorandum, July 12, 1943, *FRUS 1943*, 606.

[94] See reports in *FRUS 1943*, 232–33, 238–40, 344–45; John S. Service, "The Political Situation in Kansu," July 18, 1943, in Esherick, *Lost Chance in China*, 20–25; see also *SLGB* 53:281, 283, 287 (April 24, 25, 26, 1943); Gong'anbu, *Tang Zong riji*, 352, 358.

Chiang's diaries express concern over the spreading student unrest and attacks on Nationalist Party organizations in the schools.[95] It was presumably these challenges, as well as the larger threat from the Communists, that induced the Generalissimo to propose a transition to constitutional government (chapter 8).

There was, however, no threat of greater concern to Chiang Kai-shek than the Communists, and 1943 saw dramatic developments on that front. As noted above, the United Front joining the Communists and Nationalists in the fight against Japan had broken down with the New Fourth Army incident of 1941. The Communist armies operated with total autonomy and relative impunity behind Japanese lines, their guerrilla forces avoiding major battles with the better-armed Japanese, but engaging in periodic harassment that helped to keep the enemy contained in urban centers and safely away from the rural population. Despite their minimal contribution to the military struggle against Japan, the Communists were gaining significant support among the peasants of north China. Their programs of rent and interest reduction, highly progressive taxes that exempted many of the poorest peasants, and village elections (even if tightly controlled) appealed to the rural majority. In addition, Communist cadres tended to live simply, and their troops were better disciplined than either the Nationalists or the puppets. For these reasons, the Communist armies found it easier to survive and even prosper as guerrillas behind Japanese lines than did their Nationalist adversaries.[96]

Through much of 1942–1943, Chiang hoped and expected that relief

---

[95] *SLGB* 53:466 (May 20, 1943), 545 (June 1, 1943).

[96] On the much-debated question of how much the Communists contributed to the War of Resistance, see Yang Wu, "CCP Military Resistance during the Sino-Japanese War: The Case of Beiyue and Jidong," *Twentieth-Century China* 29, no. 1 (November 2003): 65–104; also Yang Kuisong, "Nationalist and Communist Guerrilla Warfare in North China," in Peattie, Drea, and van de Ven, *Battle for China*, 308–27. For an overview of Communist-Nationalist relations in this period, see Yang Kuisong, *Guomindang*, 461–84. Important studies of Communist wartime base areas include Tetsuya Kataoka, *Resistance and Revolution in China: The Communists and the Second United Front* (Berkeley: University of California Press, 1974); Yung-fa Chen, *Making Revolution: The Communist Movement in Eastern and Central China, 1937–1945* (Berkeley: University of California Press, 1986); Odoric Y.K. Wou, *Mobilizing the Masses: Building Revolution in Henan* (Stanford, CA: Stanford University Press, 1994); Kathleen Hartford and Steven M. Goldstein, *Single Sparks: China's Rural Revolutions* (Armonk, NY: M.E. Sharpe, 1990).

from the Communist menace would come from a Japanese attack on the Soviet Union. In Chiang's eyes, the Chinese Communist Party was entirely a creature of the Soviet Union.[97] He disdained the Communist armies as "rabble" (literally, "a flock of crows"—*wuhe zhi zhong*), and was convinced that without Soviet aid, they would crumble before his forces.[98] Accordingly, the optimal solution to Chiang's predicament was a Japanese attack to weaken or even (together with Germany's invasion) destroy the Soviet Union, an attack that would also deflect Japanese forces from their aggression against China. Chiang had been confidently predicting such an attack since 1941, encouraged by the Anti-Comintern Pact that Japan had signed,[99] but by 1943 there was a renewed urgency to his wishful thinking. When Roosevelt's speech in February said that Japan could not be defeated from the Pacific alone, that China would also play a role, Chiang complained, "our strategy for the past three years has been almost completely destroyed by [FDR]. The result is that Japan will not dare attack Russia."[100] His strategy, it seems, had been to keep the China front quiet so that Japan would be emboldened to attack the Soviets. A few months later, hopes revived with "clear intelligence" of a June attack on Russia.[101] By June, he was losing sleep worrying about this, calling it "the key to our nation's survival."[102] And when in the end it seemed the Japanese would not attack, he found this unhappy development "the greatest danger to our country."[103] Chiang could not, it seems, escape the conception of China as a victim, whose fate lay entirely in the hands of untrustworthy foreign powers.

As prospects faded for Japanese assistance in solving his Communist problem, Chiang was presented with another source of hope, Moscow's May 1943 announcement that it was disbanding the Communist Interna-

---

[97] *SLGB* 54:496, 499 (September 9, 1943). This theme would later become the thesis of Chiang's book, *Soviet Russia in China: A Summing Up at Seventy* (Taipei: China Publishing, 1969), and a persistent theme of anti-Communist propaganda.

[98] *SLGB* 54:512–13 (September 11, 1943).

[99] Vincent to Secretary of State, April 24, 1943, *FRUS 1943*, 50–51; Davies to Stilwell, July 5, 1942, *FRUS 1942*, 99–101. Cf. Davies, *China Hand*, 95.

[100] *SLGB* 52:491 (Weekly review, February 14, 1943).

[101] Cable to Mme. Chiang, May 16, 1943, *SLGB* 53:439.

[102] *SLGB* 53:610 (June 12, 1943).

[103] *SLGB* 53:650 (Weekly review, June 20, 1943).

tional. Chiang called it a "historic watershed," the "only great event of the early twentieth century."[104] Immediately he started planning to attack the Communist base in northern Shaanxi. "The Communist bandit problem," he wrote, "can only be resolved by force."[105] In the area surrounding Yan'an, he ordered airfields prepared, roads and bridges repaired, maps drawn, and extra funds allocated to nearby Nationalist armies.[106] In August, he prepared a major policy document on the Communist problem. Clearly pleased with his product, he called it "one of the great scholarly achievements of my entire revolutionary career."[107] The plan called for ten armies to attack the Communist base and turn the Reds into roving bandits, who could then be pursued by Chiang's troops. Timing was essential. Yan'an must be attacked before the defeat of Germany so that Soviet forces could not intervene.[108] American victories in the Pacific were another important consideration. In Chiang's mind, they reduced the Japanese threat to manageable proportions. As a result, he said, "the problem for the future is entirely internal: how to eradicate the Communist bandits."[109]

September would bring a critical meeting of the Nationalist Party's Central Executive Committee. Chiang sent special planes to bring each of the leading northwest warlords to the conclave, and on September 11, a wide range of central and regional leaders met to decide on measures to address the Communist problem. Military plans had been drawn up earlier that day, but in the end, Chiang reversed course, abandoning the military option and choosing instead to treat the Communists' independent strategy as a matter of disobedience to central authority requiring legal and constitutional remedies. Accordingly, the Central Executive Committee issued a strong condemnation of Communist insubordination, but declared that the issue would be resolved by political, not military, means.[110]

---

[104] *SLGB* 53:498 (May 25, 1943), 531 (Monthly review, May 1943).

[105] *SLGB* 54:261 (August 9, 1943).

[106] *SLGB* 53:634 (June 17, 1943), 54:122 (Weekly review, July 18), 319–20 (August 17), 341–42 (August 19), 347–48 (August 20), 366, 368 (August 24), 404 (August 29), 415 (August 29); Gong'anbu, *Tang Zong riji*, 365 (June 29, 1943), 374 (August 17), 378 (September 9).

[107] *SLGB* 54:410 (Weekly review, August 29, 1943).

[108] Chiang Kai-shek memo on CCP and USSR policy, *SLGB* 54:378–89.

[109] *SLGB* 54:431 (Monthly review, August 1943).

[110] *SLGB* 54:485 (September 8, 1943), 509–16 (September 11), 55:724–25 (1943 annual review).

Divisions in the Guomindang leadership played a role in this decision, as well as fears that an attack would only unify the Communists. Of greatest concern, however, were American warnings against civil war, though Chiang was convinced that the United States and the White House in particular had been misled by Communist propaganda.[111] That was one problem that he hoped to clear up at the coming Cairo summit.

A Politics of "Trusting One's Own"

The sudden cancelation of military action against the Communists was not the only time in 1943 that Chiang changed his mind at the last minute. It would occur again in the context of Chiang's longstanding conflict with General Stilwell. Although this time it was not foreign pressure that brought the reversal but domestic politics that bore all the hallmarks of a family feud, it also illustrates important characteristics of Chiang's regime.

As one reads Chiang's diary or the daily chronology of his activities, the small circle of close associates is notable. Again and again he meets with the same people: his secretaries, especially the talented Chen Bulei; Dai Li, the sinister head of the secret service; He Yingqin, his chief of staff; Chen Lifu, the minister of education and leader of the Nationalist Party's powerful C.C. Clique; H.H. Kung (Kong Xiangxi), Chiang's brother-in-law and acting head of the Executive Yuan; his other brother-in-law, the foreign minister T.V. Soong, on the rare occasions when Soong was in Chongqing; and of course his wife, Soong Mayling. This reliance on a close circle of trusted associates was not just a matter of Chiang's aloof personality but an explicit aspect of his governing philosophy. He believed that effective governance required "trusting one's own" (*xin qi suo si*) and giving them authority within their areas of responsibility. If one were to rely on capable people from society, he believed, the result would be discord and obstruction as they formed self-interested bureaucratic

---

[111] Atcheson to Secretary of State, July 14 and September 17, 1943, *FRUS 1943*, 283–84, 340; Gauss to Secretary of State, October 14, 1943, *FRUS 1943*, 351–60; *SLGB* 52:480 (February 12, 1943) and 54:276–77 (August 11, 1943); Gong'anbu, *Tang Zong riji*, 380 (September 12, 1943).

cliques.[112] Beyond this small circle of trusted associates, Chiang repeatedly complained of his officials' "incompetence and stupidity."[113] In some cases, the problem probably was incompetence, but more commonly it was their failure to correctly discern and carry out Chiang's wishes. At one point he moaned, "Nobody understands my intentions."[114] Most importantly, Chiang demanded loyalty, and nothing was more apt to provoke his anger than signs of independence, which were inevitably interpreted as selfishness and arrogance. In these cases, the only way to regain the favor of the autocrat was to offer an abject apology.[115]

The problematic consequences of this style of governance based on personal relations, trust, and loyalty were illustrated in a dramatic confrontation in the fall of 1943. As noted above, Chiang Kai-shek had long been frustrated by his troubled relations with the American commander in China, General Joseph Stilwell. The two men openly despised each other, Stilwell describing Chiang as "a vacillating, tricky, undependable old scoundrel, who never keeps his word,"[116] and Chiang complaining of Stilwell's "stubbornness, stupidity, and despicable manners."[117] In the spring of 1943, Chiang actively pressed for Stilwell's removal, working through T.V. Soong and Mme. Chiang, who were both in Washington at the time. After Mme. Chiang's return, T.V. Soong aggressively continued the effort, using all his connections in Washington and eventually receiving Roosevelt's agreement to replace Stilwell.[118] Soong returned to Chongqing in

---

[112] Chiang Kai-shek diary, August 23, 1943. The *SLGB* version (54:363–64) changes this term to *qinxin* (亲信), avoiding the unorthodox endorsement of *si* (私). The alert reader will note the contrast to Abraham Lincoln's approach to governance described in Doris Kearns Goodwin, *Team of Rivals: The Political Genius of Abraham Lincoln* (New York: Simon and Schuster, 2012).

[113] *SLGB* 53:290 (April 27, 1943); cf. *SLGB* 52:228 (January 10), 301 (January 12), 54:240 (August 4).

[114] *SLGB* 53:430 (May 14, 1943).

[115] See Chiang's pleasure at Bai Chongxi's apology, *SLGB* 54:256–57 (August 8, 1943); cf. *SLGB* 53:126 (March 31), 54:345 (August 20), 55:717 (1943 annual review).

[116] Cited in Chennault, *Way of a Fighter*, 226.

[117] *SLGB* 53:686 (June 28, 1943); cf. *SLGB* 53:639–41 (June 18, 1943, cable to Mme. Chiang).

[118] *SLGB* 54:418–20 (T.V. Soong August 30 cable on meeting with Roosevelt), 532 (T.V. Soong September 15 cable on meeting with Hopkins), 607 (Soong September 29 cable on meeting with Roosevelt); see also T.V. Soong memoranda of May 10, August 20, and October 13, 1943, in T.V. Soong Papers, Box 60, Folios 3–4; *FRUS 1943*, 135–37.

Figure 1.4: Chiang Kai-shek, Mme. Chiang, and General Joseph W. Stilwell in 1942. *Source:* Joseph W. Stilwell Papers, Hoover Institution Archives.

October to join the meetings with the new commander of the China-Burma-India Theater, the dashing young British Lord Louis Mountbatten. In the meantime, however, Mme. Chiang was having second thoughts about the consequences of Stilwell's removal. Accordingly, together with her sister, the wife of T.V. Soong's rival H.H. Kung, minister of finance and acting head of the Executive Yuan, she began maneuvering to save the general's career.[119]

In many ways, T.V. Soong was the odd man out in Chiang Kai-shek's inner circle. Wealthy, intelligent, Harvard-educated, with a firm grasp of economics (he had overseen the modernization of China's currency and banking system in the 1930s), he was thoroughly Westernized in his man-

---

[119] Tuchman, *Stilwell and the American Experience*, 388–95; Qi Xisheng, *Jianba nuzhang*, 386–408; Davies, *China Hand*, 170–73. T.V. Soong returned on October 11, the day after Chiang's inauguration, and one wonders if Chiang might have been irritated that Soong had not hurried to arrive in time for the ceremony (*SLGB* 55:84 [October 11, 1943]).

ners. He wore expensive Western suits, preferred Western food, and typically addressed his Foreign Ministry associates in English. Simplistic
American accounts analyzed Chongqing politics as a contest between the
"modern" T.V. Soong and the "reactionary" H.H. Kung, the latter condemned as much for his Chinese scholar's gown as his corruption.[120]
Soong had been extraordinarily successful in Washington, lobbying for
aid for China, gaining support for Chennault in his battles with Stilwell,
and now getting Roosevelt's agreement to replace Stilwell. Kung, by contrast, was wildly unpopular, and stories of his family's extravagance and
his own corruption constantly circulated in both Chongqing and the
provinces.[121]

For reasons that are not clear, relations between Chiang and his wife
were not entirely harmonious after her return from the United States. By
August, she was staying in the nearby house of her sister, the wife of H.H.
Kung, returning only briefly in the evening for dinner with the Generalissimo.[122] This made it easier, in September, for the two sisters to work actively against Stilwell's recall, meeting several times with him and convincing him that "they [were] a pair of fighters." According to Stilwell,
"May [Soong Mayling] let out that she has a hell of a life with Peanut: no
one else will tell him the truth so she is constantly at him with disagree-
able news."[123] Clearly the two women were playing a desperate game, and
there is some evidence that their determination was motivated, in part, by
perceived threats to H.H. Kung's position.[124]

The whole affair finally came to a head with T.V. Soong's return to
Chongqing in mid-October. There he continued to spearhead the campaign to remove Stilwell, even translating for Chiang Kai-shek in the first

---

[120] Joseph W. Alsop with Adam Platt, *"I've Seen the Best of It": Memoirs* (New York:
W.W. Norton, 1992), 162–63, 213; Wu, Huang, and Liu, *Wu Guozhen zhuan*, 371–76.

[121] Gong'anbu, *Tang Zong riji*, 252 (January 22, 1942), 327–28 (December 29, 1942);
Peck, *Two Kinds of Time*, 357–60, 556.

[122] Gong'anbu, *Tang Zong riji*, 373 (August 15, 1943), 384 (October 3), 387 (October
16). For a taste of the rumors circulating in Chongqing regarding the Chiangs' domestic
discord, see John S. Service, "Domestic Troubles in the Chiang Household," May 10, 1944,
in Esherick, *Lost Chance in China*, 93–96.

[123] White, *Stilwell Papers*, 223–38, quotes from 229, 232.

[124] Gong'anbu, *Tang Zong riji*, 373 (August 15, 1943).

meetings with the American general Brehon Somervell about replacing Stilwell. Suddenly the whole deal fell apart. Chiang's own account is noteworthy:

> On the question of whether or not to remove Stilwell, my intent was to follow the analysis of October 15 [to state my clear objections to Stilwell but leave the decision to the United States]. In the first two meetings with Somervell, I proceeded in this way to effect the changes necessary to achieve our objectives. But T.V. insisted on sticking to his own hatred of Stilwell and his personal opinions. So in translating he did not convey my views. In his telling, Stilwell would definitely have to be removed. After Somervell left, I considered carefully and decided to endeavor to save the situation and make a 180 degree turn.

Mme. Chiang was sent to warn Stilwell of his fate unless he offered a sincere apology and promised to reform. This was done, and the next day Chiang met Somervell to announce the reversal.[125] Stilwell had dodged another bullet and would stay on for another year before one final crisis in U.S.-China relations would at last bring about his removal. T.V. Soong was not so lucky. On the morning after Stilwell made his apology, Soong held a stormy meeting with the Generalissimo in which both sides lost their tempers, Chiang smashed teacups, and T.V. ended up in disgrace, banned from attending the Cairo Conference, removed from power, and allowed to return only months later when friends found someone with better Chinese than his own to pen an appropriately contrite apology.[126]

Two points are particularly notable in this incident. First, T.V. Soong's crime had been to adhere to his own position—though in this case, the position was originally Chiang's own. The problem was, in presenting it to

---

[125] *SLGB* 55:106–23 (October 15–17, 1943), quoted passage pp. 118–19.

[126] Wu, Huang, and Liu, *Wu Guozhen zhuan*, 399–406; Alsop with Platt, *"I've Seen the Best of It,"* 223–27; *SLGB* 55:122 (October 18, 1943) cleans up the diary a little, changing Chiang's order that Song "get the hell out" (*gundan*) to "leave" (*likai*); Gong'anbu, *Tang Zong riji*, 386 (October 16, 1943).

the American representative, Soong had spoken more forcefully than Chiang wished: Chiang had long hoped that expressing his dissatisfaction with Stilwell would suffice to persuade Roosevelt to remove him. He was, after all, used to a politics in which subordinates readily discerned his position and adopted it as their own. Soong was wiser to American ways and recognized the need for a more direct statement of Chiang's wishes. When they had their final fight, Soong protested that his failing was that he had been "too loyal" in carrying out Chiang's wishes, but this only further enraged the Generalissimo.[127] Chiang compared Soong's behavior to an obscure incident in 1921 when Sun Yat-sen's lieutenant Hu Hanmin had deliberately ignored several of Sun's orders that he deemed unwise. Sun had forgiven Hu and later entrusted him with even more important positions. But Chiang took a dimmer view of the incident, saying that Soong's conduct in 1943 threatened "another catastrophe like 1921." Soong was "holding his own personal views and treating our party-state's foreign policy like his personal plaything."[128] Chiang so identified himself with the Chinese nation that views even slightly different from his own were regarded as self-interested and contrary to the national interest.

Second, the lesson that Chiang drew from his sudden change of mind was that "in deciding and changing policy, success or failure depends completely on the last five minutes."[129] Although the Allies were certainly glad that Stilwell, a trusted commander for all his faults, would remain in China to direct the Burma campaign, the process that led to this result could hardly have encouraged them. One constant complaint against the Generalissimo was his unpredictability, his indecision, his tendency to vacillate. Now, on the eve of the Cairo Conference, Chiang had not only removed T.V. Soong, his most experienced foreign affairs deputy, he had changed his stance "180 degrees" in successive conversations with Somervell and raised last-minute policy change to the status of an essential governing principle.

---

[127] *SLGB* 55:122 (October 18, 1943).

[128] *SLGB* 55:119–20, 122 (October 17, 18, 1943).

[129] *SLGB* 55:118 (and again, 121) (October 17, 1943); cf. Huang, "Chiang Kai-shek and His Diary," 105 (diary entry of April 2, 1939).

CAIRO

Hsiao-ting Lin has provided an excellent discussion of Chiang Kai-shek at the Cairo Conference (chapter 13), so it is not necessary to repeat the narrative here. Nonetheless, the conference encapsulated so many of the successes and failings of 1943 that a few words on the issues raised in this prologue are required. Most importantly, one must admit the historic significance of including China among the Great Powers in 1943. From the perspective of the present, it seems obvious that China should be considered a Great Power, but in the early twentieth century, poor, weak, and internally divided China certainly did not look like a Great Power. In this respect, Roosevelt's insistence that China's size and the energy of its people made its rise in the postwar world inevitable was an act of considerable foresight. Churchill, of course, resisted, describing China as a "faggot vote" for the United States in the United Nations; and Stalin, understandably given his own nation's sacrifices, thought China had not fought well enough to deserve such recognition.[130]

We should not imagine that it was only prescience or altruism that drove Roosevelt to treat China in this way. As FDR told his son after his first meeting with Chiang in Cairo, "The job in China can be boiled down to one essential: China must be kept in the war, tieing [*sic*] up Japanese soldiers."[131] To this end, it was essential to boost Chinese morale. Unable to supply much material assistance over the perilous Hump lifeline, the United States offered symbolic gestures: the termination of the "unequal treaties," the inclusion of China in the Four Powers, and now the summit in Cairo.[132] At Cairo, the Allies could make cost-free promises that would be welcome to China and boost Chiang's standing—most notably the return of Taiwan and Manchuria. They could pose for the photographs of Roosevelt, Churchill, and Chiang—photos that are perhaps the most en-

---

[130] Sainsbury, *Turning Point*, 61–62, 138–39, 143–47; Bohlen minutes on Roosevelt-Stalin conversations at Tehran, *FRUS Cairo*, 484, 530–31, 566. American readers should be alerted that the term "faggot vote" is not a homophobic slur. See "What Is Faggot Votes?," Law Dictionary, accessed February 2, 2014, http://thelawdictionary.org/faggot-votes/.

[131] Elliott Roosevelt, *As He Saw It* (New York: Duell, Sloan and Pearce, 1946), 143.

[132] Brown memorandum, May 21, 1943, *FRUS 1943*, 55.

during legacy of the conference. Indeed, in reading the official conference record, one gets the impression that, putting aside the heated debates over the Burma campaign, for Roosevelt the confab was largely about atmospherics and taking the measure of Chiang Kai-shek. In contrast to the Tehran Conference with Stalin that would follow, the Cairo record is incredibly sparse, with no American minutes on Roosevelt's key conversations with Chiang.[133]

As for the measure of Chiang, the inescapable conclusion is that he came off poorly. Above all, he was seen as indecisive, vacillating, constantly changing his mind.[134] Some have blamed this on Mme. Chiang's translation,[135] but it must be remembered that T.V. Soong was banned from the conference precisely for his failure to properly interpret the Generalissimo's intentions. Mme. Chiang would not have made the same mistake. The more plausible explanation is that the Americans and British had been meeting in these strategic conferences for almost two years. They knew how to debate and bargain with each other and did so in their native language. The Chinese were outsiders in this club. Chiang was utterly unused to negotiation among equals and felt limited by his poor English.[136] In his first summit outing, he was simply not up to the task.[137]

His stock would fall even further after Churchill and Roosevelt met with Stalin. In contrast to Chiang's "characteristic myopia" in seeing Burma as the key to the struggle for Asia, Stalin quickly appreciated the conflicting demands of the Burma campaign, the Pacific War, Mediterranean options, and the planned invasion of northern France. Indeed, the British chief of staff found Stalin a better strategic thinker than either Roosevelt or Churchill.[138] This judgment was no doubt colored by the fact

---

[133] *FRUS Cairo*, passim, but esp. 322–23, 334–35. At Tehran, Charles Bohlen from the State Department translated and left detailed minutes and analysis of the meetings with Stalin, but at Cairo, Mme. Chiang translated, and no State Department representative was present. See also Davies, *China Hand*, 149–51.

[134] Ronald Ian Heiferman, *The Cairo Conference of 1943: Roosevelt, Churchill, Chiang Kai-shek and Madame Chiang* (Jefferson, NC: McFarland, 2011), 72–102; Sainsbury, *Turning Point*, 165–216; *FRUS Cairo*, 338–50.

[135] Taylor, *Generalissimo*, 248–50.

[136] *SLGB* 55:470 (November 23, 1943).

[137] Qi Xisheng, *Jianba nuzhang*, 412–13; Davies, *China Hand*, 144–47.

[138] Sainsbury, *Turning Point*, 184, 226.

that Russia and Britain agreed on the low priority of the Burma campaign. More importantly, when Stalin repeated his promise to enter the war against Japan once Germany was defeated, an alternative was provided to a costly campaign through the jungles of Burma.[139] In the run-up to Cairo, Chiang Kai-shek had insisted that he meet Roosevelt before the president met Stalin.[140] Obviously he wanted to state his case to Roosevelt first, but the unhappy result was that Stalin got the last word on the critical strategic issues of the war.

In September, when Chiang abandoned his plan to solve the Communist problem by force, he resolved to do his utmost to disabuse his American allies of any illusions they had of the CCP as a potential partner in the war against Japan.[141] The need for this had been brought to him forcefully when, on the first day of the Guomindang Central Executive Committee meetings that would decide policy toward the Communists, Stilwell had presented him a military plan that involved a combined Communist-Nationalist offensive in north China.[142] In Chiang's planning for Cairo, relations with the Communists were a matter that he expected the Americans to raise, and there is no question that they came up in the Generalissimo's private talks with the president. The precise nature of those conversations is not known, but Roosevelt told his son Elliott, who accompanied FDR to Cairo, "Chiang would have us believe that the Chinese Communists were doing nothing against the Japanese. Again, we know differently."[143] So Chiang, as he intended, had used the opportunity to press his argument that the Communists were not, in fact, resisting Japan.

Roosevelt, obviously, was not convinced. The predicament that this presented for Chiang was that whether or not the Communists were resisting Japan was a matter of fact that could be investigated. This is precisely what the Americans started requesting soon after the conference in

---

[139] Heiferman, *Cairo Conference*, 121–28; Sainsbury, *Turning Point*, 110, 250.

[140] *SLGB* 53:594–95 (June 9, 1943), 55:38 (October 7, 1943).

[141] See also Hurley to Roosevelt, November 20, 1943, *FRUS 1943*, 163–66.

[142] *SLGB* 54:519 (Weekly review, September 12, 1943). Naturally, Stilwell's suggestion only confirmed Chiang's conviction that Stilwell was a "despicable, stupid little man." See also Stilwell diary, October 5, 1943, Stilwell Papers, Box 39, Folder 10.

[143] Roosevelt, *As He Saw It*, 163.

Cairo: permission to send a mission to Yan'an to better understand the Communist movement. Eventually, in June 1944, Chiang was forced to agree, and the Dixie Mission of U.S. military and foreign service experts was sent to investigate the Communist resistance. Their reports were uniformly favorable to the Communists, and while there has been much subsequent debate on whether the American observers were hoodwinked by their Communist hosts, the undeniable fact is that the Dixie Mission together with simultaneous visits by Chinese and Western newsmen brought back reports of a powerful political and military movement growing in north China and independent of Chiang's control. Their reports left no doubt that China's destiny no longer lay exclusively in Chiang Kai-shek's hands.[144]

The approval of the Dixie Mission came just as Chiang's own troops were reeling before Japan's Ichigo offensive. Stilwell had long argued that if Chennault was successful in his air offensive against Japanese supply lines, Japan would respond by taking the Chinese airfields. Chiang Kai-shek promised that his ground forces could defend the airfields,[145] but he was wrong. The Japanese rolled over his forces and opened a land corridor that stretched all the way from Korea and northeast China to Vietnam and Southeast Asia. Chiang lost 750,000 men in the fight, and his prestige suffered a crushing blow.[146] In domestic politics, as discussed in chapter 8, his constitutional preparations were overtaken by growing support for the rival Communist call for a coalition government—an idea that Roosevelt had also pressed at Cairo.[147] In the famous words of an earlier era, "Things fall apart; the centre cannot hold."[148] And in many respects, the seeds for the collapse were planted in 1943.

---

[144] David D. Barrett, *Dixie Mission: The United States Army Observer Group in Yenan, 1944* (Berkeley: University of California Center for Chinese Studies, 1970); Esherick, *Lost Chance in China*; Kenneth E. Shewmaker, *Americans and Chinese Communists, 1927–1945: A Persuading Encounter* (Ithaca, NY: Cornell University Press, 1971).

[145] *SLGB* 53:312 (April 30, 1943), 331–32 (May 1, 1943).

[146] Peattie, Drea, and van de Ven, *Battle for China*, 392–418. For contemporary accounts, see White and Jacoby, *Thunder out of China*, 179–98; Peck, *Two Kinds of Time*, 551–83.

[147] Roosevelt, *As He Saw It*, 164.

[148] William Butler Yeats, "The Second Coming," in *Selected Poems and Four Plays of William Butler Yeats*, ed. M.L. Rosenthal (New York: Scribner Paperback Poetry, 1996) 89–90.

2

Madame Chiang's Visit to America

GRACE C. HUANG

After the Japanese bombing of Pearl Harbor in December 1941, the United States and China formalized their alliance by signing the Declaration of the United Nations on January 1, 1942, along with twenty-four other countries. This group of signatories now regarded China as one of the four Great Powers of the war. Franklin Roosevelt and his administration, by treating China as an equal ally in the war, were also in keeping with the internationalist "one world" philosophy championed by Wendell Willkie, who had lost the presidential election to Roosevelt in 1940 but was invited by Roosevelt to serve as his personal representative abroad to signal U.S. unity regarding the war effort.[1] Yet this sudden elevation of China's status, according to Zhang Baijia, would nevertheless "create excessive expectations in both countries and obscure many difficulties."[2] This gap between expectations and self-interest was all too evident in the

---

[1] Willkie accepted the status of personal representative rather than ambassador-at-large because it gave him official status without the constraints on his freedom of expression. See Steve Neal, *Dark Horse: A Biography of Wendell Willkie* (Lawrence: University Press of Kansas, 1989), 232, 236.

[2] Zhang Baijia, "China's Quest for Foreign Military Aid," in *The Battle for China: Essays on the Military History of the Sino-Japanese War of 1937–1945*, ed. Mark Peattie, Edward Drea, and Hans van de Ven (Stanford, CA: Stanford University Press, 2010), 294.

1943 visit of Mme. Chiang Kai-shek (Song Meiling) to America a year later.

In the wake of Pearl Harbor, advisors in Roosevelt's administration felt that a visit by Mme. Chiang would signal to the world and the American public that the U.S. alliance with China could form a viable alternative to Japan's vision of pan-Asian unity. Not only was she the wife of China's leader, Generalissimo Chiang Kai-shek, but her extensive U.S. education would allow her to connect easily with the American public. In a letter to Mme. Chiang in 1942, Eleanor Roosevelt invited her to the White House, stating that she and Franklin felt that her visit would enable them to get to know her better, become more familiar with China's problems, and "serve the ends of publicity" by demonstrating the close bond between China and the United States to the American public. During Willkie's visit to China at the end of 1942, he enthusiastically pressed family members to encourage Mme. Chiang to visit, calling her the "perfect ambassador."[3] Coupled with Mme. Chiang's desire to consult doctors in the United States about her health, she was persuaded in favor of a visit.

Measured by Eleanor's goal of serving the ends of publicity, Mme. Chiang's trip appeared to exceed all expectations. According to *Life* magazine, on February 19, 1943, Mme. Chiang "captivated," "amazed," and "dizzied" members of the U.S. Congress in back-to-back speeches to the Senate and then the House "without a single bobble or ill-timed pause, in a rich, concise voice that clipped off the words better than most Americans can pronounce them."[4] After her speech, a House member stood up to say that he would introduce a bill, which passed by the end of the year, to repeal the Chinese Exclusion Act of 1882.[5] By her tour's end two months later, she was a celebrity, received by enthusiastic crowds in New York, Boston, Chicago, San Francisco, and Hollywood. Her stage presence

[3] Wendell L. Willkie, *One World* (New York: Simon and Schuster, 1943), 141.

[4] Frank McNaughton, "Mme. Chiang in the U.S. Capitol," *Life*, March 8, 1943, Henry S. Evans, clippings file, Hoover Institution Archives, Stanford, California.

[5] Hannah Pakula, *The Last Empress: Madame Chiang Kai-shek and the Birth of Modern China* (New York: Simon and Schuster, 2010), 422.

on tour, her reception in the media, and the recent American and British renunciation of the unequal treaties all projected a picture of China joining the Allied community on an equal footing and laid to rest its image as the "sick man of Asia."

With the support of the American media and the Roosevelt administration, Mme. Chiang presented herself to the American public as a confident, cosmopolitan Chinese woman, suggesting that by extension, the Sino-American alliance was a friendship between equals and that Americans could embrace the Chiangs as the benevolent and popular rulers of China. Nonetheless, this chapter contends that while making a persuasive impression upon the American public as the first lady of a junior Great Power following in the footsteps of the United States, Mme. Chiang's visit would have unintended consequences. Most importantly, the success of the trip further inflated what John Fairbank later described as the Free China bubble, when Americans and, even more troubling, Chiang Kaishek and Mme. Chiang largely ignored the shortcomings and disturbing trends emerging within Chiang's Nationalist regime. As we shall see, this bubble also led to excessive expectations on both sides of the alliance: China felt that it deserved more aid from the United States for the war effort, and the U.S. government felt no need to meet China's request even as citizens across the United States opened their pocketbooks to help. Another unintended consequence, the chapter argues, was that the trip also inflated Mme. Chiang's own sense of power. She not only acted more aggressively in issues related to America upon her return to China, which would have important consequences for Sino-American relations, but appeared to undergo a change of heart within herself, leading to a more pessimistic assessment of China's fate. In essence, Mme. Chiang's tour can be viewed as a high point in both China's and the Chiangs' international prestige, but one that neither would be able to sustain for long. To understand this great irony of the tour, this investigation focuses specifically on how her deployment of gender, race, and democratic values contributed both to her success in improving China's status in the world and to masking tensions within the Sino-American alliance and contradictions in the Chiang leadership that would later lead to the decline of both.

Mme. Chiang, the American Media, and the Sino-American Relationship

Willkie, confident that Mme. Chiang's visit would take the United States by storm, attempted to persuade Mme. Chiang and her family to accept Eleanor Roosevelt's invitation: "Someone from this section with brains and persuasiveness and moral force must help educate us about China. ... We would listen to her as to no one else."[6] Indeed, the oratorical and inter-personal skills that she brought to this task and her determination to ensure that her health issues would not get in the way of her public message successfully portrayed China as a robust country with which Americans could happily ally.

Although the sheer force of her personality would serve Sino-U.S. relations well, the American media helped magnify her effectiveness by representing China as a country that was following in America's democratic footsteps. Henry R. Luce, editor of the widely read and influential *Time* and *Life* magazines, clearly viewed China as a vessel for American evangelicalism and economic cooperation.[7] He also saw the Chiangs as ideal Christian leaders and put them on the cover of *Time* in 1937 as International Man and Wife of the Year. His paternalistic understanding of China resonated with a broader American mission to spread liberty and democracy to the world.[8] Mme. Chiang's background squared easily with Luce's view. Not only had her father traveled to America at the age of fifteen and eventually received a theology degree from Vanderbilt University in 1885, but Mme. Chiang and her siblings also all received American educations. Mme. Chiang, the fourth of six children, began her education in America at the age of nine and graduated from Wellesley at nineteen. Her English was so fluent that upon her return to China, she had to re-learn Chinese.[9] Her excellent command of English, familiarity with Amer-

---

[6] Willkie, *One World*, 141.

[7] T. Christopher Jespersen, *American Images of China, 1931–1949* (Stanford, CA: Stanford University Press, 1999), 1.

[8] Ibid., 25, 87.

[9] Laura Tyson Li, *Madame Chiang Kai-shek: China's Eternal First Lady* (New York: Grove Press, 2007), 19, 26–43.

Figure 2.1: Madame Chiang addresses House of Representatives from the speaker's rostrum. Editorial, *LIFE*, March 1, 1943. Online at http://cbi-theater-1 .home.comcast.net/~cbi-theater-1/life030143/life030143.html, accessed June 16, 2015.

ican culture, and Christian faith appeared to narrow the differences between the two countries. Indeed, even before Mme. Chiang uttered a single public word on American soil, she had already drawn significant attention from the American public. Despite opening her tour in "icebox frosty" February conditions, nearly 6,000 requests for tickets were received to fill the 673 available seats in the House galleries in anticipation of her speeches to the U.S. Congress.[10]

In her addresses to Congress, Mme. Chiang personified the Sino-American bond and persuasively argued that America needed to aid China by drawing on its understanding of American political culture. In her opening salutations, Mme. Chiang immediately underlined her knowledge of the American democratic process by making clear that her intended audience was not simply the legislators but the American people at large, announcing to the Senate that she was "literally speaking to the American people" and saying to the House, "I am overwhelmed by the warmth and spontaneity of the welcome of the American people, of whom you are the representatives."[11]

Unafraid to present an agenda that differed from that of the American president, Mme. Chiang urged America to adopt an Asia First strategy for fighting the war instead of the administration's Europe First policy. To persuade Congress, she reminded the members of the friendship between China and America with the story of one of General Doolittle's aviators who had been forced to bail out in the interior of China after a bombing run in Tokyo. The downed airman was greeted by Chinese villagers who "laughed and almost hugged him, and greeted him like a long lost brother," making him feel like "he had come home when he saw our people" despite never having been to China before. Like this American serviceman in China, Mme. Chiang told members of Congress, she too felt that she was coming home on this trip to America. Through such anecdotes, she infused personal warmth and not just political calculation into the U.S.-China relationship.[12]

Mme. Chiang also advocated for a global, universalist, and humanist point of view before Congress, declaring that "peace should not be punitive in spirit and should not be provincial or nationalistic or even continental in concept, but universal in scope and humanitarian in action, for

---

[10] McNaughton, "Mme. Chiang in the U.S. Capitol."

[11] "Mme. Chiang, House Speech." The text of Mme. Chiang's speeches to both the House and Senate appeared in the *New York Times*, February 19, 1943, 4, hereafter cited as "House Speech" or "Senate Speech."

[12] Mme. Chiang, "Senate Speech."

modern science has so annihilated distance that what affects one people must of necessity affect all other people."[13] With vivid language highlighting mutual friendship and universal values, Mme. Chiang's ultimate goal was to urge Congress and the American people to provide China with military aid and support. Just as the previous Congress had declared war on the Japanese aggressors, she asserted, the job of the current Congress was to "help win the war and create and uphold a lasting peace."[14]

Time's Washington correspondent, Frank McNaughton, observed that members of Congress, many of whom were skilled orators themselves, believed that Mme. Chiang's delivery had been unequaled in twenty years.[15] Following his wife's tour closely from China, her husband, delighted by her performance, wrote in his diary, "The warm reception by the audience of Congress has been unprecedented. Ten years of hardship to perfect her scholarly and ethical endeavors are realized today, finally fulfilling her life's aspiration."[16] In important ways, this personal apogee in Mme. Chiang's career coincided with the high point of American perceptions of China's significance on the international stage.

Just as forthright as she had been in her speech to Congress, Mme. Chiang continued to hold her own during an exchange with Roosevelt at a joint press conference the following day. In response to a reporter's criticism that China could be using more of its manpower in the war effort, Mme. Chiang replied that more men could fight if more munitions were sent over. Roosevelt then explained that America would supply its ally with such support "just as fast as the Lord will let us," to which Mme. Chiang quickly rejoined, "The Lord helps those who help themselves." Her response elicited much laughter in the room and was widely reported in the papers.[17] Via humor and wit, Mme. Chiang demonstrated her ease in going head to head with a great power and that by extension, China was rightly a partner of equal standing. (Her husband was less amused by

---

[13] Mme. Chiang, "House Speech."

[14] Ibid.

[15] McNaughton, "Mme. Chiang in the U.S. Capitol."

[16] Chiang Kai-shek diary, February 20, 1943, Box 43, Folder 1, Hoover Institution Archives, Stanford, California.

[17] "Press Conference Number 881," in *Complete Presidential Press Conferences of Franklin D. Roosevelt*, vol. 21, February 19, 1943, 165, 168.

the exchange, writing in his diary that the president's "words were close to ludicrous, making excuses" to avoid a direct commitment for American aid to China, although he was unsure "if his meaning was truly like this."[18])

Mme. Chiang next traveled to New York, where she addressed a crowd of 17,000 at Madison Square Garden and an audience of 3,000 Chinese Americans at Carnegie Hall. In Boston, she addressed her alma mater, Wellesley. Her next stop was Chicago, followed by San Francisco and finally Los Angeles, where Henry Luce and David O. Selznick, producer of *Gone with the Wind*, gave Mme. Chiang a Hollywood-style welcome, including a parade and reception attended by 200 Hollywood stars in her honor.[19] Her speech on April 4 at the Hollywood Bowl to 30,000 people, the largest audience of her tour, marked the end of her speaking tour.

Several of Mme. Chiang's qualities reinforced her portrayal of China as an emerging Great Power. As noted earlier, she had impeccable English diction and an eloquence that sent reporters scrambling for their dictionaries. The three-time Pulitzer prize–winning Carl Sandburg praised Mme. Chiang as a natural orator, "a marvel at timing her pauses and making each word count in relation to what goes before and comes after. Yet she doesn't know how she does it any more than Ty Cobb knew which one of his eleven ways of sliding to second he was using."[20] Another reporter remarked that after having trouble understanding Willkie's Midwestern accent as he was introducing Mme. Chiang at Madison Square Garden, he was relieved when Mme. Chiang finally began speaking, as she had the "finest diction America has heard through the air."[21]

Another strength was her knowledge of American history. As one letter to the editor noted, "Madame Chiang knows more about American history than most Americans; speaks better American than most Americans; understands the genius of American liberty better than most Amer-

[18] Chiang Kai-shek diary, February 21, 1943, Box 43, Folder 1.

[19] Jespersen, *American Images*, 101–2.

[20] Carl Sandburg, "Sandburg: 'Mayling' Chiang Co-operation and Humility," *Galesburg Post*, March 18, 1943, Henry S. Evans, clippings file.

[21] Herb Graffis, "Graffis: Mme. Chiang, Teacher," *Chicago Times*, March 5, 1943, Henry S. Evans, clippings file.

Figure 2.2: A crowd of 20,000 gathered in the Chicago Stadium to hear Mme. Chiang Kai-shek. A ticket stub for entry is shown in the corner, dated March 13, 1943. *Source* (stadium): Kaufman & Fabry photograph, Henry S. Evans, clippings file, Hoover Institution Archives, Stanford, California. *Source* (ticket stub): Henry S. Evans, clippings file, Hoover Institution Archives, Stanford, California..

icans. I know not what course others may take, but for me I'm going to learn more about my country. This I owe to Madame Chiang—a great teacher."[22]

Another much-praised personal quality was her excellent memory for people, which allowed her to personalize her interaction with others and imbue the alliance with a sense of warmth. In one reported incident, she was on her way to a waiting car after receiving a key to Chicago from the mayor when she spotted in the crowd a classmate from Wellesley whom she had not seen in twenty-six years. Calling out to her classmate by her nickname, Rommie, and grasping her hand for a minute before she was pressed forward toward the waiting car moved her former classmate to tears.[23] Another newspaper account noted that at a Hollywood reception for two hundred film folk, Mme. Chiang was able to say something personal to almost every individual, such as asking after Joan Bennett's children and thanking Claudette Colbert for reading her letter to American children on a China relief broadcast.[24]

Americans were also impressed by her ability to persevere through the tour despite suffering from severe health problems. Mme. Chiang had taken advantage of her American visit to consult American doctors regarding longstanding health problems, including debilitating outbreaks of hives, severe abdominal pain, and sinus problems. Immediately upon her arrival in the country on November 27, 1942, Mme. Chiang had checked into New York Presbyterian Hospital, where she convalesced until early February 1943. Her condition was serious enough that she was forced to decline several invitations, such as one to receive an honorary degree from Princeton University.[25] Upon her release, her physician, Dr. Robert Loeb, urged her to maintain a light schedule to prevent a relapse.[26]

---

[22] "Madame Chiang" [Letter to the editor], *Chicago Times*, March 2, 1943, Henry S. Evans, clippings file.

[23] Eddie Doherty, "Mme. Chiang Thrills Throng; Makes Dull Day Memorable," *Chicago Sun*, March 20, 1943, Henry S. Evans, clippings file.

[24] Marjorie Driscoll, "Mme. Chiang Chats with Screen Stars," *Los Angeles Examiner*, April 2, 1943, Henry S. Evans, clippings file.

[25] "Department of State: Division of Foreign Affairs, Memorandum of Conversation," February 16, 1943, Stanley K. Hornbeck, Box 49, Folder 1 of 4, Chiang Kai-shek and Mme. Chiang, Hoover Institution Archives, Stanford, California.

[26] Li, *Madame Chiang Kai-shek*, 207.

But despite her doctor's vigorous objections, Mme. Chiang kept up a grueling schedule on her American tour. At times, her illness led to cancelations and delays. She arrived in Chicago a week later than planned, for instance, and had to present a battle flag to representatives of Chinese air cadets, who were in training at Thunderbird, Arizona, while convalescing in her hotel suite in Los Angeles. Yet according to the press coverage, her American audiences admired her efforts to soldier on.[27] The well-known celebrity gossip columnist Hedda Hopper, noting that Mme. Chiang sometimes appeared in pain when delivering her speeches, reported that her demonstration of self-discipline was such that, Hopper said, "For the first time since I've lived in Hollywood I've seen our personalities willing and anxious to take a back seat—to Mme. Chiang Kai-shek."[28] Although her husband's diaries revealed a twinge of guilt that he had "examined the matter carelessly and allowed her to struggle forward alone" despite her health, he nevertheless believed that her efforts would "result in a fine outcome for our country's future."[29]

Finally, virtually everyone responded to her beauty. During a reception at the Drake Hotel in Chicago, Mme. Chiang's entrance was reportedly met with applause and gasps of "Isn't she lovely!" and "Isn't she beautiful—much prettier than her pictures!" The society editor of the *Chicago Daily News*, June Parsons, felt that "no photograph could ever capture the charm of that friendly smile. ... She looks much sweeter, much more feminine than any camera has ever shown her."[30] Her sense of style also inspired American fashion designers such as Maurice Rentner, whose collection that summer included sprays of Chinese embroidered flowers and black silk braids.[31]

Despite the numerous tensions simmering below the surface of Sino-American relations, Mme. Chiang's public persona suggested equal stand-

---

[27] E.g., wire photo, *Kansas City Star*, April 7, 1943, Henry S. Evans, clippings file.

[28] Hedda Hopper, "Super Woman," *Chicago Tribune*, April 2, 1943, Henry S. Evans, clippings file.

[29] Chiang Kai-shek diary, March 2, 1943, Box 43, Folder 2.

[30] June Parsons, "Mme. Chiang Even Lovelier Than Her Pictures Show, Guests at Reception Find," *Chicago Daily News*, March 20, 1943, Henry S. Evans, clippings file.

[31] Susan Barrett, "ChinaNote: Introduced by Rentner," *Chicago Sun*, March 29, 1943, Henry S. Evans, clippings file.

ing with those with whom she interacted, and, by extension, of China with the other members of the alliance. Perhaps the editor of the *Chicago Sun Times*, Turner Catledge, summed up her representation of China best: "Chicago loves Mme. Chiang, above all, because it honors China—the immense sacrifice and courage of China in our war; the key role China has played and the increasing role she means to play for victory; and the 20th century Chinese revolution which ... made it possible for women to be leaders in their country's fight for freedom, a fact of which Mme. Chiang is a symbol."[32] To understand why this image of Mme. Chiang, China, and the Chinese leadership would not withstand prolonged scrutiny by Americans and Chinese alike, we must examine tensions within her deployment of gender, race, and democratic values, and their eventual consequences for the Sino-American alliance.

MME. CHIANG'S INSPIRED NAVIGATION OF GENDER EXPECTATIONS

Although Mme. Chiang's gender might have communicated a subordinate status to the American public and policymakers, she deftly circumvented many of the constraints typically imposed by gender. Despite the paternalistic attitudes of the period, Mme. Chiang's savvy deployment of gender further reinforced the credibility of her portrayal of China as an equal partner and led by a progressive Chinese couple.

According to T. Christopher Jespersen's study of American images of China, Mme. Chiang, as only the second woman in history to address Congress (the first being Queen Wilhelmina of the Netherlands), was perceived by American women from all walks of life as someone who represented the potential for where gendered relations could go.[33] Eleanor Roosevelt, for instance, felt that Mme. Chiang's reception in Congress "marked the recognition of a woman who through her own personality and her own service, has achieved a place in the world, not merely as a wife

---

[32] Turner Catledge, "Why Chicago Loves Her," *Chicago Sun*, March 21, 1943, Henry S. Evans, clippings file.

[33] Jespersen, *American Images*, 97.

… but as a representative of her people."[34] At the other end of the social spectrum, old Mrs. Moy of Chicago's Chinatown told a reporter that Mme. Chiang's visit finally gave her the courage to wear the "newest fashion" from China, making her feel "emancipated" and as belonging to the "New China."[35]

Mme. Chiang's personal relationship with her husband also appeared congruent with her public persona and her projection of the progressive nature of the Chiangs' reign over China. From the beginning of her marriage, according to biographers, Mme. Chiang insisted upon maintaining a degree of autonomy. Approximately a month after their marriage, for instance, Mme. Chiang wrote to her college classmate, Emma Mills, "Marriage should [not] erase or absorb one's individuality. For this reason I want to be myself, and not as the General's wife."[36] Although during the early years of their marriage Mme. Chiang avoided the spotlight and appeared in public only with Chiang, she eventually came into her own as a public figure in China, leading fund-raising campaigns for a military hospital and establishing schools for the "warphans" of Chiang's soldiers. Her persistent efforts to ensure some autonomy within her marriage was no doubt helped by her education in America and the prominence of her birth family.

Particularly in the area of Sino-American relations, Mme. Chiang was a true partner with her husband. Working on behalf of Chiang during her visit, she translated his intentions in ways that would resonate with American audiences. In her speech to Congress, Chiang had instructed her to emphasize the five points of traditional friendship between China and America, the peril of Japanese ambitions, and the importance of strong leaders like Washington, Lincoln, Jesus, Confucius, and Sun Yat-sen.[37] Rather than slavishly list the Generalissimo's points, however, Mme. Chiang brought his message to life. Instead of simply reminding Congress

---

[34] Rochelle Chadakoff, ed., *Eleanor Roosevelt's My Day* (New York: Pharos, 1989), 283.

[35] Rose Hum Lee, "Chinatown Welcomes Madame Chiang," *China Monthly*, June 1943, 21.

[36] Thomas A. DeLong, *Madame Chiang Kai-shek and Miss Emma Mills: China's First Lady and Her American Friend* (Jefferson, NC: McFarland, 2007), 77, quoted in Pakula, *The Last Empress*, 184.

[37] Pakula, *The Last Empress*, 420.

of the dangers of Japan's ambitions, she deftly wielded her words and understanding of Western culture to make the point memorable: it was not in Congress's interest, she declared, to "allow Japan to continue not only as a vital potential threat but as a waiting sword of Damocles, ready to descend at a moment's notice."[38]

Although some China watchers, such as Owen Lattimore, a personal adviser to Chiang, had their doubts about how much clout Mme. Chiang had in domestic affairs,[39] she appears to have been one of Chiang's more important advisors. She was indisputably part of the inner circle of family advisers that included her siblings, T.V. Soong (Song Ziwen) and Mme. Kung (Song Ailing), and brother-in-law, H.H. Kung (Kong Xiangxi).[40] Although Mme. Chiang was no coequal in every aspect of Chiang's rule, at least in the area of Sino-American relations she played an active, assertive, and sometimes independent role from her husband. Indeed, she was probably more effective as an international spokesperson than as a domestic adviser—and an even more important one after her U.S. tour than before.

Despite the widespread perception of Mme. Chiang as a powerful and progressive woman, other portrayals in the American press threatened to distract from the strong female presence that she projected during her visit. First, male reporters and observers tended to emphasize Mme. Chiang's sensuality to the point of diminishing her abilities. Regarding Mme. Chiang's physical appeal and choice of dress, for instance, *Newsweek* honed in on her choice of the traditional *qipao* or cheongsam dress, noting that "she wore a long, tight-fitting black gown, the skirt slit almost

---

[38] Mme. Chiang, "House Speech."

[39] Lattimore believed that Mme. Chiang had no influence over the planning or execution of Chiang's international or domestic policy, claiming that he and Chiang got down to business only after Mme. Chiang retired for the evening. Owen Lattimore, *China Memoirs: Chiang Kai-Shek and the War against Japan*, comp. Fujiko Isono (Tokyo: University of Tokyo Press, 1999), 138–39. In any case, an important exception in terms of domestic policy was her efforts during Chiang's kidnapping in 1936. Mme. Chiang risked her life to come to Xi'an, took part in high-level talks to secure his release, and likely played a critical role in saving Chiang's life. Samuel C. Chu, ed., *Madame Chiang Kai-shek and Her China* (Norwalk, CT: Eastbridge, 2005), 161.

[40] Lattimore, *China Memoirs*, 142.

to the knee," which John Gittings of the *Guardian* later observed "was, of course, as revealing of American orientalising fancies as of the garment that they praised."[41] Female reporters noted her physical appeal, too. As one claimed, "In a few short minutes, Mme. Chiang had Congress in the palm of her hand. ... Petite as an ivory figurine, Mme. Chiang stands barely five feet tall in her high-heeled American slippers."[42] But despite the sexism of such comments, the sensual and fashionable dimensions of her appearance ultimately appeared to work in her favor, attracting attention without obscuring her message. True to Luce's view of China as an aspirant to American-style democracy, the *Time* editorial response to her addresses before Congress asserted that Mme. Chiang was not just some "glamor-queen" whose goal was "to charm Congress away," but rather an eloquent and important voice from Asia "propounding the very principles that the Fathers had been at such pains to develop."[43]

Ironically, Mme. Chiang also played into the trope of the damsel in distress. Her argument for aid to China fit into the larger picture of what Emily S. Rosenberg has characterized as the masculine assumptions about women where "wartime exaltation of family ... and of male bonding amid danger and violence widened the gulf between social constructions of femininity and masculinity."[44] These assumptions would spill into the international arena with portrayals of U.S. relations with weaker nations in gendered terms: Latin American countries, for instance, were often depicted as "fair maidens" in need of Uncle Sam's protection.[45] In a variation of this trope, an American businessman, Carl Crow, depicted the Sino-American alliance as Uncle Sam wooing a Chinese damsel in a cheongsam and carrying a parasol with American wares. In Mme. Chiang's case, the American media portrayed her as the petite Chinese fair maiden sur-

---

[41] John Gittings, "Obituary: Madame Chiang Kai-shek," *Guardian*, October 24, 2003.

[42] Pakula, *The Last Empress*, 421.

[43] "Speech to Congress: Madame Chiang Kai-shek Calls upon the U.S. to Join China in War and Peace" [editorial], *Life*, March 1, 1943.

[44] Emily S. Rosenberg, "Gender," *Journal of American History* 77, no. 1 (1990): 120.

[45] Michael H. Hunt, *Ideology and U.S. Foreign Policy* (New Haven, CT: Yale University Press, 2009), 142; Jespersen, *American Images*, 88.

rounded by tall American men who could rescue her and China from their enemies.[46]

Another gendered characterization of Mme. Chiang was as China's first lady, a position that Eleanor Roosevelt was already elevating and redefining in what Maurine Beasley describes as a "struggle between the Victorian idea of womanly subordination and the modern concept of self-actualization."[47] By representing herself as her husband's helpmate rather than as a public figure in her own right and by defining her involvement in public affairs in moral rather than political terms, Eleanor was able to deflect or defend herself against charges that she was stepping outside her place. Mme. Chiang similarly signaled that she was upholding the Victorian ideal of womanhood through her appearance and publicized activities such as her work with war orphans and in the New Life Movement, even as both women were at the same time redefining women's roles. In any case, Mme. Chiang seemed to have a knack for not being trapped by these roles or censured for stepping out of them. She could easily transition from being the "mother" of war orphans to discussing military logistics and aid.

Mme. Chiang's varied activities all contributed to what Jespersen describes as "her image as a woman who had moved beyond the traditional confines placed upon women by both Chinese and American societies."[48] The impact of her 1943 U.S. visit on this image cannot be overstated. None of the subsequent first ladies of the People's Republic of China or the Republic of China has come close to Mme. Chiang's international stature. Beyond the personal acclaim it earned her, the perception that Chiang Kai-shek rightly valued his wife's opinions and respected her talents with regard to international issues suggested an enlightened leadership and country that could stand on an equal footing with the United States.

---

[46] Carl Crow, *Four Hundred Million Customers: The Experiences—Some Happy, Some Sad of an American in China and What They Taught Him* (New York: Harper and Brothers, 1937), 283; Jespersen, *American Images*, 88.

[47] Maurine H. Beasley, *Eleanor Roosevelt and the Media: A Public Quest for Self-Fulfillment* (Urbana: University of Illinois Press, 1987), 190.

[48] Jespersen, *American Images*, 97.

COMPLICATING TENSIONS IN MME. CHIANG'S
DEPLOYMENT OF RACE

Race, however, was a harder issue for Mme. Chiang to navigate than gender, in large part because much of Sino-American relations prior to the bombing of Pearl Harbor was based on racism against the Chinese and Chinese Americans. Although she was sharply aware of this, her overriding concern with seeking American aid for China sometimes made her complicit in reinforcing the racial status quo. In her speech to Congress, for instance, she avoided mentioning imperialism or racial injustice within the context of Sino-American relations. Mme. Chiang knew that her allusion to 160 years of Sino-American friendship was inaccurate—for one thing, the Americans (jointly with the British) had operated a foreign concession in her home city of Shanghai—but she supported this public fiction so as not to alienate those whose help her country now needed.[49] Although Mme. Chiang felt comfortable calling for racial equality in off-the-cuff remarks to reporters,[50] in more formal settings, she adhered to a tacit diplomatic agreement that the two countries would eschew challenging each other's national myths: Mme. Chiang would not talk about American race relations, and American officials would refrain from exposing the authoritarian nature of the Nationalist regime.

This diplomatic understanding curtailed Mme. Chiang's ability to advocate for racial equality. Thus, when the secretary of the NAACP, Walter White, invited her to participate in a panel discussion on "the question of skin color and 'white supremacy' both as a factor in winning the war and in winning the peace," she declined the opportunity.[51] Pearl S. Buck, an

---

[49] Mme. Chiang, "House Speech"; Li, *Madame Chiang Kai-shek*, 197.

[50] One reporter asked whether she had a message for "Negro" Americans. He paraphrased her words: "I need give no message to Negroes because I consider them part and parcel of the nation. When I speak to America, I feel that the Negroes are a vital segment of the country, not to be differentiated from any other America." The reporter was clearly impressed by her response. Deton J. Brooks, Jr., "Mme. Chiang Sees Race Vital in U.S. Democracy," *Chicago Defender*, March 27, 1943, 1.

[51] Karen J. Leong, *The China Mystique: Pearl S. Buck, Anna May Wong, Mayling Soong Chiang, and the Transformation of American Orientalism* (Berkeley: University of California Press, 2005), 138–39.

American writer and novelist, was disappointed that Mme. Chiang chose not to make a public statement on the repeal of the Chinese exclusion laws at the congressional hearings during her visit. Her silence, Buck feared, would serve the purposes of a coalition that wanted the laws intact: the American Legion, some labor unions, and Southern politicians. Instead, Buck herself served as the chief spokesperson for Chinese interests at the hearings, voicing what was no doubt Mme. Chiang's own position that "democracy demanded equal treatment for Chinese with other foreign nationals; and success in the Pacific war depended on China's belief in American solidarity."[52] Mme. Chiang's silence in instances such as these prevented her from broadening her base of support in America and acknowledged the subordinate position of China—she could ill afford to alienate those who had the power to aid China.[53]

Further complicating Mme. Chiang's presentation of race was that after Pearl Harbor, Americans could justify racism toward the Japanese because they were at war but not toward their "friends," the Chinese. Yet Americans could still exercise another kind of racism toward China in the form of "ethnocentric paternalism." Ignoring history and the differences between the two countries, Americans now viewed the Chinese not as alien others but as would-be Americans. Observing someone like Mme. Chiang who knew their culture so well, many Americans might be misled into believing that all Chinese were similar to themselves in valuing freedom and democracy. The American media and the president did nothing to dissuade the public from this perception, as bolstering China's role as America's ally was an important goal. In Mme. Chiang's last official stop at the Hollywood Bowl, the spectacular pageantry of the occasion focused in large part on her gender, but rendered her race invisible—never once was she referred to as a "Chinese."[54]

Mme. Chiang's selective silence over race issues and the American tendency to render racial tensions and inequality invisible allowed the racial status quo to go unchallenged during her visit. By the end of her

---

[52] Peter Conn, *Pearl S. Buck: A Cultural Biography* (New York: Cambridge University Press, 1996), 274.

[53] Leong, *The China Mystique*, 139.

[54] Ibid., 143.

speaking tour, when it became clear that the sought-after aid from the U.S. government would fall far short of what was requested, the editorial page of the African American newspaper the *Chicago Defender* reinterpreted her initial speech to Congress along different lines: "Mme. Chiang knows that ... right now the Japanese 'sword of Damocles' is not killing white men in any great number; that for the moment, at least, it is destroying, for the most part, the Chinese, the Burmese, the Malayans, the Javanese, and the Indians. Mme. Chiang knows that these are the darker races of this world. She knows that THEY are the REAL expendable of this war. ... Official Washington rose to its feet, doffed its hat, clapped its hands—and winked its eye."[55]

In playing into the public fiction that the Chinese were aspiring Americans, Mme. Chiang's presentations allowed her American listeners to ignore the racial dimensions of their government's Europe First policy. And without a more realistic picture of conditions in China, whether the needs and treatment of soldiers on the ground or the authoritarian tendencies of the Nationalist government, Americans were little inclined to demand accountability from China's leaders or able to make accurate and appropriate decisions about how much aid should be given. As a result, the inflation of the Free China bubble in American opinion allowed American policymakers to rationalize that whatever aid they gave China would be adequate.

Despite reinforcing the racial status quo in the formal aspects of her visit, Mme. Chiang's informal efforts to ensure the repeal of the Chinese Exclusion Act of 1882 and the participation of the Chinese and Chinese Americans in the war effort made important contributions to the advancement of domestic and international racial equality in 1943. America's entry into the war in 1941 inspired a conspicuous shift in how Chinese Americans thought of themselves, and many went on to make notable contributions in the war effort.[56] A total of 13,499, or 22 percent, of Chinese American adult males were eventually drafted or enlisted in the U.S.

---

[55] "Chinese Realism and Nordic Hypocrisy," *Chicago Defender*, April 17, 1943.

[56] Ronald Takaki, *Strangers from a Different Shore: A History of Asian Americans*, updated and rev. ed. (Boston: Little, Brown, 1998), 370–71.

armed forces.[57] The new work opportunities available because of the war allowed many Chinese Americans to break out of the ethnically prescribed occupations in the restaurant and laundry business, which had negatively stereotyped them, and enter into war-related employment. One member of the New York Chinatown community noted that for the first time, he felt part of an American dream and proud of Chinese heroes such as Chiang Kai-shek and Mme. Chiang Kai-shek: "It was just a whole different era and in the community we began to feel very good about ourselves."[58]

This new political reality had brought into sharp relief the hypocrisy of the Chinese Exclusion Act that barred Chinese laborers from coming to America. Within these changing racial dynamics, Mme. Chiang appeared on the American stage to give voice to the injustices of discrimination against Chinese, which she and her family had experienced firsthand. Her family may have excelled during their time in America, but they still faced discrimination, and Mme. Chiang was sensitive to these slights. Although her father had been ordained as a missionary in America, his American sponsors nonetheless changed his status to "native preacher" upon his return to China, a demotion that gave him lower pay than his expatriate counterparts. Mme. Chiang confided to Owen Lattimore that when her father would report back to American missionaries in Shanghai after proselytizing in remote areas of China, they never invited him to sit. She felt that this oversight spoke volumes; the Americans had treated her father more like a servant than a colleague.[59]

No matter how Americanized Mme. Chiang and her siblings appeared to be, they had also been on the receiving end of discrimination during their years in the United States. In a speech to a Chinese audience in New York's Chinatown, she noted that as a child, she and her two older sisters had been barred from attending public schools in Georgia because of their race and had to be tutored in the home of Dr. W.N. Ainsworth.[60]

---

[57] Ibid., 373–74.

[58] Diane Mei Lin Mark and Ginger Chih, *A Place Called Chinese America* (Dubuque, IA: Kendall and Hunt, 1982), 97–98.

[59] Lattimore, *China Memoirs*, 141.

[60] Mary Hornaday, "The Greatest Woman in the Public Eye," *Christian Science Monitor*, April 10, 1943.

She remarked to Lattimore that Americans had a racist and condescending attitude toward her, describing their judgment of her: "Oh yes, she is clever, of course, but after all she is only a Chinese."[61]

Perhaps because of her sensitivity to such slights, Lattimore noted that Mme. Chiang always insisted upon top ceremonial protocol when visiting the United States.[62] This insistence was especially true in Mme. Chiang's interactions with someone like Winston Churchill, who, unlike Roosevelt, had a frankly imperialist understanding of the world order. Churchill's personal physician, Lord Moran (Charles McMoran Wilson), noted that when Churchill spoke of India or China, one was readily reminded that Churchill was prone to Victorian orientalizing. After listening quietly to Roosevelt about the need to be China's friend, Churchill later spoke privately and derisively to Moran of the Chinese as "little yellow men."[63] In public, Churchill also made clear that he did not consider China an equal partner in the alliance. The night before Mme. Chiang was to address an audience in Chicago, Churchill gave a radio address in which he stated that the aim of the war in Asia was to reclaim the lost imperial territories taken by the Japanese—a pointed insult to China and to critics of colonialism. Furthermore, he made no mention of China's participation in postwar plans, saying only that China would be "rescued" from Japan.[64]

It is within such a context that Mme. Chiang's insistence on protocol should be understood. In May 1943, Churchill requested a meeting with Mme. Chiang at the White House. At the time, Mme. Chiang had finished her cross-country tour and was staying at the Waldorf Astoria in New York. Rather than accepting Churchill's request, Mme. Chiang asked that Churchill travel to see her in New York instead. Churchill likewise declined. Roosevelt tried to solve this impasse by inviting Mme. Chiang to dine with himself and Churchill at the capital. Although the Generalissimo encouraged his wife to meet Churchill as a political courtesy and to avoid bearing grudges or bargaining with the prime minister, she never-

[61] Lattimore, *China Memoirs*, 141.

[62] Ibid.

[63] Lord Moran, *Winston Churchill: The Struggle for Survival, 1940–65* (London: Constable, 1966), 599.

[64] Li, *Madame Chiang Kai-shek*, 222.

theless refused, leading Chiang to criticize her for "stubbornly sticking to her position and paying no heed to [our] policy."[65] To the consternation of the British government, Mme. Chiang also never responded to its open invitation to visit that year. While Chiang had initially urged her on March 26 not to visit, he reversed position on May 15, asking her to accept if Churchill asked, yet Mme. Chiang continued to cite health reasons for declining the visit.[66] Although some, including T.V. Soong himself, may have interpreted her actions as spoiled behavior, another interpretation was that Mme. Chiang insisted on equal treatment or better, especially from those who took for granted a hierarchical view of race in the world order.[67]

In a letter to Roosevelt's White House economic advisor, Lauchlin Currie, in May 1942, Mme. Chiang had voiced her concerns that the "Democracies," and specifically the British, had yet to accept China as an equal partner. If China was treated this way even though China was necessary for final victory, she worried about her country's treatment after the war, when it was no longer needed. She warned, "Unless China after the war is accepted as an equal in international affairs, the Chinese people will rise in such indignation that there may be another war far more terrible than the war which we are now passing through."[68] In this regard, Mme. Chiang gave voice to her compatriots' own desire to be treated as an equal by other nations. Konshin Shah, a pilot for Chiang and a protégé of Mme. Chiang, was representative of the Chinese admirers of the Chiangs when he stated, "For me, Generalissimo and Madame Chiang rescued us from being a downtrodden country. ... My generation regards the Chiangs as a godsent couple for uplifting our country to an equal status in the world."[69]

Fittingly, in response to Mme. Chiang's speech to the House of Rep-

---

[65] *Jiang Zhongzheng zongtong dang'an: Shilüe gaoben* [President Chiang Kai-shek's archives: The *shilüe* manuscripts] (Hsintien: Guoshiguan, 2011), vol. 53, 428, 456.

[66] Ibid., vol. 53, 101–2, 433.

[67] Leong also analyzes this exchange through the lens of gender in *The China Mystique*, 146–47.

[68] Mme. Chiang's letter from Chongqing, May 18, 1942, Lauchlin B. Currie, Box 1, Folder, Correspondence: Mme. Chiang Kai-shek, Hoover Institution Archives, Stanford, California.

[69] Li, *Madame Chiang Kai-shek*, 468.

resentatives, the Democratic representative Martin J. Kennedy of New York noted that he would "take this auspicious occasion, in [Mme. Chiang's] gracious presence" to introduce his bill to repeal the Chinese Exclusion Act.[70] Mme. Chiang made sure to build on this momentum during her visit, if only on an informal basis. At a dinner party several months later when Congress was holding hearings about the act, she stressed the importance of its repeal to several key congressmen, impressing upon them that the repeal would boost Chinese morale and support the war effort.[71] In the end, Roosevelt would sign the law into effect on December 17, 1943, after the Cairo Conference had concluded. In some ways, the repeal was merely symbolic, as it allowed only 105 Chinese to enter annually, and an average of only 59 per year came during the first ten years. Nonetheless, it was an important step toward racial equality. One Chinatown resident remarked, "Now that I have become a naturalized citizen, I am going to change my birthday. Henceforth, it will be on the Fourth of July."[72]

Shifting American attitudes about the Chinese and Mme. Chiang's sensitivity to racial discrimination worked in tandem to open a path for an understanding on American aid to China on the basis of mutual respect. One letter to the editor, for instance, remarked that the "talented and accomplished Mme. Chiang Kai-shek" only brought into sharp relief "our bad treatment of the Chinese people in the past," and made clear that "no amount of lend-lease goods to the Chinese can now atone for such past treatment,"[73] thereby agreeing with Chiang Kai-shek's assessment that his wife had conveyed the appropriate meaning on her American trip: "That China's request for American aid and materials is not a gift [to China] but a basic responsibility."[74]

Despite taking care not to embarrass Americans by publicly criticizing their racism toward people of color at home and internationally, Mme. Chiang credibly pushed for racial equality during her visit. Her speeches

---

[70] Leong, *The China Mystique*, 150.

[71] Takaki, *Strangers from a Different Shore*, 376.

[72] Ibid., 378.

[73] F.M. Shureman, "Letter to the Editor," *Chicago Times*, March 25, 1943, Henry S. Evans, clippings file.

[74] Chiang Kai-shek diary, February 27, 1943, Box 43, Folder 1.

to members of the Chinatown community reflected this desire publicly; her interactions with Churchill reflected it privately. Much of the out-pouring of private aid to China that resulted from her visit was given in the spirit of admiration and respect for Mme. Chiang and China. The Toledo and Milwaukee Chinese communities, for instance, contributed $2,500 (which, adjusted for inflation, would be almost $35,000 today). Mrs. Emmons Blaine, daughter of Cyrus McCormick, the founder of the International Harvester Company, contributed $100,000 and told Mme. Chiang that the money was to be used at the Chiangs' discretion.[75] A likely estimate of the large and small monetary gifts from across the coun-try is more than $1.3 million.[76] Despite the complicated terrain of race, the repeal of the Chinese Exclusion Act and Mme. Chiang's efforts on behalf of the Chinese and Chinese Americans increased the possibility of full equality among the Allied Powers.

THE DEMOCRATIC VALUES OF
MME. CHIANG AND AMERICA

From the opening line of her speeches to Congress and throughout her tour, Mme. Chiang appeared to enthusiastically embrace democratic val-ues, confirming Luce's vision of China as an eager acolyte of America. Nevertheless, the trip revealed a distinct gap between the positive image the American public had of Mme. Chiang's democratic values and the negative image about those same values that was emerging privately. Al-though the Roosevelt administration and American media kept these negative representations largely out of the public eye in the interest of

[75] Thomas J. Watson, "The Crossroads of America," in *The First Lady of China: The His-toric Wartime Visit of Mme. Chiang Kai-shek to the United States* (New York: International Business Machines, 1943).

[76] After Mme. Chiang's New York speech, Henry Luce noted that gifts had totaled $300,000 and $1 million was on its way. See T. Christopher Jespersen, "Madame Chiang Kaishek and the Face of Sino-American Relations: Personality and Gender Dynamics in Bilateral Diplomacy," in Chu, *Madame Chiang Kai-shek and Her China*, 137. Since Mme. Chiang was still in the early stages of her tour, this suggests that the total amount of aid was likely much higher.

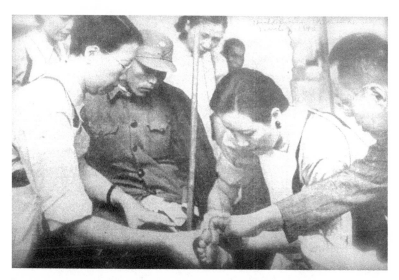

Figure 2.3: Praising Mme. Chiang, the Herald noted: "A woman whose word has changed the lives of 450,000,000 Chinese people, Mme. Chiang still has time to minister to the needs of just one of them." *Source:* Herald American Pictorial Review, March 3, 1943. Henry S. Evans, clippings file, Hoover Institution Archives, Stanford, California.

maintaining the relationship with a dependable ally in the Pacific, turning a blind eye to Mme. Chiang's undemocratic behavior when out of the spotlight would have unintended consequences for Mme. Chiang, her husband's regime, and China.

In keeping with Roosevelt's vision of a democratic international order in which "cooperation was not a one-way street" and no nation could assume that it had "a monopoly of wisdom or of virtue," Mme. Chiang vigorously conveyed an image to the American public of herself as a woman of her people, which implied, by extension, that the Nationalist leadership could be viewed in a democratic light.[77] She had, for instance, set up a boys' and girls' school on a thousand-acre lot at the foot of the Purple Mountains in Nanjing, and her "warphans" came from the poorest fami-

---

[77] Tony McCulloch, "Franklin D. Roosevelt in US Foreign Policy and Democracy Promotion," in *US Foreign Policy and Democracy Promotion*, ed. Michael Cox, Timothy J. Lynch, and Nicolas Bouchet (New York: Routledge, 2013), 82.

lies and called her "Mama."[78] During the war years she administered first aid to soldiers, tested medical supplies sent from the United States, and sewed Red Cross bandages. A photo of her published in the *Herald American Pictorial Review* in 1943 captured her diligently bandaging a soldier's wounded foot.[79] These examples projected a credible image of Mme. Chiang as a woman with a common touch.

In her speeches across America, Mme. Chiang spoke admiringly of the Chinese people's wartime sacrifices in the face of what appeared to be impossible odds. The Japanese Prince Konoye, she reported in her Madison Square Garden address, had believed that Japan would beat China within three months. She then explained why so many "three months" had gone by without his prediction coming true. Although the Nationalist government had set up food centers in Chongqing for people whose homes were destroyed by the Japanese bombings, many declined the help. They felt that they had suffered no more than others. Only after being told that they were entitled to the food because of their contribution to the war effort did they accept.[80] In contrast to the "arrogant pride" of Prince Konoye, this "rightful pride" of her people, according to Mme. Chiang, was what allowed China to persevere in the face of the Japanese threat.

Mme. Chiang even extended her connection with ordinary people to American workers. When the mayor of San Francisco, Angelo Rossi, neglected to invite representatives from the Longshore and Warehouse Union to meet with her during her stay, Mme. Chiang took matters into her own hands and visited them. These union members had supported China's boycott of Japanese goods in 1932 and had allowed Chinese Americans to picket on the docks at great cost to members and their families. Mme. Chiang showed her appreciation by repeatedly addressing them as "fellow workers" in her speech. One reporter described her impassioned back-and-forth exchange with workers:

> "Do you want to lose this war?" cried Mme. Chiang.
> As a voice the answer came: "No!"

---

[78] Li, *Madame Chiang Kai-shek*, 87–88.

[79] *Herald American Pictorial Review*, March 3, 1943, Henry S. Evans, clippings file.

[80] Watson, "In the City of Skyscrapers," in *The First Lady of China*.

"Do you want to increase production?" she asked.

"Yes! Yes! Yes!"

"Then," she shouted, "let all labor cooperate and increase production."[81]

A rather different picture of Mme. Chiang and the Nationalist regime, however, emerged outside of the public eye. That Mme. Chiang was an aristocrat did not automatically undermine her democratic image, but she was less than vigilant about how others would perceive her words and actions, especially given wartime exigencies. During her eleven-day stay at the White House (February 17–28), for instance, instead of using the bells or telephones with which their rooms were equipped, Mme. Chiang and her niece and nephew would repeatedly clap their hands to summon the staff. According to one observer, she treated "virtually everybody below Cabinet rank as coolies." According to another, her visit posed more problems for the Roosevelts than that of any other guest during their twelve-year tenure in the White House.[82] When U.S. Customs delayed a shipment of cigarettes, calls from Mme. Chiang's staff continued all day to the Treasury until an agent was instructed to "get them off the boat and fly them" to the White House. Sufficiently concerned that his guest's "private manners might gain unfavorable publicity to spoil her public image," Roosevelt hoped that Mme. Chiang would return to China at the end of February.[83] But Mme. Chiang did not leave until July 4, and such behavior continued unabated throughout her tour.

Given Mme. Chiang's fastidious cultivation of her image, her familiarity with American customs, and her position as a guest in another country hoping to garner aid for China, her behavior seems puzzling. One plausible explanation was that her illness had exacerbated her imperious side and hampered her ability to manage potential misunderstandings. Stanley Hornbeck, the special adviser to the secretary of state, Cordell Hull, noted

---

[81] Leong, *The China Mystique*, 147–48.

[82] Doris Fleeson, "Mme. Chiang Gave Roosevelts a Record Number of Headaches," *Buffalo Evening News*, December 14, 1945.

[83] Barbara W. Tuchman, *Stilwell and the American Experience in China, 1911–45* (New York: Macmillan, 1971), 352–53.

that Mme. Chiang's uncertain schedule was partly due to illness, and although "Americans are habituated to demanding precision," he suggested that incorporating flexibility into the schedule was highly desirable in Mme. Chiang's case.[84] Adjusting the expectations of Mme. Chiang's American security guards, for instance, may have lessened their complaints about long waiting times and her unpredictable schedule.[85]

Such behavior might have been overlooked except that it appeared to have a darker side, revealing a profound insincerity about Mme. Chiang's embrace of democratic values. Unaware of this in the beginning, Eleanor Roosevelt soon discovered "a certain casualness about cruelty" in Mme. Chiang. During one of their dinners together during her stay at the White House, Franklin Roosevelt mentioned that a labor leader, John Lewis, was giving him trouble and asked Mme. Chiang how she would handle such a leader in China. Eleanor observed that she responded with "a most expressive gesture": a "beautiful, small hand came up very quietly and slid across her throat." Franklin then gave Eleanor a look before continuing the conversation and later teased her, "Well, how about your gentle and sweet character?"[86]

This "casualness about cruelty" was on full display in her reaction to an article published in *Time* on March 22 about a terrible famine occurring in Henan Province (see chapter 10). Author Theodore H. White blamed the Nationalist army for insisting on collecting grain taxes when there was no food to be collected, and faulted the Nationalist government for not sending grain to the affected area when there was still time. Compounding the tragedy, according to White, was the veritable feast officials gave him before his departure from the area.[87] Mme. Chiang's reaction to the article was telling. Outraged that White criticized the Nationalist government, she demanded that he be fired. To his credit, Henry Luce refused.[88] Expressing not an iota of sympathy for her suffering compatri-

---

[84] Correspondence to Mr. Hamilton and Mr. Welles, March 4, 1943, Stanley K. Hornbeck, Box 49, Folder 3 of 4: Chiang Kai-shek and Mme. Chiang, Hoover Institution Archives.

[85] Pakula, *The Last Empress*, 428.

[86] Eleanor Roosevelt, *This I Remember* (New York: Harper and Brothers, 1949), 284.

[87] Theodore H. White, "Until the Harvest Is Reaped," *Time*, March 22, 1943, 21–22.

[88] Li, *Madame Chiang Kai-shek*, 219.

ots, Mme. Chiang appeared more concerned about maintaining the legitimacy of her husband's regime. Even a symbolic gesture of empathy toward those suffering in the famine would have gone a long way. Instead, this apparent absence of a felt connection with her people revealed a fundamental difference between the Chiangs and the Roosevelts (who also came from an aristocratic background) and reflected an elitist view of nationalism that lacked the critical element of a shared or imagined community.

Mme. Chiang's seeming disconnection from ordinary people may be explained in part by the clannish political environment to which she had grown accustomed. Chiang Kai-shek often encouraged feuds and withering criticisms among his subordinates while prohibiting criticism of himself and his wife and family members. Over time, Parks M. Coble suggests, this protection from criticism may have given Mme. Chiang a view of democracy in which the rule of law did not apply to her.[89] Her sense of difference from ordinary people may also have been exacerbated by her belief that she and her husband were among a Christian elect and "had been divinely chosen to rule China."[90] The American public's wholehearted adulation of her likely further reinforced this feeling. Graham Peck, who worked for the Office of War Information in China, felt that with her celebrity reception in America, it "would have taken a woman of the most austere character not to become addled."[91] In any case, Eleanor Roosevelt perceptively observed that although Mme. Chiang spoke highly of democracy, she found the ideas too abstract and was thus uncertain as to how they would work in practice in China.[92] By the end of the war, Roosevelt concluded that Mme. Chiang "can talk beautifully about democracy, but she does not know how to live democracy."[93]

Even as Mme. Chiang's tour continued to wide acclaim, her lack of democratic values began to draw concern from other quarters. In a March

---

[89] Parks M. Coble, "The Soong Family and Chinese Capitalists," in Chu, *Madame Chiang Kai-shek and Her China*, 76–77.

[90] Li, *Madame Chiang Kai-shek*, 475.

[91] Graham Peck, *Two Kinds of Time* (1950; reprint, Seattle: University of Washington Press, 2008), 477.

[92] Roosevelt, *This I Remember*, 283.

[93] "Mme. Chiang Chided by Mrs. Roosevelt," *New York Times*, December 5, 1945.

22, 1943, letter to Eleanor Roosevelt urging her to visit China,[94] Pearl S. Buck noted, "Not a few Chinese have said to me, 'She has behaved like an empress or a queen. ... We would have been better pleased had she behaved more democratically.'" Buck regretted that Mme. Chiang's eldest sister and the widow of Sun Yat-sen, Mme. Sun (Song Qingling), had not been sent to represent China in America, as she truly "made the cause of common Chinese people hers and they know it." Tellingly, Mme. Sun was at the time virtually under house arrest in China because of her outspoken criticisms of the Chiang regime and her identification with the Chinese Communist cause.[95]

Buck made her criticisms public in *Life* two months later, albeit in a milder tone that focused on the dangers of the Free China public relations bubble. In "A Warning to China," Buck observed, "American friendship for China has at this moment reached a popular height which brings it to the verge of sentimentality" and warned that "those who have rushed to give gifts ... are going to wake up one morning condemning China and all Chinese. ... One of the major paradoxes of this war is that although Madame Chiang is our most eloquent wartime evangelist, the Chinese people themselves are voiceless."[96] Buck had come to the ironic conclusion that Mme. Chiang appeared to have more in common with Churchill's hierarchical worldview than with Roosevelt's democratic worldview.

Paralleling the tensions in Mme. Chiang's portrayal of democratic values were similar tensions within the U.S.-China partnership. Despite Roosevelt's democratic vision of a world order and Mme. Chiang's successful celebrity tour, the United States was not forthcoming with significant aid to China. In fact, when China needed the greatest assistance during this most difficult stage of the war (1941–1944), American aid totaled

---

[94] Franklin turned down Eleanor's request for a reciprocal visit to China in the middle of 1943 due to worries that he would receive extra pressure to give the China front a higher priority. According to her close friend and biographer, Joseph P. Lash, Eleanor "accepted his decision uncomplainingly." Sensing her disappointment, Franklin encouraged her to visit Australia and New Zealand instead. See Joseph P. Lash, *Eleanor and Franklin: The Story of Their Relationship, Based on Eleanor Roosevelt's Private Papers* (New York: W.W. Norton, 1971), 679–80.

[95] Theodore F. Harris, *Pearl S. Buck: A Biography*. Vol. 2, *Her Philosophy as Expressed in Her Letters* (Omaha, NE: John Day, 1971), 321–22.

[96] Pearl S. Buck, "A Warning about China," *Life*, May 10, 1943.

only $280 million. As a mere "side show" compared to Europe in the war and not an "important American priority," the goal was only to ensure that China had just enough aid to keep fighting, but not necessarily to win. By contrast, in 1945, China received $1.1 billion in American aid because the goal and function of aid had shifted to defeating the Communists.[97]

Just as the American public's esteem for China was at an all-time high, U.S. decision makers and observers of China's situation were beginning to have doubts about Chiang Kai-shek and his Nationalist regime. Nevertheless, the strategic, if secondary, importance of having China as an ally made ignoring Mme. Chiang's treatment of staff workers, intolerance of criticism, and other undemocratic behavior politically expedient, and this collective averting of the eyes occurred all the way to the top. Heeding the praise and not picking up on the criticism or uneasiness that Mme. Chiang's tour engendered may have contributed to Chinese overconfidence about its standing within the alliance. This overconfidence would ill serve the Nationalist regime and China in the aftermath of the tour.

AFTER THE TOUR: TIPPING POINTS FOR THE ALLIANCE AND MME. CHIANG

The success of the American tour translated into a more confident Mme. Chiang upon her return to China in July. Perhaps most crucially, her new international influence helped her to persuade her husband to retain Joseph Stilwell, the controversial American general in charge of the China-Burma-India theater, who had often clashed with Chiang over the use of Chinese troops. Furthermore, by accompanying her husband to the Cairo summit, where she was captured on camera with Chiang, Roosevelt, and Churchill, she helped reinforce the image of China as a Great Power and of a progressive Chinese leadership. Yet her newfound influence would also have unintended consequences for the Nationalist regime and for Mme. Chiang herself.

---

[97] Zhang Baijia, "China's Quest for Foreign Military Aid," in Peattie, Drea, and van de Ven, *The Battle for China*, 303–4.

In September 1943, just a few months after her triumphant return, Mme. Chiang's brother, T.V. Soong, persuaded Chiang to remove Stilwell and began taking the necessary steps on Chiang's behalf. At this point, however, Mme. Chiang and her sister, Mme. Kung, allied to keep Stilwell, a move apparently influenced at least in part by a family power struggle between the sisters and their brother. Yet Mme. Chiang recognized that the removal of Stilwell, as Rana Mitter points out, would make public "a fundamental divide between the Americans and the Chinese at a time when Japanese forces still threatened to conquer Free China," as removing him would be unpopular among the American military leaders and public, who considered Stilwell a hero.[98] In October, following further interventions by General Somervell and Lord Mountbatten, Chiang ultimately accepted his wife's counsel and changed his mind. Soong, whom Chiang then blamed for having put him in the awkward position of having to back down from an official request to remove Stilwell, disappeared from the Generalissimo's inner circle for most of the following year.[99]

The consequences of Mme. Chiang's influence on retaining Stilwell and her part in her brother's removal would have far-reaching effects. Her influence not only helped to prolong a difficult relationship for another year but temporarily forced Soong out of Chiang's inner circle at a crucial time in preparations for the Cairo Conference the following month (see chapter 13). As a result, the most capable person slated to attend the conference with Chiang was now also prevented from going, replaced by Mme. Chiang.[100] Mme. Chiang's increased confidence and influence was still on full display during the Cairo Conference in November, leading the English general Alan Brooke to ultimately (if probably wrongly) conclude in his diaries a dozen years later that Mme. Chiang was the "leading spirit" of the Chiangs.[101] Unfortunately, Mme. Chiang was far less capable than her brother would have been in stage-managing the Chinese side of the

---

[98] Rana Mitter, *The Forgotten Ally: China's World War II, 1937–1945* (New York: Houghton Mifflin Harcourt, 2013), 303.
[99] Tuchman, *Stilwell and the American Experience in China*, 395.
[100] Ronald Ian Heiferman, *The Cairo Conference of 1943: Roosevelt, Churchill, Chiang Kai-shek and Madame Chiang* (Jefferson, NC: McFarland, 2011), 48.
[101] From Alanbrooke's diaries, quoted in Pakula, *The Last Empress*, 472.

negotiations. To make matters worse, her persistent illness and the fact that the very capable public relations master Hollington Tong was relegated to a minor role at the summit, because of his association with Soong, meant that the China contingent was hardly working at its fullest capacity. As a result, the Chiangs' performance in Cairo was a public relations disaster that within the span of a week managed, according to Ronald Heiferman, to undo "much of Soong's previous efforts to cultivate a favorable image of the Kuomintang regime and its leaders." Chiang Kai-shek sensed that Roosevelt now perceived China as a liability rather than an asset, a change in perception that may have actually begun during Mme. Chiang's American tour and would have serious implications for the Sino-American alliance moving forward.[102]

Despite seeing a more assertive and confident Mme. Chiang upon her return to China, observers also began to notice a change in her faith in herself and her country's possibilities. Peck observed that she had "become a pathologically pretentious woman who, under the surface, was so distraught, uneasy, and at odds with herself that she could no longer make much sense on either a political or personal level."[103] Along similar lines, John Fairbank, who interviewed Mme. Chiang in September, reported that she appeared tired and unhappy and despite her philosophical remarks about keeping to one's ideals and meeting circumstances as they came up, Mme. Chiang ultimately could not make peace with the reality that "China [was] backward, the material backwardness being associated with spiritual backwardness, each causing the other."[104] In the absence of the American adulation that had supported her optimistic portrayal of China, the contradictions in the China she returned to must have been painfully evident to Mme. Chiang, taking a heavy toll on her. Her biographer, Laura Tyson Li, thought that a turning point occurred around this time in which Mme. Chiang changed from someone relatively well intentioned to a brittle, rigid, self-righteousness, and dogmatic woman. By her 1948 visit to the United States, according to Li, her noticeable lack of

---

[102] Heiferman, *The Cairo Conference*, 159–60.

[103] Peck, *Two Kinds of Time*, 477.

[104] John King Fairbank, *Chinabound: A Fifty-Year Memoir* (New York: Harper and Row, 1982), 245–46.

self-reflection struck a serious blow to her subsequent role in elite politics.[105]

During her American tour, Mme. Chiang's rhetoric was not substantively overblown, but reflected the actual possibilities for a viable and mutually respectful Sino-American alliance. While it is easy to judge her undemocratic in retrospect, as Eleanor Roosevelt did in 1945, putting her squarely in this category in early 1943 would have been unfair. Indeed, 1943 had begun well for Mme. Chiang, the Nationalist regime, and China. Her speeches to Congress and across the United States were genuine high points in the prospects of all three. Had more regard been given for her health than to political expediency, and had the Free China mania been leavened with more critical reporting and counsel, perhaps Mme. Chiang might have returned to China with a renewed sense of her initial ideals and maintained her star quality for decades more.[106] Instead, Mme. Chiang returned to China in illness and with a somewhat broken spirit even as she worked tirelessly for the betterment of China's position within the Sino-American alliance. In the end, the politics of the alliance, the inflation of the Free China bubble, and the Chiangs putting their own power considerations over the general good of China would set the stage for the downturn of the Nationalist regime, making Mme. Chiang's 1943 American tour but a shooting star in the night sky—beautiful, memorable, and fleeting.

---

[105] Li, *Madame Chiang Kai-shek*, 471.

[106] Had Mme. Chiang been less ill, for instance, she may have had the fortitude to reduce her imperious behavior and to resist the cynical turn of her personality. The combination of strong sleeping medications, gastrointestinal distress, and chronic and acute urticaria, on top of a lengthy, grueling tour schedule, would have affected the steeliest of minds (Li, *Madame Chiang Kai-shek*, 477–78).

3

Xinjiang and the Promise of Salvation in Free China

JUDD C. KINZLEY AND JIANFEI JIA

In 1942, control of China's westernmost province of Xinjiang changed hands. After more than a decade of nearly exclusive Soviet oversight, that summer, the province's long-term governor (*duban*) switched allegiances away from his erstwhile Soviet patrons to Chiang Kai-shek's Nationalist government. The moment was one of triumph for Chinese officials cooped up in their wartime capital of Chongqing. As Chiang Kai-shek gushed in December, "This is our greatest achievement since the founding of the Republic."[1] For Chiang and other officials, the events in Xinjiang, an arid, isolated region in the far northwestern corner of the republic, offered the promise of national unification and even national salvation.

The view from China's northwestern periphery suggested that 1943 would be a turning point for the battered Chinese nation. The reacquisition of Xinjiang was, in many respects, a counterbalance to Japan's annexation of Manchuria in 1931 and was a much-needed morale boost for

---

[1] Quoted in Sheng Shicai, "Si yue geming de huigu yu qianzhan" [Reviewing the April Revolution and a look forward], *Xin Xinjiang*, April 12, 1943, 14.

a Nationalist Party struggling to reclaim territories held by their Qing dynasty (1644–1911) predecessors (see chapter 13).[2] Yet the Nationalist victory in Xinjiang was by no means only psychological. Bottled up by Japanese forces in China's mountainous southwest (a region commonly referred to as Free China), the National Government was largely cut off from the world, reeling from a series of catastrophic famines and epidemics, and suffering severe shortages of the natural resources needed to maintain the war effort. The recovery of Xinjiang appeared to be the answer to nearly every one of their problems. Its territory could open an international supply line through the Soviet Union, Iran, and British India; its land could serve as a refuge for China's growing number of displaced famine victims; and the region's rich natural resources could help alleviate the critical shortages of minerals needed to maintain the war effort and serve as an important source for future development. For Chiang Kai-shek and other Nationalist officials, the foreboding clouds hanging low over Chongqing appeared to be dissipating in the face of this unexpected light from the west.

If republican officials wanted to take advantage of this unexpected territorial gift, they needed to undertake the difficult task of more clearly incorporating Xinjiang into the Chinese Republic. In late October 1942, the geologist Huang Jiqing received orders from his superiors in China's Central Geological Survey to locate and assess Xinjiang's mineral wealth and begin sketching out plans for its extraction and transport to the southwest: "Go to Xinjiang, the quicker you leave the better."[3] Similar orders were issued in government offices throughout Free China in late 1942 and 1943, as Chinese state agents undertook an ambitious campaign of integration and state expansion without historical precedent in Xinjiang. Drawing on a wide array of Nationalist Party sources including many from underutilized archives in China and Taiwan, this chapter examines the efforts of these Chinese political figures, geologists, and eco-

---

[2] Ibid. In the same speech in December 1942, Chiang Kai-shek noted that "the area [of Xinjiang] was in fact double that of Manchuria."

[3] Huang Jiqing, *Tianshan zhi lu* [Foothills of the Tianshan] (Urumqi: Xinjiang renmin chubanshe, 2001, reprint), 2.

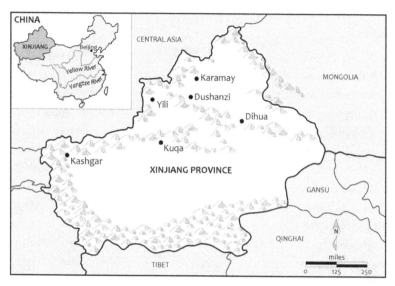

Figure 3.1: Map of Xinjang. Cartography by Debbie Newell.

nomic planners as they sought to bind Xinjiang to the Chinese Republic in 1943.

The efforts of these state representatives were imbued with a sense of optimism that stands in stark contrast to the bleak narratives that scholars of the wartime period have penned for other parts of China in 1943. This chapter, like others in this volume, suggests that in fact the republic's wartime experiences were not all rooted in battlefield casualties, refugees, destruction of property, corruption, famine, and suffering, which has characterized much of the scholarship on this period. In China's far west, Nationalist officials were presented with an opportunity in 1943 that appeared to herald their wartime salvation as well as a glorious postwar future for the Chinese Republic. The optimistic exuberance of Nationalist Party officials as they contemplated this long-lost territory points toward a far more complex narrative of China's wartime experience and also helps reveal the need to expand studies of wartime beyond the political and economic centers of Nationalist China or the Communist base areas in the north.

A RUSSIAN HINTERLAND IN CHINA

Xinjiang Province (today's Xinjiang Uighur Autonomous Region) lay on the farthest western edge of the Republic of China. This arid region, with a population in the 1920s that was more than 95 percent non-Han Chinese (the majority population of China) and overwhelmingly Muslim, had a long history of strong economic, political, and cultural connections to Central Asia. The region's political connections to China can be traced back to the second century BCE, when the Han dynasty emperor Wudi conquered the region in order to help shore up the empire's western borders. A number of subsequent dynasties followed Wudi's lead and sought to maintain the region as a buffer against powerful neighbors from the Eurasian steppes. China's last imperial dynasty, the Qing, conquered the region in 1759 and named it Xinjiang, or New Dominion, shortly thereafter.

New threats to Xinjiang from the Russian and British empires during the latter half of the nineteenth century prompted the imperial court in Beijing to undertake an aggressive and historically unprecedented policy of incorporation and integration.[4] Yet these policies ran up against political and economic realities. The financial crisis that pounded the Qing Empire in its last two decades short-circuited the ambitious plans to construct transportation infrastructure, develop political institutions, and invest in resource extraction enterprises in the province. The inauguration of the Republic of China in 1912 did little to alleviate the economic and political factors obstructing the integration of Xinjiang into the emergent nation-state.

Fearful of being drawn into the political turmoil of warlordism that was sweeping across central and eastern China in the late 1910s and 1920s, the first republican governor of Xinjiang, Yang Zengxin, sought to

---

[4] For more information on this process, see Joseph Esherick, "How the Qing Became China," in *Empire to Nation: Historical Perspectives on the Making of the Modern World*, ed. Joseph W. Esherick (Berkeley: University of California Press, 2006); Judd Kinzley, "Turning Prospectors into Settlers: Gold, Immigrant Miners and the Settlement of the Frontier in Late Qing Xinjiang," in *China on the Margins*, ed. Sherman Cochran and Paul G. Pickowicz (Ithaca, NY: Cornell University East Asia Program, 2010), 17–41.

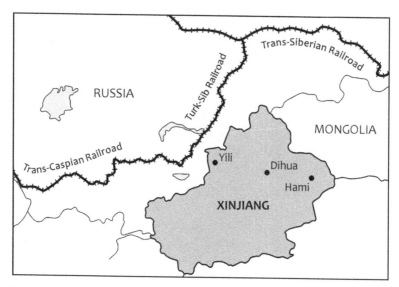

Figure 3.2: TransSiberia railroad.

maintain the province's status as a land apart. Despite the republic's new leaders' keen interest in Xinjiang's tax revenues, natural resources, and arable land for refugees from overcrowded eastern and central China, Governor Yang denied calls to construct new transportation infrastructure binding the province to the east, held off attempts to send out migrants from crowded provinces in eastern China, and rejected any attempt by the central government to stake a claim to the province's mineral wealth. From Yang's ascension in 1912 until his death by an assassin's bullet in 1928, Xinjiang was officially a province of the Chinese Republic, but lacked all but the most superficial connections to political and economic centers in the east.

At the same time, the willingness of the Russian Empire and later the Soviet Union to invest in infrastructure served to undermine first the Qing court's and later the Republic of China's attempts to more clearly integrate this border province. The Russian rail network stretched nearly up to Xinjiang's western border by 1899. This transportation infrastructure allowed Russian state agents to cheaply import large volumes of manufactured goods and dominate Xinjiang's markets, project Russian military power into the province, and facilitate the extraction of Xinjiang's natural resource wealth. After seeing Soviet plans for yet another rail line in the region, the Chinese consul in Irkutsk sent a worried telegram to his superiors in 1927: "On the surface they have stated that the purpose [for building the rail line] is to develop commerce in border regions," the consul wrote. "But in reality their plans contain a political end," he said, referring to the potential domination and ultimate annexation of the province.[5] Indeed, with the completion of the new line in 1928 that ran parallel to Xinjiang's western border, the concentration of rail lines on the other side of the border served to transform Xinjiang's connections to the Soviet Union. By the late 1920s, Soviet products dominated Xinjiang's markets; rubles were the preferred currency of exchange; and Soviet geologists and engineers sketched out plans to incorporate Xinjiang's natural resource wealth into Soviet economic plans. Facilitated by superior infrastructure, the Soviet Union inexorably dragged China's erstwhile westernmost province into its own vast economic hinterland.

Finally, in 1933, a succession crisis in Xinjiang resulted in the centralization of Soviet control over the province. That year, the Soviet Union offered direct military aid to help Sheng Shicai, a Han Chinese military officer from Manchuria, eliminate his political opponents and rise to power in Xinjiang. Throughout the 1930s, the Soviet Union dispatched help in the form of loans, shipments of grain and weapons, and outright military support to Xinjiang, even deploying a garrison of Red Army troops to the eastern Xinjiang town of Hami in 1938 to support Sheng's ultimately successful bid to become the province's supervisor. As a result of the Soviet support, Sheng announced his "six basic policies," which included a reliance on Communist ideology and maintaining a close Soviet-Xinjiang relationship as his top priorities.[6] What Sheng was able to gain

---

[5] "Su'e shixing jianzhushang Xitielushi cheng song Sulian jiaotongbuzhang zhi baogao ji luxian tushi," April 1927, Foreign Affairs Collection: 03-17-059-02-001, Academia Sinica, Institute of Modern History, Taipei, Taiwan.

[6] For more information, see Andrew Forbes, *Warlords and Muslims in Chinese Central Asia: A Political History of Republican Sinkiang, 1911–1949* (New York: Cambridge University Press, 1986).

in military and financial support from the Soviets was made up for in trade agreements and lucrative mining and oil-drilling concessions that directly benefited Moscow and Soviet heavy industry.

At various points, seeking to demonstrate his strong allegiance to Stalin and the Soviets, Sheng Shicai called for the outright Soviet annexation of Xinjiang Province and in 1936 even urged Stalin to conquer China itself. Pushed by Sheng's enthusiasm and his need for a deep-pocketed patron, throughout the late 1930s and early 1940s, Xinjiang became a colony of the Soviet Union in all but name. On the eve of Germany's invasion of the Soviet Union in 1941, Soviet geologists were actively incorporating Xinjiang's mineral wealth into Soviet national economic planning; Soviet merchants dominated the trade in Xinjiang's local products; Soviet advisors shaped Xinjiang's foreign and domestic policy; Red Army troops were active in the province; and the activities of all non-Russians, including Chinese, in the province were heavily restricted. Despite diplomatic protests and periodic bluster from Nationalist officials about the unusual relationship between the Soviet Union and this Chinese province, Xinjiang remained beyond the reach of Chiang Kai-shek and the National Government.

By 1942, however, the Soviet Union's role as Xinjiang's primary patron and ally was losing its luster. Sheng Shicai saw Adolf Hitler's invasion of the Soviet Union in June 1941 as a dark portent. From September 30 to December 5, 1941, the Soviet Union suffered 500,000 casualties, had 673,000 soldiers captured, and lost 1,242 tanks and 5,412 artillery pieces. During the spring of 1942, the seemingly decisive battle of Stalingrad teetered and it was unclear who would emerge victorious.[7] As a consequence, Soviet aid payments and investments in Xinjiang slowed at the same time that Soviet officials began seeking to mobilize Xinjiang's resources for their war effort. Faced with growing obligations to repay their earlier support and little prospect of military and financial aid for the foreseeable future, Sheng Shicai began casting around for other potential pa-

---

[7] Data from Cai Jinsong, *Sheng Shicai zai Xinjiang* [Sheng Shicai in Xinjiang] (Zhengzhou: Henan renmin chubanshe, 1998), 325. The Russian scholar Barmin argues that Sheng's shift was largely a product of Sheng's greed and ambition. See V.A. Barmin, *SSSR i Sin'tszian, 1941–1949* [The USSR and Xinjiang, 1941–1949] (Moscow: Barnaul, 1999), 13.

trons who could underwrite his political and military power in this region
that remained, on paper at least, a province of China. Chiang Kai-shek
and the Nationalists, having acquired a seemingly unbeatable ally in the
United States after the Japanese attacked Pearl Harbor in December
1941, seemed to be the obvious choice.

Throughout the summer of 1942, Sheng Shicai and Chiang Kai-shek
executed a delicate *pas de deux*, as each sought to determine the motives
and intentions of the other. Sheng was eager to quickly end his relationship with the Soviet Union without jeopardizing his own position of authority within the province, while Chiang Kai-shek hoped to rapidly incorporate Xinjiang into the Republic of China without alienating the
Soviet Union. The details of Sheng's planned about-face were worked out
in a series of meetings with various high-level members of the National
Government who traveled to the provincial capital of Dihua (present-day
Urumqi) that summer. By late August, following a trip to the province by
Chiang's wife, Song Meiling, the two sides reached an informal deal.
Throughout the fall and winter, supported by the Nationalist Party politi-
cally, financially, and militarily, Sheng moved to arrest pro-Soviet figures
(including Mao Zedong's brother) in the provincial administration and
force all Soviet military and civilian personnel from the province.

By early 1943, the border crossings out of Xinjiang were jam-packed
with Soviet technicians, advisors, soldiers, and diplomats. Following
closely on their heels were trucks loaded down with industrial equipment,
military hardware, and reams of files and reports accumulated over the
nearly ten years of Soviet patronage. Abandoned Soviet industrial sites,
military installations, and mining operations dotted Xinjiang's vast landscape in early 1943. At one Soviet oil-drilling enterprise, which had been
booming the year before, witnesses described a scene in which only the
steel frames and piping for wells, a few boilers, and assorted abandoned
buildings remained.[8]

Nationalist officials from Chongqing eagerly stepped into this post-
apocalyptic landscape. They focused their efforts on extending the political

---

[8] Liu Yuehua, "Minguo Xinjiang shiyou kaifa yanjiu" [Research into the development of
Xinjiang's oil], master's thesis, Xinjiang University (Urumqi), 2002, 32.

infrastructure of Free China into Xinjiang: expanding transportation networks into the province, incorporating its mineral wealth into China-centered national economic planning, and importing large numbers of Han immigrants. These efforts, intended to transform Xinjiang into a fully integrated province of China, were undertaken with an eye toward rescuing the deteriorating war effort. Yet before they could undertake the process of saving China, they needed to fully reorient the province toward China, and in late 1942 and throughout 1943 officials sought to lay the political infrastructure that would make Xinjiang Chinese once and for all.

REORIENTING XINJIANG

In a July 9, 1942, meeting in Chongqing, the Soviet ambassador to the Republic of China sought to undermine Sheng Shicai by presenting Chiang Kai-shek a letter that detailed all of Sheng's machinations, including his calls for the outright Soviet annexation of the province, his calls for the Soviet conquest of China, and his suggestion in 1936 that Soviet agents assassinate Chiang. Without reaction, Chiang accepted the letter and politely informed the ambassador that in the future, "regarding the Xinjiang problem, the Soviet government should directly consult China's central government and not the Xinjiang provincial government."[9] Chiang Kai-shek's firm declaration belied the fact that the Nationalists had almost no way of enforcing their newly acquired authority in this province where they lacked all but the most rudimentary political institutions. The year 1943 would be witness to a vast political reorientation, as Chiang and Nationalist Party officials sought to lay the political infrastructure that would bind Xinjiang more closely to the republic.

In the summer of 1942, Chiang created a "special office" in the provincial capital of Dihua that was charged with handling Nationalist interests

---

[9] "Panyouxin yu Jiang Jieshi huitan jiyao: Xinjiang diqu wenti" [A summary of the minutes of Pushkin's conversation with Chiang Kai-shek: The Xinjiang problem], July 9, 1942, reprinted in Shen Zhihua, ed., *Eguo jiemi dang'an: Xinjiang wenti* (Urumqi: Xinjiang renmin chubanshe, 2013), 123–24. All of the sources included in Shen's book are Chinese translations of Soviet-era Russian-language sources uncovered in Russian archives.

in the province. At the center of their activities was overseeing Xinjiang's relationships with the Soviet Union. Chiang and many high-ranking officials maintained a deep mistrust of the Soviet Union and its intentions in China that stretched back to the party's violent confrontation with the Soviet-backed Chinese Communist Party in the late 1920s and early 1930s, and continued through Stalin's decision to renege on his pledges of support for the National Government in their War of Resistance by signing a neutrality pact with Japan in 1941. Yet due to their prominent place in the broader alliance against the Axis powers, Chinese leaders needed to maintain a working relationship with Stalin and the Soviet Union, and the new office in Dihua was charged with managing Xinjiang's break with the Soviet Union without provoking an outright Sino-Soviet rupture.

The first permanent liaison appointed by Chongqing to head up the office was the London-educated diplomat Wu Zexiang. Wu's task was to eliminate Sheng's foreign policy autonomy by taking over all negotiations with the Soviet Union and recalling or exerting central government control over the consuls stationed in Soviet Central Asia whom Sheng had personally appointed during his tenure. The Ministry of Foreign Affairs asserted, "In any matter relating to provincial sovereignty or economic profit, the case must be brought to the attention of the central government, regardless of the gravity of the affair."[10] Throughout 1943, Wu and the Ministry of Foreign Affairs worked to ensure that Chongqing held the monopoly on all diplomatic communications.[11]

In addition to creating a new liaison in Chongqing, Chiang Kai-shek also sought to find a counterbalance to Soviet military power in the region. For this, the Nationalist regime mobilized four full divisions from the New Second Army stationed in Gansu Province for duty in Xinjiang. Troops continued to flow in throughout 1943, and scholars estimate that by 1944 and 1945, approximately 100,000 Nationalist troops were sta-

---

[10] Quoted in Justin Jacobs, "Empire Besieged: The Preservation of Chinese Rule in Xinjiang, 1884–1971," PhD diss., University of California, San Diego, 2010, 361.

[11] Old habits were hard to break, however, and when Sheng himself responded to a Soviet diplomatic protest in late 1942, the Ministry of Foreign Affairs felt compelled to remind Wu, "In the future, whenever a similar case arises it would be best not to issue a reply from the provincial government. Instead, our reply to the Soviets should come directly from our special agent for foreign affairs." Quoted in ibid., 361–62.

tioned in the province.[12] To further undermine Soviet power in Xinjiang, Chiang Kai-shek sought to cultivate a population of non-Soviet foreigners within the province. By April 1943, at the encouragement of China's Ministry of Foreign Affairs, the British and American governments had both set up consulates in the provincial capital of Dihua. In their wake followed American and British traders, political figures, and missionaries who Chiang hoped would serve to reorient the province away from the Soviet Union.

Paralleling actions within the Xinjiang provincial government, Nationalist officials sought to begin laying local Nationalist Party political infrastructure throughout the province. At the beginning, officials from Chongqing sought to lay this party infrastructure on top of that already in place, simply swapping out Sheng's Anti-Imperialist Society Party organization with Nationalist Party institutions throughout the province. The society, which was created in 1934, had large-scale popular membership throughout the province, a monthly publication that reinforced Sheng and the Soviet Union's position within the province, and a network of local party offices. Throughout 1943, Chinese officials worked to strengthen the political power of the Nationalist Party within Xinjiang and lay the institutional foundation that would allow them to weather future political, economic, and social turmoil, and hold off any future attempts by the Soviet Union to again exert control over the province.

On January 16, 1943, the official opening of the Xinjiang Nationalist Party headquarters in Dihua was commemorated with flag-raising ceremonies in small towns scattered throughout the province.[13] Not far behind, a flood of party cadres, teachers, and officials streamed into the province. They were energized by new slogans such as "Open the great northwest" and "Establish the foundation of the nation in the northwest" as well as patriotic appeals to ethnocultural Han pride through the use of historical figures like Zhang Qian and Ban Chao, who had played a central role in integrating the northwest during the Han dynasty over 2,000 years earlier.

---

[12] Forbes, *Warlords and Muslims*, 168.

[13] In his memoir, Huang Jiqing recalls one such ceremony in the oil town of Dushanzi in northern Xinjiang. See Huang, *Tianshan zhi lu*, 40.

Part of this political reorientation entailed a sharp rejection of Soviet and Marxist ideology and symbols. Provincial and National Government officials undertook an aggressive campaign to rip out the ideological roots fostered by the decade of Soviet oversight within Xinjiang. Soviet diplomats complained in communications to Moscow that throughout late 1942 and 1943, provincial officials were violently purging the province of Soviet symbols. Portraits of Lenin and Stalin were ripped from the walls of classrooms, government buildings, and private homes, and books of Marxist writings were seized and destroyed.[14]

To sustain this mission over the long term and eliminate the potential for any future ideological waffling by Sheng or any governor, Chiang sought to recraft the ideological foundation of the province. Provincial schools were given a new curriculum centered around Sun Yat-sen's "Three Principles of the People." He funded cadre and party training institutes equipped to train the 3,000 new cadres and 20,000 new party members who were to serve as the backbone for an unshakeable Nationalist presence in the province. In addition, essay and research competitions in knowledge of the Three Principles were funded and regularly held; a network of forty-three Sun Yat-sen Rooms was established around the province to spread the gospel of the Three Principles of the People and the good news about the Father of the Country (Guofu) Sun Yat-sen, and a new party press was established, which by 1944 was already publishing seven new magazines on topics hand-picked by the provincial party apparatus.[15]

The construction of Nationalist political infrastructure, the dissemination of Sun Yat-sen's Three Principles of the People, and the co-option of previous political institutions in the province were all central components of a process of political integration being undertaken by Chinese state agents in Xinjiang. In some cases, their actions were piecemeal and in others ineffectual, but overall their attempts were part of an ambitious process

---

[14] See Barmin, *SSSR i Sin'tszian*, 30.

[15] See Huang Jianhua, *Guomindang zhengfu de Xinjiang zhengce yanjiu* [Research into the Nationalist government's Xinjiang policy] (Beijing: Minzu chubanshe, 2003), 89; see also Zhang Dajun, *Xinjiang fengbao qishinian* [Xinjiang's seventy-year storm], vol. 10 (Taipei: Wenhai chubanshe, 1980), 5837–41.

of incorporation that officials hoped would reorient the province toward China.

SAVING THE REPUBLIC

The acquisition of Xinjiang was hailed as a real victory in Chongqing. To many it seemed as if the province had been dropped like a gift from some benevolent god. Newspapers hailed it as a miracle in gushing articles about the northwest. The official Wu Aichen, who had played a prominent role in the province's tumultuous early 1930s, noted, "Every sector of society is beside itself with joy."[16] This joy was tinged with optimism about the future of the republic. Indeed, acquiring Xinjiang not only served to energize Chinese nationalism in a dark period of the war, but it also appeared to be the medicine needed to cure the various ills that plagued the wartime republic. The acquisition of the province could end the international isolation of Free China, allow Chinese officials to gain access to the minerals they needed to maintain the war effort, and simultaneously open new grain-producing areas and serve as a place to resettle refugees from the increasingly overcrowded regions of the southwest.

Transportation Connections

By early 1942, Japan's isolation of China was nearly complete. After the initial invasion of China in 1937, the invading Imperial Japanese Army drove the government deep into China's rugged and long-unexplored southwest. The Japanese navy exerted control over all of China's major Pacific harbors. The surrender of French Indochina to the Japanese in September 1940 closed off China's southern border, and the signing of the Japan-Soviet neutrality pact in April 1941 and the subsequent cooling of Sino-Soviet relations appeared to isolate China to the west and north. Even the hope inspired by the American entry into the war in late 1941

---

[16] See Jacobs, *Empire Besieged*, 364. For the original, see Wu Aichen, *Xinjiang jiyou* [Travels in Xinjiang] (Shanghai: Shangwu yinshuguan, 1944), preface.

was mitigated by Japan's successful assault on Burma and the closing of
the so-called Burma Road that connected China to the major port of
Rangoon in early 1942.

For Nationalist officials, the exertion of control over Xinjiang appeared
to resolve the regime's pressing isolation by reopening desperately needed
connections to the outside world. "There is not one person who does not
hope to improve transport in the northwest in order to overcome the enemy's plan of sealing off our country," wrote one Nationalist planner undertaking a survey of transport facilities in Xinjiang in the summer of
1942.[17] The hope for officials was that the acquisition of the province
would allow the regime to resume importing the equipment and supplies
needed to continue waging the war. Pushed by the enthusiasm of Nationalist officials, Allied planners decided that the trans-Xinjiang supply corridor should begin at the docks at Karachi, continue along the rail line
crossing eastern Persia to the Soviet border, and connect up to China's
western border via the Soviet Trans-Caspian rail network.[18] Throughout
1942 and 1943, from their headquarters in the War Cabinet in London
and the Department of State in Washington, DC, planners undertook the
delicate diplomatic negotiations and the complicated logistical legwork
needed to open the route.

For their part, Nationalist economic planners placed a priority on
firming up the transport infrastructure crossing Xinjiang in 1943. Surveying teams blanketed Xinjiang in 1942 and 1943, and began the arduous
task of laying the foundation for a new transportation network in the
province. According to archival sources, in 1943 alone, five surveying
teams operating with a budget of 4 million yuan set out to lay plans for a
new rail line connecting western Gansu Province to Xinjiang's border

---

[17] "Gong Xuezhu guanyu Xinjiangsheng jiaotong yunshu yanjiu baogao" [A research
report from Gong Xuezhu on Xinjiang Province's transport] (July 1942), in *Zhonghua Minguoshi dang'an ziliao huibian* (caizheng jingji 10), ed. Zhongguo di er lishi dang'anguan
(Nanjing: Jiangsu guji chubanshe), 1991, 371–87.

[18] The planning for this route was spearheaded by the British War Cabinet's Subcommittee on Chinese Oil Supplies, which later changed its name to the Executive Subcommittee on Supplies to China. The subcommittee was charged with overseeing the complex
multilateral U.S.-China-Soviet negotiations and navigating the knotty logistical problems of
long-distance international transport. The complete records of the subcommittee are held in
the British Library in the India Office Collection, file numbers L/PS/12/4618 and L/
PS/12/4617.

town of Tacheng.[19] The longest of these expeditions was undertaken in 1943 by a group from the Academia Sinica, which surveyed more than 2,300 kilometers of territory in an expedition that spent more than 170 days in the field.[20]

The plans these teams drew up focused on the construction of a trunk route that would link, by either rail or road, all of the northwest into one broad transport network. The line would begin in Xi'an or Baoji in Shaanxi Province, continue into Tianshui in eastern Gansu Province, cross through the major northwestern transport hub Lanzhou, travel north through the Jade Gate in western Gansu, traverse the arid Hexi corridor into Xinjiang, travel along the Tianshan north road through Hami, pass through the capital of Xinjiang Province Dihua, cross the old Soviet oil fields at Dushanzi, and end at the northwestern border town of Tacheng. The entire route traversed a rugged nearly 3,500 kilometer route across northwestern China.[21] The ambitious plan crafted in 1942 and 1943 also included lines integrating Baotou in Inner Mongolia and a line to Xining in Qinghai Province, as well as a line stretching south into Chengdu in northwestern Sichuan Province. The entire network covered a total distance of 5,840 kilometers (the longest stretch of which was the line linking eastern Gansu to Tacheng). According to a report from the Ministry of Transport, the rail network could be completed in no less than ten years. The plans called for the final phase of construction to be completed in 1953, when the line connecting eastern Gansu Province and Tacheng would be opened to traffic.[22]

---

[19] See "Jiang Jieshi guanyu jianshe xibei tielu jinhou buzhu yu Zhang Jia'ao deng laiwang daidian" [Chiang Kai-shek on the construction of the steps forward for a northwestern rail system and Zhang Jiao'ao's official message] (October 1942), in *Zhonghua Minguoshi dang'an ziliao huibian* 5, 2 (Caizheng jingji 10), ed. Zhongguo di'er lishi dang'anguan (Nanjing: Jiangsu guji chubanshe, 1997), 192–94.

[20] Xinjiang weiwuer zizhiqu defang zhi bianmu weiyuanhui, ed., *Xinjiang tongzhi, di jiu juan (xia), dizhi kuangchan zhi* [Xinjiang gazetteer, vol. 9, no. 2, Geological mineral production] (Urumqi: Xinjiang renmin chubanshe, 1999), 818.

[21] "Jiang Jieshi guanyu jianshe xibei tielu jinhou buzhu yu Zhang Jia'ao deng laiwang daidian," 192.

[22] "Jiaotongbu guanyu nifa 'xibei shinian jiaotong jianshe jihua' zhi zhongyang shejiju mishu gonghan" [Official letter to the Central Planning Office Secretariat from the Ministry of Transport regarding the planned issuance of the "Northwest Ten Year Construction Plan"] (October 10, 1942), in *Kangzhan shiqi xibei kaifa dang'an shiliao xuanbian*, ed. Ma Zhendu, Lin Ningmei, and Chen Guang (Zhongguo shehui kexue chubanshe, 2009), 220.

Mineral and Oil Extraction

For Nationalist officials, minerals and oil held the key to maintaining China's war effort. In addition to using minerals in domestic industries, the sale of minerals like tungsten and antimony on international markets served as a critical source of revenue for the embattled regime. They used ores as collateral for cash loans and as a down payment to ensure the smooth flow of aid from allies such as the United States and the Soviet Union. Looking beyond the war, officials saw Xinjiang's ore wealth as the foundation for China's postwar prosperity. In the months immediately following the reacquisition of Xinjiang, large numbers of geologists and surveyors were dispatched to the province to begin the task of integrating its mineral wealth into national economic development plans.[23]

One geologist, in a 1945 report, remembered the high tide of geologists and other surveying teams sweeping the province in the months immediately following Sheng Shicai's change of allegiance: "Every type of investigative group was organized and sent out to Xinjiang to undertake on-the-ground surveys."[24] Sheng himself petitioned for the establishment of a Xinjiang branch of China's Central Geological Survey in December 1942, a request that the National Government's National Resource Commission had no problem granting. This provincial branch was established in March 1943, and that year twenty-one geological teams were tapped to survey Xinjiang's established mineral and ore sites.[25] Various reports outlining oil, tin, tungsten, copper, and bitumen ore deposits in the province flowed regularly into the offices of government agencies located through-

---

[23] For more information, see Judd Kinzley, "Staking Claims to China's Borderlands: Oil, Ores and Statebuilding in Xinjiang, 1893–1964," PhD diss., University of California, San Diego, 2012, 238–43.

[24] The author estimated that four different ministries and organs of government sent out their own surveying teams to understand Xinjiang's mineral wealth. See Mi Taiheng, *Xinjiang kuangchan jilue* (1942), Central Geological Survey Information Room, Document 2857, Central Geological Survey of China, Beijing.

[25] "Gedi cheng qing kaicai kuangchan" (December 24, 1942), Mining Industry Management Collection: 003-010307-0026, Academica Historica, Taipei, Taiwan, 25–27; see also "Cha guanyu Xinjiangsheng choushe dizhidiaochasuo yi shi qiangfeng" (October 11, 1943), Economic Affairs Collection: 18-24C, 14-4, Institute of Modern History, Academia Sinica, Taipei, Taiwan, 3.

out Chongqing.[26] An early 1943 report from the Ministry of Economics, Commission of Inquiry on Industrialization in the Northwest, noted, "The territory of this province is broad, its products are fruitful, and the conditions for economic development are even more promising than Shaanxi, Gansu, Qinghai and Ningxia."[27]

For Nationalist officials, Xinjiang's rich oil wealth was of particular interest. The Soviet Union had invested substantial amounts of capital into one prominent oil field in north-central Xinjiang, at a place called Dushanzi. The minister of economic affairs, Weng Wenhao, investigated the field in the summer of 1942 after being personally invited by Sheng Shicai. Weng's initial report, which he wrote in late July shortly after returning to Chongqing, provides a detailed analysis of the production capacity of the oil field and offers optimistic suggestions for dramatically increasing production and aiding the transport of oil for use in China's war effort.[28]

In addition to oil, Nationalist economic planners also focused their efforts on tungsten, another mineral that Soviet officials had had some success in mining. Tungsten served as a critical component of Nationalist wartime finances. An extremely valuable component of the steel alloy used in the production of armaments, the metal was used as collateral for loans

---

[26] Mi, *Xinjiang kuangchan jilue*; Huang Jiqing, *Wusu Dushanzi youtian* (1942), Central Geological Survey of China Information Office: Document 4565, Central Geological Survey of China, Beijing; Huang Jiqing, *Xinjiang Wusuxian Dushanzi shiyou ji meiqi kuangchuang shuomingshu* (1942), Central Geological Survey of China Information Office: Document 743, Central Geological Survey of China, Beijing; Wen Long, *Xinjiang Tacheng Katushan jinkuang baogao* (1942), Central Geological Survey of China Information Office: Document 935, Central Geological Survey of China, Beijing; Wang Hengsheng, *Xinjiang dizhi diaocha gaikuang ji kuangchan gongbu* (1943), Central Geological Survey of China Information Office: Document 1142, Central Geological Survey of China, Beijing.

[27] "Lin Jiyong guanyu xibei gongye gaikuang de kaocha baogao" [An investigative report by Lin Jiyong on northwestern industrial situation] (February 18, 1943), in *Zhonghua Minguoshi dang'an ziliao huibian* 5:2 (caizheng jingji 6), ed. Zhongguo di'er lishi dang'anguan (Nanjing: Jiangsu guji chubanshe, 1997), 167–72.

[28] His plans are exceedingly optimistic, suggesting that a sizable investment in production and refining would enable the Nationalists to increase the production of oil from 1,000 gallons of oil daily to 7,000 gallons, all of which would be shipped to the front lines along the new transport network for use in the war effort. Weng Wenhao, *Xinjiangsheng Dushanzi youkuang shicha baogao* (July 1942), Central Geological Survey of China Information Office: Document 3684, Central Geological Survey of China, Beijing.

and was an important commodity for international trade.[29] In 1943, the
National Government established a Xinjiang Tungsten Mine Engineering
Office that was charged with identifying Soviet mining operations and
surveying the province's tungsten reserves. The next year a fifteen-man
surveying team set out from Lanzhou to survey western Xinjiang's tungsten fields and begin sketching out plans to incorporate the ores into national development plans.[30]

Resettlement of Refugees

Famine and overcrowding in Free China were critical obstacles facing Nationalist officials in 1942 and 1943. After the Japanese invasion in 1937,
large numbers of agricultural workers fled their lands in northern and central China to the relative safety of the southwest. The exodus created a
crisis of overcrowding in the arable lands of Free China. The outbreak of
famine and a wave of epidemics in northern China in 1942 and 1943 only
compounded this problem, as a surge of 4 million additional refugees
flooded out of the region and into Shaanxi and the southwest (see chapter
10). The acquisition of Xinjiang appeared to be an answer to the prayers of
Nationalist officials. The province could provide agricultural land and employment opportunities for refugees, and the rich unoccupied steppe of
northern Xinjiang could also produce food for Free China. Indeed, only
weeks after throwing his lot in with Chongqing, Sheng, along with the
Nationalist general Zhu Shaoliang, who commanded the neighboring
province of Gansu, put together a plan in which 30,000 to 50,000 settlers
would be immediately sent to Xinjiang and an additional one million settlers would be shipped in over the long term.[31]

At the beginning, the acquisition of Xinjiang was seen as a golden opportunity for the Chinese government to cull its swollen bureaucracy. In a

---

[29] By 1944, China's wartime economy was fully dependent on mineral exports for generating revenue, and, in many cases, sacks of tungsten were exchanged directly with international trading partners like the United States for essential sundries like cloth and medicine.
See September 3, 1944, Mining Industry Management Collection: 001-113100-0004, Academia Historica, Taipei, Taiwan, 94.

[30] See Kinzley, "Staking Claims to China's Borderlands," 241–42.

[31] Cited in Cai, *Sheng Shicai zai Xinjiang*, 363.

September 1942 report, Chiang Kai-shek put forth a plan to cut party and military personnel and employ them in development activities in the northwest.[32] A drought, which took hold of central China in the summer of 1942 and created a massive mobile population of refugees, presented itself as an opportunity for central government officials looking for the strong backs needed to develop the northwest. These settlers were to be the vanguard in an economic transformation of the province and played a central role in the development of Free China's "rear area." As one official pointed out in a report to Chiang Kai-shek, "the construction of roads and irrigation canals in the northwest lacks a large number of people, and so do other construction jobs."[33] One high-ranking official submitted a report to Chiang that suggested that the answer to the "population problem" was to be found in the resettlement of refugees from Henan Province in Gansu Province's Hexi corridor and eastern Xinjiang. His report called for the government to resettle 50,000 famine victims in the northwest at a total cost of 30 million yuan to pay for transportation, housing, equipment, clothing, and various start-up costs. As the official above noted, these refugees "would preserve the vitality of the nation, and increase its productive and construction capabilities."[34]

Energized by the opportunity to simultaneously increase the pool of labor in the northwest and also find a way to handle at least part of central China's refugee problem, central government officials quickly upped the ante on the resettlement plans. In one early proposal, Chiang Kai-shek himself suggested that 50,000 was far too low. He argued that the amount of arable land in the tiny province of Ningxia alone could accommodate an additional 200,000 families or an additional one million settlers from famine-affected regions. As the desire to kill two birds with one stone

---

[32] "Jiang Jieshi guanyu zhongyang dangjunzheng ge jiguan caiyuan san fenzhi yi yiju xibei shi shi Kong Xiangxi, He Yingqin ling" [Orders given to Kong Xiangxi and He Yingqin from Chiang Kai-shek regarding plans in which central party members, military, and bureaucrats of every level should be reduced by one-third and sent to settle the northwest] (September 22, 1942), in *Kangzhan shiqi xibei kaifa dang'an shiliao xuanbian*, 166.

[33] "Jiang Jieshi guanyu Zhang Fang cheng ni yizhi Xiangsheng huomin dao Hexi anzhu zhi Kong Xiangxi deng kuaiyou dai dian" [Special delivery to Kong Xiangxi from Chiang Kai-shek regarding a plan from Zhang Fang to resettle Henan refugees in the Hexi corridor] (September 27, 1942), in *Kangzhan shiqi xibei kaifa dang'an shiliao xuanbian*, 167–72, 168.

[34] Ibid.

took hold, officials became more and more convinced of the benefits of shipping large numbers of refugees and demobilized party members and soldiers into the northwest.

Throughout 1943, officials in the Ministries of Transport, Economic Affairs, and Agriculture and Forestry crafted plans that enabled the shipment and resettlement of large numbers of immigrants in the northwest. In the end, the logistical burdens of resettling large numbers of refugees in Xinjiang meant that the final plan was to send 30,000 refugees to Xinjiang beginning in 1943.[35] Agricultural experts were sent out to increase the amount of arable land in the province with the construction of a network of irrigation canals to accommodate the settlers. In 1943, plans for five large industrial farms were sent to Chongqing.[36] According to a production plan from the Ministry of Agriculture and Forestry, by 1944 more than one million *mu* of land in Xinjiang had been surveyed and was ready for broad-based reclamation activities undertaken by the new settlers.[37]

THE END OF OPTIMISM

The year 1943 was one of ambitious planning for Xinjiang. Blueprints, maps, and surveys were compiled by the legions of Chinese state agents unleashed on the province. On paper, Xinjiang appeared well positioned to transform the Chinese war effort and lay the foundation for a powerful postwar China. Yet, by 1944, these plans were crashing against hard realities. If indeed Xinjiang was key to China's wartime salvation and postwar rejuvenation, precious national resources would need to be redirected to the province; central government control would need to be clearly exerted

[35] "Guanyu yimin Xinjiang sanwan ren yi an" (April 5, 1943), Economic Affairs Collection: 20-26, 52-8, Institute of Modern History, Academia Sinica, Taipei, Taiwan, 3.

[36] The farms would be worked by settlers and would cost nearly 15 million yuan to complete. "Xinjiang sheng zhengfu jiansheting minguo sanshi'ernian shuili nongchang jianshe jingfei jihua zongbiao" (March 3, 1944), Economic Affairs Collection: 20-00-61, Institute of Modern History, Academia Sinica, Taipei, Taiwan, 1–3.

[37] "Sanshisan nian nonglinbu jianshe jihua" (May 1, 1944), Economic Affairs Collection: 20-00-61, 1-4, Institute of Modern History, Academia Sinica, Taipei, Taiwan, 4–5.

and a peaceable agreement reached with the Soviet Union in Xinjiang. Absent these three factors, the Nationalists' position within the province remained tenuous at best. None of these goals were accomplished by the end of 1943 and Nationalist authority in Xinjiang was indeed shaken by both internal and external forces the next year.

If the National Government was going to integrate Xinjiang into the Chinese nation-state, it had to inexorably centralize its control over the province. The inability of the central government to control Xinjiang's provincial governors had been an obstacle to central control since the overthrow of the Qing in 1912. To be successful where their predecessors failed, Nationalist officials needed to be much more aggressive in establishing lines of power binding Dihua to Chongqing. It quickly became clear to Nationalist officials that the appointment of a liaison from Chongqing and the establishment of local Nationalist Party organs were not sufficient to bring Xinjiang into the Free China fold, as Sheng proved reluctant to cede any real authority in Xinjiang. Even on the fairly straightforward question of foreign policy, in late 1942, in direct opposition to Nationalist Party policies in the region, Sheng himself, rather than Chongqing's liaison, responded directly to a Soviet diplomatic protest.[38] Sheng's intransigence continued throughout 1943, as he sought to resist attempts by Nationalist officials to subvert his authority over Central Asian consulates, worked to ensure that his allies operated in positions of authority throughout the province, and aggressively held off any inroads into his stranglehold on the reins of power in Xinjiang.

The clearest indicator of the National Government's failures in laying political infrastructure was its inability to hold off a campaign of terror against Soviet citizens and personnel by Sheng Shicai. Throughout late 1942 and 1943, fearing a Soviet backlash against his political about-face, Sheng actively sought to drive all Soviet citizens out of the province. He undertook a vicious campaign of imprisoning Soviet experts and citizens, as well as anyone affiliated with Soviet administration of the province.[39]

---

[38] See Jacobs, *Empire Besieged*, 285–386.

[39] Soviet officials recounted that Soviet citizens were being regularly berated in the streets, were not being sold food or other sundries by local merchants who were forbidden to do so on pain of immediate imprisonment, and were subjected to humiliating searches by

As one 1943 Soviet diplomat complained to Chiang Kai-shek, "In April and May of this year the attitude at every level of government in the province toward Soviet citizens and organizations has taken a rapid turn for the worse."[40] Fearing the long-lasting impact on Sino-Soviet relations, officials from China's Ministry of Foreign Affairs urged Sheng to be more circumspect in his dealings with the Soviet Union. In negotiations with their Soviet counterparts, Chinese officials desperately sought to distance themselves from Sheng's actions and minimize the diplomatic damage by insisting that his days in power in the province were numbered. Despite these efforts, Sheng's bull-in-a-china-shop policy toward the Soviet Union continued throughout much of 1943, severely undermining Nationalist policy and ultimately jeopardizing its control over the province.

The Soviet threat to Xinjiang and Sheng Shicai's ability to operate with relative autonomy in the region could have been mitigated if Chiang Kai-shek and the Nationalists were able to simply incorporate the province into a China-centered infrastructure. However, questions remained about how a government mired in a seemingly endless war of attrition would be able to foot the astronomical bill to construct a new infrastructural network in this long-isolated region. Indeed, as economic planners in Chongqing sat down to examine the large volume of reports and blueprints outlining the new China-centered infrastructure network in the province that were crossing their desks in 1943, they were paralyzed by the massive cost. As their Qing and early republican counterparts had come to understand, the price tag on the railroad lines, highways, and irrigation canals that would integrate Xinjiang into the nation-state were sky high.[41] The cost for constructing the northwestern rail network was so substantial that in its ten-year construction plan, the Ministry of Transport chose to calculate only the first year, which would cost a staggering 657 million yuan. Additional lines crossing southern Xinjiang were estimated to cost

---

overly eager policemen and border guards. "Asitahuofu zhi Jiekazuofu han: Xinjiang de fan-Su huodong" [A letter from Asitahuofu to Jiekazuofu: Xinjiang's anti-Soviet movement] (June 15, 1943), reprinted in Shen, *Eguo jiemi dangan*, 152–55.

40 Ibid.

41 See Kinzley, "Staking Claims to China's Borderlands," chapters 1 and 2.

444 million.[42] The plans to resettle refugees from northern China were likewise substantial. In 1944, the annual price tag on transport and seed money to set up these communities in Xinjiang was 150 million Chinese yuan.[43] Mining and drilling enterprises likewise cost money and, as officials sketched out their mineral extraction priorities, it was unclear when and indeed if those capital investments would pay off.

The long list of financial obligations for the central government in Xinjiang continued to mount throughout 1943. The problem for Nationalist economic planners was not their desire to integrate Xinjiang more completely, but rather to come up with the means. The financial situation in Free China was dire by 1943: tax revenues were plummeting, wartime expenditures were increasing, and the economy appeared to be gripped in an inflationary death spiral (see chapter 9). As a result, the investments in Xinjiang in 1943 and after were piecemeal. A paved highway linking the province to China proper was not completed; ground was not even broken on the northwestern railroad;, and despite grand plans to open new arable lands in Xinjiang, the limited investment in large-scale reclamation doomed the communities of former refugees who had been sent out to the province. In 1947, officials in the Ministry of Agriculture and Forestry were deluged by telegrams from former refugees resettled in Xinjiang begging to return home. As one disgruntled settler wrote in his request, "If you do not undertake and complete irrigation works, there surely will be no reclamation sites to speak of."[44]

The inability of the Nationalists to come up with the investment needed to more clearly incorporate Xinjiang into the transport, commodity, and labor markets of Free China allowed the Soviet Union to play the role of spoiler in the province. Without a firm infrastructure binding Xinjiang to China, Sheng's about-face was nearly meaningless, as the Soviet

---

[42] "Jiaotongbu guanyu nifa 'xibei shinian jiaotong jianshe jihua' zhi zhongyang shejiju mishu gonghan," 220.

[43] "Zhonghua Minguo sanshisan nian er yue yi ri qizhi sanshisannian shiyue sanshiyi zhi" (1944), Economic Affairs Collection: 20-26, 33-8, Institute of Modern History, Academia Sinica, Taipei, Taiwan, 1.

[44] "Weicheng qing zhengfu yuanhui yuanji shi" (December 10, 1947), Economic Affairs Collection: 20-26, 33-12, Institute of Modern History, Academia Sinica, Taipei, Taiwan, 1.

Union could derail all of the grand plans and pop the gilded fantasies being dreamed up by Nationalist officials. Despite the efforts of Nationalist officials in Chongqing to reorient the province, their hopes and aspirations, and indeed China's very salvation in 1943, remained fully in the hands of the Soviet Union.

Even the hope that Xinjiang would serve as a life-saving international conduit ran up against geopolitical realities. In late September 1943, after more than a year of intense diplomatic negotiations, the Soviet Union blocked a convoy of trucks loaded down with 500 tons of American equipment that was bound for Free China via Soviet Central Asia and Xinjiang.[45] Soviet opposition, which stemmed from Stalin's fear that a Chinese shipping route might siphon off supplies needed for the Soviet war effort, might jeopardize their already tense nonaggression pact with Japan, and might also serve as an avenue for an American military buildup in western China, ended Chinese officials' hopes that Xinjiang could act as the international transport conduit.

Shipments of American equipment were not the only things blocked by the Soviet Union. Cross-border trade between Xinjiang and the Soviet Union, which the province had depended on completely since the late nineteenth century, dropped by 85 percent from 1942 to 1943.[46] The move crippled Xinjiang's economy overnight, as the volume of goods that could be shipped to and from China proper on the subpar transportation infrastructure could by no means make up the shortfall. The closing of the border prompted shortages of various critical items such as cloth, metal goods, tea, and sugar in Xinjiang's markets and led to massive price increases.[47] More troublingly for Nationalist officials was the fact that Xin-

---

[45] The decision to block the trans–Central Asia shipping route served as a shock to British, American, and Chinese officials. After extensive negotiations with the Soviet Union throughout 1942 and 1943, they were under the mistaken impression that Soviet permission for the transshipment had been obtained. See "Prospects of Opening the Sinkiang Route" (January 24, 1944), India Office Collection: L/PS/12/4918, British Library, London. For a more general account based on Chinese sources, see David Wang, *Under the Soviet Shadow: The Yining Incident, Ethnic Conflicts and International Rivalry in Xinjiang, 1944–1949* (Hong Kong: Chinese University Press, 1999), 81 n. 96.

[46] Li Sheng, *Xinjiang dui Su (E) maoyishi, 1600–1990* [A history of Xinjiang's trade with the Soviet Union (and Russia)] (Urumqi: Xinjiang renmin chubanshe, 1992), 511.

[47] According to an analysis by Owen Lattimore, the market prices for these commodi-

jiang's raw materials lost their primary market when the Soviet Union halted cross-border trade. In 1943 and 1944, local products such as skins, furs, and animal parts piled up in markets around the province and prices dropped sharply, in a few cases as much as 90 percent.[48] As a result, the livelihoods of various nomadic groups around the province had collapsed by 1944 and unrest swept across the province. The economic turmoil prompted a predictable surge in dangerous anti-Nationalist China and anti–Han Chinese sentiments within the province. Hoping to avert a crisis and establish control, Chiang Kai-shek removed Sheng from power in September 1944. Yet the damage had already been done.

The Soviet Union, energized by having successfully turned back the German invasion in 1943, sought to capitalize on the unrest for which they themselves were in large part responsible and once again stake a claim to Xinjiang. Led by a policy shift crafted in the Soviet Union's Politburo in May 1943, the former pro–Han Chinese Soviet ethnic policy that had shaped relations with the province since the 1910s was scrapped in favor of one that supported those non-Han peoples plotting to overthrow Sheng and Han Chinese rule in Xinjiang. Beginning in 1943, but continuing through 1944, agents of the Soviet government undertook a whisper campaign in the province to undermine Sheng and his Nationalist patrons. They began covertly distributing weapons to various local nomadic groups and even began military training for expatriate Turkic Muslims from Xinjiang under the guidance of Red Army officers in Soviet Central Asia.

In November 1944, units of well-equipped Kazak and Uighur soldiers marched on the western Xinjiang city of Yili. Aided by substantial support from the Soviet Union, the small, localized rebellion morphed into a large-scale anti-Chinese and pro-Soviet uprising that threatened all of Xinjiang. In the end, the so-called Three Districts Rebellion, undertaken beneath the mantle of a new government with aims to create a new independent Turkic Muslim state in the region, swallowed up the three districts hugging the Soviet border in northern Xinjiang (which, perhaps not

---

ties increased by 750 times from 1942 to 1945. See Owen Lattimore, *Pivot of Asia: Sinkiang and the Inner Asian Frontiers of China and Russia* (Boston: Little, Brown, 1950), 179.

[48] Li, *Xinjiang dui Su (E) maoyishi*, 500.

coincidentally, was Xinjiang's most mineral-rich region). The armies of the East Turkestan Republic, as the government was called, were halted in their quest to seize the rest of Xinjiang only by fears among their Soviet patrons that ongoing unrest would jeopardize the Soviet-American relationship. The East Turkestan Republic would hold onto the region until the collapse of the Nationalist government in 1949.

In stark contrast to the optimism of late 1942 and 1943, the year 1944 was one of shattered hopes in the northwest. The uprising ended any belief that the province would be central to China's salvation and postwar rejuvenation. Indeed, the uprising completely ended any hope of opening the international supply corridor, led to the seizure of Xinjiang's most mineral-rich lands, and threw the most promising refugee settlements in northern Xinjiang into chaos. Almost as quickly as it appeared, the light from the west was snuffed out. If China was to be saved, its salvation would not come from Xinjiang.

CONCLUSION

There is no question that the failed integration of Xinjiang in 1943–1944 was a missed opportunity for Nationalist China. Chiang Kai-shek was able to muster neither the economic capital to integrate the province into China's trade, commodity, and labor networks, nor the political capital to develop new, lasting political institutions binding Xinjiang to Chongqing. In the end, Xinjiang did not save China. This missed opportunity not only undermined the postwar rejuvenation of the republic but also condemned Xinjiang to the periphery of the Chinese nation-state well into the era of the People's Republic. Nevertheless, the reports, surveys, and maps carefully drawn up by the agents of the Nationalist state in 1943 served as an important blueprint for postwar and indeed post-1949 Chinese Communist Party planning in the province.[49] These plans, implemented by party

---

[49] The geologists Huang Jiqing and Weng Wenhao both went on to serve in both the republican and Chinese Communist Party governments. These connections across 1949, especially among scientists and technocrats, were the rule, rather than the exception. See Morris Bian, *The Making of the State Enterprise System in Modern China: The Dynamics of Institu-*

officials in the late 1950s and early 1960s, served to reorient Xinjiang once and for all, transforming it into an integral part of the Chinese nation-state.

The frenetic activity of Nationalist officials in Xinjiang in 1943 points to the fact that China's border regions were not merely supporting actors in a play set in China's political, economic, and cultural capitals of Chong-qing and Yan'an. Chinese peripheries were not simply part of a "great rear area" (*dahoufang*), as Chiang Kai-shek referred to them, but instead, in an expanded view of wartime China, were a front line. Sheng Shicai recog-nized as much, remembering that in 1943 he and other provincial officials felt that Xinjiang was no longer the back door to the republic, instead saying, "We felt that Xinjiang had become the front door of China."[50] Chiang Kai-shek's statement heralding the acquisition of the province in 1942 as the "greatest achievement" since the Republican Revolution of 1912 suggests that for at least one moment, he might have agreed.

Whether or not we want to put it on the front line, the story of Xin-jiang in 1943 suggests the relevance of border regions to the broader war-time narrative. This chapter suggests that any integrated focus on China at war cannot rest on the experiences of those in so-called China-proper alone. While nation-centered scholarship has long tended to a Nationalist Party narrative of wartime that focuses on central China, the lessons of Xinjiang in 1943 point toward new scholarly approaches to the wartime period in which national narratives are merged with regional or subna-tional narratives in which the experiences of seemingly peripheral regions such as Xinjiang are neither dismissed nor relegated to the "rear area" of a battle centered in central and eastern China.

---

tional Change (Cambridge, MA: Harvard University Press, 2005); Judd Kinzley, "Crisis and the Development of China's Southwestern Periphery: The Transformation of Panzhihua, 1936–1969," *Modern China* 38, no. 5 (September 2012): 559–84; William Kirby, "Continuity and Change in Modern China: Economic Planning on the Mainland and on Taiwan, 1943–1958," *Australian Journal of Chinese Affairs* 24 (1990): 121–41.

   [50] Allen Whiting and Sheng Shih-ts'ai, *Sinkiang: Pawn or Pivot?* (East Lansing: Mich-igan State University Press, 1958), 155.

4

Codifying the
Three People's Principles
Judicial Reform and the
End of Extraterritoriality

THOMAS R. WORGER

Henceforth, every legal institution, law and regulation, decree, code, everything that could take the form of law, regardless of whether its aspect is of creating, implementing, studying or interpreting law, must not only thoroughly take the Three People's Principles as its main idea, but must also take the Three People's Principles as its guiding principle.

> —Ju Zheng, "Why Must We Reconstruct the
> Chinese Legal System?" September 1946[1]

I swear to faithfully fulfill the sacred mission of legal workers in socialism with Chinese characteristics. I swear my loyalty to the Motherland, to the people, to uphold the leadership of the Communist Party of China and the socialist system, and to protect the dignity of the Constitution and the laws. I swear to practice law for the people; to be diligent, honest, professional, honest and corruption free; safeguard the lawful rights and inter-

---

[1] Ju Zheng, "Weishenme yao chongjian Zhongguo faxi" [Why must we reconstruct the Chinese legal system?], in *Ju Zheng wenji xiace* [The collected writings of Ju Zheng, vol. 2] (Wuchang: Huazhong shifan daxue chubanshe, 1989), 507.

ests of clients, maintain the right implementation of the law, uphold social fairness and justice, [and] diligently strive for the cause of socialism with Chinese characteristics.

—"Lawyer's Oath," Ministry of Justice, People's Republic of China, March, 21, 2012[2]

In March 2012, the Ministry of Justice of the People's Republic of China issued a notice requiring that all Chinese lawyers practicing at Chinese law firms take an oath of loyalty as part of their annual licensing procedure. Only a single paragraph in length, the oath required lawyers to pledge to practice law honestly, justly, and—most controversially—in accordance with the leadership of the Chinese Communist Party in furtherance of the cause of socialism with Chinese characteristics. The vagueness of the language was compounded by the lack of accompanying procedural instructions detailing what constituted breaking the code or the punishments for doing so. China watchers abroad, and legal professionals within China, characterized the oath as yet another sign of the increasing infiltration of party control into a nascent Chinese judiciary.[3] The Ministry of Justice, for its part, explained that the oath would promote the importance of developing "correct professional values" and instill in the legal profession a "sense of proper social responsibility."[4] While some view the oath as a particularly troubling feature of a new Chinese authoritarianism, cur-

---

[2] Translation provided by James Zimmerman, "News and Views from Beijing," *China Law Deskbook Monthly*, April 2012, 1–4.

[3] Attorney Li Zhuang reacted by saying, "Lawyers should only have the law in their sights, not parties or politics." Edward Wong, "Chinese Lawyers Chafe at New Oath to Communist Party," *New York Times*, March 22, 2012, World/Asia Pacific, http://www.nytimes.com/2012/03/23/world/asia/chinese-lawyers-chafe-at-new-oath-to-communist-party.html. Li Zhuang is a defense attorney from Chongqing, who served eighteen months in prison beginning in 2010 for inciting a client to provide false testimony. The incident has been considered by many who followed the case as something of a kangaroo trial and a personal attack by the instigator of the investigation, Bo Xilai. Prominent Beijing lawyer Pu Zhiqiang commented, "I don't see the legal basis for adding these procedures. On what basis is the Ministry of Justice doing this?" He Weifang, "A Letter to Chongqing Colleagues," *China Media Project*, April 12, 2011, http://cmp.hku.hk/2011/04/12/11481/. Sui-Lee Wee, "China Orders Lawyers to Pledge Allegiance to Communist Party," *Reuters* (Beijing), March 21, 2012.

[4] "Jinru lüshi duiwu bixu jinxing xuanshi" [Entering the ranks of lawyers requires swearing an oath], *Zhonghua renmin gongheguo sifabu* [People's Republic of China Minis-

rent policy is consistent with a historic and problematic role of a separate judicial branch within a one-party Chinese state.[5]

Over seventy years ago, in the war-torn Nationalist refuge of Chongqing, the Republic of China, the United States, and Great Britain set the stage for the creation of a legal system controlled by Chinese political interests when they signed treaties that brought an end to the hundred-year practice of extraterritoriality: a system of foreign legal jurisdiction on Chinese soil. The practice of extraterritoriality had been introduced in the nineteenth century in response to arguments by foreign powers that China's existing legal system was primitive and arbitrary. By the beginning of the twentieth century, the reform of the nation's legal system to mirror those of the West was believed to be the best means of convincing foreign nations to end extraterritoriality. Intellectuals vying for an independent judiciary based on Western neoliberal ideals of apolitical legal professionals had argued that these reforms were necessary to end foreign concessions and privileges. Nevertheless, following the abrogation of extraterritoriality in 1943, a decades-long ideological battle came to a head. The ruling Nationalist Party (Guomindang) was less interested than leading legal intellectuals in creating an independent judiciary and sought instead to create a judicial branch based on adherence to party doctrine. Though judicial reform had been leading to greater party control for the preceding two decades, the end of extraterritoriality and China's resumption of judicial sovereignty definitively extinguished any remaining hope for a politically independent judiciary.

The practice of extraterritoriality, widely resented by the Chinese, allowed the extension of legal jurisdiction over nationals beyond their home territory. Under extraterritoriality, individuals from one state may enter the territory of another and bring with them all the rights, immunities,

---

try of Justice], March 21, 2012, http://www.moj.gov.cn/index/content/2012-03/21/content _3445267.htm?node=7318.

[5] Most recently, there has been substantial movement toward greater inclusion of party rhetoric in regulations concerning the practice of law in the years since the promulgation of the 2007 Lawyers Law. Elizabeth M. Lynch, "China's Rule of Law Mirage: The Regression of the Legal Profession since the Adoption of the 2007 Lawyers Law," *George Washington International Law Review* 42 (2011): 535; see also Leland Benton, "From Socialist Ethics to Legal Ethics: Legal Ethics, Professional Conduct, and the Chinese Legal Profession," *UCLA Pacific Basin Law Journal* 28 (2011): 218–20. Carl F. Minzner, "China's Turn against Law," *American Journal of Comparative Law* 59 (2011): 949–55, 959–64.

and privileges afforded them within their own territory, while simultaneously enjoying exemption from local jurisdiction. Far more extreme than the immunities commonly associated with diplomats, the practice of extraterritoriality elevated the nationality principle of prescriptive justice above the territorial principle. In effect, the venue and controlling law of any case would be determined by the nationality of the defendant. For example, an American national appealed his conviction of vagrancy by the consular court in Shanghai in 1909, a crime then under U.S. law, by arguing that the court had no jurisdiction over him, as he had "taken an oath of allegiance" to the Boer Republic of South Africa ten years earlier. Though the court upheld the conviction, it did so only because the appellant could not provide sufficient documentation of his naturalization as a citizen of the Boer Republic.[6] Under this system, crimes ranging from vagrancy to murder would be adjudicated by foreign courts applying foreign law as long as the perpetrator was one of their citizens.

Efforts to end foreign extraterritorial privileges became entangled in attempts to reform the entire Chinese judicial system until the practical demands of wartime judicial administration in World War II ended the practice. Reformers involved in the government's Law Codification Commission—a late Qing attempt to modernize the legal code and reform the court system—advocated for an independent judiciary both as a prerequisite for constitutional government and as a means to avoid the easy corruption of local judicial actors who were simultaneously vested with administrative power. In the aftermath of the 1911 Revolution that founded the Republic of China, the influence of political parties was viewed as an additional impediment to fair and independent judicial practice. By this time, foreign powers had already stipulated the goal of judicial independence as a prerequisite for ending their extraterritorial privileges. Despite reforms to the legal system and the creation of a new civil code, the potential for interference from the political branches of government was often given as the primary reason for the refusal to end the practice. However, despite the increasingly politicized nature of judges throughout the 1930s, the practice of extraterritoriality ended by 1937 in reality and in 1943 in

---

[6] Rufus Thayer, "Robert W. Sexton v. United States," in *Extraterritorial Cases*, ed. Charles Lobingier (Manila: Bureau of Printing, 1920), 183–85.

law. As a result, extraterritoriality came to an end not from any achievement of judicial autonomy, but because the entire wartime environment—including the loss of the coastal treaty ports—made maintaining the system no longer practical.

In consequence, the abrogation of extraterritoriality made politically viable the establishment of a Chinese judiciary based exclusively on the moral precepts of Sun Yat-sen's Three People's Principles and the centralization of judicial power under the party-controlled state. The Program for the Training of Judicial Personnel (*sifa renyuan xunlian dagang*) was announced in the pages of the Ministry of Justice's official bulletin in August 1943, redefining judicial education as inherently political and requiring the inclusion of political content by legal mandate. With the promulgation of these new training guidelines for judicial officers, giving equal weight to Nationalist Party political doctrine and practical legal training, what had previously been implied by ministry practice now became law. Though judicial curricula had increasingly included political content throughout the prewar period, the institutional and rhetorical changes of 1943 mapped out the party's postwar plans for a nationwide judiciary staffed with officials educated primarily in adherence to the moral precepts of the Three People's Principles and Nationalist Party doctrine, rather than a strong theoretical understanding of judicial practice and codified law.

Although there has been little scholarly study of this period, there had been continual official debate over the form, function, and essence of a new Chinese legal system starting in the last decade of the Qing dynasty. The desire for institutional reform that would lead to an internationally recognized rule of law had to be balanced with the practical limitations of the Chinese state. Ultimately, the twin goals of building an effective and modern judiciary and satisfying the standards set by foreign powers for recognition of sovereign equality would prove themselves contradictory. Ending the practice of extraterritoriality had always been a prime motivator in the rhetoric of reform and the promulgation of regulations and codes.[7] Reform based on Western legal concepts had become the required

---

[7] Jeremy Murray, "'A Dream Deferred': Obstacles to Legal Reform and Rights Reclamation in Early Republican China," in *China on the Margins*, ed. Sherman Cochran (Ithaca, NY: Cornell East Asia Program, 2010), 95–96; Douglas Reynolds, *China, 1898–1912: The*

vocabulary until the abrogation of extraterritoriality in 1943. Consequently, most sources related to judicial modernization from this period were published in English with the hope that international audiences would take notice of the strides in legal reform that the Chinese government publicized.

Scholars have already examined important changes in the legal system from the end of the Qing dynasty up to the events during World War II. Progressive judicial reform in the last decade of the Qing dynasty has been rescued from the overshadowing narrative of Sun Yat-sen and the 1911 Revolution by scholars arguing that the New Policy reforms were representative of China's transformation from "tradition to modernity."[8] However, the early reformers that emerged after the fall of the Qing have been marginalized in scholarly work by what Jeremy Murray termed the "darkness" of the warlord period, stripped of any substantial intellectual agency or relevance.[9] Before Xu Xiaoqun's 2008 monograph, *Judicial Reform in Twentieth-Century China: 1901–1937*, the only English-language studies focused primarily on republican era Chinese legal reform had been Philip Huang's 2001 comparison of the Qing and republican legal codes in *Code, Custom, and Legal Practice in China* and Frank Dikötter's 2002 study of republican prison reform in *Crime, Punishment, and the Prison in Modern China*.

Both Xu and Huang focus on the question of judicial independence, particularly as an aspect of the larger subject of the rule of law. Unfortunately, the concept itself remains nebulous. Comparative law scholar Tom Ginsburg has commented, "Judicial independence has become like freedom: everyone wants it but no one knows quite what it looks like, and it is easiest to observe in its absence."[10] Xu contends that government policy

---

Xinzheng Revolution and Japan (Cambridge, MA: Council on East Asian Studies, Harvard University, 1993), 180–81; Xu Xiaoqun, *Trial of Modernity: Judicial Reform in Early Twentieth-Century China, 1901–1937* (Stanford, CA: Stanford University Press, 2008), 18.

[8] Quotation from Reynolds, *China, 1898–1912*, 1. Another example, among many, is Meribeth Cameron, *The Reform Movement in China, 1898–1912* (New York: Octagon, 1963).

[9] Murray, "'A Dream Deferred,'" 93.

[10] Tom Ginsburg, "Judicial Independence in East Asia: Lessons for China," in *Judicial Independence in China: Lessons for Global Rule of Law Promotion*, ed. Randall Peerenboom (Cambridge: Cambridge University Press, 2010), 248.

after 1927 did not abandon judicial independence, but favored what he terms a "narrow" view of the concept, which only applied to the fear of local power structures influencing judicial decisions. Under the regime's logic, strengthening party control at the local level promoted greater judicial independence from local interests. This masks the abandonment by the National government of the previous ideal of the separation of politics from judicial practice, in favor of the Guomindang-backed "partyization of the judiciary" (*sifa danghua*).[11] Huang, however, disagrees with Xu's depiction of party-led judicial governance, and distinguishes the Guomindang's politically powerful rulers from the lower-level technocrats assigned to independently reform the nuts and bolts of judicial practice.[12] Murray contends that the politically charged reforms following the Northern Expedition (1926–1928) were an intellectual regression that caused true judicial reform, namely reforms modeled on Western legal practices, to become a "dream deferred."[13] However, Huang believes that this identification of perceived Western concepts as the only path to judicial modernity represents a deeply orientalist view shared by contemporary academics both in China and abroad.[14] Unfortunately, both Xu and Huang extend their studies only to the point at which republican law reached its prewar height, shortly after the promulgation of the Civil and Criminal Codes in the early 1930s but well before the end of extraterritoriality and the Guomindang wartime reforms.

   Work by Chinese scholars has examined legal reform through the wartime period, much of which portrays the changes made by the Nationalist Party as despotic and corrupt.[15] Similar in tone to many critics of the

---

[11] Xu Xiaoqun, "The Fate of Judicial Independence in Republican China, 1912–37," *China Quarterly*, no. 149 (March 1, 1997): 27; Xu, *Trial of Modernity*.

[12] Philip Huang, *Code, Custom, and Legal Practice in China: The Qing and the Republic Compared* (Stanford, CA: Stanford University Press, 2001), 51. The two principle reformers Huang notes in constructing the Civil Code are Hu Hanmin and Wang Chonghui, neither of whom he argues were particular adherents to the specific political ideologies of Chiang Kai-shek and the party's core leadership.

[13] Murray, "'A Dream Deferred,'" n. 1.

[14] Philip Huang, *Chinese Civil Justice, Past and Present* (Lanham, MD: Rowman and Littlefield, 2010), xvi–xvii.

[15] Zhang Renshan, *Sifa fubai yu shehui shikong (1928–1949)* [Judicial corruption and lost control over society, 1928–1949] (Beijing: Shehui kexue wenxian chubanshe, 2005).

Republican government during this time, Zhang Qingjun has argued that legal practice under the Guomindang was a complete failure of "rule of law" (*fazhi*) and instead exemplified "rule of man" (*renzhi*), speaking specifically of the autocratic rule of Chiang Kai-shek.[16] The theme of similar studies is that changes to judicial practice after 1927 were merely forms of corruption, both professional and intellectual. Refreshingly, Li Zaiquan has argued that though ultimately unsuccessful and affected by power struggles within the Nationalist Party, the goal of partyization was to use party loyalty and indoctrination to counter local economic and political influences in order to unite a fractured judiciary.[17] Ingrained obedience to the central party leadership would create a cohesive judicial system, rather than a loosely connected series of self-interested local fiefdoms. Furthermore, Li characterizes partyization as a process beginning as early as 1924 and evolving alongside (not in spite of) Beiyang Era (1912–1927) reforms.

By 1943, the pressures to reform an inefficient and unreliable judiciary and to free China from foreign judicial control led to a moment in which the government could attempt to refashion the legal system to wrest control from local officials as well as foreign governments. This effort was ambitious and ultimately unsuccessful, yet an examination of the Nationalists' wartime judicial efforts provides a timely context for the ongoing efforts by the People's Republic of China to reform, and control, the judicial system.

JUDICIAL REFORM AND THE SHADOW OF EXTRATERRITORIALITY

The abrogation of extraterritoriality brought an end to what had popularly been termed the hundred years of humiliation. Following its loss in the 1842 Opium War, China spent the following half century unwillingly entering into a series of unequal treaties extending extraterritorial privileges to foreign powers spanning the globe from Japan to Brazil. While these

---

[16] Zhang Qingjun, *Minguo sifa heimu* [Dark secrets of the republican judiciary] (Nanjing: Jiangsu guji chubanshe, 1997).

[17] Li Zaiquan, *Fazhi yu dangzhi: Guomindang zhengquan de sifa danghua (1923–1948)* [Rule of law vs. rule of party: The partyization of the Guomindang regime's judiciary, 1923–1948] (Beijing: Shehui kexue wenxian chubanshe, 2012).

treaties were not the first instances of China granting such privileges to foreign states, they became the basis for an alternative court system within Chinese territory previously unrivaled in complexity and size.[18] One year after the Treaty of Nanking ended the Opium War, China and Great Britain signed the Treaty of the Bogue on October 8, 1843. Article 13 of the treaty's General Trade Regulations provided that British nationals who committed crimes within Chinese territory would be tried by British officials according to British law. No such reciprocal practice was required for Chinese citizens in British territory. By the end of 1844, both the United States and France had secured similar rights in treaties of their own. Although the theory of jurisdiction based on the laws of the defendant's country of origin does not appear inherently unequal on its face, theory did not often match reality. The most basic inequality of this system was that it was not applied to Chinese citizens living abroad. Within Chinese territory, there were two prominent concerns with the adjudication of foreigners under this evolving system. First, instead of extraditing their citizens for punishment, foreign powers established consular courts within China to administer justice. These courts were largely political organs, often staffed by consular officials rather than judges. Second, Chinese charged with crimes involving foreigners were often subject to a mixed court system where representatives of the involved foreign power could attend and often applied political pressure for favorable outcomes for their citizens.[19]

The flaws of the consular administration of justice were well known by foreign powers, and its practice more often a source of embarrassment than a shining light of judicial modernity. In 1906, a report to the U.S. Congress described American consular activities in China as not merely incompetent but criminal. The report charged the previous U.S. consul general of Canton with numerous crimes, including gross drunkenness

---

[18] The 1689 Treaty of Nerchinsk with Russia provided that citizens of either nation who committed crimes in the territory of the other would be extradited home for punishment. See Wesley Fishel, *The End of Extraterritoriality in China* (Berkeley: University of California Press, 1952), 2.

[19] Ibid., 19–21. Though foreign representatives exerted no official authority in these courts, they retained the ability to protest decisions. In many contexts, such crimes never went to trial but were negotiated between Chinese and foreign consular officials.

during a speech with numerous Chinese officials in attendance at the opening of a train station (which included his threatening to beat a member of the audience), and ordering the American consular court to arrest and jail a man for purposes of personal revenge.[20] Nonetheless, foreign rhetoric still maintained that Chinese law remained far too "antiquated" and "barbaric" for Chinese courts to retain jurisdiction.[21] In reaction to the 1906 report, instead of ending the practice of extraterritoriality, the United States chose to establish the United States Court for China, which was the only example of a U.S. federal court established in the sovereign territory of another recognized state. The court continued to operate in Shanghai until the abrogation of extraterritoriality in 1943. However, no cases were tried by the court after Shanghai was occupied by Japanese troops in 1941.

By the beginning of the twentieth century, bringing an end to extraterritoriality became the unreachable brass ring for successive Chinese governments and legal reformers. The imperial edict of January 29, 1901, called for new policies that would "blend together the best of what is Chinese and what is foreign."[22] This edict further called for the study of Western law and governance practices with particular attention to the abstract moral principles that guided them. China's weakness was characterized as having originated in the inability of corrupt officials and petty bureaucrats to administer with benevolence, instead twisting the letter of the law to serve their own interests. In a word, selfishness (*si*) was blamed as the cause of the nation's failures and its subjugation by foreign powers.[23] Modernization of the legal system along these lines was prioritized after the 1902 and 1903 commercial treaties with the United States, Great Britain, and Japan.[24] All three powers stated that they were prepared to relinquish their extraterritorial rights "when satisfied that the state of the

---

[20] *Report on Inspection of United States Consulates in the Orient*, 59th Cong., 1st sess., H. Doc. 665, serial 5037, Session vol. no. 97, 13–14, 20.

[21] Thomas Millard, "Why Criminals in the Foreign Settlements Are Fighting the United States Court in China," *Washington Post*, March 22, 1908, M4.

[22] Translation provided by Reynolds, *China, 1898–1912*, 202.

[23] Ibid.

[24] Cameron, *Reform Movement in China*, 171; Yang Honglie, *Zhongguo falü fada shi* [A history of the development of Chinese law] (Shanghai: Shanghai shudian, 1930), 886.

Chinese laws, the arrangements for their administration, and other considerations warrant it in doing so."[25] With this in mind, in 1902 the Qing government established the Law Compilation Commission (renamed the Law Codification Commission in 1907) to begin developing the framework for a new legal system.

Shen Jiaben, a *jinshi* degree holder and deputy chairman of the Board of Punishment, and Wu Tingfang, a British-trained attorney who had practiced law in Hong Kong, were two of the first to serve as commissioners of law codification.[26] Shen maintained the need for strict separation of judicial and executive power at all levels of government based on the premise that such independence was a prerequisite for constitutional government. The partition of executive duties and judicial responsibility was a radical shift from the existing practice of the Qing state, which at the most basic level had charged a single office, the county (*xian*) magistrate, with the dual responsibilities of local government administrator and judicial officer.[27] In 1906, a government edict adopted this approach by advocating the separation of judicial responsibility from administrative organs based on Western notions of separation of powers.[28] Government reformer Zai Ze argued in a 1907 memorial that the mixing of local administrative power with judicial responsibility led administrators to provide unjust verdicts, and that "revolutionary storms in various countries all stemmed from the miscarriage of justice."[29] Couched in the language of judicial modernity—including the introduction of "protecting human rights" (*baohu renquan*) into Chinese official discourse—Zai's argument implied a top-down bifurcation of local Chinese governance for the purpose of achieving a legitimate rule of law.

---

[25] "TS 430," *Treaties and Other International Agreements of the United States of America 1776–1949,* (Bevans 6, 1968): 704.

[26] Xu, *Trial of Modernity*, 27; Cameron, *Reform Movement in China*, 172.

[27] Madeleine Zelin, *The Magistrate's Tael: Rationalizing Fiscal Reform in Eighteenth-Century Ch'ing China* (Berkeley: University of California Press, 1984), 120; Sybille Van der Sprenkel, *Legal Institutions in Manchu China: A Sociological Analysis* (New York: Athlone, 1966), 42–43.

[28] Zhao Yuhuan, "Qingmo sifa gaige de qishi" [The inspiration of late Qing judicial reform], *Shandong shehui kexue* 8 (2009): 142–44.

[29] Xu, *Trial of Modernity*, 29.

Shen and his commission worked toward splitting the Qing code into separate civil and criminal codes, each with its own accompanying procedural law. Though completed and presented in draft form by 1907, the new codes were never promulgated due first to conservative opposition and then to the fall of the dynasty. Many of the codes were, however, directly adopted by the postrevolutionary government of President Yuan Shikai, while others strongly influenced judicial practice and organization throughout the Beiyang era, as their authors continued to work with the new government. There was no direct adoption of the civil code and the related procedural laws drafted by the Law Codification Commission, but the new government did promulgate the draft criminal code as the Provisional New Criminal Code. Many other drafted provisions and regulations managed to survive the transition without direct promulgation, but in the form of administrative directives. Despite its failure to be officially established, much of the Civil Procedure Law managed to survive in this way.[30]

The Organic Law of Judicial Courts inherited from the Qing government echoed the ideals and paranoia of the dynasty, as well as those of the new government, in barring serving judges from joining political parties and organizations. In 1914, Yuan Shikai again called on practicing judicial officials to stop being selfish and uphold the spirit of judicial independence.[31] This prohibition was extended in the following year to any magistrates with judicial responsibilities, and even covered police and military personnel.[32] The provisional constitution adopted by the new republican government in 1912 provided codified protection for judicial independence. Article 51 of the constitution stated, "Judges shall adjudicate independently, and without interference from higher officials."[33] The following provision specified that judges could neither be transferred nor have

---

[30] Huang, *Code, Custom, and Legal Practice in China,* 31.

[31] Xu Xiaoqun, *Chinese Professionals and the Republican State: The Rise of Professional Associations in Shanghai, 1912–1937* (Cambridge: Cambridge University Press, 2001), 117.

[32] Xu, "The Fate of Judicial Independence in Republican China," 5–6.

[33] In the provisional constitution, the term used for "judge" is *faguan*. However, later laws passed by the Guomindang-controlled government use the term *tuishi*.

their pay docked unless they had been convicted by law, and could not be dismissed unless convicted of a crime or offense warranting dismissal.[34] Unless caught and tried for abuse of power, judges were for the most part statutorily protected from interference by the administrative arms of the local and central governments.

Systemic local corruption and abuse of power was a long-recognized, though detested, facet of Qing governance.[35] The risk that consolidated local power posed to the creation of a new constitutional government was evident in the aftermath of the end of the rule of avoidance—where government officials could not serve in their home province. The rule's abandonment and limited adoption of local governance structures in the late Qing quickly led to political instability for the republican era National Government. Local governance was described as "local bullies and evil gentry" more likely to incite rebellion than pacify it. By 1934, five counties were told to appoint their ward-level headmen from outside counties, essentially resurrecting the rule of avoidance.[36]

Xu Xiaoqun has found in his study of Jiangsu that following the establishment of separate local judicial offices after 1911, there was an immediate problem of local elites attempting to control the appointment of new judicial officers. Local elites, who had long enjoyed a great deal of political influence at the county level, feared the threat that local judicial institutions might not render verdicts in their interest. Magistrates had traditionally relied on local elites for help in local governance, including tax collection and militia recruitment. Faced with the possibility of an independently financed judicial branch of government that could empower local nonelites to seek retribution, or even justice, for past wrongs was a dramatic penetration of the central government into local society. Local elites formed voluntary associations that regularly petitioned for the removal of judges who were "not compatible with local opinion" or who

---

[34] Art. 51, 52, "Zhonghua minguo linshi yuefa" [Republic of China provisional constitution], 1912.

[35] Zelin, *The Magistrate's Tael*, 220.

[36] Philip Kuhn, "The Development of Local Government," in *The Cambridge History of China*, vol. 13: *Republican China, 1912–1949*, part 2, ed. John Fairbank and Albert Feuerwerker (Cambridge: Cambridge University Press, 1986), 351.

were in "dereliction of duty."[37] Judges were generally protected from dismissal by the constitution. However, in some cases, local elites attempted to preempt the process by appointing judges themselves before being blocked or overruled by the provincial government.[38]

The role and character of judges was a perennial subject in discussions of Chinese judicial modernization. Wang Chonghui, former minister of justice and in 1918 president of the government's Law Codification Commission, stated in an English-language interview for *Millard's Review* that the current code revisions would result in the end of extraterritoriality within five years. Giving a four-thousand-year history of Chinese legal reform in brief, Wang played to the Western narrative of a linear evolution from barbarity to civilization—one common among advocates of extraterritoriality—by illustrating China's past as one based on the subjective application of highly punitive statutory law. Discussing the statutory punishments of 2000 BCE, Wang stated, "These, to be sure, were primitive and vindictive, mostly consisting of forms of mutilation." Wang continued, "Chinese judges had always been in the habit of interpreting law by analogy, that is, if the law did not exactly cover a given case, he would so adapt it as to make it apply." Such judicial practice "not infrequently caused the punishment of the innocent."[39] Not only was codified law historically punitive, it was callously enforced. While using the stereotype of Chinese legal barbarity, Wang argued that the newly reformed code not only abandoned previous punitive savagery but also required judges to adhere to what he described as the "Western rules of strict interpretation."[40] The personal qualities of judges were to be of no significance outside their ability to dispassionately apply the letter of the law as written. This reflected the faith that Wang and other members of the Law Codification Commission had that a modern legal code would be sufficient to end extraterritoriality.

In the following issue of *Millard's Review*, a foreign observer critiqued

---

[37] Xu, *Trial of Modernity*, 123.

[38] Ibid., 122.

[39] Hollington K. Tong, "China's Progress toward Legal Reform," *Millard's Review* 6, no. 2 (September 14, 1918): 53–56.

[40] Ibid., 55.

Wang by saying, "After the laws have been codified, the material question arises as to the training and personal character of the men who are to preside in the Chinese courts."[41] Wang's argument that codified law could safeguard against the subjective will of individual judges appeared to fall on deaf ears. The issue of judicial education was particularly sensitive in the context of the drive for the abrogation of extraterritoriality. While the modernization of China's legal codes was a matter of legislative action, the training of a new class of judicial professionals required qualified and interested candidates. Between 1915 and 1921, the Ministry of Justice's Judicial Education Institute (*sifa jiangxi suo*) graduated a total of 437 judicial officials, not all of whom became judges.[42] By 1925, only 995 judicial officials were in office in the entire country.[43]

The desire to end the practice of extraterritoriality continued through 1926 when two events changed the course of judicial reform: the failure of the Commission on Extraterritoriality in China to recommend the return of judicial sovereignty, and the military conquest of the Northern Expedition. The commission was the creation of the Washington Conference of 1921, although it did not meet until 1926. Wang Chonghui served as the honorary president of the commission, composed of representatives from numerous nations holding extraterritorial rights in China. Ultimately, the commission did not believe that China had modernized sufficiently for full judicial sovereignty. Echoing the response to Wang's optimism in the pages of *Millard's Review*, the principal reason Britain and the United States refused to end extraterritoriality concerned the application of laws and not their codification. The failure of the uniform application of codified law throughout the nation, there existing only one operational modern court for every 4,400,000 citizens, and an understaffed judiciary all contributed to the decision, but the primary recommendation put forth

---

[41] T.R. Jernigan, "Observations," *Millard's Review* 6, no. 3 (September 21, 1918): 88.

[42] Glenn Tiffert, "The Chinese Judge: From Literatus to Cadre (1906–1949)" (October 23, 2011), in *Knowledge Acts in Modern China: Ideas, Institutions, and Identities*, ed. Eddy U. and Robert Culp (forthcoming) (available at SSRN: http://ssrn.com/abstract =1948259), 15

[43] Chang Yao-tseng, "The Present Conditions of the Chinese Judiciary and Its Future," *Chinese Social and Political Science Review* 10 (1926): 175.

was to create a judiciary protected against "interference by the executive or other branches of the Government, whether civil or military."[44]

This blow came at the same time the National Government was vastly expanding its power and reconquering many areas that had fallen under the control of local warlords after the fall of the Qing. In this geographical expansion of the Guomindang-controlled government, an ideological conquest was at play as well. The concept of partyization of the judiciary became the new guiding principle of state governance and the force behind judicial reform. Broadly defined as an adherence to Sun Yat-sen's Three People's Principles and Nationalist Party doctrine in legislation and judicial practice, the president of the Judicial Yuan, Ju Zheng, explained in 1934 that "Partyizing the Judiciary is not to make a judiciary of 'party members,' but to make a judiciary of 'party doctrine.'"[45]

Nationalist doctrine was thus one of social responsibility and creating a rule-of-law system that would benefit society rather than individuals. In the introduction to the 1930 Civil Code, Fu Bingchang explained, "The [Guomindang] doctrine considers therefore men not as self-contained entities, but in relation to the society which they form."[46] The social and political focus of partyization moved away from the reform rhetoric of Wang Chonghui, which advocated an apolitical and neutral legal code based on Western forms, toward a judicial structure focused on moral guidance and broadly imagined social welfare based on the political ideals of the increasingly centralized party-state. Including such language in the laws of the republic was not difficult, but the character of the individuals applying those laws had to conform as well. Ju Zheng explained, "Partyization of the judiciary absolutely requires the partyization of judicial officials."[47]

---

[44] Commission on Extraterritorial Jurisdiction in China, *Report of the Commission on Extraterritoriality in China* (Washington, DC: Government Printing Office, 1926), 97, 100, 107.

[45] Ju Zheng, "Sifa danghua wenti" [The question of partyizing the judiciary], in *Weishenme yao chongjian Zhongguo faxi: Ju Zheng fazheng wenxuan* [Why must we reconstruct the Chinese legal system? Selected writings on law and politics by Ju Zheng], ed. Fan Zhongxin (Beijing: Zhongguo zhengfa daxue chubanshe, 2009), 169.

[46] Fu Bingchang, "Introduction," in *The Civil Code of the Republic of China*, trans. Jinlin Xia (Shanghai: Kelly and Walsh, 1930), xx.

[47] Ju, "Sifa danghua wenti," 169.

The Judiciary at War

During the War of Resistance against Japan, the men who represented and administered the judicial power of the Republic of China were the president of the Judicial Yuan, Ju Zheng, and the minister of justice, Xie Guansheng. Both were seasoned veterans of the Nationalist Party and wielded considerable power before and during the war. However, in contrast to Xie, Ju Zheng's credentials were more political than academic. Despite his prolific writings on judicial practice, he had studied law only for a brief time at the Tokyo Law College in 1907. Ju had been a member of Sun Yat-sen's Revolutionary Alliance (Tongmenghui) starting in 1905, giving him an elder statesman status in the Nationalist Party by the time of his appointment to the Judicial Yuan in 1932. His dedication to Guomindang ideology was pronounced in his writings, and his political ambition was demonstrated by his failed, though surprisingly strong, 1948 bid for president against incumbent Chiang Kai-shek.[48]

Xie's background was more similar to those of other officials of the Nationalist judiciary. An academic and polyglot, Xie's first book was a complete Chinese-French dictionary compiled before he was twenty-four. He spent 1922–1924 earning his *docteur de droit* at the Université de Paris—his thesis being a history of Chinese law—before returning to China to serve concurrently as senior secretary of the Ministry of Foreign Affairs and dean of the Law School at National Central University until 1932. At the beginning of the war in 1937, Xie was brought in as minister of justice.[49] The juxtaposition of Ju and Xie was representative of the changing nature of the judiciary prior to 1943, as the focus of its officers gradually shifted from the ivory tower of academia to the practical administration of party doctrine.

The legal system that these men administered in 1943 cannot be understood without considering the context of the war with Japan. Military conflict endangered the entire judicial system that consecutive reformers

---

[48] Howard Boorman, *Biographical Dictionary of Republican China* (New York: Columbia University Press, 1967), 469–75.
[49] Jerome Cavanaugh, ed., *Who's Who in China, 1918–1950* (Hong Kong: Chinese Materials Center, 1982).

had attempted to build over the previous thirty years. The creation and maintenance of a single high court for each province was not a difficult task, and these courts continued to operate as long as the province remained under the control of the central government. However, the number of functioning branch high courts and district courts varied wildly throughout the republican period. In the first year of the republic (1912), 124 branch courts and 179 local courts operated in the country.[50] This number soon fell dramatically, as many either faced government retrenchment or failed outright in their first few years. These jurisdictions quietly reverted back to the practice of having magistrates serve as judges.[51] By 1913, the number of branch courts and local courts had quickly fallen to 103 and 134. The number of courts was further limited by provincial and local political and economic conditions. Dozens of courts were established in wealthier places such as Zhejiang, Jiangsu, and the city of Beijing, while remote and poor interior provinces such as Xinjiang and Yunnan could barely manage eight each.[52]

On the eve of the Northern Expedition in 1926, further institutional changes and the redefinition of jurisdictional boundaries had reduced the number of officially recognized courts to only 23 high (that is, provincial) courts, 26 branch high courts, and 64 district courts.[53] Ju Zheng later estimated that of the 1,950 basic-level judicial institutions across the country in that year, less than 5 percent could be considered "modern courts."[54] By 1936, this would increase to 17 percent, though the numerical increase of courts (now 301) was accompanied by an overall reduction in operating judicial institutions (1,790).[55]

Before July 1937, the National Government had established over 417 courts of different grades throughout the country. With a total of 1,469

---

[50] Chang Yao-Tseng, "Present Conditions of the Chinese Judiciary and Its Future," *Chinese Social and Political Science Review* 10 (1926): 172.

[51] Huang, *Code, Custom, and Legal Practice in China*, 40.

[52] Glenn Tiffert, "An Irresistible Inheritance: Republican Judicial Modernization and Its Legacies to the People's Republic of China," *Cross-Currents* 7 (June 2013): 89.

[53] Chang, "Present Conditions of the Chinese Judiciary," 174.

[54] Ju Zheng, "Ershiwu nianlai sifa zhi wenti yu zhanwang" [Problems in the administration of justice over the past twenty-five years and prospects], in Fan, *Weishenme yao chongjian Zhongguo faxi*, 334.

[55] Ibid.

counties, less than a third had an established court, and even fewer were fully staffed.[56] While still too few to meet the needs of the nation, the increased number of courts reflected a dedication to increase the number of jurisdictions where cases would be tried by courts independent of local government administration. However, the geographical distribution of these reforms was soon shaped by the war at hand. Early Japanese military encroachment in 1938 forced the Guomindang out of southeastern China and their capital of Nanjing, where the greatest number of new courts had been established, into the southwest and the new wartime capital of Chongqing, where there had been the fewest new courts. Many judicial officers fled their home districts when occupied by the Japanese, and the policy of the National Government was to reassign them to new or understaffed courts in areas still under government control. However, many were unable, or unwilling, to escape and in several cases continued serving their district under the supervision of Japanese occupying forces.[57] Whether collaborators or refugees, many of these legal professionals found their careers at an end by 1945.[58]

Faced with this situation, Ju Zheng stated in 1938, "Now that China's war of resistance is being prosecuted from these strategic regions, the Judicial Yuan has taken the necessary steps to establish more courts in the provinces concerned."[59] Indeed, during the period from 1938 to 1942, 85 new courts were established, most in the interior provinces.[60] Government statistics for these years indicate that by the end of 1942 the National Government claimed 516 courts at all three levels, though due to the war and other difficulties only 373 were actually functioning.[61] By July 1944, these numbers would increase to 399 functioning courts and 152

---

[56] Hollington K. Tong, ed., *China Handbook, 1937–1943: A Comprehensive Survey of Major Developments in China in Six Years of War* (New York: Macmillan, 1943), 106.

[57] For examples of cases handled by Chinese courts in occupied areas, see Zhao Ma, "On the Run: Women, City, and the Law in Beijing, 1937–1949," PhD diss., Johns Hopkins University, 2007.

[58] Tiffert, "An Irresistible Inheritance," 94.

[59] Ju Zheng, "War-Time Judicial Administration," *China Quarterly* 4, no. 1 (Winter 1938): 12.

[60] Tong, *China Handbook*, 291.

[61] Ibid., 292.

suspended ones.[62] The total population of the provinces in which courts were actually trying cases in 1941–1942 was estimated at 338,466,910.[63] Even assuming that the 1942 operational courts were evenly distributed, this would mean roughly one court for every 900,000 people, and not all of these courts were necessarily fully staffed. These numbers portray a legal system hopelessly outmatched by the exigencies of war and the needs of the nation's vast population. It most certainly failed to adjudicate the large number of existing and potential criminal and civil cases, and those that were tried did not always receive the same level of procedural due process.[64] More important than the actual number of courts functioning is their surprising, though modest, wartime expansion.

The question thus becomes, who was staffing these courts or, more precisely, who did the government intend to staff them? As previously stated, the ongoing difficulty of training a whole class of technocratic officials to staff China's burgeoning legal system had been a long-unfulfilled goal. The realities of war made this even more unattainable under the current framework. Staffing newly established courts seemed unimaginable with existing courts failing or being captured by the Japanese. In the face of consistent court failure, basic "judicial sections" had been allowed during the war to act in the place of courts at the local level when the court responsible for the county had ceased to function. Government policy decreed that if a court was no longer functioning, then cases under its jurisdiction could be adjudicated by the judicial sections of the county government involved.[65] Unlike organizationally independent courts, judicial sections merely involved the appointment of a judge to handle local cases in the place of the magistrate under the latter's authority.[66]

Intended as a temporary fix for an extraordinary situation, these judi-

---

[62] H.P. Tseng and Jean Lyon, eds., *China Handbook, 1937–1944: A Comprehensive Survey of Major Developments in China in Seven Years of War* (Chungking: Chinese Ministry of Information, 1944), 179.

[63] Tong, *China Handbook*, 2, 293.

[64] For an example of the failure of courts to enforce procedural norms, see Xu Xiaoqun, "The Rule of Law without Due Process: Punishing Robbers and Bandits in Early-Twentieth-Century China," *Modern China* 33, no. 2 (April 1, 2007): 230–57.

[65] Ju, "War-Time Judicial Administration," 11.

[66] Ch'ien Tuan-sheng, *The Government and Politics of China, 1912–1949* (Stanford, CA: Stanford University Press, 1950), 254.

cial sections would take on the bulk of judicial responsibility during the war. The use of county governments as temporary courts was itself a regressive step, as the government had been carrying out a specific policy since 1936 (and similar ones before) to create county judicial sections as an intermediary step before founding local courts. At the beginning of the war, 711 such county-level judicial sections had been established. While the exact staffing of each of these judicial sections is difficult to surmise on anything larger than a case-by-case basis, they were intended to have at least one qualified judge to preside over cases. Though the separation of judicial and administrative power could not be guaranteed in these sections, the understanding was that local magistrates would not wield both judicial and executive power.[67]

Functioning National Government courts had strict requirements on the qualifications of judges and judicial officers. The 1938 Law on Court Organization expanded the list of possible qualifications by the start of the war to include individuals with practical experience who, however, had not passed through the official judicial examination system.[68] Nonetheless, the Chinese justice system was hopelessly understaffed in terms of qualified judicial officers. By October 1938, the number of registered judicial officers totaled only 1,270 (485 judges and procurators, 639 clerks, and 126 prison officers).[69] The Ministry of Information listed a total of 1,393 trained judicial officials by the end of 1941.[70] That being said, in 1943, the combined caseload of all Chinese courts and county judicial sections was 516,468 civil and criminal cases, with all but 2,914 supposedly being decided within the year.[71] It should be remembered that these statistics were self-reported by the Ministry of Information for English-language audiences, and the number of total and undecided cases may have been much higher.

Orders from the Judicial Yuan in 1937 and 1938 attempted to prevent

---

[67] Tseng and Lyon, *China Handbook*, 178.

[68] Art. 33, "Fayuan zuzhi fa" [Law on court organization], 1938.

[69] Ju, "War-Time Judicial Administration," 14. The principal difference between a procurator and a prosecutor in Anglo-American law is that a procurator is charged with both investigation and prosecution, whereas a prosecutor is responsible only for the latter.

[70] Tong, *China Handbook*, 299.

[71] Tseng and Lyon, *China Handbook*, 179.

the loss of qualified judicial officers by forbidding their resignation with-out good cause, and threatened severe punishments for those deserting their posts while their assigned courts still functioned.[72] However, simply preventing the further drain of judicial talent would not staff the expand-ing system, so new officials needed training to fill these posts. The Nation-alist rhetoric was particularly heavy in the context of the ongoing war with Japan. Over the previous decade, the National Government had trained its judicial officials in the Training Institute for Judicial Officials (Faguan xunlian suo, hereafter called the Institute). Varying levels of political edu-cation had always been involved in this training, but by the early days of the war this aspect of judicial education had expanded prolifically. From 1929 to 1941, the Institute held six training sessions for prospective judi-cial officers and six shorter courses for their already-serving counterparts. Judges were trained in odd-numbered sessions and procurators in even-numbered sessions, with their final classes graduating in 1939 and 1941, respectively.[73] From 1941 to 1943, four sessions were convened to train county-level trial officers.[74]

Those chosen for judicial training would need to be ready to try not only the banal cases of peacetime, but the extraordinary cases of wartime, "in examining spies and arresting traitors and apprehending all who may threaten to endanger the security of the State."[75] For this specialized train-ing two sessions were convened beginning in April 1938 (one of judges and the other of procurators), where a total of 169 students—all Nationalist Party members with five years' judicial service experience—were selected as the wartime class.[76] While earlier classes trained for six and eighteen months respectively, training during the war would range from only two months to one year.[77]

---

[72] Ju, "War-Time Judicial Administration," 12.

[73] Sifayuan bianyi chu, *Sifa nianjian* [Judicial yearbook] (Changsha: Shangwu yinshu-guan, 1941), 347–65. For a more detailed discussion of the particular history of judicial edu-cation, see Tiffert, "The Chinese Judge," 26.

[74] Xie Guansheng, *Zhanshi sifa jiyao* [Summary of the wartime judiciary] (Taibei: Sifa-yuan mishu chu, 1971), 401–2.

[75] Ju, "War-Time Judicial Administration," 14.

[76] Ibid. Previous classes had been admitted through a judicial exam.

[77] Ibid.; Tong, *China Handbook*, 298.

In the drive to train more judicial officials, the requirements for admission were broadened to include groups with no prior legal education, including party workers chosen for training by central authorities.[78] Following the end of extraterritoriality in 1943, the Ministry of Justice openly characterized the purpose of the Institute in English as "instilling [Guomindang] principles in the trainees."[79]

The Plan for Training Judicial Personnel had evolved into a complex and expansive political curriculum. The primary goal of the Institute, as explained in the 1941 *Judicial Yearbook* (*sifa nianjian*) was to train judicial officials for a "partyized" judiciary (see Appendix 5.1).[80] The importance of the training at the Institute only increased as the requirement for prior legal education was removed. Advanced training in legal knowledge and skills was only one of the plan's six guiding principles, among which included extensive study of party doctrine and military training. The amount of time dedicated to the study of each subject shows a clear move away from a strong understanding of codified law toward political and moral training. Categories of study were defined as substantive (criminal and civil), procedural, and "other." In the six sessions of judicial training convened beginning in 1929, with the final class graduating in 1941, the amount of time spent on "other" steadily increased from 15.9 percent to 44.44 percent. This was largely to the detriment of procedural law, the time spent on which plummeted over the same period from 63.8 percent to 25.26 percent.[81] These other categories involved topics such as "spiritual training," which focused on the guiding principles of Nationalist reconstruction and the purpose of the partyization of the judiciary, and the study of party principles.

In an address to the class of 1939, Ju Zheng made clear that this program was meant to provide its students with more than a technical education. The philosophy of the program was to articulate and replicate a morality based on Nationalist Party doctrine that would serve as the basis for the new China they were hoping to build. The Institute thus "aim[ed] on

---

[78] Ibid., 299.
[79] Ibid., 298.
[80] Sifayuan bianyi chu, *Sifa nianjian*, 347.
[81] Ibid., 349.

the one hand to establish judicial specialists for the nation, and on the other hand to temper the mind and body of these specialists, to be a school for cultivating the teaching of loyalty and the encouragement of diligence." The material needs of the moment were not lost on Ju Zheng when he further stated, "In times of war in our country, human resources all belong to the nation, and intellectual will must be used in the interests of the nation."[82] The creation and staffing of a new legal system to protect the interests of the people was key to the construction of a new China, "a Three People's Principles rule of law nation [*sanmin zhuyi zhi fazhi guo*]."[83]

THE END OF EXTRATERRITORIALITY AND
THE CODIFICATION OF POLITICAL EDUCATION

It was not China's legal modernization that brought an end to extraterritoriality, but the military threat of Japan. By late 1941, U.S. relations with Japan were rapidly deteriorating as the latter mocked the Western powers for their feigned friendship with China while refusing to undo the damage of the unequal treaties.[84] On November 26, 1941, the United States proposed a draft mutual declaration to Japan that promised the abolition of both nations' extraterritorial rights in China and to jointly endeavor to obtain similar agreements from other nations "including rights in international settlements and in concessions and under the Boxer Protocol of 1901."[85] Less than two weeks later Japan declared war on the United States, and the practice of extraterritoriality became moot. The day following the attack on Pearl Harbor, Japanese troops in Shanghai took control of the United States Court for China and temporarily interned presiding

---

[82] Ju Zheng, "Di liu jie faguan xunlian ban tongxue lu xu" [Introduction to the yearbook of the sixth training session for judicial officials], in Fan, *Weishenme yao chongjian Zhongguo faxi*, 419–20.

[83] Ju Zheng, "Fazhi qiantu zhi zhanwang" [Future prospects of rule of law], in *Ju Zheng wenji xiace* [The collected writings of Ju Zheng, vol. 2] (Wuchang: Huazhong shifan daxue chubanshe, 1989), 678.

[84] Fishel, *The End of Extraterritoriality in China*, 208.

[85] "Outline of Proposed Basis for Agreement between the United States and Japan," in *Foreign Relations of the United States Diplomatic Papers: Japan 1931–1941*, vol. 2 (Washington, DC: Government Printing Office, 1943), 769.

Judge Milton Helmick.[86] With Japanese control of the foreign concessions in Shanghai, the bulk of the extraterritorial court system came to an abrupt end, and by 1943 there was little left to abolish.

Both British and American documents from the war concede that the abrogation of extraterritoriality was motivated by a desire to show support for the Nationalist regime and appreciation for China's continued war with Japan rather than a reflection of judicial modernization. In 1942, U.S. State Department Division of Far Eastern Affairs analyst Walter Adams acknowledged murmurings that "China has grown up," but believed the only accurate reason to end the practice of extraterritoriality was to show appreciation for the Chinese effort in the war.[87] It was argued that had the United States relinquished their extraterritorial rights in 1942—rights that their "citizens [could] not … now exercise"—the Japanese would cite this empty gesture as a sign of Allied weakness.[88] Though internal U.S. reports indicated that the system would not survive long after the war, retention of extraterritoriality on paper would postpone the revision of new treaties until the United States had a better sense of its potential interests in postwar China.[89]

British political reports confirmed the lack of any strategic significance for the continuance of extraterritoriality, which in the context of the war had "come to have little practical importance to foreigners."[90] The same reports also stated that the original intention of their negotiations was only to offer the abrogation of judicial rights (currently worthless with Japanese control of the consular and mixed courts), but that the "Chinese press, public and Government had chosen to give the offers a much wider

---

[86] Eileen Paula Scully, "Crime, Punishment, and Empire: The United States District Court for China, 1906–1943," PhD diss., Georgetown University, 1993, 355.

[87] Walter Adams, "Memorandum by Mr. Walter A. Adams of the Division of Far Eastern Affairs, March 19, 1942," in *Foreign Relations of the United States Diplomatic Papers: 1942 China* (Washington, DC: Government Printing Office, 1956), 268.

[88] Stanley Hornbeck, "Memorandum by the Chief of the Division of Far Eastern Affairs (Hamilton), March 27, 1942," in *Foreign Relations of the United States Diplomatic Papers: 1942 China*, 271.

[89] Ibid., 272–73.

[90] Correspondence from Seymour to Eden, June 22, 1943, in *Foreign Relations of the United States Diplomatic Papers: 1942 China*, 145.

interpretation," calling for the end to the unequal treaties in total.[91] With the exception of the question of Hong Kong, the U.S. and British governments agreed to end all extraterritorial privileges and return foreign concessions in the ports.

Chinese ambassador to the United States Wei Tao-ming agreed that the system had lost all justifiable utility, describing its abrogation as the ending of "an outdated and outworn system," but hoped this would finally confirm China as an equal among other nations.[92] U.S. Senator Arthur Vandenberg—a prominent voice of American support for Chiang Kai-shek after the war—proclaimed, "It is an act of faith in the destiny of China, an ally who has never faltered in the fight for freedom."[93] Recognition of China's modern legal system does not appear in this discourse.

In the pages of Chiang Kai-shek's 1943 opus, *China's Destiny*, the consular courts and special privileges of extraterritoriality were transformed from a symbol of lost sovereignty to the root cause of all of China's current ills. Chiang argued that the application of foreign law delegitimized Chinese law in the eyes of its people, leading to a lack of respect for the rule of law and increased criminality. He continued, arguing that the concessions further became havens for foreign spies intent on harming China, and consular courts and police regularly violated the human rights of Chinese nationals through unlawful arrests and torture. Their abolition created an opportunity for the rejuvenation of the Chinese legal system in both form and substance. Expanding on the principle of partyization through adherence to the Three People's Principles, Chiang's new path to modernization echoed the imperial edict of 1901 by calling on the best of what he saw as traditional Chinese culture (which the Nationalists claimed to fervently support and manifest) to be incorporated with aspects of Western thought. However, Chiang was quick to caution that wholesale Westernization would lead to selfishness (*si*) and "violate the intrinsic

---

[91] Correspondence from Seymour to Eden, January 4, 1943, in *Foreign Relations of the United States Diplomatic Papers: 1942 China*, 91.

[92] Tong, *China Handbook*, 181.

[93] "Senate Approves Treaty Giving Up Rights in China," *New York Times*, February 12, 1943, 1.

spirit of Chinese civilization."[94] Modernization not only meant formaliza-
tion and codification, but had to include proper moral training to uphold
the traditional spirit of the Chinese people.

The structural reforms of the judicial system beginning in 1943 were
the most holistic since the last decade of the Qing dynasty. Rather than
promoting gradual changes to the existing system, a paradigm shift in how
the judiciary would be defined and operate began in 1943. Two fundamental changes followed the abrogation of extraterritoriality: the recod-
ification of judicial education as now being inherently political, and the
realignment of the judiciary within the executive arm of the central government.

In February 1943, the Training Institute for Judicial Officials closed its
doors for the last time. In August of that year, a new program was rolled
out in the pages of the Ministry of Justice's official publication that would
be the first step in the reformation of judicial education after the war. In
the August issue of the *Ministry of Justice Bulletin* (*Sifa xingzheng gongbao*), the 1943 Program for the Training of Judicial Personnel (*sifa renyuan
xunlian dagang*) was published, relocating the specialized training of judicial workers in the Nationalist Party's own central party school, Central
Politics School (*Zhongyang zhengzhi xuexiao*, which would become National Chengchi University in 1947). No longer placed in their own separate training institutes, judicial officials received their education alongside
party cadres. This program would be expanded and codified into the postwar legal order as the Law on the Training Course of Judicial Officials
(*sifaguan xunlian banfa*), promulgated in August 1946.

Article 1 of the 1943 program stated its mission as the incorporation
of political education into the training of judicial officials.[95] As evidenced
in the 1941 curriculum of the Institute, political content had been gradually introduced into judicial education over the previous decade. However,
the program now mandated its inclusion as foundational for judicial prac-

---

[94] Chiang Kai-shek, *Zhongguo zhi mingyun* [China's destiny] (Chongqing: Zhengzhong
shuju, 1943), 40, 46.
[95] Sifa xingzhengbu [Ministry of Justice], "Sifarenyuan xunlian dagang" [Program for
the training of judicial personnel], *Sifaxingzheng gongbao* [Ministry of Justice bulletin] 1, no.
8 (August 1943): 33–34.

tice. In the expanded 1946 Law on the Training Course for Judicial Officials, this directive was officially codified into postwar expectations and requirements for judicial officials.[96] The requirement of all officials to have between six months and one year of combined "political training and practical judicial training" left little room for any focus on abstract legal principles. Combined with the lowering of admission requirements to accept individuals with no formal legal training, this meant that individuals could become judicial officials with as little as a few months of formal legal education. The power to decide the courses offered and selection of teaching staff was to be determined between the school and the Ministry of Justice, according to Article 3 of both documents.

Central Politics School hosted three training sessions over the following four years, training 131 students from March to October 1944, another 84 from March to November 1945, and a final class of 174 beginning in October 1947.[97] The first class underwent two months of specifically defined political training and six months of professional training.[98] The school itself had evolved from the Central Party School (*Zhongyang dangwu xuexiao*) in 1929, and continued to train cadres for the Nationalist Party and offer special training courses for those wishing to enter the government bureaucracy throughout the war. Reflecting its pedigree for Nationalist political training, the school's chancellor was Chiang Kai-shek himself. Much of this is reflected in a British government report on the status of wartime universities based on a tour made by a British national in late 1942 and again in 1943. The school was the only university visited that did not complain of lost equipment, missing staff, or a lack of funds. However, the political nature of the school is not lost in the report: "Discipline is very strict and men and women are both subjected to a course on military training. It may be argued that this institute is not sufficiently liberal to train future leaders, and that it is too much the child of the [Guomindang]."[99] The observer goes on to disagree with this conclusion,

[96] "Sifaguan xunlian banfa" [Law on the training course for judicial officials], reproduced in Xie, *Zhanshi sifa jiyao*, 406–7.

[97] Ibid., 402–3.

[98] Tseng and Lyon, *China Handbook*, 188.

[99] John Blofeld, "Report on Universities in War-time China, August 18, 1942," *British*

noting that the students were allowed to read the works of Karl Marx, if they so chose.

Ultimately, it was the strict requirements of judicial education (whether political or legal in nature) and the related judicial exam that sabotaged Chiang's postwar vision of a national judicial class loyal to the Nationalist Party.[100] The years beginning in 1943 saw a sharp rise in undergraduate education, and law continued to be a popular subject. Between 1943 and 1947, undergraduate institutions across China granted law degrees to 19,612 students.[101] Despite this flood of new talent supplementing existing legal professionals and party officials, the required doctrinal education monopolized by the program at Central Politics School, guarded by a difficult entrance exam, created a very narrow path for judicial appointment. From 1944 to 1947, the school graduated a total of only 389 judicial officials.[102]

In addition to the educational changes made in the wake of the abrogation of extraterritoriality, the bulk of the nation's judicial institutions were brought under the direct control of the Executive Yuan, ending the separation of executive and judicial authority. With the transfer of the Ministry of Justice from the Judicial Yuan to the Executive, authority and administration of the courts, judges, and procurators now fell under the control of the president of the Executive Yuan, Chiang Kai-shek. In their 1944 supplement to the English-language *China Handbook*, the Ministry of Information was quite candid about the reasoning behind this: "The Ministry of Justice was transferred to the Executive Yuan as a result of the abrogation of extraterritoriality."[103]

This shift in the dynamic of judicial power was not adequately reflected in the 1946 constitution since that document made no mention of

---

Documents on Foreign Affairs: Reports and Papers from the Foreign Office Confidential Print, Part III, 1940–1945, Series E, Asia, vol. 6 (Bethesda, MD: University Publications of America, 1997), 12.

[100] Tiffert, "The Chinese Judge," 41.

[101] Tang Nengsong et al., *Tansuo de guiji: Zhongguo faxue jiaoyu fazhan shilue* [Exploring the trajectory: A brief history of the development of Chinese legal education] (Beijing: Falü chubanshe, 1995), 318.

[102] Xie, *Zhanshi sifa jiyao*, 402–3.

[103] Tseng and Lyon, *China Handbook*, 177.

individual ministries, but only of the powers and duties granted the five branches of government. The independence of judges and authority of the Judicial Yuan would continue as stipulated in the 1912 and 1923 provisional constitutions. However, the application of the requirement of judicial independence to judges under the authority of the Executive Yuan is unclear. The Judicial Yuan continued to carry higher nominal judicial authority through its control of the Supreme Court, through which it retained the power to interpret the constitution, and the Administrative Court. However, the functioning of the nation's provincial and local courts and authority over the education and appointment of judicial officials was transferred with the Ministry of Justice to the purview of the Executive Yuan.

CONCLUSION

The notion of an independent judiciary has been fundamental to any discussion of the rule of law in the twentieth century. In the non-European context it has also been a point of contention in the nationalist goal of becoming a modern state in the eyes of the world. This debate continues today, as the People's Republic of China builds its legal system according to its own interests and set of principles, while also attempting to portray a level of professionalism and formalism acceptable to the international community.[104] The events of 1943 provide an instance of clarity when the pressure of foreign approval was momentarily replaced with the ambition to create a new form of judicial governance. The National Government sought to counter the evils of local corruption and political fragmentation through the establishment of a professional class of legal workers who could nominally remain organizationally separate from the political branches of government while representing the interests of the one-party state. Judicial officers were free to make their own decisions, but were trained to frame their answers in the language of Nationalist Party doc-

---

[104] Randall Peerenboom, ed., *Judicial Independence in China: Lessons for Global Rule of Law Promotion* (Cambridge: Cambridge University Press, 2010).

trine. Ultimately, the burden of carrying out such a training regime was too much for the postwar government to accomplish, and the narrow road to judicial office left the legal system starved of new, competently trained judicial talent. The People's Republic of China is markedly less ambitious in requiring an oath of loyalty. Although the Lawyer's Oath is not as rigorous as the Plan for Training Judicial Personnel, it remains a powerful reminder of what the state regards as proper professional behavior.

Both 1943 and 2012 manifest the contradictions between the perceived requirements of internationally recognized judicial modernism and what each regime believed to be the ideological needs for the development of a practical and professional legal system. Faced with the threat of local political opposition and social instability, judicial independence remains palatable only if the independent decisions of judges and the behavior of attorneys reflect the greater goals of the party in power. Seven decades later, China remains caught between its desire for central control of the judiciary and the foreign pressure to maintain a separation of powers as a prerequisite for equal standing.

Plan for Training Judicial Personnel (Procuratorial), 1941

Guiding Principles:

1. To supplement their legal knowledge, judicial practices, and investigatory skills to cultivate procurators of exceptional ability.

2. To develop their intrinsic devotion to party work and obedience to judicial procedures, and to engage in procuratorial affairs so as to promote the effectiveness of the procuratorial system under party rule.

3. To promote their comprehension of our partyist (*dang-zhuyi*) programs and policies, the spirit of the Nationalist government's legislation, and the governing policies of the Ministry of Justice to produce an understanding of the foundations of Three People's Principles Rule of Law.

4. To promote their understanding of international law, politics, economics, and cultures to produce an understanding of the relationships between law and various social sciences, and their trends.

5. To explain the theory of national construction during the War of Resistance, and direct judicial personnel in the responsibilities they should shoulder during this period so as to assist in the mission of total national mobilization.

6. To implement military training, impart military learning, cultivate the discipline and life of military culture, and the spirit of bravery, loyalty, hard work and honesty.

Spiritual Training (subjects of weekly lectures and activities): The Chinese Nationalist Party and the national revolution; essentials of national construction during the War of Resistance; the main idea of partyification of the administration of justice (*danghua sifa yaozhi*); the official duties and self-cultivation of judicial officials.

Academic Lectures (subjects of weekly lectures): comparison of Eastern and Western cultures and the construction of a new culture; general trends in international politics and economics; strategy and foreign policy in the War of Resistance; schools of modern legal science and their trends.

Academic Training: party principles; criminal law; special criminal laws; criminal procedure; criminal trial and procuratorial practice; civil law; essentials of civil litigation; essentials of special civil laws; civil trial practice; criminal policies; criminology; penology; forensic medicine; fingerprinting; jurisprudence; law on court organization; official documents; foreign language (English or Japanese).

Military Training skills: individual drills; unit drills; shooting drills; non-combatant battlefield service. Academic: army affairs; military protocol; infantryman's manual; field service regulations; fortifications manual; firing manual.

Study of Party Principles: philosophical foundations of the Three People's

Principles; the Three People's Principles and the national revolution; the essential properties of the Three People's Principles; the legal foundations of the Three People's Principles.

Small Group Training: discuss legislative questions in the Three People's Principles; discuss current questions in the judicial system; practical questions in criminal laws and regulations; technical questions in procuratorial practice.

Source: Sifayuan bianyi chu, *Sifa nianjian* [Judicial yearbook] (Changsha: Shangwu yin-shuguan, 1941), 363–64.

5

Empire versus Nation

Hong Kong between Allies

NOBCHULEE (DAWN) MALEENONT

It was September 1945. British warships cruised into port at Hong Kong, anticipating the formal recovery of the colony from the control of Japan. However, the returning conquerors were not greeted with a warm welcome by their long-suffering Hong Kong subjects; instead, they were met with an overwhelming outburst of Chinese nationalism: "on every junk and on nearly every house there flew the flag of China." The people of Hong Kong were expecting an early return of the colony to Chinese sovereignty.[1] Decades later, the authors of Chiang Kai-shek's *Critical Biography* described the postwar status of Hong Kong as "the greatest irony of the new equal treaty" of 1943, which was designed to reconfigure the relationship between China and her imperialist ally, Great Britain.[2]

HONG KONG IN WARTIME STRATEGY

Hong Kong occupied a rather peculiar position during World War II. The colony was certainly not the vibrant metropolis retroceded to the People's

---

[1] F.S.V. Donnison, *British Military Administration in the Far East, 1943–46* (London: Her Majesty's Stationery Office, 1956), 202.

[2] Wang Rongzu and Li Ao, *Jiang Jieshi ping zhuan* [Critical biography of Chiang Kai-shek] (Taipei: Shangzhou wenhua shiye gufen youxian gongsi, 1995), section 3.

Republic of China in 1997. In the early 1940s, materially, and especially within the grand scheme of war, the colony appeared most unimportant. It held no strategic significance whatsoever to the Allied war effort. And yet in late 1942, at a time when the colony was under Japanese occupation, the Chinese and British were already bickering over who would own it after the war. During negotiations for the treaty abrogating British extra-territorial rights in China, Hong Kong served as the final hurdle to agreement, playing a critical role in the fate of the Sino-British alliance. The sudden importance of Hong Kong's future may on the surface appear an anomaly, but a closer look at the negotiations over the colony within the context of the war reveals that such an anomaly typifies the very nature of Sino-British wartime diplomacy: the future of Hong Kong and the relations between the two allies were intricately tangled with the prosecution of the war, conflicting histories and ideologies, and divergent visions for security in and influence over the postwar Asia-Pacific region.

To the Chinese Nationalist Party, Hong Kong under British rule represented both the beginning and the enduring symbol of the unequal relationship between foreign imperialists and China. In 1842, the Chinese lost Hong Kong Island to the British in the first "unequal treaty," the Treaty of Nanking, which followed China's defeat in the First Opium War. After the Second Opium War in 1860, the Chinese ceded the Kowloon Peninsula, a small piece of land at the tip of the Chinese mainland, across the harbor from the original colony. Finally, in 1898, in the Second Convention of Peking, Britain extended Hong Kong's territory by acquiring, through a ninety-nine-year-lease, the third and largest chunk of land, the New Territories, also known as the Kowloon leased territory. In 1898, the Great Powers' "scramble for concessions" marked the darkest period in Chinese international relations, as foreign powers threatened to tear China apart. Yet it also signified the golden age of British imperialism, when Great Britain acquired the largest empire in the world.

By the second half of the 1930s, however, the sun was beginning to set on the once-great empire, and British imperial power had lost much of its luster. With their homeland preoccupied with the aggression of Nazi Germany, a threat also loomed over British colonies in Asia as Japanese influence spread over Asia and the Pacific. By the end of the decade, with

China and Japan already at war, the outbreak of a broader war in the Pacific seemed imminent. The British government quickly, albeit reluctantly, abandoned hope of defending Hong Kong, as Prime Minister Churchill decided that it was "indefensible."[3] With the Nazis terrorizing Europe, the British could no longer afford to protect their Asian empire. On Christmas Day 1941, less than three weeks after it was invaded, Hong Kong fell to Japan. It was the first domino to fall in Britain's Asian empire: Singapore, the Malay Peninsula, and Burma fell in the subsequent months, completely shattering the myth of British superiority. Great Britain's power and prestige in the Asia-Pacific region crumbled.

In contrast, China's stature among the United Nations was rising. The Western Allies' disastrous campaigns in the Pacific in late 1941 to early 1942 further enhanced the image of China's prowess, bravery, and tireless resistance against the common enemy. A surge of support for Chinese national sovereignty followed, particularly among Americans who more and more became advocates for the independence of countries and peoples enslaved, subjugated, or colonized. The Americans' friendship and generosity toward the Chinese was, in addition, driven by their war strategy. The United States needed to keep China in the war, preoccupying Japanese forces while it prepared for offense; it also planned to rely on China for the eventual attack on the enemy homeland, effectively dismantling the Japanese empire.[4]

Meanwhile, an ambivalent and contradictory mentality arose among the Chinese as the result of the Western Allies' declaration of war on Japan, defeat in the Pacific, and overall war policy. Even though exaggerated propaganda on China among the Allied nations—fabricating Chinese victories, valor, and perseverance for the purpose of rallying support abroad and bolstering morale in China—infected the Nationalist government with a dangerous superiority complex and the Allies with the illu-

---

[3] Churchill to Maj. Gen. Ismay, January 7, 1941, quoted in Winston Churchill, *The Second World War.* Vol. 3, *The Grand Alliance* (London: Cassell, 1950), 157.

[4] For excellent general histories of China at war, see Rana Mitter, *Forgotten Ally: China's World War II, 1937–1945* (Boston: Houghton Mifflin Harcourt, 2013); Mark Peattie, Edward J. Drea, and Hans van de Ven, *The Battle for China: Essays on the Military History of the Sino-Japanese War of 1937–1945* (Stanford, CA: Stanford University Press, 2011).

sion of China's enormous breathing room, it was undeniable that China could not win the war alone. After the Allies joined the war, China's leaders became more confident that Japan's defeat was only a matter of time. Nevertheless, the Western Allies' initial failure in the Pacific and, even more, their decision to devote resources to the European front first, provoked substantial Chinese concern over their allies' commitment in the war against Japan. In May 1942, the British embassy in Chongqing reported that the Chinese were not "convinced that the United States and British Empire [were] determined to carry on the war with Japan to a finish if the war against Germany [was] won."[5] This anxiety was further aggravated by the fall of British Burma, the loss of which effectively cut China off from Allied supplies. As a result, despite the image of China's relentless resistance propagated by the Allied press, rumors began to multiply that the National Government might be considering the numerous peace proposals it had received from the Japanese.[6]

While support for China grew stronger in 1942, Allied confidence in the British was rapidly waning, especially where Asia was concerned. A British official in China wrote with great alarm: "Our stock is low and is in danger of falling still lower." Even Foreign Secretary Anthony Eden recognized "the necessity of doing everything possible to counter [Chinese] pessimism."[7] The British decided that the abrogation of British extraterritoriality, which the Chinese had long resented, would have the most effect on China's attitude toward Britain while incurring a minimum loss for the British. Eden realized, "At the end of the war there could ... be no question of our maintaining our extra-territorial privileges," and it would serve to greatly improve the relationship between the two countries if the "Chinese Government realise[d] that the initiative came from us."[8]

[5] Seymour to Eden, tel. 764, May 28, 1942, in Paul Preston, Michael Partridge, and Antony Best, eds., *British Documents on Foreign Affairs: Reports and Papers from the Foreign Office Confidential Print. Part III, Series E (Asia)*, vol. 5, *Far Eastern Affairs, January 1942–September 1942* (Bethesda, MD: University Publications of America, 1997), 129. Henceforth cited as *BDFA*.

[6] Halifax to Eden, tel. 165, May 15, and Seymour to Eden, tel. 975, July 11, 1942, *BDFA* 5:128, 229.

[7] A. Clarke Kerr to Eden, January 28, 1942, *BDFA* 5:13.

[8] Eden to Clarke Kerr, tel. 410, March 28, 1942, *BDFA* 5:37.

Thus on October 10, 1942, the British government joined the Americans in announcing its intention to relinquish extraterritorial rights in China. The British did not realize, however, that the National Government would demand more than what Britain offered, indeed more than the British were willing to give: the cancellation of the lease on the New Territories, which would in effect render the Hong Kong colony useless to the British Empire.

Scholarship on wartime Hong Kong has never been scarce. Important works, such as G.B. Endacott's *Hong Kong Eclipse* and Philip Snow's *Fall of Hong Kong*, describe life under Japanese occupation, while others like Tony Banham's *Not the Slightest Chance* focus on the experiences of British officers and civilians interned during the war. Nonetheless, few works seriously explore the wartime deliberations over Hong Kong's postwar status in any depth. Andrew Whitfield's *Hong Kong, Empire and the Anglo-American Alliance at War* considers only the British point of view and opinion, almost completely removing the Chinese factor from the equation. Whitfield views the Hong Kong problem as part of the struggle of British imperialism against America's new world order, which Whitfield describes as a "hegemonic agenda" cloaked under the rhetoric of democracy and freedom.[9]

Steve Tsang's *Appointment with China* presents a more balanced analysis of the issue in the context of Sino-British relations. However, the book's main focus is the relationship between the British and Communist governments after 1960 and its significance in determining the fate of post-1997 Hong Kong. Finally, K.C. Chan's *China, Britain and Hong Kong* explores the postwar question as part of the longer history of Sino-British relations on Hong Kong from 1895 to the end of World War II. Chan argues that following the signing of the new treaty on January 11, 1943, Britain became significantly more adamant about regaining con-

---

[9] Andrew Whitfield, *Hong Kong, Empire and the Anglo-American Alliance at War, 1941–1945* (Houndmills, UK: Palgrave, 2001), 3. Whitfield's understanding of the U.S. postwar goals is mirrored by the analysis of E.B. Reynolds, who terms American postwar policy in Asia as "'free world' imperialism …, one that recognized independence and offered financial aid in return for the economic 'open door' and military facilities." See E. Bruce Reynolds, *Thailand's Secret War: OSS, SOE, and the Free Thai Underground during World War II* (Cambridge: Cambridge University Press, 2005), 457.

trol over Hong Kong than in 1942, while Nationalist China made "less
clamour about [the colony]."[10] Largely unexplored, however, is the critical
question of why Chiang Kai-shek's regime became less aggressive on the
issue in 1943.

Without disputing Chan's conclusion that British policy to regain
Hong Kong "stiffened" while the Chinese did not, this chapter seeks to
explore both the decision-making process that led to China's policy on
Hong Kong, and the domestic and strategic environment that shaped that
policy.[11] Accordingly, in addressing China and Britain's contention for
Hong Kong during the negotiations over the Sino-British treaty in late
1942 and the year that followed, my analysis reaches beyond the surface of
diplomatic negotiations and explores what went on behind the scenes:
What was each side's strategy? What were their views and attitudes toward one another and toward Hong Kong's future? What did that future
mean or imply for either side? Above all, this chapter explores the themes
of British imperialism and Chinese nationalism during and after the negotiations, and the ideology, opinion, and perceptions that served as un-
dercurrents shaping policies.

STALEMATE IN THE NEW TREATY NEGOTIATIONS

Though known as one of the proudest imperialist nations in the world, the
British were not so conceited as to assume that everything in their Asian
empire would go back to the status quo ante at the end of the war. When
he decided to abandon Hong Kong, Churchill understood that he was
going to have to address the colony's future "at the peace conference."[12]

Congruently, as early as the spring of 1942, the officers in the British
Colonial Office in London already acknowledged the certainty of "very
radical alterations in the position of the Colony and its Government vis à

---

[10] Chan Lau Kit-ching, *China, Britain and Hong Kong, 1895–1945* (Hong Kong: Chinese University Press, 1988), 310–11.

[11] Ibid.

[12] Churchill to Maj. Gen. Ismay, January 7, 1941, quoted in Churchill, *The Second World
War*, 3:157.

vis China after the war."[13] At the same time, the Foreign Office also began to discuss the postwar fate of Hong Kong, including contemplating retrocession to China of part or all of the colony. In the meantime, the British government had a much more pressing issue to deal with in its relations with China, its standing in Asia, and its reputation as a Great Power and a great empire in the eyes of the world. With the rapid surge of sympathy and support for China among Allied nations, the British no longer had a choice but to cooperate with the Chinese, a people they had oppressed, exploited, and forced into one "unequal treaty" after another. For this reason, in 1942, they decided that relinquishing their special legal rights and privileges in China would serve as a grand gesture symbolizing their generosity and sincere feelings of friendship toward their up-and-coming ally.

On October 30, 1942, the British presented the first draft of their new equal treaty to the Chinese government. In addition to extraterritoriality and the special rights accorded to a most favored nation, the British also gave up concessions in Tianjin and Canton, along with privileges in their major trading port, Shanghai. In return for this, many in the British government expected from the Chinese gratitude, reciprocating amity, and a sense that all their past animosity had been wiped clean. What they did not expect was that the Chinese would present them with a list of additional demands, including relinquishing control over the leased land in Kowloon, a vital part of their Hong Kong colony.

The typical British reaction was illustrated by Viscount Halifax, British ambassador to the United States, who deemed the request unreasonable, saying that it was "last minute."[14] But any China veteran would know that the Chinese demand for the return of the Kowloon leased territory, and even the colony itself, was neither last minute nor spontaneous. The British government had in fact received warnings from its officials in China before the treaty was even drafted. John Keswick, commanding officer in the British Special Operations Executive, warned in the summer of 1942, "The Chinese have their eye on Hong Kong, and it is delusion to

[13] Gent Memorandum, February 14, 1942, The National Archives of the UK (hereafter TNA): CO 825/42/15. London, UK. Documents collected in compact disc held at Geisel Library, University of California San Diego.
[14] Halifax memorandum, January 13, 1943, TNA: FO 371/35680/F 412/G.

deny it."[15] After the British announced their intention to abrogate extraterritorial rights in October, Sir Horace Seymour, British ambassador in
Chongqing, who handled the negotiations with the National Government, reported back to London the response of the Chinese public as
summarized by the *Dagongbao*, a top independent newspaper in the wartime capital: the article heralded the announcement as the beginning of a
"new epoch," in which America and Britain "realized that China [was]
capable of sharing equal responsibilities of the world with other Allied
nations" and therefore "should no longer be treated as a quasi-colony." Accordingly, the Chinese public expected that "any right or interest held by
the powers which [was] not in keeping with the principle of equality in
international law should be entirely eliminated." This included any consular jurisdiction, concession, or leased territory (i.e., the New Territories).
The article especially noted that Hong Kong proper "may be held apart
from the present discussion," indicating that, while the Chinese recognized that the treaty being negotiated was not about the colony, which had
been ceded to Britain in perpetuity, they expected the British to return it
to China eventually.[16]

T.V. Soong (Song Ziwen), the Chinese foreign minister, argued that in
demanding the return of the leased territory, the government was simply
acting on the popular demand of the Chinese public and the People's
Political Council, who viewed the abolition of extraterritoriality not only
as the end of foreign jurisdictional rights in China but, more importantly,
as the long-awaited "end of the unequal treaties, root and branch."[17] For
that reason, the Chinese demanded that the British make clear that all
rights enjoyed under the "unequal treaties" were to be abolished, and the
relations between Britain and China from this point on were to be established on the principle of equality and reciprocity.[18] This meant that the

---

[15] Keswick memorandum, enclosed in E. Teichman to Edgcumbe, July 30, 1942, *BDFA*
5:252.
[16] *Dagongbao*, October 19, translation enclosed in Chungking tel. 1444, October 21,
1942, TNA: FO 381/31662.
[17] T.V. Soong to Seymour, as reported in Seymour to Eden, November 13, 1942, and tel.
543, December 7, 1942, *BDFA* 6:66–67, 107.
[18] The Chinese first counterdraft, in Seymour to Eden, tel. 1550 and 1551, November 13
and 14, 1942, *BDFA* 6:58–60.

New Territories, and implicitly even Hong Kong proper, were included as one of the privileges Britain should relinquish. Unfortunately, such a demand became a colossal roadblock to the negotiations between the two countries. By mid-December 1942, the British had already settled all other outstanding issues in the new treaty by acquiescing to virtually every Chinese demand. Yet neither side was willing to give in on the leased territory. Both threatened to refuse to sign the treaty altogether.[19]

The key to understanding the significance of Hong Kong during World War II is to determine why both sides were so adamant about the New Territories during the negotiation. Unlike British colonies elsewhere in Asia, Hong Kong had little potential in terms of natural resources or production.[20] Commercially, Shanghai, which Britain willingly relinquished, was a much more important base for Sino-British trade. Furthermore, both the British and Chinese saw no strategic significance in Hong Kong—in contrast to Singapore, for example, with its major naval base.[21] Therefore, it is safe to say that in every practical aspect, Hong Kong in World War II was neither the most prominent nor the most essential of British possessions in East Asia. But the back-and-forth arguing and stalemate between the two sides during this negotiation showed that the significance of Hong Kong lay not in its material or physical value, but rather in its symbolic and sentimental status.

From the earliest point in the negotiations, Ambassador Seymour warned Anthony Eden that the Chinese were unlikely to budge on the question of the New Territories because they believed they deserved to have an equal relationship with Great Britain, and thus were determined to have the British recognize China's sovereignty over all concessions and

---

[19] See Seymour to Eden, tel. 1651, December 7, and Eden to Seymour, tel. 1641, December 8, 1942, *BDFA* 6:77, 99. See also Chiang Kai-shek diary entry of December 22, 1942, in Gao Sulan, ed., *Jiang Zhongzheng Zongtong dang'an shilüe gaoben*, vol. 52 (Taipei: Academia Historica, 2011), 102, hereafter cited as *SLGB*. For its relative accessibility, this source is cited in lieu of the Chiang Kai-shek diaries in the Hoover Institution Archives. However, all direct quotes have been checked against the original diary.

[20] N.L. Smith memorandum, August 2, 1942, TNA: CO 825/42/15.

[21] T.V. Soong to Chiang Kai-shek, June 1943, in Wu Jingping, ed., *Song Ziwen zhumei shiqi dianbao xuan, 1940–1943* [Selected telegrams of T.V. Soong while stationed in the U.S.] (Shanghai: Fudan daxue chubanshe, 2008), 535–36. Hereafter cited as *Song Ziwen dianbao xuan.*

leased Chinese land. Seymour recommended giving up the leased territory. This way, he argued, Britain would have a much greater chance of retaining the Kowloon Peninsula and Hong Kong Island.[22] However, Chinese and British officials with even a little knowledge of Hong Kong's terrain knew that the colony would be virtually unsustainable without the natural resources and facilities in the New Territories, among which the most important were fresh water and the airfield. If the leased land was returned to China, it would be only a matter time before Hong Kong proper followed. Moreover, Eden and his staff understood that the true intention of the Chinese was to drive British influence from China. Therefore, many in the Foreign Office believed, "regardless of what we may or may not think it desirable to do concerning Hong Kong after its recovery, the present proposal [by the Chinese] should be resisted."[23] A. Cadogan and M. Peterson, Eden's undersecretaries, agreed. They argued that it was "unwise and unsafe to give way," and the British should "resist even at the cost of sacrificing the treaty as a whole."[24] Eden thought similarly. He believed, "the Chinese invariably try to stretch any concession offered. In this case, I would prefer to offer none."[25] But the Foreign Office knew that an outright refusal would cause conflict with the Chinese, and possibly the Americans. Their best solution was to postpone the matter until after the war.

For this reason, Ambassador Seymour told the Chinese that the Kowloon leased territory was outside the scope of the treaty under discussion. The British further argued that they had already given way on a lot of other issues and were reserving Hong Kong for the use of the United Nations in postwar reconstruction. The Chinese retorted that they had also relented by refraining from bringing up Hong Kong Island and the Kowloon Peninsula together with the leased territory. They further pointed out that the treaty would not serve its full purpose of eliminating all misunderstanding between China and Britain without the New Territories.[26]

---

[22] Seymour to Eden, tel. 1564, November 17, 1942, *BDFA* 6:69.
[23] Ashley Clarke to Monson, November 25, 1942, TNA: FO 371/31663 F 7822.
[24] Ashley Clarke minute, December 28, 1942, TNA: FO 371/31665 F 8482.
[25] Eden minute, December 3, 1942, TNA: FO 371/31663 F 7822.
[26] Seymour to Eden, tel. 1678, December 15, 1942, *BDFA* 6:88–89.

In mid-December, Han Liwu, a pro-British member of the National Government, privately suggested a compromise to Seymour. He proposed that China recognize the Kowloon leased territory as outside the scope of the present treaty and, in exchange, that the British promise to discuss the matter at a later date.[27] Seymour feared that at this point Chiang Kai-shek would not be satisfied with anything less than a guarantee that Britain would return the leased land at the end of the war,[28] and he was probably correct. Chiang wrote in his diary on December 22, "I maintain my position to recover [the Kowloon leased territory]. If not, I would prefer not to ratify the new treaty."[29] Seymour nonetheless passed along Han's suggestion to Eden and urged the foreign secretary to accept the compromise, since, he believed, the Chinese had gotten themselves into a position from which they found it impossible to withdraw.[30]

On December 22, Wellington Koo (Gu Weijun), Chinese ambassador to Britain, stepped in to persuade the British.[31] He stressed that given the Generalissimo's temperament, a British expression in writing of their intention to return the New Territories was most likely the only way Chiang would sign the treaty.[32] However, Eden refused to back down. He took the line proposed by Cadogan and Peterson and asserted that if China refused to sign, Britain would just do without the treaty.[33] In truth, Britain under Churchill and Eden's leadership had arrived at exactly the same position as Chiang Kai-shek. Neither Britain nor China was willing to give in because it was the matter of national (or for the British, imperial) pride. The British further expressed resentment that they were being censured for not doing something they had not promised, while they were never appreciated for their unsolicited initiative to relinquish extraterritorial rights.[34] Because of the Hong Kong issue, the treaty that was supposed to improve

---

[27] Ibid.

[28] Seymour to Eden, tel. 1651, December 7, 1942, *BDFA* 6:77.

[29] *SLGB* 52:106 (December 22, 1942).

[30] Seymour to Eden, tel. 1678, December 15, 1942, *BDFA* 6:88–89.

[31] Koo came back to China at that time, accompanying the British parliamentary delegation (nonpolitical).

[32] Seymour to Eden, tel. 1709, December 22, 1942, *BDFA* 6:93.

[33] Eden to Seymour, tel. 1641, December 8, 1942, *BDFA* 6:99.

[34] Seymour to Eden, tel. 1732, December 27, 1942, *BDFA* 6:97–98.

Sino-British relations now threatened to bring a major rupture between the Allies.

BREAKING THE STALEMATE

From a diplomatic standpoint and in terms of global public opinion, the British were in a much more disadvantageous position than the Chinese. Of course, a breakdown in negotiations might cost China a friendly wartime ally and any aid that ally might have provided. On the other hand, Nationalist Free China, with its sovereignty now restored and with support from the United States, did not really need British approval to retake their ancestral land from Japanese control or unilaterally cancel British extraterritoriality. In the Cabinet meeting of December 21, many members of the British government voiced such a concern:

> The failure to sign the treaty will not mean that we can retain extra-territorial rights, which the Chinese will take over from us as soon as the treaty with America is signed; it does mean that we shall receive none of the countervailing safeguards and rights for our nationals in China which the treaty was designed to secure. The Chinese will argue that the Kowloon leased territory is at least analogous to the concessions at Tientsin and Canton: this … will probably carry weight in some sections of opinion in this country and certainly in the United States, from whom we can expect little support.[35]

If this were to happen, the British would lose not only territory and interests in China, but also prestige and respect as a world power.

By the end of December 1942, external pressure was setting in for both the Chinese and the British, making them increasingly anxious to settle the treaty. China and Britain were essentially playing a game of diplomatic

---

[35] Ashley Clarke, "Extraterritoriality Negotiations: Kowloon Leased Territory," December 28, 1942, TNA: FO 371/31665 F 8482.

chicken, one with serious domestic and global consequences, for the breakdown in relations between China and Britain could severely hamper the Allied effort in the war against Japan. At that time, the United States essentially set United Nations war strategy, and the U.S. leadership believed that China, in terms of both human resources and geography, was essential to defeating the Japanese empire. On the other hand, before that could happen, the Chinese army desperately needed to be resupplied and reinforced, and rescuing China from the isolation it had suffered since the fall of British Burma depended on the contribution of Britain, particularly its naval power.

Meanwhile, negotiations had already concluded between the United States and China for their parallel treaty. The U.S. government and the Chinese both wished to announce the Sino-American treaty on New Year's Day; indeed, much to the annoyance of Chiang Kai-shek, the Nationalists' *Central Daily News*, on December 27, had leaked news of the planned New Year announcement.[36] Now all sides were waiting for the negotiations between Britain and China to reach agreement. The British, in order to keep in line with the Americans, had already acquiesced on most other points in the treaty, including giving in on the "national treatment" for commerce, which they deemed one of the most important issues.[37] In addition, in order to make the deadline proposed by the Americans, the British agreed, along the lines suggested by Han Liwu, to discuss the future of the leased territory after victory had been won.[38] But refusing to be pushed any further than this, Eden sought the Americans' help in persuading the Chinese to agree to the proposed compromise.[39]

On their part, the Chinese were also under tremendous pressure to sign the treaty, partly because they did not want to cause any misgivings among the British or Americans, and partly because on December 20,

---

[36] *SLGB* 52:126 (December 28, 1942), 187 (January 3, 1943).

[37] Eden to Seymour, tel. 1616 and 1629, December 22 and 24, 1942, *BDFA* 6:93–94. The "national treatment" meant favorable terms would be granted to British nationals engaged in trade within China.

[38] Extract from War Cabinet Conclusions 171 (42), December 21, 1942, TNA: FO 371/31665 P8397.

[39] Eden to Seymour, tel. 1641, December 8, 1942, and Eden to Halifax, tel. 8264, December 29, 1942, *BDFA* 6:99, 110–11.

they learned that Wang Jingwei, leader of the Japanese-supported Nanjing government, had flown to Tokyo to discuss with Prime Minister Hideki Tojo's cabinet the abrogation of Japan's special rights in occupied China.[40] Chiang Kai-shek was greatly disturbed to learn that the signing date for the Sino-American treaty would be pushed back. He blamed the British, accusing them of "despicably" (*kewu*) using their influence to make the Americans postpone the treaty.[41] T.V. Soong and Wellington Koo, however, were more worried about how to settle the negotiations quickly. Soong confessed that he had wanted to push the British as far as possible on the subject of the leased territory, but not to the point of sacrificing the entire treaty.[42] As December drew to a close, the foreign minister was now desperately trying to convince Koo to help him persuade Chiang.

In his memoir, Wellington Koo recalled visiting the Generalissimo in an attempt to allay his wrath. He told Chiang that the British considered the new treaty to be a gift to China, and suggested that the polite thing to do was to accept this gift first; they could always revisit the question of the Kowloon leased territory later. Koo indicated that he was confident, from his conversations with officials in London, that the British were sincere about returning Hong Kong to China.[43]

On December 30, Soong and Koo again went to see the Generalissimo to report that the British still held their ground, and now wished an explicit statement that the New Territories were outside the scope of the treaty. Chiang was furious when he heard this, declaring that "nobody could endure this." Nonetheless, China, the United States, and Britain were simultaneously in talks about the joint invasion of Burma, which was slated to take place in the coming months. The National Government was receiving increasing pressure from the Chinese press to recapture Burma.[44] Chiang knew that upsetting the British at this time could jeopardize the

---

[40] *SLGB* 52:93 (December 20, 1942), 149 (1942 annual review).

[41] *SLGB* 52:174 (January 1, 1943).

[42] Wellington Koo, *Gu Weijun huiyilu*, Chinese ed. (Beijing: Zhonghua shuju, 1983), 16–18.

[43] Wellington Koo, *Reminiscences of Wellington Koo*, original English ed. (Glen Rock, NJ: Microfilming Corp. of America, 1978), 32–34. Cf. *SLGB* 52:122–23 (December 27, 1942).

[44] Seymour to Eden, tel. 543, December 7, 1942, *BDFA* 6:104.

operation to reopen supply routes into China. Thus, on the same day, he finally decided to give up on including the leased territory in the treaty, writing in his diary, "Kowloon and Hong Kong will certainly be occupied by our troops [at the end of the war]. That will establish the facts. Although there is no written declaration, what's to prevent this?"[45] On January 11, 1943 (two days after a similar agreement between Japan and the Nanjing government), the treaty abrogating British extraterritoriality in China was signed, and the negotiations that had dragged on for over two months were finally concluded.

Why were the British so adamant about Hong Kong? Partly it was the matter of face and pride. More importantly, the postwar status of Hong Kong symbolized the position and strength of the British Empire vis-à-vis China, and in some respects vis-à-vis America. The British feared that if they gave way to Chinese pressure, they would be laying themselves "open to serious pressure from China on other matters."[46] N. Butler of the Foreign Office North American Department argued similarly with regard to the United States, "We should on no account get into the position of seeming to give way to American pressure ... [I]t would be most undesirable that Americans should come to believe that they have compelled us 'to do justice to China,' and this might lead them to draw all sorts of undesirable conclusions elsewhere."[47] "Other matters" and "undesirable conclusions" meant the influence Britain still had over China, and the postwar status of the rest of the British Empire. What the British feared, above all, was to reveal the vulnerability of their empire and risk any chance of recovering it after the war. Giving in on the question of Hong Kong could encourage the Chinese and Americans to push further toward the disintegration of the British Empire once the war was over. The thought of the end of British imperialism was devastatingly frightening to Britain under the leadership of the unapologetic imperialist Winston Churchill.

Similarly, Hong Kong meant little to the Chinese in terms of material

---

[45] *SLGB* 52:138–39 (December 30, 1942).

[46] Ashley Clarke, "Extraterritoriality Negotiations: Kowloon Leased Territory," December 28, 1942, TNA: FO 371/31665 F8482.

[47] M. Butler minute, January 22, 1943, TNA: FO 371/35680 F412/G.

value. But regaining all territories lost under the unequal treaties was an integral part of the Nationalist Party agenda. This was underlined by Chiang Kai-shek's attitude in *China's Destiny*, published to celebrate the signing of the new treaties (see chapter 6). The book revealed that the Chinese goal was not only to become one of the powerful nations shaping the fate of the postwar world; more importantly, Chiang was determined to drive out foreign imperialist influence from China. *China's Destiny* credited foreign influence, particularly imperialism, for essentially all the wrongs that had emerged within the Chinese nation in the modern era. The imperialists were responsible for "prolonging China's internal disorders," preventing economic reconstruction essential to national defense, and, through the importation of opium, turning China "into a sick nation," among many other horrible things.[48] Accordingly, regaining Hong Kong would mean that the Chinese had made one more successful step toward the expulsion of foreign evils and curing China's ills.

On the other hand, this attitude was in contradiction to the reality the Chinese were facing at the time. While declaring independence, sovereignty, and equality with other nations, Nationalist China was not self-sufficient. In fact, the nation under the current regime was unlikely to survive the war without aid from its Western allies. Therefore, until China strengthened its position to the level that it no longer needed help from foreign powers, it could not afford to be unyielding about its long-term goals. Unfortunately, this put China in quite a bind, for while the National Government relied on the power of foreigners to survive the war, according to *China's Destiny*, it was precisely these foreign powers that had weakened China in the first place. This was a painful paradox the Nationalists continued to face throughout the war. But as the Nationalists' position weakened, both domestically and in regard to Great Britain, their anti-foreign and anti-imperialist attitude became more and more secondary to their survival.

---

[48] Chiang Kai-shek, *China's Destiny and Chinese Economic Theory*, trans. Philip J. Jaffe (New York: Roy, 1947), 78–79, 86, 91.

The Roots of Compromise

As the treaty negotiations came to a compromised conclusion, the British were able to avoid prematurely settling the postwar fate of Hong Kong. But the question still remained: who would take possession of the leased territory in Kowloon, and possibly Hong Kong proper, when the war ended, and how would they go about doing so? K.C. Chan argued that after the signing of the treaty, Britain "stiffened its attitude towards" Hong Kong.[49] However, my examination of documents from the Colonial Office, the Foreign Office, and correspondence between key players in the government reveals that British policy on the future of Hong Kong in 1943 was highly inconsistent. Allied military successes and renewed imperial confidence encouraged hopes for the empire's rehabilitation in 1943. For instance, partly due to Britain's improved position and partly due to pressure from the China Association (a party of influential British merchants who were becoming increasingly anxious about their business interests in Hong Kong), the Colonial Office began to push for a more defined policy toward the future status of the colony. In the summer of 1943, the office formed the Hong Kong Planning Unit to formulate an effective administrative plan in the event the British government was to recover the colony after the war. In addition, the Colonial Office urged interdepartmental discussion to decide whether the British should retake the colony at the end of the war and, if so, design a viable plan to achieve that goal.

The Foreign Office, which had been adamant about British sovereignty over Hong Kong during the previous fall's negotiations, was much less enthusiastic in 1943. John Brenan of the Foreign Office pointed out that there was little chance of the Chinese leaving Hong Kong alone regardless of the level of unity with which China emerged from the war; even "the fact that individuals might find the colony a useful refuge in time of trouble would not weigh against the general demand for the restoration of all Chinese territory." Many in the office became increasingly

---

[49] Chan, *China, Britain and Hong Kong*, 310.

convinced that Hong Kong was after all "not worth putting up a fight for." They suggested trading Hong Kong for safeguards of British interests in the colony and the interests of the empire elsewhere in Asia. Many Foreign Office diplomats feared that stubbornly holding on to this small chunk of land would only result in putting the Chinese and the United States on one side and the British on the other. They argued that if the Hong Kong problem could be eliminated, Britain might have a better chance of "getting the United States to support [it] against any manifestations of Chinese Imperialism in Burma, Malaya or elsewhere."[50]

The attitude of the prime minister did not help in consolidating a policy on Hong Kong. Churchill declared in late 1942 that he did not become prime minister to oversee the liquidation of the British Empire. He reiterated this position in a conversation with Stanley Hornbeck of the U.S. State Department in October 1943, when he argued that Hong Kong "was British territory and he [Churchill] saw no good reason why it should cease to be such." Churchill explained that "perhaps some arrangement could be made with the Chinese whereby the question of sovereignty could be adjusted but the political control and administrative responsibility remain with Great Britain." He further declared that "he had convictions on that subject and that he was perfectly willing to say so frankly to anybody." The prime minister's imperialist convictions played a great role in shaping his Hong Kong policy as well as his attitude toward China as a whole. He told Hornbeck that even if China was stronger than it had been before, it was still "ridiculous to talk about China as a great power [or] to bracket China as a power with the United States, Great Britain, [and] Russia."[51] Perhaps his dismissive attitude toward the Chinese helps explain Churchill's nonchalance with regard to the recovery of Hong Kong. Despite his adamant stand on Hong Kong, the prime minister did not support any long-term strategy or postwar planning toward regaining Hong Kong or even toward safeguarding British imperial possessions in general. Quoting the cookbook phrase, "first catch your hare," Churchill

---

[50] M. Butler minute, January 23, 1943, TNA: FO 371/35680 F412/G.

[51] Hornbeck memorandum, November 10 and 15, 1943, Hornbeck Papers, Box 468, Folder November 1943, Hoover Institution Archives, Stanford, California.

argued, "Any conclusions drawn now are sure to have little relation to what will happen."[52]

Throughout 1943, London's official policy toward postwar Hong Kong remained fundamentally unchanged from its position during the treaty negotiations: if the Chinese wished to shorten the lease on the New Territories, which was originally set to expire in 1997, the British were prepared to discuss it after the war. Nonetheless, keeping in mind that Hong Kong proper was ceded to Britain in perpetuity, it had no relation to the matter in question.[53] The British government did not develop a more unified policy or a more substantial strategy to recapture the colony until late 1944.

Chinese policy toward Hong Kong after the signing of the new treaty was, on the surface, even more ambiguous than that of the British. While K.C. Chan has reasonably argued that the Chinese demand for the return of Hong Kong grew quiet from the beginning of 1943, it must be pointed out that, compared to the British, there is a surprising lack of documentation on Chinese policy toward the colony.[54] Even so, available documents from the Chinese Foreign Ministry largely agree with Chan's assessment. In fact, as Steve Tsang insightfully argued, "China's diplomatic machine was unprepared to exercise the right it reserved to raise the issue of New Territories with Britain at the end of the war."[55] On the other hand, the return of Hong Kong was part of the National Government's ultimate goal in gaining back lost territories and becoming an equal partner with the Western Allies. The return of Hong Kong would signify that China was no longer an inferior party at the mercy of Great Britain. Accordingly, deeper analysis is required to understand the discrepancy between Hong

---

[52] Churchill to Eden, October 18, 1942, TNA: FO 954/7B.

[53] Reiterated in Paskin's letter to Clarke, August 27, 1943, TNA: CO 825/42/15, 228–31.

[54] Chan, *China, Britain and Hong Kong*, 310–11. The published Chinese documents on the negotiations in Qin Xiaoyi, ed., *Zhonghua Minguo zhongyao shiliao chubian—dui Ri kangzhan shiqi, disan bian: Zhanshi waijiao* [Important historical materials on the Republic of China, the War of Resistance against Japan, part 3: Wartime foreign affairs] (Taibei: Zhongguo Guomindang zhongyang weiyuanhui dangshi weiyuanhui, 1981), vol. 3, 751–84, contains no documents for the critical period between December 7, 1942, and January 8, 1943.

[55] Steve Tsang, *Hong Kong: An Appointment with China* (London: I.B. Tauris, 1997), 37.

Kong's symbolic importance and China's apparent negligence toward it in 1943. In other words, one must look beyond the surface of the issue and recognize that the question of Hong Kong's future was inevitably tied to the larger context of the war. The Chinese ultimate goal did not change throughout 1943; what changed was the situation of each ally in both the domestic and global war scenes.

The lack of Chinese assertiveness on the return of Hong Kong can be partly explained by the assumptions the Chinese drew from the negotiations concluded in January 1943. Though it should be stressed that, technically, the British had never guaranteed the return of the leased territory nor included the colony of Hong Kong in the promised postwar discussion, the British had agreed to discuss the lease of the New Territories after the war. This, coupled with verbal promises from several British officials, explain the Chinese assumption that Hong Kong would somehow be recovered by China after the war with Japan ended. First of all, Wellington Koo recalled that from his survey of attitudes among British government circles in 1941–1942, Hong Kong was more of a burden than an asset to the British Empire, and British officials and even Churchill himself (contrary to what Hornbeck observed in late 1943) showed ample readiness to retrocede the colony after the war.[56] Similarly, Chiang Kai-shek recalled that Archibald Clark Kerr, the former British ambassador to China, had previously expressed a British willingness to return the colony.[57]

The structure of the National Government contributed greatly to its incoherent foreign policy. In November 1942, Seymour commented that the weakness of the Foreign Ministry had hindered Chinese diplomacy during the past year.[58] This continued to be an issue throughout 1943. T.V. Soong, the officially appointed foreign minister, remained abroad during the larger part of the war, and the ministry was often uninformed on any plan or progress he made on the issue of postwar Hong Kong because Soong usually communicated directly with Chiang.[59] Vice Minister K.C.

[56] Koo, *Reminiscences of Wellington Koo*, 29.

[57] *SLGB* 53:28.

[58] Seymour to Eden, tel. 453, November 2, 1942, *BDFA* 6:82.

[59] Wu Guozhen, Huang Zhuoqun, and Liu Yongchang, *Wu Guozhen zhuan*, vol. 2 (Taipei: Ziyou shibao, 1995), 397.

Wu (Wu Guozhen), who was left in charge of the ministry, delegated the matter of Hong Kong to the head of the European Department, Liang Long. Liang, being British educated and afraid of reprimand from his superiors, took a passive approach on the matter and formulated an unimaginative proposal, arguing, typically, that Britain should "do right by China."[60]

In the spring of 1943, the American embassy in Chongqing received from an anonymous Chinese source a draft scheme on postwar Hong Kong, detailing its potential in various aspects. Most importantly, it argued that Britain should voluntarily return Hong Kong as "the seal of goodwill and friendship between the Chinese and the British peoples in the New World," and that the former colony should then remain a free port to encourage multinational industry, shipping, and commerce, as well as cultural exchange after the war. The Americans believed that the memorandum "[typified] the attitude of many Chinese toward Hong Kong."[61] Still, no strategy was officially formulated by the National Government to regain Hong Kong until early 1945, when, in collaboration with Lt. Gen. A.C. Wedemeyer, American chief of staff to Chiang Kai-shek, who was "personally opposed to any action by the British ... directed to the reoccupation of Hong Kong," the Chinese military devised operations Icemen and White Tower for the recapture of the Canton-Hong Kong region.[62] Due to the political turmoil that loomed over China in the days before Japan's capitulation, these plans to wrest back the British colony never materialized. Nationalist military resources were redirected to winning the domestic political struggle with the Communists instead of regaining territories lost to foreign aggression.

[60] Tsang, *Hong Kong*, 37.

[61] John Carter Vincent to Secretary of State, April 2 and May 6, 1943, National Archives and Records Administration (hereafter NARA).

[62] Tsang, *Hong Kong*, 38. These plans were reworkings of an earlier plan by Stilwell, presented at Cairo, which had much angered the British and been dropped; see *Foreign Relations of the United States: Diplomatic Papers. The Conferences at Cairo and Tehran, 1943* (Washington, DC: U.S. Government Printing Office, 1961), 159–60; Keith Sainsbury, *The Turning Point: Roosevelt, Stalin, Churchill, and Chiang Kai-shek, 1943: The Moscow, Cairo and Teheran Conferences* (Oxford: Oxford University Press, 1985), 181–83.

CHINA'S WEAKENED POSITION

In 1943, the situation of the war at large was changing. The tide had turned against the Axis and in favor of the Allied Powers; the Americans gained ground in the Pacific, while the British and Russians celebrated victories in Africa and Eastern Europe. The situation took a turn in the opposite direction for China, with a significant decline in internal stability. Inflation and famine had become an uncontainable disease plaguing Chongqing and many other regions under the Nationalists' control (see chapters 9 and 10). Price fixing implemented by the government in mid-January turned into a tremendous failure that received derision and mockery from the public; even the *Dagongbao* heavily criticized the "muddle which had resulted from the price-control measures" and "enquired sarcastically if [the government] had prepared sufficient prison cells to house those operating in the black market."[63] In May, the Japanese gained control of much of the rice-producing territory between Yichang and Hankow, resulting in the price of rice in Chongqing rising by 60 percent, and with it grew stories of banditry and desertions by soldiers who were "so ill-provided and underfed as to be useless."[64]

Outside of the capital, famine prevailed in Henan and was so seriously aggravated by local officials who continued to requisition grain in the form of taxes that "whole districts [had been] depopulated, hundreds [died] daily in the towns, and the starving survivors [subsisted] on the bark of trees, grass, crushed pea-nut shells, and even human flesh."[65] A British agent tasked with intelligence and rescuing prisoners of war in Japanese-occupied Hong Kong reported on his journey through free Guangdong that the death rate surged in mid-1943. While admitting that the news reports that thousands were dying daily were an exaggeration, he wrote, "the truth is bad enough;"

---

[63] Seymour to Eden, tel. 127, February 4, 1943, *BDFA* 6:226. *Dagongbao* was then punished by Nationalist government censorship authorities and ordered to stop publishing for three days.

[64] Seymour to Eden, tel. 545 and 594, June 7 and May 29, 1943, *BDFA* 6:395, 368.

[65] E. Teichman to Eden, tel. 8, June 1, 1943, *BDFA* 6:372.

The number is at least one hundred on an average. In a short journey from Toishan to an outlying village, he saw eight unburied corpses. The worst feature is cannibalism. Human flesh sells at five dollars a plate. Parents leave their children at certain recognized points, where they are seized and butchered by the human flesh vendors.[66]

Meanwhile, civil and military unrest continued to grow in various regions of Free China, including Hunan, Guizhou, Gansu, and Sichuan, where corrupt officials, ruthless tax collection, and army conscription led to mutinies and armed revolts. What was worse, there were multiple reports that "troops sent to restore order had joined the malcontents."[67] Morale and loyalty declined rapidly even among the higher military officials. H.D. Bryan reported on his visit to Shaoguan that it was apparent that loyalty to the National Government by General Yu, who was charged with defending the region, was "merely a matter of expediency." He further noted, "There is little indication of a real intention to resist actively any Japanese attack."[68] Elsewhere, the Nationalist army was "almost as great a burden to the peasants as to the enemy."[69]

More and more, foreign officials became disillusioned about the real capability of Nationalist China, as well as its resolve in resisting and defeating the Japanese. As early as November 1942, British intelligence sent disconcerting reports that "the only serious fighting the Kuomintang Army was doing was against the Communists. ... South of Waichow all is chaos. Chungking has ordered General Cheung to carry out a sustained and ruthless attack on the Reds. He either wipes them out or he goes."[70] At the same time, a starkly contrasting image to disorderly Nationalist China began to emerge from the Communist side. M.C.A.M.

---

[66] Edwin Ride, *BAAG: Hong Kong Resistance, 1942–1945* (Hong Kong: Oxford University Press, 1981), 113–14.

[67] Seymour to Eden, tel. 545, June 7, 1943, *BDFA* 6:396.

[68] H.D. Bryan, "Report on Visit to Kwangtung, etc., from 23 March to 22 April 1943," *BDFA* 6:380.

[69] Ride, *BAAG*, 110.

[70] Ibid., 110–11.

Brondgeest, who had escaped from Beijing in early 1942, wrote of his journey and surprising encounters with the Communists as he trekked through regions controlled by the Chinese Communist Party and the Eighth Route Army to Free China: "In leaving Yenan for Chungking, I said good-bye to a country where there are no rickshaws, no squeeze, no prostitutes, no opium smokers, and no beggars. A strange China, indeed! They do not talk about a 'New Life Movement,' they have it." He also observed that the Communist leaders claimed that "they would gladly co-operate with the Kuomintang, but could not trust them." "How can we," they said, "when they blockade us, do not support us to fight the common enemy, and mass large numbers of troops on our borders?"[71]

Even among officials of the United States, sympathy as well as admiration for the Communists' effort against Japan increased significantly by mid-1943, while disappointment with the Nationalists grew exponentially. John Paton Davies, Jr., a political consultant for Gen. Joseph Stilwell, sent home increasingly critical reports on Nationalist China. In June, T.V. Soong reported Davies's views on China's situation: "Communist troops made great efforts to fight against enemy. Yet Central Government monitored Communist Party with 400,000 troops. According to *Doūmei sha* [aka the Allied News Agent] of Japan, Japanese Army has had more than twice the number of engagements with Communist troops as with central government's army troops in recent months."[72]

The image of Chiang Kai-shek as the "universally trusted, … symbol of resistance against the hated invader" that had prevailed through 1942 deteriorated rapidly in the eyes of the Chinese and of foreign officials alike.[73] At the beginning of 1942, Ambassador Kerr wrote, "It is remarkable, in these days when dictators are execrated, that a man who is so completely a dictator should command the unquestioning faith and affection of the millions he rules. To-day the Chiang Kai-shek myth remains as tenacious as ever and the immediate fate of China continues to depend

---

[71] Extracts from a report by M.C.A.M Brondgeest, enclosed in Seymour to Eden, tel. 612, December 29, 1942, *BDFA* 6:183.

[72] T.V. Soong to Chiang Kai-shek, June 8, 1943, in *Song Ziwen dianbao xuan*, 533.

[73] "Report on the Political Condition of China," *BDFA* 6:195.

upon one man alone. [The Generalissimo] continues to stand in vulgar fame immaculate and above reproach."[74]

But by 1943, while the Communists were seen calling for "central authority to enforce democracy strictly," Chiang was perceived as the stubbornly anti-Communist dictator, "China's 'Francisco Franco,'" who tried to strengthen the air forces and demanded supplies from the United States in order to ensure postwar domination over his political rivals.[75] Nationalist despotism continued to intensify to the point that the liberal elite in China, who were usually more underground and less radical in voicing their criticism of the central government, began to take more aggressive actions to express their discontent (see chapter 8). For example, Zhang Junmai, a leading figure in the China Democratic League, refused to attend a meeting of the People's Political Council "on the ground that it was undemocratic."[76] In July, Qian Duansheng, a member of the council, even wrote a letter to Churchill's cabinet, criticizing Chiang's regime. The letter reportedly included the following points: "1. Nationalist Party is autocratic; 2. nonparty elites cannot take part in government; 3. economic situation is critical, with abuses ubiquitous. Moreover, senior government officials are involved in embezzlement."[77]

More disheartening reports on the conditions in China reached the U.S. State Department from the summer through the rest of the year. George Atcheson, chargé d'affaires in Chongqing, wrote, "There is a feeling the situation in many aspects is out of control and is seriously deteriorating in practically all aspects."[78] China's allies grew increasingly concerned over its chance of survival to the end of the war. In June 1943, alarming reports from the U.S. embassy and Australian legation reached Anthony Eden's office. They indicated that the "situation [could] not endure much longer [and] that China '[could] last' not more than six months to a year."[79] While Seymour tried to dial down the panic at Whitehall,

[74] A. Clark Kerr to Eden, February 3, 1942, *BDFA* 6:139.

[75] T.V. Soong to Chiang Kai-shek, June 8, 1943, *Song Ziwen dianbao xuan*, 533–35.

[76] Seymour to Eden, tel. 24, January 4, 1943, *BDFA* 6:192.

[77] T.V. Soong to Chiang Kai-shek, July 29, 1943, *Song Ziwen dianbao xuan*, 539.

[78] Hornbeck to Leahy, June 2, 1943, Hornbeck Papers, Box 276, Folder Leahy, William D.

[79] Eden to Seymour, tel. 563, *BDFA* 6:390.

arguing that there were "no grounds for anticipating anything in the nature of such collapse in the near future," he confirmed that "the situation
[was] one of progressive deterioration." Seymour further told Eden, "More
Chinese are beginning to believe that China can do little or nothing to
help herself, and are also now wondering whether she can last long enough
to give time for her Allies ... to do much for her."[80] The ambassador
also expressed his fear that if the situation continued to decline, the National Government "would have little more than a token value, and the
greater part of the country [would] relapse into the same conditions of
un-coordinated guerilla warfare and semi-banditry as now [prevailed] in
many of the unoccupied areas."[81]

Excessive propaganda in the early war years depicting China's heroism
and vast potential played a tremendous role in exacerbating Allied disillusionment with China in 1943. Davies argued that U.S. magazines such
as *Life*, *Time*, and *Fortune* contributed greatly to the ill feelings toward the
Chinese by American officials residing in China, because they painted an
unrealistically positive picture of China under Chiang's control.[82] Even
T.V. Soong had serious concerns about the Nationalists' military propaganda, which often inflated enemy casualties to exaggerate Chinese victories. Distraught, he wrote to Chiang in July, "No wonder that US War
Department and Stilwell do not believe in fierceness of west Hubei battles, let alone enemy's intention to threaten provisional capital. Again, I
described military situation to War Department and those who concerned.
I feel our military propaganda has long been naïve, and always treated as
child's play. Moreover, its reports damaged credibility of our government
more than enemy's propaganda did. Its effect is equal to Fifth Column's
job."[83]

Whether it was due to the aftereffects of its own misleading propaganda or the abysmal conditions seen in Chongqing, Henan, Guangdong,
and elsewhere, it is clear that the way China was viewed by her allies was
increasingly negative. One secret report summarizing allegations from ob-

---

[80] Seymour to Eden, tel. 545 and 594, June 7 and May 29, 1943, *BDFA* 6:395, 368.

[81] Seymour to Eden, tel. 545, June 7, 1943, *BDFA* 6:397.

[82] T.V. Soong to Chiang Kai-shek, June 8, 1943, *Song Ziwen dianbao xuan*, 534–35.

[83] T.V. Soong to Chiang Kai-shek, July 1943, *Song Ziwen dianbao xuan*, 541.

servers of various allied nations painted an all-around depressing image of Free China, most of which was the result of the incompetent and corrupt government:

> That many of China's leaders appear to be preoccupied with the questions of gains which will come to China currently and after victory rather than with the prosecution of the war.
>
> That the Chinese people, although united in a desire to see Japan defeated, are disheartened because of economic and financial hardships which they attribute to indifference, ineptitude or preoccupation with policies of personal interest on the part of the officials.
>
> That all too little effort is being made by the Chinese Government to affect much needed military, economic and social reforms.
>
> That Chinese authorities, especially military authorities, all too frequently manifest a lack of desire or a disinclination to be cooperative; and that considerations of national and of personal "face" appear all too often to be permitted to outweigh considerations of practical needs for advancement of China and her allies.[84]

Rapid internal deterioration, coupled with the United States' new strategy of "island hopping" in the Pacific to defeat Japan, gradually led to the diminished role China would play in the final defeat of the Japanese empire. This minimized position in the war threatened China's future equality with its allies, hampered its ability to play a role in reshaping the world, and jeopardized the Nationalists' position as the supreme (and perhaps even the sole) political authority in postwar China. In view of this more important, more urgent objective, the Nationalists' first priority was to strengthen themselves—militarily, politically, and economically—fast. And in order to do this, they needed more supplies and aid from the Allies.

Though China had been granted an enormous loan and promised gen-

---

[84] "Secret Report on Conditions in China," October 1, 1943, Hornbeck Papers, Box 468, Folder October 1943.

erous material aid by the U.S. government in 1942, only a minuscule portion of the promised supplies had reached China since its ground communication and transport routes to the rest of the world had been virtually
cut off after the fall of Burma. Therefore, China's foremost diplomatic task
was to secure a coordinated plan for an Allied attack on Burma and the
reopening of the Burma Road. In addition to this, the $50 million loan
from the British was still being negotiated, and the Chinese were exploring an alternative route for nonmilitary supplies through Tibet, if an
agreement could be reached with the Tibetan government. The urgent
issue of war supplies meant that the Chinese could not afford to disrupt
Allied cooperation by bringing up such important but less immediate issues as the future of Hong Kong.

The Chinese mind-set of first appeasing the aid-providing Allies was
clearly demonstrated by T.V. Soong's visit to London in late July through
early August 1943. Despite the British anticipation, the issue of Hong
Kong's postwar status was absent from Soong's agenda during his talks
with various leaders of the British government, including Eden and
Churchill. Chiang Kai-shek had emphasized to his foreign minister that
the prime objective of this visit was the reopening of the Burma Road and
that Soong was to prioritize the joint attack on Burma above all other issues. Chiang was even willing to be more flexible on the issue of Tibet. He
promised to refrain from sending spy planes or putting any more pressure
on the region. Chiang reflected that the most important thing at that time
was to avoid antagonizing the British or doing anything that would give
them an excuse to back out from their agreement on the Burma Road.[85]
The Chinese most likely felt that broaching the subject of the British colony at that point would not only be fruitless but probably also detrimental
to the negotiations at hand. Soong later explained in his telegram to
Chiang and in his private, handwritten memo on the meetings, "[The]
only person who [could] influence the British Government is President
Roosevelt," and therefore, the foreign minister "purposely avoided discussing Hong Kong ... [and] since President Roosevelt has his ways I did not
raise question."[86] This illustrates three points. First, even though the Na-

[85] *SLGB* 54:155–56.
[86] Soong's handwritten note on his and Wellington Koo's meetings in London, August
1943, T.V. Soong Papers, Box 29, Folder 17, "Great Britain: Foreign Relations with China,"

tional Government "made less clamor" on the subject of Hong Kong after the treaty, they did not give up their aim to regain it once the war was over. Second, during 1943 the Chinese strategy to recapture the British colony rested mostly on the support of the U.S. government or, more accurately, Roosevelt. And third, the future of Hong Kong, though very important, was not as urgent as war supplies or internal stability, which were ultimately more necessary for the Nationalists' goal to emerge with glory and power as one of the postwar world leaders. Unfortunately, this in turn contributed to their eventual failure to regain Hong Kong at the end of the war.

THE AMERICAN ROLE

While intentionally avoiding the issue with the British, China's leaders often pressed the U.S. government for their guaranteed support on Hong Kong throughout 1943. Whereas the State Department tended to be circumspect on the issue, Roosevelt openly expressed his support to the Chinese. In March, the president advised Chiang to compromise with the British by keeping Hong Kong a free port and promising to protect British rights and interests in the former colony. Though he accepted Roosevelt's suggestion, Chiang asserted as a matter of pride that this could not be the condition for the British returning Hong Kong. His desire was to have Britain recognize China's equal status and return Hong Kong without argument; then the Chinese government would itself declare Hong Kong a free port.[87] In May, Roosevelt and Soong discussed the matter again and made plans to declare Hong Kong an open port, as if the British had agreed and the return of the colony to China had already been decided.[88] In June, Soong and Roosevelt expressed surprising confidence about securing the British territory for China.

Three factors explain such conceit in spite of Britain's adamant refusal to relinquish even the leased territory during the treaty negotiations in late

Hoover Institution Archives; cf. T.V. Soong to Chiang Kai-shek, August 17, 1943, *Song Ziwen dianbao xuan*, 548.

[87] *SLGB* 53:28–29.

[88] T.V. Soong to Chiang Kai-shek, May 1943, *Song Ziwen dianbao xuan*, 522.

1942. First, in addition to Kerr's indication while he was in Chongqing and the impression Wellington Koo got from the British officials he met, Soong presumptuously believed that during the previous year's negotiations, "Britain expressed that the hand-over of Kowloon would be negotiated after the war." Again, technically, the British had only agreed to discuss the "lease" or the "question of" the Kowloon leased territory and not the "hand-over." Nonetheless, Soong confidently argued, "If China regards Hong Kong as a foreign territory, Hong Kong will inevitably go bankrupt."[89] Thus, Soong believed, the British would probably realize sometime before the end of the war that there was no point in stubbornly retaining Hong Kong out of pride. Second, in April 1943, the U.S. State Department received word from an influential Chinese that negotiations with the British for the return of the colony were already well under way.[90] This may have led the U.S. government to assume that the British were more inclined than previously to relinquish the colony if the Chinese agreed to British conditions, though Hornbeck's meeting with Churchill suggested otherwise.

Third, as indicated by Elliot Roosevelt's book on his father, *As He Saw It*, the president simply took it for granted that the future of Hong Kong, and in fact the future of the whole British Asian empire, was up to him to decide. Elliot Roosevelt recalled that at the Cairo Conference at the end of the year, his father made a deal with Chiang that if the Generalissimo "agreed to form a more democratic government in China," he would in return promise to "support [China's] contention that British ... no longer [enjoyed] special Empire rights to Hong Kong." Elliot cautioned the president against making such promises, accurately pointing out that it would be "tough to get agreement from Churchill on any part of that one." The senior Roosevelt retorted, "There can't be much argument, inasmuch as it's ninety-nine per cent American matériel and American men bringing about the defeat of Japan. ... American foreign policy after the war must be along the lines of bringing about the realization on the part

---

[89] T.V. Soong to Chiang Kai-shek, June 1943, *Song Ziwen dianbao xuan*, 536.

[90] Memorandum dated May 6, 1943, enclosed in John Carter Vincent to Secretary of State, April 2, 1943, Dispatch 1044, File 846g.01, Central Decimal File, 1940–1944, Box 5098, Record Group 59, NARA.

of the British and the French and the Dutch that the way we have run the Philippines is the only way they can run *their* colonies."[91]

It is difficult, if not impossible, to pinpoint the influence Roosevelt had on the future of the British colony. The anti-imperialist president died before the war was over, and substantial military planning toward recapturing Hong Kong only took shape during the final months of the war. In addition, most promises Roosevelt made on Hong Kong were mere verbal agreements between him and the Chinese. While aware of American influence in the Pacific, the British never acknowledged any of these agreements, nor did the United States have legal claims over Hong Kong. What is more, Roosevelt's sense of superiority and confidence in American control over the world often led him to make promises arbitrarily. While in Cairo, Roosevelt supported the return to China of territories acquired by foreign powers during the century of unequal treaties, yet he also took the liberty of promising Dalian (then known as Dairen or Port Arthur) to Stalin at the Tehran Conference, which immediately followed the Cairo meeting.[92]

Moreover, the U.S. president's policy toward China was congruent with the embellished propaganda in America; accordingly, it was increasingly contradictory to the reality in China. This is demonstrated by Roosevelt's own conversation. While promising Hong Kong to Chiang at Cairo, the president at the very same conference asked Stilwell, "How long … do you think Chiang can last?" Despite the fact that Stilwell had been urging throughout the war for the president to form a more realistic policy toward China and to demand results for the aid the United States had given, Roosevelt chose to give the National Government support, all the while knowing the dire conditions in the territories under Nationalist control.[93] After all, America's objectives "were to keep China in the war and aligned with the United States in the future." And if worse came to worst, "if there was no alternative to Chiang Kai-shek capable of holding

[91] Elliott Roosevelt, *As He Saw It* (New York: Duell, Sloan and Pearce, 1946), 164–65.

[92] Whitfield, *Hong Kong, Empire and the Anglo-American Alliance*, 161.

[93] Tang Tsou, *America's Failure in China, 1941–1950* (Chicago: University of Chicago Press, 1963), 92–95.

China united (the Communists were out of the question), then Chiang had to be supported regardless."[94]

Cairo probably represented one of the cruelest ironies in the history of republican China. When 1943 came to a close, China gained symbolic momentum by being invited to sit side by side with the two other world powers and participate in discussions on important world problems (see chapter 13). If Roosevelt's words could be taken for granted, the Generalissimo could feel at ease that the retrocession of Hong Kong and ergo the full expulsion of British imperial privilege in China were already guaranteed. It was, however, not guaranteed that Chiang or even Nationalist China would survive to see the day when China returned to its pre–unequal treaties glory.

China and Britain's policies toward the postwar status of Hong Kong were intricately linked to developments in the war and Britain and China's position internally and in relation to one another. The controversy surrounding the question of Hong Kong's future and the seemingly disproportionate importance accorded to it during the 1942–1943 treaty negotiation signifies a common symptom in Allied diplomacy during World War II: the foreign policies of each of the Allies faced an impossible dilemma in which they attempted to balance immediate wartime needs and long-term goals and ideals—which were different for each of the Allies. On the one hand, the stubborn British and Chinese designs on the leased territory, and implicitly but more importantly Hong Kong, represent the struggle between waning but obstinate British imperialism and rising but unstable Chinese nationalism. On the other hand, each party's considerable disinterest in the issue in the subsequent months showed that principles and ideologies often had to be subordinated to the urgent realities of war. In the end, it was the outcome of the war that determined whose foreign policy yielded more favorable results. Because China's situation began to deteriorate and continued to spiral downhill, it became impossible for the Chinese to balance both the things they wanted to bargain for during the war, and those they wished for in the long run. British triumph

---

[94] Barbara W. Tuchman, *Stilwell and the American Experience in China, 1911–45* (New York: Macmillan, 1970), 353, 355, 410.

on the Hong Kong issue, on the other hand, was not the result of persistence or a "stiffened" policy, but resulted from the improvements in the British war situation, the death of the anti-imperialist President Roosevelt, and the disintegrating order in China.

In September 1945, when the Japanese finally surrendered, the Nationalists had at least two large contingents of troops that could have outrun the British to Hong Kong. But by this time, their war reality had completely changed. Without President Roosevelt, the United States no longer prioritized China over Britain; more importantly, Chiang Kai-shek's regime was about to embark on another major crusade against their formidable countrymen and enemy, the Chinese Communists. Given Chiang's decision to squash Mao and his flock before anything else, the return of Hong Kong was no longer a priority or even a practical possibility.

6

Debating China's Destiny

Writing the Nation's Past and Future in Wartime China

DANIEL D. KNORR

On October 9, 1942, Chiang Kai-shek received word that the United States and Great Britain had decided to abrogate their unequal treaties with China as a sign of good will toward their mutual ally. The renegotiation of these treaties, which stretched back to the 1842 Treaty of Nanjing, had been a common goal of Chinese nationalists even before Sun Yat-sen coined the term "unequal treaties" (*bu pingdeng tiaoyue*) in 1924.[1] In private, Chiang gushed with self-congratulation, writing in his diary, "To have achieved by my own hand the great goal of Sun Yat-sen's revolutionary struggle leaves me without words to express the gratification in my heart."[2] He wasted no time in making this accomplishment an integral part of the ongoing propaganda effort in support of his own political prestige and the continued governance of the Nationalist Party. The next day, October 10, he announced this good news to the Chinese people as

---

[1] Dong Wang, *China's Unequal Treaties: Narrating National History* (Lanham, MD: Lexington, 2005), 64–70.

[2] Qin Xiaoyi, ed., *Zongtong Jiang gong dashi changbian chugao* [Draft of the major events of President Chiang Kai-shek] (Taipei: Zhongzheng wenjiao jijinhui, 2005), vol. 5, 209 (October 10, 1942).

part of the National Day celebrations. He also instructed one of his secretaries, Tao Xisheng, to begin drafting a book that would elaborate on the pivotal place of these renegotiated treaties in the history of the Chinese nation. Published six months later, in March 1943, this book would be called *China's Destiny* (*Zhongguo zhi mingyun*).

The publication of *China's Destiny* came at a critical time for Chiang and the Nationalist Party. With the entry of Britain and the United States into the Pacific War in late 1941, China found itself with new allies and an unprecedented degree of international prestige derived from its stubborn resistance to Japan. This resistance appeared all the more impressive after the shocking defeats Japan inflicted on the United States and Britain in the weeks following the attack on Pearl Harbor. Despite domestic problems such as inflation and famine (see chapters 9 and 10), Chiang could point to China's hard-earned respect as just reward for the sacrifices made by its people and as an indication that the nation was heading in the right direction under his guidance.

To make this argument to the Chinese people and, to a lesser extent, his foreign allies, Chiang invested a great deal of time and energy in writing *China's Destiny*. Although this book is widely and correctly understood to have been ghostwritten by Tao Xisheng, Chiang's personal participation was integral to the writing process. Its successes and failures should be attributed in no small measure to him. Unfortunately for Chiang, *China's Destiny* proved to be a squandered opportunity and a tremendous liability. Its history unequivocally reveals Chiang's failure to anticipate that his friends and foes alike would converge on a series of devastating and thorough critiques of the book that bore his name.

In many ways, the criticisms of *China's Destiny* were predictable, especially those of the Communists and liberal intellectuals. However, a close reading of its text and these responses shows that Chiang failed to anticipate the damage the book would inflict on the political legitimacy of him and his party. While Chiang could hardly expect to win over diehard Communists or liberals, *China's Destiny* actively prejudiced even moderate readers against the Nationalist Party. Students and intellectuals interpreted Chiang's enthusiastic support for the values of traditional Chinese society and culture, along with his bent toward political authoritarianism, as a recapitulation of the worst elements of the imperial era. Moreover, the Communists strategically made *China's Destiny* the centerpiece of their anti-Guomindang propaganda both in China and abroad from mid-1943 on. While the Nationalist and foreign governments' cooperation in suppressing English translations of the book succeeded in muting foreign criticism during the war, postwar reactions demonstrate Chiang's naïveté in thinking that *China's Destiny* could ever boost his standing with a foreign audience.

Beyond these groups, the Japanese response to *China's Destiny* has received no attention at all from scholars. An analysis of pro-Japanese writers' responses to *China's Destiny* serves two main purposes. The first is to expose how the book opened the door for critics to claim that certain aspects of Chiang's ideological program bore an affinity to ideas being promoted by Japan, while others were even more extreme than the Japanese brand of fascism. The second is to demonstrate that by echoing Communist claims about *China's Destiny*, especially that Chiang's ideology resembled that of Japan, the pro-Japanese response magnified the impact of Communist propaganda, especially in areas where both critiques were disseminated side by side.

This narrative of failure and missed opportunity contradicts the thrust of some scholars' recent attempts to rehabilitate Chiang Kai-shek's wartime administration from the ravages of postwar critiques by American journalists and scholars.[3] Part of this disagreement is no doubt due to differences in focus: for example, Hans van de Ven's focus on Nationalist military strategy and mobilization leads him to sympathize with the Nationalist administration on account of the material constraints it faced by 1943. By comparison, as far as *China's Destiny* is concerned, material constraints were of little relevance. Nothing was forcing Chiang to write this book, or any book at all for that matter. Chiang was positively enthusiastic about *China's Destiny* and honestly surprised when it failed. External cir-

---

[3] See, for instance, Jay Taylor, *The Generalissimo: Chiang Kai-shek and the Struggle for Modern China* (Cambridge, MA: Harvard University Press, 2009), 141–335; Stephen MacKinnon, "Conclusion," in *Negotiating China's Destiny in World War II*, ed. Hans van de Ven, Diana Lary, and Stephen MacKinnon (Stanford, CA: Stanford University Press, 2015), 239–44.

cumstances were certainly unfavorable, but Chiang's failure to appreciate the context in which *China's Destiny* would be published and the liabilities he was creating as he flooded Tao Xisheng's draft with red ink was his own. To make this point, this chapter returns to the original Chinese sources—*China's Destiny* itself and the critiques of it—and relies on foreign accounts only sparingly. Thus, if it falls within the White-Stilwell paradigm of Chiang Kai-shek critiques that van de Ven disparages, then it is because Chiang's own words put it there.[4]

The primary focus of this chapter is how short-term considerations shaped the writing of *China's Destiny* and how this book had an immediate impact on the course of history. *China's Destiny* was very much a product of its immediate circumstances. Its singular focus on the abrogation of the unequal treaties and its assumption that victory over Japan was a matter of when, not if, grew out of the course of events leading into 1943. Likewise, the concurrent events of 1943 shaped each party's responses to *China's Destiny*. By demonstrating these links, I correct previous scholars' inattention to the relationship between *China's Destiny* and the events of 1942–1944.[5]

The long-term significance of *China's Destiny* is more difficult to assess. On the one hand, it belongs to a long tradition of Chinese nationalist literature as well as a more narrow current of fascist thought. In both regards, *China's Destiny* was more exemplary than exceptional. Its authorship and wide dissemination at a very particular point in time are what make it integral to the study of wartime China. Throughout this chapter and especially in the notes, I have alluded to works that explore these ideological issues that, while certainly relevant to a com-

---

[4] Hans van de Ven, *War and Nationalism in China, 1925–1945* (New York: Routledge-Curzon, 2003), 3–12.

[5] In his biography of Chiang, Jonathan Fenby places his brief discussion of *China's Destiny* in a chapter about Madame Chiang, making no reference to the connection to the unequal treaties or the Communist response in the summer. Jonathan Fenby, *Chiang Kai-shek: China's Generalissimo and the Nation He Lost* (New York: Carroll and Graf, 2003), 400. Jay Taylor, Chiang's other biographer in the 2000s, misdates the completion of *China's Destiny* to late 1943, perhaps being confused by the revised edition that Chiang prepared over the course of 1943. Needless to say, he does not account for the role *China's Destiny* played in the events of the summer of 1943. Taylor, *The Generalissimo*, 259–61. Li Yang and Deng Ye, cited in the subsequent section, are exceptional in this regard.

prehensive understanding of *China's Destiny*, are less germane to our focus on 1943.[6]

The other side of the long-term significance of *China's Destiny*—its impact on subsequent Chinese history—is equally difficult to assess. Up through the Cultural Revolution, the veneration of China's past, on which *China's Destiny* hinged, seemed unlikely to hold much sway on the mainland. Following the fading of Marxist-Leninist ideology with China's "reform and opening" under Deng Xiaoping, the 2000s in particular have seen a resurgence of official appeals to China's past (both ancient and revolutionary) for national legitimation. While forty years ago *China's Destiny* seemed destined to become a mere footnote in Chinese history, it now appears that the final chapter of its history remains to be written, which is all the more reason to understand its origins.

WRITING AND CRITICIZING *CHINA'S DESTINY*

From start to finish, *China's Destiny* was Chiang Kai-shek's pet project. After the National Day celebrations on October 10, 1942, Chiang instructed one of his secretaries, historian Tao Xisheng, to draft a manuscript, using as a basis the text of his speech announcing the impending abrogation of the unequal treaties.[7] Chen Bulei, Tao's friend and Chiang's close confidante, assisted. (Had Chen not been ill at the time, he might well have been in charge of drafting the book himself.[8]) Tao's prior col-

---

[6] Some of the more useful works on the place of *China's Destiny* in Nationalist and Communist ideology include Raymond Wylie, *The Emergence of Maoism: Mao Tse-tung, Ch'en Po-ta, and the Search for Chinese Theory, 1935–1945* (Stanford, CA: Stanford University Press, 1980), 195–225; Thomas Mullaney, *Coming to Terms with the Nation: Ethnic Classification in Modern China* (Berkeley: University of California Press, 2010), 27–30; James Leibold, *Reconfiguring Chinese Nationalism: How the Qing Frontier and Its Indigenes Became Chinese* (New York: Palgrave Macmillan, 2007), 143–44; Lin Hsiao-ting, *Tibet and Nationalist China's Frontier: Intrigues and Ethnopolitics, 1928–1949* (Vancouver: University of British Columbia Press, 2011), 140–44, 155–56; Liu Xiaoyuan, *Frontier Passages: Ethnopolitics and the Rise of Chinese Communism, 1921–1945* (Stanford, CA: Stanford University Press, 2004), 123–26.

[7] Li Yang, "Tao Xisheng yu *Zhongguo zhi mingyun* xinjie" [A new understanding of Tao Xisheng and *China's Destiny*], *Zhongguo shehui daokan*, no. 19 (2008): 44.

[8] Tao Xisheng, *Chaoliu yu diandi* [Tides and drips] (Taibei: Zhuanji wenxue chubanshe, 1964), 204. On Chen's knowledge about the *China's Destiny* project, see Gu Weijun, *Gu*

laboration with Wang Jingwei, who now headed the Japanese puppet government in Nanjing, had left him in a precarious political position, even after his return to Chongqing. Fearing for his life and his family's safety, Tao made sure to follow Chiang's instructions exactly as he prepared the draft.[9]

Chiang continued to exert his influence throughout the drafting process. Tao met repeatedly with Chiang over the course of November and December, and his original 30,000-character draft eventually ballooned into a text of over 100,000 characters.[10] By the end of the revision process, not a single character from Tao's original draft, written in black ink, could be discerned beneath the sea of red that Chiang left on the manuscript.[11] On Christmas Eve, 1942, Chiang wrote in his diary that the previous night he had put so much energy into revising the draft of *China's Destiny* that he had difficulty falling asleep.[12]

The initial motivation for and guiding theme of *China's Destiny* was, of course, the end of China's "century of humiliation" under the unequal treaties. Chiang's concern was both to explicate the importance of the treaties' abrogation and to bolster the nationalist credentials of the Nationalist Party amid fears that the Communists were drawing support from patriotic but ideologically vulnerable youth.[13] Chiang positioned the National-

---

Weijun huiyilu [The memoirs of Wellington Koo] (Beijing: Zhonghua shuju, 1987), vol. 5, 208. On the basis of this source, Deng Ye suggests that Chen Bulei himself was the author of *China's Destiny*, but without any explicit claim by Chen himself, there is no reason to doubt the sources cited here that identify Tao Xisheng as the author. Deng Ye, "Jiang Jieshi guanyu 'Zhongguo zhi mingyun' de mingti yu Guo Gong de liangge kouhao" [Chiang Kai-shek's selection of the topic for *China's Destiny* and the slogans of the Nationalist and Communist Parties], *Lishi yanjiu*, no. 4 (2008): 88–90.

[9] Shen Ning, *Yige jiazu jiyizhong de zhengyao mingliu* [One family's memory of famous politicians and celebrities] (Beijing: Zhongguo qingnian chubanshe, 2008), 131.

[10] Li Yang, "Tao Xisheng," 45.

[11] Shen Ning, *Yige jiazu jiyizhong*, 131.

[12] Qin Xiaoyi, *Zongtong Jiang gong dashi*, 248 (December 24, 1942). For further references on Chiang's personal involvement with the composition of *China's Destiny*, see Guoshiguan, ed., *Jiang Zhongzheng zongtong dang'an shilüe gaoben* [The Chiang Kai-shek collections: The chronological events] (Taibei: Guoshiguan, 2011), vol. 52, 148, 203, 211, 223, 229–30, 325, 357. He continued to work on revising the text after its publication. See, for example, Guoshiguan, *Jiang Zhongzheng zongtong*, vol. 53, 460–61; vol. 54, 112, 116; Qin Xiaoyi, *Zongtong Jiang gong dashi*, 409.

[13] Deng Ye, "Jiang Jieshi," 88–90; Qin Xiaoyi, ed., *Zhonghua Minguo zhongyao shiliao*

ist Party as the bearers of the great traditions of the Chinese nation and the vanguard that promised to return China to its rightful status as a rich and powerful world leader. This was in contrast to the Communists, who had abandoned China's great traditions in favor of their neo-imperialist or warlord politics. (These charges stemmed from the Communists' foreign ideology and their demands for political and military autonomy under the Second United Front.)

By the end of December 1942, Tao had distributed two hundred copies of a full draft to party officials for comment and assumed responsibility for compiling their responses. Along with a number of positive comments and suggestions that Chiang willingly incorporated, he rejected four opinions. These opinions are significant because they anticipated the critiques that others would levy against the book. Chiang's responses demonstrate his own myopia. First, some comments suggested that the book not dwell so much on the ills of imperialism, which would likely offend China's new allies, Britain and the United States. Since the abrogation of the unequal treaties provided both the historical context and narrative fulcrum of *China's Destiny*, Chiang dismissed this suggestion. Second, some criticized Chiang's indication that the war would be over within two years, but Chiang replied that this was based on the objective conditions of the war and ought to motivate and encourage the people. (*China's Destiny* had hardly anything to say about how the war would be won.) Third, there was a proposal to change the title of the book from *China's Destiny* (*Zhongguo zhi mingyun*) to *China's Future* (*Zhongguo zhi qiantu*) or something different altogether. Chiang reasserted the appropriateness of this title, as it was inspired by a quote from Sun Yat-sen ("China's destiny will be decided by its citizens") and accurately reflected the theme of the book. Fourth, some argued that Chiang, as head of state, ought to strive to transcend party politics, instead of trumpeting the special role played by the Nationalist Party in China's destiny. (This suggestion was echoed by one of Chiang's

---

chubian—duiRi kangzhan shiqi: Zhonggong huodong zhenxiang [Important historical documents of the Republic of China—Anti-Japanese war period: The true facts of the Communist Party's activities] (Taipei: Zhongguo Guomindang zhongyang weiyuanhui dangshi weiyuanhui, 1985), vol. 5, 136–42 (October 13, 1942).

foreign advisors, Reverend Frank Price.)[14] Chiang replied that without the Guomindang there would be no revolution, reaffirming the book's message that the Guomindang was the indispensable actor in China's modern history.[15]

Chiang's responses to these initial criticisms reflected his motive for writing *China's Destiny* in the first place. *China's Future* was an inadequate title because this book had to be about the past as much as the future. The past was so important because it provided the pedagogical impetus for the playing out of China's national essence on the blank slate of its future after the end of the unequal treaties.[16] The present avatar of this timeless national essence was the Nationalist Party; to suggest otherwise would be to contradict not only political exigency but also Chiang's fundamental belief in the Chinese nation.

China's Destiny was released to the public on March 10, 1943, two months after the signing of the new treaties. Regardless of its merits, it was guaranteed a wide audience. Chiang made the book required reading for political and military officials and for middle school, high school, and college students alike.[17] Its remarkably low price, given the shortage of high-quality paper, made it affordable for the public. (This fueled speculation that the book's printing was subsidized by the government.)[18] The day after *China's Destiny* was released, *China Central Daily News (Zhongyang ribao)* ran an editorial exhorting readers to read this book as soon as pos-

---

[14] Li Yang, "Tao Xisheng," 46.

[15] Tao Xisheng, *Chaoliu yu diandi*, 204–5.

[16] See Prasenjit Duara, *Rescuing History from the Nation: Questioning Narratives of Modern China* (Chicago: University of Chicago Press, 1995), 17–50; Homi Bhabha, "DissemiNation: Time, Narrative, and the Margins of the Modern Nation," in *Nation and Narration*, ed. Homi Bhabha (New York: Routledge, 1990), 298–99.

[17] Chongqing peidushi shuxi bianweihui [Committee on the History of Chongqing as Temporary Capital], *Guomin zhengfu Chongqing peidushi* [The history of Chongqing as the temporary capital of the Nationalist government] (Chongqing: Xinan shifan daxue chubanshe, 1993), 443–44; Zhang Zhihong, "Disanci fangong moca shijian yanjiuzhong de liangge yiwen" [Two doubts from researching the third anti-Communist campaign], *Langfang shifan xueyuan xuebao* 21, no. 3 (September 2005): 76.

[18] Tao denied these rumors, but at a price of five yuan, *China's Destiny* was sold at half the price of other government-printed books, and it was longer and printed on the best paper available. Tao Xisheng, *Chaoliu yu diandi*, 210; Shen Ning, *Yige jiazu jiyizhong*, 132.

sible; the editorial's author explained that he had read the whole thing in only half a day.[19] Two days later, the newspaper reported that a second printing was already underway because demand was outstripping supply.[20]

Besides additional printings and new editions,[21] Wang Chonghui was entrusted with overseeing the book's translation into English. However, apprehension among Chiang's advisers, including Wang, about how foreigners would react to the book led Chiang to table this plan. Neither Chiang nor his advisers were enthusiastic about issuing an edition specially edited for foreign audiences.[22] Madame Chiang (Song Meiling) may well have been decisive in persuading Chiang not to pursue a foreign translation. She had been touring the United States while the book was being written and revised, but on her return she told Owen Lattimore that she had advised against circulating *China's Destiny* in the United States.[23] American readers would, no doubt, have been shocked by the contradictions between the Generalissimo's antiforeign rhetoric and the pro-American, prodemocratic platitudes that had filled Madame Chiang's speeches during her U.S. tour. No full foreign translation appeared until 1947, when both the authorized translation by Wang Chonghui and an unauthorized translation edited by the left-wing editor Philip Jaffe were released within days of each other.[24]

---

[19] "Du *Zhongguo zhi mingyun*" [Reading *China's Destiny*, or Read *China's Destiny!*], *Zhongyang ribao*, Chongqing, March 11, 1943, 2.

[20] "*Zhongguo zhi mingyun* chuban gongbuyingqiu, zaiban yi zai yinzhi" [The supply of the first printing of *China's Destiny* unable to meet demand, additional printing already underway], *Zhongyang Ribao*, Chongqing, March 13, 1943, 2.

[21] Contrary to expectations, these new editions did not significantly alter the content or organization of the book. See "Report by Maj. V.F. Meisling, Enclosing a Digest by John S. Service of Chiang Kai-shek's Book *China's Destiny*, March 25, 1944," in Committee on the Judiciary, U.S. Senate, *The Amerasia Papers: A Clue to the Catastrophe of China*, ed. Anthony Kubeck (Washington, DC: Government Printing Office, 1970), vol. 1, 409–15.

[22] Tao Xisheng, *Chaoliu yu diandi*, 204; Gu Weijun, *Gu Weijun huiyilu*, 207–8.

[23] Owen Lattimore, *China Memoirs: Chiang Kai-shek and the War against Japan* (Tokyo: Tokyo University Press, 1990), 186.

[24] See the *New York Times* for coverage of these publications: "Books—Authors," September 10, 1946, 5; "Books and Authors," January 14, 1947, 23; "Books—Authors," January 17, 1947, 21; "People Who Read and Write," January 19, 1947, BR 8; Orville Prescott, "Books of the Times," January 28, 1947, 21; "2 Chiang Volumes Stir Controversy," January 28, 21." John King Fairbank capped this coverage with a scathing review of the book. See "Introducing a Skeleton from the Kuomintang Closet," February 9, 1947, BR 3.

The Guomindang's tight censorship of the press (including foreign correspondents in Chongqing) and the decision to delay a translation of *China's Destiny* succeeded in preventing a hostile response from appearing publicly in newspapers in China and, for the most part, abroad.[25] Although they could not publicly criticize it, Chinese intellectuals vented their frustrations behind closed doors.[26] (The reasons for and content of these criticisms are explored below.)

The Communists published the most public and best-known critique of *China's Destiny*. The book's anti-Communist bent would lead the Chinese Communist Party (CCP) to later term it "ideological preparation" for the "third anti-Communist upsurge" of the summer of 1943.[27] *China's Destiny* identified Communism as one of many foreign ideologies (including liberalism) that had infiltrated China since the onset of its century of humiliation.[28] Chiang also ignored Sun Yat-sen's alliance with the CCP in the first United Front of 1924–1927 and blamed the 1927 purge on the Communists and Wang Jingwei.[29] Paying lip service to the United Front, Chiang avoided mentioning the Communists by name but unmistakably criticized them as "warlords in disguise" and "new-style feudalists" who controlled their own armies and territories.[30]

---

[25] On censorship, see Lee-hsia Hsu Ting, *Government Control of the Press in Modern China: 1900–1949* (Cambridge, MA: East Asian Research Center, 1974), 126–47. Foreign news agencies were only allowed to print English quotes from a summary of *China's Destiny* provided by the Chinese Bureau of Information. Unauthorized English excerpts were published by the *West China Missionary News*, however, and Edgar Snow quoted these excerpts in his critical review of *China's Destiny* in his 1944 book *People on Our Side*. See "China's Destiny," *West China Missionary News* 45, nos. 1–4 (1943): 2–3, 36–52; Edgar Snow, *People on Our Side* (New York: Random House, 1944), 280–82. On the response of the foreign diplomatic corps, see Liu Xiaoyuan, "Reshaping China: American Strategic Thinking and China's Ethnic Frontiers During World War II," in *Negotiating China's Destiny in World War II*, 161–64.

[26] John King Fairbank, *Chinabound: A Fifty-Year Memoir* (New York: Harper and Row, 1982), 252.

[27] These scholars included Li Xin, Chen Tiejian, and Huang Lingjun. See Zhang Zhihong, "Disanci fangong moca shijian," 75.

[28] Jiang Zhongzheng, *Zhongguo zhi mingyun* [China's destiny] (Chongqing: Zhengzhong shuju, 1943), 72.

[29] Ibid., 86–88.

[30] Ibid., 198–99. Chiang was quite pleased with himself for adding these phrases to the text. Qin Xiaoyi, *Jiang gong dashi*, 268 (January 25, 1943). After the dissolution of the Comintern, he determined to be even more explicit in the revised edition. Gong'anbu

By the end of April, Mao had already instructed Chen Boda to write a response.[31] Chen recounted, "As Chairman Mao was talking with several of us cultural workers, he said, 'Look, Chiang Kai-shek has given you a topic [to write about].' From this I understood that Chairman Mao's intention was for us to write a critical essay."[32] Chen's rise to prominence as an intellectual and writer can be attributed to one degree or another to his authorship of this essay and his other contributions to the Rectification Campaign. Mao himself not only reviewed Chen's essay but also added a paragraph at the beginning specifically noting Chiang's use of Tao Xisheng, a known collaborator, as a ghostwriter.[33]

The CCP only published Chen's essay several months later, after the dissolution of the Comintern in May and a planned Nationalist invasion of Yan'an precipitated a political crisis and a new round in the propaganda war between the two parties. Following Guomindang calls to dissolve the CCP, Mao criticized the reactionary fascism of the Guomindang at a June 16 Politburo meeting and said that since the publication of *China's Destiny* it had become highly improbable that relations between the Nationalists and Communists would improve.[34] For his part, Chiang ordered General Hu Zongnan to initiate a plan to invade Yan'an by early July. After learning about these plans through a spy who had infiltrated General Hu's staff, the CCP reacted by adopting a policy of "using propaganda to deal with anti-Communist propaganda and using military force to deal with a military invasion" at a Politburo meeting on July 7. Liu Shaoqi went a step further at a Politburo meeting on July 13 (by which time Yan'an knew that the invasion had been called off), advocating a new, more aggressive direction for propaganda and arguing that the CCP should "sharply refute

---

dang'anguan, ed., *Zai Jiang Jieshi shenbian banian: Shicongshi gaoji muliao Tang Zong riji* [Eight years at Chiang Kai-shek's side: The diaries of a high-ranking war room advisor, Tang Zong] (Beijing: Qunzhong chubanshe, 1991), 359–60 (June 1, 1943).

[31] Pang Xianzhi, ed., *Mao Zedong nianpu: 1893–1949* [Chronological biography of Mao Zedong: 1893–1949] (Beijing: Zhongyang wenxian chubanshe, 2002), vol. 2, 434 (April 22, 1943).

[32] Chen Boda, *Chen Boda: Zuihou koushu huiyi* [Chen Boda: The final dictated memoirs], ed. Chen Xiaonong, rev. ed. (Hong Kong: Sun Global, 2005), 70.

[33] Li Yang and Fan Hong, *Chongshuo Tao Xisheng* [Revisiting Tao Xisheng] (Taibei: Xiuwei zixunkeji gufen youxian gongsi, 2008), 161.

[34] Pang Xianzhi, *Mao Zedong nianpu*, 446 (June 16, 1943).

Chiang's *China's Destiny*." The Politburo then commissioned Liu to hold a meeting with cadres to write this critique.[35] Criticism of *China's Destiny* was central to the anti-Nationalist rhetoric in Kang Sheng's speech "Rescuing Those Who Have Lost Their Footing" on July 15, which initiated the Rescue Campaign to root out and "save" supposed Guomindang agents in Yan'an (see chapter 6).[36]

Even after Chiang called off the planned attack on Yan'an, the CCP continued with a public propaganda campaign against the Nationalists, with criticism of *China's Destiny* playing a central role. Chen Boda's critique of *China's Destiny* was published in *Liberation Daily* on July 21 and was followed by essays written by other intellectuals such as Fan Wenlan and Ai Siqi. These essays attacked Chiang's fascistic political program, his ineffective and even traitorous military strategy, and his absurd views about the history and nature of the Chinese nation. Mao ordered Chen's essay to be published as a separate booklet and distributed in Nationalist-controlled areas. His critique was also translated into English and published abroad in early 1944, demonstrating the confidence the Communists had in the international appeal of their propaganda, unlike the Nationalists.

By August 1943, Chiang's plans to uproot the Communists through propaganda and political pressure had come to nothing. Nevertheless, Chiang continued to believe that by maintaining military pressure he could hasten the demise of the Communists, writing on August 25, "The mentality of the Communists is already splintering, and I believe that if my army adds a little bit of pressure or invades, then their internal military dissension will immediately come to the surface."[37] Chiang's impression

---

[35] Liu Chongwen and Chen Shaochou, eds., *Liu Shaoqi nianpu* [Chronological biography of Liu Shaoqi] (Beijing: Zhongyang wenxian chubanshe, 1996), vol. 1, 427 (July 7, 8, 13, 1943). My own interpretation is that the participants in this meeting read and perhaps revised the essay Chen had been ordered to write in April and that other writers, such as Ai Siqi and Fan Wenlan, were instructed on how to write their own essays.

[36] Kang Sheng, "Qiangjiu shizuzhe" [Rescuing those who have lost their footing], in *Zhonggong dangshi jiaoxue cankao ziliao* [Chinese Communist Party history educational material], ed. Zhongguo Renmin Jiefangjun Guofang daxue dangshi dangjianzhenggong jiaoyanshi [China's People's Liberation Army National Defense University Party History and Establishment Research and Education Section] (Beijing: Guofang daxue chubanshe, 1985), vol. 17, 380–84.

[37] Qin Xiaoyi, *Jiang gong dashi*, 361 (August 25, 1943).

was that the CCP had interpreted *China's Destiny's* call for a solution to China's political situation as a declaration of war. This suggested to him that the CCP did not believe that a purely political solution was possible and that military conflict was inevitable.[38]

Meanwhile, *China's Destiny* also caught the attention of the pro-Japanese press. Newspapers in occupied China began reporting on *China's Destiny* only after the summer crisis between the Guomindang and the CCP, and the nature of their commentary demonstrates that this was not a coincidence.[39] An essay titled "Chongqing's Destiny" played on the Guomindang-CCP tensions to contend that Chiang's best chance for political survival was to ally with Japan.[40] The most substantial of these critiques was published in early 1944 by Li Bo'ao, who argued that *China's Destiny* and Chiang's near invasion of Yan'an were evidence of the Generalissimo's preference for fighting the Communists and allying with the Japanese, in contradiction to his stated policies.[41] While the immediate goal of pro-Japanese authors was to bolster the position of the Nanjing government, to the extent that they echoed Communist critiques, they reinforced the imputation of pro-Japanese sympathies to Chiang.

Chiang could not have foreseen the contingencies leading up to the dissolution of the Comintern, the launching of the Rescue Campaign, and the CCP's well-prepared assault on *China's Destiny*. Nevertheless, his advisers had already noted the aspects of *China's Destiny* that would make it such a liability. Chiang certainly anticipated a critical reaction from the CCP (and even found this reaction useful for gauging its attitude),[42] but he was sincerely surprised by the harshness of the criticism that *China's Destiny* evoked from the Communists and foreigners. In spite of this crit-

---

[38] Ibid., 362–63.

[39] See "Zhongguo zhi mingyun jiyu xinsheng Yazhou" [China's destiny is tied up with newly born Asia], *Shi bao*, Beiping, August 14, 1943, 1.

[40] Yoshida Tōsuke, "Chongqing zhi mingyun" [Chongqing's destiny], *Shen bao*, Shanghai, November 24–26, 1943, 1.

[41] Li Bo'ao, "Jiang zhu *Zhongguo zhi mingyun* de pipan" [Criticism of Chiang's *China's Destiny*], *Zhengzhi yuekan* 7, no. 5 (1944): 2–27.

[42] Gao Sulan, ed., *Shilüe gaoben* 54, no. 387 (August 25, 1943).

icism, Chiang refused to yield any ground to his critics or make significant alterations to the revised edition of *China's Destiny*, believing instead that "the influence of this book on the country and the nation will only grow with time. Were a sage to rise again, he would surely agree with what I have said!"[43]

This final exclamation was a quote from Mencius and appears several times in the classic named after him. Although we cannot know what Chiang was thinking when he cited this phrase, it is easy to imagine him identifying with Mencius (whom he frequently quoted) in the following passage, which closes with the same exclamation:

> If the way of Yang and Mo does not subside and the way of Con-
> fucius does not shine forth, the people will be deceived by heresies
> and the path of morality will be blocked. When the path of moral-
> ity is blocked, then we show animals the way to devour men, and
> sooner or later it will come to men devouring men. Therefore, I am
> apprehensive. I wish to safeguard the way of the former sages
> against the onslaughts of Yang and Mo and to banish excessive
> views. Then there will be no way for advocates of heresies to arise.
> For what arises in the mind will interfere with policy, and what
> shows itself in policy will interfere with practice. Were a sage to
> rise again, he would surely agree with what I have said.[44]

Like Mencius, Chiang was concerned with rooting out heresies, establish-
ing the "path of morality," filling the mind with correct thoughts, and implementing proper policies. Although Chiang monitored the reactions of others to *China's Destiny*, these critiques never influenced the book as much as his own convictions. His self-identification as a hero in an age of turmoil was a source of great personal strength, but it also contributed to the debacle of *China's Destiny*, the text of and responses to which I now explore in more detail.

---

[43] Qin Xiaoyi, *Jiang gong dashi*, 409 (October 7, 1943).
[44] D.C. Lau, trans., *Mencius*, rev. ed. (New York: Penguin, 2003), 73.

DEFINING THE NATION

As discussed above, *China's Destiny* was about China's past as much as its future; this was true of criticisms of it as well. To understand these criticisms and why they mattered so much in wartime China, we first have to examine Chiang's own ideology of the Chinese nation (*Zhonghua minzu*) and how this ideology laid the basis for his political program for building China's future. In the first place, Chiang described the Chinese nation as a lineage race, related through descent from a single ancestor,[45] from which different "racial stocks" or clans (*zongzu*) had emerged. Through a centuries-long process of intermarriage and mutual assimilation, these clans had then grown (back) into a single nation. James Leibold refers to this model of the nation's racial unity (first introduced by Guomindang racial nationalists in the 1930s) as a "diamond-shaped paradigm."[46] Chiang's elaboration of this model involved a redefinition of the word *minzu* to mean the nation as a whole, rather than individual ethnicities.[47] In this way, *China's Destiny* seemed to repudiate Sun Yat-sen's early republican formulation of the relationship between the Han majority and the major ethnic minorities as "five nationalities, one country" (*wuzu yijia*).[48] Chiang's nationalist ideology incorporated China's ethnic minorities and their lands into the greater Chinese nation by historical necessity. This left no room for ethnic

---

[45] Chiang, somewhat surprisingly, did not put much emphasis on members of the Chinese nation having a single ancestor in the 1943 edition of *China's Destiny*. This was made much more explicit, however, in the 1944 revised edition and in supplementary texts. See Jiang Zhongzheng, *Zhongguo zhi mingyun*, 2; Chiang Kai-shek, *China's Destiny*, trans. Wang Chonghui (New York: Macmillan, 1947), 4.

[46] Leibold, *Reconfiguring Chinese Nationalism*, 143. One point of the diamond represented the presumed national ancestor, the widest point(s) the branching out into multiple *zongzu*, and then the last point the convergence of these *zongzu* into a single unified nation. Prasenjit Duara refers to this more generally as "discent," *Rescuing History*, 66.

[47] In Chinese, the word *minzu* could (and still can today) refer to either an ethnic nationality, such as the Mongol *minzu*, or the nation as a whole, that is, the Chinese *minzu*. I follow Mullaney in translating the word *minzu* as "nation" or "nationality/ethnicity," depending on the context and by whom it is being used. Mullaney, *Coming to Terms*, 16.

[48] For more on the *wuzu yijia* formulation, see Joseph Esherick, "How the Qing Became China," in *Empire to Nation: Historical Perspectives on the Making of the Modern World*, ed. Joseph Esherick, Hasan Kayali, and Eric Van Young (Lanham, MD: Rowman and Littlefield, 2006), 245–47.

self-determination and suggested that the alienation (or even autonomy) of any part of the Chinese nation would fundamentally undermine the integrity of the national body as a whole.[49]

Coupled with this unity through blood, Chiang argued that the Chinese nation was motivated by a common national spirit that consisted of China's inherent traditional (*guyou*) culture. Chiang argued that this moral essence was the spiritual force behind the development of the Chinese nation and imbued its history with a pacific tendency, which he contrasted to the imperialism of Western countries and Japan. The Confucian virtues of loyalty (*zhong*) and filial piety (*xiao*) represented the epitome of the Chinese nation's moral essence, and Chiang emphasized that the recovery of these values was absolutely essential to restore China to its past glory.[50] In a supplemental study guide, one author enumerated more than ten special qualities of the Chinese nation, including equal treatment of all ethnic groups (*pingdengxing*), capacity for conciliation (*tiaohexing*), conservatism (*baoshouxing*), resilience (*jianrenxing*), peacefulness (*hepingxing*), absorptivity (*xishouxing*), independence (*dulixing*), unity (*tongyixing*), and cohesiveness (*tuanjiexing*). On the basis of China's supposed racial and cultural unity, the author asserted that all of its "clans" were essentially identical except for geographic and religious differences. He described classifications like Han, Manchu, Mongolian, Tibetan, and Hui as more of a convention than a scientific taxonomy. Because of their fundamental similarities, he argued, once these clans came into greater contact with each other, which was especially possible with modern transportation, they would blend together naturally. The example par excellence was the recent (re) assimilation of the Manchus, who by now were "ninety-nine percent" assimilated.[51] Chiang summarized this view of China's ethnic diversity (or lack thereof) by proclaiming that "China's history of five thousand years is but a record of the common destiny shared by the different racial stocks of the Chinese nation."[52]

---

[49] Jiang Zhongzheng, *Zhongguo zhi mingyun*, 5.

[50] Ibid., 7, 133.

[51] Yu Jianhua, *Zhonghua minzushi* [China's national history] (Nanping: Guomin chubanshe, 1944), 9–10, 8–22.

[52] Jiang Zhongzheng, *Zhongguo zhi mingyun*, 8.

The Communist Critique

Like *China's Destiny* itself, Chen Boda's critique focused heavily on the seemingly abstract topic of how to define the Chinese nation. He began his essay by criticizing Chiang's narrative of the origins and development of the Chinese nation. Objecting to Chiang's assertion that China consisted of a single *minzu* (composed of multiple *zongzu*), Chen appealed to the authority of Sun Yat-sen, who had embraced the idea of China as a multi-*minzu* nation-state. He proceeded to argue that it was absurd to think that different nationalities could be combined through the intermarriage of a few elite families. If this were the case, then wouldn't China already have become a *zongzu* of the Japanese *minzu* through the marriage of a few Chinese men to Japanese women? Moreover, Chen argued, if all ethnicities were members of a single *minzu*, then invasions and uprisings like the Taiping Rebellion and the 1911 Revolution were not wars for national liberation but actually civil wars, as both sides (Han and Manchu) were, according to Chiang, both inherently members of the same Chinese nation. In Chen's view, if Chiang's idea of the Chinese *minzu* held, "then the totality of Chinese history must be repudiated."[53]

Chen went on to critique Chiang's description of the moral and cultural qualities that supposedly facilitated the amalgamation of the various *zongzu* into a cohesive national body. Chen argued that the Confucian values heralded by Chiang were merely "magic spells" used by the elite to control the masses, often in collaboration with invaders. It was the masses, according to Chen, who persevered in true nationalistic fervor while the elite pursued their own interests. Chen pointed out that the Japanese invaders were employing the same Confucian values trumpeted by Chiang to pacify areas under their control.

While invoking the Marxist theory of class struggle, Chen was by no means abandoning belief in the objective existence of the Chinese nation. His basis for this belief, though, was the orthodox Stalinist definition of nationality, whereby material conditions that could be scientifically stud-

---

[53] Chen Boda, "Ping *Zhongguo zhi mingyun*" [Criticizing *China's Destiny*], *Jiefang ribao*, Yan'an, July 21, 1943, 1.

ied—language, geography, economic life, and cultural psychology—gave rise to different nationalities. The occasional blending of nationalities, Chen said, was based on specific historical conditions (not a general historical pattern), and conflict between nationalities was not an unavoidable feature of human history. Chen contrasted this scientific theory of national difference to the idealist ethnonationalism propagated by Chiang, which was precisely the tool used by fascists to justify their invasions of other countries and which would ultimately lead to the downfall of those who espoused it.[54]

Chen sought to replace this ethno-nationalism with a class-based national consciousness located in the masses (*minzhong*), without whom, he claimed, "there is no Chinese nation."[55] As the CCP had done since its early years, Chen associated class struggle with defending national interests. Whereas *China's Destiny* was dedicated to Zeng Guofan[56]—a traitorous Han elite who supported China's foreign oppressors, the Manchus— Chen (like Sun Yat-sen and most left-wing intellectuals) claimed the Taiping as both class and national heroes. Chiang's failure to heed the needs of the masses and to grant them political representation thus constituted an affront to the Chinese nation itself.[57] Liberating China from imperialism, recognized by both Chiang and Mao Zedong in *On New Democracy*[58] as essential to China's national development, necessitated the democratic reforms decried by *China's Destiny*. Given this view of the Chinese nation, it was impossible to dismiss Chiang's views on how to govern China as merely political errors; rather, Chiang's political program threatened to undermine the Chinese nation just as much as the Japanese invasion did.

---

[54] Ibid. Also see Fan Wenlan, "Chi suowei Zhongguo wenhua de tongyixing" [Refuting the so-called unity of Chinese culture], *Jiefang ribao*, Yan'an, July 10, 1943, 4.

[55] Chen Boda, "Ping *Zhongguo zhi mingyun*," 2. Of course, the masses invoked by the CCP were and continue to be predominantly Han masses. Self-determination for ethnic minorities thus became just as problematic under the CCP as it was for the Nationalists.

[56] June Grasso, Jay Corrin, and Michael Kort, *Modernization and Revolution in China* (Armonk, NY: M.E. Sharpe, 1991), 103.

[57] Chen Boda, "Ping *Zhongguo zhi mingyun*," 2–3.

[58] Chen stated that since the Communists had yet to answer Guomindang attacks on Mao's *On New Democracy*, published in 1940, his essay would serve as a rejoinder to those criticisms.

The View from Nanjing

The Nanjing government's response to Chiang's positions on the nature of the Chinese nation indicated that Chen had a point in comparing the ethno-nationalism of Chiang and the Japanese. If anything, Chiang's positions were more extreme than those of the Japanese. Furthermore, Li Bo'ao's attempt from occupied Nanjing to open a dialogue with Chiang in his essay on *China's Destiny* was damaging to Chiang's credibility in itself.

Li, who quoted extensively from both Chiang's book and Chen Boda's essay, summarized Chiang's view of the Chinese nation in three main points: (1) that the Chinese nation was completely formed by the Qin and Han dynasties; (2) that China's territory constituted a natural and inviolable geographic unit; and (3) that all of China's *zongzu* were united by a single moral spirit. Ironically, Li agreed with Chen in his criticism of the first two points, saying that Chiang's view that China's borders were a historical birthright did not correspond to reality and appeared to be influenced by the expansionist national visions of Mussolini and Hitler. Like Chen, Li rejected Chiang's theory of *minzu*. Unlike Chen, though, Li accepted the existence of natural cultural and genetic affinities among different nationalities. These pan-Asian affinities were the ideological basis for Japan's East Asia Co-prosperity Sphere.[59] Li's essay reflected the official Japanese position that China ought to be a monoethnic (Han) nation but also a member of an East Asian community of nations, with whom China shared a common bloodline and culture. This theory undergirded Japan's policy of creating monoethnic puppet states, such as Manchukuo, and encouraging ethnic minorities to agitate for national independence while simultaneously absorbing them into Japan's cultural and political sphere.[60]

Li agreed wholeheartedly, though, with *China's Destiny*'s emphasis on China's inherent moral spirit (*guyou dexing*), contending that this was the most correct thing Chiang had said about China's premodern history. Li's rebuttal of the Communists' criticisms of this part of the book only bol-

---

[59] Li Bo'ao, "Jiang zhu *Zhongguo zhi mingyun* de pipan," 4–5.

[60] See Kevin Doak, "The Concept of Ethnic Nationality and Its Role in Pan-Asianism in Imperial Japan," in *Pan-Asianism in Modern Japanese History: Colonialism, Regionalism, and Borders*, ed. Sven Saaler and J. Victor Koschmann (New York: Routledge, 2007), 168–82.

stered the CCP's assertion that in this respect the ideologies of Chiang and the Japanese invaders were not so different. The one deficiency Li saw in this aspect of Chiang's thought was that China's moral system had not developed in a vacuum but had influenced and been influenced by a broader East Asian culture. The nations who shared this culture all possessed the ability both to maintain their moral qualities and to draw on Western science in order to defeat Western utilitarianism (*gongli zhuyi*). Japan was showing the way to do this in its current struggle against Anglo-American and Soviet imperialism.[61]

China's Destiny, of course, expressed Chiang's disdain for foreign imperialism, blaming the unequal treaties for the deterioration of morality in China, especially under the influence of liberalism and Communism (i.e., Anglo-American and Soviet ideological imperialism). "On this point," Li said, "Chiang's opinion is completely without mistake." While praising Chiang's candor given his current dependence on the very nations he was criticizing, Li suggested that Chiang would be better off siding with Japan, itself a victim of Western imperialism.[62] On one hand, this argument was obviously a propaganda ploy, but it was also profoundly logical, at least on the basis of what Chiang had written in *China's Destiny* and the criticisms the Communists were leveling against him.

The Response of Intellectuals

As suggested above, the response of intellectuals is essential for understanding the history of *China's Destiny* because Western-educated technocrats played an important role in Chiang's administration, and they were a group that Chiang needed to accomplish economic modernization. Unlike the Communists, Chiang could have avoided alienating them. Given the ongoing war and China's newfound equality with its allies, 1943 could have been a grand occasion to rouse the May Fourth spirit of nationalism and reform, which were, after all, the two central concepts of *China's Destiny*. But Chiang failed or chose not to do this. Instead, by dwelling on a

---

[61] Li Bo'ao, "Jiang zhu *Zhongguo zhi mingyun* de pipan," 5.
[62] Ibid., 18.

particular conception of what the Chinese nation was and promulgating a
politically narrow vision of China's future, he alienated many of China's
best and brightest.

The alienation of intellectuals began with Chiang's insistence that
the Chinese nation was transhistorically coherent in terms of ethnicity
and culture. On ethnic issues, *China's Destiny*'s stringent denial of self-
determination for minority peoples actually belied flexible Nationalist
policies on the ground.[63] Politically, then, the book's extended pseudo-
history was of only dubious necessity, especially when it was bound to
touch the raw nerves of scholars who disagreed, such as the well-known
historian Gu Jiegang and the ethnologist Wu Wenzao.[64]

Even more problematic for intellectuals was Chiang's culturalist definition of the Chinese nation. This emphasis on traditional Chinese virtues
entailed a rejection of both Communism and liberalism, whose increasing
popularity since the May Fourth Movement he regarded as an unsavory
by-product of imperialism. Chiang repeatedly criticized Chinese scholars
who had blindly followed these foreign ideologies, selling out their national heritage in the process. Wen Yiduo, then a professor at National
Southwestern Associated University (Xinan Lianda) wrote later, "The
publication of *China's Destiny* was an important point for me personally. I
was simply frightened by the 'Boxer spirit' contained in it. Had our wise
leader always thought like this? The May Fourth Movement had had a
deep impact on me, and *China's Destiny* was a public declaration of war
against the May Fourth Movement. No matter what, there was no way I
could accept this."[65] Rather than uniting the populace under a large ban-

    [63] Lin Hsiao-ting, *Tibet and Nationalist China's Frontiers*, 140–41, 155–56; Liu Xiao-
yuan, *Frontier Passages*, 123–24; Leibold, *Reconfiguring Chinese Nationalism*, 143–44; Mullaney, *Coming to Terms*, 27–29.
    [64] Leibold, *Reconfiguring Chinese Nationalism*, 138–41, 144; Mullaney, *Coming to Terms*,
56–57, 73–80; Wang Jianmin, *Zhongguo minzuxue shi* [The history of ethnology in China]
(Kunming: Yunnan jiaoyu chubanshe, 1997), vol. 1, 226. However, the book did avoid some
of the more extreme aspects of racial nationalism, like eugenics. See Frank Dikkoter, *The
Discourse of Race in Modern China* (London: Hurst, 1992), 184–85.
    [65] Wen Yiduo, "Banian de huiyi yu ganxiang" [Reflections and feelings on eight years],
in *Wen Yiduo nianpu changpian* [Draft chronicle of the life of Wen Yiduo], ed. Wen Liming,
Hou Jukun, and Wen Lidiao (Wuhan: Hubei renmin chubanshe, 1994), 662.

ner of nationalism, *China's Destiny* drew attention to the different brands of nationalism in play—"Boxer" nationalism or May Fourth nationalism. In place of the intellectual efflorescence of the May Fourth era, Chiang's brand of nationalism entailed submission to his authority and a rejection of foreign ideas, precisely the ideas embraced by China's allies. Intellectuals saw Chiang installing himself as a sage-ruler, hearkening back to the imperial era, when both political and ideological authority were consolidated in the person of the emperor.[66] Sun Yat-sen's son, Sun Ke (Sun Fo), described the ironic and unsettling ideology expressed in *China's Destiny*: "The book criticizes communism; communism is the state philosophy of our ally, Soviet Russia. It criticizes liberalism; liberalism is the state philosophy of our allies, the United States and Great Britain. The book does not criticize Nazism and Fascism; these are the state philosophies of our enemies, Germany, Japan and Italy."[67]

One did not have to belong to the CCP to appreciate Chen Boda's critique of *China's Destiny*'s definition of the Chinese nation. At least in rhetoric, the CCP upheld the May Fourth celebration of progressive thinking and openness to foreign (nonfascist) ideas. The accusation of Chen Boda and Li Bo'ao that Chiang's emphasis on traditional Confucian virtues was essentially identical to the thinking of the Japanese drew support from Chiang's choice of Tao Xisheng, a conservative intellectual and former collaborator, as his ghostwriter. Even the right-leaning intellectual Lei Haizong declared that *China's Destiny* was the worst of the Nationalist Party's many mistakes and that its errors were "so numerous that even American sinologists could spot them."[68] Some intellectuals were so aggravated that they simply refused to read *China's Destiny*.[69]

---

[66] Fairbank, *Chinabound*, 252; Atcheson (Chongqing) to the Secretary of State, May 31, 1943, in U.S. Department of State, *Foreign Relations of the United States, Diplomatic Papers: China, 1943* (Washington, DC: Government Printing Office, 1957), 246.

[67] Atcheson to the Secretary of State, May 31, 1943, in U.S. Department of State, *Foreign Relations of the United States*, 246.

[68] John Israel, *Lianda: A Chinese University in War and Revolution* (Stanford, CA: Stanford University Press, 1998), 148.

[69] Fairbank, *Chinabound*, 252; John S. Service, "Resentment of Censorship and Cultural Control by the Kuomintang," June 2, 1943, in *Lost Chance in China: The Wartime Despatches of John S. Service*, ed. Joseph W. Esherick (New York: Random House, 1974), 106.

IMAGINING THE NATION'S FUTURE

Intellectuals feared that *China's Destiny* represented a signal of intent to revive a form of despotism reflected in the book's political program. By constituting the nation (*minzu*) as the subject of China's history and the Nationalist Party as the only true representative of the nation in the present day, Chiang denied the political agency (in any robust sense) of any individual or group independent of the party. In contrast, the Communists' rhetoric in 1943 depicted the Communist Party as a willing, democratic partner with anyone who shared the interests of the nation, especially China's masses. Even the Nanjing government, which could more plausibly be accused of fascism through its association with Japan, criticized the undemocratic bent of *China's Destiny*.

In the fifth chapter of *China's Destiny*, Chiang laid out his plan for national reconstruction under the same five headings he had used to describe the effects of the unequal treaties: psychological, moral, social, political, and economic. Chiang prioritized psychological reform because he believed China's people needed to eliminate their dependence on foreign ideas while simultaneously cultivating their intrinsic spirit of wisdom (*zhi*), humaneness (*ren*), and courage (*yong*). This would promote greater creative energy and the pursuit of truth through science. Chiang viewed secondary school teachers as "anonymous heroes" who were responsible for instilling this revolutionary and patriotic psychology in students.[70]

Chiang clarified the importance of traditional Chinese culture and renewed his criticism of foreign ideals in his sections on moral and social renovation. He claimed that individuals should put the values of loyalty and filial piety into action by subordinating their own interests to those of the nation, something youths could do in practice by joining the military. He also explained that Chinese intellectuals obsessed with foreign ideas had ignored the traditional values that supported the longstanding hierarchical organization of Chinese society, and so these social structures (like the village and *baojia* system) had disintegrated. To strengthen the cohe-

---

[70] Jiang Zhongzheng, *Zhongguo zhi mingyun*, 130–32.

sion of Chinese society, Chiang encouraged people to engage in work at the local village level rather than remaining in the capital.[71]

Chiang's criticism of foreign ideologies reached a crescendo when he discussed China's political destiny. Chiang's idea of democracy and constitutionalism entailed not the guarantee of individual rights but the rational delineation of state power through a constitution (see chapter 7). Liberal individualism had no place in China. Later in the book, Chiang cited Sun Yat-sen's contention that China's problem under imperial rule was not that the people lacked freedom but that they enjoyed too much of it, which necessitated a revolution to transform China from a "sheet of loose sand" into a strong nation capable of its own defense.[72] *China's Destiny* made it clear that Chiang believed that this process of political coalescence was not yet complete and that the need for national strengthening far outweighed the demands of individual freedom.

Chiang placed special emphasis on economic development, arguing that it was central to the principle of the people's livelihood. However, other than very specific and wildly ambitious ten-year goals for industrial and raw material production and numbers of trained workers, his economic plan provided few details about how this would be achieved. His main point of encouragement was that a correct and unified national spirit, which would ostensibly be achieved through his first four points of national reconstruction, would enable China to overcome seemingly insurmountable obstacles and achieve these unrealistic goals. He had little to say about more immediate problems like rampant inflation and corruption.

Chiang's silence about the practical steps necessary to build China into a strong and independent nation betrayed his attitude toward the agency of the common people. Constantly reiterating Sun Yat-sen's motto, "To know is difficult, to act is easy" (*zhi nan xing yi*), *China's Destiny* demanded sincere (*cheng*) loyalty to the direction of the Nationalist Party. (Sincere loyalty to those who knew best would make action easy.) Chiang argued in the seventh chapter that the party and its youth corps were de-

---

[71] Ibid., 133–37.
[72] Ibid., 137–39, 181–83.

cisive in the struggle to realize the destiny of the Chinese nation. According to him, every youth and adult had the right and responsibility to join the youth corps and the party, respectively.[73] This culminated in the slogan, "Without the Nationalist Party there would be no China" (*Meiyou Zhongguo Guomindang ... meiyoule Zhongguo*).[74]

Communist Democracy

In reality, the CCP was just as capable of demanding absolute loyalty from its followers and would soon claim that "without the Communist Party there would be no [new] China."[75] But the CCP did not make bold requirements to join their party part of their public propaganda. Instead, the CCP employed rhetoric that appealed to those who were unwilling to sincerely subordinate themselves to Nationalist Party dictatorship and who were more aware of the ideological repression they suffered at the hands of the Nationalists than of what they might have endured had they fled to Yan'an.

In this sense, the CCP enjoyed a peculiar advantage in responding to Chiang's plan for national reconstruction by virtue of not being a national government itself. Instead of laying out a centrally administered plan for the entire nation, the main thrust of the CCP's critique of Chiang's political stance in *China's Destiny* was to argue that it deserved to participate in planning the future, especially since it represented the needs of the vast majority of the "people" (workers, peasants, the petit bourgeoisie, and revolutionary intellectuals). The CCP also put a democratic mask on its political system by mandating that other political parties be given a representative stake in the border region government.

Chen Boda refuted Chiang's argument that achieving China's destiny required loyalty to a single party by claiming that the vision shared by Sun

[73] Ibid., 189.

[74] Ibid., 195.

[75] This now-famous slogan was only later altered to say, "Without the Chinese Communist Party, there would be no *new* China," out of a concern for the same sort of historical anachronism of which the CCP accused Chiang.

Yat-sen and the CCP necessitated the end of absolutism in China, not the dictatorship of a single party. Chen specifically condemned the oppression of youth by the Guomindang's secret service.[76] For Chen's readers who were unfamiliar with the CCP's rounding up of young students suspected of being spies in the border regions, the contrast between the two parties was clear (see chapter 7).

The Communists also criticized Chiang's claim to privileged knowledge about China's destiny and how to realize it. The CCP claimed to found their theory and practice of democracy on a "scientific" knowledge of the true material conditions of the lives of the masses. Chiang's slogan "To know is difficult, to act is easy" was idealist and unscientific, they argued. Ai Siqi, another Communist intellectual, argued that Chiang's philosophy of "without sincerity there is nothing material" (*bucheng wuwu*) was fundamentally backward and that sincere ideology had to be founded on the basis of a clear understanding of material conditions (*wuwu bucheng*).[77] Ai argued that Chiang's fallacious idealism was evident in how he ordered his five-point plan for national reconstruction. In Ai's view, the primary obstacles facing the Chinese nation were not the psychology and morality of the average person but the corruption of the small class of officials and magnates who had broken the economic and political system. Chiang's conceptual bifurcation of knowing (*zhi*) and acting (*xing*) implied that people should blindly follow the orders of their superiors; Ai argued that this made a scientific examination of past revolutionary mistakes impossible.[78] The Communists countered this philosophical separation of knowing and acting with an emphasis on combining knowledge and action (*zhixing heyi*). (This philosophy was also promoted by the Ming dynasty scholar Wang Yangming and was explicitly repudiated by Chiang in *China's Destiny*.)[79]

A little over a month after Chen Boda's critique of *China's Destiny* was

---

[76] Chen Boda, "Ping *Zhongguo zhi mingyun*," 4.

[77] Ai Siqi, "*Zhongguo zhi mingyun*—Jiduan weixinlun yumin zhexue" [*China's Destiny*: Extreme idealism and deluding philosophy], *Jiefang ribao*, Yan'an, August 11, 1943, 2.

[78] Ibid., 4.

[79] Jiang Zhongzheng, *Zhongguo zhi mingyun*, 162.

first published, *Liberation Daily* printed a front-page article that turned Chiang's statement about the indispensability of the Nationalist Party to the Chinese nation and revolution on its head: "Without the Communist Party There Would Be No China" (*Meiyou Gongchandang, jiu meiyou Zhongguo*).[80] Unlike Chiang, the Communists justified their new slogan by reference to their contributions to the current fight against Japan and their struggle on behalf of the Chinese people. While wording their slogan similarly, the CCP, in sharp contrast to Chiang, claimed to be indispensable on the basis of its service to the nation in the war against Japan and left the door open for individuals and other groups to cooperate with it as equal partners.

While justifying its own value to the nation, the CCP launched a series of attacks accusing Chiang of being fascistic and even in league with the Axis powers. In response to Chiang's assertion that until the CCP gave up its territorial and military independence there could be no "leniency," Chen Boda asked who had ever benefited from the Guomindang's so-called leniency: was it anyone except bad gentry, corrupt officials, counterrevolutionaries, and traitors who had defected to the Japanese, such as Tao Xisheng? Even those without direct ties to the Communist Party were unable to enjoy basic freedoms under Chiang's dictatorship.[81] In the weeks that followed the publication of Chen's article, CCP propaganda increasingly cast Chiang as in league with the fascist Axis powers, especially associating him with Mussolini, who had just been toppled in Italy. *China's Destiny* appeared in political cartoons as the textbook of Chiang's dictatorial aspirations and fascist utopian vision. One such cartoon depicted a man in disguise (a moustache indicated the figure could be Tojo, Hitler, or Chiang) standing next to a chest labeled "China's Destiny," which contained a diorama of a prosperous future. A swastika emblazoned on the side of the box betrayed the fascist reality behind this utopian vision of China's future (Figure 6.1).[82]

---

[80] "Meiyou Gongchandang, jiu meiyou Zhongguo" [Without the Communist Party there would be no China], *Jiefang ribao*, Yan'an, August 25, 1943, 1.

[81] Chen Boda, "Ping *Zhongguo zhi mingyun*," 4.

[82] *Jiefang Ribao*, Yan'an, August 21, 1943, 4.

Figure 6.1: Disguised fascist sells seemingly prosperous future labeled "China's Destiny."

Nanjing's Critique of Fascism

Writers who critiqued *China's Destiny* from Japanese-occupied China had less to say than the Communists about Chiang's plans for national reconstruction, but they did echo the Communists' critiques in striking ways. Li Bo'ao seemed to agree wholeheartedly with Chiang about the need for reforming China's morality, psychology, and social and academic environment. Li and another author also generally agreed with Chiang's economic plan.[83] The problem, of course, was how Chiang advocated carrying out this plan, especially his political aims and alliances. Hu Lancheng (the former director of propaganda for the Nanjing government and the first husband of Zhang Ailing) referred to the economics of *China's Destiny* as "empty talk" since Chiang had no answer for how to resist the pressures of the international capitalist system and to free China from reliance on foreign capital.[84] This criticism complemented Li Bo'ao's argument that by allying with the British and Americans instead of the Japanese, Chiang was confusing friends and enemies.[85]

The other major problem with Chiang's plan for reconstruction, from Li and Hu's perspective, was his political intentions. Li Bo'ao concurred with Chiang on the importance of the rule of law and his account of how feudalists and warlords (and Communists) had undermined it, but he wondered if Chiang really intended to follow the law himself or if he merely meant to use it as a mechanism to secure his own power.[86] Hu Lancheng argued that the entire purpose of *China's Destiny* was to solidify Chiang's authority and that his proposed postwar political reforms had little vitality, comparing them to the constitutional reforms undertaken near the end of the Qing dynasty.[87] The message was essentially the same as the Communists': Chiang was a despotic leader near the end of

---

[83] Li Bo'ao, "Jiang zhu *Zhongguo zhi mingyun* de pipan," 22; Zhou Yuying, "Zhongguo zhi mingyun yu dongya zhi mingyun" [China's destiny and East Asia's destiny], *Taipingyang zhoubao*, no. 91 (1943): 20–30.

[84] Hu Lancheng, "*Zhongguo zhi mingyun* de pipan" [Criticism of *China's Destiny*], *Xin Dongfang zazhi* 9, no. 2 (1944): 7.

[85] Li Bo'ao, "Jiang zhu *Zhongguo zhi mingyun* de pipan," 9.

[86] Ibid., 24.

[87] Hu Lancheng, "*Zhongguo zhi mingyun* de pipan," 7.

his rope whose democratic rhetoric was empty at best and duplicitous at worst.

Some readers may have quickly dismissed Li Bo'ao and Hu Lancheng's political critiques of *China's Destiny* as a case of the pot calling the kettle black, but the consonance of the CCP and the Nanjing regime's political critiques of *China's Destiny* suggests the possibility of a compound effect of Communist and Nanjing anti-Nationalist propaganda. Even readers who were suspicious of both the Communists and the Wang Jingwei regime in Nanjing would have been struck by their agreement that Chiang's democratic intentions were suspect. Moreover, both the Communists and the Nanjing government emphasized that Chiang was not really interested in fighting the Japanese. For example, a cartoon in *Liberation Daily* commemorated the anniversary of the Mukden Incident (September 18, 1931) by depicting Chiang and the Japanese as covillains: while the Japanese made off with the four northeastern provinces, Chiang maintained his policy of pacifying internal politics (dealing with the Communists) before resisting the Japanese, stabbing the great figure of the Chinese people in the leg and holding it back from fighting the Japanese (Figure 6.2).[88] Li Bo'ao said essentially the same thing, arguing that Chiang had always been more concerned with fighting the Communists and had only feigned resisting the Japanese after the Xi'an Incident in 1936 while using the War of Resistance as a slogan to boost his political credibility.[89]

Discouraged Dissent

Students and intellectuals echoed these critiques of Chiang's reactionary authoritarianism and false patriotism. In 1944 a student from Fudan University delivered to the U.S. embassy in Chongqing a letter addressed to Vice President Henry Wallace. Among other things, the letter stated:

> In addition to political and military affairs, culture and education also show the effects of the reactionary administration, and the

---

[88] "*Jiuyiba* shibian de zhenxiang" [The truth of the Mukden Incident], *Jiefang ribao*, Yan'an, September 25, 1943, 4.

[89] Li, "Jiang zhu *Zhongguo zhi mingyun* de pipan," 15–16.

Figure 6.2: Chiang holds the Chinese people back from defending against Japan.

Kuomintang has issued orders to persecute, arrest, and kill all liberals and left-wing elements. The book *China's Destiny*, an evil book "full of lies and absurdities," is required reading for all university and high school students in the country. Chiang Kai-shek's Kuomintang Government and Wang Ching-wei's puppet government are essentially analogous, the only difference being that the former pretends to be patriotic while the latter has sold out openly to the enemy.

While the embassy noted a clear pro-Communist bias in the letter, it expressed the opinion that the number of Communist sympathizers in Chinese universities was quite small and that this letter was written "more in protest of the refusal of the Kuomintang to adopt democratic procedures than in support of the Chinese Communist Party."[90]

---

[90] Ambassador in China (Gauss) to Secretary of State, Chongqing, July 11, 1944, in U.S. Department of State, *Foreign Relations of the United States, Diplomatic Papers: Volume 6, 1944* (Washington, DC: Government Printing Office, 1967), 472–74.

Regardless of these students' political sympathies, it is evident that *China's Destiny* had failed to win them over to the Guomindang's cause and, in fact, had turned them even more against it. The students' concerns echoed those of intellectuals who saw Chiang as setting himself up as a sage as well as a ruler, monopolizing political and ideological authority. John King Fairbank (who worked for the U.S. Office of War Information at the time) observed,

> The professors here are discouraged, and foresee the growth of an unbreakable police control over all China, with liberal education extinguished and economic life regimented as well as thought. They see nothing to stop the process. I have argued in return that the regime lacks the personnel to do the job it wants to do, and hence will have to compromise with the people who seek the development of the country, rather than mere political control over it.[91]

Here again we see the effect of *China's Destiny* on intellectuals who, in the spirit of the May Fourth Movement, wanted so badly to contribute to China's destiny. Their only form of protest against what they saw as Nationalist authoritarianism was not to read this book, referred to by multiple sources as the bible of the Guomindang and by others as Chiang's own *Mein Kampf;* they were forced either to sit idly by while China's destiny played out under the control of the Guomindang or to defy limits on public discourse in order to expound their own version of China's destiny.

CONCLUSION

If reading *China's Destiny* was a turning point in the life of the intellectual Wen Yiduo, then it was a fateful one. From 1943 on, he increasingly participated in politics and became involved with the Democratic League over the course of 1944 and 1945. He "made speeches and published ar-

---

[91] Fairbank, *Chinabound*, 252.

ticles demanding that the Nationalist Government adopt 'democratic measures' and mobilize 'the masses of the people' to strengthen resistance to the Japanese."[92] When his colleague Li Gongpu was assassinated in July 1946, Wen gave a eulogy at his funeral in which he accused Guomindang agents of murdering Li, despite warnings that he might be next. The warning was warranted. On his way home from the funeral, Wen was assassinated. He was forty-six years old and left behind a wife and five children.

On April 23, 1945, a year before Wen Yiduo's murder, Mao Zedong claimed, "There are two versions of China's destiny: one has already been written by someone in a book; our congress is representing a different version of China's destiny, and we too will produce a book."[93] Mao's pronouncement reflected the ongoing ideological battle between the CCP and the Nationalists, including his personal rivalry with Chiang Kaishek,[94] but his insistence that there were precisely two versions of China's destiny—a right one and a wrong one—also foreshadowed the ideological repression that would continue to characterize CCP rule. To write the history of *China's Destiny* as merely a battle between the Nationalists and Communists would simply reproduce the discursive and physical violence perpetrated throughout this period. This chapter has addressed this problem by engaging voices that have been repressed for a variety of reasons, specifically those of intellectuals and pro-Japanese writers. These voices not only broaden our understanding of the controversy surrounding *China's Destiny* but also shed new light on the importance of this book in its

---

[92] Howard L. Boorman, ed., *Biographical Dictionary of Republican China* (New York: Columbia University Press, 1970), vol. 3, 410–11.

[93] Mao Zedong, "Liangge Zhongguo zhi mingyun" [Two versions of China's destiny], in *Mao Zedong zai qida de baogao he jianghuaji* [Collection of Mao Zedong's reports and speeches at the Chinese Communist Party's Seventh National Representative Congress], ed. Zhongguo zhongyang wenxian yanjiushi [Chinese Communist Party Central Committee Document Research Unit] (Beijing: Zhongyang wenxian chubanshe, 1995), 17. This was part of Mao's opening speech at the Seventh National Congress of the CCP. The book Mao said would be produced by the CCP was *On Coalition Government*, which was promulgated at this congress.

[94] Lyman Van Slyke, "The Chinese Communist Movement during the Sino-Japanese War 1937–1945," in *The Cambridge History of China*, ed. John King Fairbank and Albert Feuerwerker (New York: Cambridge University Press, 1986), vol. 13, part 2, 692.

immediate context. They enable us to see *China's Destiny* as having truly national significance during a momentous year in China's history.

Seventy years after the publication of *China's Destiny*, it is more timely than ever to remind ourselves that, in Prasenjit Duara's words, "In place of the harmonized, monologic voice of the Nation, we find a polyphony of voices, contradictory and ambiguous, opposing, affirming, and negotiating their views of the nation."[95] This is all the more the case since the accession of Xi Jinping, who has presided over the ongoing resurgence of nationalist rhetoric that appeals to the same traditional values embraced by Chiang Kai-shek and roundly criticized by the CCP in 1943. To take a narrow view of this turn of events is to confront the bewildering possibility that the two versions of China's destiny mentioned by Mao have now resolved themselves into a single arch-narrative of the Chinese nation; it is to wonder if China's Destiny has become the China Dream (*zhongguo meng*).[96]

The parallels between the nationalist ideology of *China's Destiny* and contemporary CCP rhetoric are striking and more than superficial. Increasingly, the CCP has embraced China's past and encourages the Chinese people to embody traditional values, especially a respect for order.[97] The party condemns the espousal of ideals that it deems foreign and not in accord with China's past and current reality, or at least not with the government's agenda. Even socialism must be qualified with the phrase "with Chinese characteristics." Ethnic autonomy is a taboo subject. The narrative of a transcendent, racially unified *minzu* carries so much weight that some publishers are even squeamish about discussing the anti-Manchu discourse that catalyzed the 1911 Revolution.[98] Chen Boda would tell us that history has been "overturned." In the twenty-first century, though, there is no Chen Boda or Mao Zedong to assert an alternative vision of China's destiny on behalf of a recognized political party.

---

[95] Duara, *Rescuing History*, 10.

[96] Taylor considers the increasing complexity of Chiang's legacy in light of the PRC's post-Mao transformation. Taylor, *The Generalissimo*, 589–95.

[97] There are many indications of this, but the most striking for me was a propaganda sign I saw in Jinan in August 2014 that stated, "Order is life. Order is a kind of justice" (*zhixu— jiu shi shengming, jiu shi gongping*).

[98] Joseph Esherick, "On Dealing with Chinese Censors," ChinaFile, October 14, 2014, http://www.chinafile.com/reporting-opinion/viewpoint/dealing-chinese-censors.

Yet, as in 1943, nationalist discourse will inevitably be populated by a "polyphony of voices," even if they appear marginal or marginalized. Even unwelcome or inconvenient voices such as the pro-Japanese discourse in wartime China warrant study since, as this chapter has shown, they may interact with more historically conventional narratives in unpredictable and consequential ways. Moreover, it is impossible to know in the long run which so-called failed nationalisms might become politically viable again, as seems the case with the nationalist ideology espoused by Chiang. As in 1943, China's destiny is written on paper, not set in stone.

7

Yan'an's Iron Bodhisattva

Hunting Spies in the Rectification Campaign

Yidi Wu

We have the heart of a bodhisattva in saving the young who have lost their
footing, but we have an iron will to suppress confirmed agents.
—Kang Sheng, "Rescuing Those Who Have Lost
Their Footing," July 15, 1943[1]

On July 15, 1943, Kang Sheng gave the speech that signaled the start
of the Rescue Campaign. This speech, given at the Central Auditorium in Yan'an, the rural and isolated Communist wartime headquarters
in northwestern China, launched one of the most chilling and coercive
periods of the Yan'an Rectification Campaign, which had begun more
than a year earlier in February 1942. Focusing on actual and suspected
spies from both the Nationalist Party (Guomindang) and the Chinese
Communist Party (CCP), this chapter shows how perceived threats from
the Nationalist military and intelligence services influenced the inception
of the Rescue Campaign.

---

[1] Kang Sheng, "Qiangjiu shizuzhe" [Rescuing those who have lost their footing], in
Zhonggong dangshi jiaoxue cankao ziliao (Beijing: Guofang daxue chubanshe, 1985), 384,
translation from John Byron, *The Claws of the Dragon: Kang Sheng, the Evil Genius behind
Mao and His Legacy of Terror in People's China* (New York: Simon and Schuster, 1992), 180.

Figure 7.1: Kang Sheng. *Source:* Cheng Mo, *Yong jingtou jujiao lishi* (Beijing, 2012).

Multiple factors led to the Rectification Campaign of 1942–1944. Internally, most newly recruited Communist Party members were either illiterate peasants who had little understanding of Marxism-Leninism, or young students and intellectuals who had fled from the Japanese-occupied and the Nationalist-controlled urban areas and were more nationalistic and liberal than Marxist. From such heterodox elements, Mao had to build a party with a unified ideology. Externally, the Communists faced the dual pressures of Japanese advances and "mopping up" campaigns in 1941–1942 and the Guomindang blockade of the border regions. Due to the deteriorating United Front against the Japanese, the Nationalists withheld previously promised subsidies to local governments in the border regions. Thus a lack of material support coupled with military threat required a boost of party morale and discipline.[2]

---

[2] Frederick Teiwes, *Politics and Purges in China: Rectification and the Decline of Party Norms, 1950–1965*, 2nd ed. (Armonk, NY: M.E. Sharpe, 1993), 52–53.

Figure 7.2: Qiangjiu Shizuzhe pamphlet. *Source:* Kongfuzi website
(http://m.kongfz.com/book/item_pic_43869_295772914).

As a carefully orchestrated campaign, the Rectification Movement is
often viewed as a crucial turning point contributing to the eventual success of the Chinese Communist revolution.[3] However, the darker side of
this movement included an elite-level power struggle between Mao Zedong and the Russian-returned "Internationalist" group represented by
Wang Ming, as well as a ground-level thought-reform campaign implemented through political study of party documents linked to intense personal self-criticism sessions. The thought-reform campaign eventually
developed into a more aggressive campaign of cadre screening and spy
hunting.

The Rescue Campaign in China echoed the Stalinist purges and terror
of 1930s Russia. The two periods resemble each other in that they both

---

[3] Joseph W. Esherick, "Ten Theses on the Chinese Revolution," *Modern China* 21, no. 1
(January 1995): 67.

involved forced confession, distrust between comrades, and intense anxiety.[4] Kang Sheng's role may account for the similarities. Before coming to
Yan'an with Wang Ming in late 1937, Kang had learned secret-police
techniques during four years in Moscow, where he witnessed Stalin's Great
Purge and may himself have persecuted "enemies" in the Chinese ranks.[5]
He brought Stalin's methods back to Yan'an when he became the chief of
the Social Affairs Department in charge of security and intelligence. He
was appointed chairman of the Cadre Investigation Commission in August 1941, and vice chairman under Mao of the General Study Commission overseeing the Rectification Movement in July 1942.[6] Simultaneously
holding these three titles, Kang unsurprisingly conflated cadre screening
and document studies with spy hunting.

The Yan'an Rectification Campaign has long been studied in the West,
but its relation to the Rescue Campaign has been contested.[7] Studies on

---

    [4] See studies on the Great Purge: Robert Conquest, *The Great Terror: A Reassessment*
(New York: Oxford University Press, 1990); J. Arch Getty, *Origins of the Great Purges: The
Soviet Communist Party Reconsidered* (New York: Cambridge University Press, 1985); and
Robert Thurston, *Life and Terror in Stalin's Russia, 1934–1941* (New Haven, CT: Yale Uni-
versity Press, 1996).
    [5] Byron, *Claws of the Dragon*, 18.
    [6] Ibid., 173, 174.
    [7] An early English study is Merle Goldman, *Literary Dissent in Communist China* (Cam-
bridge, MA: Harvard University Press, 1967), which includes one chapter on literary intellectuals' criticisms of life in Yan'an and campaigns against them in the early stage of the
Rectification Movement. Mark Selden, *The Yenan Way in Revolutionary China* (Cambridge,
MA: Harvard University Press, 1971), presents a more positive picture of the era that goes
beyond elite politics to explore economic development and social transformation through six
secondary campaigns. Frederick Teiwes, *Politics and Purges in China: Rectification and the
Decline of Party Norms, 1950–65* (Armonk, NY: M.E. Sharpe, 1979; reprint with new introduction, 1993), introduces the "persuasive-coercive continuum" that can place any Chinese
Communist rectification campaign on the spectrum. His model provides a theoretical connection between the Rectification Movement and the Rescue Campaign and also explains
why the Yan'an rectification was relatively successful while campaigns later in the 1950s
caused so much trouble. Raymond Wylie, *The Emergence of Maoism: Mao Zedong, Chen Boda
and the Search for Chinese Theory* (Stanford, CA: Stanford University Press, 1980), not only
details power struggles surrounding Mao but also considers domestic and international circumstances. David Apter and Tony Saich, *Revolutionary Discourse in Mao's Republic* (Cambridge, MA: Harvard University Press, 1994), is based on interviews with survivors of the
Yan'an experience, and seeks to explain why rectification was attractive to many cadres and
also effective in building the party as an organization capable of taking over China. Tony
Saich and Hans van de Ven, eds., *New Perspectives on the Chinese Communist Revolution* (Ar-

the latter did not appear in English until 1986, when Peter Seybolt wrote a seminal article, "Terror and Conformity: Counterespionage Campaigns, Rectification, and Mass Movements, 1942–1943," showing that campaigns to uncover spies during the war were a response to real dangers from the Japanese and Guomindang, as well as an effective tool for party unification and mass compliance.[8]

The current official CCP narrative blames Kang Sheng for all of the Rescue Campaign's evils while confining Mao's role to initiating the "correct" Rectification Campaign and bringing a halt to the Rescue Campaign's excesses, but Kang could not have single-handedly carried out the campaign without support from Mao. This narrative intentionally separates the two campaigns in order to preserve a positive portrayal of the Rectification Campaign while treating the Rescue Campaign as excess. Speaking against the official narrative, some scholars view the Rescue Campaign as an integral part of the overall Rectification Campaign. Chen Yung-fa's *Yan'an de yinying* (Shadow of Yan'an) reviews Kang Sheng's responsibility in the Rescue Campaign and the problems arising from relying on the mass line in counterespionage.[9] Dai Qing's *Wang Shiwei and "Wild Lilies"* argues for a connection between the two campaigns by linking Kang Sheng's speeches.[10] Gao Hua's *How Did the Red Sun Rise over Yan'an?* traces the origins of the Yan'an rectification as early as 1930, and stresses Mao's central role in the Rectification Campaign as a part of intraparty struggles.[11]

Previous studies of the Rescue Campaign have rarely taken the rhetoric regarding secret agents seriously because survivors and scholars of this movement assume that most of the "spies" were falsely charged and later found innocent. Similar to Stephen Averill's study of the Futian Incident

---

monk, NY: M.E. Sharpe, 1995), includes essays by Apter, Saich, and Teiwes, all using new sources made available in the 1980s to explore more aspects of the Rescue Campaign.

[8] Peter J. Seybolt, "Terror and Conformity: Counterespionage Campaigns, Rectification, and Mass Movements, 1942–1943," *Modern China* 12, no. 1 (January 1986): 39–73.

[9] Chen Yung-fa, *Yan'an de yinying* [Shadow of Yan'an] (Taibei: Zhongyang yanjiuyuan jindaishi yanjiusuo, 1990).

[10] Dai Qing, *Wang Shiwei and "Wild Lilies": Rectification and Purges in the Chinese Communist Party, 1942–1944* (Armonk, NY: M.E. Sharpe, 1994).

[11] Gao Hua, *Hongtaiyang shi zenyang shengqi de: Yan'an zhengfeng yundong de lailong qumai* [How did the sun rise over Yan'an] (Hong Kong: Zhongwen daxue chubanshe, 2000).

in 1930, I am interested in the "atmosphere of fear and tension" that motivated the suppression.[12] While acknowledging the irrationality and injustice of the Rescue Campaign, my research shows that real Nationalist spies had infiltrated the Communist border regions, compelling the Communists to intensify cadre screening and spy hunting.[13] Another relatively ignored factor is the Guomindang military threat after the dissolution of the Comintern in May 1943. I argue that the Nationalist military threat was real, but top leaders in Yan'an knew most details thanks to their own spies, and they intentionally used the excuse of an imminent civil war to implement spy hunting among Communist comrades. Overall, the Communists were justifiably sensitive to the Nationalist military and intelligence threats, but they knowingly exaggerated the civil war crisis and overestimated the number of potential spies in initiating their intraparty screening campaign.

Spies in Yan'an: Nationalist Agents from the Dai Case

The Japanese bandits and the Guomindang trained many secret agents to destroy us ... [The Nationalist agents] did not save Chinese youth from the Japanese bandits' poisoning, but dragged those promising Chinese youth into this evil quagmire to serve the Japanese bandits' fifth column.
— Kang Sheng, "Rescuing Those Who Have Lost Their Footing," July 15, 1943[14]

The Guomindang Bureau of Investigation and Statistics (Juntong) dreamed of infiltrating the Communist Party to destroy it from within.[15] Though

---

[12] Stephen Averill, "The Origins of the Futian Incident," in Saich and van de Ven, *New Perspectives on the Chinese Communist Revolution*, 86, 110.

[13] For more on the Nationalist infiltrations in the Communist regions, and the correlation between the anti-Communist tides and Yan'an cadre screening, see Lu Yi, "Yan'an shengan yundong zhong de Guomindang yinsu" [Guomindang factors in Yan'an cadre screening], *Dang de wenxian* 140, no. 2 (2011): 80–85.

[14] Kang Sheng, "Qiangjiu shizuzhe," 380. "Fifth column" refers to spies who undermine a larger group from within.

[15] Zhang Yanfo, "Kangzhan qianhou Juntong tewu zai xibei de huodong" [Junton spies' activities in the northwest before and after World War II], in *Tegong miwen: Juntong huodong jishi* [Secret information of special agents: A record of Junton activities], ed. Chen Chujun (Beijing: Zhongguo wenshi chubanshe, 1990), 235.

this goal was never realized, the Nationalist intelligence apparatus tried every conceivable method to infiltrate the Communist border regions and to set up a station in Yan'an. Juntong established a Northwestern Regional Office in Xi'an in October 1935, headed by Zhang Yanfo. The following year, Dai Li, Chiang Kai-shek's spymaster in charge of Juntong, asked his staff to initiate a special police training unit to produce agents who could enter Yan'an.[16] Trained and sent out half a year later, all the trainees returned because they could not bear the hard conditions in Yan'an.[17] In 1938, Zhang arranged for Wang Keyi to work at the Yan'an telegraph bureau, but Wang came back after a few months complaining that being surrounded by Communists made him feel suffocated.[18] In 1942, Dai Li selected three assassins for missions in Yan'an, but none managed to assassinate any Communist leaders.[19] Tang Zong, who worked on intelligence issues at the side of Chiang Kai-shek, revealed in his diary on August 31, 1942, "[We should] reflect on the fact that we have no agents among the Communists."[20]

Despite all the failed attempts, the Communist border regions were not completely sealed off from Guomindang intelligence. In October 1940, a Qingyang middle school teacher named Wu Nanshan confessed to his Communist colleague that Juntong had trained him at the Hanzhong Special Training Unit (HSTU),[21] founded by Dai Li in 1939 to train agents to infiltrate Yan'an. It trained eight groups of thirty trainees each before its relocation to Xi'an in 1942.[22] The executive manager was

---

[16] See more about Dai Li in Frederic Wakeman, *Spymaster: Dai Li and the Chinese Secret Service* (Berkeley: University of California Press, 2003).

[17] Ma Zhendu, *Guomindang tewu huodong dang'an dajiemi* [Disclosure of archives of Guomindang special agents' activities] (Taibei: Linghuo wenhua shiye youxian gongsi, 2010), 147.

[18] Zhang Yanfo, "Kangzhan qianhou," 237.

[19] Shen Zui, *Shen Zui huiyi zuopin quanji* [A complete work of Shen Zui memoir] (Beijing: Jiuzhou tushu chubanshe; Jingxiao xinhua shudian, 1998), 172–73.

[20] Tang Zong, *Tang Zong shiluo zai Dalu de riji* [Tang Zong's diaries lost in the mainland] (Taibei: Zhuanji wenxue chubanshe, 1998), 272.

[21] Hao Zaijin, *Zhongguo mimi zhan: Zhonggong qingbao, baowei gongzuo jishi* [China's secret war: A recounting of CCP intelligence and security work] (Beijing: Jincheng chubanshe, 2010), 244.

[22] Liang Xiong, *Dai Li zhuan* [A biography of Dai Li] (Taibei: Zhuanji wenxue chubanshe, 1985), 110; see also Xu Enzeng et al., *Xishuo Zhongtong Juntong* [A detailed account of Zhongtong and Juntong] (Taibei: Zhuanji wenxue chubanshe, 1992), 342.

Cheng Muyi, whom Dai Li trusted because he had previously destroyed a Communist underground organization in Jiangsu.[23] Dai Li had high expectations for this training unit. When he visited and gave a speech in the autumn of 1940, he ordered trainees to "bring back the masses from the Communists and bring back traitors from the Japanese."[24]

Having HSTU students infiltrate the border regions was an amazing achievement for Nationalist intelligence. One factor contributing to their success was that instead of relying on police or merchants as undercover agents, Juntong changed its focus to training young students. This was done in response to the Communists' new policy of welcoming intellectuals to Yan'an. In his essay "On the Decision to Attract Intellectuals" in December 1939, Mao acknowledged that the Communists had formerly disregarded intellectuals, but he now claimed that without them the revolution would not achieve victory.[25] Young students and intellectuals brought the Communists renewed energy, but also provided Nationalist intelligence a new opportunity for infiltration. At some checkpoints, Guomindang inspectors confiscated the school acceptance letters of some progressive students on their way to Yan'an, and indoctrinated others before sending them on.[26] Another reason for HSTU's success was that the trainees were local middle school students who had relatives or friends in the border regions, making it easier for them to get in and out.[27]

According to Hao Zaijin's research, HSTU trainee Wu Nanshan had graduated from high school and became an elementary school principal before getting fired due to a conflict with local Guomindang authorities. As a patriotic youth in his twenties seeking a job, he went to the training site only to find that the so-called wartime guerilla tactics cadre training unit was actually an anti-Communist spy training camp.[28] Along with

---

[23] Shen Zui, *Shen Zui huiyi zuopin quanji*, 169. Cheng Muyi had started a similar training unit at his hometown in Wenzhou, Zhejiang, before moving to Hanzhong.

[24] Hao Zaijin, *Zhongguo mimi zhan*, 248.

[25] Mao Zedong, "Zhonggong zhongyang guanyu xishou zhishi fenzi de jueding" [On the decision to attract intellectuals] (December 1, 1942), in *Mao Zedong nianpu* [Chronology of Mao Zedong], ed. Pang Xianzhi (Beijing: Zhongyang wenxian chubanshe, 2002), vol. 2, 145.

[26] Shen Zui, *Shen Zui huiyi zuopin quanji*, 168.

[27] Hao Zaijin, *Zhongguo mimi zhan*, 248.

[28] Jiang Wei, *Hongse Fu'ermosi: Bu Lu yu gong'an xitong diyi qi'an* [Red Sherlock Holmes:

strict discipline, the indoctrination included studying Sun Yat-sen and Chiang Kai-shek's works, professional agent techniques, and, most importantly, knowledge about the Communists imparted through a textbook written by Zhang Guotao, a longtime leader of the CCP and recent defector to the Guomindang. Wu pretended to be enthusiastic, but he did not believe the instructors' demonization of the Communists. He fabricated an excuse to graduate early and returned home. Meanwhile, Wu's hometown of some three thousand people had kicked out the Guomindang local government and replaced it with Communist officials, who assigned Wu a middle school teaching position.[29]

After local Communist security leaders heard of Wu's confession to his colleague in late 1940, they did not arrest or kill him. Instead, they used him as a "hook" to fish for his peers from the same training unit. Bit by bit, the training unit's network functioned as a road map to discover more Guomindang spies. Starting in 1941 and lasting for over half a year, the Communist security apparatus accumulated a list of HSTU attendees. In October 1941, Wu unexpectedly encountered his former classmate Qi Sanyi, who remained to teach at HSTU after graduation and therefore knew all the students from HSTU after Wu left.[30] On that same day, Qi was arrested. He became a crucial informant in the search for other students. By May 1942, all Nationalist agents had been located.[31]

Soon, CCP security services started arresting these agents from HSTU. Some were still studying at schools, while others worked in various Communist bureaus where they had been promoted as cadres. Three agents in particular worked at the military intelligence bureau.[32] Most cooperated after being detected, partly because they did not want their families, who also lived within the border regions, to be persecuted, and

---

Bu Lu and the top mysterious case in public security system] (Shanghai: Xuelin chubanshe, 2003), 103; Hao Zaijin, *Zhongguo mimi zhan*, 242.

[29] Hao Zaijin, *Zhongguo mimi zhan*, 243–44.

[30] Xiu Lairong, *Chen Long zhuan: Zhongguo yinbi zhanxian de zhuoyue zhihuiyuan* [Biography of Chen Long: An excellent commander in China's invisible front]. (Beijing: Qun zhong chubanshe, 1995), 134.

[31] Hao Zaijin, *Zhongguo mimi zhan*, 255.

[32] Xiu Lairong, *Chen Long zhuan*, 135.

partly because the CCP was lenient toward agents who confessed.[33] Many of them later became double agents working for the Communists. By the end of 1942, most Nationalist agents were exposed. Estimates of the total number of spies ranged between thirty-two and fifty-six, the higher estimates having been made at later dates for wider regions.[34] It was not until the spring of 1943 that Dai Li learned that HSTU students who had penetrated the border regions had been discovered. Angry and frustrated, Dai Li fired Cheng Muyi and suspended the training unit.[35]

The large number and wide range of Nationalist agents alarmed the Communists. They named the incident Hanzhong Special Training Unit Case or simply the Dai Case because of its association with Dai Li. Bu Lu, a cadre in the security bureau, was in charge of the case, earning him the nickname Sherlock Holmes.[36] Although Kang Sheng was not in charge of this case, he most likely communicated with Bu Lu, and he requested all of the case files by December 1941.[37] Kang later reported the case to Mao, who said, "This case gives us a lesson, especially for those who still have illusions about Chiang Kai-shek. It is a pity that we have so few Bu Lus, and in the future we need more cadres like him to strengthen Yan'an's security."[38] Kang described the case as "ringing an alarm in our minds."[39] He reflected, "Since these spies were all youths, the Communist cadre screening should target the same group, especially those from outside the Communist regions. Since these spies permeated various bureaus and positions, their activities must be extensive and thorough, and therefore our cadre screening should be extensive as well."[40]

In the Rescue Campaign, young students and intellectuals from the Nationalist-controlled regions became the main suspects. It would be an

[33] Zhu Hongzhao, *Zhongshuo fenyun hua Yan'an* [Yan'an from various accounts] (Zhaoqing: Guangdong renmin chubanshe, 2001), 109.

[34] Hao Zaijin, *Zhongguo mimi zhan,* 258; Jiang, *Hongse Fu'ermosi,* 108.

[35] Ma Zhendu, *Guomindang tewu huodong dang'an dajiemi,* 148.

[36] Jiang Wei, *Hongse Fu'ermosi,* 108.

[37] Hao Zaijin, *Zhongguo mimi zhan,* 250; Shi Zhe, *Zai lishi juren shenbian: Shi Zhe huiyilu* [Next to historical giants: Shi Zhe's memoir] (Beijing: Zhongyang wenxian chubanshe, 1991), 248.

[38] Jiang Wei, *Hongse Fu'ermosi,* 109.

[39] Zhu Hongzhao, *Zhongshuo fenyun hua Yan'an,* 110.

[40] Shi Zhe, *Zai Lishi juren shenbian,* 249.

exaggeration to say the Dai Case by itself led to cadre screening in the Rectification, but the concurrency of this specific espionage case and the shift in the political movement might not be accidental. The Dai Case reminded the Communists that Nationalist spies existed in the border regions, and that rectification should go hand in hand with cadre screening as a way to detect agents.

Although the Dai Case alerted the Communists to the need for rigorous cadre screening and the threat of espionage, what happened in the Rescue Campaign was more of a witch hunt. Security agents investigated the Dai Case secretly while the Rescue Campaign relied on the "mass line," mainly people without any intelligence skills. Many Nationalist agents from the Dai Case ended up being trusted and recruited to work for the Communists, but "spies" from the Rescue Campaign could not escape their tainted records and were often targets of later political campaigns. In the end, while the threat of Guomindang espionage was real, the Dai Case served as a bogeyman that helped provoke the excesses of the later witch-hunt.

MYTH AND TRUTH OF THE ZHANG KEQIN CASE

Many people who were salvaged and renewed [by the Confession Campaign] said, "The Communist Party is [our] reincarnated parents." These grateful voices prove the greatness of the Communist Party's lenient policy and that the collective power of the Party is truly the engineer of spiritual transformation.

—Kang Sheng, "Rescuing Those Who Have Lost
Their Footing," July 15, 1943[41]

As the Dai Case's investigation drew to a close, the Rectification Movement shifted to cadre screening and spy hunting. In a talk on cadre screening on June 19, 1942, Mao hinted that the targets of counterespionage should be intellectuals. In his opening remarks to the Northwest Bureau

---

[41] Kang Sheng, "Qiangjiu shizuzhe," 381.

High Cadre Conference on October 19, Mao harshly criticized liberals for being blind to enemy agents.[42] In November, during the same conference, Mao reminded people of the counterespionage struggle, and distinguished the half-hearted (referring to those with both bourgeois and proletarian sympathies) from the double-hearted (referring to counterrevolutionary and revolutionary hearts).[43] Simultaneously, as if Kang Sheng read Mao's mind, Kang reported that the Social Affairs Department had discovered a spy: Zhang Keqin.[44]

A nineteen-year-old student from Gansu Province, Zhang Keqin had joined the Communist underground in 1937 and came to Yan'an in 1939. He studied at the Northwest Public School run by the Social Affairs Department to train agents. However, starting in the summer of 1942, the school was turned into a cadre screening institution. In November, Kang Sheng asked the school vice president, Li Yimin, who had previously headed the intelligence bureau, to investigate all "problematic" students.[45] Zhang became a natural suspect: he was a student from the Guomindang-controlled region, and the Guomindang had arrested his father and wife, both of whom converted to the Guomindang after Zhang left for Yan'an. To make matters worse, an informant reported that Zhang was a spy.[46]

According to Li Yimin's memoirs, in November 1942 the interrogation of Zhang started with three questions and a statement: "How did you come to Yan'an? What did you come here to do? Do you know what your problem is? Someone already told us that you came here for intelligence gathering." Zhang was shocked, yet remained cool headed. He revealed that his father was a doctor, whose patients sometimes included Nationalist officials. This fact became Zhang's Achilles heel, as the interrogation continued for three days nonstop, focusing on his father's relationships

---

[42] Gao Hua, *Hongtaiyang*, 479–80.

[43] Hua Shijun, *Yan'an zhengfeng shimo* [Yan'an Rectification Campaign from beginning to end] (Shanghai: Shanghai renmin chubanshe, 1985), 66.

[44] Song Xiaomeng, *Li Rui qiren* [Li Rui as a person] (Zhengzhou: Henan renmin chubanshe, 1999), 197.

[45] Chen Yung-fa, *Yan'an de yinying*, 69.

[46] Wang Suyuan, "Shaan-Gan-Ning bianqu 'qiangjiu yundong' shimo" ["Rescue Campaign" in Shaan-Gan-Ning border regions], *Zhonggong dangshi ziliao* 37 (1991): 209.

with Guomindang officials. At five a.m. on the third day, Zhang agreed to confess: he had joined Nationalist intelligence via his father's connection to Guomindang officials disguised as patients. More strikingly, he described Gansu's underground Communist Party as a "red flag party," which Nationalist agents had infiltrated to conduct anti-Communist activities although it superficially maintained a progressive Communist cover.[47] If his charge was true, all underground Communist parties in Nationalist-controlled areas were in danger of infiltration from agents, making an extensive investigation necessary.

The next day the Northwest Public School held a meeting with all students and faculty, as well as representatives from other organizations in Yan'an. Introduced as a model confessor, Zhang talked through tears about how he had joined the fake Communist Party and had come to Yan'an on an intelligence mission, and how he appreciated being saved and given a chance to be reborn as a true Communist.[48] This confession from an enemy agent who was saved by the party emotionally moved many attendees, and some revealed themselves as spies while others went back to their work units and initiated campaigns to discover other Zhang Keqins.[49] Zhang also toured Yan'an with his testimonial of confession and rebirth, allowing more people to copy his model as well as to seek out enemy agents. More red flag parties came to the surface, along with more suspected underground party cadres.[50]

Not everyone believed what Zhang confessed, though no one dared to speak out against it. Chen Long, who worked in intelligence, did not trust the coerced confession, but he could not openly challenge Kang Sheng's authority. When Chen ran into Zhang Keqin, he asked, "What nonsense did you talk about? Did it really happen?" This surprised Zhang, since nobody else had questioned his confession.[51] Xie Juezai, who was acquainted with Zhang's father in Lanzhou, also found Zhang's story unre-

---

[47] Li Yimin, *Li Yimin huiyilu* [Li Yimin's memoir] (Changsha: Hunan renmin chubanshe, 1986), 113–15. "Red flag party" refers to those who pretend to wave the red flag but in fact oppose the red flag.

[48] Ibid., 115.

[49] Chen Yung-fa, *Yan'an de yinying*, 63, 66.

[50] Wang Suyuan, "Shan-gan-ning bianqu 'qiangjiu yundong' shimo," 210.

[51] Xiu Lairong, *Chen Long zhuan*, 142, 144.

liable and denied that the Lanzhou underground Communist Party was completely infiltrated.[52] Zhou Enlai, who was in charge of all underground Communist branches in Nationalist-controlled regions, believed that red flag parties did not exist, though he had little leverage to stop the spy hunt since he did not return to Yan'an until July 1943.[53] None of these doubts were publicly expressed at the time.

For Kang Sheng, the Zhang Keqin Case was a heavenly gift coming at the right moment. He did not care whether Zhang was a real spy, nor did he bother to investigate the truthfulness of the red flag parties. The simple fact that Zhang confessed to being an agent sent by the Gansu red flag party left enough room for Kang to elaborate: "This enabled us to acquire a new knowledge of the Guomindang's secret service policy, to make a reappraisal of our Party organs in the rear provinces, and to learn more about the influx of numerous espionage agents into Yan'an."[54] In Kang's view, the "red flag policy" was a Guomindang secret service strategy to infiltrate the party with spies that had only been discovered thanks to the Zhang Keqin Case, and anyone who still doubted Guomindang agents' existence in Yan'an was himself viewed with suspicion.

In December 1942, during the Northwest Bureau High Cadre Conference, Kang Sheng gave a report, "On the Issue of Counter-espionage." It was the first time that he declared that "spies in Yan'an were as thick as weeds," and he categorized two types of spies: "Those who infiltrated [Yan'an], such as spies sent by Dai Li; and those who were pulled out, in other words, they [the Guomindang] developed agents in our team."[55] Kang was referring to the Dai Case and the Zhang Keqin Case, respectively. The contrast between the two cases was ironic: the real Guomindang agents were dealt with secretly, whereas the alleged Guomindang spy

---

[52] Xie Juezai zhuan bianxiezu, *Xie Juezai zhuan* [Biography of Xie Juezai] (Beijing: Renmin chubanshe, 1984), 292–93.

[53] Yang Shangkun, *Yang Shangkun huiyilu* [Yang Shangkun's memoir] (Beijing: Zhongyang wenxian chubanshe, 2001), 218–19.

[54] Wang Suyuan, "Shan-gan-ning bianqu 'qiangjiu yundong' shimo," 210. translation from Warren Kuo, *Zhongguo gongchandang shilun* [Analytical history of the Chinese Communist Party] (Taipei: Institute of International Relations, 1968), 399.

[55] Gao Putang and Zeng Luping, *Yan'an qiangjiu yundong shimo: 200 ge qinlizhe jiyi* [Yan'an Rescue Campaign: Memories from 200 witnesses] (Hong Kong: Shidai guoji chuban youxian gongsi, 2008), 79.

was presented publicly as a confession model. In this conference, Kang also claimed that "rectification will inevitably shift to cadre screening, and cadre screening will inevitably shift to anti-subversion. The three are intrinsically connected as an iron principle."[56] It was after this conference that the Rectification Campaign moved on to cadre screening and counter-espionage.[57] Even though the name Rescue Campaign only appeared after Kang Sheng's report on July 15, 1943, the practice of interrogation and confession based on the Zhang Keqin model started much earlier, in December 1942.

HU GONGMIAN'S VISIT TO YAN'AN AND THE APRIL ARREST IN RESPONSE

> After April 10 the central Party organs once again adopted a lenient policy and called on young people to renew and reform themselves to break away from the special agents' trap. In the last three months the efforts of the Party and non-Party members have spurred many of those who had lost their footing and been injured to accept the Party's call to rise and speak out against the Japanese bandits and the Guomindang for their murder of China's youth.
>
> —Kang Sheng, "Rescuing Those Who Have Lost
> Their Footing," July 15, 1943[58]

Unlike elsewhere in China, wartime Yan'an was mostly peaceful, yet occasional Nationalist military threats were enough to cause their rivals to panic. Yan'an had been expecting a "third anti-Communist high tide" as early as May 1942. On May 3, Mao proposed military preparation for any surprise attack on the Shaan-Gan-Ning border region. On May 19, Mao drafted a telegraph to Hu Zongnan, the Nationalist general at Xi'an in

---

[56] Zhongguo renmin gong'an shigao bianxie xiaozu, *Zhongguo renmin gong'an shigao* [A historical record of Chinese people's public security] (Beijing: Jingguan jiaoyu chubanshe, 1997), 117.

[57] Kuo, *Analytical History of the Chinese Communist Party*, 398.

[58] Kang Sheng, "Qiangjiu shizuzhe," 380, translation from Byron, *Claws of the Dragon*, 179.

charge of military activities against the Communists, warning him not to attack Yan'an.[59] Starting from March 1942, however, Hu was busy with his "western expedition" dealing with the recovery of Xinjiang (see chapter 3). Thus, he had no time to fight the Communists.[60]

It was probably not until February 1943 that Chiang Kai-shek started to make concrete military plans against the Communist border regions. Chiang approved a "Military Plan to Attack the Shaanbei Bandit Region," which he sent not only to Hu Zongnan but also to Nationalist generals in Gansu, Ningxia, and Qinghai provinces, which encircle the Shaan-Gan-Ning border region. Chiang ordered Nationalist troops to stay at their current positions and wait for a turning point.[61] In April 1943, Hu moved his troops from southwest Shanxi to Shaanxi and west to the Communist border region. Though rumors spread that Chiang would attack the Shaan-Gan-Ning border region, it was likely that he was only attempting to avoid confrontations with Japanese forces.[62]

To carry out Chiang's military plan to attack the CCP, Hu Zongnan had to know his rivals. In late March 1943, he chose Hu Gongmian as his representative to visit Yan'an for three months. It was not a random choice: Hu Gongmian had served as a commander in the Communist Red Army but was arrested by the Guomindang in 1932.[63] After being released from jail four years later, he became a senior staff member under Hu Zongnan, who respected Hu Gongmian as his former teacher from the Whampoa Military Academy.[64]

Prior to Hu Gongmian's visit, Yan'an's political atmosphere had already slightly shifted. At the Politburo meeting on March 16, 1943, Mao suggested, "The Rectification Movement should not

[59] Pang Xianzhi, *Mao Zedong nianpu*, 379, 381 (May 3 and 19, 1942).

[60] Yang Zhesheng, *Zai Hu Zongnan shenbian de shier nian: Qingbao yingxiong Xiong Xianghui* [Twelve years with Hu Zongnan: Intelligence hero Xiong Xianghui] (Shanghai: Shanghai renmin chubanshe, 2007), 188.

[61] Xiong Xianghui, *Wo de qingbao yu waijiao shengya* [My intelligence and foreign relations career] (Beijing: Zhonggong dangshi chubanshe, 1999), 14.

[62] Shi Zhe, *Feng yu gu: Shi Zhe huiyilu* [Hump and valley: Shi Zhe's memoir] (Beijing: Hongqi chubanshe, 1992), 7.

[63] Chen Yung-fa, *Yan'an de yinying*, 176.

[64] Yang Zhesheng, *Zai Hu Zongnan shenbian de shier nian*, 189.

only target the petit bourgeois, but also counterrevolutionaries. ... Since the anti-Japanese war, the Guomindang has practiced a secret agent policy against our party, and thus the Social Affairs Department and the Central Party School has discovered many spies. Now we need to tell spies apart from talent. In Yan'an, we should finish cadre screening and the purge of bad people within a year."[65]

Mao probably learned of the Guomindang's secret agent policy from Kang Sheng, who made Mao believe spies existed in Yan'an. Besides, Mao implied that cadre screening and spy hunting would be part of the rectification. Then on March 20, Kang Sheng reported on cadre screening. He confirmed the Guomindang secret agent policy as recently discovered from cadre screening, and said, "We should prioritize cadre screening in our work in 1943, and we should inform all border regions of the Yan'an cadre screening experience."[66] That same day Kang's report was approved, meaning the Zhang Keqin model was officially recognized and spread throughout Yan'an and beyond. After that, cadre screening was intensified and leaned toward counterespionage.[67]

Starting on the night of April 1, Kang Sheng took Hu Gongmian's impending visit as an excuse to arrest suspected Guomindang agents in Yan'an to prevent them from meeting with Hu. Shi Zhe, a security officer under Kang Sheng, remembered that night: "Holding a list of suspects in his hand, Kang Sheng talked with us, while marking on the list with circles and dots. He mumbled, 'This is [a member of the] "Renaissance Society," that is [a member of the] "CC clique," "traitor," "rebel," "Japanese spy."' Then he wanted us to arrest those whom he circled, and send those with dots to the Border Region Administration College to undergo investigation."[68] When Shi asked Kang whether he had any concrete evidence to arrest those people, Kang replied, "If there is evidence, why do you

[65] Hu Qiaomu, *Hu Qiaomu huiyi Mao Zedong* [Hu Qiaomu's memory of Mao Zedong] (Beijing: Renmin chubanshe, 1994), 276.

[66] Wang Xiuxin, "Yan'an 'qiangjiu yundong' shuping" [A review of Yan'an rescue campaign], *Dang de wenxian* 3 (1990): 71–72.

[67] Gao Hua, *Hongtaiyang*, 487–88.

[68] Shi Zhe, *Feng yu gu*, 241. Both the Renaissance Society and the Central Club clique were Guomindang intelligence groups.

bother to interrogate?"[69] In other words, without clear evidence, Kang expected to extract confessions through interrogation. Shi saw that his brother's name was circled and told Kang, who immediately crossed it out. Then Shi said, "Anyone should be arrested if he deserves it, including my brother." Without explanation, Kang changed the circle to a dot.[70] Chen Long, another staff member under Kang, was familiar with many people on the list. In 1941, Chen had cleared many suspects and declared their innocence. Now they reappeared on the list, not as suspects but as spies.

Within two days, 260 people were arrested in Yan'an. Similar arrests took place in other areas within the border region. Some were held in police detention, while some went to security offices, and others were interrogated at the Northwest Public School.[71] One of them was Li Rui, who came to Yan'an for three years and who later became Mao's secretary. At first Li's wife thought he would be back within days, but he was not released until June 1944.[72] When Peter Vladimirov, the Soviet representative in Yan'an, asked about the arrests, Kang explained, "[The] order to isolate the Guomindang and Japanese henchmen has been given by the CCP leadership."[73] The "CCP leadership" probably referred to Mao, who would certainly hear about the arrests from Kang, or who would even authorize the arrests.

While tension in Yan'an was aggravated by the arrests, another heavy blow came on April 3, 1943, when the Party Central Committee announced the decision to continue the Rectification Campaign. It was not merely to continue the same movement for one more year, but to change focus and rhetoric. The annoucement first recognized the recent exposure of spies: "Since the founding of the united front against Japan and our party's growth with new members, the Japanese bandits and the Guomindang practiced secret agent policies on a large scale. Our party organiza-

---

[69] Shi Zhe, *Zai lishi juren shenbian*, 250.

[70] Shi Zhe, *Feng yu gu*, 241.

[71] Xiu Lairong, *Chen Long zhuan*, 143.

[72] Li Nanyang, ed., *Fumu zuori shu 1938–1949* [Parents' past correspondences, 1938–1949] (Guangzhou: Guangdong renmin chubanshe, 2008), 418–19, 463.

[73] Peter Vladimirov, *The Vladimirov Diaries: Yenan, China, 1942–1945* (Garden City, NY: Doubleday, 1975), 112.

tion in all places was infiltrated by a large number of secret agents. The tactic was ingenious, and the number of agents was alarming."[74]

After reading Kang Sheng and Mao's speeches on the discovery of agents through cadre screening, it is unsurprising to see confirmation from the CCP official documents. In response to these alleged secret agents, the Rectification Campaign adjusted its aims: "The main target of rectification is to correct nonproletarian thoughts (including feudal, bourgeois and petit bourgeois thoughts) among cadres and to purge counterrevolutionaries hiding within our party. ... Rectification is not only the best method to correct cadres' incorrect thoughts, but also to discover and purge secret agents."[75] In other words, cadre screening and spy hunting were added to the rectification, and did not diverge from the rectification as the official narrative portrays. The connection between correcting thoughts and purging spies meant that the Rescue Campaign was integral to the Rectification Movement and the two could not be separated. In order to clarify the relationship, the April 3 decision stated:

> Correcting incorrect thoughts and purging secret agents are interconnected in the process of the rectification, but in nature they are distinct from each other and should not be confused. ... At the beginning and middle part of the rectification, except for the main deputies who should pay particular attention, in public announcements, absolutely do not mention the tasks of cadre screening and spy purging. ... Do not declare them as spies in a hurry, but treat them as comrades with incorrect thoughts, so as to let them expose as much as they can.[76]

The April 3 decision sounds like a scheme to invite people to air their opinions, not publicly mentioning spy hunting at first, and then to label them as spies. Though the decision allocated five months to correcting the

---

[74] Zhongyang dang'anguan, *Zhonggong zhongyang wenjian xuanji* [Selected documents of CCP Central Committee] (Beijing: Zhonggong zhongyang dangxiao chubanshe, 1989), vol. 14, 30.

[75] Ibid., 29, 30.

[76] Ibid., 30, 31.

incorrect thoughts before purging spies, that agenda was never followed. Soon afterward, cadre screening and spy hunting dominated the campaign.

On April 5, Mao proposed a meeting with all party members, encouraging secret agents to confess.[77] Between April 9 and 12, a public gathering was held with more than 20,000 participants from all units in Yan'an. Zhang Keqin was brought there as a model and confessed again. Ren Bishi, a member of the Central Committee Secretariat, introduced the party's lenient policy toward the misled youth, but maintained that if they were still unwilling to confess, then this was "a profound evil, and a dead end."[78] By this point, people were presumably well aware of, if not shocked by, the arrests after April 1. They knew the campaign was serious.

With the April 3 decision and the mass meeting, cadre screening and spy hunting turned from private to public, and from a handful of cadres and organizations to a mass Confession Campaign involving everyone in every working unit in Yan'an. On April 24, Mao decided to dedicate three months from May to July for counterespionage education with Kang Sheng in charge.[79] Then, on April 28, Mao warned against forced confession through torture and the importance of evidence over confession, although what was really happening and what happened later would contradict this directive.[80]

DISSOLUTION OF THE COMINTERN AND RENEWED NATIONALIST THREAT

This time the invasion of the border regions is not out of Hu Zongnan's will, but Chiang Kai-shek's order and command. Please consider the following: if the Japanese bandits along with Wang Jingwei's converts attempt to exterminate the Communists, and Chiang Kai-shek also mobi-

---

[77] Pang Xianzhi, *Mao Zedong nianpu*, 433 (April 5, 1943).

[78] Wang Xiuxin, "Yan'an 'qiangjiu yundong' shuping," 72.

[79] Pang Xianzhi, *Mao Zedong nianpu*, 434–35 (April 24, 1943).

[80] Hu Qiaomu, *Hu Qiaomu huiyi Mao Zedong*, 276.

lizes his troops to exterminate the Communists, then what on earth is the difference between the two?

> —Kang Sheng, "Rescuing Those Who Have Lost
> Their Footing," July 15, 1943[81]

While Chiang Kai-shek intended to exert more military pressure on the Shaan-Gan-Ning border region, and Mao was convinced that a counter-espionage campaign was necessary, a turning point came from an ally that sent weapons to the Nationalists and Marxism-Leninism to the Communists. It was news that the Soviet Union was dissolving the Comintern that shaped both parties' next steps. Initiated in 1919, the Comintern aimed to promote proletarian revolution and overthrow the international bourgeoisie in developed nations. Once Russia became entangled in World War II, the Comintern would potentially handicap Russia from allying with the very countries where it was intended to initiate proletariat revolutions. Thus Stalin "decided to make a gesture of good will (to the United States in particular)" by dissolving the Comintern. This announcement came on May 15, 1943.[82]

The Comintern representative in Yan'an, Peter Vladimirov, expected that the news "would be a very joyous piece of information for the Mao group," which was competing with Wang Ming's internationalist Communist group. Mao did not seem surprised or bewildered by the news, but instead seemed as though "he had it all thought out."[83] During the Politburo meeting on May 21, Mao expressed his total agreement with the dissolution, and he instructed Zhou Enlai to publish the news in *Xinhua Daily*, the CCP's voice in Chongqing. Three days later, he telegraphed Zhou, asking him to return to Yan'an, ideally by plane, to discuss the CCP's policies in response to the Comintern's dissolution.[84]

The official CCP statement on the dissolution was issued on May 26

---

[81] Kang Sheng, "Qiangjiu shizuzhe," 383.

[82] Raymond Wylie, *The Emergence of Maoism: Mao Tse-tung, Ch'en Po-ta, and the Search for Chinese Theory, 1935–1945* (Stanford, CA: Stanford University Press, 1980), 201.

[83] Vladimirov, *Vladimirov Diaries*, 116–17.

[84] Pang Xianzhi, *Mao Zedong nianpu*, 440 (May 24, 1943).

and further clarified Mao's stand: the CCP fully endorsed the Comintern's decision; the Comintern had completed its historical mission, including invaluable assistance to the Chinese people; and the CCP was a creation of modern Chinese history and could function independently based on its specific national conditions.[85] If the first two points were more rhetorical, the last one contained the statement's real message: "It is necessary to steadfastly and consistently fight for the genuinely national and independent character of the CCP."[86] Such a confident response, as historian Raymond Wylie has written, was not "a brave face on a fait accompli" but "a genuine statement of relief and satisfaction."[87]

In comparison to Mao's enthusiastic embrace of the dissolution, Chiang Kai-shek's reaction expressed his persistent distrust for Stalin. While recognizing that the dissolution superficially united the Allies, he still doubted whether the news was true, assuming that the Comintern must have changed its form without truly dissolving and that the dissolution was a political tactic and propaganda ploy of Stalin.[88] He also realized that it would be a key moment for domestic policy, especially regarding the Communists.[89] Thus, he sent a secret telegraph to Hu Zongnan at the end of May: "The subversive party has carried out rectification for years and has suffered intensive internal struggles. The Comintern's dissolution must be a heavy blow to the subversive party. You should take advantage of this good opportunity to attack Yan'an and occupy the Shaan-Gan-Ning border region. Preparations should be finished by the end of June, and actions should be kept in absolute secrecy. ... Do not publicly comment on the Comintern's dissolution."[90] In comparison with

---

[85] Zhongyang dang'anguan, *Zhonggong zhongyang wenjian xuanji*, vol. 14, 38–40 (May 26, 1943).

[86] Vladimirov, *Vladimirov Diaries*, 117.

[87] Wylie, *Emergence of Maoism*, 202.

[88] Qin Xiaoyi, ed., *Zongtong Jiang gong dashi changbian chugao* [First draft of President Jiang's major events chronology] (Taibei: Caituan faren zhongzheng wenjiao jijinhui, 1978), 323.

[89] Gao Sulan, ed., *Jiang Zhongzheng zongtong dang'an: Shilüe gaoben* [Archives of President Chiang Kai-shek: Draft chronology], (Taipei: Guoshiguan, 2003), vol. 53, 497, 498 (May 24 and 25, 1943), (hereafter cited as *SLGB*).

[90] Xiong Xianghui, *Dixia shi'er nian yu Zhou Enlai* [Twelve years underground with Zhou Enlai] (Beijing: Zhonggong zhongyang dangxiao chubanshe, 1991), 22. See also Yang

Chiang's original plan in February, this telegram indicated a change from attacking the edges of the border regions to directly attacking Yan'an, thanks to the "good opportunity" provided by an ally that Chiang never liked.[91]

Though Chiang Kai-shek miscalculated the impact of the Comintern's dissolution on the Communists, the news triggered his ambition to attack Yan'an. However, Chiang did not leave any detailed record of his plan in his diaries, except in a passing sentence on June 17, when he telegraphed Hu Zongnan asking for an update on preparations for the attack on the border regions.[92] The next day, Hu held a military conference and decided to position the Thirty-Seventh and Thirty-Eighth regiments to invade the border regions from the west and the south, respectively.[93] However, this plan was never put in motion, because the Nationalists had other concerns at the same time and the CCP utilized its intelligence and propaganda power to put the civil war on hold.

A major factor distracting the Nationalists was the Gannan Incident. Southern Gansu was a multiethnic region with a historical record of uprisings. Since the spring of 1942, a multiethnic peasant force of 50,000 to 60,000 people had been mobilized in southern Gansu under the slogan "Gansu people ruling Gansu; oppose conscription and the grain levy; kill all southern bandits."[94] Tang Zong, a Nationalist intelligence official, confessed that the Gansu crowds were not bandits but protesters, who were pushed to rebel against the grain levy because of a severe drought that year.[95] The chaos got worse in April 1943, when troops sent by Hu Zongnan and Zhu Shaoliang, a Guomindang general in Gansu, failed to put down the uprising.[96] Chiang Kai-shek showed extreme concern over this

---

Zhesheng, *Hu Zongnan zhege ren* [This person called Hu Zongnan] (Shanghai: Shanghai renmin chubanshe, 1996), 252.

[91] Yang Zhesheng, *Zai Hu Zongnan shenbian de shi'er nian*, 193.

[92] *SLGB* 53:634 (June 17, 1943).

[93] Yang Zhesheng, *Hu Zongnan zhege ren*, 253.

[94] Hu Zongnan shangjiang nianpu bianzuan weiyuanhui, ed., *Hu Shangjiang Zongnan nianpu* [General Hu Zongnan's chronology] (Taibei: Wenhai chubanshe, 1978), 118–21.

[95] Tang Zong, *Tang Zong shiluo zai dalu de riji*, 320.

[96] Hu Zongnan shangjiang nianpu bianzuan weiyuanhui, *Hu Shangjiang Zongnan nianpu*, 119.

situation, sending two consecutive telegraphs to Zhu on April 25 and 26, emphasizing the absolute necessity to suppress the uprising.[97]

In response to Chiang's orders, Hu sent the Thirty-Seventh regiment to help Zhu's troops. Starting on June 5, battles lasted forty days until July 15, during which there were eleven major confrontations, and Nationalist forces killed 14,000 peasants, arrested 18,000, disbanded 20,000, and captured 3,000 horses.[98] Though the peasant uprising failed, it interrupted Hu's plan to attack Yan'an, because it went on longer than expected and Hu's Thirty-Seventh regiment could not participate in two battles simultaneously. Hu had to withdraw part of the Thirty-Fourth regiment from the anti-Japanese front line to join the Yan'an invasion.[99] Hu disliked being labeled as only anti-Communist and not anti-Japanese, but now he had to ignore the Japanese to deal with the Communists. Hu sent very few troops in advance, and most stayed in defense until two days before the planned attack date of July 9.[100]

On the Communist side, Mao did not believe a civil war was imminent. In a telegram of June 1, Mao said he expected that the anti-Japanese war would go on for three more years, during which the Communists should avoid military conflicts with the Nationalists, so as to let them focus on the Japanese. At the Politburo conference on June 16, Mao speculated that the Guomindang was weak internally and did not have the energy to launch a large-scale attack on the Communists. The following day, Mao half-jokingly said, "[Even if] Hu Zongnan's troops surround the Shaan-Gan-Ning border region, he is doing nothing more than selling two baskets of eggs. If we throw two stones at him, everything will be smashed."[101]

However, the joke turned more real on the night of July 3, when Yan'an received a telegram from Xiong Xianghui via the Eighth Route Army's office in Xi'an detailing Hu Zongnan's military plan and scheduled date of

[97] *SLGB* 53:283, 287.
[98] Hu Zongnan shangjiang nianpu bianzuan weiyuanhui, *Hu Shangjiang Zongnan nianpu*, 119, 121.
[99] Yang Zhesheng, *Hu Zongnan zhege ren*, 253.
[100] Yang Zhesheng, *Zai Hu Zongnan shenbian de shi'er nian*, 200.
[101] Pang Xianzhi, *Mao Zedong nianpu*, 443, 446, 447 (June 1, 16, 17, 1943).

attack.[102] Xiong was a Communist agent who had worked as an intelligence secretary for Hu since 1939.[103] Thanks to Xiong, all the Nationalist military moves were exposed to the Communists, who gained a decisive advantage in the intelligence war. With this advantage, the Communists earned a few days to change the course of a potential civil war.

The Communists initiated a propaganda war by warning the Guomindang of a potential civil war and by informing Britain, the United States, and the Soviet Union, who would not tolerate a civil war before the defeat of Japan.[104] Mao proposed that only by revealing Chiang Kai-shek's military plans to a domestic and international audience could he demonstrate that the CCP was not exaggerating the Nationalist threat.[105] On July 4, Zhu De, the commander in chief of the Red Army, telegraphed Hu: "It is generally said that the Central Government plans to utilize the opportunity offered by the dissolution of the Comintern to attack the Communists. ... There is danger that civil war may break out at any time. ... At a time when our war against Japan is at a difficult stage, everything should be done to maintain unity. National unity and national resistance would suffer irreparable harm from a civil war which will benefit only Japan."[106] The telegram directly quoted what Xiong Xianghui reported to Yan'an and completely shocked Hu Zongnan, who asked Xiong, "Who leaked out the news? Should we continue the attack plan?" Xiong was prepared for the question, as he answered, "Maybe we have been infiltrated by Communist spies. You should assign someone to investigate everyone who knew the secret, including me." Hu followed the suggestion, but he trusted Xiong too much to suspect him. Because of Zhu De's telegram, Hu had to drop the original plan. Otherwise, the Japanese would attack the weakened Na-

[102] Xiong Xianghui, *Wo de qingbao yu waijiao shengya*, 15.

[103] Yang Zhesheng, *Hu Zongnan zhege ren*, 185.

[104] Fan Shuo, *Ye Jianying zhuan* [Biography of Ye Jianying] (Beijing: Dangdai zhongguo chubanshe, 1995), 187.

[105] Yang Di, *KangRi zhanzheng zai zongcanmoubu: Yiwei zuozhan canmou de lishi huimou* [Anti-Japanese war at the headquarters: A general's historical review] (Beijing: Jiefangjun chubanshe, 2003), 184.

[106] Zhongyang dang'anguan, *Zhonggong zhongyang wenjian xuanji*, vol. 14, 68 (July 4, 1943), translation from *Foreign Relations of the United States: Diplomatic Papers, China 1942–1943* (Washington, DC: U.S. Government Printing Office, 1956), 278.

tionalist position and the Allies would condemn the Guomindang, just as the CCP expected, for fighting the Communists rather than Japan.[107]

International allies also received information regarding the tense Nationalist-CCP situation, but neither the American nor British officers in Chongqing believed that the Guomindang military threat would turn into an actual conflict.[108] Only the Soviet embassy expressed concern and was eager to exchange views with the other two allies before declaring that its military assistance was for "furthering the national liberation struggle of the Chinese people and not for unleashing a civil war."[109] Chiang would not sacrifice foreign aid for a civil war and ultimately decided that open conflict with the CCP had to be postponed until after the war against Japan. Thus, on July 7, Chiang approved Hu Zongnan's suggestion to withdraw, but he asked Hu to investigate if spies had leaked military secrets. Starting on July 8, Hu Zongnan withdrew his troops.[110]

On July 9, Yan'an gathered 30,000 people for a public meeting, which was ostensibly in commemoration of the sixth anniversary of the anti-Japanese war but was more importantly a demonstration against civil war. As Vladimirov wrote, "All this demonstration of good will which was meant for Chungking [Chongqing] was playacted seriously and conscientiously."[111] People in Yan'an were divided about the nature of this potential Guomindang attack: some believed that it was the start of a civil war, while some thought the opposite was true. Xiao Jun, a left-wing author from Northeast China, reflected in his diary that this periodic military threat from the Nationalists was weaker each time, but the Communists should propagate it in order to stop the conflict through domestic and international media.[112]

---

[107] Yang Zhesheng, *Hu Zongnan zhege ren*, 256–57.

[108] *Foreign Relations of the United States*, 279; Kenneth Bourne, *British Documents on Foreign Affairs: Reports and Papers from the Foreign Office Confidential Print* (Frederick, MD: University Publications of America, 1983), vol. 7, 22.

[109] Vladimirov, *Vladimirov Diaries*, 129.

[110] Yang Zhesheng, *Hu Zongnan zhege ren*, 257. The withdrawal of Nationalist troops at this time does not mean that Chiang had no intention to attack the Communists in the future. In his diary entry of August 13, 1943, Chiang felt he had to defeat the Communists before the end of war in Europe. But any Nationalist military threat after July 15, 1943, is no longer relevant to the inception of the Rescue Campaign, and thus not included in this chapter.

[111] Vladimirov, *Vladimirov Diaries*, 129.

[112] Xiao Jun, *Yan'an riji* [Yan'an's diaries] (Hong Kong: Oxford University Press, 2013), 176.

Besides the anti-Nationalist propaganda, a different agenda was taking shape. On July 11, the General Study Commission issued a notice, "Mass Education on Anti–Civil War and Protecting the Border Regions in Yan'an." It clarified the education campaign's goals as "mobilizing and educating the masses, actively fighting against the civil war and protecting border regions, and continuing counterespionage." Although the last goal seemed out of place, according to the notice, "The education of cadres and the masses must go hand in hand with cadre screening and the Confession Campaign. [We should] take the opportunity of the imminent Guomindang attack to strengthen the counterespionage struggle."[113] For the first time the Communists confirmed the connection between the Nationalist threat and Communist internal spy hunting. This July 11 notice was a harbinger of the Rescue Campaign that officially started four days later. At this point, even though the Nationalist threat was no longer real, the Communists still acted as if it was real in order to launch their own ideological campaign. At the Politburo meeting on July 13, Mao echoed the notice by listing widespread spy hunting and counterespionage education as one of five tasks in response to the Nationalist threat.[114] Consequently, prior to Kang Sheng's speech on July 15, Yan'an was already primed for an intensive spy-hunting campaign.

RESCUING THOSE WHO HAVE LOST THEIR FOOTING

> Today's meeting comes at a time of emergency, a time of military mobilization … when the Guomindang … is tightly enveloping our southern front and awaiting the order to attack.
>
> —Kang Sheng, "Rescuing Those Who Have Lost Their Footing," July 15, 1943[115]

The sun was shining on July 15, 1943, in Yan'an, though for people who heard Kang Sheng's report, it was remembered as a gloomy day.[116] At the

---

[113] Zhongyang dang'anguan, *Zhonggong zhongyang wenjian xuanji*, vol. 14, 74–75 (July 11, 1943).

[114] Pang Xianzhi, *Mao Zedong nianpu*, 456 (July 13, 1943).

[115] Kang Sheng, "Qiangjiu shizuzhe," 380, translation from Byron, *Claws of the Dragon*, 179.

[116] Xie Juezai, *Xie Juezai riji* [Diaries of Xie Juezai] (Beijing: Renmin chubanshe, 1984),

Central Auditorium where the meeting was held, above the front stage hung a banner that read "Mobilization meeting to rescue those who have lost their footing." Along the side walls were slogans often seen in prisons, such as, "Tell the truth and you will receive a lighter sentence. Refuse to acknowledge your crime and you will receive severe punishment!"[117] More than a thousand people filled the auditorium, but they were too nervous even to greet those they knew.[118]

Peng Zhen, Mao's close ally in the General Study Committee and vice president of the Central Party School, opened the meeting. He first described the Nationalist military threat as if it were still imminent, and the fact that a large number of "Guomindang spies" had been exposed and arrested. He then said, "The special department cannot catch all the agents teeming in Yan'an. That is why the department has appealed to Communist cadres and members for help in this matter of great importance."[119] In contrast to the Soviet secret purge, which was implemented almost entirely by the security bureau, in the Rescue Campaign the mobilized masses became responsible for counterespionage.

After the opening remarks, a group of twelve "spies" went on stage one by one, confessing how they infiltrated Yan'an and committed various crimes. As the best-known spy, Zhang Keqin came out again to introduce the Nationalist red flag policy. Though he had confessed many times on different occasions, Zhang's example was still effective. Another model spy was Xu Manli, a female student at Suide Normal School, who condemned the Nationalists for forcing her to enter into sexual relationships to gain access to intelligence.[120]

Kang Sheng's report, "Rescuing Those Who Have Lost Their Footing," took the bulk of the meeting. He started by declaring that it was "a time of emergency, a time of military mobilization," and went into great

---

512. Zhu Hongzhao, *Yan'an richang shenghuo zhong de lishi, 1937–1947* [History of daily life in Yan'an] (Guilin: Guangxi shifan daxue chubanshe, 2007), 185.

[117] Lin Qingshan, *Kang Sheng zhuan: Yige yinmoujia de faji shi* [Biography of Kang Sheng: History of an intriguer] (Changchun: Jilin renmin chubanshe, 1996), 100.

[118] Zhu Hongzhao, *Yan'an richang shenghuo zhong de lishi*, 155.

[119] Vladimirov, *Vladimirov Diaries*, 130. The special department he referred to was the Social Affairs Department under Kang Sheng.

[120] Zhu Hongzhao, *Yan'an richang shenghuo zhong de lishi*, 156.

detail listing all the participating Nationalist troops.[121] However, the Guomindang troops had withdrawn on July 8, and both Chiang Kai-shek and Hu Zongnan had informed Yan'an on July 11, several days before Kang Sheng's report. As head of the Communist intelligence apparatus, Kang would have known better than anyone else that the Nationalist military threat was no longer imminent. Thus, it appears that he intentionally exaggerated the situation by using the potential civil war as a convenient excuse for spy hunting. In order to capitalize as much as possible on the military conflict, he said,

"Now the troops and people in border regions are all mobilized. Consequently, our Yan'an bureaus and schools should intensify cadre screening, consolidate [party] organizations, and purge spies. These are our current missions that cannot be postponed."[122]

The message was clear to the audience: correlated with the Guomindang threat, this rescue campaign was an opportunity for self-incrimination.[123] After associating the Nationalist military threat with spy hunting, Kang Sheng reviewed his accomplishments over the past three months, during which 450 people had confessed to being spies.[124] It was not clear if these people were all arrested in early April or if they had all been forced to confess. Nevertheless, they were all considered "youth who had lost their footing," a term Kang had never explicitly defined. The term generally refers to people who have made serious mistakes, but here it specifically indicated people who were Nationalist or Japanese spies who had confessed and were waiting to be rescued. Kang exhorted every cadre and party member to search for people who had lost their footing, yet did not give a concrete standard for identifying these people. Consequently, anyone and everyone could be accused of being a spy with no evidence at all. Once someone was charged as a spy, others had the responsibility to save him or her, but not to openly raise doubts about the accusation or sympathize with the charged spy.

Kang Sheng differentiated the Nationalist spy policy from the Com-

---

[121] Kang Sheng, "Qiangjiu shizuzhe," 380.

[122] Ibid., 380.

[123] Xiao Jun, *Yan'an riji*, 179.

[124] Kang Sheng, "Qiangjiu shizuzhe," 380.

munists' lenient policy toward confessed spies. He named several Guo-
mindang spies, none of whom was later found guilty. He also charged
Wang Shiwei, an intellectual who had been imprisoned for writing criticisms of party cadres, as a triple agent for Trotsky, the Nationalists, and
Japan.[125] Kang further described the Guomindang's nature not as anti-
Japanese but anti-Communist, portraying Chiang Kai-shek not as one of
the four Allied leaders but one of the four fascist leaders. He interpreted
Chiang's version of the Three People's Principles as contrary to Sun Yat-
sen's and described colonial and feudal fascism as the core of Hitler and
the cover of Sun Yat-sen. Kang based his argument on Chiang's book
China's Destiny (see chapter 6) and summarized it as a book of theories for
traitors ghostwritten by Tao Xisheng.[126] Kang spent half of his 20,000-
word speech trying to persuade those working as Nationalist agents to
side with the Communists and abandon any illusions they might hold
about the Guomindang, Chiang Kai-shek, and his version of the Three
People's Principles. However, based on participants' memoirs, no one recalled what Kang Sheng actually criticized about *China's Destiny*, while
everyone remembered the intimidating, if not terrorizing, effect he created. As Vladimirov described, "An oppressive silence descended on the
hall and the visibly frightened audience. People suddenly became aware of
what unlimited power the intelligence office chief wielded and what
would become of anyone who dared to raise his voice in defense of
truth."[127] Just like *China's Destiny*, Kang Sheng's report was later published
as a pamphlet and distributed to each unit for study, one copy per cadre.

By the end of Kang's speech, he played the role of an iron bodhisattva:
on the one hand, he encouraged people to confess actively, as if it was their
last chance; on the other hand, he warned those who would not confess
that repression would follow. He concluded with a couplet: "Pull back
before it is too late, being repentant is to be saved; drop the butcher's knife
and become a Buddha immediately."[128] It sounded like he was speaking to

---

[125] Kang Sheng, "Qiangjiu shizuzhe," 381. For books on Wang Shiwei, see Dai, *Wang Shiwei and "Wild Lilies."*
[126] Kang Sheng, "Qiangjiu shizuzhe," 38183.
[127] Vladimirov, *Vladimirov Diaries*, 130.
[128] Kang Sheng, "Qiangjiu shizuzhe," 384.

a group of prisoners who were already charged with being spies but had not yet confessed. Afterward, the audience instinctively applauded for a long time, though they felt terrified. When Peng Zhen was about to close the meeting, Zhu De unexpectedly went onstage and asked Kang Sheng in a calm tone of voice, "Do you mean to say that after this meeting I should lose faith in my friends and comrades-in-arms? Does this mean that from now on I should live in fear of arrest or expect to see my friends arrested? How dare you treat the party activists in this way, the best men of the party and its backbone?"[129] As a member of the Politburo, Zhu held the most power in terms of military rank, but Kang Sheng's spy-hunting campaign seemed strange to him. Zhu was brave enough to raise objections, but he did not get answers right away. Peng Zhen ended the meeting, and the attendees dispersed in silence. The afternoon meeting had lasted until after sunset.[130]

Kang Sheng's report initiated the Rescue Campaign and sparked a series of rescue meetings for the purpose of spy hunting at schools, military, administrative, and party units in and outside of Yan'an. At first, both party cadres and ordinary members genuinely believed that secret agents had infiltrated the Communist lines and it was necessary to use cadre screening to get rid of any potential spies. As a party veteran, Xie Juezai acknowledged that coming from a nonproletarian background, he had little experience with proletariat struggles and therefore learned class struggle from this counterespionage campaign. He felt more sympathy than hatred toward those youth who lacked experience and proletarian background and had therefore lost their footing.[131]

Besides wholeheartedly following party indoctrination, competition existed among cadres in different units to report the most spies and surpass the expected quota.[132] Kang Sheng certainly contributed to such competition, and he even set up an incredibly high quota for hunting spies:

---

[129] Vladimirov, *Vladimirov Diaries*, 131. See also Zhu, *Yan'an richang shenghuo zhong de lishi*, 184.

[130] Shi Lan, *Wo yu Shu Tong sishi nian* [My forty years with Shu Tong] (Xi'an: Shaanxi renmin chubanshe, 1997), 94.

[131] Xie Juezai, *Xie Juezai riji*, 521.

[132] Zhu Hongzhao, *Yan'an richang shenghuo zhong de lishi*, 189.

"Seventy to eighty percent of party members and cadres in Yan'an are politically unreliable. They are made up of all sorts of spies, traitors and bad elements! Each unit should follow this quota to rescue those who have lost their footing! Whoever cannot reach that quota is either apathetic or has some problem himself."[133] As a result, cadres were not only persuaded to actively engage in spy hunting but also warned against falling behind. If they were not active enough, they would be questioned.

As the number of accused spies accumulated, the campaign went awry rather quickly. Though Mao decided to cut back the rescue meetings from ten days to three, the Rescue Campaign continued anyway.[134] Li Weihan recalled that after the first meeting for confession and the second meeting for persuasion, the third meeting for accusation became so intense that if someone had suggested the death penalty, people would have supported it.[135] One of the suspects, He Fang, reflected on his changing opinion about the Rescue Campaign: Initially, I believed it was real, assuming that the Party must be correct and must have evidence against those suspects. When it came to rescuing myself, I still half-believed and half-doubted, thinking there must be a misunderstanding. Later when I looked around, seeing more and more people who had become crestfallen, I was convinced that the Rescue Campaign was nonsense.[136]

Within ten days after July 15, the number of suspects surpassed the total number of those accused within the past few months, and by the end

---

[133] Zhong Kan, *Kang Sheng pingzhuan* [Biography of Kang Sheng] (Beijing: Hongqi chubanshe, 1982), 90.

[134] Chen Yung-fa, "Yan'an de zhengfeng, shengan yu sufan" [Yan'an's rectification, cadre screening and suppression], in Zhongyang yanjiuyuan jindaishi yanjiusuo, *Kangzhan jianguo shi yantaohui lunwenji, 1937–1945* (Taibei: Zhongyang yanjiuyuan jindaishi yanjiusuo, 1985), vol. 2, 782–83.

[135] Li Weihan, *Huiyi yu yanjiu* [Memory and analysis] (Beijing: Zhonggong dangshi ziliao chubanshe, 1986), vol. 2, 512.

[136] He Fang, *Cong yan'an yilu zoulai de fansi: He Fang zishu* [Reflection of the way from Yan'an: He Fang's narrative] (Hong Kong: Mingbao chubanshe, 2007), vol. 1, 112–13.

of July, over 1,400 people were charged as spies.[137] Within 1943, the number of "spies" reached 15,000 out of 40,000 cadres and students in the border regions.[138] Most came from Nationalist-controlled areas, were former underground Communist members, had been arrested by the Guomindang, or were intellectuals.[139]

When the number of spies became the only thing that mattered, it was no longer important who the accused were and whether they were real spies. Anti-Japanese Military and Politics University invented "photo taking" as one way to expose spies en masse. During a meeting, a group of people would be asked to stand on stage and let others "take photos" by looking at them. If people on stage did not change their facial expressions, they would be fine; if their facial expressions changed, they would become suspects.[140]

During the Rescue Campaign, forced confession along with torture was almost inevitable. In order to be saved, suspects came up with creative reasons for being Nationalist spies. Sometimes a group of inmates would collude by assigning roles to each person. After one confessed, the others would verify the same plot in their own confessions to make it convincing.[141] Sometimes even without coercion, people would confess at public meetings. *Liberation Daily* covered a rescue meeting at Suide Normal School in northern Shaanxi, far from Yan'an, in which all the students were teenagers. By the end of a nine-day meeting, 230 students, 73 percent of the school, had confessed to being spies, including girls who described themselves as "sex spies," and a boy who claimed that he used a bag of stones as a murder weapon.[142]

Why would people confess things that they had never done? Partly

[137] Hua Shijun, *Yan'an zhengfeng shimo*, 68.

[138] Gao Putang and Zeng Luping, *Yan'an qiangjiu yundong shimo*, 105.

[139] Gao Xinmin, *Yan'an zhengfeng shilu* [A record of Yan'an rectification] (Hangzhou: Zhejiang renmin chubanshe, 2000), 374.

[140] Xu Xiangqian, *Lishi de huigu* [Review of history] (Beijing: Xinhua shudian, 1984), 462.

[141] Shi Zhe, *Zai lishi juren shenbian*, 252.

[142] Suide shifan shizu qingnian huiguo [Regrets from youth who have lost footing at Suide Normal School], *Liberation Daily*, September 21, 1943. Author unidentified.

because of material benefits after confession: no matter whether the confession was true or not, one could move to a warmer room with a comfortable bed, have a nice meal (usually noodles), and receive congratulations and a red paper flower signifying rebirth.[143] Concrete rewards were particularly appealing to young students: a fourteen-year-old boy said he confessed to being a spy because he wanted to eat noodles. When asked what spies were, he said, "some ate pancakes, and some ate noodles."[144] Thus, paradoxically, those "spies" who cheated in confession were honored and well treated, whereas those who remained honest were distrusted and tortured.

For better-educated intellectuals, it was not practical concerns but psychological terror and isolation that forced them to write their confessions. After her husband was taken from home in the middle of the night, He Xiang was left with her daughter and was forced to write a confession about her "spy" husband. She was terrified that her husband would be killed and her daughter left an orphan. She felt extreme isolation living in a cave on the top of a hill, especially during freezing winter nights with the sounds of wolves howling in the wild.[145] The writer Liu Baiyu was not accused of being a spy during public meetings, but he still needed to write an autobiography to clear himself. After his work was rejected four times, his fifth autobiography was approved and he was asked to talk with a cadre. Feeling anxious, Liu was already in tears when welcomed by the smiling cadre.[146]

Within a short period, the Rescue Campaign achieved what the Nationalists had failed to do: make everyone feel insecure and suspicious of each other until their spy charges were cleared.[147] Through forced confessions, youths and intellectuals in Yan'an created policies that Guomindang

[143] Shi Zhe, *Feng yu gu*, 14, 243.

[144] Xiu Lairong, *Chen Long zhuan*, 148.

[145] He Xiang, in Yan'an Zhongguo Nüzi Daxue Beijing xiaoyouhui, *Yanshui qing: Jinian Yan'an Zhongguo Nüzi Daxue chengli liushi zhounian* [Feeling of Yan'an's water: Commemoration of sixty years anniversary of Chinese Women College] (Beijing: Zhongguo funü chubanshe, 1999), 449–52.

[146] Liu Baiyu, "Xinling de licheng" [Journey of the soul], in *Liu Baiyu wenji* [Collected essays of Liu Baiyu] (Beijing: Huayi chubanshe, 1995), vol. 9, 372–82.

[147] Wang Ruowang, *Wang Ruowang zizhuan* [Autobiography of Wang Ruowang] (Taibei: Xingguang chubanshe, 1992), vol. 2, 294.

intelligence had never thought of, yet the Communist cadres took serious-ly.[148] The Rescue Campaign was intended to physically and mentally con-trol party members by disconnecting them from the Nationalists, and it was indeed a bitter mockery when a large number of determined CCP members confessed that they were Guomindang spies. The Nationalists never acknowledged these "spies," nor did the Communists feel ashamed of having been so heavily infiltrated, but they celebrated the victory of discovering and rescuing so many "people who had lost their footing."

CONCLUSION

In terms of the counterespionage struggle, we should analyze from two sides. From a positive perspective: 1. Cleared out a group of spies. 2. Dis-covered and cultivated a group of capable cadres. 3. Broke bureaucratism and improved working efficiency. 4. Exposed many people's mistakes (such as corruption). 5. Deepened class education. From a negative per-spective: 1. Exaggerated agent organizations and assumed spies were as thick as weeds. 2. In some departments and some places the masses were terrified. 3. Some departments were taken advantage of and obstructed by spies. 4. Widespread suspicion of new intellectuals. 5. Disregarded the united front, as many cadres lowered their opinions of it.

—The CCP Central Secretariat's meeting on the
counterespionage struggle, December 22, 1943[149]

It was easier to start the Rescue Campaign than to stop it from getting out of control. In the official narrative, Mao reined in the campaign before it caused too much damage. As early as July 1, 1943, Mao asked Kang Sheng to publish the right and wrong ways of counterespionage, in which Mao warned against "applying torture, extracting a confession and believ-ing it."[150] In other words, before Kang Sheng's report on July 15, Mao had

---

[148] Wei Junyi, *Si tong lu* [Record of thinking about pains] (Beijing: Beijing shiyue wenyi chubanshe, 1998), 13.

[149] Pang Xianzhi, *Mao Zedong nianpu*, 487 (December 22, 1943). The evaluation was proposed by Kang Sheng and approved by Mao. See also Hu, *Hu Qiaomu huiyi Mao Zedong*, 278–79.

[150] Pang Xianzhi, *Mao Zedong nianpu*, 448 (July 1, 1943).

expected that the campaign might go wrong, and torture and forced confessions might be unavoidable.

Mao's warning proved ineffective. When the same lines appeared again on August 15, 1943, in the CCP Central Committee's "Decision on the Screening of Cadres," it was meant to bring the campaign to a halt, but instead the campaign further evolved into a widespread, massive antisubversion movement throughout the border regions.[151] The decision confirmed the necessity of spy hunting: "The fact that there are large numbers of espionage agents is nothing to be surprised about."[152] With this assumption, the campaign had to continue. The decision was consistent with the Communists' lenient policy toward treatment of suspects: The only way to avoid error is to arrest and kill as few people as possible. For when the suspected are kept alive there is the opportunity to vindicate the innocent and rehabilitate the wrongly persecuted. To arrest and kill as many people as possible can definitely cause irretrievable mistakes.[153]

A minimal number of killings differentiates the Rescue Campaign from the Soviet Great Purge, but it remains unclear how many people were killed or committed suicide: estimates range from three to one hundred.[154] The problem with this policy was that by relying on ex post facto vindication and rehabilitation, cadres did not worry about arresting too many suspects at first, believing that mistakes could be corrected later. In July and October, Mao twice emphasized the principle: "arrest few, kill no one," but many arrests and killings occurred beyond his reach.[155]

On December 22, 1943, the CCP Central Secretariat held a meeting on the counterespionage struggle, which signaled the concluding stage of spy hunting. As the meeting pointed out, "From being apathetic to spies to having spies as thick as weeds, now is time to evaluate right and wrong."[156] The meeting consisted mainly of Kang Sheng's report on the

---

[151] Zhongyang dang'anguan, *Zhonggong zhongyang wenjian xuanji*, 89–90 (August 15, 1943).

[152] Ibid., 89, translation in Kuo, *Analytical History of the Chinese Communist Party*, 488.

[153] Zhongyang dang'anguan, *Zhonggong zhongyang wenjian xuanji*, 94, translation in Kuo, *Analytical History of the Chinese Communist Party*, 493–94.

[154] Apter and Saich, *Revolutionary Discourse in Mao's Republic*, 363 n. 20.

[155] Pang Xianzhi, *Mao Zedong nianpu*, 460, 475 (end of July, and October 9, 1943).

[156] Ibid., 487 (December 22, 1943).

counterespionage struggle, in which he presented a seemingly impartial view of the campaign.[157] During the discussions afterward, Ren Bishi delivered a speech that almost totally contradicted Kang's ambivalent evaluation: According to Zhou Enlai, by 1943 the Guomindang had over a million Party members, including 30,000 student members, who joined after 1940. The Guomindang would never send 30,000 student party members to Yan'an, not to mention that intellectuals in Yan'an mostly arrived in 1937 and 1938. ... 80 to 90 percent of intellectuals who came to Yan'an after the War of Resistance were good-willed, and they came for revolution. The view that 80 percent of new intellectuals are spies should be denied.[158]

Later, a more critical evaluation of the Rescue Campaign came from Jiang Nanxiang, a leader of the anti-Japanese December 9 Movement of 1935, who worked at the Central Youth Committee. In March 1945, he wrote a letter to Liu Shaoqi titled "Opinions on the Rescue Campaign," reflecting his experience as a cadre.[159] He first acknowledged his mistake in forcing people to confess without considering whether his view was correct.[160] He believed that the Rescue Campaign, in his unit at least, certainly failed to result in positive effects but instead caused severe harm: Comrades were not more unified, but more divided. Under the intense atmosphere, party members' relations were not brought closer, but pushed farther apart. Our work enthusiasm and efficiency were not increased, but withered.[161]

Jiang spoke directly against Kang Sheng's report at Northwest Bureau High Cadre Meeting on March 29, 1944, which had basically repeated his ambivalent view from December 1943.[162] Jiang argued that as a completely failed campaign, "It was absolutely (I dare to say absolutely!) wrong to be self-deceiving and claim more achievements than pitfalls."[163] The achieve-

---

[157] Ibid.

[158] Hu Qiaomu, *Hu Qiaomu huiyi Mao Zedong*, 279.

[159] Gao Putang and Zeng, *Yan'an qiangjiu yundong shimo*, 406–25.

[160] Jiang Nanxiang, "Guanyu qiangjiu yundong de yijianshu" [Opinions on the Rescue Campaign], *Zhonggong dangshi yanjiu* 4 (1988): 64.

[161] Ibid., 65.

[162] Kuo, *Analytical History of the Chinese Communist Party*, 412–23.

[163] Jiang Nanxiang, "Guanyu qiangjiu yundong de yijianshu," 66.

ment of discovering so many "spies" came at a cost. He used war as an analogy: The mobilized and armed soldiers were looking for enemies, which were very few and under cover, making it inevitable to find wrong targets and fight among comrades. During this blind battle, a few enemies might be hit by accident, but more often we hurt ourselves.[164]

For Jiang, the cost of the Rescue Campaign was not only friendly fire, but also wasting almost two years doing nothing but cadre screening, spy hunting, and breaking down party members' revolutionary enthusiasm. Considering the historical context of the Rescue Campaign, although the Guomindang did not open fire on Yan'an, the Communists launched a war among themselves.

If there were any positive consequences of the Rescue Campaign, they were unanticipated. Apter and Saich argue that the campaign led Red Army soldiers and cadres from poor peasant backgrounds, who were less affected, to feel more sympathy for the intellectuals, thus diminishing their resentment of the intellectuals while gaining more confidence in their own class backgrounds.[165] But how did the party survive the Rescue Campaign and win over most intellectuals' hearts again after 1943? Many memoirs have answered that Mao's sincere apologies were key. Between 1944 and 1945, Mao publicly apologized on several occasions and took responsibility for all the mistakes in the Rescue Campaign.[166] Thus, wrongly accused spies felt relieved and moved on, and Mao gained even more trust among the Communists, though he was probably behind the spy hunt.

In conclusion, during the Yan'an Rectification Campaign, cadre screenings and spy hunting eventually culminated in the Rescue Campaign, which represented a shift from persuasive education to coercive confession. It was a brief yet terrifying episode for the purpose of counterespionage, though in retrospect it was more of a witch hunt. The campaign was partly triggered by the infiltrations of actual Nationalist agents, as well as

---

[164] Ibid., 66–67.

[165] Apter and Saich, *Revolutionary Discourse in Mao's Republic*, 167, 171, 177.

[166] Hu Qiaomu, *Hu Qiaomu huiyi Mao Zedong*, 280–81. See also Li Yimin, *Li Yimin huiyilu*, 118–19; and Shi Zhe, *Zai lishi juren shenbian*, 259.

the Guomindang military threat. However, the Communists overestimated the number of potential agents and intentionally exaggerated the civil war crisis, resulting in many more spies than the Nationalists could ever have boasted. It was not the first time that the Communists confused their comrades with enemies and, unfortunately, it was not the last. Lessons from the Rescue Campaign were disregarded until after the Cultural Revolution, when the price was even more costly.

8

Debating Constitutionalism and Democracy

The Constitutional Movement during Late Wartime China, 1943–1944

XIAO CHEN

W hen Robert Payne, a thirty-one-year-old English writer, started to teach his English literature course at National Southwest Associated University (*Guoli xinan lianhe daxue*, hereafter, Lianda) in Kunming in September 1943, he found a common theme planted in his students' minds: "A new, humane China was about to be born, and the intellectual elite was going to play a major part in it."[1] John K. Fairbank, who worked for the U.S. government in China from September 1942 to the end of 1943, later mentioned in his memoir that from late 1943, Chiang Kai-shek and the National Government began to lose Chinese intellectuals' trust and loyalty.[2] Several months later, in July 1944, the U.S. ambassador

---

[1] Interview of Robert Payne by John Israel, cited in John Israel, *Lianda: A Chinese University in War and Revolution* (Stanford, CA: Stanford University Press, 1998), 333.

[2] John K. Fairbank, *Chinabound: A Fifty Year Memoir* (New York: Harper and Row, 1982), 264.

to China, Clarence Gauss, reported that even liberals who a year earlier had staunchly supported Chiang Kai-shek saw "no hope for China under Chiang's leadership."[3]

Curiously, of the three American observers' views on the relationship between Chinese intellectuals and the National Government in 1943, Fairbank's comment seems the most negative. Payne's view, however, reveals hope and confidence. Both Payne and Fairbank had lived in China for a long time and had close connections with intellectual circles in Chongqing and Kunming: Payne was close with numerous professors at Lianda, including the liberal poet and literature scholar Wen Yiduo, while Fairbank had frequent conversations with several leading Chinese intellectuals.[4] The different assessments of Payne and Fairbank were probably more a matter of nuance and perspective than of fact. Fairbank had lived in China before the war and now returned during the most oppressive time for Chinese intellectuals since the war began. Payne, however, had just embarked on a new path in late 1943 and sensed hope among Chinese intellectuals. What exactly had happened during this period in China's domestic politics to affect the mood of Chinese intellectuals? Such questions lead us back to the historical context. What was the "new, humane China" that Payne's students envisioned? And why was hope lost by mid-1944, as Gauss concluded?

In 1943, the war between China and Japan entered its sixth year. The Chinese press was confident about the increasingly favorable international situation: the Allied forces were making strategic victories in both Europe and the Pacific, and the U.S. and U.K. governments had abolished the unequal treaties with China and offered increasing amounts of military

---

[3] *Foreign Relations of the United States: Diplomatic Papers, 1944, China* (Washington, DC: Government Printing Office, 1957), 492, cited in Lloyd Eastman, ed., *The Nationalist Era in China, 1927–1949* (Cambridge: Cambridge University Press, 2001), 176.

[4] The connotations of the term "intellectual" (*zhishi fenzi*) in the context of twentieth-century China are subtle and may cause confusion. In this chapter, I largely adopt Zuo Shunsheng (左舜生)'s contemporary definition of intellectuals, articulated in an article published in 1944. His definition was threefold: first, intellectuals have concerns and aspirations in Chinese politics; second, intellectuals understand China's past and present and have knowledge about the world; third, intellectuals are not only able to lead the Chinese people but also to instruct those in power. Zuo Shunsheng, "Tan shishi xianzheng de xianjue tiaojian" [Prerequisites of constitutionalism], *Xianzheng yuekan* 2 (1944): 5.

and financial aid. The domestic situation, however, was less hopeful: the Nationalist armies were making little progress in battles with Japan,[5] but were involved in more clashes with the Chinese Communist Party (CCP); the high rate of inflation in the cities had exhausted the professional class, and widespread corruption had infuriated the people as well (see chapter 9). Growing criticism in the Western press of the Nationalist Party (Guomindang) and the National Government was beginning to tax Chiang Kai-shek's patience.[6]

For those still attentive to domestic politics in spite of the oppressive political environment after the armed clash between the Nationalist and Communist armies in the New Fourth Army Incident of January 1941,[7] one piece of positive news was the Nationalist Party's renewed promotion of constitutionalism. In September 1943, at the fifth plenum of the eleventh Central Executive Committee of the Nationalist Party, Chiang Kai-shek declared that the National Assembly (*guomin dahui*) should be convoked within one year after the war. A few weeks later, an official advisory institution called the Commission for the Inauguration of Constitutionalism (*xianzheng shishi xiejinhui*, hereafter referred to as the commission) was established. The main purposes of this institution were to advise on constitutional matters, including amending the Draft Constitution of 1936 (*xiancao*)[8] and preparations for the establishment of local self-governments

---

[5] Theodore White mentioned that that the so-called great victories in western Hubei province in 1943 were merely "testaments of disillusion and despair." See Theodore White, *Thunder out of China* (New York: William Sloane, 1947), 139.

[6] Chiang Kai-shek mentioned several times in his diary how he disliked the "libel on China" in the U.S. press. Gao Sulan, ed., *Jiang Zhongzheng zongtong dang'an shilüe gaoben* [Archives of President Chiang Kai-shek: Draft chronology] (Taipei: Guoshiguan, 2011), vol. 54, 88. Hereafter cited as *SLGB*.

[7] The New Fourth Army Incident took place in January 1941 and was the most serious military conflict between the Nationalist and Communist armies during World War II. After the military clash, the National Government imposed stricter censorship on domestic publications.

[8] The Draft Constitution of 1936 was initiated in 1932 under pressure from Sun Ke, the son of Sun Yat-sen and the head of the Legislative Yuan (*lifa yuan*), and was finally published in 1936 for the preparation of constitutionalism. The Draft Constitution featured a strong presidency, in which the president can convoke the National Assembly and the five yuan of the government should be responsible to him. The Draft Constitution also empowered the National Assembly to elect the president and vice president, and the heads of the five yuan. As Zhang Junmai, a key member of the Democratic League and a legal expert, once com-

(*difang zizhi jiguan*).[9] Another important platform was the People's Political Council (*guomin canzhenghui*), a quasi-representative consulting institution for the National Government. Both agencies were mainly staffed by Nationalist Party members, but non-Guomindang members, such as the Democratic League (*minzhu tongmeng*), CCP, and independent political leaders were also included.[10] But prodemocracy intellectuals' activities were not confined to discussions and proposals within these official platforms. After Chiang's talk, newspapers, journals, public speeches, and university wall posters were soon flooded with discussions of constitutional issues and political rights. This wave of discussions on constitutionalism and democracy lasted until late 1944 and has been referred to as the

---

mented, the Draft Constitution of 1936 "provided for a system in which people had few rights and the president was omnipotent." Zhang Junmai, "Baozhang sanxiang jiben quanli" [Guarantee three basic human rights], *Zaisheng zazhi* 94 (1944): 36–42.

[9] Chinese Ministry of Information, ed., *China Handbook, 1937–1945* (New York: Macmillan, 1947), 119. At the central level, the National Assembly (*guomin dahui*), composed of over 2,000 elected representatives from each county, should exercise the four rights on behalf of the people. At the county or city level, the county council (*xian yihui*) or city council (*shi yihui*) should be elected by local residents. During the period of political tutelage prior to the final stage of constitutionalism, the Nationalist Party should help people establish local self-governance, such as a county council or city council. After the establishment of local governance, the National Assembly should be convened and the constitution drafted and introduced, both of which would mark the realization of constitutionalism. Sun Zhongshan, *Sun Zhongshan quanji* [Collected works of Sun Zhongshan] (Beijing: Zhonghua shuju, 1984), vol. 9, 227–28, 325. Neither Sun Yat-sen nor the later National Government provided a time schedule for convening the National Assembly. Under increasing pressure for the end of political tutelage, the fifth plenum of the third Central Executive Committee of the Nationalist Party on February 15, 1937, announced that the National Assembly should be convened in November of that year, but the outbreak of full-scale war between China and Japan in July interrupted this process.

[10] The China Democratic League was established in 1941 as a coalition of several minor political parties and organizations. A member of the Democratic League was first a member of a political organization other than the CCP or the Nationalist Party (Guomindang). The Democratic League was formed as a response to the increasingly severe conflicts between the Guomindang and the CCP. Its main aims were to realize democratic politics and unified national military forces in China. The Democratic League played an important role in mediating tensions between the CCP and the Nationalist Party, especially with regard to the New Fourth Army Incident, which took China to the brink of civil war in 1941. The league's official name was the China Democratic League of Parties and Organizations (*Zhongguo minzhu zhengtuan tongmeng*) until September 1944, when it was reorganized and named the China Democratic League (*Zhongguo minzhu tongmeng*). The purpose of this reorganization was to admit nonparty members. In this chapter I simply use the terms China Democratic League or Democratic League to refer to this organization.

Second Constitutional Movement (*dierci xianzheng yundong*) in CCP historiography.[11] In this chapter, I adopt the term "constitutional movement" to describe these political and social activities related to constitutionalism.

This chapter covers the short but critical period from late 1943 to the end of 1944.[12] Many intellectuals were willing to cooperate with the government to realize constitutionalism at the beginning of the constitutional movement in 1943 and early 1944. Their democratic conceptions and demands, however, were different from the official and leftist Nationalist Party's discourse in the movement. The Nationalist Party activists in the movement, such as Sun Ke (Sun Fo), the head of the Legislative Yuan and son of Sun Yat-sen, stuck closely to Sun Yat-sen's ideology. They believed that the establishment of local self-governments and the convening of the National Assembly were the essence of constitutionalism. The intellectuals emphasized democracy, including the protection of human rights such as freedoms of the press, speech, and body (*shenti de ziyou* or habeas corpus).[13] Intellectuals became disillusioned with the one-party rule of the Nationalist Party when the National Government failed to fulfill their democratic demands and simultaneously suffered a series of military defeats in the Japanese Ichigo campaign of 1944.

This chapter attempts to shed new light on the constitutional movement of 1943–1944 in the following aspects. First, by using newly published sources, I reveal that Chiang Kai-shek announced the constitutional

---

[11] The term was first used by CCP leaders in 1944 to differentiate it from the First Constitutional Movement in the early 1940s. From 1939 to 1941, Chinese intellectuals of minor parties and groups (the Democratic League) and some leftist Guomindang members demanded that the government end political tutelage immediately and convene the National Assembly. This was later called the First Constitutional Movement.

[12] Among existing scholarship, Edmund S.K. Fung and Wen Liming have contributed the most to the topic. Yet both works do not highlight the significance of 1943 in terms of the high expectations of the constitutional movement, and also fail to notice the transformation from confidence to criticism during this critical period. See Edmund S.K. Fung, *In Search of Chinese Democracy* (Cambridge: Cambridge University Press, 2000); Wen Liming, *Di san zhong liliang yu kangzhan shiqi de Zhongguo zhengzhi* [The third force and politics during wartime China] (Shanghai: Shanghai shudian, 2003).

[13] The phrase "freedom of the body" (*shenti de ziyou*) was frequently used in intellectual discourse at the time. It generally means "protection against unlawful imprisionment." I discuss this idea in detail in the following section.

movement mainly to contain the CCP and to gain advantage over it in the press. Second, intellectual discourse on democracy and human rights fundamentally challenged the framework of the constitutional movement conceived by the Nationalist Party. Third, the constitutional movement failed as the Nationalist Party neither achieved its own goal of constitutionalism nor fulfilled intellectuals' demands for human rights. Last but not least, while Chinese intellectuals played pivotal roles in the constitutional movement, this chapter does not aim to produce an intellectual history of intellectual discourse (intrinsic factors) of the time. Instead, it attempts to unpack the complex interactions between the Nationalist Party and intellectuals during the constitutional movement. Unlike most existing studies concentrating on intellectuals' roles in the constitutional movement, I take the role of the state (extrinsic factors) into consideration, showing how the state launched the movement and later responded to intellectuals' democratic demands.

ORIGINS OF THE MOVEMENT

Why did Chiang Kai-shek suddenly announce the postwar constitutional plan in September 1943? Many contemporary Chinese, be they members of the Nationalist Party or not, hardly believed Chiang's promises, even after the movement had progressed for several months. In a series of speeches in early 1944, Sun Ke repeatedly tried to dispel people's doubts that the Nationalist Party was serious about achieving constitutionalism.[14] Around the same time, Zuo Shunsheng, head of the China Youth Party (*Zhongguo qingnian dang*) and chief secretary of the China Democratic League, wrote that many of his friends in Kunming and Guilin were also highly doubtful of the Nationalist Party's commitment to constitutionalism.[15]

These suspicions are understandable since the Nationalist Party had previously failed to live up to expectations on the schedule for constitu-

---

[14] Sun Ke, *Sanmin zhuyi xin Zhongguo* [New China under the three principles of China] (Chongqing: Shangwu Yinshuguan, 1946), 47.

[15] Zuo Shunsheng, "Xianjue tiaojian," *Xianzheng yuekan* 2 (1944): 5.

tionalism. A decision to convoke the National Assembly on November 12, 1940, was made at the fifth plenum of the eleventh Central Executive Committee of the Nationalist Party in 1939. By the end of that year, the Constitutional Promotion Committee (*xianzheng qichenghui*), composed of members of the People's Political Council, was established to advise on the Draft Constitution of 1936. Lei Zhen, who worked in the secretariat of the People's Political Council, mentioned that most members of the council were committed to the discussion of the Draft Constitution. However, in mid-1940, the Nationalist Party abruptly announced that, owing to transportation difficulties and the worsening military situation, the scheduled convocation of the National Assembly was suspended. Disappointment raged among members of the People's Political Council, especially the intellectuals.[16] The political climate became even more depressing after the New Fourth Army Incident. Before the constitutional movement in late 1943, articles on democracy or constitutionalism rarely appeared in major newspapers and journals. From 1941 to early 1944, even college students at Lianda, which enjoyed a reputation as a "democratic fortress," seemed to lack interest in domestic politics: no large gatherings of that nature were organized.[17]

Members of the People's Political Council, the major platform for wartime political participation by intellectuals, were disappointed in the National Government after it refused to convoke the National Assembly and after the New Fourth Army Incident. Chen Qitian, a key figure of the China Youth Party and a member of the People's Political Council, related the extent of concern for constitutionalism within the People's Political Council to the changing political environment. From its establishment in 1938 to the New Fourth Army Incident in 1941, members of the council were highly committed to constitutional issues. After October 1943, Chen claimed, "members of the Council revived their interests in democratic demands but the wartime democratic movement gradually shifted from

---

[16] Lei Zhen, *Zhonghua minguo zhixian shi* [The history of constitutionalism in republican China] (Taipei: Daoxiang, 2010), 117–51.

[17] Xinan lianda chuxi fukan, ed., *Lianda banian* [Eight years in Lianda] (Beijing: Xinxing chubanshe, 2010), 65.

the People's Political Council to the outside."[18] Chen seemed to suggest that members of the council devoted themselves to promoting constitutionalism to the public rather than continuing their activities in the official platform (I elaborate on this point below). Chen's observations reveal that the Nationalist Party's attitude toward constitutionalism limited the options of non-Guomindang members.

No clear and direct evidence has been found to clarify Chiang Kaishek's 1943 plan for postwar constitutionalism. Most existing studies casually brush over the origins of the constitutional movement in 1943. Historiographies of the CCP, without providing any solid evidence, argue that Chiang's decision was made in the face of growing demands for democracy from the Chinese people.[19] In fact, it was only after Chiang's speech that a number of such demands appeared in the press. According to Huang Yanpei, one of the founders of the China Democratic League, President Roosevelt exerted pressure on Chiang, suggesting that he implement constitutionalism as soon as possible. But this evidence is drawn solely from Huang Yanpei's diaries, in which Huang claimed that he learned the news from one of his friends who relayed the message from another official in the Nationalist Party.[20] Huang's words may seem reliable since he was a former member of the Revolutionary Alliance (*Tongmeng hui*) and maintained close connections with many high-ranking Nationalist officials. Acording to my knowledge, so far no direct evidence indicating Roosevelt's words to Chiang on constitutional issues is to be found either in the *Records of the Foreign Relations of the United States* or in correspondence between Chiang and T.V. Soong, who served as the main liaison between Chongqing and Washington from 1940 to 1943.

More recently published sources may shed light on the origins of the constitutional movement. Xiong Shihui, a high official in the Nationalist Party who was very close to Chiang Kai-shek, wrote in his diaries that on

---

[18] Chen Qitian, *Jiyuan huiyilu* [Memoirs] (Taipei: Shangwu Yinshuguan, 1965), 186.

[19] Li Rong, *Kangzhan shiqi dahoufang de minzhu yundong* [Wartime democratic movements in Guomindang-ruled areas] (Beijing: Huawen chubanshe, 1997), 89.

[20] Huang Yanpei, *Huang Yanpei riji* [Huang Yanpei's diary] (Beijing: Huawen chubanshe, 2008), vol. 8, 58.

August 4, 1943, Chiang told him in a breakfast meeting about the two decisions to be announced at the next month's Nationalist Party Central Executive Committee meeting. The first was that Chiang himself had decided to replace Lin Sen as the president of China (Lin had just died). Second, the National Assembly would be convoked and the Draft Constitution introduced around October 10, 1944, if the "military and political situations are unified by then" (which implied that the CCP would have to place its government and army under national government control).[21] Chiang emphasized that this decision must be known to the public prior to his scheduled meeting with Roosevelt during the fall, so that people would not misunderstand and think that the decision was made because of the influence of the American president. Chiang also added that he could merely announce the decision without implementing it. Three days later, Xiong met with Wang Shijie, a legal expert and Chiang's close advisor, and discussed Chiang's plans in detail. They both disagreed with Chiang and believed that constitutionalism was not merely a matter of procedure but required sincere determination and careful preparation. Two days later, on August 9, Wang and Xiong discussed constitutional issues again and reached two conclusions. First, if the convoking of the National Assembly was declared but not implemented as scheduled, public sentiment would turn strongly against the government. Second, Chiang's intention to use constitutionalism as a means to press for the disarmament of the CCP and the unification of its armies seemed both impractical and unnecessary.[22] If Xiong's account is to be believed, then Chiang Kai-shek probably promised constitutionalism as an anti-CCP tactic, seeking to gain some advantage over the CCP in the press.

We are not sure when in 1943 Chiang came to this idea, but indirect evidence suggests that Chiang may have already formed this plan in early July.[23] According to Chiang's diary, as early as July 8, 1943, Chiang accepted Roosevelt's offer to meet but asked to meet after September. Chiang

---

[21] Xiong Shihui, *Hai sang ji* [Xiong Shihui's memoirs] (Hong Kong: Mingjing chubanshe, 2008), 418.

[22] Ibid., 418–19.

[23] By July, constitutionalism was probably among Chiang's several options against the

further requested that he be notified at least two weeks in advance if Roosevelt changed the time to before September.[24] Five days later, on July 13, 1943, according to Huang Yanpei's diary, Chiang specially invited fifteen members of the People's Political Council, including Huang himself, and solicited their comments on domestic and international issues. During dinner Chiang expressed his wish that constitutionalism should be accelerated.[25]

Overall, from existing evidence, we can conclude several points about the origin of the constitutional movement. Chiang made the decision to initiate the movement in haste. He did not thoroughly discuss the coming constitutional movement with his close advisors, nor did they fully prepare or plan the movement in advance. Although Chiang was certainly aware of U.S. criticism of his party's antidemocratic tendencies, there is no direct evidence of Roosevelt's pressure on Chiang for constitutionalism in mid-1943. The dissolution of the Comintern in May 1943 may have contributed to Chiang's decision. As Chiang always believed in close connections between the Comintern and the CCP, he probably assumed that the dissolution of the former must be a heavy blow to the latter. CCP historiography regards a series of Nationalist Party propaganda and military operations during mid-1943 as the "third anti-Communist high tide" (*di sanci fangong gaochao*). Finally, as inferred from Xiong Shihui's account, Chiang intended to maneuver the constitutional movement to press the CCP to abandon its independent military power.

Thus we can conclude that Chiang's hasty decision on constitutionalism was in accord with his anti-Communist agenda. Whether or not Chiang Kai-shek made up his mind to launch the constitutional movement based on pressure from Roosevelt seems less important than Chiang's intention to use the constitutional movement to manipulate public opinion against the CCP.

CCP. As chapter 7 reveals, at least in July, Chiang was still actively planning military operations against Yan'an.

[24] *SLGB* 54:57.

[25] Huang Yanpei, *Huang Yanpei riji*, vol. 8, 50.

INSTITUTIONS FOR THE DISCUSSION OF CONSTITUTIONAL ISSUES

In late 1943 and early 1944, discussions of constitutional issues arose in major cities of Free China. Apart from the monthly gathering of the official Commission for the Inauguration of Constitutionalism, other constitutional symposia were established, mostly by members of the China Democratic League and other organizations like the monthly journal *Constitutionalism (Xianzheng yuekan)*. Leading newspapers and journals also published at great length on constitutional topics. At the very beginning, these symposia and articles largely focused their discussions on the 1936 Draft Constitution and suggestions for its revision to be submitted to the National Government.

Members of the Democratic League played key roles in the discussion and in the dissemination of constitutional ideas. In early January 1944, Zuo Shunsheng and Zhang Junmai (a U.K.-educated intellectual and head of the National Social Party) organized the first monthly constitutional symposium in Chongqing. The symposium soon gained popularity among Chongqing intellectuals. During its fifth meeting in May 1944, more than sixty people participated, including many influential figures in the Democratic League, and even one representative from the CCP. In September 1944, the symposium reached its zenith and was transformed into an enthusiastic mass gathering: more than eight hundred people of different backgrounds met in a big assembly hall in a Chongqing factory. Participants included senior members of the Nationalist Party like Feng Yuxiang and Shao Lizi, and key members of the Democratic League. Some young participants passionately kneeled and knocked their heads bloody as they fiercely shouted their democratic demands.[26]

Another influential constitutional symposium was set up by Huang Yanpei in the name of the journals *Constitutionalism* and *National Bulletin (Guoxun)*, gathering a number of influential intellectuals, especially legal experts. Summaries of each meeting appeared in influential newspapers in

---

[26] "Zhaokai guoshi huiyi chengli lianhe zhengfu" [Meeting for national issues, establishing a coalition government], *Xinhua ribao*, September 25, 1944.

Chongqing including the *Dagongbao, Xinhua Daily,* and *Xinmin Daily.* According to the memoir of a senior editor of the two leading journals of the constitutional movement (*Constitutionalism* and *National Bulletin*), the symposium was initially organized like a salon: apart from contributors to the journal, most participants were industrial and business leaders and they met in a luxurious meeting room on the second floor of the Bank of Communication (*Jiaotong yinhang*) in Chongqing.[27] In Chengdu, Zhang Lan, the president of the China Democratic League, organized the Constitutional Democracy Promotion Council (*Minzhu xianzheng cujinhui*) in February 1944, primarily made up of members of the China Youth Party and other non-Guomindang people.[28]

Vigorous discussions of constitutional issues also took place in Kunming. Two important constitutional symposia were established in Kunming: one was founded by the Yunnan branch of the Nationalist Party and joined by its proconstitutionalism members as well as other intellectuals; the other symposium included mostly members of the China Democratic League and university professors.[29] Available sources provide little information on discussions of constitutional issues in cities other than Chongqing, Kunming, and Chengdu.

Above all, constitutional symposia offered intellectuals and other public personages a platform for public voices on constitutionalism and the current situation, a rare opportunity since 1941. Although Chiang regarded the ongoing constitutional movement as one of the best social phenomena of recent years (the other was the recruitment of young students into the army), at the beginning of the movement he was still concerned about the increasing number of public lectures and symposia on constitutional issues. On January 8, 1944, in a lecture delivered to Nation-

---

[27] Shang Ding, *Fangcao xieyang yi xingzong* [Shang Ding's memoirs] (Shanghai: Wenshi chubanshe, 1997), 7–10.

[28] "Yu xianzheng shouci zuotan" [The first constitutional symposium in Chongqing], *Yunnan ribao,* January 3, 1944; "Xianzheng yundong zai Chengdu" [Constitutional movement in Chengdu], *Yunnan ribao,* February 12, 1944.

[29] "Xianzheng taolunhui zuokai chengli dahui" [The establishment of a constitutional symposium], *Yunnan ribao,* January 12, 1944; "Kunming xueshujie zuo chengli xianzheng yanjiuhui" [A constitutional symposium established in the academia of Kunming], *Yunnan ribao,* February 7, 1944.

alist Party cadres in the Central Training Corps (*Zhongyang xunlian tuan*), Chiang stated:

> Recently members of some cultural communities in Chongqing have established several symposia and public lectures. Since our party branches failed to take the lead in the movement and have already fallen behind them, we can only try to participate in these activities and try hard to save the situation. It is relatively easy to master the information of such activities in Chongqing. In other places, party branches should be well informed of the circumstances of such symposia and activities. If we cannot control the situation, then these organizations should not be allowed to exist at all.[30]

Chiang acutely sensed that constitutional discussions (via printed media or symposia) might sway public opinion and be used against the Nationalist Party and the government. Probably authorized by Chiang, some pro-Guomindang intellectuals did join the constitutional discussion by writing articles in official or semiofficial journals or newspapers on a rather limited scale. Despite Chiang's dislike of these public gatherings by non-Guomindang members, it is worth noticing that no such symposia or lectures were suspended by the government in late 1943 and 1944.

As for the official platform, the Commission for the Inauguration of Constitutionalism had three main functions: first, it should advise the government on the preparation of constitutionalism; second, its members should investigate the establishment of local self-governments; and third, it served as a means of communication between the public and government in preparing for constitutionalism.[31] According to an interview with several of its members, the agenda of the commission for January to May 1944 primarily focused on discussion of the main articles of the Draft

---

[30] Qin Xiaoyi, ed., *Xian zongtong Jianggong sixiang yanlun zongji-yanjiang* [Collected works of Chiang Kai-shek: Speeches] (Taibei: Zhongyang wenwu gongying she, 1984), vol. 15, 302–8.

[31] "Xiejinhui" [Commission for the Inauguration of Constitutionalism], *Xinmin bao*, October 12, 1943.

Constitution and eliciting suggestions from the public.[32] By October 1944, 269 suggestions on the Draft Constitution had been submitted to the commission by the public and thirty-two amendments were formulated. Some researchers argue that, compared to the Constitutional Promotion Committee in 1940, the members of the 1944 commission were too conservative in their revisions.[33] Lei Zhen made this point in his memoir: he wrote that in 1943–1944 members of the commission were much less serious in discussions, and Huang Yanpei and Zuo Shunsheng constantly complained about the meaningless meetings.[34] It seems that the official commission failed in its original aim to motivate the public to offer suggestions on the Draft Constitution. As Chen Qitian has argued, interest in democratic rights was indeed reviving at this time, but the center of the wartime democratic movement gradually shifted from the People's Political Council (the official agency) to the social realm.[35]

Participating in an Elitist Movement

Members of the China Democratic League and some other nonparty intellectuals actively engaged in the constitutional movement, although possibly not in the ways hoped for and expected by the Nationalist Party. More importantly, intellectuals saw themselves as leaders and essential figures of the movement. In early January 1944, Zuo Shunsheng wrote that the fate of the ongoing constitutional movement lay in the hands of Chinese intellectuals. Zuo criticized Chinese intellectuals (whether in office or opposition) for the consistent failures to establish constitutional government since the founding of the Republic of China. Without intellectuals' support, he argued, it would have been difficult for Yuan Shikai to restore the monarchy and proclaim himself emperor in 1915–1916. Ac-

---

[32] "Xianxiehui gongzuo jinkuang" [Recent situations of the commission], *Yunnan ribao*, January 9, 1944.

[33] Ma Qihua, *Kangzhan shiqi de zhengzhi jianshe* [Political building during wartime] (Taipei: Jindai zhongguo chubanshe, 1986), 473.

[34] Lei Zhen, *Zhonghua minguo zhixian shi*, 231.

[35] Chen Qitan, *Jiyuan huiyilu*, 186.

cording to Zuo, as Chinese intellectuals had failed to indoctrinate the Chinese people with "correct political values," the belief that "Chinese people had a deficient level of political consciousness" lasted from the late Qing era to the 1940s. Zuo's intellectual elitism is far from new in modern Chinese political history, but it is worth noting that Zuo was one of the leaders of the Democratic League. He was certainly not alone in believing that Chinese intellectuals should be the main leaders and contributors to the constitutional movement. Zuo also emphasized that most of the advocates of the constitutional movement were not "figures in political eclipse who were merely trying to obtain some political capital for themselves under the disguise of democracy."[36] Clearly, Zuo attempted to dispel views that intellectuals from minor parties were merely using the opportunity to gain influence in politics.

Pan Guangdan, a key member of the Kunming branch of the Democratic League and a sociology professor at Lianda, also projected a strong sense of elitism regarding the constitutional movement. He regarded the essence of constitutionalism as a kind of "wise-men politics" (*xianren zhengzhi*). According to Pan, people were divided into three levels—top, middle, and bottom—in terms of their virtue and ability (*caipin*). The wise man arises from at least the middle level and stands for only part of the public opinion. Pan believed that the representation of overall public opinion was unattainable, and that the absolute idea of the rule of the people existed only in theory. So he argued that wise men with enough virtue and ability were best able to represent the people.[37]

Zuo and Pan's writings and speeches reflect the common belief that intellectuals were obliged to lead the constitutional movement. Who, then, were considered intellectuals in their eyes? Zuo Shunsheng characterized intellectuals in three aspects: first, they should be committed to Chinese politics; second, they understood China's past and present and had knowledge of the world; third, they were not only able to lead the Chinese people but also instruct those in power.[38]

---

[36] Zuo Shunsheng, "Xianjue tiaojian," *Xianzheng yuekan* 2 (1944): 5–9.

[37] Pan Guangdan, "Minzhu zhengzhi yu Zhongguo shehui beijing" [Democracy and Chinese society], *Ziyou luntan* 2, no. 3 (1944): 8–16.

[38] Zuo Shunsheng, "Xianjue Tiaojian," *Xianzheng yuekan* 2 (1944): 5.

Obviously, Zuo's definition was rather broad and elastic. It helped the movement reach a wider audience by bringing in business leaders and professionals who otherwise might not have considered themselves intellectuals. Huang Yanpei and Zhang Zhirang's monthly symposia held in the Chongqing offices of the Bank of Commerce included many such men. In March, May, and June 1944, for example, the topics of discussion centered on the protection of private capital, and many industrial and commercial figures attended these meetings.[39] Another example is the August symposium on the protection of the freedom of the body, which drew many experienced lawyers.[40]

A CONSTITUTION OF NO SIGNIFICANCE
IN THE CONSTITUTIONAL MOVEMENT

The term "constitutional movement" was not created by later historians, but was already used from the movement's inception in 1943. It was accepted by both government officials and intellectuals and widely used in public speeches, newspaper editorials, and journal articles. Although propaganda frequently announced that Nationalist Party authorities or Chiang himself had initiated the constitutional movement, the Nationalist Party's original goals for the constitutional movement were unable to constrain the way the movement later unfolded.

Discussing and revising the 1936 Draft Constitution was the most important goal conceived by the Nationalist Party in the constitutional movement. Although the term "constitutional movement" was widely used in the commercial press, in the official press the movement was more often termed "the movement on the discussion of the Draft Constitution" (*yantao xiancao yundong*). In his speeches Chiang frequently mentioned that one of the goals of the movement was to inform the Chinese public

---

[39] "Siren qiye yu xianzheng" [Private enterprise and constitutionalism], *Xianzheng yuekan* 7 (1944): 13; "Minsheng zhuyi zhong de baohu siren qiye" [Protection of private enterprises in Three People's Principles], *Xianzheng yuekan* 6 (1944): 15; "Benkan di san ci xianzheng zuotan" [The third symposium], *Xianzheng yuekan* 2 (1944): 12.

[40] "Benkan di ba ci luntan" [The eighth symposium], *Xianzheng yuekan* 9 (1944): 20.

about the Draft Constitution and gather their suggestions to improve it.[41] In December 1943, a month after the establishment of the commission, the Nationalist Party's Central News Agency (*Zhongyang tongxun she*) stated that the movement had already started nationwide, and the commission called upon all universities, public organizations, and Nationalist Party branches to study and discuss the Draft Constitution, and to submit their suggestions on it to the commission by May 5, 1944.[42]

The establishment of local governments such as the county council (*xian yihui*) was another important goal in the constitutional movement. According to Sun Yat-sen's doctrines, the National Assembly should be composed of over 2,000 representatives elected by each county council. Chiang promised members of the People's Political Council that the establishment of local self-governments should be finished by 1944.[43] Also, during the fifth plenum of the twelfth Central Executive Committee of the Nationalist Party in May 1944, an Executive Yuan (*xingzheng yuan*) report on the progress of the constitutional movement stated that "the establishment of local self-governments was the most basic and practical work in the preparation for constitutionalism."[44]

It is thus clear that the establishment of local governments and the revision of the Draft Constitution were the two main goals of the constitutional movement as conceived by Nationalist authorities. In addition, the National Government conceived itself as the leader of the movement. Propaganda Minister Liang Hancao said in a press conference that the ongoing constitutional movement was different from those in Europe or the late Qing dynasty in that the constitutional movement was launched and led by the National Government while the earlier European and Qing movements primarily originated from the people's demands for constitutional government.[45]

---

[41] "Jiang zhuxi xunci" [The speech of Chiang Kai-shek], *Xinhua ribao*, September 19, 1943.

[42] "Faqi taolun xiancao yundong" [The launch of the constitutional movement], *Dagong-bao*, December 17, 1943.

[43] "Jiang zhuxi xunci," *Xinhua ribao*, September 19, 1943.

[44] "Shierjie quanhui xianzheng baogao" [Constitutional reports in the twelfth Central Executive Committee], *Xin Zhonghua zazhi* 2, no. 7 (1944): 2.

[45] "Liang buzhang tan xianzheng" [Minister Liang on constitutionalism], *Xinmin bao*, February 19, 1944.

However, the constitutional movement soon deviated from the official road map, as the main issues of public discussion went far beyond the revision of the Draft Constitution and the establishment of local councils. A series of intriguing topics proposed by intellectuals became the main agenda of the movement: the difference between constitutionalism and democracy, the combination of political democracy and economic democracy, the relationship between constitutionalism and contemporary Chinese politics, and how constitutionalism related to wartime mobilization. These topics were widely discussed by intellectuals of various backgrounds in journals, public gatherings, and speeches. It is important to understand how these democratic demands from the intellectuals' perspective came to supplant the two goals for the constitutional movement set by the National Government. The official Commission for the Inauguration of Constitutionalism played a minimal role in the constitutional movement. As noted above, in 1939 the National Government had promised the People's Political Council that constitutionalism would be realized soon. A quasi-representative institution called the Constitutional Promotion Committee, which included many intellectuals, was established by the National Government at the end of 1939, and a series of radical suggestions on the Draft Constitution was proposed. The 1939 committee and the 1943 commission differed in two aspects. First, the Constitutional Promotion Committee of 1939 was mostly made up of non-Guomindang members, including members of the People's Political Council and other intellectuals, while the 1943 Commission for the Inauguration of Constitutionalism was composed of a great number of high-ranking Nationalist Party officials, including Chiang Kai-shek himself. In fact, many "troublemaking" intellectuals (in the eyes of the Nationalist Party) were not included in the commission.[46]

Second, compared with the 1939 committee suggestions on the revision of the Draft Constitution, the 1944 commission's suggestions were much more conservative in that they generally preserved the main structure and articles of the Draft Constitution. For example, since the National Assembly was convened at an interval of three years, the 1939 committee suggested that a standing committee be established during the long

---

[46] Wen Liming. *Di san zhong liliang yu kangzhan shiqi de zhong Zhongguo zhengzhi*, 49.

periods of recess. The standing committee and the Legislative Yuan would jointly assume the functions of parliament. The Judicial Yuan should serve as the Supreme Court instead of its previous status as an executive institution.[47] Thus the revisions suggested in 1939 embodied the Western system of checks and balances and fundamentally challenged the basic structure of Sun Yat-sen's design of constitutional government. These revisions suggested by intellectuals in 1939 were too radical in the eyes of the Nationalist Party and were discarded. In the end, the 1946 version of the constitution did not adopt such suggestions and differed only slightly from the 1936 Draft Constitution. In other words, the 1943 commission contributed little to any substantial revisions of the Draft Constitution.

Despite the media attention to the establishment of the commission and public expectations for improvements in the rule of law, its members, officials of the Nationalist Party and intellectual alike, seemed to pay little attention to the discussions during the meetings, according to Lei Zhen's accounts. Some important Nationalist officials like H.H. Kung (Kong Xiangxi, head of the Executive Yuan) and Xiong Shihui never attended the meetings at all. Sun Ke (head of the Legislative Yuan) and Wu Tiecheng (chief secretary of the Nationalist Party) each attended only one meeting. Intellectuals like Zuo Shunsheng and Huang Yanpei told Lei Zhen that they went to the meetings only to give face to the National Government. Zuo Shunsheng believed that the commission was useless, based on the earlier futile efforts of the Constitutional Promotion Committee in 1939 and 1940.[48] The commission soon ceased to convene at regular intervals and failed to formulate final suggestions on the Draft Constitution until March 1946. According to Huang Yanpei's diaries, at its last meeting on December 26, 1944, the commission did not have a quorum to hold an official meeting.[49]

In fact, merely discussing and advising on the revision of the Draft Constitution held little appeal to intellectuals. A typical view among intellectuals in the constitutional movement was that it would be futile to attempt to realize constitutionalism by simply introducing a constitution.

---

[47] Ibid., 59.

[48] Lei Zhen, *Zhonghua minguo zhixian shi*, 195.

[49] Huang Yanpei, *Huang Yanpei riji*, vol. 8, 132.

For example, Wu Zhichun, a famous professor of political science in Lianda, argued that in the West the spirit of constitutionalism in the social realm (rule of the people) actually predated the adoption of a political constitution. He listed a number of nations that had introduced a constitution but still had authoritarian regimes including Spain, Poland, and Argentina.[50]

Intellectuals unanimously agree that improving the rule of law in China was one critical step to constitutionalism. Wu and other intellectuals noted that laws were not strictly observed or enforced in China. The people's rights stipulated in law were not guaranteed in reality at all. These intellectuals wanted to use the constitution as a tool to reform society: "Unless people have equal political, economic, and educational opportunities, a constitution would not last long."[51] Thus participants in the constitutional movement were not only busy discussing and promoting constitutional issues but also pressed the government to take practical actions to improve the rule of law. Huang Yanpei, in the symposium held by the journal *Constitutionalism*, stated that discussions and suggestions should not be vague and general. The discussion in the symposium then centered on people's liberties, especially the freedom of the body. Many intellectuals in the meeting agreed with Huang Yanpei's more practical attitude. Huang proposed that the National Government should first observe the Provisional Constitution (*linshi yuefa*) before moving to full constitutionalism. During a lecture on May 17, 1944, Huang called on the government to stir from its inaction and clear the obstacles to democracy.[52]

Yu Jiaju, a senior member of the China Youth Party and the People's Political Council, shared a similar practical approach and argued that the enactment of the constitution was by no means a crucial step toward constitutionalism. Instead, several important laws, such as an administrative code to curb the abuse of government power, should be drafted immedi-

---

[50] Wu Zhichun, "Zhuanbian shehui zhong de Zhongguo xianfa yu xianzheng" [Chinese constitutionalism in a changing society], *Ziyou luntan* 2 no. 3 (1944): 15.

[51] Ibid., 16.

[52] "Xianzheng yuekan shedeng erci zuotanhui" [The second symposium of the journal *Constitutionalism*], *Yunnan ribao*, February 12, 1944; "Women gongtong xiezhu zhengfu cucheng quanguo shangxia jinli fengxing yuefa" [Assisting the government to observe the Provisional Constitution], *Xianzheng yuekan* 6 (1944): 1–3.

ately and strictly observed before the introduction of constitutionalism.[53] Zhang Zhirang, a legal expert and editor-in-chief of the journal *Constitutionalism*, recommended that the government should legislate to fulfill several urgent democratic demands, such as the guarantee of human rights, including personal freedom and freedom of publication. Zhang even quoted from Sun Yat-sen to affirm that constitutionalism in fact should predate the enactment of a constitution.[54]

Readers might find it paradoxical that many intellectuals did not regard the enactment of a constitution as the central task of the constitutional movement. They were instead pressing the Nationalist government to observe existing laws and pass new laws to guarantee the human rights of the people. As we shall see in the following section, the disagreement on the goals of the constitutional movement between intellectuals and the Nationalist government became more evident as the government failed to fulfill intellectuals' democratic demands.

BUILDING LOCAL SELF-GOVERNMENTS: A CASTLE IN THE AIR

From the perspective of the Nationalist Party, apart from the revision of the Draft Constitution, the other important goal of the constitutional movement was the establishment of local self-governments. However, this goal proved elusive as leaders of the Nationalist Party like Sun Ke lacked practical solutions to resolve the problems in local election and administration.

According to Sun Yat-sen's doctrines, constitutionalism should be achieved from the bottom up. The foundation of constitutionalism lay in the success of local self-governments in each county since establishing local self-government was the means to train people in how to exercise their rights.[55] During the period of political tutelage, the Nationalist Party

---

[53] Yu Jiaju, "Xianzheng de jineng" [The function of constitutionalism], *Xianzheng yuekan* 3 (1944): 8.

[54] Zhang Zhirang, "Xunzheng xianzheng yu xianjieduan jianguo gongzuo" [Constitutionalism and the founding of our nation], *Xianzheng yuekan* 2 (1944): 1–6.

[55] The term "local self-government" originated in the Western context and had been

was to help each county become self-governing as the embodiment of public opinion. The preparation for constitutionalism would begin only when over half of the nation's counties had established local self-governments. Sun Yat-sen did not mean to decentralize power into each county. Instead, the core of the theory was to train people to exercise the four rights in a practical way.[56]

Sun Ke was maybe the keenest figure among high-ranking Nationalist officials in the constitutional movement and also the main advocate of building local self-governments. In a nationwide radio address on New Year's Day in 1944, Sun Ke criticized several popular "false ideas" about the constitutional movement. He stated that "the ongoing constitutional movement was fundamental to China's political development" and the construction of constitutionalism during wartime could offer motivation for people to better fight the war. He called on every citizen to study the Draft Constitution of 1936, since it was not yet widely discussed, and the domestic situation had changed after eight years to an extent that a revision had become necessary.[57]

Sun Ke was a loyal disciple of his father in terms of the construction of constitutionalism. Sun Ke thus firmly advocated the consolidation of local self-governments as critical to constitutionalism.[58] He proposed that the Commission for the Inauguration of Constitutionalism investigate local "public opinion" on constitutional matters. He was also invited to discuss local constitutional matters in the city council of Chongqing, a newly established self-governing institution.[59]

---

familiar to Chinese since the late Qing. Sun borrowed the term to better explain his theories to the Chinese people. Zhang Shenfu, ed., *Minzhu yu xianzheng* [Democracy and constitutionalism] (Chongqing: E mei chubanshe, 1944), 37.

[56] Sun Zhongshan, *Sun Zhongshan quanji*, vol. 9, 127–28. Sun Yat-sen believed in the separation of rights (*quan*) exercised by the people and abilities (*neng*) possessed by the government. He claimed that the four basic rights of the people—election (*xuanju*), recall (*bamian*), initiative (*chuangzhi*), and referendum (*fujue*)—should be exercised at both the central and county levels.

[57] "Renshi xianzheng yu yanjiu xiancao" [Learning constitutionalism by studying the Draft Constitution], *Yunnan ribao*, January 8, 1944; "Youguan xianzheng zhu wenti" [Problems related to constitutionalism], *Xianzheng yuekan* 3 (1944): 32.

[58] Sun Ke, *Sanmin zhuyi xin Zhongguo*, 48, 112.

[59] "Xianzheng xiehui tongguo liu yaoan" [Six important resolutions in the commission], *Yunnan ribao*, February 1, 1944; "Chongqingshi linshi canhui zuzhi difang zizhi xiejinhui"

Sun Ke openly criticized the National Government for ignoring the training of the people and admitted that much political training was far from being finished.[60] Although some county-level political councils were already established, Sun pointed out that the representatives of these councils were not elected by the local people but were instead appointed by higher authorities. Thus the rights of the people were not fully exercised.[61] He also argued that in order to catch up with the world trend of democracy, it would be far too late to launch constitutionalism only after more than half of the two thousand counties in China had well-established local self-governments.[62] Sun further stated that many government institutions below the county level were staffed with powerful local people or evil gentry (*lieshen*), and corruption was rampant in local administration.[63] Sun complained that these corrupt local figures who were originally "the targets of ... revolution had now become officials carrying out orders of the government!"[64]

However, Sun Ke in his lectures on constitutionalism failed to provide any practical solutions to establish local self-governments, except for calling on his listeners to revive the "revolutionary spirit" of the Nationalist Party. Here I agree with the historian Gao Hua's view that Sun Ke's foreign educational background and his lack of local working experience had left him with limited insight into the problems of rural China.[65]

How did Sun Yat-sen's design of "local self-government" work in practice during the constitutional movement? It should be remembered that the establishment of local self-governments had not begun until the early 1940s, but the constitutional movement definitely accelerated this process. Local self-governments were in fact established through a series of local elections based on residency or vocation. Through these institu-

---

[Local official constitutional commission established in Chongqing], *Yunnan ribao*, February 13, 1944.

   [60] Sun Ke, *Sanmin zhuyi xin Zhongguo*, 111.

   [61] Ibid., 32, 112.

   [62] Ibid., 34.

   [63] Ibid., 50, 86.

   [64] Ibid., 88.

   [65] Gao Hua, "Lun kangzhan houqi Sun Ke de zuoqing" [Sun Ke becoming a leftist during late wartime], *Minguo yanjiu* 2 (1995): 45.

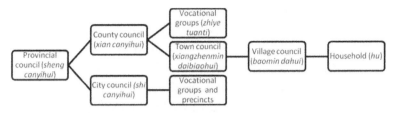

Figure 8.1: Structure of local self-government. Xiao Gongquan, *Xianzheng yu minzhu* [Constitutionalism and democracy] (Beijing: Qinghua daxue chubanshe, 2006), 84.

tions, people were able (mostly indirectly) to exercise the two important rights of election and recall. Xiao Gongquan, a U.S.-educated professor of political science and a non-Guomindang member of the Commission, included a flow chart in his investigative report on local self-governments (Figure 8.1).

According to the chart, only the city and village councils were directly elected by local people. Each household could only have one vote. Other self-governing institutions like provincial, county, and town councils were elected by representatives from lower institutions. Government officials below the county level were elected by the self-governing institutions of that level, but the candidates were nominated by a higher level of government. For example, a county magistrate (*xianzhang*) was elected by members of the county council, although candidates for county magistrate were nominated by the provincial government. There were several restrictions regarding the eligibility of the candidates. Only the bottom-level *jiazhang* (village constable) was directly elected by the village council.

Zhang Pengzhou, a senior journalist for the *Dagongbao*, published a half-page in-depth investigative report titled, "The Road to Constitutionalism in Sichuan," in which he elaborated on the election of the first twenty-six county and city councils in Sichuan province by August 1944.[66] Zhang in this long report focused on the election of chief and vice *qu-zhang* (district administrator) of the eight districts (equivalent to a county) affiliated with Chengdu. The election received nationwide attention since

---

[66] Zhang published his article under the pen name Yang Ji.

these were "the first elected *quzhang/xianzhang* in the history of republican China." However, there were several serious problems in the election.
For example, the government nominated only three candidates for each
position. Also, the representatives of the town council were informed of
the nominees only one day prior to the election, while according to election rules they should have been given five days' notice. In short, according
to Zhang's observation, what the government did was to "gradually and
partially return the power back to the people" but it was still "a long way
from democracy."[67] Discrepancies in the local election were also mentioned in the investigative reports made by members of the Commission
for the Inauguration of Constitutionalism.[68]

Although Chiang announced the constitutional movement in haste
and mainly used it as a means to contain the CCP, the Nationalist Party
still had its road map. From the perspective of the National Government,
the constitutional movement should mainly consist of the two preparatory
works for constitutionalism in Sun Yat-sen's ideology: the revision of the
Draft Constitution and the establishment of local self-governments. However, as Chiang and his officials in the party were either half-hearted or
lacked practical solutions, neither goal was attained.

INTELLECTUALS' DEMOCRATIC DEMANDS
AND THE GOVERNMENT'S RESPONSE

Intellectuals' conception of the constitutional movement differed greatly
from the Nationalist Party's vision. The movement could not gain momentum without the active participation of intellectuals and non-
Guomindang parties. Even Chiang Kai-shek admitted that the Nationalist Party had fallen behind and failed to take the lead in the constitutional
movement. The range and scope of the democratic and constitutional demands made by various intellectuals and non-Guomindang political parties during the constitutional movement are so broad as to be impossible

---

[67] Yang Ji, "Sichuan maixiang xianzheng zhitu" [Sichuan's path to constitutionalism],
Dagongbao, September 20, 1944.
[68] Xiao Gongquan, *Xianzheng yu minzhu*, 89.

to cover in a single chapter. Here I choose several recurring themes that received serious discussion in the press to highlight the disagreements between intellectuals and the Nationalist Party. Finally, I examine how the Nationalists responded to the intellectuals' democratic pleas.

As noted in the previous section, from the very beginning of the constitutional movement, most intellectuals realized that the movement could not be limited to offering suggestions on the Draft Constitution. This can be seen in subtle variations in the use of the terms "constitutionalism" (*xianzheng*) and "democracy" (*minzhu*) by intellectuals. In public discourse these terms were usually interchangeable. Some intellectuals, however, painstakingly elaborated on the difference between democracy and constitutionalism, the latter of which was frequently used in the Nationalists' discourse on the constitutional movement. Xiao Gongquan argued in an article published in late 1943 that the "essence of democracy" is the "rule of people," while the "essence of constitutionalism" is the "rule of law."[69] In a long article titled "The Chinese Road to Constitutionalism" published in mid-1944, Liang Shuming, a key figure in the Democratic League, agreed with Xiao on the distinction between the two ideas. Liang emphasized two aspects of democracy: the protection of individual freedom and public engagement in national affairs. He further claimed that democracy (the rule of people) is the advanced form of constitutionalism (the rule of law). For example, Liang argued that constitutionalism in Britain had originated during early modern times and had been established for hundreds of years, but many democratic rights such as universal suffrage were not introduced until the early twentieth century. He concluded that constitutionalism serves to gradually foster the spirit of democracy.[70]

The fastidious use of the two terms was not a word game. Both Xiao and Liang highlighted the differences between constitutionalism and democracy because they believed that the pursuit of constitutional or democratic goals was more urgent than the mere discussion and introduction of the Draft Constitution or the convening of the National Assembly. Shen Zhiyuan, a member of the Democratic League and a Marxist economist,

---

[69] Ibid., 190.

[70] Zhongguo wenhua shuyuan, ed., *Liang Shuming wenji* [Collected works of Liang Shuming] (Beijing: Zhongguo wenhua shuyuan, 1993), vol. 6, 473–75.

criticized views that overly concentrated on constitutionalism but ignored democracy. Shen argued that the wartime governments of Japan and Germany seemed constitutional in form but were fascist in nature. Shen suggested that the government should guarantee basic freedoms of the people such as the freedom of speech, assembly, and body.[71] Overall, regardless of their political inclinations (Xiao seemed close to the government; Liang was neutral and stayed in remote Guangxi; Shen was a leftist), important intellectuals like these men all hoped that China would use the constitutional movement to establish the rule of law and secure more rights and freedoms for the Chinese people. From this perspective, the movement could not confine itself to discussions of the Draft Constitution.

More intellectuals and members of the Democratic League shared Shen's view on human rights. In fact, calls for human rights and people's freedoms remained one of the most important themes throughout the constitutional movement. At the first meeting of the commission in 1944, Zhang Junmai proposed the protection of three basic human rights. First, the right to freedom of the body: only a court could issue orders to detain people; a suspect's family must be notified within twenty-four hours of arrest; detainees would have the right to appeal; detention should have a time limit; and any limitations placed on these rights must be based in law. Second, the freedom of association and assembly, and third, the freedom of speech and publication, including the tolerance of criticism of the government, religious organizations, and the economic situation (e.g., rampant inflation).[72] Zhang emphasized that guaranteeing the freedoms of the body, speech, and publication distinguished a democratic regime from a dictatorship. He specifically proposed that prepublication censorship (*shiqian jiancha*) should be abolished and a new law on publication should be introduced as soon as possible.[73]

Freedom of speech and publication was viewed as a necessary condition of constitutionalism and became an urgent demand for intellectuals. Luo Changpei, a linguist and professor at Lianda, discussed the statutes regarding the protection of freedom of speech and publication that had

---

[71] "Youguan xianzheng zhu wenti de shangque" [Questions about constitutionalism], *Guoxun*, 360 (1944): 2–3.

[72] "Xianzheng xiehui tongguo liu yaoan," *Yunnan ribao*, February 1, 1944.

[73] Zhang Junmai, "Baozhang sanxiang jiben quanli," 36–42.

existed since the founding of the republic. He offered several suggestions on the freedom of speech: first, the government should ease censorship on publications; second, a publication should be banned only if its contents went against existing law; finally, legislative bodies should draft the law on publication.[74]

> The National Government, on the one hand, justified censorship as a national security measure during wartime, but on the other hand, slowly moved to improve the freedom of speech in response to intellectuals' pressing demands. On October 12, 1943, at the beginning of the constitutional movement, Chiang Kai-shek addressed the commission on the freedom of speech and suggested a possible change in censorship policies: "The current regulations on publications are certainly necessary in wartime, especially when the war is still fought in our homeland. This should be the consensus of all insightful Chinese people. But in terms of the statutes regarding checks on freedoms of speech and publication in the Draft Constitution, is there anything that should be modified? Also, in terms of the degree [of censorship], is there anything we can change so that people's speech and behavior are more in accord with constitutionalism? These should be among your considerations."[75]

The commission soon proposed more latitude in publication and speech to the Executive Yuan. In fact, one of the resolutions of the commission during its very first meeting on November 13, 1944, was to change current regulations on publication.[76] At the fifth plenum of the twelfth Central Executive Committee of the Nationalist Party in May 1944, the Central Executive Committee suggested reform to the current method of censorship: prepublication censorship would be partially abolished; the different censorship institutions should be merged into one division under the Executive Yuan.[77] In June 1944, an act on freedom of speech and pub-

---

[74] Luo Changpei, "Yanlun ziyou zai xianzheng zhong de baozhang" [The protection of the freedom of speech], *Ziyou luntan* 2, no. 3 (March 1944): 20–25.

[75] Ibid., 23.

[76] "Diyici dahui jueyi" [Resolutions of the first meeting], *Xinmin bao*, November 13, 1943.

[77] "Shi'erzhong quanshui tongguo sixiang yaoan jingshen yaodian" [Four important

lication was passed, but prepublication censorship was not abolished as expected. The enactment of the law was disappointing since it stipulated that only books and journals with neither military nor political content were exempt from prepublication censorship.[78]

Due to a lack of research on wartime censorship, we are not sure if the censorship situation improved (or to what degree it improved or worsened) after mid-1944. On the one hand, more coverage of government malfeasance seemed to appear in the press after mid-1944 than before. On the other hand, censorship certainly continued. The editor of *Freedom Forum*, which was one of the most influential journals on constitutionalism by mid-1944, complained that an article discussing the wartime censorship law was censored. The editor reminded its readers that the government had failed to live up to its promise to improve the freedom of publication.[79]

Tensions between the government and media escalated in the late wartime period. Some newspaper offices in Chengdu and Chongqing were searched by the government. For example, from late 1944 to the end of the war in 1945, it was said that the Communist *Xinhua Daily* offices in Chongqing were raided over three hundred times by law enforcement agencies or secret police. Many newspaper issues were confiscated and the staff were beaten. Though wartime raids resulted in beatings and property damage, at least they did not escalate to the level of repression reached during the civil war period, when many journalists were brutally murdered by secret police.[80]

From the perspective of Chinese intellectuals, the National Government's response to demands for greater personal freedom was just as disappointing as the actions to limit freedom of speech. The "regulation on the guarantee of freedom of the body" (*baozhang renmin shenti ziyou banfa*) took effect in August 1944. The enactment of the regulation was a Na-

---

resolutions on the Twelfth Central Executive Committee], *Xinzhonghua* 2, no. 7 (1944): 162–64.

[78] "Zhanshi chubanpin shukan shencha liangxiang fagui" [Two laws on wartime censorship], *Xinwen zhanxian* 4, no. 3–4 (1944): 10–11.

[79] "Bianhouji" [Afterword], *Ziyou luntan* 2, no. 3 (March 1944): 35.

[80] Jiang Pei, "Nanjing zhengfu shiqi yulun guanli pingxi" [Regulation of the press in republican China], *Jindaishi yanjiu* 3 (1995): 105, 107, 108.

tional Government response to intellectuals' pressing concern about unlawful detention. However, when the act was discussed at the August 31, 1944, meeting of the constitutional symposium held by Huang Yanpei, the lawyers and legal experts in attendance were unsatisfied, as the regulation failed to address their concern over unlawful detention. Three professional lawyers were invited to the symposium: Shen Junru, a member of the Democratic League who was close to the CCP; Fang Zhongying, an experienced judge; and Wu Yuheng, an experienced lawyer and a secret member of the Democratic League. Shen, Fang, and Wu had three main criticisms of the regulations. First, apart from law enforcement agencies, military agencies also had the right to detain people. Second, specific agencies that possessed the right to arrest were not mentioned in the regulation (according to the regulation, the Executive Yuan should release an updated list of such agencies every half year). Many non-Guomindang people worried that military and the notorious Guomindang intelligence agencies were authorized to make arrests. Third, according to the regulations a person could be in custody for forty-eight hours at most without charge, a period longer than the common limit of twenty-four hours.[81] On the same day as the symposium, the Executive Yuan released the list of agencies that possessed the right to make arrests, including assorted military divisions such as the headquarters of each military war zone (*zhanqu zhangguanbu*) and garrison forces (*weishu zongsilingbu*).[82] Obviously, the power to arrest and detain people was not restricted to law enforcement agencies as was expected by the intellectuals.

Promises to end unlawful detention and partially abolish prepublication censorship were made at the fifth plenum of the twelfth Central Executive Committee of the Nationalist Party in May 1944. In response to public demand for human rights, the Nationalist government enacted the above-mentioned two regulations on the protection of personal freedom, speech, and publication. In these regulations, however, the government yielded little expansion of people's freedoms, a situation that severely disappointed the intellectuals.

---

[81] "Benkan di ba ci zuotan" [The eighth symposium], *Xianzheng yuekan* 10 (1944): 30–32.

[82] "Queding youquan buren jiguan" [Agencies authorized to arrest], *Dagongbao*, August 30, 1944.

Socialism as an Alternative Model of Constitutionalism: Economic Democracy

The idea of economic democracy (*jingji minzhu*) was another important theme in the intellectual discourse of constitutionalism. A senior editor of the *National Bulletin* later admitted in his memoir that the term "economic democracy" was a substitute for the censored word "socialism."[83] In fact, economic democracy had a broader connotation in the context of the 1940s, and socialist thinking was only a part of it. Socialist economic thinking, such as theories of a planned economy, social equality, and justice can be found in the writings of Sun Yat-sen and had long been popular among many Western-educated Chinese intellectuals and leftists in the Nationalist Party. Many young Chinese students who would later become influential intellectuals, such as Zhang Junmai, Luo Longji, Wang Zaoshi, and Fei Xiaotong, studied at the London School of Economics in the 1920s, where they were influenced by the teachings of Harold Laski, a British socialist thinker well known for his Fabian thinking on political pluralism and social equality. During 1930s and 1940s, at least eight translations of Laski's works were published in Chinese.[84]

Harold Laski was even invited to write a long article titled "Several Points on the Outlook for Victory in China" for the *Dagongbao*, published in Chongqing on October 8, 1944. Laski claimed that unless postwar China established institutions of economic democracy, wartime victories would not last long. Laski offered several suggestions to the National Government, most of which were socialist in nature and already in practice in the Soviet Union. Laski suggested that "important industries such as banks, land, communication, and national defense should be state-owned. … Foreign investment should be based on the principle of non-interference in domestic politics. … Peasants and small producers should cooperate to prevent exploitation by middle-men." Laski reiterated that a capitalist

---

[83] Shang Ding, "Minzhu xianzheng de xianfeng zhanshi Zhang Zhirang yu Xianzheng yuekan" [Zhang Zhirang and the journal *Constitutionalism*], *Wenshi ziliao xuanji*, no. 85 (Beijing: Wenshi ziliao chubanshe, 1983), 33.

[84] Xiao Yanzhong, "Xiandai Zhongguo feibian zhuyi de sixiang qishi" [Fabianism in modern China], *Twenty-First Century* [Er shi yi shiji] 108 (2008): 39.

China would not become a democratic country. He concluded, "What was achieved in the Soviet Union was also possible in China. ... The first [step] is massive industrialization under state control. ... The second is cooperation and collectivization in agriculture."[85] Huang Yanpei wrote in his diary that he found resonances with Laski's arguments, which further confirmed his faith in economic democracy.[86]

Socialist economic thinking was popular among Chinese intellectuals, including Western-trained liberals, largely due to the fast development of the Soviet Union. In 1936, the Soviet Union claimed the establishment of socialism and the vast improvement of society such as universal education and the rise of people's living standards. In fact, the liberal intellectuals' consensus was that despite one-party rule, the people of the Soviet Union enjoyed considerable equality in economic status.[87] Liang Shuming believed that economic democracy was a necessary step in the pursuit of democracy. Liang anchored his hope for democracy on the improvement of universal education through the increase of the productive forces. Inspired by Marx's socioeconomic theories and by Soviet practice, Liang considered the Soviet Union an alternative model of constitutionalism, juxtaposing it with Western models such as Britain.[88] Luo Longji, an American-trained intellectual and active member of the Democratic League, published an article in the first issue of *Democratic Weekly* titled "The Significance of Democracy," in which he emphasized that political democracy should go hand in hand with economic democracy. Luo argued that the French Revolution represented political democracy, while the Soviet Union represented economic democracy.[89] Zhang Shenfu, another important liberal intellectual, summarizing several democratic trends, claimed, "Any democratic development without economic democracy is only pseudo-democracy."[90]

---

[85] Harold Laski, "Zhongguo shengli de jidian zhanwang" [Several points on the outlook for victory in China], *Dagongbao*, October 8, 1944.

[86] Huang Yanpei, *Huang Yanpei riji*, vol. 8, 122.

[87] "Fangyingtuan guilai" [The U.K. mission is back], *Ziyou luntan* 2, no. 3 (1944): 2.

[88] Zhongguo wenhua shuyuan, *Liang Shuming wenji*, vol. 6, 444.

[89] Luo longji, "Minzhu de yiyi" [The significance of democracy], *Minzhu zhoukan* 1, no. 1 (1944): 3–8.

[90] Zhang Shenfu, ed., *Minzhu yu xianzheng*, 9.

Xiao Gongquan, in an article written in 1947 titled "On Democracy" (*Lun minzhu*), argued, "Political democracy emphasized personal freedom while economic democracy focused on equality." Xiao admitted that it was hard to reconcile the two since equality of wealth would necessarily jeopardize the freedom of certain people, but only through the combination of the two values could China achieve "democracy for the people."[91]

Despite lively discussions, demands for economic democracy remained largely theoretical. Few intellectuals mentioned how to put theories of economic democracy into practice in China. Soon, however, the deteriorating economic and military situation brought new demands for coalition government, eclipsing the calls for constitutional reform.

MILITARY DEFEAT, CALLS FOR A COALITION GOVERNMENT, AND THE FAILURE OF THE CONSTITUTIONAL MOVEMENT

During the early constitutional movement, many intellectuals held high expectations for the National Government. Both officials of the Nationalist Party and intellectuals attempted to dispel people's doubts about the ongoing movement. For example, Chu Fucheng, a senior member of the Nationalist Party and a constitutional activist since the 1930s, openly expressed his confidence in the ongoing movement and in the government's attitude toward constitutionalism.[92] Key members of the Democratic League such as Zuo Shunsheng and Huang Yanpei all shared Chu's view in public. An editorial published in March 1944 in the liberal journal *Freedom Forum* stated, "We are currently optimistic about the future of constitutionalism. ... Discussions of constitutional issues fill the air."[93]

By mid-1944, however, it seems that some intellectuals were already impatient and unsatisfied with the government, as the latter failed to put serious efforts into constitutionalism. In May 1944, the Democratic

[91] Xiao Gongquan, *Xianzheng yu minzhu*, 161–70.
[92] "Chufu lao tan xianzheng" [On constitutionalism], *Yunnan ribao*, January 12, 1944.
[93] "Bianjihouji," 35.

League released a stern statement in which it claimed that China should accelerate its transformation into a democratic country, and this process must be finished before the end of the war.[94] The statement warned that if democracy was not achieved during wartime, then the Chinese people after the war would be left with a divided and devastated nation. In the statement the Democratic League expressed its utmost dissatisfaction with almost every aspect of the Nationalist Party's rule and urged the Nationalist Party to hand state power over to the people.[95] Zhang Youyu, a legal expert and news commentator, dedicated his article titled "Constitutionalism and War" to the upcoming fifth plenum of the twelfth Central Executive Committee of the Nationalist Party in May 1944. Zhang pointed out two critical issues that needed to be solved: launching constitutionalism and improving the economic situation. Zhang complained that in the six months since the last Central Executive Committee meeting, when the government declared its support of constitutionalism, neither of these two goals had been achieved. He suggested that, instead of waiting until the end of the war, the government should begin constitutionalism as soon as possible in order to better mobilize people and resources to win the war.[96]

Apart from the Nationalist Party's reluctant and inept actions on constitutionalism and people's rights, a series of military defeats contributed to the intellectuals' disappointment. In late April 1944, the Japanese army launched the Ichigo offensive in Henan Province. The campaign attempted to destroy American air bases in China and to establish a north-south transportation line to Southeast Asia.[97] By May, Henan Province was lost. By August, as more cities in central and south China were taken,

---

[94] To what extent this statement was known to the public remains unclear since I have not found it in major newspapers in Chongqing and Kunming.

[95] "Shiju xuanyan" [Declaration of current situation], in *Documents on the Democratic League*, ed. Zhongguo minzhu tongmeng (Washington, DC: Center for Chinese Research Materials, Association of Research Libraries, 1969), 18.

[96] Zhang Youyu, "Kangzhan yu xianzheng" [The war and constitutionalism], *Guoxun* 368 (1944): 111.

[97] Mark Peattie, Edward J. Drea, and Hans J. van de Ven, eds., *The Battle for China: Essays on the Military History of the Sino-Japanese War of 1937–1945* (Stanford, CA: Stanford University Press, 2010), 392–418.

the military defeats caused widespread panic in Free China. It was said that the price of a train ticket out of Guilin skyrocketed to over 100,000 yuan.[98] The press was filled with editorials on "salvaging the crisis" or "looking for China's solution."

In September 1944, Lin Boqu, the CCP representative on the People's Political Council, proposed the establishment of a coalition government (*lianhe zhengfu*) after the war. The proposal proved to be a huge political success, at least among many intellectuals, since it aimed at ending one-party rule and allowed the participation of other non-Guomindang parties, including the China Democratic League.[99]

As the Chinese army suffered more losses on the battlefield and lost more cities in southern China, intellectuals put forward more radical demands. In October 1944, an editorial in the liberal journal *Freedom Forum* even argued, "Democracy is the key. Once we get it, every problem will be solved. Victory and a bright future will be ahead."[100]

In November, Zhang Shenfu, a philosopher and member of the Democratic League, wrote that there were three main ways to achieve democracy. The first was the Nationalist official way, establishing local self-governments and then convening the National Assembly. He referred to this way as a "detour" under the current critical domestic situation. The second way was to guarantee a series of people's freedoms, including freedom of the body, speech, publication, assembly, and so forth. This was exactly the way proposed by intellectuals for months since the beginning of the movement. But Zhang Shenfu argued that it was impossible for the government to yield these freedoms to people, and that they would become possible only after the establishment of democracy. Finally he pointed out the timely and logical third way: as democracy should be based on public opinion of the overall population of China (not just a portion of it), the political and military unification of the nation was necessary. Different representatives of various parties should be included in the

---

[98] Zeng Zhaolun, "Lengjing yu zhenjing" [composure], *Ziyou luntan* 2, no. 6 (1944): 4.

[99] Deng Ye, "Lianhe zhengfu de tanpan yu kangzhan moqi de zhongguo zhengzhi" [Coalition government and late wartime politics], *Jindaishi yanjiu* 5 (2002): 200.

[100] "Zhengzhi shang de silu yu huolu" [Dead end and way out in politics], *Ziyou luntan* 3, no. 2 (1944): 12.

government so that their respective interests would be represented. Zhang did not use the term "coalition government," but he clearly was echoing its meaning.[101]

Around the same time, an editorial published in *Freedom Forum* titled "Looking Forward to China's Democracy" appealed to the government to remove the ban on (non-Guomindang) political parties. The anonymous author, who claimed to be a university professor, mentioned that one of the preconditions of democracy was that the Nationalist Party must allow the activities of other legal parties instead of merely acknowledging the heads of these parties as public personages.[102] Huang Yanpei, who was a centrist in the Democratic League, mentioned in an unofficial meeting of the commission in November 1944 that constitutional issues should give way to the unification of state power. Sun Ke agreed with Huang and even declared that non-Guomindang parties should also participate in political tutelage, which was theoretically monopolized by the Nationalist Party. Huang also mentioned that other members present all agreed with Sun Ke and his proposals.[103]

In late 1944, intellectuals' demands for personal freedoms gave way to a more urgent claim—the immediate reform of the government and quick establishment of a national unity government. But this also suggested the decline of the constitutional movement as intellectuals of minor parties and groups, at least temporarily, seemed to give higher priority to political participation than to democratic demands. This perhaps reminds us that intellectuals' democratic demands in the constitutional movement were as much liberal as political: liberal as they pressed the government to promote human rights; political as intellectuals from minor parties and groups viewed democracy as "a means of survival" since their legal status was not fully recognized by the government during wartime.[104] Calls for a coalition government held particular appeal for intellectuals from minor

---

[101] Zhang Shenfu, "Minzhu yu zhexue" [Democracy and philosophy], *Xianzheng yuekan* 10 (1944): 10.

[102] Cheng zhi, "Zhanwang zhongguo minzhu" [Looking forward to China's democracy], *Ziyou luntan* 3, no. 3 (1944): 11–12.

[103] Huang Yanpei, *Huang Yanpei riji*, vol. 8, 132.

[104] Edmund S.K. Fung, "Chinese Nationalism and Democracy during the War Period, 1937–1945: A Critique of the Jiuwang-Qimeng Dichotomy," in *Power and Identity in the*

parties and groups partly as it offered them a possibility for political participation.

Concluding Thoughts

The constitutional movement of 1943–1944 was launched at the highest
level of the Nationalist Party. The longstanding scholarly neglect of the
role of the Nationalist Party in the constitutional movement has led to
an underestimation of the complex relationship between the Nationalist
Party and intellectuals. In CCP historiography, as well as more recent
works, the movement was always believed to have "originated from the
minority parties and groups."[105] Without Chiang's initiative, however, it
would have been impossible for intellectuals to carry out widespread discussion and promotion of constitutional and democratic ideas in the press.
Ironically, Chiang probably made his decision to launch the constitutional
movement out of his desire to mount public pressure on the CCP.

One of the main goals of this chapter has been to elaborate on the
Nationalist Party's involvement in the constitutional movement, not to
give it political credit. The Nationalist Party and intellectuals disagreed in
their separate discourses on the constitutional movement: the former had
its own road map to constitutionalism according to Sun Yat-sen's doctrines, while the latter were more concerned with personal freedoms and
human rights.

That the Nationalist Party failed to fulfill the democratic demands
pressed by intellectuals in the constitutional movement undoubtedly contributed to the alienation of Chinese intellectuals in the late wartime period. In terms of rhetoric, many articles in early issues of Huang Yanpei's
National Bulletin dating from late 1943 and early 1944 attempted to convince readers to have patience and confidence in the authorities. By late
1944, however, Huang himself wrote a foreword calling for the realization

---

Chinese World Order: Festschrift in Honour of Professor Wang Gungwu, ed. Billy K.L. So (Hong
Kong: Hong Kong University Press, 2003), vol. 1, 211.
    [105] Wen Liming, *Di san zhong liliang*, 24.

of constitutionalism as soon as possible.[106] This is noteworthy since among members of the Democratic League Huang appeared centrist, or at least was much less a leftist than members like Shen Junru. The deteriorating military and economic situation contributed to intellectuals' ever-increasing disappointment toward the National Government after mid-1944. Eventually they chose to support the CCP's proposal to establish a "coalition government" in which all political forces could participate.

From the perspective of the National Government, despite the convoking of the National Assembly and the enactment of a constitution in 1946, the constitutional movement from 1943 failed to fulfill its two main goals. Especially, the problematic establishment of local self-governments, which was the core of Sun Yat-sen's constitutional theories, left constitutionalism only a castle in the air. From the intellectuals' perspective, the constitutional movement also failed as their democratic demands achieved so little. In early 1945 some intellectuals admitted that little improvement had been made during the previous year.[107]

While this chapter attempts to reveal the historical contingencies of the constitutional movement and contextualize intellectuals' discourse on rights and freedoms, it is necessary to examine briefly the place of the short-lived constitutional movement in the long-term struggle between the Nationalist Party and Chinese intellectuals. As early as 1928, when the new National Government was just established, Hu Shi (one of the leading public intellectuals at the time) criticized a series of unlawful arrests made by the Nationalist Party in the purge of CCP members. Hu urged the government to place its own power under the law. He also pressed the government to draft a constitution and adopt certain laws or guidelines to protect the rights of the people.[108]

During the wartime constitutional movement, Chinese intellectuals voiced democratic claims similar to those of Hu Shi, except the demand

---

[106] "Qianyan" [Foreword], *Guoxun* 378 (1944): 2.

[107] "Suishou bianyan" [Words in the beginning of the year], *Xianzheng yuekan* 12 (1945): 1.

[108] Yeh Wen-shin, "Discourse of Dissident in Post-imperial China," in *Realms of Freedom in Modern China*, ed. William C. Kirby (Stanford, CA: Stanford University Press, 2005), 180–81.

for a constitution (which lacked appeal to intellectuals). It may seem paradoxical that intellectuals on the one hand showed little interest in discussing the "fundamental" Draft Constitution but on the other hand hoped that the government could introduce several "practical" laws to secure human rights. It seems to me that this reflects the compromises made by intellectuals in facing both the powerful Nationalist Party and the imperatives of war. As Wen-hsin Yeh has argued, Chinese intellectuals had been "fashioned through vigorous encounters with the growing power of the state" and did not enjoy the security of free speech in public.[109] This was especially the case during wartime: from 1941 through most of 1943, intellectuals were completely silenced. Also, the imperatives of war left most intellectuals in a dilemma: they by no means demanded a weak state, nor did they sacrifice their longing for democracy. Edmund Fung in his latest study of wartime intellectuals argues that they attempted to reconcile "saving the nation" with "enlightening the people."[110] Both Fung and Andrew Nathan notice that several intellectuals including Shen Junru, Luo Longji, and Liang Shuming claimed the utilitarian ends of democracy by linking the protection of human rights with sustaining the war effort.[111] Such a strategy, as Nathan points out, certainly ran a risk that "it would fail to persuade those who were skeptical about the value of individual liberty for strengthening the state."[112]

As noted in the previous section, calls for political participation grew stronger as the military and economic situation grew worse. Intellectuals' democratic demands gave away to urgent calls for a national unity government. In early 1944, while many intellectuals were optimistic about the constitutional movement, Liang Shuming, in his article "On China's Constitutional Issues," surprisingly expressed pessimism. Liang's article appeared in at least two major publications—*Democracy and Constitutionalism (Minxian)* and the *Yunnan Daily*—but it seems to have received little

---

[109] Ibid., 196.

[110] Fung, "Chinese Nationalism and Democracy during the War Period," 211–15.

[111] Ibid., 212; Andrew J. Nathan, "Redefinitions of Freedom in China," in *The Idea of Freedom in Asia and Africa*, ed. Robert H. Taylor (Stanford, CA: Stanford University Press, 2002), 256.

[112] Nathan, "Redefinitions of Freedom in China," 256.

attention from either contemporaries or later historians.[113] Liang maintained that every Chinese constitutional movement since the late Qing dynasty was different from "genuine" constitutional movements in the West because China's movements were always launched during a time of national crisis. Those movements (in China) all failed because they were not aimed at true constitutionalism, but were instead a means of "saving the nation." He then predicted that the constitutional movement would inevitably flounder under the political slogan "saving the nation comes first." Unfortunately, Liang Shuming's prophetic words came true.

---

[113] Zhongguo wenhua shuyuan, *Liang Shuming wenji*, vol. 6, 455; "Tan Zhongguo xianzheng wenti" [On China's constitutional issues], *Yunnan Daily*, January 14, 1944.

9

Chongqing 1943

People's Livelihood, Price Control, and State Legitimacy

MATTHEW T. COMBS

Every morning the water carriers filled their buckets with water from the flowing rivers, hung them from their poles, and started the trek up the path of seven hundred stairs that tracked along the cliffside and back within the walls of Chongqing. Just outside of Chongqing, the Jialing and Yangzi rivers come together, inscribing and carving out over time two sides of a triangular outcropping of land. By 1943 the rivers had carved down an average of 230 feet from the plateau they had left above.[1] The city of Chongqing occupied the pinnacle of this plateau, although the primary water source for the city was the rivers below.[2] As the rivers were also the primary route for external commerce, the paths and riverbanks were often blue and white with the cloth covering countless moving bodies.[3] Once inside the city, trudging along the main thoroughfares and

---

[1] Lee McIsaac, "The City as Nation: Creating a Wartime Capital in Chongqing," in *Remaking the Chinese City: Modernity and National Identity, 1900–1950*, ed. Joseph Esherick (Honolulu: University of Hawai'i Press, 2000), 174.

[2] Theodore Harold White and Analee Jacoby, *Thunder out of China* (New York: William Sloane, 1946), 6–7.

[3] Brooks Atkinson, "Chungking's Mood Kindles New Hope," *New York Times*, August 20, 1943.

splashing "great black slabs of water on the dusty pavement,"[4] the carriers would pass by merchant shops, restaurants, peddlers, and food stalls with every seller singing out their wares for sale, with the smell of food; the sound of merchant calls mixing with blacksmiths' hammerings, tailors' sewing machines; pigs; chickens; people gossiping and yelling; babies bawling; and the occasional rumble of the rare army truck or Red Cross ambulance. Peddlers would stay long into the night, continuing to sell their wares by dim lamplight in the otherwise "humid darkness" of Chongqing.[5] Thousands of alleyways split off from the main roads and twisted and turned all over the hilltop that was Chongqing. Most native residents lived in these alleys.[6] Like fresh water from the rivers, most goods in Chongqing were transported by the muscle power of "coolies" who "trot[ted] in a slave's gait" and "never seem[ed] to rest except for a moment or two to ease their shoulders or recover their wind."[7]

In the summer, Chongqing is hot and humid, yet for the six months of winter "a pall of fog and rain overhangs [Chongqing] and coats its alleys with slime."[8] Yet the fog also protected the city from Japanese bombing during the winter months. Regular and intense summertime bombings of Chongqing, the wartime capital of the Republic of China (ROC), took place between 1939 and 1940—killing several thousand people in all. The final bombing, the first in over a year, came at midday on August 23, 1943, killing fifteen and injuring thirty-two.[9]

In 1937, before the war began, approximately 261,000 people lived in Chongqing. Lee McIsaac calculates this as a population density of 104,400

    [4] Robert Payne, *Chinese Diaries, 1941–1946* (New York: Weybright and Talley, 1970), 186.

    [5] Brooks Atkinson, "Chungking—Battered but Unbowed," *New York Times*, June 6, 1943; White and Jacoby, *Thunder out of China*, 7; Brooks Atkinson, "Chungking Is Calm as Usual in Alert: Narrow Paths to Shelters Are Clogged by Persons Carrying Bundles of Treasures," *New York Times*, May 24, 1943.

    [6] White and Jacoby, *Thunder out of China*, 6–7.

    [7] Atkinson, "Chungking—Battered but Unbowed."

    [8] Brooks Atkinson, "Heat in Chungking Is Likened to Hell," *New York Times*, August 1, 1943; White and Jacoby, *Thunder out of China*, 5–6.

    [9] Xinan shifan daxue lishi xi, Chongqing shi dang'an guan, *Chongqing da hongzha, 1938–1943* [The bombing of Chongqing, 1938–1943] (Chongqing: Chongqing chubanshe, 1992), 212–13.

Figure 9.1: Chongqing bombing from above. *Source:* Library of Congress.

people per square mile, making Chongqing "one of the world's most crowded cities" at the time.[10] By the end of 1939 when the ROC capital had moved to the city and civil servants and refugees began swarming into Chongqing, the population of the already crowded city swelled to over one million people.[11] Due in part to the crowding, people suffered from a lack of water (rationed at only one basinful per day) and all the effects on health and hygiene of the shortage of clean water: dysentery, cholera, rashes, internal parasites, and sewage pileup.[12] Although Chongqing's municipal public health authorities were successful in using inoculations to prevent cholera epidemics in 1943,[13] other diseases prevailed. Epidemics

---

[10] McIsaac, "The City as Nation," 175.

[11] White and Jacoby, *Thunder out of China*, 8.

[12] Ibid., 16.

[13] Nicole Barnes, "Protecting the National Body: Gender and Public Health in South-

of malaria swept the city each autumn,[14] and a rabies epidemic in 1943 led to new regulation of dogs.[15] Rats were a major problem as well: "Sometimes they were bold enough to swarm about your ankles as you walked at night, and the press reported that they killed babies in their cribs."[16] The rat problem led the Municipal Bureau of Sanitation to launch a "rat-catching movement," offering a reward of two *fen* (2/100 of a Chinese dollar or yuan) for each dead rat; however, the bounty was ended "when it was discovered that people were breeding rats in order to collect the money."[17]

In crowded wartime Chongqing, disease spread more widely and more rapidly than it had before. The general population of Chongqing experienced a high rate of malaria infection, even though there had been almost no malaria there before the start of the war. Additionally, "a large percentage of the infected persons are chronic sufferers with repeated relapses."[18] Tuberculosis was also spreading in Chongqing, especially among the college and high school student population, among whom the disease spread rapidly due to the cramped living conditions in their hastily constructed temporary dormitories. Yet while Chongqing required a tuberculosis ward with a capacity for five hundred patients, only sixty beds were available.[19] Often the sick could not afford medicine or could not work to support their families. In late 1943 at a Chongqing bus stop, "a well-dressed woman approached the crowd and in a low, embarrassed tone asked for help. She showed her identification card, such as every resident of Chong-

---

west China during the War with Japan, 1937–1945," PhD diss., University of California, Irvine, 2012, 104. Barnes further recounts that in later years as inflation increased, cholera cases also increased.

[14] Y.T. Yao, "Present Status of Malaria in Free China," *Chinese Medical Journal* 61, no. 1 (January 1943): 38–46.

[15] Chongqing shi difangzhi bian zuan weiyuanhui, *Chongqing shi zhi di shiyi juan* [Chonqing city gazetteer vol. 11] (Chongqing: Chongqing chubanshe, 1999), 448.

[16] White and Jacoby, *Thunder out of China*, 16.

[17] McIsaac, "The City as Nation," 183.

[18] K.T. Chen, I.L. Tang, and M.C. Wang, "Congenital Malaria: Report of a Case," *Chinese Medical Journal* 62, no. 2 (April–June 1944): 199.

[19] C.K. Chu, "The Modern Public Health Movement in China," in *Voices from Unoccupied China*, ed. Harley Farnsworth MacNair (Chicago: University of Chicago Press, 1944), 29.

qing had to have, and said that her husband was a government employee, but had been sick for months."[20]

The city itself, or at least the long-term viability of its buildings, suffered during the war, not just because of bombings but also due to the inflation crisis. By 1943 Chongqing was a boomtown rapidly and shoddily constructed and reconstructed after bombings. Structures that looked fairly stable from the outside were "really built with a bare skeleton of thin timber to support the roof, with hollow walls made of woven split bamboo plastered with a coat of mud and whitewash, in expectation of more bombings."[21] A cartoonist depicted how a new building could be put up within three hours after a bombing raid.[22] Since building materials were limited and prices high, most new buildings were impromptu affairs because if they were bombed the loss would not be too great, and, it was said, "When the government moves down river after the war most of them will not be needed."[23] The rapidly escalating building costs led to the strange juxtaposition of two buildings next door to each other, each built at the exact same expense: "A three-story brick and cut stone modern broadcasting studio built in 1939" and "a one-story mud and bamboo temporary structure" built in 1943.[24] This jumble of architecture led Lin Yutang, with his famous knack for a turn of phrase, to describe Chongqing thus: "Neither town nor country, neither city nor suburb, it was just guerilla architecture born out of this war."[25] The lack of space and high construction costs also meant that the hundreds of thousands of refugees that came to Chongqing during the war, especially the civil servants, teachers, and students, were almost all housed in difficult conditions: "Many persons, accustomed to comfortable standards of living, are now packed into overcrowded, unheated houses

---

[20] Lin Yutang, *The Vigil of a Nation* (New York: John Day, 1945), 39.

[21] Ibid., 37, 38.

[22] Huang Yao, *Chinese People in Wartime* (Guilin: Guilin keji daxue chubanshe, 1943), 88. Also available at http://huangyao.org/assets/files/1938Cple_wartime.pdf. Hereafter cited as *CPIW*.

[23] Atkinson, "Chungking—Battered but Unbowed."

[24] Brooks Atkinson, "China Must Regain Some Areas Soon," *New York Times*, September 2, 1943.

[25] Lin Yutang, *Vigil of a Nation*, 38.

Figure 9.2 Downtown Chongqing. *Source:* Library of Congress.

with dirt floors."[26] Yet after the end of the bombings in the summer of
1943, what most affected people's daily life in Chongqing was persistent
inflation, which caused hunger, anxiety, and the erosion of wealth, and also
exacerbated health crises and poor housing conditions.

EXPERIENCING INFLATION

Inflation provides a lens for exploring the daily life experiences of people
in Chongqing during the year 1943. Inflation was omnipresent—to varying degrees it affected all classes. Chongqing's residents had collectively
experienced pervasive bombing, but this was limited to the summer, and
raids were less frequent after 1940. By that time, people reacted to air raid
warnings by moving to bomb shelters with routine calm and few casual-

---

[26] Brooks Atkinson, "Economic Issues Critical in China," *New York Times*, January 21,
1943.

ties,[27] and, as mentioned above, the last Japanese bombing of Chongqing took place in August 1943. Inflation, on the other hand, did not stop: month-to-month price increases in 1943 averaged almost 10 percent. Whether one was buying rice, cooking oil, a bus ticket, or a new hat, increasing prices were a fact of life. In fact, in January 1943 an unnamed "authority" in Chongqing said, "The problem of inflation is graver than the war."[28] An examination of people's daily experiences with inflation clarifies both the extent of some people's suffering and highlights the government's failure to provide more than the basic survival-level sustenance of its people.

As the wartime capital of the refugee government of the ROC, Chongqing became the power center of the Nationalist Party (Guomindang). Yet the ROC government was not the only refugee in Chongqing; the city was a magnet for Chinese fleeing fighting in other parts of the country. Refugees fled to Chongqing because they saw it as a symbol of resistance against Japan and of hope for the nation, as seen in Lao She's (1899–1966) 1942 drama *Who First Arrived in Chongqing.* Lao She's central characters seek to escape occupied Beijing and flee to Chongqing. By the end of the play, Chongqing has taken the place of heaven, as the dying Wu Fengming utters his final words: "It is I who first arrived in Chongqing."[29]

Over 80 percent of Chongqing's wartime population was made of up such refugees from all corners of China. This created a melting pot of Shanghainese, Cantonese, northerners, and others that contributed to a perception that Chongqing was a microcosm of the nation.[30] The daily anguish of inflation was not unique to wartime Chongqing—and Chongqing was not even the worst-affected city.[31] But because the city was full of temporary wartime refugees, tales of the misery there would spread all

---

[27] Atkinson, "Chungking Is Calm as Usual in Alert."

[28] Atkinson, "Economic Issues Critical in China."

[29] Lao She, *Shei xian daole Chongqing* [Who first arrived in Chongqing], in *Lao She quanji* [The complete works of Lao She], vol. 9, 537–615 (Beijing: Renmin wenxue chubanshe, 1999), quotation on 615. Original published in serial, May–September 1942, *Zhongguo qingnian.*

[30] McIsaac, "The City as Nation," 176.

[31] Li Choh-Ming, "Inflation in Wartime China," *Review of Economics and Statistics* 27, no. 1 (February 1945): 24. Kunming was the worst off in terms of runaway inflation.

over China when people returned home. And because Chongqing was the capital, people would naturally hold the government more accountable for its perceived failures there.

DEFINITIONS AND COMPARISONS

Inflation originally referred to a "blowing out" of the money supply;[32] the term generally means an ongoing rise in price levels, the rate of which is usually determined by calculating the yearly percentage growth in the average price of a "basket of goods" such as food, clothing, housing, construction materials, transportation, and fuel or heating oil. Most modern-day central banks consider a "low but positive" inflation rate of between 1 and 3 percent annually to be healthy.[33] Inflation can also be seen as a tax, since declining currency value transfers wealth from the money-holding public to the money-printing government.[34] While wartime China's inflation was not the worst in history, it met two criteria established by economists for categorizing severe cases of inflation: (1) chronic inflation, defined as five (or more) consecutive years of inflation rates over 20 percent; and (2) acute inflation, defined as "episodes of one or two (or more) years during which rates of inflation reached 80–100 percent or more."[35] In fact, from 1939 through 1945 the city of Chongqing experienced seven years of inflation rates over 100 percent.[36]

---

[32] Carl-Ludwig Holtfrerich, *The German Inflation, 1914–1923*, trans. Theo Balderston (Berlin: Walter de Gruyter, 1986), 11.

[33] Lawrence H. White, "Inflation," in *The Concise Encyclopedia of Economics*, ed. David R. Henderson (Liberty Fund, 2008), Library of Economics and Liberty, http://www.econlib.org/library/Enc/Inflation.html.

[34] Michael K. Salemi, "Hyperinflation," in *The Concise Encyclopedia of Economics*, ed. David R. Henderson (Liberty Fund, 2008), Library of Economics and Liberty, http://www.econlib.org/library/Enc/Hyperinflation.html.

[35] Arnold C. Harberger, "Fiscal Deficits and the Inflation Process," in *Inflation and Growth in China: Proceedings of a Conference Held in Beijing, China, May 10–12, 1995*, ed. Manuel Guitian and Robert Mundell (Washington, DC: International Monetary Fund, 1996), 66.

[36] Annual inflation rates calculated by the author from semiannual wartime price indexes for Chongqing reported in Arthur N. Young, *China's Wartime Finance and Inflation, 1937–1945* (Cambridge, MA: Harvard University Press, 1965), 351.

The most widely studied historical inflation is the case of Weimar Germany after World War I, which is often linked to political instability and the rise of Nazism.[37] In Germany, while inflation had risen steadily throughout World War I and the postwar period, it was not until 1922–1923 that the most dramatic inflation occurred, with an inflation rate of over 300 percent per month.[38] As the German and Chinese cases illustrate, inflation is often (if not always) associated with wartime, and is not necessarily bad in each case. A consensus in German historiography is that the wartime inflation was not bad for World War I Germany, as it helped absorb some costs of the war, pay pensions for widows, and so forth; and inflation did not begin to undermine the government until the inflationary spiral intensified around 1922.[39]

A useful comparison for China's World War II inflation is other nations at war. During the same era, the U.S. annual inflation rate was approximately 9.6 percent, with an overall wartime increase in wholesale prices of 70 percent.[40] The U.S. government financed its war effort more through debt spending (expanding the money supply) than through taxation, and managed inflation through price controls and rationing.[41] The United Kingdom, on the other hand, largely at the urging of John Maynard Keynes, adopted higher taxation, compulsory savings, and price controls in order to fund the war and rein in inflation.[42] The resulting rate of

---

[37] See, for example, Lewis E. Hill, Charles E. Butler, and Stephen A. Lorenzen, "Inflation and the Destruction of Democracy: The Case of the Weimar Republic," *Journal of Economic Issues* 11, no. 2 (June 1977): 299–313; Holtfrerich, *German Inflation*; Adam Fergusson, *When Money Dies: The Nightmare of the Weimar Collapse* (London: William Kimber, 1975).

[38] Salemi, "Hyperinflation"; Holtfrerich, *German Inflation*, 192.

[39] I thank Frank Beiss for sharing his insight into this matter.

[40] Lee. E. Ohanian, "The Macroeconomic Effects of War Finance in the United States: World War II and the Korean War," *American Economic Review* 87, no. 1 (March 1997): 25, 26.

[41] Ibid., 25, 33; U.S. Office of Price Administration, *What Inflation Means Today* (Washington, DC: Government Printing Office, 1945), World War II Posters Collection, Illinois State Library Digital Archive, http://www.idaillinois.org/cdm/ref/collection/isl5/id/156; U.S. Office of Price Administration, *Rationing Means a Fair Share for All of Us* (Washington, DC: Government Printing Office, 1943), World War II Posters Collection, Illinois State Library Digital Archive, http://www.idaillinois.org/cdm/singleitem/collection /isl5/id/65/rec/2.

[42] Thomas F. Cooley and Lee E. Ohanian, "Postwar British Economic Growth and the Legacy of Keynes," *Journal of Political Economy* 105, no. 3 (June 1997): 443–45.

inflation in the cost of living in the U.K. was 4.4 percent annually, and overall the U.K. experienced only a 28.4 percent increase in the cost of living from 1939 to 1945.[43] Germany saw an increase of only 10 percent in general prices from 1939 to 1943, but there were shortages of most civilian consumer goods, and inflation was controlled through "rigorous" rationing of foodstuffs and consumer commodities. Due to price controls and rationing, Franz Neumann reported in October 1944, that for "all practical purposes, there is at present no price inflation in Germany."[44]

In contrast to these inflation rates in wartime Europe and America, from 1937 to 1945 the city of Chongqing experienced an average annual inflation of over 150 percent, and by 1945 prices had risen to over 2,000 times prewar (1937) levels. The average monthly price rise in Chongqing was on par with (or greater than) annual inflation rate of the United States (see Table 9.1). To rein in and control this inflation, the Nationalist government instituted a series of policies that in fall 1942 culminated in the announcement of the Program for Strengthening Price Control, which was to be instituted on January 15, 1943.

THE GOVERNMENT'S RESPONSE TO INFLATION

Under the new and ambitious Program for Strengthening Price Control, all commodity prices, transport charges, and wages were to be capped at November 1942 levels.[45] This was not the first time that the National Government had attempted price control, but the government placed great importance on this new policy, and there was real hope for its success. In the weeks leading up to implementation, there were almost daily

---

[43] Adapted from figures given in Mark Harrison, ed., *The Economics of World War II: Six Great Powers in International Comparison* (Cambridge: Cambridge University Press, 1998), 51.

[44] Franz Neumann, "The Problem of Inflation in Germany (October 16, 1944)," in Franz Neumann, Herbert Marcuse, and Otto Kirchheimer, *Secret Reports on Nazi Germany: The Frankfurt School Contribution to the War Effort*, ed. Raffaele Laudani (Princeton, NJ: Princeton University Press, 2013), 365, 366–67, 382. Neumann's reports were made to the American Office of Strategic Services.

[45] "Shishi xianjia jinri kaishi" [Implementation of price controls begins today], *Dagongbao*, January 15, 1943; "Xianjia zai gedi zhankai" [Price controls launched in all areas], *Qunzhong*, January 16, 1943, 6; Li Choh-Ming, "Inflation in Wartime China," 28, 29–30.

announcements about it in major newspapers.[46] This policy was authorized by the National General Mobilization Act and directly ordered by Chiang Kai-shek in his capacity as president of the Executive Yuan. His order included regulations for enforcement of the price control program.[47] This was a major government undertaking, and at the time it was reported by newspapers, "If the price ceiling program does not succeed the entire Chinese economic system will collapse."[48]

Chiang Kai-shek understood the seriousness of the inflation problem. In his diary for October 29, 1942, he noted that current prices were tumultuous, and that both military supplies and people's livelihoods were suffering harm.[49] He continued, writing that all departments overseeing economic matters should cooperate in controlling prices, and indicating that he believed the economic problems were a matter of life and death for the Chinese people (*guojia minzu*).[50] A week earlier, in his opening address to the Third People's Political Council on October 22, Chiang had highlighted the importance of economic issues for the war effort:

> Modern warfare is by no means merely a matter of military operations; economic affairs constitute another factor of the first importance. The implementation of the National General Mobilization Act and the advancement of economic policy will therefore have an immense influence on the course of the war. If we fail to mobilize our manpower, to effect complete economic control, to stabilize prices, to adjust production and distribution, success at the front will not free the nation from its peril.[51]

---

[46] See, for example, *Dagongbao* and *Zhongyang ribao* for January 1–15, 1943.

[47] H.P. Tseng and Jean Lyon, eds., *China Handbook, 1937–1944: A Comprehensive Survey of Major Developments in China in Seven Years of War* (Chungking: Chinese Ministry of Information, 1944), 385.

[48] Atkinson, "Economic Issues Critical in China." Atkinson cited the *Dagongbao* for this statement.

[49] Gao Sulan, ed., *Jiang Zhongzheng zongtong dang'an shilüe gaoben* [Archives of President Chiang Kai-shek: Draft chronology] (Taibei: Guoshiguan, 2011), vol. 51, 501–5. Hereafter cited as *SLGB*.

[50] *SLGB* 51:507, 514–15.

[51] Chiang Kai-shek, *The Collected Wartime Messages of Generalissimo Chiang Kai-shek,*

Here Chiang placed the control of inflation on a par with military operations in guaranteeing the safety of the nation. The topic remained on his
mind at the end of November 1942, as the program for strengthening
price control was announced, and Chiang returned to the issue in his diary.[52] Yet after this, Chiang seems to have decided that he had taken care of
the issue, as for the rest of 1943 his diary records only attention to the
economic problems but no new action to solve the crisis.[53]

The Program for Strengthening Price Control directed local governments from the provincial and municipal levels down to the county and
village levels to implement price controls and to create new bureaus for
the implementation of commodity regulations. These government organs
were empowered to fix price ceilings to be applied to the production,
wholesale, and retail prices of selected commodities; suppress black markets; and confiscate commodities if the market price was higher than the
price ceiling. The "eight essential commodities" under price control were
food, salt, cooking oil, cotton, cotton yarn, cotton piece goods, fuel, and
paper.[54] However, when this policy was implemented in Chongqing, 1,000
different commodities were selected for control, including various types of
grains, oils, and cloth.[55] Additional stipulations called for thrift among the
people and in government expenditures, the readjustment of taxation to
increase government revenue, the improvement of transportation, and further controls on commercial loans.[56]

Regulations for the enforcement of this price control program were
approved the same day as the program itself. The government allocated at
least 3 percent of the 1943 budget to funding enforcement measures.
Local governments were to enforce the price controls and to work with
local trade guilds and merchants to set prices based on the November 30,
1942, rates. Sellers were required to post government-approved prices either on a list in their place of business or on the commodities themselves,

---

1937–1945, compiled by the Chinese Ministry of Information (New York: Kraus Reprint, 1969), 714.

[52] *SLGB* 51:633, 645.

[53] *SLGB* vols. 52–55 cover 1943.

[54] Tseng and Lyon, *China Handbook*, 385–86, 389.

[55] Young, *China's Wartime Finance and Inflation*, 147.

[56] Tseng and Lyon, *China Handbook*, 386–87.

and were not allowed to change prices without approval. Black market activities were strictly prohibited, and "any one violating the laws and orders or arbitrarily raising the prices shall be immediately checked by the competent authorities and court-martialled [*sic*]."[57] Those selling foodstuffs at prices other than those set by the government or in amounts other than those specified could be punished with fines between one-half and all of the proceeds of the sale.[58] Part of the punishment of one group of violators was actually a bit of street theater as they were forced to march in a parade of shame through the street.[59]

Hoarding was also outlawed and stiff penalties were established, especially for the hoarding of foodstuffs. Hoarding small amounts could be punished with detention and a 1,000-yuan fine. Hoarding large amounts of rice or wheat could be punished with anything from six months to life imprisonment (or even capital punishment).[60] Yet with all these strict punishments and price control regulations, inflation continued apace. And some blamed hoarding for continued inflation in the prices of commodities "under control."[61]

In some respects this price control program was doomed from the start. The average price index for Chongqing had already increased by 10 percent from November 1942 to January 1943, and increased another 12 percent in February after price controls had been implemented.[62] How were commodity prices to be capped at November 1942 rates? The answer is that they were not. The *China Handbook* of 1944 claims that, as a result of this Program for Strengthening Price Control, by June 1944 "commodity prices had become considerably stabilized due both to the improved

[57] Ibid., 388. The *Dagongbao* also reported that courts martial would be used to punish violators: "Xianjia bi qi guanche" [Price controls must be carried out at this time], *Dagongbao*, January 23, 1943.

[58] Tseng and Lyon, *China Handbook*, 392.

[59] "Crowds in Chungking Boo Price Violators," *New York Times*, March 13, 1943.

[60] Tseng and Lyon, *China Handbook*, 392. The minimum amount required for convicted hoarders to receive the light sentence of six months to one year in prison was over 5,000 lbs of rice. Hoarding of more than 68 metric tons (over 130,000 lbs) would be met with life imprisonment or execution.

[61] Jiang Pengxiang, "Xianjia zhengce zhi jiantao" [A discussion of price control policy], *Dongfang zazhi* 39, no. 7 (June 15, 1943), 28–34.

[62] Young, *China's Wartime Finance and Inflation*, 351.

war situation and to the government's policy of controlling the prices and increasing the production of needed materials."[63] This description is clearly inaccurate. In Chongqing, the city that was "a model for the new price control measure," commodity prices did not stabilize in June 1944. Although food prices remained flat for the second half of 1944 (but flat at 477 times prewar price levels), they had increased 155 percent from December 1943, and the price indexes for all other commodities increased between 28 percent and 174 percent from June to December 1944.[64] These rates cannot be considered "stabilized."

The failure of the Program for Strengthening Price Control can be seen in the cases of two commodities: cloth and pork. Cloth was the most-cited example of the unrealistic requirements of the price ceiling policy. The price ceilings created an absurd situation in which the fixed price for a unit of cloth was less than the total stipulated price for all the cotton required to make that much cloth. This of course meant that manufacturers who stuck with the legally set price would already be selling their goods at a loss even without factoring in the additional cost of processing the cotton into cloth. This led some producers to be unwilling to make cotton cloth, which decreased the available supply and put upward pressure on prices.[65] The influx of refugees into Chongqing increased the demand for consumer goods, especially clothing and food. Thus in 1943 the price ceiling program actually exacerbated the inflation of cloth prices, driving clothing costs to unaffordable levels.

The case of pork is an instructive example of how people avoided commodity restrictions. Pork disappeared from the official market when the price was fixed because it was not sufficient to pay farmers to bring their pigs into Chongqing. This evident failure of the price control policy led to

---

[63] Tseng and Lyon, *China Handbook*, 381. Actual inflation figures from Young, *China's Wartime Finance and Inflation*, 351.

[64] Young, *China's Wartime Finance and Inflation*, 147. Statistics calculated from numbers given in ibid., 353. The increase in the average price index for this time period was 38 percent.

[65] This problem was already pointed out by several articles from the first half of 1943; see "Xianjia shishi hou de gongzuo" [The work after implementing price control], *Qunzhong*, April 16, 1943, 114; Wang Yunwu, "Cong xianjia dao pingjia" [From price control to price fairness], *Dongfang zazhi* 39, no. 1 (March 15, 1943): 58–61; Jiang Pengxiang, "Xianjia zhengce zhi jiantao."

pork being banned, yet restaurants still served it and people ate it, putting pork in the strange situation of being "both banned and eaten."[66] The fixing of pork prices in Chongqing was even more curious since there was no shortage of the meat in Sichuan, and due to transportation deficiencies it could not be transported anywhere else. Thus, as in the case of cloth, the price controls on pork had the effect of causing shortages where there were none before—and also drove people into the black market in defiance of government regulations.[67]

The Program for Strengthening Price Control failed both in implementation and in its basic precepts. One reason for the failure was the bureaucratic shuffling of administrative responsibility for price control. In February 1942, commodity price control was entrusted to the newly created Commodity Administration under the Ministry of Economic Affairs. But this agency was dissolved in December of the same year and replaced with the Daily Commodities Administration. But control of cotton and its products was placed under the Cotton Yarn and Cloth Administration in the Ministry of Finance. Then Chiang Kai-shek's regulations for price control stipulated that the standing committee of the National General Mobilization Council would be "temporarily designated as the highest policy-making organ for price control throughout the nation"[68] However, while this standing committee was responsible for planning, it had to coordinate between several different state organs that were placed in charge of various aspects of commodity control and price stabilization. Transport costs were the responsibility of the Ministry of Communications; foodstuffs were under the Ministry of Food, but salt was regulated by the Ministry of Finance; daily necessities and mining and manufacture were overseen by the Ministry of Economics. This byzantine administrative hierarchy was actually codified in the regulations for price control authorized by Chiang Kai-shek: each type of commodity under price control was to be regulated by a specific government agency; other govern-

---

[66] Lin Yutang, *Vigil*, 44.

[67] Arthur Young, "Letter to Mrs. Young," March 14, 1943, cited in Young, *China's Wartime Finance and Inflation*, 148.

[68] Tseng and Lyon, *China Handbook*, 383, 385. The National General Mobilization Council was made up of representatives from almost every government ministry.

ment organs were not to interfere. But enforcement was left to provincial, municipal, and other local governments. The central government must have found enforcement lax, as in mid-1944 they passed a series of emergency measures aimed at forcing provinces to comply with the price control directives issued from the center.[69]

Another likely reason for the program's failure is corruption of government officials, especially low-paid civil servants at the local level.[70] The tendency of civil servants to resort to "squeeze" as a way to make ends meet is documented below.

With the air of one explaining how foreigners could not properly understand China, the economist Li Choh-Ming attributed the price-fixing failure "to the very nature of the Chinese economy."[71] Lin Yutang attributed the failure not specifically to the nature of the Chinese economy, but rather to the nature of Chinese people:

> The answer to the problem of inflation in China can be only through the individualistic, and not through the collectivistic approach. The Chinese are either not educated enough, or not regimented enough, to submit to price control: besides, printing ration books for the three hundred million people would use up all the available paper in Free China. Things are just not done that way, and the Chinese would resist it.[72]

John King Fairbank and his contacts saw this as another example of Chiang Kai-shek's ill-conceived and failing policies. Recounting events of early 1943, he wrote how Chiang tried "to counter the inflation by fixing meat prices by decree. It didn't work, and Li Chi remarked to me that: 'It was most unsound for [Chiang Kai-shek] to put himself behind the price-fixing fiasco, as though his personal request would change the laws of

---

[69] Ibid., 386, 388–89; Li Choh-Ming, "Inflation in Wartime China," 30.

[70] Long Dajun, "Ruhe shishi pingquan guowu zhi" [How to implement a system of ration coupon purchasing], *Dongfang zazhi* 39, no. 7 (June 15, 1943): 25–26. Long does not explicitly make this criticism himself, but rather reports it as the type of criticism leveled at the price control policy by its opponents.

[71] Li Choh-Ming, "Inflation in Wartime China," 30.

[72] Lin Yutang, *Vigil of a Nation*, 43–44.

economics.'"[73] In the end, the dire predictions of economic collapse if the price ceiling program failed were false, but inflation did continue unchecked, only bringing more suffering to the people and further undermining confidence in the government.

In January 1943, Dr. Wang Chonghui, of the National Defense Council, stated that the government was "thoroughly awake to the dangers of the present situation" and was doing everything it could to stabilize the currency and reduce inflation, but "it was apparent to everyone that the government [could] not reduce the war budget [nor] bring any volume of goods to China until land communications [were] opened."[74] In September 1943, with the economic situation getting worse, a government official stated (off the record), "Unless China can take back some of the occupied territory within a year the difficulties of the Government will be greatly increased."[75] In addition to the price control program, the National Government attempted to combat its economic difficulties through food allocations to workers, taxation, attempts to secure foreign loans, and calls for frugality.

One stipulation of the 1943 price control law was that people should live frugally, as "befitting wartime": banquets, wedding and funeral feasts, festival and New Year presents, and even birthday parties as well as "other activities of unnecessary spending" were to be suppressed and prohibited.[76] In a speech commemorating the ninth anniversary of the New Life Movement on February 19, 1943, Chiang Kai-shek urged frugality among the population. He said that by following the principles of the New Life Movement, China would be able to improve its living conditions and become an equal of the advanced nations.[77] In line with this call, bans were instituted on permanent waves for women's hair and on the sale of luxury items. Army officers were forbidden from riding in rickshaws or sedan chairs, and playing cards became a penal offense.[78]

[73] John King Fairbank, *Chinabound: A Fifty-Year Memoir* (New York: Harper and Row, 1982), 252.
[74] Atkinson, "Economic Issues Critical in China."
[75] Atkinson, "China Must Regain Some Areas Soon."
[76] Tseng and Lyon, *China Handbook*, 386.
[77] "Chiang Urges Frugality," *New York Times*, February 20, 1943.
[78] "Chungking to Ration Meat, Sugar and Oil," *New York Times*, March 8, 1943.

The National Government's deficit spending habit was one of the causes of the inflationary spiral. Chiang Kai-shek's constant appeals for financial assistance from the United States and Britain, all while implying that he might seek a separate peace with Japan if funds were not forthcoming, have sometimes led to his vilification in historical scholarship. In fact, however, government leaders in part sought foreign aid as a solution to the problem of inflation, as any way the Guomindang could get more war supplies without printing more money would reduce both the government deficit and potential inflation.[79] Yet despite all government efforts to control inflation through price fixing or other measures, it continued without pause.

INFLATION BY THE NUMBERS: CHONGQING, 1937–1945

Wartime China saw a rapid rise in inflation. Chongqing was no exception. Before the National Government completed its relocation to Chongqing at the end of 1938, the city had already experienced a 40 percent rise in the cost of living compared to before the war. From January 1939 to December 1942, the average cost of living in Chongqing increased over forty-eight-fold.[80] Over the course of 1943, the cost of living in China's wartime capital would yet again triple, rising to 208 times the prewar level.[81] The logarithmic graph in Figure 9.3 charts price increases in Chongqing during the wartime period. The graph was constructed to show the doubling of prices. The first doubling, when the price index reached 2, did not occur until July 1939, when thirty months had gone by. For the first two years of the war, inflation was already high by any modern standard: an increase of 11 percent over the year 1937, and 34 percent inflation for 1938 (remember, 1–3 percent is considered healthy). From mid-1939 onward, prices doubled on average every six and a half months, ranging from April 1940,

---

[79] Chang Kia-Ngau, *The Inflationary Spiral: The Experience in China, 1939–1950* (New York: MIT Press and Wiley, 1958), 15.

[80] Young, *China's Wartime Finance and Inflation*, 352. This represents an increase of 4,703 percent.

[81] Ibid.

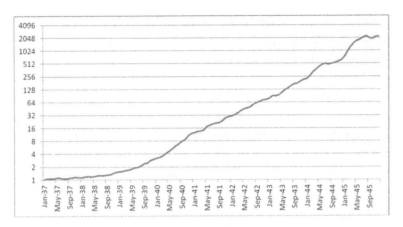

Figure 9.3: Wholesale price and cost of living increases in Chongqing, 1937–1945. The X-axis is time, reflecting monthly price data. The Y-axis is on a log base 2 scale. In the numeric values, the monthly price indexes for the prewar year of July 1936–June 1937 were averaged and that number was set as the base value for prewar prices, or 1. This graph is based on monthly reports of the inflation rate in Chongqing. Lin-log graph generated by author based on average of wholesale price and cost of living indexes produced by Nankai University, as reported by Arthur Young. Values given in table 52, Wholesale Prices and Cost of Living in Chungking, 1937–1945, in Young, *China's Wartime Finance and Inflation*, 352.

when prices reached four times prewar levels, to July 1945, when the price index hit 2,048 times the 1937 level.

The annual inflation rates are stupefying: prices at the end of 1939 were 99 percent higher than they were at the end of 1938; those of 1940 301 percent higher than in 1939; 1941 saw a 144 percent increase; 1942 a 154 percent increase; 192 percent in 1943; 186 percent in 1944; and 256 percent in 1945. Table 9.1 shows average price indexes and average month-to-month inflation growth in Chongqing, broken down by year from 1937 to 1945.[82]

Many conclusions can be drawn from all these numbers. One is that 1943 marked the beginning of runaway inflation that continued, with

---

[82] Table 9.1 also based on values given in table 52: Wholesale Prices and Cost of Living in Chungking, 1937–1945," Young, *China's Wartime Finance and Inflation*, 352.

Table 9.1: Average Price Indexes and Average Monthly Inflation Growth in Chongqing, 1937–1945

	1937	1938	1939	1940	1941	1942	1943	1944	1945
Average price index	1.08	1.27	2.09	6.37	19.38	51.36	137	446	1,735
Average monthly growth in price index (%)	1.01	2.49	5.98	12.41	7.87	8.16	9.45	9.42	11.93

only a brief pause in the autumn of 1945, all the way through the end of the Chinese Civil War until the new Communist government brought inflation under control in the early 1950s. Of course, inflation was already extremely high in 1939, and 1940 saw the worst annual increase in prices of the entire anti-Japanese war period. But relative to 1940, inflation slowed in 1941 and 1942. However, from 1943 the inflation rate picked up significantly and did not slow for the rest of the war years. Additionally, in 1943 the Chongqing price index hit both 100 and 200 times prewar levels.

But the average person would not know the exact inflation rate, unless he regularly consulted statistical publications such as the "Index Numbers of Retail Prices in Leading Cities of China," published by the Farmer's Bank of China, access to which was actually restricted.[83] Regular people instead would have experienced inflation rates when they went to the market or shops to buy their daily food or other needed items.

CAUSES OF WARTIME INFLATION

With varying degrees of significance, multiple causes of China's rampant wartime inflation can be identified: supply problems, increased demand, hoarding and speculation, expansion of the money supply, and government deficits. These causes are also all interrelated and can in many respects be attributed to the war.

Supply problems were almost entirely due to the war, with the Japanese strategy of capturing coastal provinces, port cities, and important transportation hubs and networks cutting off the flow of goods into unoccupied areas of Nationalist China.[84] Demand rose largely due to the influx

---

[83] *Zhongguo ge zhongyao chengshi lingshou wujia zhishu yue bao* [Index numbers of retail prices in leading cities of China], Zhongguo nongmin yinhang jingji yanjiuchu [Farmer's Bank of China Economic Research Division], June 1943. Published primarily in Chinese but with some English (including the title) and chart headings, the cover of the issue is prominently stamped with both the Chinese *mi* (secret, confidential) and the English "Restricted."

[84] Chang Kia-Ngau, *Inflationary Spiral*, 12–14, 34–36, 44–45. For a discussion of Guangzhouwan, see chapter 12.

of people from occupied territories, which by 1940 was said to have already increased the population of Free China by about 25 percent. The flood of refugees particularly increased inflationary pressure on the price of food and clothing.[85]

The Chinese press discussed hoarding as a major cause of price inflation. Small-scale hoarding was practiced by farmers, merchants, and families, but these practices were considered by some to be amateur efforts in comparison to the hoarding and price speculation conducted by rich people, and especially by private financial institutions, which engaged in professional speculation and hoarding.[86] As National Government financial advisor Arthur Young observed, "Most of the business of banks, other than the four government banks, consisted of financing and engaging in hoarding and speculation."[87]

While all of the above causes clearly contributed to China's pervasive wartime inflation, the main cause of inflation was the expansion of the money supply. As the Nationalist government lost revenue due to its shrinking tax base after Japanese conquests, wartime needs, including massive infrastructure projects in China's underdeveloped interior, put a huge drain on the government's coffers. The National Government paid for this deficit by printing money.[88] However, whatever the relative weight given to the causes of inflation, people experienced its effects, not its causes.

INFLATION: WINNERS AND LOSERS

Based upon his experiences living in Chongqing in late 1943 and early 1944, Lin Yutang described inflation as bringing the war home to the rear: "It is brought home to the people in their food, their dwelling, their trans-

---

[85] Chang Kia-Ngau, *Inflationary Spiral*, 14, 25–27.

[86] Ibid., 42; Young, *China's Wartime Finance and Inflation*, 325–26; Li Choh-Ming, "Inflation in Wartime China," 28; Chou Shun-hsin, *The Chinese Inflation, 1937–1949* (New York: Columbia University Press, 1963), 257.

[87] Young, *China's Wartime Finance and Inflation*, 326.

[88] Ibid., 299, 302, 315; Li Choh-Ming, "Inflation in Wartime China," 27–28; Chang, *Inflationary Spiral*, 15, 17, 27, 37, 42, 47, 58.

portation, and their habits of living."[89] With the dwindling of Japanese bombings of the city after 1941, and the final bombing of the area coming in late August 1943, inflation was the only effect of the war that reached into the daily lives of Chongqing's people. Examination of people's actual experiences with inflation, however, shows that different groups had divergent outcomes: some suffered; some saw little change; and some even benefited from inflation.

The Losers

"These days who doesn't live hand to mouth? Just surviving is considered good already."[90] These words from Wang Wenxuan, the protagonist of Ba Jin's novel *Cold Nights*, set in 1944 Chongqing, encapsulate the life situation for many real-life denizens of that city. The best-documented suffering during the wartime inflation spiral was that of the salaried class of public employees: professors, teachers, civil servants, and military officers. But before probing their situation, let us first consider the biggest losers, the unemployed. Unsurprisingly, the unemployed found it hard to provide for themselves and their families. Those who had lost their jobs or who fled to Chongqing from occupied areas and were not placed in new positions would quickly see inflation erode away their savings. The 200 percent price increase over the course of 1943 would reduce the value of any savings by two-thirds. Several criminal cases from the Chongqing Municipal Court in 1943 show the lengths that some went to in order to survive. Yet these cases also display the extent of sympathy some judges held for the suffering of the people.

The thirty-three-year-old poor and unemployed kitchen worker Huang Boming stole quilts and clothes from unknown persons and sold them for cash. Finding that he had stolen only to survive, the court took pity on him and only sentenced him to forty days detention as a "warning."[91] Since

[89] Lin Yutang, *Vigil of a Nation*, 42. Lin didn't arrive in Chongqing until September 1943, thereby missing the last Japanese bombing of the city.

[90] Ba Jin, *Hanye* [Cold nights] (1955; reprint, Shanghai: Shanghai wenyi chubanshe, 1980), 72.

[91] Sichuan Chongqing defang fayuan xingshi panjue [Chongqing Municipal Court

by mid-1943 cloth prices had increased over 20,000 percent from 1937 levels, Huang probably thought that stealing clothes would be a good source of income.[92] Zheng Jigang also thought stealing clothes would be a good way to make money. Zheng was sentenced to a 200-yuan fine and labor service.[93]

Some people just stole cash. On May 2, 1943, twenty-three-year-old Xu Hailin and thirteen-year-old Wang San were arrested and accused of pickpocketing 400 yuan on the street. Xu was convicted and given three months detention. Wang, however, was considered too young to punish and found not guilty.[94] The court also claimed it was showing leniency in the case of sixteen-year-old Zhu Jiaju when he was convicted of the March 31, 1943, break-in and attempted home robbery of 800 yuan. He was caught by the owner and taken to the police station, where he confessed. Citing his young age (under eighteen) and his poverty, the court sentenced him to "only" three months in prison—the same sentence received by twenty-three-year-old Xu Hailin (above) for successfully pickpocketing only 400 yuan.[95] In a final case reminiscent of earlier "Spanish prisoner" letter scams and our more modern "Nigerian prince" and "Trapped in London" e-mail scams, thirty-four-year-old Wang Jingruo was convicted of forging documents to attempt to gain money by fraudulently pretending to be a family member writing to request funds. Since Wang was very poor and caring for both an elderly mother and young children at home, the court sentenced him to only four months in prison.[96]

Each of these court decisions claimed to be granting a more lenient punishment to the convicted offenders. While some of the sentences are clearly not very lenient, it is likely that the judges just took pity on these people who faced difficulty in a time of economic hardship. Perhaps the judges empathized with them since as civil servants, the judges were part

Criminal Case files], May 16, 1943. Unpaginated bound volume in Stanford University Library. Hereafter cited as CQMC.

[92] For statistics on commodity price increases, see Young, *China's Wartime Finance and Inflation*, 353.

[93] CQMC, May 8, 1943.

[94] Ibid., June 25, 1943.

[95] Ibid., May 29, 1943.

[96] CQMC, June 14, 1943.

of the class whose salaries did not keep up with inflation and who could afford to eat only because of employee subsidies.[97]

While in general the salaried public employees suffered under inflation as the purchasing power of their monthly income failed to keep up with rapidly rising prices, the government provided food disbursements or sold rice, salt, coal, and other essentials to their employees at low rates.[98] The government also provided rice allowances to students.[99] In his June 1943 book *Chungking in Cartoons*, cartoonist Huang Yao depicted a poor professor saving money by carrying home his own rice ration (Figure 9.4).[100] Professors were forced to economize in other ways, as Huang Yao depicts in another cartoon of a professor skipping an umbrella in favor of a (cheaper) bamboo hat (Figure 9.5).[101]

Yet while food subsidies provided enough staples to survive, many people still had difficulty maintaining a balanced diet and were threatened with malnourishment. For one manager of a government manufacturing plant, his salary was only enough to buy rice for himself and his daughter.[102] Another government servant recounted how he could rarely afford meat and could afford neither books nor magazines.[103] Chinese professors had gone from being comfortably middle class to a condition of poverty: "none of them pretends to keep well-clothed and many are insufficiently fed."[104] A joke from the time preserves the apprehension people felt over securing enough to eat in a time of high inflation: A doctor conducted an autopsy on a corpse and declared the man died from swelling. The judge was confused and asked, "But this man is so skinny that all that remains is

---

[97] Brooks Atkinson, "Chungking Prices Bar New Clothing," *New York Times*, June 10, 1943; Young, *China's Wartime Finance and Inflation*, 320; "China Curbs Students," *New York Times*, September 25, 1943; Li Choh-Ming, "Inflation in Wartime China."

[98] Jiang Pengxiang, "Xianjia zhengce zhi jiantao"; Atkinson, "Chungking Prices Bar New Clothing." Factories and businesses also provided these types of subsidies to their employees. These cases are discussed below.

[99] "China Curbs Students," *New York Times*, September 25, 1943.

[100] *CPIW*, 11.

[101] *CPIW*, 6.

[102] Atkinson, "Chungking Prices Bar New Clothing."

[103] Atkinson, "Economic Issues Critical in China."

[104] Atkinson, "Chungking Prices Bar New Clothing."

節省人力物力的緩語下教授自
担"平價米"回家

To cconomize man-power, the professor
himself carries his chcap-ration rice home.

Figure 9.4: Poor professor carrying rice. *Source: Chinese People in War-time.*

bone. How did he die of swelling?" The doctor replied, "He died of commodity price swelling!"[105]

Part of the food anxiety stemmed from the fact that most Chinese had already been suffering from undernourishment before the inflation began. The primary reason for this was the "low purchasing power of the average person or family."[106] On average, Chinese diets were largely vegetarian and deficient in animal proteins, minerals, and vitamins.[107] Yet wartime government and employer food subsidies only provided staple foods like

---

[105] Wang Zhikun, Gu Lejin, and Yuan Jiahong, eds., *Xiaolin jiqu* [Record of interesting jokes] (Chonging: Chongqing chubanshe, 2006), 26.

[106] J. Heng Liu and C.K. Chu, "Problems of Nutrition and Dietary Requirements in China," *Chinese Medical Journal* 61, no. 2 (April–June 1943): 95.

[107] Ibid., 96.

6

冒雨去上課的教授戴了笠帽

（ 戴人的笠帽比雨傘經濟與方便，大學私授
冒雨去上課也怕用了這個。 ）

Th: professor goes to class in a bamboo
rain hat, more economical and convenient
than umbrella and rain coat.

Figure 9.5: Professor in
bamboo rain hat. *Source:
Chinese People in War-
time.*

rice—people were expected to use their own income to purchase meat and
other nonstaples.[108] As increasing costs continuously made these nonsta-
ple foodstuffs more difficult to purchase, "the lack of a balanced diet
among salaried people at home and among soldiers at the front gradually
sap[ped] vitality and [was] serious for the entire nation."[109]

   The inevitable consequence of this general undernourishment was, as
a medical study found at the time, "prevalence of deficiency diseases, lowered resistance against infections and very much lowered expectation of
life."[110] In other words, high inflation led to low nutrition, which led to

---

[108] Young, *China's Wartime Finance and Inflation,* 319–20.
[109] Atkinson, "Economic Issues Critical in China."
[110] Liu and Chu, "Problems of Nutrition and Dietary Requirements," 95. Studies of
daily food intake among different classes in Chongqing conducted in 1941 and 1943 showed
that people were eating 10–15 percent less than their recommended daily calories. For a table

increased vulnerability to disease. But if one did get sick, medicine was also scarce and expensive. Lin Yutang observed, "One just cannot afford to be ill."[111] Furthermore, as Ba Jin illustrates in *Cold Nights*, when one was sick not only was medicine expensive, but one could not afford to take time off to recuperate.[112] Although strenuously denied by Red Cross representatives, there were rumors that Red Cross medicines were being hoarded too. There were also reports of soldiers selling medicines proscribed by the Army Medical Corps.[113]

In addition to facing undernourishment, civil servants and educators saw their purchasing power dramatically decrease due to an erosion of over 80 percent of their real income.[114] In *Cold Nights*, the main character's mother suggests they relax and go see a movie, to which Wang Wenxuan replies, "Intellectuals are a lower class now. Watching movies requires money which only drug dealers and smugglers can afford."[115] Or, as described in cartoonist Huang Yao's 1943 cartoon: "Everyone is so busy for earning his rice that he has no time to enjoy" (Figure 9.6).[116]

Loss of income resulted in "many good men" leaving the civil service due to their inability to maintain their standard of living. Of those who stayed in the service, many lost their entire life savings. They sold furniture and other belongings, and concentrated all of their household expenses on food and other vital necessities. One extreme case was a family that had been diligently saving "a substantial amount" each year for their son's education: "When toward the end of the war he had his 18th birthday, they took all the funds and bought him a cake."[117]

The focus on survival and the high cost of cloth made new clothing an extreme rarity. An observer reported that since a new dress might cost a

---

summarizing these studies, see ibid., 97. For a table of recommended daily caloric intake, see ibid., 105.

[111] Lin Yutang, *Vigil of a Nation*, 42.

[112] Ba Jin, *Hanye*, 52.

[113] Brooks Atkinson, "Red Cross in China Find Relief Able," *New York Times*, May 16, 1943.

[114] Li Choh-ming, "Inflation in Wartime China," 26.

[115] Ba Jin, *Hanye*, 81.

[116] Huang Yao, *Manhua Chongqing* (Guilin: Guilin Keji daxue chubanshe, 1943), 73. Also available at http://huangyao.org/assets/files/1940/1943_chungking_in_cartoons_web.pdf.

[117] Young, *China's Wartime Finance and Inflation*, 320–21.

73

每個人連人生樂趣也顧不了地忙着這
碗"帽兒頭"("上尖兒白飯"的四川名字)

Everyone is so busy for earning his
rice hat he has no time to enjoy.

Figure 9.6: Too busy working
to enjoy life. *Source: Manhua
Chongqing.*

month's wages, and a new white-collar worker's business suit might cost
the month's salary of a bank manager, "almost no one buys clothes in
Chungking."[118] One civil servant told a reporter that he was wearing sec-
ondhand clothing from a friend who had entered the army, and that he
"could replace worn-out shirts, stockings and underwear only with the
greatest difficulty."[119] Ba Jin's novel *Cold Nights* highlights the concern that
salaried people would have felt about rising cloth prices: while repairing a
coat, one character complains that her poor grandson has worn the coat
for three years already and it will be too small the following year, yet they
do not have the money to buy a new one.[120] Huang Yao's cartoons also
showed how people adopted cheaper methods of clothing themselves: a
college student who switches to sandals rather than the leather shoes he is
used to (Figure 9.7), and old tires that become shoe soles (Figure 9.8).[121]

---

[118] Atkinson, "Chungking Prices Bar New Clothing."
[119] Atkinson, "Economic Issues Critical in China."
[120] Ba Jin, *Hanye*, 36.
[121] *CPIW*, 5, 20.

5

大學生穿舊跳舞皮鞋的腳

（大學生穿舊舞皮鞋的腳，後穿了厚實

簡輕跟的草鞋。）

The college student puts sanda's on feet
which are used to leather dancing shoes.

Figure 9.7: College student in sandals. *Source: Chinese People in Wartime.*

The inflationary situation prompted tendencies toward inefficiency and corruption in civil servants, who often left their offices for long periods of time every day to "engage in outside remunerative activities." There was also "constant stimulus to engage in irregularities and accept graft or squeeze."[122] One instance of this corruption can be seen in the early 1943 Chongqing Municipal Court conviction of a judicial official. Forty-six-year-old Li Peng was discovered charging a fee of one and a half yuan for filing documents in the local court where he worked. In a telling example of how widespread this type of corruption was, Li's defense was that he did not know his actions were illegal.[123] Regarding this type of corruption, one government advisor explained, "When an ordinary man is faced with a choice between irregular activities and seeing his family gradually starve,

---

[122] Young, *China's Wartime Finance and Inflation*, 321.

[123] CQMC, February 23, 1943.

20

周上汽車(車——汽車胎做鞋底

(利用廢了(車胎來做堅固的鞋底。)

Old tyres become shoe-soles.

Figure 9.8: Tires become shoes. *Source: Chinese People in Wartime.*

he is likely to consider that society owes him and his family a living and to feel that it is not wrong to supplement his income in devious ways."[124] The morale difficulties of the Sichuan Provincial Health Administration employees can be illuminating here as well. The staff was not concerned with war developments but rather with the economic situation: "When every member of an institution is constantly worried about his daily life, one may readily appreciate the task of doing constructive work through that institution."[125] These workers were concerned with the economic livelihood of themselves and their families and were thus distracted and inefficient at work.

---

[124] Young, *China's Wartime Finance and Inflation,* 321.

[125] C.C. Chen (Chen Zhiqian) in a letter to Marshall C. Balfour (officer of the Rockefeller Foundation, 1939–1944), November 6, 1940, Szechuan Provincial Health Administration files, 1939–1942, Folder 161, Box 18, Series 601, Record Group 1.1, Rockefeller Foundation Archives, Rockefeller Archive Center, New York. I thank my colleague Nicole Barnes for sharing this information.

From these stories we catch a glimpse of how the salaried class of public workers truly was living "an austere, Spartan life with a roof over-head but no luxuries," many of them sharing that roof overhead by moving in together three or four to a room in order to save money.[126] According to a government spokesman at the time, "China's war has brought about some leveling of social strata. ... The rich are poorer, and the poor are richer."[127] Huang Yao depicts this sort of leveling in his cartoon of a general and a modern girl eating at a public dining hall (*gonggong shitang*).[128] But according to a Chinese sociologist of the time, while the rapid inflation had led to a redistribution of wealth among classes, "The burden of war is solely on the shoulders of those whose income is controllable by the government. Those who are free from the burden of war are mostly the less-educated people."[129]

Not Losers, But Not Quite Winners

Perhaps "free from the burden of war" is not the most accurate description of China's less educated. But in wartime Chongqing, "relatively free from the burden of inflation" may be an apt description. Farmers, manual labor-ers, factory workers, and other private business employees all experienced only slight deterioration in their standard of living—and in some cases even saw modest gains.

Like public employees, factory workers also received monthly rice al-lotments, with skilled workers receiving more food than unskilled workers (including meat).[130] Factory workers' wages also failed to keep up with inflation.[131] And some factory workers only received a token monthly sal-

---

[126] Atkinson, "Chungking Prices Bar New Clothing."

[127] Atkinson, "China's Taxes Explained," *New York Times*, July 22, 1943.

[128] *CPIW*, 41.

[129] Fei Hsiao-T'ung, "Some Social Problems of Free China," in *Voices from Unoccupied China*, ed. Harley Farnsworth MacNair (Chicago: University of Chicago Press, 1944), 62. The chapters in this volume were originally talks given by the authors at the University of Chicago Harris Foundation Lectures, 1943.

[130] Li Danke, *Echoes of Chongqing: Women in Wartime China* (Urbana: University of Illinois Press, 2010), 123–27.

[131] Li Choh-Ming, "Inflation in Wartime China," 24.

ary of two or three yuan in addition to their food supplements, making their monthly income lower than that of professional laborers like carpenters and rickshaw pullers.[132] In the words of Lin Yutang, "The managers of the factories must see to it that the workers and their families do not starve. But to say that they are thriving is a travesty."[133]

Businesses could both generally pay salaries that kept up with inflation and also provide food and lodging for their staff. However, "many enterprises suffered so severely from the fighting, economic deterioration, uncertainty, and confusion, that this limited what they could do to meet the problems of inflation."[134] One compelling example of this is the case of Ji Cairong. In January 1943, this thirty-seven-year-old boat captain was under contract to transport a load of coal for the government. Instead, he absconded with the entire cargo, selling it for cash, which he spent to feed his own employees. This Robin Hood figure was caught and prosecuted. After an investigation confirmed not only that Ji had indeed used his ill-gotten cash to feed his sailors but also that Ji himself was in debt 3,000 yuan, the judge, in a show of "sympathy," sentenced Ji to six months in prison.[135]

Yet not everyone received allotments of rice or other staples. Farmers, laborers such as water carriers and rickshaw pullers, and the unemployed all had to fend for themselves when it came to food. Farmers of course grew their own food, and with the decreasing real value of their contractually stipulated rent and the increasing numeric value of the prices they received for their crops, it is possible that the situation of farmers actually improved with inflation.[136] However, as their prewar income was so low, "one can say only that they are feeling less the pinch of poverty."[137] A court case from May 1943 gives an example of tension that could arise between landowners and tenant farmers. On April 27, 1943, when for an unknown

[132] Li Danke, *Echoes of Chongqing*, 123–27; Li Choh-Ming, "Inflation in Wartime China," 24.

[133] Lin Yutang, *Vigil of a Nation*, 40.

[134] Young, *China's Wartime Finance and Inflation*, 321.

[135] CQMC, March 26, 1943.

[136] Fei Hsiao-T'ung, "Some Social Problems of Free China," 53.

[137] Lin Yutang, *Vigil of a Nation*, 40.

reason one landlord sought to cancel a contract with the tenant farmers on his land—perhaps to sell the land, or to renegotiate a contract that would pay him higher rent—the farmers attacked the landlord and broke his ribs. While this was a serious attack on the landlord, when the farmers were brought to trial the judge took pity on the men who had to work to support their families and only sentenced them to twenty days in detention, which he suspended for two years.[138]

Like farmers, the situation of some laborers improved during the war. In the words of one contemporary, "Before the war they had trouble finding work, now there is plenty of work and they can demand higher wages."[139] A curious example of this is the case of the city's rickshaw pullers. In October 1943, for a ten-minute run they collected a fare of about 15 yuan, the equivalent of a bowl of noodles or perhaps a pack of cheap cigarettes.[140] This seems like a small amount, yet multiple accounts report that they refused fares as often as nine times out of ten.[141] One writer described these laborers as "of the royal line," for "[they] accept passengers only when the distance is short, the destination agreeable and the fee satisfactory."[142] During hot weather, the average rickshaw puller spent most of the day sleeping under the canopy of his rickshaw, and "if you are impudent enough to poke him awake he starts shaking his head 'no' before he is fully conscious."[143] This regal abstention from hard work is attributed to the ease with which they regularly earned money.[144] Huang Yao's cartoon of a rickshaw puller bringing home a large slab of meat, "more than his family used to eat in a month before the war," depicts, if not necessarily reality, at least a common perception of the newfound well-being among these laborers (see Figure 9.9).[145]

The root cause of the ease with which rickshaw pullers earned money

[138] CQMC, May 26, 1943.
[139] Fei Hsiao-T'ung, "Some Social Problems of Free China," 54.
[140] Lin Yutang, *Vigil of a Nation*, 40, 41.
[141] Ibid., 39; "U.S. Envoy in China Has Car Troubles," *New York Times*, August 15, 1943.
[142] Atkinson, "Chungking—Battered but Unbowed."
[143] "U.S. Envoy in China Has Car Troubles."
[144] Ibid.
[145] CPIW, 31.

31

昔日有"牛角掛書" 今日有 "車角掛肉"

(膂力的黃包車夫，在戰時中搵天工作後
都能買着肉，掛在車前上回家用羹。)

Figure 9.9: Rickshaw puller   The rickshaw man brings a piece of
bringing home meat. *Source:*   pork bigger than all the meat his family
Chinese People in Wartime.   used to eat in a month before the war.

was likely their ability to set their own wages through the act of negotiating the fare before transporting a passenger. This would allow their wages to keep up with inflation on a daily basis, so they could avoid burning excess calories by working only as much as necessary. Yet rickshaw pullers were evidently a cut above the average transport "coolie." The most massive transport undertaking Chongqing saw in 1943 was likely the June 2 move of the American embassy. This near-herculean effort required 550 laborers and five "dingy, battered junks" that sailed down the Yangzi from the old embassy, and then poled back up the Jialing River to the beach nearest the new embassy compound. For a move that began at five-thirty in the morning and took all day, the Americans paid 38,000 yuan.[146] Assuming all that money went directly and evenly to the 550 workers, each received slightly more than 69 yuan. Recalling that a ten-minute rickshaw fare was 15 yuan, the men who moved the American embassy seem poorly paid.

Winners

Aside from the government, which benefited from the "inflation tax" or wealth transfer from the money-holding public to the money-printing government, those who gained most were the wealthy, bankers, and powerful people who could either use their own capital or secure bank loans to engage in commodity speculation.[147] The fact that hoarders got richer during a time of war and national sacrifice while the rest of the people seemed to get poorer or saw no real improvement in their situation was resented by many. One writer argued that the government should not be tolerant of hoarders, people who lived rich lives in wasteful and luxurious fashion while simultaneously destroying the economic base of the country during war. Blaming them for the inflation, he called them "degenerate scum" (*bailei*).[148] The public evidently agreed, and consequently many government policies aimed at stopping inflation targeted bank lending and other activities thought to contribute to hoarding and commodity speculation.[149]

LOSS OF PUBLIC CONFIDENCE

Analysts thought at the time that the greatest danger of inflation was that people would lose confidence first in the currency and next in the government.[150] Underpaid teachers and public employees were demoralized by

---

[146] Brooks Atkinson, "550 Coolies Move American Embassy," *New York Times*, June 9, 1943.

[147] Chou Shun-Hsin, *Chinese Inflation*, 256–57.

[148] Jiang Pengxiang, "Xianjia zhengce zhi jiantao," 34.

[149] Chang Kia-Ngau, *Inflationary Spiral*, 39.

[150] Atkinson, "Economic Issues Critical in China."

the burden of inflation, which they felt rested solely on their shoulders. Chou Shun-hsin, another analyst of Chinese wartime inflation, wrote in 1963 that the "inequitable distribution of the burden produced widespread graft and corruption among the civil servants, and it undoubtedly was an important factor in the downfall of the Nationalist government."[151]

This sentiment is reflected in Ba Jin's *Cold Nights*. The main character's friend, who was a writer, is despondent after his wife has died in childbirth. He looks to drink and death to escape and laments, "We are law-abiding and suffer, while others get rich and become high government officials at our expense."[152]

Some, like economist Li Choh-ming and author Lin Yutang, argued that people were not demoralized. Li felt that since inflation only adversely affected the salaried class, "the question of morale under inflation does not arise for the great majority of the population." He believed that those who faced the "hardships and deprivations" of inflation were the well-educated citizens "whose deep conviction in continued resistance cannot be easily shaken."[153] Lin Yutang wrote that since inflation had been going on like that for the previous "three years," everyone knew "inflation is part of the war, and since everyone wants to carry the war to the bitter end, they do not see how the inflation can be avoided." He also said, "The Chinese people do not grumble, but are more likely to smile at their misfortunes."[154]

Yet some Chinese people did grumble, if not in the censored press then to their friends. One disgruntled citizen wrote that while it was "the sacred duty of every person and the country to endure all sufferings for the nation's good," it was distressing to see government officials "make profit from the muddled situation and thus further their private purses so as to live a comfortable life."[155] In 1943, John King Fairbank found that "the

---

[151] Chou Shun-Hsin, *Chinese Inflation*, 258.

[152] Ba Jin, *Hanye*, 42.

[153] Li Choh-Ming, "Inflation in Wartime China," 32.

[154] Lin Yutang, *Vigil of a Nation*, 42.

[155] Letter from T.T. Chang, *China Weekly Review*, Shanghai, October 25, 1941, cited in Young, *China's Wartime Finance and Inflation*, 323–24.

government was peculiarly dependent on its reputation ... its public image."[156] Yet as inflation got worse and "malnutrition and despair riddled the salaried class," the situation reached a point where scholars began to feel alienated from the government.[157] Fairbank recalled a conversation with his university professor friend he had recorded in early 1943: "The intellectuals would not mind starving if they felt they were mobilized or if all classes were taking it together. But they see gross inequality and lavish spending in high places."[158] When leading officials imported fresh foreign food by air while common people subsisted hand-to-mouth on rice allotments, it was only natural for people to feel a sense of injustice.[159] This feeling could only be compounded in the case of Fairbank's friends by the fact that one friend had lost two children to malnutrition, and another friend had lost his wife. It was this spirit among the intellectuals that led Fairbank to conclude, "A lot of intellectuals will therefore get lost, some will die, and others will become revolutionaries."[160]

The National Government's wartime minister of communications believed that Chiang Kai-shek was "overconfident of his ability to surmount the financial obstacles of a war economy."[161] He saw that government leaders followed a "strange combination of traditional Chinese beliefs and modern authoritarian ideas: 'Where there is land, there is money,' and 'Where there is absolute power, there are goods,'" meaning that their territory would provide them with sufficient cash and that money would then "be able to command the real resources required for the conduct of war."[162] As we have seen, this was unfortunately not the case as inflation grew largely unchecked.

In the epilogue to *Cold Nights*, Shu-sheng, the wife of the main character, overhears two men worriedly talking about how to get home from

[156] Fairbank, *Chinabound*, 247.

[157] Ibid., 244, 252.

[158] Ibid., 252.

[159] Letter from T.T. Chang, cited in Young, *China's Wartime Finance and Inflation*, 323–24.

[160] Fairbank, *Chinabound*, 252.

[161] Chang Kia-Ngau, *Inflationary Spiral*, 18.

[162] Ibid.

Chongqing before they starve, as common people cannot get steamer tickets back downriver. They say, "[This] victory is their victory, not ours."[163]

Conclusion

The rapid and severe price inflation in Chongqing during the anti-
Japanese war was part of a larger inflationary spiral that affected all of
China. By focusing on the experiences of people living within one city
within the time span of one year, I hope that the extent of suffering caused
by uncontrollable price increases has been made clear. After the sporadic
Japanese bombing of Chongqing ended in August 1943, inflation was
truly what brought the war home to citizens far from the front lines.
While some profited from the inflation, it brought many of them hunger,
anxiety, shoddy housing, and disease. It destroyed their savings and undermined their standard of living.

The inflation was caused by commodity hoarding and speculation, lack
of supply due to transportation difficulties and the Japanese blockade,
high demand because of dramatically increased population, and, most significantly, by the government printing money to cover its wartime deficit
spending. In these respects, the Chinese inflation is quite similar to that
experienced in Weimar Germany. The Weimar inflation also eroded real
income, evaporated savings, and engendered desperation, disease, and
hunger among the German population.

However, unlike the case of Germany, many Chinese were malnour-
ished before the onset of inflation. A significant proportion of Chongqing
lived through the inflation only because their employers (the government,
factories, or other businesses) provided food (especially rice) allotments or
subsidies in addition to regular salaries, or they grew their own food (e.g.,
farmers). However, while factories and other businesses could provide for
their staff, the government found it more difficult to provide enough for
all the civil servants—many of whom could afford to buy nothing more

---

[163] Ba Jin, *Hanye*, 277.

than food for their families, and even then at bare subsistence levels. This led to an exacerbation of the underlying problem of malnourishment and increased the populations' susceptibility to disease. Of particular political importance was the malnourishment and consequent suffering and disaffection experienced by the small but politically active middle class. Malaria, tuberculosis, and many vitamin deficiency diseases became common in wartime Chongqing.

The government's success rate in responding to the crisis was mixed, but largely failing. The taxation of rice and grain production in kind rather than in cash was successful in allowing the government to collect cereals it could distribute directly to soldiers and civil servants. The basic rice allotments that came from this probably kept the majority of Chongqing civil servants from the brink of starvation. Unfortunately this could be considered a case of robbing Peter to pay Paul, since the confiscation of grain contributed to famine conditions in Henan Province (chapter 10). The successes of the Guomindang government in procuring foreign financial assistance also lessened the potential extent of the inflation. If it can be considered a coherent government policy, rather than just the humane compassion of municipal court judges, the leniency shown to some offenders who lived in poverty surely helped ameliorate their sufferings.

However, the government's failure to curb deficit spending only continued the vicious cycle of spiraling inflation. When viewed as a wealth-transferring tax that put purchasing power in the hands of the government as it printed money at the expense of ordinary people who held ever-depreciating currency, the impact of the government's failure to halt inflation is only underscored further. If the abject poverty and hunger of citizens selling furniture to scrape together enough funds to feed their families is juxtaposed with the government's print-and-spend policies, Chiang Kai-shek's February 1943 call for frugality becomes both bizarrely absurd and supremely hypocritical.

The government's final failure to control inflation can be placed squarely within 1943. Price ceilings boldly enacted in January with great publicity and public fanfare proved utterly ineffective and was more evaded than followed. By December 1943, not only had price controls failed, but the average price index had increased over 200 percent from the November 30, 1942, levels at which prices were supposedly capped. The government's complete failure here could not but contribute further to the suffering salaried class's loss of confidence in their leaders. As they looked to the top and perceived inefficiency, incompetency, corruption, and waste, the salaried class felt that the burden of war was solely on their shoulders. Morale was low and corruption high as average civil servants constantly worried about the difficulties of daily life and sought ways to supplement their incomes and food consumption.

By mid-1943, "informed Chinese" in Chongqing were all convinced that Japan would eventually be defeated. However, the war remained "on a dead level," and "the beginning of the end [was] not in sight."[164] Arthur Young has argued that the government's failure to plan for postwar financial stability and its "inability to deal with the inflation" played a major role in "making China ripe for revolution" and the fall of the Guomindang on the mainland.[165] After 1943 the government deficit only continued to grow, thus "generating the inflation that was to bring Free China near economic collapse in the later stages of the war."[166] The stories recounted herein have detailed the hardships of many Chongqing residents, especially the salary-earning civil servants and teachers, in the face of rapidly rising inflation that, despite attempts at price controls, accelerated through 1943 and by and large did not slow down until after the final Communist victory. As a result, the newly poor intellectuals and former middle-class teachers and civil servants lost faith in the Guomindang government's ability to manage the economy.

---

[164] Brooks Atkinson, "China's Arms Low but Spirits High," *New York Times*, July 8, 1943.
[165] Young, *China's Wartime Finance and Inflation*, 316, 328.
[166] Chang Kia-Ngau, *Inflationary Spiral*, 18.

10

Saving the Nation, Starving the People?

The Henan Famine of 1942–1943

KATHRYN EDGERTON-TARPLEY

Who knew that of our thirty million compatriots [in Henan], most are already trapped in the hell of death by famine. The exposed corpses of those who starved to death become meat; families who flee bringing along the old and young are scattered; refugees packed together in a crowd are beaten with rods yet are still unable to obtain a relief committee registration card. ... Particularly incomprehensible is [the fact that] the central authorities long ago took note of the disaster conditions in Henan, and the high officials sent by the central authorities to inspect the disaster also long since concluded their work and returned. We also heard that the central authorities allocated a considerable sum for relief funds. Now half a year has passed, but up until the time this newspaper's correspondent sent his report on the 17th of last month [January 17, 1943], we still have not seen relief funds provided, and millions of disaster victims are still anxiously waiting. What is the reason for this?

—*Dagongbao*, February 2, 1943

Concerning the Henan famine, after the government sent high ranking officials from the central authorities to inspect disaster conditions last year, it has long since actively provided relief. ... If those in charge of relief,

323

vowing diligence and care and working hard regardless of criticism, receive and carry out the central government's directives, then the outcome of the test posed by the Henan disaster is sure to prove the strength of our ability to relieve disaster.

—*Zhongyang ribao*, February 4, 1943

The Henan famine of 1942–1943 provides an important window on possible tipping points in China during the War of Resistance against Japan. Over the course of the disaster, between 1 and 3 million of the North China province's prefamine population of 30 million people died of starvation and famine-related diseases, while another 3 million fled the province.[1] "It was the greatest disaster of the war in China, one of the greatest famines in the world," wrote the American journalist Theodore H. White after touring the famine-stricken province in 1943.[2] To commemorate the seventieth anniversary of the disaster, in 2012 the famine was drawn back into public memory on a grand scale by the big-budget war epic *Back to 1942* (Yi jiu si er). Directed by the celebrated Chinese director Feng Xiaogang, based on a 1990 novella by the Henan native Liu Zhenyun, and starring high-profile American actors, the film brings the plight of individual famine refugees into vivid visual relief while also exploring the wartime political context that exacerbated famine conditions.[3]

The immediate catalyst for the famine was the serious drought that struck Henan in the spring and summer of 1942. Provincial newspapers

---

[1] Wang Tianjiang et al., *Henan jindai dashiji, 1840–1949* [Major events in modern Henan, 1840–1949] (Zhengzhou: Henan renmin chubanshe, 1990), 418. Most Chinese- and English-language publications on the Henan famine estimate that the famine led to approximately 3 million deaths. In contrast, Anthony Garnaut's newly published quantitative study puts the number of excess deaths caused by the famine at under 1 million. Garnaut derives this lower estimate by using a survey of the impact of the famine organized by the Nationalist government in 1943, in concert with analysis of the relative size of age cohorts born during the famine years versus that of cohorts born in the surrounding nonfamine years. Anthony Garnaut, "A Quantitative Description of the Henan Famine of 1942," *Modern Asian Studies* 47 (2013): 2009, 2032–45.

[2] Theodore H. White and Annalee Jacoby, *Thunder out of China* (New York: William Sloane, 1946), 176–77.

[3] Feng Xiaogang, dir., and Liu Zhenyun, screenplay, *Back to 1942* [Yi jiu si er] (Beijing: Huayi Brothers, 2012).

began to sound the alarm in July, after the winter wheat crop planted the previous autumn and harvested in May and June failed and the roads began to be filled with beggars and people praying for rain.[4] Exceptionally hot temperatures and continued lack of rain then decimated the summer crops, including sorghum, millet, maize, black beans, and sweet potatoes, which were normally planted in June and harvested in autumn. "The Henan summer crop in 1942 failed spectacularly, with yields at only one-third the pre-war average," writes Anthony Garnaut. When combined with the poor winter wheat harvest, "average crop yields in Henan in 1942 were in fact 40 percent below the pre-war average."[5] By September, missionaries stationed in Henan were reporting famine conditions. "Famine is hitting this district this year, for after the long drought of summer which fairly dried things up, much of the wheat has been commandeered for the military and people are already getting down to their last resources," wrote Helen Mount Anderson, a China Inland Mission missionary stationed in eastern Henan.[6] On October 20, President Chiang Kai-shek sent two high-level Guomindang officials to Henan to investigate the situation. Late in 1942 the Nationalist government on both the central and provincial levels began relief work. The central government gave Henan 200 million yuan (half of it as a loan) for relief expenditures, and Chiang also ordered a reduction in Henan's grain taxes.[7] The relief provided did not begin to meet the enormous need. According to the *Henan Minguo ribao* (Henan republican daily), a leading provincial

---

[4] "Zaixiang yicheng, xun mou jiuji" [Disaster is already occurring; quickly begin relief], *Qianfengbao*, July 24, 1942, in Song Zhixin, ed., *1942: Henan da jihuang* [1942: The great Henan famine] (Wuhan: Hubei renmin chubanshe, 2005), 120–22.

[5] Garnaut, "A Quantitative Description," 2020–23. The Nationalist government's wartime agricultural production data used by Garnaut cover only those counties in Henan that remained under Nationalist control. His quantitative analysis does not include the roughly one-third of the province under Japanese or Communist control during the famine.

[6] Letter from Helen Mount Anderson to her mother, Louise Wadsworth Mount, September 11, 1942, Folder 7, Box 1, Collection 231, Papers of Ian Rankin and Helen Mount Anderson, Archives of the Billy Graham Center, Wheaton, Illinois.

[7] Song Zhixin, *1942*, 6, 145. The grain levy required farmers to submit part of their grain harvest to the state. The *Henan Minguo ribao* reported that Chiang Kai-shek ordered Henan's grain levy to be reduced to 2 million large sacks (*da bao*) of grain. "Henan sheng jiuzai gongzuo zhi jiantao," [Self-criticism of disaster relief work in Henan], *Henan Minguo ribao*, August 2, 1943.

newspaper, the severe drought affected 82 percent of all arable land in Henan, and left more than 12 million people in need of relief.[8] Moreover, the pressure to feed the nearly 1 million soldiers stationed in Henan was intense, and officials continued to extract grain from farmers by force.[9] The situation reached a crisis point in the spring of 1943, when food prices skyrocketed and famine refugees who had run out of grain during the winter starved to death en masse.

This chapter examines the Henan famine through Chinese and foreign media coverage of the disaster, reports by Guomindang and Communist relief officials, accounts by Henan-based missionaries, and narratives published in China after 1949.[10] I argue that the disaster represents a turning point for China both domestically and abroad. In the approximately two-thirds of Henan Province under Nationalist control, the government's decision to prioritize feeding the military over nourishing the people during a time of intense crisis meant that the Nationalists lost the hearts and minds of a significant proportion of the rural population. The central government's delayed and inadequate response to the famine also played a role in diminishing the faith of some of China's influential American backers in Chiang Kai-shek and the entire Nationalist regime. For the Chinese Communists, who organized relief campaigns in their base areas behind Japanese lines, on the other hand, the famine provided an opportunity to attract popular support with the promise that under Communist rule, "not one person would starve to death."[11]

---

[8] "Henan sheng jiuzai gongzuo zhi jiantao" [Self-criticism of disaster relief work in Henan], *Henan Minguo ribao*, August 2, 1943.

[9] Zhang Gaofeng, "Yuzai shilu" [Memoir of the Henan disaster], *Dagongbao*, February 1, 1943; White and Jacoby, *Thunder out of China*, 174–75.

[10] This chapter focuses on Guomindang and Communist Party responses to the famine. For a discussion of Japanese responses, see Odoric Y.K. Wou, "Food Shortage and Japanese Grain Extraction in Henan," in *China at War: Regions of China, 1937–1945*, ed. Stephen R. Mackinnon, Diana Lary, and Ezra F. Vogel (Stanford, CA: Stanford University Press, 2007), 175–206.

[11] Jin-Ji-Lu-Yu Border Area Government, "Taihang qu sier, sisan liangnian de jiuzai zongjie" [Summary of disaster relief in the Taihang area in 1942 and 1943, dated August 1, 1944], in *Jin-Ji-Lu-Yu kang Ri genjudi caijing shiliao xuanbian, Henan bufen* [Selected historical materials on the finance and economy of the Shanxi-Hebei-Shandong-Henan anti-Japanese base, Henan section], ed. Henan Finance Department and Henan Provincial Archives (Beijing: Dangan chubanshe, 1985), 137. Hereafter shortened as JJLY *caijing shiliao*.

CAUSES OF FAMINE IN WARTIME CHINA

Although the severe drought that hit Henan in 1942 was the immediate trigger for the disaster, the drought alone would not have resulted in such a serious famine. Recent scholarship on the disaster identifies wartime decline in food production, transportation difficulties caused when Chinese and Japanese troops cut Henan's main railroad lines for strategic reasons, the destruction caused by the Chinese military's strategic breaching of a Yellow River dike in 1938, soaring food prices due to inflation, the requisitioning of grain to feed the troops stationed in Henan, and insufficient relief from the government as key reasons why the drought led to such a devastating famine.[12] Most recently, Micah Muscolino has examined famine causation in Henan through the lens of environmental history. Employing an innovative "social metabolism" approach that "traces energy flows through and between societies and environments," he argues that wartime ecological damage, in combination with the sharp reduction in human labor power caused by wartime displacement and conscription, significantly reduced food production in Henan, while the military's "voracious appetite for energy" intensified pressure on food supplies and took calories away from the civilian population. "Satisfying the metabolism of the military required extracting energy from agro-ecological systems in Henan that were already in a highly degraded condition due to war's devastating impact," he writes.[13]

Henan was an important battle theater throughout the war. Within a year of Japan's invasion of China in July 1937, Japanese forces had seized roughly one-third of the province. By the time the drought began in the

---

[12] For overviews of famine causation in Henan, see Song Zhixin, *1942*, 3–5; White and Jacoby, *Thunder out of China*, 172–77; Li Wenhai, Cheng Xiao, Liu Yangdong, and Xia Mingfang, *Zhongguo jindai shida zaihuang* [The ten great disasters of China's modern period] (Shanghai: Shanghai renmin chubanshe, 1994), 268–300; Micah S. Muscolino, "Violence against People and the Land: The Environment and Refugee Migration from China's Henan Province, 1938–1945," *Environment and History* 17 (2011): 291–311; Wou, "Food Shortage and Japanese Grain Extraction in Henan," 176–79.

[13] Micah Muscolino, *The Ecology of War in China: Henan Province, the Yellow River, and Beyond, 1938–1950* (New York: Cambridge University Press, 2014), 4, 19–20, 89–90. My sincere thanks to Micah for generously providing me with a draft of his book a few months before its December 2014 release.

spring of 1942, the Japanese were occupying 43 of Henan's 111 counties, while the Nationalists controlled 68 counties south of the Yellow River, west of the Jialu River, and north of the Huai River, and the Chinese Communists were active in their bases behind Japanese lines in northern and eastern Henan[14] (see Map 10.1, Henan during the Famine, 1942–1943).[15] The war created a "tri-polar struggle among the Japanese, Nationalists, and Communists," writes Odoric Y.K. Wou, and threw Henan into a "state of anarchy." The ensuing chaos led to a sharp decline in food production in Henan that emptied local granaries and left farmers increasingly vulnerable to drought.[16] "The poor yields experienced in 1942 were not isolated," states Garnaut. According to his analysis of Nationalist agricultural production data from the prewar and wartime periods, total agricultural production in Henan counties that remained under Nationalist control was 10 percent below the prewar average in 1941, and 40 percent below average in 1942. In 1943 both spring and autumn yields improved, but the total crop was still 20 percent below average. Crop yields did not approach normal levels until 1944.[17]

Severe and recurring flooding caused by the strategic breach of a major Yellow River dike in 1938 also increased Henan's vulnerability to famine in crucial ways. As Diana Lary has narrated, by May 1938, China's military situation was utterly desperate. All but two of the country's major cities were lost, and the Japanese were racing to take Wuhan, where the Chinese government had relocated, before the Nationalists could evacuate west. This bleak situation convinced Chiang Kai-shek and the Chinese military command to breach the Yellow River dike near Zhengzhou, a

---

[14] Compilation Committee, *Henan kangzhan shilue* [A brief history of the Sino-Japanese War in Henan] (Zhengzhou: Henan renmin chubanshe, 1985), 50–55; Wang Guozhen and Xi Ge, comp., *Shuihan huangtang beige* [Elegy of floods, droughts, locusts and Tang (Enbo)] (Beijing: Renmin chubanshe, 2010), 153. This volume reproduces a useful array of disaster-related documents held by the Henan Provincial Archives.

[15] I would like to express my sincere gratitude to Yelena Granovskaya for her invaluable assistance in designing the maps for this essay.

[16] Odoric Y.K. Wou, *Mobilizing the Masses: Building Revolution in Henan* (Stanford, CA: Stanford University Press, 1994), 166, 170, 172; Wou, "Food Shortage and Japanese Grain Extraction in Henan," 176–77.

[17] Garnaut, "A Quantitative Description," 2021–23, 2028–30.

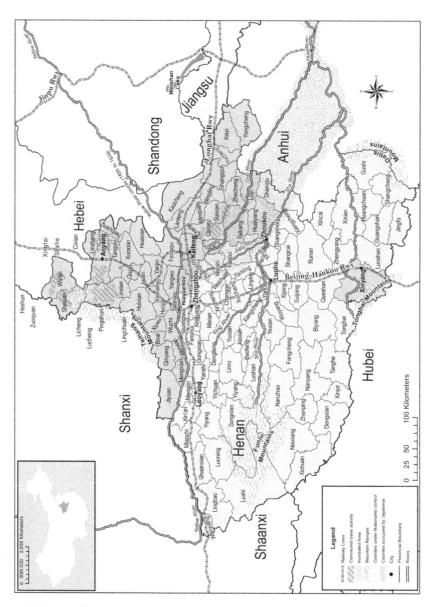

Map 10.1: Henan During the Famine, 1942–1943.

major city in Henan Province and the locus of a key railway junction that the Chinese military was desperate to hold, in an attempt to buy time by "using water in place of soldiers."[18] The breach caused a major change in the Yellow River's course that led to catastrophic flooding in Henan, Anhui, and Jiangsu provinces, and kept nearly 2 million acres of good farmland out of dependable production for close to a decade.[19] Although the Nationalists attempted to repair the breach, the chaos of war kept this goal out of reach until 1947. Areas along the river's unstable new southeastern course thus experienced flooding and famine conditions not only in 1938, but almost every summer for the next eight years.[20]

The chronic flooding had catastrophic effects in Henan. In addition to taking the lives of more than 325,000 people in eastern Henan and displacing at least 1,172,000, explains Muscolino, the flooding "crippled agricultural production" by destroying the "agricultural landscapes that Henan's rural residents had expended labor and energy to construct and maintain." Floodwaters "inundated 32 percent of the fields in eastern Henan" and buried "vast tracts of cultivated land" with silt, he continues.[21] Farmers in the inundated areas were thus forced to migrate to other places; within a year of the 1938 breach, 900,000 refugees from Henan had fled west into Shaanxi Province. This sudden and drastic loss of population meant that even after the floodwaters receded each winter, it proved almost impossible for counties in the inundated area to recruit enough laborers to protect villages and farmland from the river's new and ever-

---

[18] Diana Lary, "The Waters Covered the Earth: China's War-Induced Natural Disasters," in *War and State Terrorism: The United States, Japan, and the Asia-Pacific in the Long Twentieth Century*, ed. Mark Selden and Alvin Y. So (Lanham, MD: Rowman and Littlefield, 2004), 143–48; Diana Lary, "Drowned Earth: The Strategic Breaching of the Yellow River Dyke, 1938," *War in History* 8, no. 2 (2001): 198–99. Seizing Zhengzhou, where the east-west Longhai Railway and the north-south Beijing-Hankou Railway connected, would have allowed the Japanese to use the north-south line to rush their troops to Wuhan.

[19] O.J. Todd, "The Yellow River Reharnessed," *Geographical Review* 39, no. 1 (1949): 39–45.

[20] Li Wenhai et al., *Zhongguo jindai shida zaihuang*, 249–54.

[21] Muscolino, "Violence against People and the Land," 295–96, 298. For Muscolino's most recent work on the catastrophic impact of the flood, see *The Ecology of War in China*, chap. 1.

shifting course. The "devastation of Henan's hydraulic infrastructure" left the population of eastern Henan wholly unprepared to deal with the drought and locusts that arrived in 1942.[22]

Another causal factor was wartime inflation. According to Zhang Guangsi, a Nationalist official sent to investigate famine conditions in Henan over the summer of 1943, as food shortages worsened due to the drought, the rapid increase in the price of grain made it increasingly difficult for people to afford to purchase grain imported from other provinces. Wheat had been sold at 0.6 yuan per *shidou* before the war, he wrote, but before the wheat harvest of 1942 the price had risen to over 20 yuan per *shidou*, and before the spring harvest of 1943 the price soared to over 300 yuan per *shidou*.[23] Li Wenhai and his colleagues give additional figures on wartime inflation in Henan. The retail price index in Luoyang was 100 in the spring of 1937, they explain, but by December of 1941 it had reached 2,029.5, which was roughly twenty times its prewar number.[24] Rampant inflation was a serious concern in 1943 even in China's wartime capital.[25] In drought-stricken Henan, inflation meant that the cash relief provided by the government was of less and less use in the face of soaring grain prices. Inflation constrained missionary relief efforts as well. "During former famine years, when the prices of grain and other products only rose a certain percent, or were doubled at the most, and when the cost of living only amounted to several dollars a month per individual, it was comparatively easy to relieve the starving," wrote William Nowack, a missionary stationed in Henan's Biyang County, in January 1943. "But with things as they are at present, when it takes from two to three hundred per month to feed one individual, it is entirely beyond us to meet their need."[26]

---

[22] Muscolino, "Violence against People and the Land," 299–301.

[23] Zhang Guangsi, "Zhang Guangsi guanyu Henan sheng hanzai qingkuang ji jiuzai qingxing de diaocha baogao" [Investigative report from Zhang Guangsi concerning drought conditions in Henan Province and the disaster relief situation], *Zhonghua minguo shi dang'an ziliao huibian* [Collection of archival materials on the history of the Republic of China], vol. 8, issue 5:2:3 (Nanjing: Jiangsu guji chubanshe, 1991), 560. One *shidou* is equivalent to 2.2 gallons.

[24] Li Wenhai et al., *Zhongguo jindai shida zaihuang*, 286.

[25] See chapter 9, this volume.

[26] William Henry Nowack, "Echoes from Inland China" (January 1943), 3, Folder 3,

Inflation thus compromised the efficacy of relief funds and made it more difficult for people to survive the drought.

The requisitioning of grain to feed the nearly one million soldiers stationed in Henan played a particularly important role in exacerbating famine conditions. Concerned that purchasing large amounts of food grain for the military on the open market was leading to more inflation, in July 1941 the central government made the decision to feed the troops by collecting the land tax in grain rather than in cash. It also authorized the compulsory purchase of grain, usually at below market value, when the land tax alone could not feed the army in a particular area. "The new system shifted an even greater responsibility for the war effort to the countryside," writes Rana Mitter. "Suddenly, the burden of feeding the armies fell directly on the peasants."[27] Even missionaries who were generally supportive of the Nationalist state commented on the impact of the grain tax policy. As Dr. Catherine Simmons observed when describing the famine from her station in Xihua County in 1943, "Military grain taxes have been getting heavier and heavier, and ever since I have been in Honan strings of carts have been streaming out of the Province, loaded with military wheat. So there were no reserves."[28] Accounts published in the People's Republic of China (PRC) after 1949 offer more pointed critiques. Zhang Zhonglu, for instance, who served as the director of the Henan Provincial Construction Department during the famine, includes "corrupt and gangster-like troops" sent to Henan by Chiang Kai-shek, and the exploitative policies of Tang Enbo, a leading Nationalist general in Henan, in his list of factors that made the famine so severe. People in Henan listed Tang Enbo as one of Henan's "four great calamities," right behind floods, droughts, and locusts, he writes.[29] PRC scholar Song Zhixin notes that by early

---

Box 1, Collection 632, Papers of William Henry Nowack, Archives of the Billy Graham Center, Wheaton, Illinois.

[27] Rana Mitter, *Forgotten Ally: China's World War II, 1937–1945* (Boston: Houghton Mifflin Harcourt, 2013), 265–66; Muscolino, *The Ecology of War*, 96.

[28] Catherine Simmons, "Sidelights on the Famine," *China's Millions* 49 (July–August 1943): 32.

[29] Zhang Zhonglu, "1942 nian Henan dazai de huiyi" [Recollections of the great Henan disaster of 1942], in Song Zhixin, *1942*, 145–47. Dated December 1961 and originally published in *Henan wenshi ziliao* 1 (1995).

1943, the Guomindang state had collected 340 million *jin* of wheat from Henan in order to feed the army. That amount dwarfed the 20 million *jin* of grain that the state's allocation of 200 million yuan for famine relief could purchase.[30] The film *Back to 1942* brings military grain requisition to life for a mass audience. Early in the film, the commander of Nationalist troops in Henan requests 750,000 tons of grain from the province. When Henan's governor, Li Peiji, begs him to cancel that request due to the drought, the commander justifies his request bluntly. "There are tens of millions of men marching to the front," he reminds the governor. "If it's a matter of choosing who will starve, a dead refugee won't lose the war for us; a soldier starving to death is another matter entirely."[31]

Government inspectors writing during the famine also recognized that feeding so many troops was a struggle for Henan's population. In his investigative report dated September 27, 1943, Zhang Guangsi identified the following four reasons for Henan's dire situation: the rapidly increasing price of grain, the heavy burden of provisioning the many troops stationed in Henan, the falling price of land that made it difficult for farmers to survive by selling their land, and the malpractice of local leaders who misused or embezzled relief funds and grain.[32] Even representatives of the Nationalist state, then, acknowledged that the crisis in Henan was not simply a natural disaster (*tianzai*).

REPORTING THE FAMINE

As stories about the situation in Henan began to reach Chongqing, both Chinese and foreign correspondents traveled to Henan to investigate the disaster. In early February 1943, one of Nationalist China's most independent and well-respected newspapers, the *Dagongbao* (The Impartial),[33]

---

[30] Song, *1942*, 6–7. One *jin* is equivalent to 1.102 pounds.

[31] Feng and Liu, *Back to 1942*.

[32] Zhang Guangsi, "Zhang Guangsi guanyu Henan sheng hanzai qingkuang," 560–61.

[33] Stephen R. MacKinnon, "Press Freedom and the Chinese Revolution in the 1930s," in *Media and Revolution: Comparative Perspectives*, ed. Jeremy Popkin (Lexington: University Press of Kentucky, 1995), 174–78.

published two incendiary pieces that sought to raise awareness of the Henan famine and move the state and the Chinese public to expand relief efforts. The first piece, "Memoir of the Henan Disaster" (Yuzai shilu), offered *Dagongbao* correspondent Zhang Gaofeng's vivid account of his travels through Henan in December 1942 and January 1943.[34] Zhang's essay brought the suffering of Henan's 30 million people into stark relief. He described the swollen faces and blackened eyes of famine refugees sickened when they consumed poisonous herbs in an attempt to survive, and the horror of seeing hungry dogs eat the corpses of their starved masters. Zhang depicted government relief efforts as incompetent and often cruel. Most of the tens of thousands of refugees he saw crowding into railway stations along the Longhai Railway to board government-sponsored trains to Shaanxi were illiterate, he explained, so they could not read the complicated refugee registration procedures posted on the walls of the stations. Unable to figure out how to obtain the required permit and uncertain which train to board, many refugees tried to slip onto whatever train appeared without following procedures, and were beaten by police and separated from family members (see Figure 10.1).[35] Zhang went on to flatly contradict newspaper reports that the government was reducing the grain tax in Henan and providing relief. "They say the pressure was even greater than last year," he wrote. People who could not pay the required grain tax were detained in county offices without food, beaten, and forced to sell their land in order to pay the tax, he claimed, and many disaster victims had yet to receive any relief grain or cash at all.[36]

One day after Zhang's article appeared, the *Dagongbao*'s editor in chief, Wang Yunsheng, published a critical editorial on the disaster titled "Looking at Chongqing, Thinking of the Central Plains" (Kan Chongqing, nian Zhongyuan). Wang's editorial, which is quoted above, asked why the people of Henan had received no relief and were forced to pay heavy grain taxes in spite of the fact that the central government had known about the disaster for half a year. Wang made the point that while the people of Chongqing were busy celebrating the revision of the unequal treaties and preparing for Spring Festival, they were also experiencing ris-

---

[34] Song Zhixin, *1942*, 42–44.
[35] Zhang Gaofeng, "Yuzai shilu," *Dagongbao*, February 1, 1943.
[36] Ibid.

Figure 10.1: Henan Province, refugees fleeing famine on train, 1943. *Source:* The Henan Famine images: Harrison Forman collection. From the American Geographical Society Library, University of Wisconsin-Milwaukee Libraries.

ing prices exacerbated by the government's failure to tax the assets of the rich and control their purchasing power. Chongqing citizens should reduce their guilt by curbing their desire for food and drinks and economizing in order to send relief to Henan disaster victims, he concluded.[37]

The Guomindang government's response to these critiques was quick and telling. The state ordered the *Dagongbao* to cease publication for three days, February 3 through 5, thus signaling to China's wartime media that critical coverage of the famine was off-limits to newspapers that wanted to stay in circulation. This had a chilling effect on national newspapers, but the American media, as well as provincial newspapers in Henan, continued to cover the disaster throughout the spring and summer of 1943. The state also hurried to provide an alternate interpretation of the famine in the official newspaper of the Guomindang, the *Zhongyang ribao* (Central daily news).[38]

---

[37] Wang Yunsheng, "Kan Chongqing, nian Zhongyuan," *Dagongbao*, February 2, 1943.
[38] "Zhenzai nengli de shiyan" [A test of our ability to relieve disaster], *Zhongyang ribao*, February 4, 1943. *Back to 1942* includes a scene in which Chiang Kai-shek asks the secretary

The Chinese government's decision to punish the *Dagongbao* for covering the famine "acted like a barb on the foreign press," states Theodore White, the American journalist whose reports transformed the Henan famine into an issue of international concern. Such blatant suppression of "the most independent Chinese paper in Chungking" convinced White to travel to Henan to conduct his own investigation.[39] It is difficult to overstate the influence of White's searing account of his journey through the famine-stricken province. In her 2004 article about war-induced disasters in China, Diana Lary, a leading scholar of World War II in China, writes of the famine, "It remains almost unknown, the best account of it still one written by a young journalist, Theodore White, fifty-five years ago."[40] Song Zhixin, whose 2005 compilation offers the widest array of famine sources to date, also credits White's influence. It was the introduction of White's famine accounts to China in the 1990s, she explains, that "drew the attention of the domestic cultural sphere" to the famine.[41] Liu Zhenyun, the novelist whose 1990 book provided the basis for the film *Back to 1942*, also turned to White to gain a better understanding of the famine.[42] Given the reach of the film, it is likely that White's account of the famine will continue to dominate for the foreseeable future.

Before his experience in Henan, White held a fairly positive view of Chiang Kai-shek and the Nationalist government. His first article about the famine, which appeared in *Time* magazine in October 1942, praised the government's relief efforts and blamed the disaster on the Japanese and the drought. White described how the government was "rushing 1,000,000 piculs of seed grain from Shensi Province and the same amount from Anhwei" and had already "appropriated $10,000,000 Chinese for direct relief and ordered the Food Ministry to rush seed grain to the threat-

---

general of the Executive Yuan to read aloud the opening line from Wang Yunsheng's critical editorial. Chiang then accuses Wang of "poisoning people's minds," orders the *Dagongbao* to be shut down, and commands the secretary to have the *Zhongyang ribao* "set the record straight with an editorial."

[39] White and Jacoby, *Thunder out of China*, 166.
[40] Lary, "The Waters Covered the Earth," 160.
[41] Song Zhixin, *1942*, 216, 15.
[42] Liu Zhenyun, "Memory, Loss," *New York Times*, November 30, 2012.

ened areas."[43] His October piece reflected the type of upbeat coverage of Nationalist China that *Time's* publisher, Henry Luce, was determined to provide. Luce, who had grown up in China as the son of Presbyterian missionaries, "was one of Chiang Kai-shek's most ardent American admirers" and believed that increasing American support for Nationalist China was *Time's* "journalistic duty."[44]

After the Chinese government suppressed the *Dagongbao* for its coverage of the famine, in late February 1943 White and photojournalist Harrison Forman of the *Times* of London flew to Shaanxi and took the Longhai Railway into Henan. They spent two weeks there visiting rural areas, orphanages, and mission compounds, and interviewing peasants, local officials, and army commanders.[45] Shocked and horrified by what he witnessed, White then wrote a second, more critical account of the disaster. Madame Chiang Kai-shek was in the United States on her widely publicized diplomatic visit when White's piece was published in *Time* on March 22, 1943. "The story infuriated her," writes White. "She asked my publisher, Harry Luce, to fire me; but he refused, for which I honor him."[46]

The tone of White's second article on the famine, "Until the Harvest Is Reaped," is strikingly different from that of his October 1942 article. "My notes tell me that I am reporting only what I saw or verified; yet even to me it seems unreal: dogs eating human bodies by the roads, peasants seeking dead human flesh under the cover of darkness, endless deserted villages, beggars swarming at every city gate, babies abandoned to cry and die on every highway," wrote White. "Most terrible of all is the knowledge that the famine might have been averted." This time White held the Chinese government accountable for levying heavy grain taxes on Henan in spite of the famine, and for failing to send relief in time. In a harbinger of what would by 1945 become a common complaint of Americans working with the Nationalists, White charged that the relief effort was heavily de-

---

[43] Theodore H. White, "The Desperate Urgency of Flight," *Time* 40, no. 17 (October 26, 1942): 38.

[44] Joyce Hoffmann, *Theodore H. White and Journalism as Illusion* (Columbia: University of Missouri Press, 1995), 12.

[45] Theodore H. White, *In Search of History: A Personal Adventure* (New York: Harper and Row, 1978), 144–54.

[46] Ibid., 154. For more on Madame Chiang's diplomatic visit, see chapter 2, this volume.

pendent on American money and energy. "When we arrived in Chengchow the snow-covered, rubble-ruined streets seemed full of ghosts in fluttering blue rags," he wrote. "The relief committee here is supported almost entirely with American funds."[47] White would publish a more scathing indictment of the Guomindang's handling of the famine after the war, in *Thunder out of China*, which he wrote with Annalee Jacoby. Even in 1943, though, the concluding sentences of his famine essay betray his growing contempt for the Nationalist regime. "Before we left Chengchow the officials gave us a banquet. We had two soups. We had spiced lotus, peppered chicken, beef and water chestnut. ... We had three cakes with sugar frosting."[48]

After White returned to Chongqing, on April 5, he and Harrison Forman were permitted to visit Chiang Kai-shek to discuss the famine. In response to White's overview of conditions in Henan, Chiang denied that peasants were being taxed and assured them that cannibalism was impossible in China. "It was obvious he did not know what was going on," wrote White. White and Forman then produced Forman's photographs of dogs eating human corpses. "The Generalissimo's knee began to jiggle," writes White. "He took out his little pad and brush pen and began to make notes." White claims that heads began to roll after his meeting with Chiang, and that lives were saved "by the power of the American press."[49] Indeed, less than a week after White's meeting with Chiang, the *New York Times* reported that Chiang had ordered the appropriation of an additional 20 million yuan (or roughly U.S. $600,000) for famine relief in Henan, and instructed military authorities to provide the starving with grain from army stocks.[50]

Entries in the *Shilüe gaoben*, a draft manuscript of excerpts from Chiang's diary, telegrams, reports, and speeches collected by secretaries in the Office of Personal Attendants during the war and edited in the post-

---

[47] Theodore H. White, "Until the Harvest Is Reaped," *Time* 41, no. 12 (March 22, 1943): 21.

[48] Ibid., 22.

[49] White, *In Search of History*, 146, 154–56.

[50] "Chiang Aids Famine Area," *New York Times*, April 11, 1943, 14.

Figure 10.2: Henan Province, dying old man with child on side of road, 1943.
Source: The Henan Famine images: Harrison Forman collection, From the American Geographical Society Library, University of Wisconsin-Milwaukee Libraries.

war period,[51] provide a glimpse of Chiang's response to his meeting with White and Forman. In two separate entries, Chiang echoes White's claim that he had not known how serious conditions were in Henan until that meeting. A brief April 5 entry states that upon learning of the severity of famine conditions that afternoon, Chiang was, he said, "deeply pained that our country's local officials had not reported the true state of affairs in detail."[52] Then in a telegram excerpted in the April 15 entry, Chiang informed Henan's top military commanders and governor that Chinese and foreign public figures, upon traveling through Henan to inspect the situa-

---

[51] Grace C. Huang, "Creating a Public Face for Posterity: The Making of Chiang Kai-shek's *Shilüe* Manuscripts," *Modern China* 36, no. 6 (2010): 617–18.

[52] Gao Sulan, ed., *Jiang Zhongzheng zongtong dang'an shilüe gaoben* [Archives of President Chiang Kai-shek: Draft chronology] (Taibei: Guoshiguan, 2011), vol. 53, 177. Hereafter cited as *SLGB*. My thanks to Joseph Esherick for bringing this source to my attention.

tion, had reported seeing countless exposed corpses being eaten by dogs and pigs, and had noted that other bodies were buried in such shallow graves that a foul odor permeated the air. "I was not aware of this kind of situation," stated Chiang.[53]

Chiang's claim of ignorance is problematic, given that the two *Dagongbao* articles that had caused such a stir in the wartime capital had reported very similar information, including incidents of dogs devouring unburied corpses, a full two months before Chiang's meeting with White and Forman. His focus on the famine after that meeting highlights the importance he placed on projecting a positive image of Nationalist China abroad.[54] In fact, the above-mentioned telegram, and an additional telegram also delivered to top Henan authorities and excerpted in the *Shilüe gaoben* on April 15, show that Chiang was perhaps more alarmed by the bad impression White's coverage of the famine would give China's key wartime allies than by the situation on the ground in Henan. In the first telegram, Chiang lashed out at local authorities who had provided White and Forman with information damaging to China's national prestige. He accused local officials of exaggerating famine conditions in ways that revealed weak points in the Resistance War, and called them "stupid and childish" for attracting the ridicule of foreign journalists by serving them sumptuous banquets while at the same time detailing the miseries of famine victims.[55] The second telegram provides Chiang's response to the reports about unburied corpses. Rather than asking Henan officials to account for the high number of famine deaths or ordering them to find more effective ways to relieve the starving, Chiang's telegram focused on covering up the most disturbing evidence of mass starvation. He ordered provincial authorities to take responsibility for burying all unclaimed corpses, and stipulated that bodies should be buried more than

---

[53] *SLGB* 53:235–36.

[54] For extended discussion of Chiang's emphasis on China's alliance with the United States, and foreign policy dilemmas that may have distracted him from focusing on the famine, see Mitter, *Forgotten Ally*, chapter 13.

[55] *SLGB* 53:234–35.

five feet deep to avoid the problem of exposed corpses and the stench of decay.[56]

NOURISHING THE PEOPLE: FAMINE AND STATE LEGITIMACY IN CHINA

Chiang Kai-shek's willingness to downplay Chinese newspaper reports about the severity of the Henan famine until foreign journalists produced photographic evidence of the famine's toll highlights the considerable power of the foreign press and supports the contention that Chiang prioritized the war effort over famine relief until fear of losing goodwill abroad pressured him to order the military to share some of its grain.[57] At the same time, Chiang's insistence that local authorities had not informed him of the true situation in Henan shows how important it was to him to deflect the charge that he and his government had known but failed to act. Chiang's claims of ignorance, coupled with the Guomindang leadership's decision two months earlier to force the *Dagongbao* to temporarily suspend publication due to its critique of government relief efforts, demonstrate that the imperial trope of "nourishing the people" (*yangmin*) continued to be an important marker of state legitimacy in Nationalist China, even in the midst of war.

In ancient and imperial China, nourishing the people was a key way for a ruler to demonstrate his moral legitimacy and win the people's hearts. "The idea that good governance rests upon guaranteeing the livelihood of ordinary people has been a hallmark of Chinese political philosophy and practice from Mencius to Mao—and beyond," states Elizabeth Perry.[58] The

---

[56] *SLGB* 53:235–36.

[57] White, *In Search of History*, 146, 154–56. In his chapter on the Henan famine, Rana Mitter writes, "Corruption, carelessness, and callousness all played their part. But in the end there was no obviously better choice that Chiang could have made" (Mitter, *Forgotten Ally*, 273). The fact that Chiang did at last order military authorities in Henan to use some army stocks of grain for famine relief suggests that Nationalist leaders had a bit more agency than Mitter allows for.

[58] Elizabeth J. Perry, "Chinese Conceptions of 'Rights' from Mencius to Mao—and Now," *Perspectives on Politics* 6, no. 1 (2008): 39.

connection between state legitimacy and famine relief was rooted in the Confucian classics. Mencius (372–289 BCE), a foundational interpreter for Confucianism, insisted that a benevolent ruler was responsible for storing grain during times of plenty and distributing it during times of dearth.[59] Mencius, and later the Han dynasty scholar Dong Zhongshu, also popularized the idea that a ruler's heaven-granted mandate to rule (*tianming*) was not immutable and could be revoked if the ruler strayed from the path of virtue by failing to act with the good of the people at heart. Disasters such as floods and droughts were viewed as warning signs that a dynasty had displeased heaven and was in danger of losing its mandate if it did not change course. The principle that famines were caused by the negligence of rulers rather than by nature "shaped expectations of imperial and bureaucratic responsibility" throughout imperial China's long history.[60] As Pierre-Etienne Will, R. Bin Wong, and Lillian M. Li have demonstrated, the late imperial state's ability to relieve famine peaked in the eighteenth century, when the generous fiscal reserves and well-supplied granary system of the high-Qing state allowed for truly massive relief campaigns.[61] Perhaps because of the high-Qing record, both government officials and ordinary people continued to hold high expectations of the state during times of famine long after internal unrest, ecological pressures, fiscal crisis, and imperialist aggression sharply curtailed the state's ability to provide aid.[62]

After the fall of the Qing dynasty and the birth of China's new republican government in 1912, the belief that famines were a warning from heaven was rejected by many republican-era modernizers, but the state's

---

[59] *Mencius*, trans. David Hinton (Washington, DC: Counterpoint, 1998), vol. 1, 3, 7.

[60] Lillian M. Li, *Fighting Famine in North China: State, Market, and Environmental Decline, 1690s–1990s* (Stanford, CA: Stanford University Press, 2007), 2–3.

[61] Ibid., chapter 8; Pierre-Etienne Will, *Bureaucracy and Famine in Eighteenth-Century China*, trans. Elborg Forster (Stanford, CA: Stanford University Press, 1990); Pierre-Etienne Will and R. Bin Wong, with James Lee, Jean Oi, and Peter Perdue, *Nourish the People: The State Civilian Granary System in China, 1650–1850* (Ann Arbor, MI: Center for Chinese Studies Publications, 1991).

[62] Kathryn Edgerton-Tarpley, *Tears from Iron: Cultural Responses to Famine in Nineteenth-Century China* (Berkeley: University of California Press, 2008), chapter 4.

ability to feed its people remained a key marker of political legitimacy.[63] Sun Yat-sen's emphasis on the Principle of People's Livelihood (*minsheng zhuyi*) in his seminal Three People's Principles drew in important ways on the imperial ideal of nourishing the people. From the time Sun first presented his vision of modernization in 1894 to his final formulation of that vision in 1924, writes Margherita Zanasi, "the paternalistic notion that the state was responsible for ensuring the welfare of the masses as a means for maintaining political stability remained a constant aspect of Sun's idea of People's Livelihood." Since the Three People's Principles became the official platform of the Guomindang after Sun's death in 1925, the concept of People's Livelihood continued to be influential under Nationalist rule.[64]

Lillian Li argues that during the first half of the twentieth century, the political significance of famines was in fact "magnified through the lens of the newly emergent Chinese nationalism." Detailed coverage of disasters in China's modern press and increasing levels of foreign involvement in relief campaigns, she explains, made major disasters national rather than regional in significance.[65] Famine and famine relief continued to be highly politicized during the Nanjing decade (1927–1937), which began when the Guomindang reunified China under Nationalist control. In a 1928 address, Chiang Kai-shek proclaimed that the time was coming when the Nationalist state would be able to ensure the welfare of China's people during a disaster without relying on foreign aid. As Andrea Janku observes in her study of media coverage of the serious North China drought famine of 1928–1930, "China's political integrity and her place in the world were consciously renegotiated via the famine problem."[66]

---

[63] For a careful study of early republican famine relief efforts and their political significance, see Pierre Fuller, "Struggling with Famine in Warlord China: Social Networks, Achievements, and Limitations, 1920–21," PhD diss., University of California, Irvine, 2011.

[64] Margherita Zanasi, "Fostering the People's Livelihood: Chinese Political Thought between Empire and Nation," *Twentieth-Century China* 30, no. 1 (November 2004): 7, 19, 23. See also chapter 4, this volume.

[65] Li, *Fighting Famine*, 285, 302, 308.

[66] Andrea Janku, "From Natural to National Disaster: The Chinese Famine of 1928–1930," in *Historical Disasters in Context: Science, Religion, and Politics*, ed. Andrea Janku, Gerrit J. Schenk, and Franz Mauelshagen (New York: Routledge, 2012), 227–60.

PREPARING FOR *CHINA'S DESTINY*:
THE GUOMINDANG NARRATIVE OF FAMINE

The political and cosmological significance of famine in China helps to explain why the Nationalist government responded with such alarm to the *Dagongbao*'s charge that the central government had known of the severe famine in Henan for months but had failed to provide relief. On February 4, the second day of the *Dagongbao*'s three-day suspension, the *Zhongyang ribao* published an article titled "A Test of Our Ability to Relieve the Disaster." The editorial response by the *Zhongyang ribao* highlights the Guomindang leadership's determination to offer an alternative interpretation of the famine. The newspaper quoted a passage from Mencius at some length: "As Mencius said, 'whenever Heaven is about to invest a person with great responsibilities,' it must first use all sorts of methods, 'exhausting his muscles and bones, starving his body,' to temper him and polish him. 'In this way his patience and endurance are developed, and his weaknesses are overcome.'"[67]

At first glance the *Zhongyang ribao* editor's decision to frame his argument around a passage from Mencius might appear to be an appeal to tradition. In fact, the editor turned the traditional interpretation of famine upside down. Gone was Mencius's and Dong Zhongshu's view that a severe drought was a warning from heaven intended to push a ruler to examine himself and his government for faults, and adjust policies accordingly in order to retain the Mandate.[68] Instead, the *Zhongyang ribao* used the passage to introduce the famine as a test that would prepare both the Chinese state and its people for greatness. The editor compared the Chinese nation to the person described by Mencius: "A nation is also like this. China is now a country about to be invested with great responsibility. Naturally it must undergo all kinds of tempering. Amid this tempering we

[67] "Zhenzai nengli de shiyan," *Zhongyang ribao*, February 4, 1943. The *Zhongyang ribao* editor quotes some lines of the Mencius passage verbatim, but summarizes the content of other lines. For a full translation of the original passage see *Mencius*, trans. Hinton, vol. 12, 15, 230–31.

[68] See the critique of the *Zhongyang ribao* article in Li Wenhai et al., *Zhongguo jindai shida zaihuang*, 270, 282–83.

are testing ourselves. The government is being subjected to trials; the people in the same way are also enduring trials."[69] In short, the famine was a trial meant to prepare the country and its people for "China's Destiny," which Chiang Kai-shek would describe in detail in his major wartime work, published only a month after this editorial appeared.[70]

The *Zhongyang ribao* editorial acknowledged that the government should assume responsibility for relieving famine refugees, and presented a detailed account of the relief the national government had provided. The previous year (1942), Chiang Kai-shek had sent high-ranking officials to inspect famine conditions, explained the editor, and had immediately provided relief. The state had already issued 100 million yuan to fund the traditional method of stabilizing food prices by selling state grain at below-market prices (*pingtiao*), 14 million yuan for emergency relief, 6 million for work relief, 5 million for agricultural loans, and 10 million for irrigation and water conservancy loans. Moreover, the government had also given 11 million yuan for the Huanglongshan land reclamation program that resettled famine refugees in Shaanxi, 2 million to establish gruel kitchens along the Longhai Railway, 5 million for sheltering refugees in Shaanxi, and 1 million for sheltering them in Hubei. As long as those in charge of relief carried out the central government's directives, he concluded, the government was sure to pass the test posed by the famine.[71]

Unlike Mencius, the *Zhongyang ribao* editor then shifted to discuss how the Chinese people as well as the government needed to assume responsibility for relieving the disaster. "Not only will the government withstand the test, but the people must also come through their tempering," he announced. "We have heard that our brethren in the Henan army all economized in order to contribute grain and funds," he continued. Moreover, because the army could not be short of grain, even in the midst of the disaster Henan compatriots were making a great effort to hand in their full quota of grain even as the government was reducing the amount of

---

[69] "Zhenzai nengli de shiyan."

[70] See in chapter 6, this volume. *China's Destiny*, Chiang's important but controversial wartime attempt to "define the essence and character of the Chinese nation" and "explain the connection between the destiny of China and the world," was published in March 1943.

[71] "Zhenzai nengli de shiyan." These amounts come to a total of 154 million yuan.

grain requisitioned. "This kind of commendable conduct really merits the honor of having volumes written about it," he exclaimed.[72]

With this editorial, the Guomindang leadership provided a counter-narrative to both the traditional heaven-centered interpretation of famine and the critiques presented by the *Dagongbao*. According to the *Zhongyang ribao*, the famine was not a warning for the ruler but a trial that would prepare the Chinese nation for greatness. Second, far from failing to respond in a timely manner, the government had already provided an impressive amount of relief and was thus well on its way to passing the test posed by the famine. Third, the famine was a test of China's people as much as its government, so the Chinese people, including these in Henan, needed to temper themselves by withstanding the disaster. Finally and most controversially, rather than being coerced into handing over their last bit of grain to the state, the people of Henan were sacrificially choosing to do so in order to support the War of Resistance.

After giving its interpretation of the meaning of the famine, the *Zhongyang ribao* quickly returned to topics that highlighted Guomindang successes. It printed celebratory discussions of the abolition of the hated unequal treaties and the successful negotiation of a new treaty signed in January 1943, and in March it turned to championing the publication of Chiang's *China's Destiny*.[73] In Henan, on the contrary, where press censorship was not as tight as in the wartime capital, provincial newspapers such as the *Henan Minguo ribao* and the *Qianfengbao* (Vanguard newspaper), continued to cover the famine throughout the spring and summer of 1943.[74] The *Qianfengbao*, a small private newspaper based in Nanyang, published numerous famine reports that called into question the efficacy of government relief efforts. The paper called on the provincial government to lend more public grain to famine refugees to keep them alive until the May harvest, to suspend banquets for three months and contribute the

---

[72] Ibid.

[73] For articles celebrating the new treaty, see *Zhongyang ribao*, February 5–9, 1943. For more on the negotiations surrounding the treaty, see chapter 4, this volume. For *Zhongyang ribao* introductions to *China's Destiny*, see March 11 and 13, 1943.

[74] Song Zhixin, *1942*, 58–60.

money saved to relief efforts, and to find ways to force wealthy families to hand over a certain amount of their stored grain for relief. It also prodded counties in Henan to be more self-reliant by planting vegetables that could tide people over until the grain harvest and encouraging the rich to help the poor in their locale.[75] The *Henan Minguo ribao*, a larger newspaper that opened in Kaifeng in 1931 and relocated to Nanyang and then Lushan during the war, was careful to give generally positive accounts of government relief efforts. It praised by name civil and military authorities who donated relief grain and championed the work of a local official who developed three kinds of food substitutes and tested them out on himself to ensure that they were effective.[76]

Provincial newspapers also covered the disasters that extended famine conditions into the fall of 1943. Just as farmers finally began to harvest their desperately needed spring harvest, in May 1943 hastily constructed dikes along the new course of the Yellow River in eastern Henan broke in at least sixteen different places. The breaks caused severe flooding that inundated 1.3 million *mu* of land. Afraid the flooding would expand, the provincial government conscripted 500,000 civilian workers from more than twenty different counties to repair and strengthen the dikes.[77] This interrupted agricultural activities "at a pivotal time of year," before farmers had finished harvesting the spring wheat and during the time they needed to plant their autumn crops.[78] Then from June through August 1943, fifty-seven counties in Henan experienced a devastating outbreak of migratory locusts. Every plant was covered by dozens of locusts, reported the *Henan Minguo ribao*. The provincial government devised elaborate methods of exterminating the pests, but locusts still managed to consume a good por-

---

[75] *Qianfengbao*, March 16, 1943; March 28, 1943; April 1, 1943, in Song Zhixin, *1942*, 129–36.

[76] *Henan Minguo ribao*, January 25, 1943; "Jiuhuang shipin" [Foodstuff that rescues from famine], *Henan Minguo ribao*, February 14, 1943.

[77] *Henan Minguo ribao*, July 7–8, 1943; July 22, 1943; August 3, 1943; December 8, 1943. See also Zhang Guangsi, "Zhang Guangsi guanyu Henan sheng hanzai qingkuang," 564.

[78] Muscolino, "Violence against People and the Land," 301; *Henan Minguo ribao*, August 7, 1943.

tion of the autumn seedlings.[79] It was not until later in the fall that adequate rainfall and a decent harvest began to stabilize the situation.[80]

The language of *Henan Minguo ribao* editorials about the famine often mirrored the *Zhongyang ribao*'s emphasis on the national implications of the Henan disaster and the self-sacrificing character of the Henan people. "Relieving the disaster in Henan is not a kind of philanthropic action, but is a responsibility everyone should bear," warned the author of an editorial published a week after the *Zhongyang ribao* piece, for if Henan were to experience problems due to the disaster, it would negatively affect the resistance in all of North China. The famine refugees "did not blame heaven or humans, and even in the midst of hunger and cold they did not, from beginning to end, transgress the bounds of good behavior or disturb the social order," he marveled. Their patient and law-abiding spirit made them truly "worthy of the nation."[81] This narrative placed the famine squarely within what Lary terms the Guomindang's "policy of national sacrifice," according to which the only way for China to defeat the Japanese was to "use her size and her vast population to trade space and place for time without any apparent concern for human losses."[82]

COMMUNIST FAMINE RELIEF EFFORTS

The famine posed a challenge not only for the beleaguered Nationalist state but also its Communist rivals operating in base areas located primarily behind Japanese lines. The Jin-Ji-Lu-Yu (Shanxi-Hebei-Shandong-Henan) border region government was deeply concerned about the turmoil caused by famine conditions in areas under its control.[83] Within the

---

[79] "Yusheng huangzai shilu" [Record of the locust disaster in Henan], *Henan Minguo ribao*, August 15, 1943.

[80] Nowack, "Echoes from Inland China" (January 1944), 3, Folder 3, Box 1, Collection 632.

[81] "Jiuzai gongzuo zhi zai jiantao" [A reexamination of disaster relief work], *Henan Minguo ribao*, February 10, 1943.

[82] Diana Lary, *The Chinese People at War: Human Suffering and Social Transformation, 1937–1945* (New York: Cambridge University Press, 2010), 60.

[83] The Jin-Ji-Lu-Yu border region included the Taiyue, Taihang, South Hebei, and Ji-Lu-Yu base areas. The Communists claimed to have some level of activity in 148 counties

border region, the Ji-Lu-Yu (Hebei-Shandong-Henan) and Taihang bases were most severely affected (Map 10.2). In 1942 and 1943 the average harvest was only 20 to 30 percent of normal in those areas. There were roughly 1.2 million disaster victims (*zaimin*) in need of relief in the Ji-Lu-Yu base, and over 350,000 in the Taihang base (compared to 12 million in Nationalist-controlled Henan). As was also the case in Nationalist areas, grain prices rose rapidly as the disaster continued into the summer of 1943. In Ren village in northern Henan's Linxian County, for instance, the price per *jin* of millet rose from 9.37 yuan in June 1943 to between 19.5 and 21 yuan that August.[84] To make matters worse, during the famine the Japanese resorted to harsh policies in order to extract enough grain to support their troops in Henan. "The Communist base areas were the primary targets since these rural areas were located just behind the Japanese lines," explains Wou. The Japanese blockaded Communist bases to prevent grain smuggling, forced all grain stores near the bases to move to fully Japanese-controlled areas, and frequently conducted grain raids in base areas.[85]

When famine conditions first emerged in the fall of 1942, the border region government established a famine relief committee under the leadership of chairman Yang Xiufeng. Two years later, in August 1944, the border region government published a two-part account of the relief efforts it had carried out in the Taihang base from October 1942 to January 1943, and from July 1943 to June 1944. Due to prewar underground Communist activity in the area and the protection provided by the rugged Taihang Mountains, the Taihang base was the administrative center of the Jin-Ji-Lu-Yu border region, and "always contained its most secure parts."[86]

---

within the region when it was founded in July 1941. As David Goodman points out, however, "Until 1944 the CCP's hold on JinJiLuYu was fragmented and tenuous at best. The border region was certainly not united and for most of the war years the CCP was under threat even in those areas where it had its strongest bases." David S.G. Goodman, "JinJiLuYu in the Sino-Japanese War: The Border Region and the Border Region Government," *China Quarterly* 140 (December 1994): 1007, 1010.

[84] Wei Hongyun, "Commerce in Wartime: The Jinjiluyu Base Area," in Mackinnon, Lary, and Vogel, *China at War*, 260–61; Compilation Committee, *Henan kangzhan shi lue*, 95.

[85] Wou, "Food Shortage in Henan," 188, 191–92.

[86] JJLY *caijing shiliao*, 137; Goodman, "JinJiLuYu in the Sino-Japanese War," 1011, 1014.

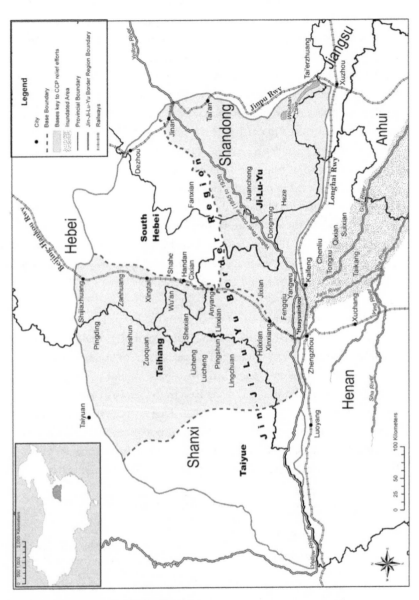

Map 10.2: Jin-Ji-Lu-Yu Border Region.

In certain ways the relief strategies employed by the Communists in their Taihang base were remarkably similar to those attempted by the Nationalists during the disaster. The parallels between the *Zhongyang ribao*'s account of the central government's response to the famine, the *Henan Minguo ribao*'s overview of provincial-level relief efforts in Nationalist-controlled Henan, and the Jin-Ji-Yu-Lu border region government's summary of its relief campaign in the Taihang base demonstrate that the rival parties were drawing on a common relief repertoire in 1942. Both parties reported that they sent high-level inspectors to investigate disaster conditions; classified disaster victims into different categories depending on the extent of their destitution; reduced the grain tax in stricken areas; provided agricultural loans; transferred in grain from other provinces in order to stabilize the price of grain; organized work relief and water conservancy projects; sought to "eradicate superstition" by teaching rural people to kill locusts rather than viewing them as divine insects; provided shelters for refugees en route to areas where they could cultivate wasteland; mobilized people to economize and donate to relief efforts; and encouraged the planting of vegetables and the use of substitute foods to make up for the acute shortage of grain.[87] Most of the above strategies were time-honored practices inherited from imperial China. Others, such as the attacks on superstition and the pronounced emphasis on work relief, show the influence of Chinese modernizers and Anglo-American famine relief methods.[88]

While many of the concrete relief strategies employed by the Communists and Nationalists were similar, particularly in 1942, in other respects the border region's approach to the famine raised suggestive alternatives. The border region government encouraged the distribution of relief via the 297 rural cooperatives (*hezuoshe*) established in the Taihang region between October 1942 and June 1943.[89] Moreover, the Taihang

---

[87] "Zhenzai nengli de shiyan," *Zhongyang ribao*, February 4, 1943; "Henan sheng jiuzai gongzuo zhi jiantao," *Henan Minguo ribao*, August 2–3, 1943; *Henan Minguo ribao*, August 15, 1943; JJLY *caijing shiliao*, 136–74.

[88] For a sustained comparison of Chinese and British famine relief practices, see Kathryn Edgerton-Tarpley, "Tough Choices: Grappling with Famine in Qing China, the British Empire, and Beyond," *Journal of World History* 24, no. 1 (2013): 135–76.

[89] JJLY *caijing shiliao*, 147. For an overview of the larger cooperative movement carried

report emphasized ideological training, mobilization, and confidence-building measures far more than Nationalist discussions of the famine. The very first measure put forward during the Taihang relief campaign, for instance, was to "reassure the public" by guaranteeing that "not one person will starve to death" (*bu e'si yige ren*).[90] The Taihang report itself provides evidence that this promise proved impossible to keep. In addition to mentioning particular individuals who starved to death, it acknowledges that in the summer of 1943 the situation in the base became so dire that old scourges, such as starving parents exchanging their children for grain or even killing their own children, resurfaced to threaten social stability.[91] Nevertheless, resolutions laid out in 1942 at the fourth conference on drought relief in the Taihang base demonstrate a degree of local accountability for famine deaths that was lacking in Nationalist-controlled areas. A regulation concerning village-level disaster relief committees stipulated that if one person in a given village starved to death because the cadre in charge had not done his best to conduct relief work, that cadre would be criticized. If two people starved, he would be warned. If more than three villagers starved to death, then the cadre in charge was to be removed from his post and punished, while his supervisor would also undergo disciplinary action.[92]

Many of the concrete relief policies pursued in the first phase of the relief campaign, such as reducing the grain tax (*gongliang*) by roughly 50 percent in the fall of 1942 and the spring of 1943, or hiring disaster victims to serve as porters who were paid double what non–disaster victim porters made for transporting grain purchased in the western part of the Taihang base into famine districts on the eastern side, aimed to heighten morale and shore up social stability as well as provide relief.[93] Some of the border region's relief policies clearly proved appealing to famished people

out in the Shaan-Gan-Ning border region in 1943–1944, see Pauline Keating, *Two Revolutions: Village Reconstruction and the Cooperative Movement in Northern Shaanxi, 1934–1945* (Stanford, CA: Stanford University Press, 1997), chapter 7.

[90] JJLY *caijing shiliao*, 137.

[91] Ibid., 153–55.

[92] Wang Guozhen and Xi Ge, comp. *Shuihan huangtang beige*, 202.

[93] JJLY *caijing shiliao*, 138–40.

living in Guomindang or Japanese-controlled areas, for by 1943 approximately 250,000 famine refugees had fled into the Taihang and Taiyue bases "from surrounding areas where there was no government-provided relief."[94] Social mobilization was an important part of the attempt to resettle those refugees. The border region government stipulated that the number of disaster refugees each nondisaster area was responsible for receiving was equal to 3 percent of its native population. When far more refugees arrived than expected, the number of refugees rose to 30 percent of the local population in places such as Heshun and Zuoquan in eastern Shanxi. Faced with such an influx, border region officials emphasized mutual aid and friendship between fellow citizens and unity between old and new settlers. "The base area is a new world," commented one recently arrived refugee upon witnessing the party's insistence that disaster refugees receive the same treatment as local residents.[95]

Although the border region government welcomed famine refugees from occupied or Guomindang-controlled areas, it also expressed fear that spies and other dangerous people might try to hide among the refugees.[96] In a directive the administrative office of the Ji-Lu-Yu base sent to all its commissioners and county heads in October 1942, for instance, each county was ordered to prepare lodgings for famine refugees and educate the public about the need to assist them. At the same time, counties were ordered to inspect these refugees to ensure that they were "good and respectable victims" (*lianghao zaimin*), and to be "strictly on guard against the activities of enemy spies and traitors among the disaster refugees."[97] The Taihang report included similar warnings. Most of the refugees had no other way to survive and left their homes temporarily to escape disas-

---

[94] David S.G. Goodman, *Social and Political Change in Revolutionary China: The Taihang Base Area in the War of Resistance to Japan, 1937–1945* (Lanham, MD: Rowman and Littlefield, 2000), 55; Li Wenhai et al., *Zhongguo jindai shida zaihuang*, 292. I have found no estimates of the number of famine refugees who may have migrated from Communist base areas into Nationalist or Japanese-controlled territory.

[95] JJLY *caijing shiliao*, 140–41.

[96] On spy hunts in the Yan'an base, see chapter 7, this volume.

[97] "Ji-Lu-Yu xingshu guanyu anzhi liuliang zaimin de zhishi" [Ji-Lu-Yu administrative office directive concerning arranging for roaming disaster refugees] (November 23, 1942), Geming lishi dang'an: G12-01-15, Henan Provincial Archives, Zhengzhou, China.

ter, stated the report, but in their midst were some who fled in order to escape their tax burden or consume low-priced grain. Also discovered were "drug peddlers, smugglers, spies, and special agents." Such people reportedly took advantage of the situation to spread rumors and incite discord. In response, the party focused on disclosing the plots of spies and special agents and educating the masses to be on guard against them.[98]

The border region government also selected famine relief methods that promoted social changes favored by the Communists. In 1942, for instance, the party sent ninety cadres to launch a "spinning and weaving campaign" in the Taihang base. The border region government loaned raw cotton to women in disaster areas, and those women could earn two *jin* of husked grain (*mi*) for each *jin* of cotton they spun into thread, and one *jin* of grain when they wove the thread into cloth. Enough women joined the spinning and weaving movement that the base no longer needed to import cloth. In Linxian, Anyang, Cixian, and Shexian counties, 23,968 women participated in the movement between fall 1942 and June 1943, and they earned 386,255 *jin* of millet (*xiaomi*) for spinning and weaving 166,090 *jin* of cotton.[99] Cadres were reminded that in addition to providing relief, the spinning and weaving movement could "lay the foundation for family industry and cooperative enterprise," raise the position of women, and promote women's work.[100] Not only did the economic position of women improve within the family, claimed the Taihang report, but earnings from their spinning work allowed some women to join newly formed rural cooperatives and become powerful shareholders in them. "In the past it was men who supported women," some elderly men reportedly exclaimed, "but today women have come to support men."[101]

The border region government displayed a willingness to intervene in other aspects of familial relations as well during the famine. When conditions deteriorated in the Taihang base over the summer of 1943 due to a combination of continued drought, locust infestation, and flooding, the number of disaster victims exceeded 350,000, and serious social problems

---

[98] JJLY *caijing shiliao*, 140–41, 136–37, 153–56.
[99] JJLY *caijing shiliao*, 142–43.
[100] Wang Guozhen and Xi Ge, comp., *Shuihan huangtang beige*, 201.
[101] JJLY *caijing shiliao*, 142–43.

emerged. Panicked people sold their agricultural implements and live-stock, devoured crops while they were still green, and stole public grain. "Each looked only to his own life," stated the Taihang report. Some women married solely to obtain food, and instances of divorce skyrock-eted. In response, divorce was temporarily banned in an effort both to save food by restricting the number of independent households and to "pro-mote friendly affection, mutual aid, and familial love between people."[102]

The border region government changed its focus significantly during the second phase of the Taihang relief campaign (July 1943–June 1944). Faced with a deepening crisis, the leadership conducted a self-criticism that drew on the experiences of 1942 to design a more effective relief plan. They concluded that because the 1942 campaign had failed to fully com-bine disaster relief work and production, much of the relief grain and loans the government distributed to disaster victims was consumed before it could be used to increase production. This gave rise to dispiriting cases such as a disaster refugee in Cixian who received 200 *jin* of relief grain and food substitutes (*daishipin*), but still starved to death in the end. In short, the 1942 campaign convinced the border region leadership that relief work that failed to mobilize the masses fostered dependence on the gov-ernment, was unsustainable in the long term, and quickly became "inactive 'charity work.'"[103]

Starting in July 1943, the government highlighted the call to "produce to provide relief for yourself" (*shengchan zijiu*). It also advertised the slo-gan, "Smash superstition; humans can conquer nature" (*dapo mixin, renli shengtian*). Taihang base cadres told the masses that praying for rain was useless and mobilized them to increase production and combat the con-tinuing drought by carrying water from wells to save young crops, partici-pating in water conservancy and irrigation projects, and rushing to plant new crops to replace those that had failed. They also disseminated "scien-tific methods" of killing locusts, and intensified efforts to eradicate the popular belief that locusts were supernatural insects that would return in ever-greater numbers if people tried to kill them.[104] The paucity of first-

---

[102] JJLY *caijing shiliao*, 153–60; Goodman, "JinJiLuYu in the Sino-Japanese War," 1023.
[103] Ibid., 169–72.
[104] Ibid., 154–57.

hand accounts written by outside or critical observers makes it difficult to evaluate the efficacy of such policies. Reports from nonstate observers are crucial to our understanding of Guomindang responses to the famine, but no such reports are cited in existing scholarly discussions of Communist efforts during the famine. Foreign correspondents like White could not travel behind Japanese lines to witness famine conditions in Communist bases once their countries were at war with Japan, while most missionaries stationed in occupied Henan had been interned by the Japanese by 1942.[105] Independent-minded Chinese journalists such as those who wrote for the *Dagongbao* or the *Qianfengbao* also appear to have lacked firsthand information about conditions in the Jin-Ji-Lu-Yu border region, since their coverage of the disaster did not include Communist relief efforts.

Given the lack of critical firsthand reports, it is worth pointing out that some of the strategies and lines of rhetoric pioneered in the Jin-Ji-Lu-Yu border region in 1943 were later used to disastrous effect when employed on a national scale during the Great Leap famine of 1958–1962. In an attempt to shore up social stability and foster the kind of self-reliance championed in the Taihang report, for instance, in the early and mid-1950s the Ministry of Civil Affairs called on peasants in disaster-stricken locales to remain in their villages to restore production rather than fleeing to other areas.[106] The PRC state's decision to inhibit temporary migration during times of disaster had lethal consequences when the Great Leap famine began a few years later.[107] The call to smash superstition and conquer nature also resurfaced in more radical and coercive ways during the Great Leap disaster. In the late 1950s, not only popular beliefs about locusts but also religious institutions and deeply held attachments to ancestral graveyards and temples were attacked as vestiges of "feudal superstition." Moreover, the massive irrigation and hydropower projects

---

[105] Erleen J. Christensen, *In War and Famine: Missionaries in China's Honan Province in the 1940s* (Montreal: McGill-Queen's University Press, 2005), 71–73.

[106] Felix Wemheuer, *Famine Politics in Maoist China and the Soviet Union* (New Haven, CT: Yale University Press, 2014), 85–87.

[107] Ralph A. Thaxton, Jr., *Catastrophe and Contention in Rural China: Mao's Great Leap Forward Famine and the Origins of Righteous Resistance in Da Fo Village* (Cambridge: Cambridge University Press, 2008), 162–67.

and wholesale cutting of forests included in the Great Leap's war against nature exhausted China's land and people to a dangerous extent.[108]

The relief campaign of 1943–1944 does not appear to have resulted in such excesses. According to the authors of the Taihang report, it was effective in fighting the famine. Because of the mass character of the campaign, they claim, even though the border region government provided comparatively fewer material resources in 1943, results were better than they had been in 1942.[109] Leading PRC famine scholars Li Wenhai and Xia Mingfang and their colleagues, writing in 1994 and drawing heavily on the Taihang report and articles published in the *Jiefang ribao* (Liberation daily), argue that the relief campaign conducted in the Jin-Ji-Lu-Yu border region represented an "unprecedented pioneering work" in the development of modern China's disaster relief system. By bringing together government relief, community mutual aid, and the people's ability to increase production to provide for themselves, they explain, the border region model moved beyond both the government-centered relief system of China's imperial past and the charitable relief activities encouraged by modern China's capitalist class and international friends to create a "community self-relief movement with genuine mass character."[110]

The Taihang report as well as Li Wenhai and his colleagues also illustrate the effective penetration of the Communist Party apparatus on the village level during the famine. In 1943, personnel working in border region party, government, military, or academic organizations were ordered to reduce the amount of time spent in their offices so that they could help famine sufferers increase production. In Cixian, for instance, the county head organized 746 people from seventeen different work units to spend ten days helping disaster victims grow vegetables, carry manure, and open up wasteland. Cadres sent to help famine refugees expand production brought their own food with them and made a point of sharing

[108] Zhou Xun, ed., *The Great Famine in China, 1958–1962: A Documentary History* (New Haven, CT: Yale University Press, 2012), 94; Judith Shapiro, *Mao's War against Nature: Politics and the Environment in Revolutionary China* (Cambridge: Cambridge University Press, 2001), chapter 2.

[109] JJLY *caijing shiliao*, 172.

[110] Li Wenhai et al., *Zhongguo jindai shida zaihuang*, 299, 295–97.

that food while eating together with the refugees. In sum, those working for the party, the government, and the army were expected to "share the comforts and hardships of the people" (*yumin tong ganku*). In the border region, as opposed to Nationalist-controlled Henan, famine relief efforts appear to have forged a bond between the rural population and Communist soldiers and cadres.[111]

Wou's study of wartime mobilization in the Communists' Rivereast (Shuidong) base examines how the famine helped forge a long-lasting relationship between the party and the peasants even in a much smaller, less secure base. The Rivereast base, which comprised five small pockets of resistance located along the borders of Chenliu, Qixian, Tongxu, Suixian, and Taikang counties in flood-ravaged eastern Henan, had far fewer resources than the Taihang base.[112] Acute food shortages during the spring of 1943 "made the party abandon any coordinated measures and adopt a laissez-faire policy of raising food provisions." Even cadres and soldiers "barely survived on yam leaves, wheat bran, and seedlings," writes Wou. "Many starved to death." Although the Communists in Rivereast were unable to relieve famine conditions, Wou argues convincingly that the collective defense operations they organized against enemy grain raids during the famine won over many villagers.[113] In 1942 and 1943, the Japanese dealt with acute grain shortages in occupied areas of Henan by making "repeated raids for grain in Communist bases and GMD-controlled areas." As the famine worsened, grain raids "became a daily affair" in the Rivereast base.[114] The Rivereast Communists, in turn, tried to obtain food by raiding Guomindang areas and by organizing defense operations against Japanese and Guomindang grain raids. "It was in common defense against enemy grain raids (*qiangliang*) that the Communists built the

---

[111] JJLY *caijing shiliao*, 160–64; Li Wenhai et al., *Zhongguo jindai shida zaihuang*, 299–300.

[112] Wou, *Mobilizing the Masses*, 234–35. The Rivereast base was incorporated into the Ji-Lu-Yu base for administrative reasons in January 1943.

[113] Ibid., 240–43, 247. See also Muscolino, *The Ecology of War in China*, 114–17. Muscolino largely agrees with Wou that Communist forces in flooded areas of eastern Henan initially struggled to obtain food during the famine, but later organized collective defense efforts that both safeguarded access to food and helped the Communists expand their influence in local society.

[114] Wou, "Food Shortage in Henan," 192.

long-lasting relationship between the party and the peasants that eventually formed a solid base for the Communist triumph in this area," writes Wou.[115]

In part because expectations of Communist guerrilla fighters in bases located behind Japanese lines were much lower than expectations of the Nationalist government in charge of "Free China," and in part because Communist cadres and soldiers appear to have shared the suffering of the famished population to a greater degree than their Guomindang counterparts, the famine bolstered rather than eroded the legitimacy of the Jin-Ji-Lu-Yu border region government. On the other hand, the wealth of new book-length studies of the Mao-era Great Leap famine that have come out since Li Wenhai et al. and Wou published their respective works in 1994 shed a darker light on some of the rhetoric and strategies employed by the Communists in response to the Henan famine. The fear that spies and provocateurs might disguise themselves as disaster refugees, the attacks on superstition, the militaristic calls to defeat the famine by warring against nature, and the decision during the second phase of the relief campaign to reduce the material resources provided by the government in favor of a fervent faith in the power of the masses to save themselves by expanding production all foreshadow important aspects of the Great Leap famine, which killed approximately 30 million people between 1958 and 1962.[116]

THE WAGES OF FAMINE: ICHIGO AND ITS AFTERMATH

The border region government's famine relief campaign of 1942–1944 appears to have convinced a quarter of a million disaster refugees that the Communists presented an appealing alternative to Guomindang or Japa-

---

[115] Wou, *Mobilizing the Masses*, 247.

[116] On the obsessive hunt for spies and counterrevolutionaries during the Great Leap famine, see Frank Dikotter, *Mao's Great Famine: The History of China's Most Devastating Catastrophe, 1958–1962* (New York: Walker, 2011), chapter 34; and Yang Jisheng, *Tombstone: The Great Chinese Famine 1958–1962*, trans. Stacy Mosher and Guo Jian (New York: Farrar, Straus and Giroux, 2012), chapter 13. For the other themes, see footnotes 104–8.

nese rule.[117] For the Nationalist state responsible for relieving two-thirds of Henan's counties, the famine had a very different effect. The central government's handling of the disaster was a turning point in terms of rural support for Nationalist troops in Henan, and ultimately in American views of Chiang Kai-shek and the Nationalist regime as well. "We knew that there was a fury, as cold and relentless as death itself, in the bosom of the peasants of Honan (Henan). Their loyalty had been hollowed to nothingness by the extortion of their government," wrote White with regard to what he and Forman had seen during their trip through Henan in March 1943.[118]

The crisis point emerged the following spring, during the Ichigo offensive that began in April 1944.[119] This offensive, "the largest military operation carried out in the history of the Japanese army," aimed to destroy American air bases in China to prevent U.S. air raids on the Japanese mainland and to open an overland transportation route from central China to Japanese-occupied French Indochina.[120] The first stage of the offensive was the Battle of Henan. In April 1944, Japanese troops attacked Chinese forces along the Beijing-Hankou Railway in Henan, the same railroad that Chinese troops had held in 1938 by breaching the Yellow River's dike. This time roughly 60,000 Japanese troops managed to "cut through the Chinese lines the way a butcher knife cuts through butter," write White and Jacoby.[121] "In nine days of the Honan Province offensive in central China below the Yellow River the Japanese have overrun about 1,800 square miles in the heart of a region where famine-ravaged millions have been hopeful of gathering a bumper wheat crop," reported the *New York Times* on April 28.[122] By late May, the Guomindang army had lost

---

[117] Goodman, *Social and Political Change*, 55; Li Wenhai et al., *Zhongguo jindai shida zaihuang*, 292.

[118] White and Jacoby, *Thunder out of China*, 177.

[119] For more on the famine and Ichigo, see Mitter, *Forgotten Ally*, 319–25; Muscolino, *The Ecology of War*, 113–14.

[120] Hara Takeshi, "The Ichigō Offensive," in *The Battle for China: Essays on the Military History of the Sino-Japanese War of 1937–1945*, ed. Mark Peattie, Edward J. Drea, and Hans van de Ven (Stanford, CA: Stanford University Press, 2011), 392–93.

[121] White and Jacoby, *Thunder out of China*, 178. See also Compilation Committee, *Henan kangzhan shilue*, 273–78.

[122] "Chengchow Falls to Japanese Drive," *New York Times*, April 28, 1944.

most of the province to the Japanese and was forced to retreat to the Funiu Mountains in western Henan.[123]

The retreating Nationalist army was not greeted with open arms by a population still reeling from the famine. When troops who fled into the Funiu Mountains began to rob and mistreat the local people, state the compilers of a short volume about the War of Resistance in Henan published in 1985, the masses in western Henan "rose in rebellion, besieged the Guomindang army that had brought calamity to the country and the people, and captured their firearms and ammunition."[124] White and Jacoby report that it was the Guomindang army's attempt to seize peasants' oxen to supplement its disintegrating supply system that pushed the peasants into armed rebellion. "They had suffered through too many months of famine and merciless military extortion," write White and Jacoby. "Now they turned, arming themselves with birdguns, knives, and pitchforks. They began by disarming individual soldiers and ended by disarming entire companies. It was estimated that 50,000 Chinese soldiers were disarmed by their own countrymen during the few weeks of the campaign."[125]

Chiang Kai-shek was appalled and humiliated by the turn of events in Henan. "The local population attacked our own forces and seized their arms, just as happened with the czar's army in imperial Russia during World War I," he lamented during the Battle of Henan. "Such an army cannot win!"[126] Indeed, by the end of May the battle was decisively lost. After pushing the Guomindang army out of all but the westernmost edge of Henan, Japanese troops moved south to conduct the second stage of the offensive, during which they occupied Hunan, Guangxi, and parts of Guangdong Province, and "cut in half the areas under Nationalist government rule."[127]

---

[123] Wou, *Mobilizing the Masses*, 329.

[124] Compilation Committee, *Henan kangzhan* shilue, 311–12.

[125] White and Jacoby, *Thunder out of China*, 177–78. See also Song Zhixin, *1942*, 143, 171. For Nationalist commander Jiang Dingwen's description of local people in western Henan attacking Nationalist troops during the campaign, see Mitter, *Forgotten Ally*, 320.

[126] Chiang Kai-shek, "Zhi chi tuqiang" [Recognizing humiliation and making our country strong], as cited in Wang Qisheng, "The Battle of Hunan and the Chinese Military's Response to Operation Ichigō," in Peattie, Drea, and van de Ven, *The Battle for China*, 417, 418.

[127] Wang, "The Battle of Hunan," 403.

The poor showing of Nationalist troops during the Japanese offensive was a turning point for American views of the Guomindang military and leadership. "The Ichigō offensive struck a massive blow against the Nationalist army, as a result of which the Americans were made painfully aware of the weaknesses of the Nationalists and lost faith in the Nationalist army," writes Hara Takeshi.[128] American views of Chiang Kai-shek also suffered. "The Generalissimo had returned to China with his prestige greatly enhanced" after President Roosevelt treated him as an equal at the Cairo Conference in November 1943, notes David Gordon, but Chinese failures during the Ichigo offensive "diminished him in American eyes." In part because of the Henan famine and its broader implications, by the end of 1944 Chiang's prestige was "declining precipitously," and his international and domestic position was increasingly precarious.[129]

In contrast, by mid-1944 the Communists were on the move in Henan, a province they considered "the key area of the liberation of central China." Japanese forces were spread far too thinly to control the large swaths of the province they seized from the Guomindang during the Ichigo offensive, explains Wou. The rapid Guomindang retreat thus "gave the CCP the chance to expand rapidly into the newly Japanese-occupied areas." In July 1944 the Communist Eighth Route Army moved out of the Taihang base to establish a new Communist base in western Henan, and decimated bases in central and southern Henan were reinvigorated.[130] Moreover, the Japanese military's decision to withdraw many of its troops stationed in eastern Henan to bolster the offensive elsewhere, explains Wou, "completely redefined the military situation there." By the end of 1944, Communist forces from the Rivereast base had moved into three additional counties and increased the number of villages under their control from 571 to 815.[131] In short, while the events of the Ichigo campaign

---

[128] Takeshi, "The Ichigō Offensive," 402.

[129] David M. Gordon, "Historiographical Essay: The China-Japan War, 1931–1945," *Journal of Military History* 70 (January 2006): 160. For more on the Cairo Conference, see chapter 13, this volume.

[130] Wou, *Mobilizing the Masses*, 329–30; Compilation Committee, *Henan kangzhan shilue*, 270–72.

[131] Wou, *Mobilizing the Masses*, 245–46.

humiliated the Nationalists, the Communists took advantage of the situation to move into former Guomindang strongholds and recover territory behind Japanese lines.[132]

CONCLUSION

The Nationalist leadership's decision to prioritize the military over the civilian population of Henan in 1942 and 1943 was a costly one. It did not in the end enable the army to defend Henan against the Japanese offensive, but it did turn many famine victims against the Guomindang, a fact that became clear in the spring of 1944. Moreover, when Chinese journalists such as Zhang Gaofeng and Wang Yunsheng of the *Dagongbao* dared to publish critical reports about the government's continued grain extraction in Henan, the Guomindang's heavy-handed response was one of many incidents of oppression that gradually chipped away at the support Chiang had initially received from Chinese intellectuals. The scope of the suffering in Henan and the spectacle of government officials forcing starving farmers to hand over their last remaining grain shocked American observers such as Theodore White as well. "Of all marks on my thinking, the Honan famine remains most indelible," he writes. In White's case, what he saw in Henan in 1943 led him to begin to believe "that the Chinese government was totally incapable of governing."[133] The disintegration of Nationalist forces in Henan during the Ichigo campaign the following year would bring other American China-hands to a similar conclusion, as well as opening the door to Communist expansion in the province.

In sum, contrary to the *Zhongyang ribao*'s expectation, the Nationalist

---

[132] Ibid., 329–30. The struggle for Henan was far from over in 1944. After Japan was defeated, Nationalist forces quickly recovered much of the territory they had lost during the Ichigo offensive, and the Communists were generally on the defensive in Henan from the fall of 1945 until mid-1947. Nevertheless, the Guomindang debacle in 1944 allowed the Communists to lay groundwork in significant areas of Henan that had been closed to them before Ichigo (see Wou, chapter 9).

[133] White, *In Search of History*, 144.

government failed the test posed by the famine. When faced with famine, Nationalist leaders did not examine policy decisions such as the heavy grain tax in Henan and change course, nor did they increase their popular legitimacy by prioritizing the livelihood of North China's rural population. Within six years of the famine, they lost control of the country and were forced to cede China's destiny to the Communists.

II

Walking the Enlightened Path

Wang Mingdao's Road to Independent Christianity under Japanese Occupation

Amy O'Keefe

On January 16, 1942, Wang Mingdao received an answer to prayer. Wang, a Chinese Christian pastor living in Beijing, was seeking divine guidance about whether or not to join the Christian umbrella organization formed by the Japanese occupation government. When Wang prayed about this question, a passage of Scripture came to his mind: "What part hath he that believeth with an infidel?" and Wang knew he should not join the church federation.[1] Who was the "infidel" with whom Wang should not associate? Not the Japanese military government, more eager to oversee church activities than support church goals; no, Wang Mingdao understood that the "infidel" referred to other Christians affiliated with the federation, Christians whose understanding of the Bible conflicted with his fundamentalist views.[2]

---

[1] 2 Corinthians 6:15.

[2] Wong Ming-Dao, *A Stone Made Smooth*, trans. Arthur Reynolds (Hants, U.K.: Mayflower Christian Books, 1981), 215–16, 224, hereafter cited as *SMS*.

For Wang Mingdao (1900–1991), the idea of cooperating with an invading nation's dictates was not as repugnant as cooperating with liberal Chinese Christians. To him, religious stance trumped political position. In this way, Wang Mingdao is different from most of the figures discussed in this volume. His crises and triumphs were not tied to the success or failure of a given regime, party, or even nation. For Wang Mingdao, 1943 was not a year of disappointed hopes, nor was it a year of crisis. After a hair-raising confrontation with the Japanese in 1942, Wang went on to have a year of blossoming confidence and expanding influence in 1943.

In 1943 Beijing, Japanese rule had been a fact of daily life for more than five years.[3] As we consider what life under occupation was like for Wang Mingdao and others, setting aside the distorting binary of collaborators and resistors will aid our understanding. A historical viewpoint weighed down by the imperative to categorize people based on their relationship with the occupation state ignores the aspects of life not involved with the military or government, and obscures people who based their primary identities elsewhere than on their citizenship. Neither a collaborator nor a resistor, Wang Mingdao was such a third-category citizen of foreign rule. He was a man whose mind was taken up in his own goals, a man not preoccupied with the occupation.[4]

Wang Mingdao was born in 1900, just weeks after his father committed suicide. Wang's father, a casualty of the Boxer Uprising, had worked for the London Mission Society. After his death, his widow received Boxer indemnity funds and bought a house, where she supported Wang Mingdao and his sister by renting out rooms to colorful lowlifes.[5] At age fourteen, Wang converted to Christianity under the influence of an older student in his school, but it was several years before he finally abandoned his dream of a life in politics and accepted that he was called by God to

---

[3] Beijing was known as Beiping starting in 1927; since "jing" indicates capital, this name change showed deference to the Nationalist capital, Nanjing. Once the Japanese established their North China regime, they changed the name back to Beijing. Many historians use "Beiping" for the whole period from 1927 to 1949. Wang Mingdao's writings echo the local regime's usage, and I have made the decision to let my usage mirror that of my protagonist: Beiping between 1927 and 1938, and Beijing thereafter.

[4] I am indebted to Christopher O'Keefe for this phrase.

[5] *SMS*, 2–6.

preach Christianity. Ill health, family responsibilities, and an unresponsive educational administrator hindered his attempts to enter a university, and Wang was forced to find employment with no higher education.[6] He took a post as a teacher and found some success using that position to lead young people to God.[7] However, upon coming to a conviction that his baptism, which had been performed by sprinkling, was not valid, Wang insisted on being rebaptized by immersion. Finding him intractable and already feeling threatened by the preacher who was to rebaptize Wang, the church that ran his school fired Wang.[8] For the next few years, Wang lived in his mother's home, studying the Bible and helping around the house. He began holding small meetings with other Christians, and in his mid-twenties he formed a congregation.[9] In 1927, Wang began publishing his Christian magazine, *Lingshi jikan* (*Spiritual Food Quarterly*); in 1933 he rented a space for his flock to congregate; and in 1936 he began building a much larger church building in Beiping.[10] He named this meeting place the Christians' Tabernacle (*Jidutu huitang*).[11]

Wang Mingdao became a very influential writer and preacher. In addition to leading his own congregation in Beiping, he was invited to speak in twenty-eight provinces of China, in churches of over thirty different denominations. Wang also wrote the vast majority of the articles in *Spiritual Food Quarterly*, which generally came to between forty and sixty pages every three months for twenty-eight years. This magazine reached tens of thousands of readers throughout China and in other parts of the world.[12]

Many scholars and Christian authors have written about Wang Mingdao, but today his fame is primarily based on his clash with the Three-Self Patriotic Movement (*sanzi aiguo yundong*), the umbrella organization aimed at oversight and control of religion that was established under the

[6] Ibid., 36–39.

[7] Ibid., 40–50.

[8] Ibid., 59–66.

[9] Ibid., 65–79.

[10] Ibid., 106, 115, 118–19.

[11] Lin Ronghong, *Wang Mingdao yu Zhongguo jiaohui* [Wang Mingdao and the Chinese church] (Hong Kong: China Graduate School of Theology, 1982), 87.

[12] *SMS*, 89, 145.

Figure 11.1: Wang Mingdao as a young preacher, standing in front of his church, the Christians' Tabernacle. *Source:* Wang Tianduo.

People's Republic of China.[13] The conflict between Wang and the Three-Self Movement came to a head in 1955, and Wang was imprisoned by the Communist regime from 1955 to 1956 for refusing to join it. To buy back

---

[13] Daniel H. Bays, *A New History of Christianity in China* (Malden, MA: Wiley-Blackwell, 2012), 160–66.

his freedom, Wang agreed to make a Communist-style self-criticism. His self-criticism left him regretful and deeply depressed, however, and he and his wife ultimately refused to take the final step of joining the Three-Self Movement. As a result, in 1958 Wang was arrested and imprisoned again. In 1963 he was sentenced to life imprisonment, having been branded a counterrevolutionary by the state, and he remained in prison for more than twenty years.[14] Finding in him a martyr, a resistor of the Communists' religious oppression, scholars and writers often gloss over Wang's earlier experiences in the wartime period.[15] To neglect this period of Wang's life or, worse, to find in it evidence that he was a political dissident, is to grossly misunderstand the man's life and goals. Such history writing politicizes him against his most strenuous objections, mutilating the meaning of his life to fit it into narratives of the nation. This chapter seeks to free Wang Mingdao from those national narratives, presenting his experience in the context of occupied Beijing and examining the changes his conflict with occupation authorities wrought in his life.

In 1937, just as events outside Beiping precipitated the Sino-Japanese War, construction on Wang's church building was completed. Wang continued to preach there as the Japanese troops drove the Nationalists out of the northern and central areas of China in 1938. A prominent member of the Nationalist Party, Wang Jingwei, formed a puppet government under the auspices of the Japanese, housed in Nanjing and called the Reorganized National Government of China.[16] Popular association of the Nanjing regime with the Nationalist Party caused some Japanese to fear an increase in nationalism in occupied areas. In addition, the North China

---

[14] Lee Ming Ng, *Christianity and Social Change: The Case in China, 1920–1950*, PhD diss., Princeton Theological Seminary, 1971. For analysis of Wang Mingdao's appeal for rehabilitation, see Xing Fuzeng, *Wang Mingdao de zuihou zibai* [The last confessions of Wang Mingdao] (Hong Kong: Logos, 2013).

[15] See Mark A. Noll and Carolyn Nystrom, *Clouds of Witnesses: Christian Voices from Africa and Asia* (Downers Grove, IL: InterVarsity, 2011), 258–62; Leslie T. Lyall, *Three of China's Mighty Men* (London: Hodder and Stoughton, 1973); Thomas A. Harvey, *Acquainted with Grief: Wang Mingdao's Stand for the Persecuted Church in China* (Grand Rapids, MI: Bazos, 2002).

[16] Lincoln Li, *The Japanese Army in North China: Problems of Political and Economic Control* (East Asian Historical Monographs) (Tokyo: Oxford University Press, 1975), viii, 11.

leadership feared that the existence of a strong Nanjing-based government would relegate them to second-tier status. So the North China Army pushed leaders in Tokyo for autonomous status for North China (Huabei), and it was granted.[17] North China was the area south of the Great Wall of China and north of the Longhai Railway,[18] including Shandong, Hebei, parts of northern Henan, and Shanxi. Its western limit was the Shaanxi border.[19] The area remained war-torn territory long after the Nationalists were driven out in 1938; the Japanese had significant counterguerrilla work to do in North China to keep down Communists and other anti-Japanese resistors.[20]

On December 7, 1941, the Japanese attack on Pearl Harbor further complicated the picture in North China, as it made all citizens of Allied powers there aliens on enemy soil. Japanese opposition to British and American imperialism in Asia included those nations' Christian workers.[21] American and British personnel and financial resources, already stretched thin by the demands of relief work before Pearl Harbor, were now disallowed altogether.[22] The change in relationship between the state and foreign-supported churches left Christians in Beijing reeling. Of course, Wang Mingdao's church was not one of these—his church was run through local donations and did not rely on the involvement of any foreigners.

---

[17] Ibid., 12.

[18] Ibid., 15.

[19] This is indicated by a map found in ibid., 154. For the Western border, my source is David P. Barrett and Larry N. Shyu, eds., *Chinese Collaboration with Japan, 1932–1945: The Limits of Accommodation* (Stanford, CA: Stanford University Press, 2001), xi.

[20] Edward J. Drea and Hans van de Ven, "An Overview of Major Military Campaigns during the Sino-Japanese War, 1937–1945," in *The Battle for China: Essays on the Military History of the Sino-Japanese War of 1937–1945*, ed. Mark Peattie, Edward Drea, and Hans van de Ven (Stanford, CA: Stanford University Press, 2011), 37.

[21] Timothy Brook, "Toward Independence: Christianity in China under the Japanese Occupation," in *Christianity in China: From the Eighteenth Century to the Present*, ed. Daniel H. Bays (Stanford, CA: Stanford University Press, 1999), 318.

[22] On pre–Pearl Harbor reorganizations, see ibid., 330. On changes after Pearl Harbor, see Daniel H. Bays, "Preliminary Thoughts on Researching the History of Protestant Christianity in Shandong Province during the War of Resistance, 1937–1945," in *Liehuo zhong de xili: kangri zhanzheng shiqi de Zhongguo jiaohui (1937–1945)* [Baptism by Fire: the Chinese church during the Sino-Japanese War (1937–1945)], eds. Lee Kam-keung and Lau Yee-cheung (Hong Kong: Jiandao shenxueyuan, 2011), 532; "Missions Transfer Their Properties to Chinese Church Organization," *Peking Chronicle*, March 17, 1942, 5.

Still, Wang's church, like most others in Beijing, did not open for services on the Sunday after Pearl Harbor.[23] They had received explicit orders to await permission from the authorities before gathering.[24] The Japanese had insisted that Christian work would be able to move ahead only in churches that could prove that they had completely cut ties with British and American organizations.[25] Wang Mingdao could logically assume that his interaction with the authorities would be brief and decisive and that he would then be allowed to go about his work, but Japanese concern about Western-linked Christian organizations placed other churches under suspicion as well.

On Saturday, December 13, the Huabei Office of Internal Affairs (*Neiwu zongshu*) called on church leaders to organize a church preservation committee. In Beijing, a committee was formed and its members held a preparatory meeting on December 15.[26] The message of that meeting was that ties with foreign churches must be cut in a spirit of independence. Pressure was also exerted to form a church union.[27] At a second meeting held on December 18, attendees chose the name North China Christian Federation Promotion Committee (*Huabei Jidujiao lianhe cujinhui*) and selected the Beijing Young Men's Christian Association (YMCA, *qingnianhui*) secretary general, Zhou Guanqing, to lead the new organization.[28] According to one missionary's account, the first conference of the promotion committee was rife with opposition to the Japanese impera-

---

[23] *SMS*, 214.

[24] From Wang's diary entry of December 20, 1941. Wang Mingdao, *Wang Mingdao riji xuanji* [Selections from the diary of Wang Mingdao] (Hong Kong: Lingshi chubanshe, 1997) (Hereafter, *WMDRJ*), 257; Song Jun, "Cong kangzhan shiqi Huabei Rijun dui Jidujiao zhengce de yanbian kan Huabei Zhonghua Jidujiaotuan chengli" [Viewing the establishment of the North China Christian Association as part of the evolution of Japanese army policy on Christianity in North China in the anti-Japanese war period], in *Liehuo zhong de xili*, 210.

[25] Brook, "Toward Independence," 333. On the Three-Self Movement's priorities, see Bays, *New History of Christianity*, 161–63.

[26] Song Jun, "Jidujiaotuan chengli," 210.

[27] Xing Fuzeng, "Wang Mingdao yu Huabei Zhonghua Jidujiaotuan: lunxianqu jiaohui renshi dikang yu hezuo de ge'an yanjiu" [Wang Mingdao and the North China Christian Union: Chinese Christians' resistance and collaboration with Japan in occupied areas], *Jiandao xuekan* no. 17 (January 2002), 10–11.

[28] Song Jun, "Jidujiaotuan chengli," 210–11.

tives. The choice of a representative from such a Westerner-heavy organization as the YMCA certainly did not indicate general agreement with the Japanese goal of independence from Western influences.[29]

Perhaps it was the resistance put up by attendees at the first meeting that led the Japanese to prohibit worship services the next weekend. On December 20, 1941, Wang Mingdao received the notification that gatherings were prohibited. Without even eating his breakfast, Wang hurried off to the branch public security office (*fenju bao'anxi*). There he was told he had to get approval from the military police to hold worship meetings. But at the office of the military police (*xianbing dui*) he was told that churches without Western members need not ask for permission to congregate. When he returned with this news, he was rebuffed by personnel in the first public security office, who told him that he did in fact need permission. After one more visit to the military police and one more trip back to the local police office, Wang finally received the go-ahead to continue holding his meetings.[30]

On January 14, 1942, Wang received a letter informing him that *Spiritual Food Quarterly* fit within one of ten categories of publications prohibited by the authorities. Wang called on friends and associates for help, seeking a way to keep publishing. His diary mentions several visits to an associate in a department store, who also looked at Wang's petition and said he would ask someone he knew for help.[31] Wang also showed the petition to a contact he had in the Special Affairs section (*tewuke*) at the police station before submitting it for formal review.[32]

On January 16, a representative of the North China Christian Federation Promotion Committee informed Wang that the YMCA leader, Zhou Guanqing, was involved in the organization. It was that evening that Wang and his associates prayed together and agreed that they must not join with "the infidel."[33] Wang had his reasons for trusting this revelation: he felt that leaders in many of the churches that had joined the federation

---

[29] Brook, "Toward Independence," 332.

[30] *WMDRJ*, 257.

[31] Ibid., 260–61, January 17, 20, and 21, 1942.

[32] Ibid., 259, January 15, 1942.

[33] Ibid., 260, January 16, 1942; *SMS*, 215–16.

were "destroying people's faith" (through liberal teachings); "they had merged with the world."[34] The liberal teachings to which Wang referred were the teachings of the Social Gospel. Wang had summed them up years earlier in an introductory letter to the first edition of *Spiritual Food Quarterly*: "What do they say? They say, 'The Christian way of life consists of service and sacrifice. Jesus is the highest pattern of personality. He is the reformer of dark society. ... Depending on the spread of learning the world will be reconstructed to become heaven. The virgin birth of Christ, His atonement, resurrection and return are myths. The Bible is no more than a history of the Hebrew religion, and not all of it is to be believed.'"[35]

Wang objected strenuously to liberal Christianity's rationalization of spiritual mysteries, but it may have been the leadership of Zhou Guanqing in particular that inspired his resolve against joining this particular organization, for he had a pronounced distaste for the YMCA. Seven years earlier, Wang had written an article titled "The Sins of the Modern YMCA," a lengthy treatise against the actions of the "clique of unbelievers" (*buxinpai*).[36] Little wonder that Wang felt he could say a single prayer and move ahead with his life, committed to his decision not to link himself to an organization led by a YMCA representative.

The next day, the man who had brought the message about Zhou Guanqing ran into Wang's closest associate, Shi Tianmin, and sent a message through him to Wang: membership in the Federation Promotion Committee was not optional. That night Xu Hongdao, Wang's other most trusted coworker in the church, came to discuss the matter in detail. Wang wrote in his diary, "Yesterday and today, these church affairs made me feel that I, [Shi Tianmin,] and [Xu Hongdao] are like the captain, first mate, and second mate in a steamship, and the safety of the whole ship is on the shoulders of we few men. The responsibility is truly heavy!"[37] But Wang did not waiver. The next day, January 18, he saw the Federation Promotion

---

[34] *SMS*, 215–16.

[35] *SMS*, 149.

[36] Xing Fuzeng, *Wang Mingdao de zuihou zibai*, 10; Wang Mingdao, "Xiandai Jidujiao qingnianhui de zui'e" [The sins of the modern YMCA], *Lingshi jikan* (*Spiritual Food Quarterly*, hereafter *SFQ*) 34, no. 2 (1935): 38–55. The article and the YMCA's eventual response are discussed in Xing Fuzeng, *Wang Mingdao de zuihou zibai*, appendix 2.

[37] *WMDRJ*, 260, January 17, 1942.

Committee representative and informed him that he would not be joining—and Wang specified that Mr. Zhou need not communicate further
with him or his church regarding this matter.[38]

The firmness of Wang's response belies the vulnerability of his church
before the occupation authorities. On the following day, the military police came to investigate the church, looking into staff, finances, and the
origins and history of the organization—but no decision was made about
the fate of the church or its publication.[39] Two days later, on January 22,
Wang went with his department store contact and another helpful associate to the military police station and was finally told that publication of
Spiritual Food Quarterly would be allowed, as long as each issue was sent
to the military police for inspection prior to publication. That day Wang
wrote in his diary, "At noon, headed toward home, and after stopping by
to tell my mother and sister, I thought [of] how it seemed we had passed
through all trials regarding *Spiritual Food Quarterly* and it had again been
resurrected. Then the tears came down."[40]

Wang's magazine had been saved, but pressure to join his church to
the federation continued. On April 30, 1942, Wang Mingdao received a
written communication from the Federation Promotion Committee, requiring the presence of a representative of Wang's Christians' Tabernacle at a branch office formation meeting the next day. Wang spent an
agonizing night alternating between thought in his courtyard and prayer
in a meeting room.[41] Finally, at two in the morning he slept. "Even in my
dreams I continued to think about this Federation business," Wang wrote
the next day. "After I got up, because I did not get enough sleep, my energy
was low. A little after seven I wrote a letter of response."[42] This is the letter
he wrote:

> I acknowledge the receipt of your letter directing me to join the
> North China Christian Federation Promotion Committee. On ex-

---

[38] Ibid., January 18, 1942.
[39] Ibid., January 19, 1942.
[40] Ibid., 261, January 22, 1942.
[41] *SMS*, 219.
[42] *WMDRJ*, 263, April 30 and May 1, 1942.

amining your statement with its references to Western missions and to the objective of becoming self-supporting, self-governing and self-propagating, I conclude that it is not necessary for us to join your group. In addition to that your Federation is made up of churches of different faith from ours, and in order to preserve an unadulterated faith it would be difficult for us to affiliate with churches of different faith. Consequently we are unable to follow your directions and to send a representative to your meeting. I hope that you will understand our position.[43]

The branch formation meeting was held, and someone who had attended came to tell Wang about it later. Seeing Wang's resolve, he did not continue to push him to join.[44]

The date for the formal establishment of the North China League of Christian Churches (*Huabei Zhonghua Jidujiaotuan*), to be modeled on Japan's church union, the Church of Christ League,[45] was set for October 15. On October 9, Wang received a Japanese visitor at his church in Beijing, who informed Wang that the investigating officer of the North China Cultural Bureau, Mr. Takeda, wanted to meet with him the next day.[46] On October 10, Wang biked off to that appointment singing "Stand Up, Stand Up for Jesus," energized to finally have a real confrontation after months in painful fear of sudden recrimination.[47] The long-awaited meeting may have been disappointingly predictable, though. Takeda urged Wang to reconsider joining the North China League of Christian Churches (NCLCC), telling him that "the Japanese and Chinese alike hope that you can exercise some leadership."[48] To make it clear that further pressure would be futile, Wang gave a refusal so direct that he felt he had caused loss of face for Takeda. He noted, though, that Takeda's manner to him

---

[43] *SMS*, 223–24.

[44] *WMDRJ*, 263, May 1, 1942.

[45] Brook, "Toward Independence," 332.

[46] In Wang's diary, he records that he went to the *xingyayuan* to meet with Takeda. *WMDRJ*, 265. This is the Japanese agency called Kōain (Sophia Lee, personal communication, November 2014).

[47] *SMS*, 229–30, 236.

[48] *SMS*, 230, October 10, 1942; *WMDRJ*, 265.

Table 11.1: North China Umbrella Christian Organizations

December 15–18, 1941	December 18, 1941–October 15, 1942	October 15, 1942–August 1945
Beijing church committee (informal)[a]	North China Christian Federation Promotion Committee (*Huabei Jidujiao lianhe cujinhui*)[b]	North China League of Christian Churches (*Huabei Zhonghua Jidujiaotuan*)[c]
[a]*SMS*, 214.	[b]Xing Fuzeng, "Huabei Zhonghua Jidujiaotuan," 11.	[c]Song Jun, "Jidujiaotuan chengli," 197.

remained remarkably warm. Nonetheless, Takeda made no definitive statement about the future of Wang's church given his refusal to join the league, and Wang's fears continued.[49]

On October 15, 1942, the Federation Promotion Committee was dissolved and the NCLCC was formed in its place. The genealogy of this organization is summarized in table 11.1.

It was perhaps his anxiety over the formation of the NCLCC and his own refusal to cooperate that kept Wang Mingdao close to home, for in 1942 he did not travel as much as usual. Ordinarily, he spent some days during each quarter in other cities, preaching in various churches by invitation from their pastors. Though the first few months of war kept him Beijing-bound in 1937, only illness and natural disasters kept Wang from traveling after that.[50] He made the modest trip to Tianjin quite often, and regularly traveled to Shandong Province.[51] In 1938 and 1939, Wang even

---

[49] *SMS*, 230–31.

[50] Wang Mingdao, "Bianzhe de xiaoxi" [Editor's message], *SFQ* 43–44, nos. 3–4 (1939): 89. Wang was unable to make a scheduled trip to Tianjin in the fall of 1939 due to flooding there. Wang, "Bianzhe de xiaoxi," *SFQ* 53, no. 1 (1940): 69; *SFQ* 54, no. 2 (1940): 73. In 1940, Wang had an extended period of ill health and was unable to travel.

[51] Visits to Tianjin to preach are noted in Wang's "Editor's message" eight times from 1937 to 1943: Wang Mingdao, "Bianzhe de xiaoxi," *SFQ* 45, no. 1 (1938): 68; *SFQ* 47, no. 3 (1938): 71; *SFQ* 49, no. 1 (1939): 69; *SFQ* 57, no. 1 (1941): 59; *SFQ* 60, no. 4 (1941): 74; *SFQ* 61, no. 1 (1942): 66; *SFQ* 63, no. 3 (1942): 60; *SFQ* 65, no. 1 (1943): 60. Visits to various places in Shandong are also mentioned eight times in Wang's "Editor's message": Wang, "Bianzhe de xiaoxi," *SFQ* 48, no. 4 (1938): 68; *SFQ* 50, no. 2 (1939): 66; *SFQ* 55, no. 3

traveled beyond the borders of occupied areas to Suiyuan Province (now part of the Inner Mongolia Autonomous Region) and Hong Kong. He also took an extended trip to Shanghai in fall 1939.[52] But changes after Pearl Harbor left Wang uncertain of his church's standing, and in the first few months after the Pearl Harbor attack, Wang traveled just once, a ten-day trip to Tianjin.[53] That spring and summer he traveled more, but all his travel was within North China.[54]

There was only one occasion on which Wang left town that fall: on October 14, 1942, the day before the inaugural meeting of the NCLCC. He went to Jinan, where he had been a student years earlier, and preached there for eight days.[55] The timing of this, his only trip that quarter, could not have been coincidental. Wang's uncertainty regarding his church's fate under the post–Pearl Harbor conditions probably accounts for it and for his restricted travel from 1942 to 1943. Just a day or two after he returned from Jinan, Wang, clearly nervous about the possibility that recriminations might cause him to weaken under pressure, told his followers, "If I one day yield and lead our church to affiliate with the North China Chinese Christian Association, then you must all immediately throw me over. Do not again listen to my preaching. You will call me Judas Iscariot."[56] Three weeks later, he received a summons from the military police.

On the day that he had been told to appear before the military police, November 18, 1942, Wang donned extra clothing and an overcoat and packed woolen socks, a toothbrush, his glasses and handkerchief, and a Bible. Having thus prepared to endure imprisonment, Wang made his way to the military police office—only to find that the summons had been a clerical error; he had been accidentally invited to the meeting in which missionary-based churches were turning their foreign-owned property

---

(1940): 59; *SFQ* 56, no. 4 (1940): 64; *SFQ* 58, no. 2 (1941): 65; *SFQ* 63, no. 3 (1942): 60; *SFQ* 64, no. 4 (1942): 60; *SFQ* 68, no. 4 (1943): 42.

[52] Wang, "Bianzhe de xiaoxi," *SFQ* 48, no. 4 (1938): 68; also *SFQ* 51, no. 3 (1939): 64–65; *SFQ* 52, no. 4 (1939): 69.

[53] Wang, "Bianzhe de xiaoxi," *SFQ* 61, no. 1 (1942): 66.

[54] Ibid., *SFQ* 63, no. 3 (1942): 60; *SFQ* 64, no. 4 (1942): 60.

[55] Ibid., *SFQ* 64, no. 4 (1942): 60.

[56] Judas Iscariot, one of the twelve Apostles, betrayed Jesus to the people who crucified him (John 6:71).

over to the Japanese puppet state. Wang went home, socks, toothbrush, Bible, and all. This event seems to have convinced Wang that he was not going to be targeted by the occupation state after all—apparently the sword over his head might actually never fall. As 1942 passed without further recrimination for his refusal to join the NCLCC, Wang's tension and fear finally dissipated.[57]

The articles Wang Mingdao published in 1943 reveal his thinking as he processed his experience with the Japanese. In late 1942, Wang had written about the need to overcome fear of men through trust in God.[58] Early in 1943, Wang wrote about great biblical figures who, trusting God, moved fearlessly into danger to do his work.[59] Later in the year, the tone of Wang's discussion of danger and deliverance changed subtly. The difference may be due to the growth in numbers that Wang's church seems to have experienced since the Pearl Harbor attack.[60] His personal prestige also seems to have grown.[61] By late in the year, as the previous year's danger became more and more a part of his success story, Wang's writings reflect a new perspective on danger—the idea that while one's enemies could attempt to harm one, their efforts could only further the work of God.

Wang opened his fall 1943 issue of *Spiritual Food Quarterly* with an article titled "Reaping Benefits from Misfortune." As he had in May 1942, Wang told the story of Joseph, who was sold by his brothers into Egypt.

---

[57] *SMS*, 234.

[58] Wang Mingdao, "Jupa ren de xianru wangluo" [Those who fear man fall into a trap], *SFQ* 63, no. 3 (1942): 51–55; "Yuren zhong zui yu de ren" [The most foolish of all foolish people], *SFQ* 63, no. 3 (1942): 59.

[59] Wang Mingdao, "Bu pasi de Zhu yu bu pasi de mentu" [The Lord who did not fear death and the disciple who did not fear death], *SFQ* 65, no. 1 (1943): 16; Wang Mingdao, "Denghou Shen" [Waiting on the Lord], *SFQ* 65, no. 1 (1943): 48–49.

[60] Daniel Bays's research indicates that while mission-based churches in Shandong floundered after Pearl Harbor, independent churches (like Wang's) drew many converts. Bays, "Preliminary Thoughts," 542–43. Growth of the independent church known as the Jesus Family during this period supports this idea. Tao Feiya, *Zhongguo de Jidujiao wutuobang: Yesu Jiating (1921–1952)* [A Christian utopia in China: The Jesus Family (1921–1952)] (Hong Kong: Chinese University of Hong Kong, 2004), 103. Wang's diary also indicates that he was considering ordaining new deacons to help care for the members of his church. *WMDRJ*, 267.

[61] Wang's diary recounts visits from prominent independent preachers who sought him out in late 1942 and early 1943. *WMDRJ*, 266–67.

But whereas in the earlier article, "Miraculous Rescues," Wang focused on the Lord's superb planning in getting Joseph out of the hands of his murderous brothers, in autumn of 1943, Wang described Joseph's brothers as tools in God's hands. By selling Joseph to the Ishmaelite traders, they put him in a position to enter Egypt, impress his employer, come to the attention of the Pharaoh, and become his official in charge of famine relief planning. Only thus could Joseph later save his entire family from starvation.

He wrote, "There are some great good fortunes that we may never receive in a lifetime, if there were not someone harming us. There are some deepest lessons that, if we did not have an enemy, we might not learn well over our whole lives. ... In the end, we see that the blessings we receive from these people are no less than those we receive from our friends, and we should say to them, 'ye thought evil against me; but God meant it unto good.'"[62]

From this article we see that by September, Wang Mingdao felt his work was seeing real benefits as a result of his confrontation with the church union.[63] By winter, his sense of victory grew, and Wang's writing took on a tone verging on triumphalism.

The Apostle Paul is the main character of one such triumphant tale. In the article "Until We Kill Paul, We Neither Eat nor Drink," Wang described Paul's escape from a band of forty Jews who made the oath referenced in the article's title: they swore not to eat or drink until they had killed the imprisoned Paul.[64] Paul's nephew, who knew of the band's plan, appealed to a Roman centurion for help. The centurion contacted his superior, who in turn arranged an armed escort to spirit Paul away. Paul rode out of town on a beast of burden, surrounded by hundreds of Roman sol-

---

[62] Wang Mingdao, "Yin huo de fu" [Reaping benefits from misfortunes], *SFQ* 67, no. 3 (1943): 3–4. Wang quotes Joseph as recorded in Genesis 50:20.

[63] This article, with nine others, was included in a book Wang published after the war. In the Introduction, Wang stated that the articles pertained to lessons he learned through his 1942 trials. Wang Mingdao, *Zai huoyao yu shixue zhong: Wang Mingdao xiansheng kunan zhong de jianzheng* [In the fiery furnace and in the lion's den: Mr. Wang Mingdao's testimony in times of trouble], 4th ed. (Hong Kong: China Alliance, 1961), 1.

[64] Wang Mingdao, "Ruo bu xian sha Baoluo jiu bu chi bu he" [Until we kill Paul, we neither eat nor drink], *SFQ* 68, no. 4 (1943): 10–12.

diers. After praising the might and power of God in saving Paul, Wang speculated about the forty disappointed Jews:

> When I read this, I really want to know if the forty people who swore to kill Paul ever ate or drank. ... At the time that they made this vow, they must have had no doubt that they would fulfill it, or they would not have dared make it. ... They did not think of the fact that God would have such great power, and such great wisdom, to destroy their plan so easily. They did not kill Paul, but were humiliated, and in failing to fulfill their vow, invited the ridicule of the people.[65]

Wang saw Paul as having the last laugh. This was no idle historical speculation, unconnected with contemporary events. Wang included this article in a volume of lessons he learned from his 1942 conflict with the authorities.[66] He, like Paul before him, had enjoyed a divinely appointed triumph, but his enemy was the YMCA, not the Jews, and the agents who helped him to safety were Japanese occupiers, not Roman soldiers.

In late 1943, the word "prophet" entered Wang's writings in a new way. Wang had written about prophets before, of course; in 1942 he told the story of Hannah, mother to the prophet Samuel, for example.[67] But in 1943, Wang began referring to "prophet" as a contemporary category, and he discussed a prophet's role vis-à-vis laymen in a new way.

In the summer 1943 issue of *Spiritual Food Quarterly*, Wang wrote of the "frightening holes" that sin creates in the lives of Christians, holes that—like those in cloth or pottery—weaken the material around them and can grow until they destroy the whole object.[68] In the next issue Wang revisited this theme, identifying prophets as "the people who stop up the holes." Using the story of Moses pleading with God not to destroy the Israelites after they made and worshipped a golden calf instead of God, Wang defined a prophet's gap-stopping, hole-filling functions as:

---

[65] Ibid., 12–13.

[66] Wang, *Zai huoyao yu shixue zhong*.

[67] Wang Mingdao, "Yige mingzhi de nüzi" [A wise woman], *SFQ* 61, no. 1 (1942).

[68] Wang Mingdao, "Kepa de liekou" [Frightful holes], *SFQ* 66, no. 2 (1943): 31.

(1) pleading with God on behalf of the people, and (2) rebuking the people and calling them to repentance.[69] Then Wang brought the term into use regarding his contemporaries, condemning them for not stepping into the roles he had outlined for prophets. He listed the problems in the church and the lives of individuals, including unbelief, timidity, disobedience, conforming to customs, treachery, greed, licentiousness, and so on.[70] The theme of sin holding back the people and the Christian church was a favorite for Wang, but now he found the solution in a good prophet, someone God could use—one who could help heal the world's wounds, a "repairer of the breach."[71] "If the world had more of this kind of person ready to close up the holes, the world's and the churches' holes, though they are many, would not be a worry. Over the enormous earth and the multitude of people's lives, everywhere there are many fearful holes. Where are the people to fill them?" Though Wang was modest enough not to answer his own question, one can almost see him raising his hand to volunteer. The prophet Wang Mingdao described is the kind of person he aspired to be, the type of person he was starting to see himself as: one who renounced wickedness fearlessly, who merited and received miraculous rescue from impossible dangers.

Wang continued to present prophet as a contemporary category in his December 1943 article, "Strong City, Iron Pillar, Impregnable Fortress." A person cannot move a strong city, or an iron pillar, or an impregnable fortress without destroying it first; it absolutely will not budge. Other people and things must go around it, for it will not give way. "God wants his prophets to be this kind of people," stated Wang.

> He wants them to be like strong cities, iron pillars, impregnable fortresses—strong, unable to give way, unable to surrender before people. God does not just want them to be like this; he gives them strength, and helps them, protects them, is with them, saves them, to the point that those who want to harm or destroy them ... not

---

[69] Wang Mingdao, "Du pokou de ren," [The people who stop up the holes], *SFQ* 67, no. 3 (1943), 5–6.

[70] Ibid., 6–7.

[71] Ibid., 9. Wang uses this phrase, quoting Isaiah 58:12.

only cannot beat them, but break their heads upon them and bleed, receiving humiliation. After God glorifies his own name through them, he will also cause them to receive glory. God has done this kind of thing in ancient times, and he continues to do this today.[72]

In the fall of 1943, Wang wrote of his own leadership role in his diary: "In all places all over the country, a certain number of people are resolving all kinds of issues, and appraising whether a thing is virtuous and good or not, using my words as a standard. Apparently this is what God has entrusted to me and what men expect of me. Bearing this heavy burden, and standing in this position, how I should exert myself, so that my every word and every act can be a model for others!"[73]

That Wang Mingdao saw himself as a prophet of God by the end of 1943 cannot be taken to mean that all his trials had been overcome and life was smooth and easy. Life in Beijing was shaped and framed by the effects of years of warfare and the added burden of occupation. By early 1943, war, bad weather, hoarding, and Japanese plundering had taken their toll on food production to such an extent that a comprehensive plan for grain relief became necessary. The grain that was distributed to every documented resident of Beijing was not top-quality flour. In fact, often it was not flour at all—the need for food relief was great, but shortages dictated that coarser and less desirable sources of grain be distributed instead of the type of flour that people preferred.[74] In addition, delays and organizational problems kept the administration of relief unpredictable; distribution was not always managed on the promised schedule and was sometimes delayed for weeks.[75] The needs imposed by the conditions of war and by the hyperinflation that had seized the city forced, according to historian Sophia Lee, a greater degree of legibility before the state. Beijing residents had to allow the state to probe into their lives, keeping tabs on the makeup

---

[72] Wang Mingdao, "Jiancheng tiezhu tongqiang" [Strong city, iron pillar, impregnable fortress], *SFQ* 68, no. 4 (1943): 20.

[73] *WMDRJ*, 270, September 17, 1943.

[74] Sophia Lee, "Official Grain Relief Distributions in Japanese-Occupied Beijing" [*sic*], paper prepared for the international conference, "Modern China in Global Contexts," Academia Sinica, August 2014, 18. Cited with permission.

[75] Ibid., 25.

of their households, so that they could obtain the documentation necessary to qualify for the much-needed, if poor-quality, food relief.[76]

Wang Mingdao was probably aided in weathering the storm of food shortage by the collective generosity of his congregation. An entry in Wang Mingdao's diary from the previous year documents how in a time of shortage one generous benefactress approached him to offer greater funds. This was a great relief to Wang, since the previous month's meager donations had all been designated for the support of workers in the field.[77] The implication of this story is that Wang's own support and/or the church's other overhead costs were dependent upon gifts from members of the congregation.

The need for food relief meant that the state was more present in people's lives in 1943 than previously. The intrusiveness of officialdom was exacerbated by the mix of agencies administering governance during the occupation. A Frankenstein-esque political structure was pieced together from Japanese and preexisting Chinese agencies, as well as a new set of agencies with origins in the occupation. The result was an ill-defined distribution of authority and responsibilities that rendered the food distribution program complex and vulnerable to abuse and corruption.[78] It also complicated other interactions with the state, as demonstrated by the confusion and mixed responses Wang received on his multiple visits to two different police stations when he was seeking permission to hold church meetings. These frustrating encounters speak to the difficulty of dealing with overlapping jurisdictions and faulty lines of communication.

By 1943, Wang's experiences with this state had taught him that frustration might be inevitable, but fear was not; the occupation state was not out to get him. There was a space within which he could pursue his goals and fulfill what he understood to be his God-given responsibilities. It was the freedom to pursue his religious goals that Wang sought; this was what drove him to defy the state's dictates and seek exemption from the

---

[76] Ibid., 39–40.

[77] *WMDRJ*, 262. The phrase is "專為工人者尚在外," and no further detail is given about who these workers were or what tasks they were engaged in.

[78] See Lee, "Official Grain Relief Distributions," 7–8, on the nature of the occupation state, and 27–30 on abuse and exploitation of the grain relief system.

Figure 11.2: Wang Mingdao and his family, pictured by the Christian's Taberna-cle in the early 1940s. *Source:* Wang Tianduo.

imperative to join the NCLCC. His attitude toward the occupation can-not rightly be termed resistance or even ambivalence; he seems (aside from some legitimate fear of recrimination) not to have wasted feeling on the occupation at all. In this, Wang was not alone; for many people, in-teraction with the occupation government was not a matter of torn feel-ings, nor a tug between the desire to resist and the imperative to collabo-rate. Rather, occupation was a background fact, a current situation. It was the furniture they had to pick their way around to move ahead in their lives.

The Buddhist monk Tanxu, like Wang Mingdao, led a life that revolved around a nonnational set of goals and imperatives. James Carter describes Tanxu's response to the new regime after they invaded his city, Harbin, in 1931: The monk was pleased with an ambitious urban planning project, in spite of the renovations interrupting construction of a Buddhist temple Tanxu was involved with. Tanxu was eager to prove that he was not part of the anti-Japanese resistance, but his eagerness to keep his name clear on that count continued after the war was past—in the time when resistance would have been admired and avowed lack of resistance might logically be strategically de-emphasized. Furthermore, while Tanxu was eager to be known as not part of the resistance himself, he was very pleased when he received the news that a monk of his acquaintance who was part of the resistance was not caught. Carter refers to Tanxu's attitude as "ambiguous." Indeed, his responses seem like data points that do not fit the curve one expects in discussing invasion. But I would suggest that Tanxu's responses to the heightened political tension map perfectly onto another equation. His attitude seems perfectly consistent once one assumes that to Tanxu, it really made no difference who governed as long as the authorities did not impede his work or hurt those he loved.[79] Tanxu, like Wang Mingdao, was not one to be riled up by politics; the state was merely one part of the backdrop to his life's drama.

Prasenjit Duara describes another population with a similar outlook—the women of the Morality Society, one of many religious "redemptive societies" in Manchuria under Sino-Japanese rule. Self-sacrificing women pursued the qualities of "good wife and wise mother" both inside and outside the home in Manchuria, and thus became seen as emblems of a national moral identity. The women of the Morality Society saw the partnership between their organization and the state as a chance to promote adherence to correct moral principles, and the state saw it as an opportunity to promote the East Asian modern model of femininity and family values, helping to build the ideological rationale for the state.[80]

Duara later interviewed an active participant in the Morality Society

---

[79] James Carter, *Heart of Buddha, Heart of China: The Life of Tanxu, a Twentieth-Century Monk* (New York: Oxford University Press, 2011), 126–27. Carter discusses collaboration and resistance with insight and nuance when presenting later events in Tanxu's life, in Chapter 9, "Life During Wartime," 154–73.

[80] Prasenjit Duara, *Sovereignty and Authenticity: Manchukuo and the East Asian Modern* (New York: Rowman and Littlefield, 2003), 133–34, 136, 141, 151.

named Mrs. Gu and was struck by her "pride and reverence for this form of self-sacrificing activism, superior to any political loyalty."[81] He points out that while the Morality Society was certainly employed as a tool of the state, describing the women involved as collaborators with the occupiers distorts the meaning of their experience. "Such a view derives from a nationalist perspective, and few of these women saw themselves from this perspective at the time. ... Mrs. Gu ... tended in fact to see the Japanese as following the *Daodehui* rather than the other way round. She saw little contradiction in serving different regimes as long as she could continue her mission."[82] Mrs. Gu's attitude parallels the feelings of Tanxu and Wang Mingdao. For them too, "nationalism was clearly less important ... than being able to pursue their religious mission and personal goals."[83]

The women of the Morality Society created or were given a reserved rhetorical space within which their activism was embraced and employed by the state. For the purposes of our discussion of Wang Mingdao, it is worth noting that self-sacrificing women were marked "safe" in the eyes of the state (and much of the rest of society, no doubt) by their prescribed gender roles, their existence within "women's spaces."[84] Though they functioned outside the home, those activities of female activists were not threatening to power hierarchies because they were oriented toward affairs traditionally considered *nei*, or inner—activities and concerns belonging to the women's quarters. The *nei* nature of these activities would not threaten or encroach upon the stability of the masculine political realm, designated *wai*, or outer.

In these "safe" female activists, I find a parallel to Wang Mingdao. Like them, he created a space apart from the realm of politics. While his work was not designated feminine, it was so carefully and completely apolitical that it could be similarly viewed as having no overlap with, and therefore presenting no threat to, the work of the occupation state. It was Wang's stance against the Social Gospel that cordoned off his religious activities so convincingly and completely from the political world.

Wang Mingdao placed the cordon around himself with great deliber-

---

[81] Ibid., 132.
[82] Ibid., 161–62.
[83] Ibid., 154.
[84] Ibid., 134.

ateness. For years, he had stated his condemnation of the Social Gospel in no uncertain terms. To Wang, Social Gospel churches, characterized by the imperative to perfect the whole of society and leaning toward nationalism, were all too vulnerable to financial and theological corruption.[85] As noted above, he vocally and irrevocably criticized the YMCA in a 1935 article. Indeed, it was his opposition to the beliefs and practices of Social Gospel churches that made it impossible for him to join the NCLCC.

In 1942, Wang's *Spiritual Food* articles carefully distinguished his brand of Christianity from Social Gospel beliefs and practices. He completely avoided discussing social reform, redrawing the lines of Christian behavior so that institutionalized charity did not factor in. In an article titled "Christians Who Bring Glory to God," Wang urged readers to respond to Jesus's injunction in Matthew 5:16: "Let your light so shine before men, that they may see your good works, and glorify your Father which is in Heaven." What Wang thought Jesus had in mind is a far cry from the type of good works done by the hospital-building, education-promoting proponents of the Social Gospel. Wang understood "good works" to mean simply "good conduct": honesty, incorruptibility, and, yes, love and labor for others, though Wang did not linger on the last point. Instead, he stressed that only through Christians' impeccably honest behavior would people's hearts be touched to listen to them.[86] Historian of Christianity Alan Harvey described Wang's stance well when he wrote that Wang believed that all social problems were caused by sin, and that bringing people to repentance was therefore the way to effect change in society. Wang worked to purify the church, writ large to include any Christian church, but did not want to deal with worldly institutions (or, as we have seen, church institutions entangled with worldly institutions).[87] Wang's definition of good works, which downplayed service to the point that it was almost relegated to a footnote, is an instance of his drawing a line between himself and proponents of the service-oriented Social Gos-

---

[85] *SMS*, 149; see also Wong Mingdao, "The Distinctive Color of Heaven," in *Spiritual Food: 20 Messages Translated by Arthur Reynolds* (Hants, U.K.: Mayflower Christian Books, 1983), 3–4.

[86] Wang Mingdao, "Rongyao Shen de Jidutu" [Christians who glorify God], *SFQ* 64, no. 4 (1942): 2–4.

[87] Harvey, *Acquainted with Grief*, 39–40.

pel stance. Wang seems to have envisioned, explicitly in contrast to a Social Gospel, a personal gospel.

Wang's opposition to liberal or Social Gospel Christianity could not have been unwelcome news to the Japanese. They were surely aware of liberal, activist Christians who viewed the Japanese as an enemy to China and to Christianity.[88] The connection between liberal Christianity and a liberal political stance also had a history in Japan, after all. In his book *Christian Converts and Social Protest in Meiji Japan*, historian Irwin Scheiner describes some Japanese Christians who credited their exposure to the religion with the enhanced sense of individual conscience that led them to seek democratic reforms. Little wonder that the occupation state brought its own Christian missionaries to China and eventually sought to unite all the Christians in North China under one easy-to-oversee organization, modeled on a similar organization that had been recently established in Japan.[89]

There were of course liberal Christians in Beijing who were seen by the occupation state as more of a threat than Wang Mingdao. Their stories represent a different side of Christian conflict with the state. Some faculty members at Beijing's Yanjing University, a missionary institution, are examples. A group of eleven faculty and others at Yanjing were arrested within forty-eight hours of the Pearl Harbor attack. Accused of resisting the Japanese, they were imprisoned for more than six months. One of those arrested was the dean of Yanjing's school of religion and recently appointed president of the Anglican Church in China, Zhao Zichen.[90]

Zhao, like several of his colleagues, wrote a memoir about his experience in prison.[91] In it he noted that he and the other five who were released at the same time were told they would be on probation for three years. If at any time in those three years they committed any act against

---

[88] Brook, "Toward Independence," 326.

[89] Ibid., 321.

[90] Wang Xiang, "Zhao Zichen yu 'jiyuji'" [Zhao Zichen and "My experience in prison"], *Shijie zongjiao wenhua* no. 3 (2008): 23, 25.

[91] E.g., Zhao Zichen, *Jiyuji* (Hong Kong: Chinese Christian Literature Council, 1969); Zhao Chengxin, *Yuzhong zaji: Yige shehuixue de jieshi* [Notes from prison: A sociological explanation] (Beijing: s.n., 1945); Zhang Dongsun, "Yuzhong shenghuo jianji" [A simple record of my time in prison], *Guancha* 7 (1947).

the Japanese, they would be sent to prison without trial.[92] Zhao kept his head down for the rest of the war, and some of his colleagues did the same. The philosopher Zhang Dongsun noted in his memoir that his greatest fear while in jail was being forced to teach on behalf of the Japanese state. To avoid this fate, he planned to run away as soon as released from prison—but when his release came, he was too ill to flee. By the time he recovered, a month had passed. Noting that the Japanese were not beating down his door asking him to teach their propaganda, he decided there was no need to leave Beijing after all.[93]

Following Zhao Zichen's release from prison in mid-1942, the Anglican Church arranged a residence for him and put him to work training clergy and writing. During this time Zhao produced two books, one on the Christian church, published in 1943, and a biography of the Apostle Paul, published in 1944. These theological treatises are considered representative examples of Zhao's mature theological work.[94] Zhao also took this time to write down the more than one hundred seventy poems he had composed while in prison.[95] Where Wang's religious work was so separated from politics as to make him immune to the state's restriction, for Zhao the threat of the state led him to the strategic choice to pursue innocuous religious work while the occupation continued.

For Zhao Zichen, as for Wang Mingdao, the main crisis of the occupation seems to have passed by 1943. Certainly the fear of reprisal caused him to constrain his activities, but his quiet time of teaching and writing was a far cry from the moral minefield of collaboration and resistance that so easily springs to mind when we think of the occupation.[96] Like Wang Mingdao, Zhao Zichen, Zhang Dongsun, and others experienced a return to normalcy—or the stabilizing of a new normal—as they made their

---

[92] Zhao Zichen, *Jiyuji*, 88–90.

[93] Quoted in Dai Qing, *Zai ru lai fo zhang zhong: Zhang Dongsun he ta de shi dai* [In the palm of the Buddha: Zhang Dongsun and his era] (Hong Kong: Chinese University Press, 2009), 289.

[94] Wang Xiang, "Zhao Zichen," 23, 26.

[95] Zhao Zichen, *Jiyuji*, 91.

[96] Great examples of scholarly work on the fraught early period of the occupation include Timothy Brook, *Collaboration: Japanese Agents and Local Elites in Wartime China* (New York: Harvard University Press, 2005).

various ways through 1942 and 1943. The occupation was part of the situation—something to be survived, to be gotten through. Certainly we can suppose that for many under the occupation the resolve to carry on with the activities that mattered most to them was paired by this time with the comforting sense that the occupation would end. Sensing that one's own crisis had passed, one could easily choose to do as Zhang Dongsun seems to have done and, perceiving the risk to be none too great, stay in Beijing to wait the occupation out.

Having found and become comfortable in his safe space under the state's purview but out of its way, Wang Mingdao resumed his active traveling schedule in 1943. That summer he spent fifty-two days away from home, his longest trip away from Beijing since the war began. Wang traveled by land beyond the borders of North China, visiting Xuzhou, Nanjing, Shanghai, and Hangzhou.[97] Wang's travels are a marker of continuity in his life. He was doing in 1943 what he had done in so many earlier years and what he felt he would be doing for many years to come.

Stories of Wang Mingdao's fearful 1942 and fruitful 1943 remind us of the partiality of national narratives. The essays in this volume paint a convincing picture of 1943 as a year of tipping points. The lost opportunities that pile up as we move through accounts of the events of this year were important and in the aggregate, they seem to have turned the fate of a nation. But beneath and behind these national stories are stories of other people and organizations on different trajectories. Only as we understand where these people and groups were going on their own power can we understand the reach and the limits of the national story.[98] Perhaps this is the never-ending process of examining history—in separating one end of a bright thread from the heavy brocade of the national picture, we are able at last to understand the pattern where the other end is woven in.

---

[97] Wang Mingdao, "Bianzhe de xiaoxi" [Editor's message], *SFQ* 67, no. 3 (1943): 42.

[98] Prasenjit Duara, *Rescuing History from the Nation: Questioning Narratives of Modern China* (New York: Routledge Curzon, 2003). The rescue Duara describes is probably best understood as a dynamic tension.

12

China's Casablanca

Refugees, Outlaws, and Smugglers in France's Guangzhouwan Enclave

CHUNING XIE

> Come to this place for brothels, gambling, drinking and opium, otherwise
> it is tough to survive; within this domain officials, merchants, soldiers, and
> outlaws can enjoy themselves at will.
>
> —Feng Lingyun, describing Guangzhouwan[1]

At 5:08 p.m. on May 24, 2012, the mayor of Zhanjiang walked out the gate of the National Development and Reform Commission with official approval for a 70 billion yuan steel production project. He could not contain his ecstasy and passionately kissed the paperwork. This fleeting moment was captured by a photographer and quickly became a hit online. "This is a dream we Zhanjiang people have had for thirty years," the mayor said in a trembling voice. The other side of the coin, however, was that due to a surplus of steel in the Chinese market, the central government had already decided to decrease steel production.[2]

---

[1] See Dai Mingguang, "Leizhou tilian xisu kao" [Textual research on couplets and customs in Leizhou], *Zhanjiang wenshiziliao* 16 (1997): 292–93. This volume lists an anonymous author for this couplet.

[2] "Zhanjiang gangtie jidi xiangmu huozhun jianshe" [Zhanjiang steel project has been approved], *Nanfang ribao*, May 25, 2012, 1; Baiyansong, "Xinwen 1+1: Gangtie shi zenyang

Zhanjiang was once known as Guangzhouwan, a name that had been used since the Ming dynasty to refer to a port situated on the Leizhou Peninsula in southern Guangdong. Guangzhouwan provides access to Guangxi, Guizhou, and Sichuan provinces to the north, and it lies just across the South China Sea from Hainan Island to the south. To the west, across the Gulf of Tonkin, are Haiphong and Hanoi (formerly part of French Indochina, now in Vietnam); and to the east Macau and Hong Kong are within three hundred miles.

In 1897, the French steamship *Boyard* lost its way in the South China Sea and accidentally sailed into the harbor of Guangzhouwan. The crew reported to Paris the discovery of this well-located deep-water port. Following more than a year of local resistance, the French occupied Guang- zhouwan, and in 1899 France signed a ninety-nine-year lease with the Qing government. Guangzhouwan was subsequently administered under the authority of the colonial government of French Indochina.

While the French hoped to take advantage of Guangzhouwan's strate- gic position and develop it by connecting to their large colony in Hanoi through Guangxi overland and across the Gulf of Tonkin by sea, their plans did not come to fruition before the outbreak of war between Japan and the Allies in 1941. It is difficult to assess how serious these plans really were at the time to the French, and Guangzhouwan probably did not oc- cupy a prominent place among France's vast overseas colonies.[3] With the cooperation of the Vichy French government, Japan occupied Guang- zhouwan on February 21, 1943, and began to promote the idea of a "Re-

lianchengde?" [News one plus one: How to make steel?], CCTV13 News Channel, May 29, 2012.

[3] The French, however, did attempt some minor construction intended to connect Guangzhouwan to the outside world. For example, in 1898 the French requested and re- ceived permission from the Qing court to build a railway connecting Guangzhouwan to Anpu (a small town less than 30 kilometers northwest of Guangzhouwan). But the railway was never built due to local opposition. See Su Xianzhang, "Faguo jinyibu yongwuli qinlue kuoda Guangzhouwan huajie de waijiao wenjian" [Diplomatic documents on the French aggression and expansion on Guangzhouwan territory by force], in *Zhanjiang wenshi ziliao*, vol. 3, ed. Literature and History Studies Committee of Zhanjiang City, Chinese People's Political Consultative Conference (1985), 140–41. In addition, many Guangzhouwan locals resisted French rule, especially in the early years of the French lease. Such resistance activities occupy one full volume of *Zhanjiang wenshiziliao*.

Map 12.1: Map of French Indochina. *Source:* La géographie documentaire, classe de fin d'études primaires, librairie classique Eugène Belin, 1947.

nascent Guangzhouwan" as a "clean" economic center, which meant that no opium, gambling, or prostitution was allowed.[4] In 1945 the Guomin-

---

[4] Tangke, "Sange shiqi de Guangzhouwan" [Guangzhouwan in three periods], *Xinya* 8, no. 4 (1943): 33–34, 41. In this article, the occupied Guangzhouwan period is classified as the third period, which is named "a period of renaissance" (*fule xinsheng de shidai*). Yinhan, "Rijun jinzhuhou zhi xinsheng didai: Guangzhouwan yipie" [A renascent domain in Japanese occupation: A glance at Guangzhouwan], *Xinya* 8, no. 4 (1943): 31–32; "Jiangnan de tu—xinsheng de Guangzhouwan: Liangbu xinwenpian cuojun daiying" [The Jiangnan soil—renascent Guangzhouwan: Two upcoming news films], *Huaying zhoukan*, no. 51 (1944): 2. Other articles published in the occupation period by the Japanese all highlight the new look of Guangzhouwan. See, for example, Lin Xinxin, "Guangzhouwan yinxiang ji" [Impressions

dang government recaptured Guangzhouwan and had a magnificent plan to build it into a huge port city and use it as a starting point for a railroad that would run from southwest to northwest China. Like the French, neither the Japanese nor the Guomindang put these plans fully in motion.[5] In 1960, Deng Xiaoping inspected the city and made waves by saying that Guangzhouwan (now renamed Zhanjiang) was an economic rival of Qingdao, another former European- (German) and Japanese-administered port in north China. In 1984, Zhanjiang was among the first fourteen coastal cities opened to the world for economic development.[6] Today, however, Zhanjiang remains a third-class city whose people still cling to the dream that a new government initiative will finally transform their city into an economic hub.

While Guangzhouwan's modern history has been marked by repeated disappointment, it actually reached a period of unprecedented, albeit temporary, prosperity during the War of Resistance against Japan. After the fall of Guangzhou, Hainan Island, and Hong Kong, Guangzhouwan became the only unoccupied port in South China through which goods could be imported to or exported from Nationalist China (besides Macau, which remained in Portuguese hands). Guangzhouwan also became an important transit point for refugees fleeing occupied Guangdong, Hainan, and Hong Kong. A well-known Hong Kong actor, Lu Dun, summed up the ironically positive impact of the war on Guangzhouwan: "To be hon-

---

of Guanghzouwan], *Xinya* 9, no. 1 (1943): 32–37. These articles all emphasize both the intention of Japanese propaganda and the actual success of the Japanese in promoting the "renascent Guangzhouwan."

[5] It would be inappropriate to say that both the Japanese and the Guomindang government did not try to carry out their plans for Guangzhouwan, but they both failed in the end, for different reasons. For the Japanese, a "clean" (morally and financially) Guangzhouwan would have conflicted with their heavy military and economic dependence on the French and the local notables, like Chen Xuetan. For example, economically speaking, both the French and Chen's interests relied greatly on "unclean" businesses that were formerly perfectly legal under the French rule. Therefore, the Japanese announcement of a "renascent Guangzhouwan" did not seem to hold much water. Clearly, for the Guomindang government, it is quite possible that their intentions and some actions in process were terminated by the political and military confrontation with the CCP.

[6] These fourteen coastal cities are Dalian, Qinhuangdao, Tianjin, Yantai, Qingdao, Lianyungang, Nantong, Shanghai, Ningbo, Wenzhou, Fuzhou, Guangzhou, Zhanjiang, and Beihai. Regarding their economic growth, Zhanjiang ranks above Beihai and Lianyungang.

est, if it had not been for the Japanese occupation of Hong Kong, I would never in my life have gone to Guangzhouwan."[7]

The fate of Guangzhouwan is exactly as Lu's statement implies: it is a place that thrived and died because of the war. To be more specific, it thrived due to others' fall as it became the only unoccupied port besides Macau, and it died by joining the fate of other ports. In an era that is generally characterized as presenting a stark choice between the National-ist Party (Guomindang) and the Chinese Communist Party (CCP), and of patriotically resisting or traitorously collaborating with Japan, Guang-zhouwan's story is an example of what Prasenjit Duara calls "bifurcated history," which cries for an alternative to the linear narrative of national history. The more bifurcated history we recover, the more complicated the grand narrative becomes.[8]

A look at the February 17, 1943, issue of the largest local newspaper, the *Daguangbao* (south Guangdong edition), reveals the ambiguous rela-tionship between wartime politics and daily life in Guangzhouwan. On the left side of the front page is an editorial with a title printed in bold font: "What Are the Japanese Trying to Do in South Guangdong (In-cluding Guangzhouwan)?" The editor analyzes the current war situation and tells local people to remain calm because the Japanese have no inten-tion of invading but are merely harassing the coast once again. As the reader's eyes shift to the middle of the page, another news item encourages local people in an even larger font: "The Enemy's Invasion of Siyi Was Repelled, and Shaping Was Recovered by the Nationalists."[9] Those two places are approximately 150 miles east of Guangzhouwan in Guangdong. On the right side of the page, two announcements jostle for the reader's attention. First is the grand opening of Huayang Hotel on Chikan School Street. Second, the Nanyang film company angrily informs the Guang-zhouwan public that a lost copy of one of its films has been shown at the

---

[7] Lu Dun, *Fengzi shengya banshiji* [Half century of a madman's career] (Hong Kong: Xiangjiang chubanshe, 1992), 69.

[8] Prasenjit Duara, *Rescuing History from the Nation: Questioning Narratives of Modern China* (Chicago: University of Chicago Press, 1995), 5, 51-82.

[9] Siyi is the general name for the four Guangdong counties of Xinhui, Kaiping, Taishan, and Enping. Shaping is approximately 60 kilometers southwest of Guangzhou, and both Siyi and Shaping are adjacent to Guangzhou.

Ping'an Theater under a different title and the company has decided to show its legal copy at half price at Wenhua Theater that same day.

The very next day, as Japanese and Nationalist forces fought on the northwestern edge of the city, *Daguangbao* halted publication. On the evening of February 19, the Japanese entered Guangzhouwan. The next day the Japanese army lined up in front of the gate to *Daguangbao*'s main office and then paraded into the center of Guangzhouwan to be welcomed by the French governor, Pierre-Jean Domec, and the head of the local gentry, Chen Xuetan.[10] On February 21, having signed a mutual defense pact with the Vichy French Indochina government, the Japanese formally occupied the French-leased territory of Guangzhouwan.[11]

Regarding the loss of Guangzhouwan, Li Hanhun, chief of the Nationalist government of Guangdong, wrote in his diary, "Over the years, the businessmen and people of Guangzhouwan have lived extremely extravagant, aimless, and self-indulgent lives. Now, it is time for them to make retribution. ..."[12] Even though Li's hometown, Wuchuan, was located not more than fifteen miles northeast of the border of the Guangzhouwan concession, he did not hesitate to express his ill feelings toward the people of Guangzhouwan. Similarly, one traveler began his travelogue of Guangzhouwan by stating, "Guangzhouwan, I read her name in history, and I love her beautiful name. But, at the same time, I resent her also for the shame that she has brought in history."[13] One person under the pseudo-

---

[10] Yun Chengshi, *Yue zhanchang* [The Guangdong battlefield] (Qujiang: Dagongbao qujiang fenguan, 1943), 112.

[11] The final pact for the common defense of Guangzhouwan was not signed until May 17, 1943. But on February 21, a ceremony was held to welcome the Japanese army's peaceful entry into Guangzhouwan. See "Ri-Fa dangju dijie, Guangzhouwan lianfang xieding" [The Japanese and the French signed the common defense treaty of Guangzhouwan], *Shenbao*, February 25, 1943, 2. The Japanese commander was received by the French in Guangzhouwan on February 17, 1943, and the negotiations between the Japanese and the Vichy French Indochina government over the Japanese control of Guangzhouwan went on for months. See all the telegrams between the Japanese and the Vichy French in Antoine Vannière, *Le territoire à bail de Guangzhouwan: Une impasse de la colonisation Française en Asie orientale, 1898–1946* [The leased territory of Guangzhouwan: An impasse in French colonization of East Asia, 1898–1946] (Lille: Atelier National de Reproduction des Thèses, 2006).

[12] Li Hanhun, *Li Hanhun jiangjun riji* [General Li Hanhun's diaries] (Hong Kong: Lianyi yinshua youxian gongsi, 1982), 419.

[13] You Hong, "Wo laidao Guangzhouwan" [I come to Guangzhouwan], *Yuzhoufeng* 106 (1941): 310.

nym Mr. Sparkling wrote to a magazine complaining about Guangzhou-wan's lack of patriotic zeal. In the letter he also fiercely attacked the women volunteers' dress code as "too modern."[14]

These sentiments are easy to understand: as both the Allies and the Japanese canceled their unequal treaties and relinquished extraterritoriality in 1943, Guangzhouwan, which remained under direct Japanese control, was among the last places where foreigners still possessed special privileges. While the Japanese and the Nanjing government trumpeted this as the end of imperialism in China, in Guangzhouwan some merchants still flew the French flag on their boats, hoping to avoid inspection.

Yet in the end, being a French concession made Guangzhouwan's name known to the rest of China. In the war against Japan, Guangzhouwan experienced a temporary prosperity in an unexpected and very ambiguous way. People did not get caught up in political loyalties but instead went about their lives and did their best to survive. While it is thought that everyone was aligned with either the Guomindang, the CCP, or the Japanese, that kind of politically oriented vision did not fit the realities of people's lives, at least not in Guangzhouwan.

GUANGZHOUWAN UNDER FRENCH RULE: A SWARM OF POWERS

The 200-square-mile French concession in Guangzhouwan was centered on the Xiying and Chikan districts. Xiying was the administrative district of Guangzhouwan where the French concession government was located, and Chikan was the main business district, housing Guangzhouwan's chamber of commerce. A six-mile rural belt separated Xiying and Chikan. The French concession extended from Chikan and Xiying in the north to two large islands, Donghai and Naozhou, in the south. The concession bordered Wuchuan County on the northeast and Suixi County on the north and west, with Lianjiang further north on the road to Guangxi (see Map 12.2).

---

[14] Zou Taofen jinianguan, ed., *Zou Taofen yanjiu* [Studies on Zou Taofen], vol. 3 (Shanghai: Xuelin chubanshe, 2008), 75–76.

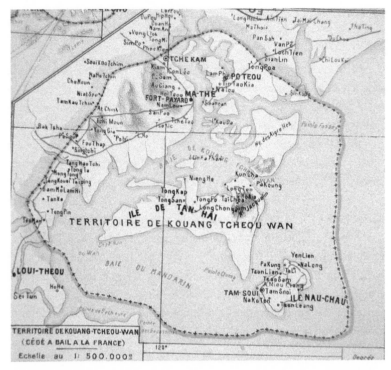

Map 12.2: Map of the leased territory of Guangzhouwan. The pinyin equivalents of the key French terms here would be: Kouang Tcheou Wan = Guangzhouwan; Tche Kam = Chikan; Fort-Payard/Ma-The = Xiying; Ile de Tan-Hai = Donghai; Ile de Nau-chau = Naozhou. *Source:* http://belleindochine.free.fr/images/Plan /1909/KouangTcheouWang.JPG. Accessed May 2, 2015.

Chikan and Xiying were filled with all kinds of businesses: restaurants, hotels, department stores, import and export corporations, travel agencies, banks, pawnshops, theaters, clubs, brothels, casinos, and opium dens. The Chikan business district had more than two thousand privately owned shops by the end of 1942.[15] This number continued to grow, as is evident from the pages of the *Daguangbao*, which were filled daily with advertisements for the opening of new stores.

---

[15] Wei Jian, *Guangzhouwan shangye zhinan nianjian heji* [Compilation of Guangzhouwan business guidebooks] (Xiguan: Dongnan chubanshe, 1943), 44–63.

Succeeding in Guangzhouwan required being able to navigate its complex political scene. The French authorities continuously provided a shield for politically controversial notables to hide behind. For example, after his military forces were defeated in 1918, Long Jiguang, a Guangdong warlord and former subordinate of Yuan Shikai, negotiated with the French and used Guangzhouwan for political asylum, moving back and forth between Guangzhouwan and Hainan to command what was left of his army.[16]

The Nationalist government had long been concerned about such "enemy" activities in Guangzhouwan. In 1939 the Guangzhouwan branch of the Nationalist government of Guangdong Province asked the municipal government for more funds for intelligence operations, claiming that there was "a swarm of traitors" in Guangzhouwan, possibly referring to both Communists and collaborators with the Japanese.[17] The CCP maintained a local branch, which it used to conduct underground activities in Guangzhouwan.[18] Even in late 1943, the Nationalist government was discovering previously unknown CCP members in Guangzhouwan.[19]

On the Japanese side, both French and Japanese sources confirm that in the summer of 1940 a Japanese control commission, aimed at keeping watch over the French supervision of smuggling into Free China, was set up in Guangzhouwan.[20] A Japanese spy branch began operations in Guangzhouwan as early as 1941.[21] On August 4, 1941, Japan took control of the

---

[16] "Guanyu junshi zhi zuijin jing wen" [Recent news from Beijing about military affairs], *Shenbao*, May 20, 1918, 3.

[17] Wang Meijia, ed., *Guomin shiqi Guangdong shengzhengfu dang'an shiliao xuanbian* [Selected Guangdong provincial government documents from the republican era] (Guangzhou: Guangdong sheng dang'anguan, 1988), 290.

[18] Zhonggong Zhanjiang shiwei dangshi yanjiushi, ed., *Zhonggong zai Guangzhouwan huodong shiliao (1926–1949)* [The activities of the CCP in Guangzhouwan (1926–1949)] (Guangzhou: Guangdong renmin chubanshe, 1994), 35.

[19] Guomindang Record (1894–1957), TE21 REEL2 1.189, 1943, 10, 13, in Hoover Institution Archives, Stanford, California.

[20] Vannière, *Le territoire à bail de Guangzhouwan*, 400; Zizhen, trans., "Guangzhouwan de jingji shikuang" [The economic situation in Guangzhouwan], *Jingji Yuebao* 3, no. 1 (1944): 58. The exact date for the establishment of the control commission is unclear: Japanese sources indicate July 1940, while French sources state August 30, 1940.

[21] Pang Fu, ed., *Qinhua Rijun jiandie tewu huodong jishi* [The record of Japanese espionage in the Sino-Japanese war] (Beijing: Beijing chubanshe, 1993), 13.

Leizhou customs administration with the consent of the French concession government. Soon after, the French government formally stopped approving the transportation of merchandise to Free China. The Japanese embassy in Indochina opened a branch office in Guangzhouwan on May 8, 1942.[22] The purpose behind the Japanese political presence in the city was primarily to prevent the import of munitions into Free China through Guangzhouwan. This was in line with Japan's larger strategy of strengthening its blockade of the Chongqing government in order to suffocate Free China's economy and diminish its ability to wage war. The Japanese took this step in Guangzhouwan in response to the Guomindang's earlier successes in transporting munitions through Guangzhouwan to Chongqing.

On November 1, 1938, the *Asahi Shimbun* reported that Chiang Kaishek had imported a large stock of munitions that could support the Guomindang troops for months. Those munitions were stored in Hong Kong, but could not be transported into the Chinese hinterland due to the fall of Guangzhou. Hence China and France reached agreement to increase steamboat shipping between Hong Kong and Guangzhouwan to carry the munitions and regularly ship additional supplies. This particular 1938 load of munitions was transported from Hong Kong to Haiphong to Guangzhouwan, and finally to Chongqing. The Japanese newspaper reported that on October 30, 1938, H.H. Kung made a speech at a press conference in Chongqing, saying, "The munitions that we have now could sustain [us] for two years." The Japanese government believed that this two-year supply had definitely been imported through Guangzhouwan.[23]

From available statistics collected during the early Sino-Japanese war period, smuggling from Guangzhouwan (and surrounding areas) to Free China was very profitable. The value of the smuggled goods the Japanese were interested in stopping may have been around 400,000 yuan per day (or approximately 146,000,000 yuan per year).[24] It was difficult to mea-

---

[22] Fang Xuechang, "Guangzhouwan ruogan shiliao bianxi" [Analyzing certain historical data from Guangzhouwan], *Guangdong shizhi*, no. 4 (2000): 45.

[23] "Hanoi e buki tennsou Hong Kong kara rennjitsu sennbin" [Weapons shipment to Hanoi from Hong Kong takes several days by boat], *Asahi Shimbun*, November 1, 1938, 7.

[24] Chang Aoding, *Jingji fengsuo yu fan fengsuo* [Economic blockade and antiblockade]

sure how many goods exactly had been transported through Guangzhou-wan to Free China, but to a certain extent, the Guangzhouwan threat of supporting Chinese resistance was shown in consistent Japanese efforts to block Guangzhouwan, and in their final capture of the city.[25] Two days after the Japanese capture, the *Asahi Shimbun* proudly announced that the route to support the Nationalist resistance to the Japanese was completely cut off.[26]

Without a doubt, in the eyes of top Nationalist leaders like Chiang Kai-shek, Guangzhouwan was important due to its role in the transport of valuable goods for the war effort. The transshipment of goods was much more important to government officials than either the vast profits that merchants made through legal and illegal trade in Guangzhouwan or the city's role as a transportation hub for refugees. While Chiang still hoped that the Burma Road could lessen Free China's reliance on Guangzhou-wan as a source for supplies, local civilians, refugees, merchants, and out-laws absolutely depended on Guangzhouwan for survival.

BLOWING WITH THE WIND: LIFE IN OCCUPIED GUANGZHOUWAN

While newspapers in Free China were fixated on the international situa-tion and hung on every detail of the war, which seemed to pose a constant existential threat, the attitude of people in Guangzhouwan was much more ambivalent. As a transit point for refugees and supplies, Guang-zhouwan was simultaneously very much a part of the war and yet some-how outside of it. In this sense, life in Guangzhouwan resembled that in the more familiar cases of Shanghai, Macau, and Casablanca. As Poshek

---

(Chongqing: 1943), 32. Areas surrounding Guangzhouwan commonly used by smugglers include Mazhang, Suixi, and Beihai.

[25] There were at least ten reports in November and December 1938 alone in the *Asahi Shimbun* regarding goods transport (ammunition and automobiles in particular) through Guangzhouwan to Free China.

[26] "Enn shoji wo kannzen shadann teki no shinnyuu kito wo sennsei" [Enemy invasion plans curbed: Route to support Chiang completely cut off], *Asahi Shimbun*, February 23, 1943, 6.

Fu says about wartime Shanghai, "Life ... seemed fixed on the present; every moment was borrowed time."[27]

Life in wartime Guangzhouwan was hardly miserable so there was no reason not to be wrapped up in the moment. Since 1938 when three marauding Japanese warships were beaten back by the French, Guangzhouwan had been "under threat."[28] Later in the same year, Nationalists tore up the northern part of the railway between Guangzhouwan and Guangxi because they feared it would be used by the Japanese in their invasion of Guangxi.[29] In January 1939, Nationalist forces began to destroy the road between Guangzhouwan and Guangxi for the same reason.[30] The next year there were rumors that the Japanese would attempt to invade southern Guangdong, but nothing came of it.[31] On March 4, 1941, a Japanese force tried to enter nearby Suixi but was repulsed by Nationalist forces.[32] After the Japanese gained control of the Leizhou customs administration in August 1941, they pulled their forces away from Guangzhouwan.[33]

Given this history of threats that never materialized, it is little wonder that *Daguangbao* claimed on February 17, 1943, as Japanese forces approached, that the Japanese still did not really intend to occupy and control Guangzhouwan. People in Guangzhouwan probably thought that they would be lucky enough to escape the fate of being occupied. When the Japanese entered Guangzhouwan on February 21, 1943, a common question may have been, had Guangzhouwan's borrowed time finally run out?

---

[27] Poshek Fu, *Passivity, Resistance, and Collaboration: Intellectual Choices in Occupied Shanghai, 1937–1945* (Stanford, CA: Stanford University Press, 1993), 125.

[28] "Fajian sansou shiwan guangzhou baohu" [Three French vessels were guarding Guangzhouwan] *Chinese Times* (Vancouver, BC), July 7, 1938, 8.

[29] "Zhongyao xiaoxi" [Important news], *Chinese Times* (Vancouver, BC), December 16, 1938.

[30] "Guangzhouwan zhi gui jing gonglu jiaotong yiduan" [The road between Guangzhouwan and Guangxi Province was cut off], *Chinese Times* (Vancouver, BC), January 27, 1939, 4.

[31] "Wo haijun pai canmou nanjin" [The Japanese navy sent a staff officer to South China], *Chinese Times* (Vancouver, BC), January 9, 1940, 6.

[32] "Wojun fenkai yuenan zengyuan" [The Nationalist government sent more troops to south Guangdong], *Chinese Times* (Vancouver, BC), April 1, 1941, 7.

[33] "Zhongyao dianbao" [Important telegrams], *Chinese Times* (Vancouver, BC), August 6, 1941.

While Japan's agreement with the colonial government of French Indochina for its forces to enter Guangzhouwan peacefully was a major success for them, the meaning of Japan's occupation of the city was far less
clear for the people who lived there. One of the major themes of Frederic
Wakeman's *The Shanghai Badlands* is "the sheer ambiguity of either resistance [against] or collaboration [with the Japanese]."[34] Much the same
could be said about Guangzhouwan, as the people there seemed adept at
maintaining loyalty to the Chongqing National Government while pursu-
ing their own personal profit. People were not willing to step forward and
openly declare their support for the Guomindang during the period of
Japanese occupation.[35] Unlike the colonial governor of Morocco, centered
in Casablanca, who feared the extreme possibility of a "local insurrection
against France" if they surrendered to the Germans,[36] this was not re-
motely a concern of the French administrator of Guangzhouwan. The
people of Guangzhouwan seemed to display an indifference toward China's future.

The most prominent of people in power in Guangzhouwan were those
in the colonial government. In the years leading up to the war, Guangzhouwan saw many government officials come and go. From 1898 to
1943, thirty-seven different colonial ministers had been in charge of the
city: on average, each official stayed for just over a year. The longest term
served by an official was four years, from 1937 to 1941.[37] One constant in
Guangzhouwan politics was the chief of the Chikan Bureau, local notable
Chen Xuetan. He had held this post for more than twenty years.[38] Unlike
other small-time local gangsters who seemed more like riffraff, Chen's
nickname was quite imposing: King of the Night, a name which reflected
the fact that Chen was without a doubt the king of Guangzhouwan's un-
derworld.[39]

---

[34] Frederic Wakeman, *The Shanghai Badlands: Wartime Terrorism and Urban Crime,
1937–1941* (Cambridge: Cambridge University Press, 1996), 4.

[35] Vannière, *Le territoire à bail de Guangzhouwan*, 418.

[36] Ibid., 247.

[37] Wei Jian, *Da Guangzhouwan* [The great Guangzhouwan] (Guangzhou: Dongnan
chubanshe, 1942), 73–74.

[38] Ibid., 77.

[39] Zizhen, "Guangzhouwan de jingji shikuang," 58.

In the film *Casablanca*, the French Captain Louis Renault states, "I have no conviction ... I blow with the wind, and the prevailing wind happens to be from Vichy."[40] Such sentiment characterized Chen Xuetan's whole life. Born into a wealthy local family, Chen had no intention of staying in school. In 1921, he worked with the Guomindang to suppress local gangs and was promoted by local warlord Deng Benyin to develop his own armed unit. In 1925, he became the leader of a local militia that fought for the Guomindang against his former patron, Deng.[41]

When Deng's local troops were defeated by the Nationalists, Zhou Guisen, one of his subordinates, was able to gather the remaining troops and continue to operate in southern Guangdong. In 1930, Zhou decided to quit, a decision facilitated by the Guomindang's offer to pay him 10,000 yuan for all of his weapons. Chen Xuetan took on the role of middleman and stored the eight hundred small arms, a dozen machine guns, and three cannons in Guangzhouwan's Chikan district, with the understanding that the small arms would be used to equip Chen's local militia, while the machine guns and cannons were handed over to the National Government. The 10,000 yuan received by Zhou did not come from the National Government, instead it was ultimately collected from three local counties near Guangzhouwan, including one where Chen was serving as a commissioner.[42] The implication here is that Chen himself probably paid a part of the money to Zhou for the guns that he received. In this way, the Guomindang inevitably became an official and legitimate middleman, allowing Chen to have a proper excuse to equip his force. Chen got what he wanted while assuring the Guomindang authorities of his loyalty and harmlessness by giving up the more powerful weapons. This case exemplifies Chen's growing local power and prestige.

Chen's great wealth derived mainly from dubious businesses, one prominent example being his casino. This casino was first named Liangli (mutual benefits), then renamed Wanli (thousands of profits) and later

---

[40] Michael Curtiz, dir., *Casablanca* (Burbank, CA: Warner Bros. Pictures, 1942).

[41] "Yuesheng nanlu zhanshi zhi xinxingshi" [Updates on south Guangdong warfare], *Shen Bao*, November 21, 1925, 6.

[42] "Shouhui nanlu Dengbu yixie" [The withdrawal of ammunition left by the troops of Deng Benyin], *Chinese Times*, October 14, 1930, 5.

Yili (millions of profits).[43] While not much involved in the War of Resistance, Chen was not reluctant to show his patriotism with money. He actively donated to support the war against Japan. In 1942 he flew to Chongqing to participate as a delegate in the opening ceremony of the "one yuan for airplanes" movement (which promoted public donations in support of the Chinese air force).[44] He was even more involved in local affairs and charities, especially for education. Along with many other primary and middle schools, the Peicai Private School was founded by Chen; his daughter later became principal and his brother the head of the school board. Peicai was one of the major schools in Guangzhouwan, with 406 students in its primary school section in 1943.[45] According to his laudatory biography (based on oral history), Chen dabbled in almost every business in Guangzhouwan, from water conservancy to shelters for refugees, hospitals, schools, hotels, department stores, cigarette companies, casinos, and even the regulation of local currency and collection of soldiers' pay.[46]

In spite of his reputation, Chen Xuetan remains a mystery. What we know of him as a person is somewhat controversial, as seen in the two views of him presented in local accounts published in the People's Republic of China. One treats Chen as a traitor to the nation for being an agent of the French and the Japanese, and a traitor to local people because of his largely illegitimate career.[47] The other admits his ill dealings but com-

[43] Chen Huakan, *Chen Xuetan xiansheng zhuanlüe* [The biography of Mr. Chen Xuetan] (Hong Kong: Zhongguo shidai chubanshe, 2009), 33.

[44] "Yiyuan xianji shouci mingming dianli" [The opening ceremony of "One yuan for airplanes"], *Chinese Times,* June 15, 1943, 8.

[45] Guo Jingsheng, "Chen Xuetan zai Guangzhouwan ban jiaoyu" [Chen Xuetan's educational endeavors in Guangzhouwan], in *Zhanjiang wenshiziliao,* vol. 21, ed. Cai Jinguang (Literature and History Studies Committee of Zhanjiang City, Guangdong Province, Chinese People's Political Consultative Conference, 2002), 124; Cai Jinguang, "Faguo zujie Guangzhouwan shiqi jijian zhuyao xuexiao jiejian" [Introduction to several main schools in French Guangzhouwan], in *Zhanjiang wenshiziliao,* vol. 12, ed. Qiu Bingquan (Literature and History Studies Committee of Zhanjiang City, Guangdong Province, Chinese People's Political Consultative Conference, 1994), 222. See also Peicai Private Middle School, *Peicai xuesheng* [Students of Peicai] (Guangzhouwan: Peicai Private Middle School, 1943), 4, 11, 14. Peicai was first founded as a primary school. In 1942, it changed its name to Peicai Private Middle School after adding a secondary section.

[46] Chen Huakan, *Chen Xuetan,* 29, 30, 34.

[47] Zhong Xia, "Fa diguozhuyi zai Guangzhouwan huanyang de Chen Xuetan" [Chen

mends Chen for his contributions to the local community and his aptness
for maintaining a neutral relationship with the CCP (a relationship that
gradually grew friendly).[48]

When the Japanese occupied Guangzhouwan, Chen accompanied
Governor Domec as the first to welcome the Japanese armies at Cunjin
Bridge, just outside Guangzhouwan.[49] Although being the first to yield to
the Japanese was not necessarily anything to brag about, Chen managed
to put a positive spin on his actions by arguing that he was trying to protect local businessmen and the poor. Reluctant to assume the official
government position that the Japanese offered him, Chen accepted the
unofficial title of "representative of West China."[50] This title was chosen
because Guangzhouwan was the only place that the Japanese had occupied in western China at that time. Chen maintained his position as chief
of the Chikan Bureau and soon volunteered to work as an agent for the
Guomindang.[51] While Guomindang records confirm that Chen did become an agent in 1943, his actual contribution is unclear.

Chen also invested in people other than upright Guomindang members. He first supported Zhang Yan, a Guomindang proponent of the
United Front, with weaponry and supplies. Yet when Zhang defected to
the CCP in 1945, Chen did not follow. When Zhang led an uprising
against the Guomindang and was finally arrested and executed by the
Guomindang in early 1945, Chen did nothing to help.[52] Chen remained

---

Xuetan, lackey of French imperialism in Guangzhouwan], in *Guangdong wenshiziliao*, vol.
14, ed. Literature and History Studies Committee of Guangdong Province, Chinese People's
Political Consultative Conference (Chinese People's Political Consultative Conference,
1964), 27. Zhong Xia worked with Chen Xuetan.

[48] Fu Ming, "Kangzhan shiqi Guangzhouwan gongjuzhang Chen Xuetan shilüe" [Biog-
raphy of wartime Guangzhouwan bureau chief Chen Xuetan], *Chikan wenshi*, vol. 3 (Zhanjiangshi Chikanqu weiyuanhui, 2011), 430–39.

[49] "Guangzhouwan yu yuenan" [Guangzhouwan and south Guangdong], *Chinese Times*,
August 24, 1943, 8.

[50] Chen Ce to the secretary of the National Government, June 10, 1943, Special Archives of the Guomindang Party Affairs 9, REEL5 35.51, *Zhongguo Guomindang Records
(1894–1957)* (microfilm). Hoover Institution Archives, Stanford, CA.

[51] Chen Su to the secretary of the National Government, January 4, 1944, Special Archives of the Guomindang Party Affairs 21, REEL1 1.24, *Zhongguo Guomindang Records
(1894–1957)* (microfilm).

[52] Zhonggong Wuchuan xianwei dangshi yanjiushi, ed., *Nanlu tewei yu Zhangyan jiang-*

on the top of the CCP's United Front list in Guangzhouwan, and the CCP realized that uniting with Chen was a "long-term job." Although Chen constantly behaved favorably toward the CCP, primarily by way of donations brokered through his subordinates, he never really joined the CCP. After the war against Japan, Chen left for Hong Kong. He came back to Guangzhouwan during the civil war only to leave for Hong Kong again, shortly before Guangzhouwan was occupied by the Communists.[53] All in all, Chen represented exactly the spirit of Guangzhouwan in wartime China, always going in whatever direction the wind was blowing, but never clearly attaching himself to any particular power.

REFUGEES AND NEW BUSINESSES

In 1931, Guangzhouwan had only 60,000 residents. By 1936, its population had reached 300,000, eventually peaking at 600,000 in 1942.[54] In the last years of the war, Guangzhouwan's population fell almost as quickly as it had risen: in 1946, when the Guomindang government took back Guangzhouwan, the annual census reported the number of residents in Guangzhouwan as 270,574.[55] In addition, it is almost impossible to count the number of refugees who had stayed in Guangzhouwan temporarily during the war. The Guomindang mayor later estimated that there may have been as many as 1,300,000 refugees in or passing through Guangzhouwan.[56]

---

jun [The South Road Special Commission and General Zhang Yan] (Guangzhou: Guangdong renmin chubanshe, 1995), 139.

[53] Zhonggong Zhanjiang shiwei dangshi yanjiushi, *Zhonggong zai Guangzhouwan*, 186–91.

[54] Qiu Bingquan, *Lieqiang zai Zhongguo de zujie* [The Great Powers' concessions in China] (Beijing: Zhongguo wenlian chubanshe), 473.

[55] Zhanjiang difangzhi bianzhuan weiyuan hui, ed., *Zhanjiang shizhi* [Zhanjiang city gazetteer] (Beijing: Zhonghuashuju, 2004), 304. The boundaries of Zhanjiang city in the republican period and the Guangzhouwan concession are almost the same. See Xu Tongshen, Wang Yi, and Zhang Chengqi, eds., *Guangxu tiaoyue* [Treaties of the Guangxu reign], vol. 60 (Taipei: Wenhai chubanshe, 1974), 10–12; Guo Shouhua, *Zhanjiang shizhi* [Zhanjiang city gazetteer] (Taipei: Dayazhou chubanshe, 1972), 7.

[56] Guo Shouhua, *Zhanjiang shizhi*, 11.

From 1938 to 1942, several waves of refugees came into Guangzhou-wan, and each wave was linked to the advance of the Japanese army in South China. In October 1938, Guangzhou and a large area of southern Guangdong came under Japanese control. Hainan Island fell in February 1939. Due in large part to Japanese attempts to conscript able-bodied men, more than 100,000 people from Hainan escaped to Guangzhouwan by the end of 1939.[57] Some local institutions also relocated, including the prestigious Qiongya Middle School, which stayed in the vicinity of Guang-zhouwan until the city fell.[58] To deal with the influx, Guangzhouwan had to establish a refugee settlement outside the city.[59] On Christmas Day in 1941, Hong Kong surrendered to the Japanese. From January 6, 1942, onward Japan launched a "return home" campaign and forced many peo-ple to leave Hong Kong and return to their hometowns in Guangdong. This movement was originally supposed to end at the close of 1942, but in October 1943, the Japanese governor of Hong Kong, Isogai Rensuke, in-creased the number of people ordered to return home. Up until June 1944, tickets for all those wanting to return home were free. By February 1943, between 800,000 and 1,000,000 people had left Hong Kong, some will-ingly, some forced out. Guangzhouwan was one of the four formal free routes out of Hong Kong that the Japanese provided.[60]

Many distinguished personages found Guangzhouwan to be the only passage to Free China, especially after Hong Kong's fall. Many went to Macau first, like Wu Chufan and many of his fellow performers. But there were also some people who went straight from Hong Kong to Guang-

---

[57] "Zhongyao xiaoxi" [Important news], *Daguangbao* (south Guangdong edition), May 14, 1941.

[58] Huang Xunyan, "Kang-Ri zhanhuo zhong de Qiongya zhongxue" [Qiongya Middle School during the Sino-Japanese war], in *Hainan wenshiziliao*, vol. 16, ed. Fan Jimin and Fu Hemin (Haikou: Nanhai chuban gongsi, 2000), 94–96. Qiongya Middle School had a long reputation and high status since it was founded on the campus of Qiongtai College, the most prestigious institution of higher learning on Hainan Island since the early Qing.

[59] "Di Guangzhouwan shang jiuji Qiong nanmin" [Discussion on how to help the Hainan refugees in Guangzhouwan], *Chinese Times*, July 19, 1939, 8.

[60] Li Heguang, "Kangzhan shiqi Rizhan xianggang de guixiang yundong pingshu" [A commentary on Hong Kong's "return home" movement in the Sino-Japanese war period], *Minguo dang'an* 2 (2012): 109–14.

zhouwan, like the historian, Chen Yinque.[61] The Dongjiang Column, one of the CCP's Guangdong guerrilla groups, made its name by rescuing intellectuals and patriots in Hong Kong around the same time. Zhou Enlai sent two urgent telegrams in December 1941 regarding the transfer of refugees in Hong Kong to Guangzhouwan, or to Guilin through Guangzhouwan.[62] Therefore, the place was pivotal in transportation of both material and human resources.

As other cities were captured by the Japanese, Guangzhouwan gained new business. The local press quickly detected the need to set up a newspaper to take the place of papers from Guangzhou and Hong Kong that were no longer printed. *Daguangbao*, first printed in a local gentry's automobile factory, became successful very quickly. In 1942, *Daguangbao* already had five branches, including a bookstore named Daguang.[63]

After the fall of Guangzhou, the four national banks (the Central Bank, the Bank of China, the Farmers' Bank, and the Communication Bank) also opened branches in Guangzhouwan. Following suit, more and more banks and bullion stores, like the Fujian Bank, opened Guangzhouwan branches.[64] Additionally, on June 26, 1939, the French Airline opened its first air route from Guangzhouwan to Hanoi, which continued until the takeover of Guangzhouwan by the Japanese.[65]

The most important business was the livestock trade. In late 1941, there was a ban on transporting livestock from Guangzhouwan to Hong Kong; the Hong Kong livestock price mounted and the supply of pigs could have sustained Hong Kong for only another four to five days if

---

[61] Liu Zheng, *Xianhua Chen Yinque* [The idle thoughts of Chen Yinque] (Tianjin: Baihua wenyi chubanshe, 2011), 189.

[62] Nanfangju dangshi ziliao zhengji xiaozu, ed., *Nanfangju dangshi ziliao dashiji* [Southern Bureau (Communist) Party history documents' chronicle] (Chongqing: Chongqing chubanshe, 1986), 180.

[63] Li Zhan, ed., *Zhongguo xinwen shi* [The history of Chinese journalism] (Taipei: Taiwan xuesheng chubanju, 1979), 504.

[64] "Zuixin Guangdong xinwen" [Recent Guangdong news], *Daguangbao* (south Guangdong edition), January 14, 1942.

[65] Sun Zhenguo, "Cong Fahang de shouhangfeng kan kangzhan shiqi de duiwai tonghang wu hangxian" [Taking Air France as an example of the five airlines with external air service in the wartime era], *Jiyou Bolan*, 2009, 11.

Guangzhouwan did not lift the ban.[66] While the export of live pigs to Hong Kong had been monopolized by Hainan Island, with the fall of Hainan, the situation changed completely in Guangzhouwan's favor, where raising pigs was already very widespread. Hong Kong actress Huang Manli noted that roast suckling pig was a famous local dish. With demand higher than ever, farmers who raised pigs benefited greatly from a rapid rise in the value of their livestock.[67]

With thousands of refugees traveling through Guangzhouwan and heading inland, mostly for Guangxi, Yunnan, and Sichuan, transportation became an increasingly profitable business venture. For instance, in 1941, it took five days to travel from Guangzhouwan to Yulin, Guangxi, on foot. Companies could charge passengers traveling by sedan chair 85 to 100 yuan per person for this trip. Taking into account the costs of a 10 yuan commission paid to the head porters, one half yuan per day for renting one sedan chair, 2 yuan per person per day for lodging and food, including two chair carriers and one traveler, the profit for a single trip could range from 40 to 55 yuan per passenger.[68] With their new connections to the wider world, local people found plenty of new ways to make money quickly.

The new riches seemed to be arising from new business opportunities Guangzhouwan seized from other ports' fall: "If life meant misery for the majority, it was a carnival for a few."[69] One newspaper wrote that travelers could notice a curious phenomenon in Guangzhouwan: people who wore short sleeves and sandals were the rich, and those who wore long gowns or Western suits had to follow them around doing as they said.[70] Even if this was not a scientific observation, it reflected the fact that in Guangzhouwan, where so many people were on their way to somewhere else, it was hard to tell who was who.

---

[66] "Guangzhouwan chijin shengkou yungang" [Guangzhouwan livestock arrive in Hong Kong after ban lifted], *Zhongyangyinhang jingji huibao* 4, no. 10 (1941): 111–12.

[67] "Guangdong xinwen yi: Yinianlai gehang shangye diaocha" [Guangdong news 1: Business surveys in different occupations last year], *Chinese Times*, January 27, 1939, 8.

[68] "Guangzhouwan kuli zhi jinkuang" [Recent situations in Guangzhouwan's coolie market], *Chinese Times*, September 9, 1941, 7.

[69] Fu, *Passivity, Resistance, and Collaboration*, 125.

[70] "Guangzhouwan kuli zhi jinkuang."

LIFE AND LOVE AS A REFUGEE IN GUANGZHOUWAN

Among the many people who fled to Guangzhouwan during the war, Wu Chufan is interesting on every account and exceptional in some respects. Wu (better known by his Cantonese name, Ng Chor-Fan) was among the many performers in Hong Kong who were reluctant to cooperate with the Japanese in the production of a movie called *The Capture of Hong Kong.* This movie was to be used as propaganda for Japan's "Greater East Asia."[71] Taking part in it could be seen as a gesture of surrender to the Japanese. Therefore, almost everyone who was approached by the Japanese to participate escaped from Hong Kong. Wu was neither brave enough to rebuff the Japanese directly nor willing to agree unconscionably so he found an excuse to leave Hong Kong: he announced his divorce from his wife, Huang Xiaoxin, who was also a performer in the Hong Kong show business, and claimed he was "devastated" and had to leave Hong Kong.[72] Of course, the divorce was a fake, but Wu found his way out of Hong Kong through much less dangerous means than some of his fellow performers, who escaped Hong Kong on small sailboats during the night, like Xue Juexian.[73] Wu left his wife and headed to Macau without worrying about her safety. He did not feel at ease in Macau, however, probably because Macau was not far enough from Hong Kong. His friends suggested that he go to Guangzhouwan because, according to them, the situation there was freer and more relaxed.[74]

Wu arrived in Guangzhouwan in the summer of 1942. At first he was afraid to be seen in public because at the time Guangzhouwan was full of both Japanese and Nationalist spies.[75] Fellow Hong Kong actor Xue

---

[71] Wu Chufan, *Wu Chufan zizhuan* [Wu Chufan's autobiography] (Taipei: Longwen chubanshe, 1994), 83–85.

[72] Ibid., 87.

[73] Shazhou, "Kangzhan shiqi xianggang yiren zai Guangzhouwan huodong suoji" [Hong Kong performers in wartime Guangzhouwan], in *Zhanjiang wenshi ziliao*, vol. 24, ed. Cai Jinguang (Zhongguo renmin zhengzhi xieshang huiyi Guangdongsheng Zhanjiangshi weiyuanhui xuexi wenshi weiyuanhui bian, 2005), 55.

[74] Ibid., 88.

[75] Ibid.

Juexian, who also escaped to Guangzhouwan, stated that Chikan belonged to the Nationalists and the local gentry, while Xiying had more Japanese spies. Since Xue had infuriated the Japanese in Hong Kong by announcing in a local Guangzhouwan newspaper his patriotic intent to "break away from the enemy and return to the motherland" to encourage resistance to the Japanese, he had to seek protection from a local notable, Dai Chao'en, whose nickname was Iron Nerve (Tiedan).[76] Another fellow actor, Lu Dun, described the situation similarly, saying that "the Japanese could enter and leave Xiying freely." Lu was protected by the head of a local gang nicknamed the "Black-eyed captain" (Heiyanyuan). Wu Chufan did not mention who promised him protection, but Chen Xuetan might have been one of his longtime patrons. The Nanhua hotel where Wu often stayed belonged to Chen, and Chen's biography describes financial support for Wu and his Hong Kong fellows.[77] Nonetheless, Wu was reassured of his safety by a local notable and resumed his performing career with other actors in the newly created Star Theater Troupe in Chikan. Wu first stayed in a local hotel, then moved out to join his troupe, which lived in a deserted middle school on a little hill near Chijin Bridge in the suburban area of Guangzhouwan. The living conditions there were terrible, especially for an actor from Hong Kong who was used to sleeping on comfortable spring mattresses. Lu Dun was a member of Star Troupe as well, and he described the living conditions in detail: no electricity, no water, no windows, and, of course, no bathtub or flush toilet. Female and male members had to take shifts showering outdoors behind the building.[78]

After a while, Wu's wife, Huang Xiaoxin, came to Guangzhouwan to join him and the troupe. The troupe performed many different plays within its first half year, but their performances were not warmly received. Wu thought this was because the local people were not very familiar with spoken drama (huaju).[79] The aforementioned Huang Manli, who had also

---

[76] Cui Songming and Wu Fusheng, Yueju wanneng laoguan: Xue Juexian [The versatile elder in Cantonese opera: Xue Juexian] (Guangzhou: Guangdong renmin chubanshe, 2009), 89–90.

[77] Chen Huakan, Chen Xuetan, 63–65.

[78] Ibid., 79–80.

[79] Wu Chufan, Wu Chufan zizhuan, 93.

joined the troupe, said that those who appreciated their performance were mainly travelers and a very small group of local intellectuals.[80] Lu Dun's suggestion to imitate a more successful local troupe was to no avail. As a result, the Star Theater Troupe continued to suffer from lack of finances and had a hard time attracting customers, and its members began to think about their own future.[81]

The failure of the Star Theater Troupe could be explained by comparing it to other troupes in Guangzhouwan. First, the playbills of the Star Theater Troupe showed plays such as the patriotically oriented *Lin Chong*; contemporary realist plays such as *Thunderstorm (Leiyu)*; and adaptations from Russian literature, such as Nikolai Gogol's *The Government Inspector*. On the contrary, the majority of the local plays were Cantonese opera. For example, Liao Xiahuai was a renowned comedian who performed his famous work *The Local Zhuangyuan*, a comedy about a leper[82] and Tan Lanqing was one of the four most famous *huadan* in Cantonese opera who performed *Yang Guifei*, which included a risqué scene of Yang taking a shower.[83] While the other troupes seemed to be more interested in humorous or sexual themes, Star Theater Troupe had a much more serious and patriotic tone to its performances. Furthermore, Liao and Tan were also given more welcome due to their well-established reputation in Cantonese opera, for which Guangzhouwan had a long history of appreciation.

Second, the target audience for Star Theater Troupe was not sufficiently large. The Troupe aimed their performances at students by giving a discounted admission price as low as 3 to 10 yuan, when the normal price was between 5 and 20 yuan.[84] But there were no universities in Guangzhouwan and only a handful of primary and middle schools. The majority of people in the city were businessmen or farmers. Gambling and opium smoking were more popular than going to the theater to become educated. The last licentiate (*xiucai*) living on a government stipend in Guangzhou-

---

[80] Huang Manli, *Wo de yanyi shenghuo*, 65.

[81] Lu Dun, *Fengzi shengya banshiji*, 74–75.

[82] See the front-page advertisement, *Daguangbao* (south Guangdong edition), September 22, 1942, 1.

[83] Ibid. *Huadan* were male actors performing sensuous female roles.

[84] Front-page advertisements, *Daguangbao* (south Guangdong edition), December 16, 1942, and September 26, 1942.

wan, Feng Lingyun, characterized the city in one of his best-known couplets, translated to read: "Come to this place for brothels, gambling, drinking and opium, otherwise it is tough to survive; within this domain officials, merchants, soldiers, and outlaws can enjoy themselves at will."[85] When the Star Theater Troupe publicized their event on the front page of the *Daguangbao* (south Guangdong edition), a personality known as "Miss Darling Flower" and her companions advertised their addresses in the same edition's supplement, targeting patrons seeking services of women.[86]

During the Star Theater Troupe's stay in Guangzhouwan, members' wives and some female members became part of the crowd of refugees who sold clothes, furniture, jewelry, and other personal belongings on the street.[87] One female member, Mei Qi, verified that one could sell a pair of new silk stockings for enough money for several days' meals.[88] The biggest problem was that no one could survive under such circumstances for long. Wu Chufan's wife, Huang Xiaoxin, could not stand the hard times in Guangzhouwan, especially since there was no end in sight. Wu told Huang to put up with it for a while and assured her that he would find another job so they could maintain their Hong Kong lifestyle but Huang missed her parents in Macau, and quarrels between this anxious couple became routine. Huang finally returned to Macau with a friend. Wu thought it might be best for them to take some time apart to work things out but after exchanging letters with Huang, Wu realized that she had no intention of coming back to him or to Guangzhouwan.[89]

At the same time, one group of members that included Lu Dun, left Guangzhouwan to head to Yulin and Guilin. They put on performances along the way to pay for travel expenses and stayed in Guilin, which was still part of Free China. A second group continued to use the troupe's

---

[85] See Dai Mingguang, "Leizhou tilian xisu kao" [Textual research on couplets and customs in Leizhou], in *Zhanjiang wenshi ziliao*, vol. 16 (1997), 292–93. This volume lists an anonymous author for this couplet.

[86] *Daguangbao* (supplement), September 21, 1942, 2. The supplement to the *Daguangbao* includes four advertisements.

[87] Huang Manli, *Wo de yanyi shenghuo*, 64.

[88] Mei Qi, *Xiju de rensheng* [Theater life] (Hong Kong: Wenzong chubanshe, 1956), 32.

[89] Wu Chufan, *Wu Chufan zizhuan*, 94–95.

name and set out for Vietnam. They traveled around Southeast Asia, visiting Haiphong, Hanoi, Saigon, Phnom Penh, Bangkok, Siam, Cholon, and Annam.[90] Wu, however, stayed alone in Guangzhouwan, waiting to see if his wife would change her mind and return.

At the end of 1942, communicating through letters, Wu and Huang decided to get a real divorce. By that time, since the Star Theater Troupe had disbanded, Wu joined his other friends in starting a small cigarette company and devoting himself totally to the business. He quickly made a decent sum of money and moved into a hotel, still unhappy because Guangzhouwan constantly reminded him of his ex-wife, whom he missed very much. This led to his gambling and drinking heavily, and his friends began introducing him to other women.[91]

One of these women was Li Zhenni, who enjoyed Cantonese opera and had dabbled in performing opera. Wu met the beautiful and witty woman while he was out with his friends from the theater troupe. Both Wu and Li's friends thought that they were a good match. At first Li was hesitant to pursue Wu and preferred the company of her female friends to Wu's constant gambling and gloomy demeanor. Wu, on the other hand, was attracted by Li's gentleness. During that time in early 1943 when the United States and Britain started bombing Guangzhouwan consistently, Wu found excuses to be alone with Li: whenever there was an air raid they would find a place to hide by themselves. Because of this, their friends would taunt them by yelling, "The airplanes are coming!"[92] This romance helped Wu through his short stay in Guangzhouwan, continuing after the Japanese occupation began in February 1943. Wu and Li finally married on May 25, 1943, leaving Guangzhouwan together the very next month for Haiphong and Cholon to rejoin the Star Theater Troupe.

The story of Wu Chufan and his theater troupe friends reveals a crucial aspect of the lives of some of the local residents of Guangzhouwan: they came to Guangzhouwan as refugees in great danger to preserve their integrity as Chinese. Back in Hong Kong, these performers rejected invi-

---

[90] Huang Manli, *Wo de yanyi shenghuo*, 66–73.
[91] Wu Chufan, *Wu Chufan zizhuan*, 96–98.
[92] Ibid., 97–100.

tation by the Japanese to act in the movie *The Capture of Hong Kong*, which ended up with a Japanese actor and actress playing the major roles.[93] These performers from Hong Kong returned to mainland China wishing to join the cultural front of the Chinese resistance. They stayed in Guangzhouwan not just for their own safety but also to raise money to travel even further. To make ends meet they performed in Guangzhouwan, Guilin, all the way to Vietnam. Many of them reached their destinations with almost nothing since they either "lost" their luggage to porters or sold their belongings for cash.

In Wu Chufan's case, when he did become a businessman in Guangzhouwan, it was only temporary. In his memoirs he wrote, "The year 1942 passed, my life had turned over an important page. It was a page filled with tears that did not just end an exceedingly sentimental love of mine, but caused me to lose a truly beautiful companion. Most importantly, it was the year that I even abandoned my unforgettable, lifetime career, which ran in my blood, as an actor."[94] Ultimately, Wu returned to his career as a performer. Right after the Japanese defeat, he returned to Hong Kong and shot his first postwar movie, *Love Fire* (*Qingyan*) in 1946. Among his more than three hundred movies, the majority were filmed after the war. When Wu died in 1993, the Hong Kong Film Awards bestowed on him the Life Achievement Award.

The story of wartime Guangzhouwan is a reminder that history is never simple and straightforward. The prosperity of the city was brought on by temporary residents such as Wu Chufan and his troupe—people who were caught up in different national agendas and who adopted the strategy of blowing with the wind in order to survive. Even though Wu worked as a merchant for a while to make ends meet, his love for an acting career never ceased and eventually it is to this career that he returned. Citizens aligning with a particular power need not signify patriotism, especially in a time marked with turmoil and filled with loss of hope for the nation's future and disappointment with the government in power, in this

---

[93] Xie Yongguang, *Sannian ling bageyue de kunan* [The tribulation of three years and eight months] (Hong Kong: Mingbao chubanshe, 1994), 262.

[94] Wu Chufan, *Wu Chufan zizhuan*, 96–97.

case, the Guomindang (see chapters 9 and 10). The possibility that the nation could be ruled by the Japanese was undeniable, since in 1943 most of China was in fact under Japanese rule (including the territory of the Nanjing government). The underlying issue was not who worked with whom, but what the local people did to carry on.

ANOTHER WORLD: OUTLAWS AND SMUGGLERS

Outlaws

Armed outlaws were a traditional problem for the Leizhou Peninsula.[95] Compared with the ideal of the Robin Hood–style outlaw who was celebrated for his brave fight against corrupt government officials, local Guangzhouwan gangsters were much less idealistic and much more self-centered. Because of the area's underdeveloped economy, poor people and landless farmers had little choice but to engage in banditry from time to time to supplement their income from farming. Phil Billingsley refers to such outlaws as "occasional."[96] While "occasionals" did not engage in banditry as often or as professionally as members of secret societies,[97] the long period of war and the area's mountainous geography provided the occasional outlaws with relatively consistent employment as gangsters. In this sense, Guangzhouwan gangsters were similar to their cohorts in Guangxi, Guizhou, and Yunnan provinces.

The Nationalists's destruction of the Guangxi roads to prevent the Japanese from moving inland greatly increased both the hardship and travel time to reach Guangzhouwan. In 1939, Xia Yan, a pro-CCP intellectual, rode in a car from Guilin to Guangzhouwan via Luzhou in thirty-

---

[95] "Leizhou tufei duduo zhi yuanyin" [The cause of Leizhou's many independent bandits], *Guangzhou minguo ribao*, January 12, 1926; "Leizhou feihuo zhi canku zhuangkuang" [The miserable state of Leizhou's bandit calamity], *Guangzhou minguo ribao*, January 25, 1926.

[96] Phil Billingsley, *Bandits in Republican China* (Stanford, CA: Stanford University Press, 1988), 5.

[97] Ibid., 8.

six hours, a route that was approximately 100 miles longer than a trip made two years later by Ling Shuhua.[98] In 1941, Ling Shuhua, a well-known writer and painter who graduated from Yenching University, also passed through Guangzhouwan with her family and some friends on their way to Liuzhou in Guangxi. She left Hong Kong for Guangzhouwan on December 2 and reached Liuzhou on the night of December 24. This prolonged trip was undertaken exclusively by foot or be carried in a sedan chair except for the journey from Hong Kong to Guangzhouwan by sea. After her trip, Ling felt the need to write a travelogue for fellow sojourners. Her main piece of advice was to seek help from local people who could use their personal connections to lessen the so-called tolls one would have to pay along the way and to keep the travelers out of harm's way.

The first checkpoint Ling had encountered was a Leizhou Customs Administration toll booth, probably installed to help deal with smuggling. One of her companions was charged 800 yuan for the new Western suits he had bought in Guangzhouwan. Another person had brought two small suitcases full of 606 vials of serum used to treat syphilis. One inspector asked in private to buy two doses, in exchange for waiving the traveler's tolls. When the traveler refused, the inspector fined him an enormous sum. This traveler with two suitcases full of syphilis medicine was not likely to use the medicine all by himself, which suggests that his travel might also have been for business.

Next, Ling's group was notified that there could be dangerous outlaws ahead, so they joined with another six people to hire three fully armed military police to accompany them. When they had to cross a wooden bridge, they encountered one robust old man and two young men who demanded toll fees. Then three people at the side of the road asked them for donations, claiming that they were raising money for the local self-protection team. Later, they encountered several old people and children asking for a one *yuan* toll fee. They were never threatened by the dangerous outlaws they had expected; though afterward, they learned that the three groups of people they had encountered were all local outlaws! If

---

[98] Xia Yan, *Xia Yan zawen suibi ji* [Xia Yan's collected essays] (Beijing: Sanlian chubanshe, 1980), 181.

passersby seemed like easy targets, the outlaws would rob them. If they seemed too strong or numerous, the outlaws would just charge them "toll fees."

When Ling's group arrived in Yulin, a Shanghai friend realized that one of his carriers had lost a piece of his luggage. This unfortunate friend was a merchant who had borrowed 20,000 yuan to buy medicine and fleece underwear that he planned to resell at a profit. He now had 200 yuan left and had lost much of his merchandise. He tried to file a lawsuit with the local government but they denied his claim, saying that he had lost his cargo outside their jurisdiction.[99]

In Ling's case, it was difficult to envision what a gangster or an outlaw looked like, whether a patriot in disguise requesting donations, or a villager who claimed to have property rights to a wooden bridge, or even children along the street begging for just one yuan. While one expected to encounter outlaws who seized goods from travelers by force, it turned out that service people such as carriers, hired bodyguards, and even toll-gate inspectors may also be considered outlaws due to their acts of extorting money and confiscating goods from travelers. The situation becomes problematic when one is unable to distinguish between outlaws and local people. The underlying problem is that both the local and the provincial governments had little means or desire to successfully control outlaws.

Smugglers

In Guangzhouwan, prostitution, gambling, and drugs had been legalized by the French government. Taxes collected on gambling and drugs made up as much as 50 percent of the government's annual revenue.[100] In addition, many residents participated in the business of smuggling, which was lucrative. Because Guangzhouwan was a free port, the French government was not supposed to collect custom taxes, nevertheless they charged mer-

---

[99] Ling Shuhua, "You Guangzhouwan dao Liuzhou ji" [From Guangzhouwan to Liuzhou], *Funü xinyun* 4, no. 8 (1942): 67–74.

[100] Guo Shouhua, *Zhanjiang shizhi*, 71; Lin Leming, *Haiguan fuwu sawu nian huiyi lu* [Thirty-five years in customs service] (Hong Kong: Longmin shudian, 1982), 25.

chants various "handling fees" based on the size of their cargo.[101] These
fees and other restrictions on trade made smuggling potentially very profitable.

The Leizhou Customs Administration installed an additional nineteen collection points in 1940, and twenty-seven more in 1942, to help
deal with smuggling, but the activities did not decrease.[102] That the leased
territory of Guangzhouwan had no natural borders separating it from the
hinterland made the search for smugglers difficult. Moreover, as is evident
from the increasing number of collection points, the job of suppressing
smugglers only became more challenging with time. After the Japanese
occupied Guangzhou, Hainan, and Hong Kong in succession, Guangzhouwan was one of the only open conduits for goods flowing into Free
China. As inflation in Guomindang-controlled areas soared, the fortune
to be made from smuggling only grew.

Over time, the boats used for smuggling increased in quantity and
became more technologically advanced. Many were equipped with firearms, and the French coastguard found their own boats outgunned. Even
if the French had possessed the capacity to clamp down on smuggling,
they were not very committed to the task. Many of the smuggled goods
were used to supply the Guangzhouwan casinos, from which the French
government drew much of its income.[103]

In 1941, the top Nationalist official in Guangdong, Li Hanhun, ordered Chen Jiadong, the commander of the No. 9 Peace Preservation
Corps in Guangdong, to secretly arrest three major smugglers in and
around Guangzhouwan: Zou Wu, Huang Jian, and Dai Chao'en. Zou was
the magistrate of Lianjiang County near Guangzhouwan and Huang was
the captain of the Lianjiang militia; both had been appointed by the
Guomindang. Huang was a local smuggler who later came under the patronage of Zou. Dai Chao'en, a member of Chen Xuetan's Chikan Bureau,
was a local administrator appointed by the French.

---

[101] Jiang Xuekai, "Guangzhouwan maoyi jiehui ji qudi zousi diaocha baogao" [Investiga-
tive report on foreign exchange trade and suppression of smuggling], *Maoyi banyuekan* 1, nos.
3–4 (1940): 1046.

[102] Ibid., 1047; Lin Leming, *Haiguan fuwu*, 26.

[103] Jiang Xuekai, "Guangzhouwan maoyi jiehui ji qudi zousi," 1047–48.

Huang Jian's smuggling business had previously come into conflict with the Nationalist central government police, since the police were engaged in smuggling activities as well. Because Huang was backed by powerful figures such as Zou Wu and Deng Xiuchuan, a local warlord and the father of the top Nationalist general in southern Guangxi, he was not deterred by the police. But the true force behind Zou and Deng's smuggling operations was the son of Deng Xiuchuan named Deng Longguang.[104]

In 1941, some of Huang's men were stopped by police on the road between Anpu and Guangzhouwan. When the police tried to seize the merchandise being smuggled, Huang's men responded by throwing twelve policemen into the sea with rocks tied to their backs.[105]

When Chen Jiadong received the order to arrest Huang, Zou, and Deng, he did not believe that Li Hanhun was serious about carrying it out. After verifying the order multiple times, Chen had no choice but to do as he was told and arrested Huang and Zou. Huang offered Chen 5 million Hong Kong dollars (half of his personal wealth) in exchange for his freedom. Because Chen hoped to curry favor with Li by carrying out this task and gain a promotion in the near future, he turned down the offer. When Li received word of Huang's arrest, he reported the good news to Chiang Kai-shek and ordered the *Daguangbao* to announce this big achievement in suppressing smuggling.[106]

Huang was executed in short order but Zou was sent to Shaoguan, the capital of the Nationalist Guangdong provincial government. Chen knew that he could not execute Zou because he was directly connected to Deng Longguang's father, Deng Xiuchuan. After Zou's arrival in Shaoguan, Deng Longguang paid a visit to Li Hanhun, and, after a few months, Zou was released and appointed a major general in the No. 35 Army Group, although it is unclear who issued the appointment orders.[107]

---

[104] Chen Jiadong, "Kangri shiqi Li Hanhun chuli nanlu sixiao neimu" [The inside story of Li Hanhun's dealing with the smugglers in south Guangdong during the Sino-Japanese war], in *Guangzhou wenshiziliao*, vol. 19, ed. Committee of Guangzhou City, Guangdong Province, Chinese People's Political Consultative Conference (Guangzhou: Guangdong renmin chubanshe, 1980).

[105] Ibid.

[106] Ibid.

[107] Ibid.

In January 1942 Chen paid a visit to Dai Chao'en (one of the men who offered protection to the refugee performers) at his mansion in Guangzhouwan. Chen's strategy was to induce Dai to cooperate with the Guomindang while at the same time planting his own agents to spy on Dai and find the right time to arrest him. But Dai turned the tables on Chen, and after a month Chen discovered that all of his agents had become loyal to Dai. He also noticed that many of them had started to wear gold rings, smoke opium, and dine in fancy restaurants. Chen realized his plan would not work, and Li did not push him to arrest Dai, in any case. At the end of 1942, Dai was appointed magistrate of Suixi County.[108]

Although this account comes from Chen Jiaodong's insider perspective, certain dynamics were at work behind the scenes. The relationships between Guomindang officials appointed by the central government, local warlords, and outlaws were extremely complicated. Li Hanhun controlled only a small part of northern Guangdong, and his authority remained largely nominal. When he tried to challenge a true local power, like the Deng family, his actions were ineffectual. Guangzhouwan was clearly beyond Li's reach.

Li's personal resentment toward Guangzhouwan and his discontent had its roots in economic conflicts in the surrounding areas as well. The Guangdong government's weekly reports dealt with proposals from Beihai city about regulating customs in Guangzhouwan. According to complaints made by Beihai city and its surrounding counties, since Guangzhouwan was leased, Beihai could no longer compete in trade due to Guangzhouwan's extremely low custom duties. Beihai officials argued that the new import and export route created by Guangzhouwan bypassed Beihai and constituted an illegal monopoly. They proposed that the Guomindang government of Guangdong establish a complete set of custom fees and tolls around Guangzhouwan to prevent the loss of government revenue.[109] This proposal was later sanctioned by both the Guangdong and national governments.[110] But all these efforts to regulate trade and smug-

---

[108] Ibid.

[109] "Nanqu chengqing sheli Guangzhouwan haiguan jizai Guangzhouwan fujin sheli shuiqia an" [South district's proposal for the establishment of Guangzhouwan custom and tolls], *Guangdong shengzhengfu bao* 59 (1928): 45–48.

[110] "Guoshui gongshu hanfu Guangzhouwan sheguanzhengshui yichengqing Guomin-

gling did not intimidate smugglers or cause them to stop their illicit dealings. Aside from the tremendous personal profit that could be made locally, Free China needed smuggling as a way to transport supplies to Chongqing, especially after the capture of South China coastal cities and the French concurrence in the Japanese blockade of the route through Indochina. What was less visible but very substantial was the need for cargo transportation between Free China and occupied China, like the livestock business between free Guangzhouwan and occupied Hong Kong, and possible military supplies shipped across Tokyo, occupied China, and Free China. Such transportation could complicate the seemingly patriotic agenda of Guangzhouwan of only transporting goods to Free China to support the Chinese resistance. It was a simple logic: some smugglers and local notables aimed at maximizing their profits without acting against the Guomindang government. As Japanese feelers reached deeper into Guangzhouwan, the weak French political attitude of compromising with the Japanese became more evident. Any real political pressure forcing Guangzhouwan residents to be patriotic was declining, especially from 1940 to 1943. It was only natural to suspect that the import and export business through Guangzhouwan was no guarantee of patriotism.

Nonetheless, these stories demonstrate how fungible the boundaries between politicians, warlords, outlaws, and beggars were in wartime Guangzhouwan. What mattered was not a person's legal status, but the power and connections that enabled him or her to survive. People did what they had to do, even if the survival strategies they adopted did not conform to nationalist or patriotic agendas.

THE LAST CHAPTER

The mechanical rhythm of the motor slowed down bit by bit to match the motion of the vessel. The passengers were all relieved. Brows that had been knitted for the last few days, no, a few months, were finally relaxed. Thank Heaven! Our motherland was close at

zhengfu chixing choubanan" [National tax office's reply to the proposal for the establishment of Guangzhouwan custom and tolls], *Guangdong shengzhengfu bao* 73–74 (1929): 46–48.

hand. Craning my neck upward, I gazed on the pure blue sky. The sunshine glistened on the ocean. There was water all around us, and we could only see the mountains far away. Where was the shore? With the boat so far out at sea, I could not tell which direction it was in. People were anxious and afraid that the boat might be delayed once again. Our suffering from being on the boat had already been extended. It was enough![111]

The author of this narrative did not specify where he and other travelers came from, but clearly they came from newly occupied areas. When this group finally arrived at Guangzhouwan, they waited for the Japanese officials to open the door and allow the passengers to disembark. Yet when the hatch opened, they were still not immediately let off the boat. For a while, no one dared say a word. Then, after an oppressive search of each passenger's luggage and a silent stare-down between the Japanese officials and the Chinese passengers, everyone was allowed to board the several small skiffs that would take them to shore. After a long journey along a rock embankment, they finally saw the vivid tricolored French flag, telling them they had at last reached their destination.[112]

This account of arriving in Guangzhouwan was written in April 1943. Even after the Japanese occupied Guangzhouwan in February of that year, quite a number of refugees still swarmed into the city. Now, however, their feelings about Guangzhouwan were tinged with anxiety and fear.

Eventually, the vitality that made Guangzhouwan such a unique place during the early years of the war ebbed. Even though Japanese military presence in Guangzhouwan was light, the abrupt change in Guangzhouwan's status meant that things could not continue as before.[113] Business was all about analysis of risks and returns. Especially after the Ichigo campaign in 1944, the transportation lines from Guangzhouwan to inner China were cut off, and so were the opportunities for profit that made a dangerous business like smuggling worthwhile.

Guangzhouwan, the small, remote port lying on the edge of southern

[111] Sun Yuan, "Zai Guangzhouwan" [In Guangzhouwan], *Zi xue* 5 (1943), 58.
[112] Ibid.
[113] Vannière, *Le territoire à bail de Guangzhouwan*, 417–18.

China, was one of the few places that truly benefited from the war (and escaped the hardships that befell other cities)— at least for a while. Harboring refugees from Hainan, Guangdong, Hong Kong, and other areas under either Japanese or Nationalist control, and serving as a key transit point for both refugees and smuggled goods, Guangzhouwan experienced an unexpected and also unprecedented boom from 1937 to 1943. As a business, smuggling had much less to do with patriotic sentiment than with profit seeking amid the complex web of local politics. To play the power game in Guangzhouwan, one had to constantly test the wind, keeping in mind the words of Louis Renault: Steady loyalty to the nation or any single political party was a luxury few could afford, and survival was what really mattered.

On June 3, 1944, Allied planes dropped three bombs on the Tongle club in Guangzhouwan, killing more than one hundred civilians who had been partying on the dance floor.[114] This rude interruption by a war that had left Guangzhouwan relatively unscathed indicated that it was time to move on. Guangzhouwan's borrowed time had run out. In 1944, Dongxing, a small port on the westernmost part of China's south coast, emerged as "the new Guangzhouwan."[115] Businesses and people packed up and moved west to one of the few coastal enclaves not yet occupied by Japan. By this time, however, the war was thankfully almost over, and Dongxing never experienced the boom of excitement, danger, and romance that had characterized wartime Guangzhouwan.

---

[114] "Zhuyu Meikongjun canwurendao, lanzha Guangzhouwan Chikanshi" [The American air force in Chongqing brutally bombed Chikan city in Guangzhouwan], *Guangdong xunbao* (Guangzhou), June 11, 1944, 4.

[115] Chen Fan, "Dongxing: Xin de Guangzhouwan" [Dongxing: The new Guangzhouwan], *Lüxing zazhi* 18, no. 8 (1944): 63–66.

13

Chiang Kai-shek and the Cairo Summit

HSIAO-TING LIN

In 1943, the Chinese National Government under Chiang Kai-shek brought about several remarkable diplomatic achievements. In January, China signed new treaties with the United States, Britain, and many of their allied nations, all of whom recognized China's contributions to the world war then in progress (see chapter 4). On February 18, Madame Chiang Kai-shek delivered a historic speech to the U.S. Congress, appealing for aid to the Chinese in their struggle against Japanese aggression, thus becoming both the first Chinese national and the second woman to address both houses of Congress (see chapter 2). In October, China was invited to sign the joint Four-Nation Declaration in Moscow that pledged a continued fight against the Axis powers. Although largely a ceremonial performance, it served to recognize China as one of the Big Four.

The Chinese National Government's most impressive diplomatic achievement that year, however, was at the Cairo summit. On December 1, 1943, the Cairo Declaration was issued by the United States, Britain, and China, which, among other historic pronouncements, pledged to return all territories that Japan had stolen from China, notably Manchuria and Taiwan. As Chiang Kai-shek wrote, "the whole world treated Cairo as

Figure 13.1: Big Four group photo of the Cairo Summit. *Source:* U.S. Army Signal Corps photo, National Archives, College Park, MD.

a huge and unprecedented victory for China."[1] A photo of Chiang and his wife sitting beside Franklin D. Roosevelt and Winston Churchill greatly impressed the Chinese people; for the first time in more than a century, the leader of China was seen as an equal to the leaders of the West, seemingly sweeping away China's longtime national humiliation.

Thus, the Cairo summit and its political legacy have long been portrayed in modern Chinese historiography as a great achievement of Nationalist Chinese diplomacy; however, a gap often exists between political image and reality. Having access to Chiang Kai-shek's personal diaries and other declassified documents allows us to reconsider several often overlooked factors. For example, what did Chiang think about the summit and

---

[1] Chiang Kai-shek's diary entry for December 4, 1943, *Chiang Kai-shek Diaries*, Box 43, Hoover Institution Archives, Stanford, California (hereafter cited as *CKSD*).

what was his initial reaction to President Roosevelt's invitation? Before arriving in Cairo, what was Chiang's game plan and what topics did he want to bring to the table? What became of Chiang's list of priorities during and after Cairo? What impact did the summit have on China's relations with the Allies? This chapter revisits the summit in an effort to address these issues.

PRELUDE TO THE SUMMIT

By the middle of 1943, Franklin D. Roosevelt had begun to warm to the idea of a meeting with Chiang Kai-shek. The reasons are manifold. In January, Roosevelt and Churchill had met in Casablanca to discuss Allied war strategy and to issue a call for the Allies to seek the unconditional surrender of the Axis Powers. Neither Chiang Kai-shek nor his representative was invited to the conference, which angered the Chinese Nationalists.[2] In the following months, both Madame Chiang and her brother, T.V. Soong (Song Ziwen), Nationalist China's foreign minister, began walking and working the corridors of power in Washington, warning of the dangers of omitting China from Allied summits, including grave consequences for China's war efforts and morale. In early June, Roosevelt asked T.V. Soong to convey an invitation to Chiang for a personal meeting, either in a Big Four summit (United States, Britain, China, and Soviet Russia) or in a bilateral discussion at a location somewhere between Washington and Chongqing, China's wartime capital. (Roosevelt's message to Chiang was also conveyed to Chongqing through Madame Chiang, before her return to China in late June.) Although at this point no details regarding the meeting were given, Chiang's initial response was positive.[3]

Roosevelt certainly had reasons to meet with Chiang in 1943. After

[2] Li Yunhan, *Zhongguo Guomindang shishu* [A historical narrative of the Guomindang] (Taipei: KMT Party Historical Committee, 1994), vol. 3, 539–40; Michael Schaller, *The US Crusade in China, 1938–1945* (New York: Columbia University Press, 1979), 120–23.

[3] *CKSD*, July 8, 1943, Box 43; Xiaoyuan Liu, *A Partnership for Disorder: China, the United States, and Their Policies for the Postwar Disposition of the Japanese Empire, 1941–1945* (Cambridge: Cambridge University Press, 1996), 116.

two years of cooperation in war, China and the United States were involved in several disputes that needed to be resolved. Nationalist Chinese leaders complained about unequal treatment by the Allies in such matters as Lend-Lease aid and inter-Allied consultation on war plans. By mid-1943, the American, British, and Chinese governments had become deadlocked over the best offensive strategy to pursue in Burma. In addition, the friction between Chiang and General Joseph Stilwell, Chiang's U.S. chief of staff in the Chinese theater, cast a shadow on the Chinese-American military collaboration.[4] Meeting with Chiang, Roosevelt hoped, would allay tensions in Sino-American wartime cooperation and possibly pave the way for his meeting with Joseph Stalin, leader of the Soviet Union.[5] On a more personal level, Roosevelt felt that his meeting with Chiang might bolster Chinese morale and keep China in its war with Japan, thus relieving Allied pressures in other theaters, and that supporting China's status as one of the Big Four would serve the U.S. postwar strategy in Asia: to oppose all forms of imperialism, including that of the British, and to favor a free, strong, and democratic China as the predominant and stabilizing force in Asia. Inviting Chiang to attend an Allied summit would thus be an important step toward incorporating China into America's global enterprise in the postwar era.[6]

The Quebec Summit of August 1943 between Roosevelt and Churchill, again lacking a Chinese representative, only further angered Chiang Kai-shek and his officials. At a meeting with T.V. Soong on August 30, a week after the summit, Roosevelt blamed China's absence on Churchill's insistence that China not be treated the same way as were the United States, Britain, and the Soviet Union. Churchill, no friend of China, did not share Roosevelt's vision of China's role in postwar Asia. Nor was the British prime minister interested in waging war in the China-Burma-India (CBI)

---

[4] David Stone, *War Summits: The Meetings That Shaped World War II and the Postwar World* (Dulles, VA: Potomac, 2005), 85–93; Christopher Thorne, *Allies of a Kind: The United States, Britain and the War against Japan, 1941–1945* (Oxford: Oxford University Press, 1978), 322–23; Bradley F. Smith, *The War's Long Shadow: The Second World War and Its Aftermath: China, Russia, Britain, America* (New York: Simon and Schuster, 1986), 42–43.

[5] Liu, *A Partnership for Disorder*, 117.

[6] Jay Taylor, *The Generalissimo: Chiang Kai-shek and the Struggle for Modern China* (Cambridge, MA: Harvard University Press, 2011), 242–43.

theater. But Roosevelt assured Soong that he disagreed with Churchill's ideas, saying that he had pointed out to his British counterpart that China would be industrialized in twenty-five years and would thus be a bulwark against Communism in Asia.[7]

China's absence at the Quebec Conference helped advance the idea of a meeting between Chiang and Roosevelt. In the weeks following Quebec, Soong discussed with Roosevelt and his top officials a wide range of topics, from the problems with Stilwell to China's place among the Allies. Also discussed was a meeting between the two heads of state, which Harry Hopkins, one of Roosevelt's closest advisers, assured Soong was "imminent." Unfortunately, Hopkins and Soong were unable to work out a concrete agenda for the proposed summit.[8] In the meantime, the new South East Asia Command (SEAC), created by a decision made at Quebec and commanded by Admiral Lord Louis Mountbatten, became a point of contention, given that the now British-dominated Southeast Asian theater overlapped with the CBI theater under Chiang's command. Roosevelt and his top aides, however, seemed convinced that such issues would be resolved at their meeting with China's top leader.[9]

According to official Chinese files, before Soong left Washington for Chongqing on October 8, 1943, he and Roosevelt had reached the following consensus: General Stilwell would be recalled from the CBI theater; a new Combined Chiefs of Staff (CCOS) to include China would be created; and China would participate in the Burma counteroffensive.[10] As for the impending meeting between Roosevelt and Chiang, Roosevelt, having discussed it with Soong and exchanging messages with Chiang in Chongqing, in early October agreed that he, Chiang, and the British would meet at a summit in Cairo, preferably attended by Stalin.[11] Accord-

---

[7] Memorandum of conversation with President Roosevelt, August 30, 1943, T.V. Soong Papers, Box 29, Hoover Institution Archives, Stanford, California.

[8] Notes on Conversation with Harry Hopkins, September 15, 1943, T.V. Soong Papers, Box 29.

[9] Memorandum of conversation with President Roosevelt, September 16, 1943, T.V. Soong Papers, Box 29.

[10] Qin Xiaoyi, ed., *Zhonghua Minguo zhongyao zhiliao chubian—dui Ri kang zhan shiqi* [First selection of historical materials on the Republic of China—the period of war against Japan] (Taipei: KMT Party Historical Committee, 1981–), vol. 3, no. 3, 267 (hereafter cited as *ZMZSC*).

[11] Ibid., 494–95.

ing to Chiang's personal diary, on October 8, Roosevelt also seemed to hint that, were Stalin to refuse to attend a summit meeting at which Chiang would be present, he might meet the Soviet leader elsewhere before meeting with Chiang. Chiang, unhappy about China again being treated as secondary, however inadvertently, bitterly suggested that there was no way for genuine cooperation to emerge among America, Britain, and the Soviet Union. In Chiang's eyes, such a summit would be nothing more than "empty talk."[12]

Chiang Kai-shek's uneasiness about participating in the upcoming summit was not alleviated when he learned on October 28 that Roosevelt was now determined to meet with Chiang (and Churchill) in Egypt regardless of whether Stalin could attend. On receiving Roosevelt's message, Chiang wrote in his diary that he "really had no intention" of accepting Roosevelt's invitation to attend the summit; however, to "decline [the invitation] would be disrespectful."[13] Chiang was equally concerned about the lack of clarity on Roosevelt's meeting with Stalin. Although unhappy that his meeting with Roosevelt was scheduled after the Roosevelt-Stalin meeting, he also worried that Stalin might become suspicious about China's intention were Chiang's meeting with Roosevelt held before Stalin's.[14] In the end, Stalin, concerned about the reaction of both Japan (with which the Soviets had signed a neutrality pact) and the Chinese Communist Party, decided not to attend the Cairo summit after learning that Chiang had agreed to attend.[15] Therefore, two conferences were scheduled, one in Egypt attended by the Americans, Chinese, and British leaders, and the other at Tehran, where Stalin would meet with Roosevelt and Churchill.

PLANNING FOR THE SUMMIT: WHAT WAS ON CHIANG'S MIND?

During late October and early November 1943, Chiang Kai-shek was becoming uneasy about attending the summit, even though it would be one of China's (and his) greatest moments in the nation's recent history.

---

[12] *CKSD*, October 7, 1943, Box 43.
[13] Ibid., October 31, 1943, Box 43.
[14] Ibid., November 3, 1943, Box 43.
[15] Stone, *War Summits*, 107–14.

What was the source of Chiang's reluctance? First, Chiang's original idea had been to hold a meeting solely with Roosevelt, hoping to build a close friendship with the president and secure additional military and economic assistance from the United States. But Chiang now faced a summit involving potential competitors for U.S. aid: Churchill, who seldom concealed his contempt for the Chinese, and possibly Stalin, whom Chiang was reluctant to meet "in the state of friendliness such a conference would require."[16] The second cause for Chiang's concern related to T.V. Soong, who, shortly after his return to Chongqing on October 11, became embroiled in a row with Chiang over Stilwell's recall, resulting in Soong's dismissal from the inner circle. Chiang had changed his mind, deciding he wanted to keep Stilwell, as he recognized Stilwell's solid connections with the U.S. War Department and his new position as Lord Mountbatten's deputy in SEAC, together with the overall situation in the CBI theater. But Chiang's decision deeply humiliated Soong, who had been working hard for Stilwell's recall in Washington.[17]

Chiang also resented Soong's independence and his propensity to make decisions without consulting Chongqing. In his personal diaries, Chiang criticized Soong as being "perverse, violent, foolish, and treacherous" and placing his personal desires and ambitions above national interests.[18] As a result of this falling out between the in-laws, Soong, who had helped plan Chiang's meeting with Roosevelt and was (supposedly) the man best able to advise Chiang at the summit, was not invited to accompany the Generalissimo to Cairo. Not only was Soong forced into seclusion in Chongqing while Chiang went off to Cairo, but he was not involved in planning the final stages of the conference agenda or in preparing Chiang for the summit.[19] Soong's fall from grace meant that the Genera-

---

[16] Ronald Ian Heiferman, *The Cairo Conference of 1943: Roosevelt, Churchill, Chiang Kai-shek and Madame Chiang* (Jefferson, NC: McFarland, 2011), 53; Taylor, *The Generalissimo*, 242–43.

[17] In his discussion of the Stilwell issue with Chiang, a furious T.V. Soong was so forceful and disrespectful that the equally agitated Chiang virtually ordered Soong to be put under house arrest. See Wu Jingping, *Song Ziwen zhengzhi shengya biannian* [A chronology of T.V. Soong's political careers] (Fuzhou: Fujian renmin chubanshe, 1998), 434–35; K.C. Wu, *Wu Guozhen huiyilu* [A memoir of K.C. Wu] (Taipei: Liberal Times, 1995), 397–99.

[18] *CKSD*, October 17, 18, 31, and November 6, 1943, Box 43.

[19] Heiferman, *The Cairo Conference of 1943*, 47–48.

lissimo now had to rely on Stilwell to prepare for the upcoming summit, a condition that Chiang might have seen as uncomfortable.

Despite Chiang's hesitation, on November 2, he officially accepted Roosevelt's invitation to the summit. On the same day, Chiang for the first time wrote down what he saw as the most critical issues to be broached at the Cairo conference table: (1) China's participation in the American-British CCOS and the retention of the "tripartite" CCOS in the postwar period; (2) the establishment of a new international organization for postwar peace and order; (3) Sino-American economic cooperation and setting up a related bilateral monetary mechanism; (4) China's minimum reparations from Japan; (5) China's disposition of Japanese naval resources after the war; (6) assistance rendered to Free France against the Axis; and (7) foreign investments in postwar China's economic reconstruction.[20] In the following days, Chiang revised his objectives to include such items as building China's air force after the war, Soviet Russia's participation in the Pacific War, a possible Anglo-Chinese alliance, and war plans and coordination for the Allied offensive against Japan.[21]

During the first weeks of November, Chiang and his top aides were indecisive about prioritizing China's conference agenda. On November 11, for example, Chiang changed his priority list again, with the following becoming (temporarily at least) the subjects he wished to discuss with Roosevelt and Churchill: China's relations with the Soviet Union; Outer Mongolia and Xinjiang; Middle Eastern questions; China's economic construction; China's railway projects; and the joint development of China's natural resources.[22] Interestingly, up to this point, only a week before his departure for Cairo, Chiang had not listed the Allied counteroffensive in Burma as a top priority at the summit. Given that Burma came to occupy much of the Allies' time and energy in Cairo, and that it evolved to become a huge controversy between China and the Allies, Chiang's initial negligence deserves our scrutiny. Perhaps Chiang thought that the issue had been thoroughly discussed and a consensus reached in Chongqing in mid-October by Lord Mountbatten, General Stilwell, and many other

---

[20] *CKSD*, November 2, 1943, Box 43.
[21] *CKSD*, November 5, 1943, Box 34.
[22] *CKSD*, November 11, 1943, Box 34.

high-ranking officers. Minutes from the official Chinese file on the meetings in Chongqing indicate that, although privately Chiang was outraged that the CCOS had sought to take Thailand and Indochina out of his theater and put them under Mountbatten, at the meetings on recapturing Burma the parties had reached agreement. The Generalissimo and the British admiral had worked out a sound plan to recover Burma: the British would provide major naval and amphibious operations in lower Burma to assure Allied supremacy in the Bay of Bengal (Operation Buccaneer); and Chiang would provide some 50,000 ground forces, which, like the Chinese X (India) and Y (Yunnan) forces of 137,000 in total, would be commanded by the British to counterattack upper Burma from Ledo and Yunnan Province to reopen the route between India and China (Operation Tarzan). Both sides agreed that sometime between January and March 1944 would be the time to launch the campaign, the ultimate goal of which would be to recapture all of Burma.[23]

As Chiang had already delegated Stilwell to take care of the Burma campaign, he most likely was paying only marginal attention to the issue. On November 12, Chiang received, reviewed, and accepted the proposals Stilwell had drawn up to recover Burma, to which the Chinese would bring ninety divisions, in three groups of thirty each, to effective combat strength. The first group was to be ready by early January 1944; the second group, reequipped after the reopening of the China-India road, by August 1944; and the third group by January 1945. Stilwell's plan also committed China "to participate according to the agreed plan in the recovery of Burma" with combined attacks from Ledo and Yunnan. Chiang's expectations were for an "all-out" Allied effort early in 1944 to reopen communications to China through Burma, using land, air, and naval forces; American equipment for the ninety divisions specified above; and 10,000 tons of material to be delivered per month to China by the Hump air transport operation.[24] Only after receiving the American general's proposals did

---

[23] Gao Sulan, ed., *Jiang Zhongzheng zongtong dang'an shilüe gaoben* [Archives of President Chiang Kai-shek: Draft chronology] (Taibei: Guoshiguan, 2011), vol. 55, 123–74 (hereafter cited as *SLGB*); *ZMZSC*, vol. 3, no. 3, 270–82; *CKSD*, October 19 and 20, 1943, Box 43.

[24] Barbara W. Tuchman, *Stilwell and the American Experience in China, 1911–45* (New York: Macmillan, 1970), 398–99.

Map 13.2: Burma map.

Chiang, for the first time, list the Burma campaign as one of the outstand-ing issues to be presented at the Cairo conference.[25]

Sifting through Chiang's personal diaries and his daily records sur-rounding the Cairo summit, one can argue that, on the eve of the sum-mit, even if Chiang was not deliberately neglecting the proposed Allied counteroffensive in Burma, his attitude toward the issue was lukewarm. Unenthusiastic as he was about sending Chinese forces to recapture Burma, perhaps Chiang did not realize that insisting on the principles and preconditions for China's participation in the Burma counteroffensive as laid out in Stilwell's plan would cost him and his government dearly in China's relations with its closest war allies. This is also evidence of Chiang's inexperience in handling global war-planning conferences.

THE LOST TERRITORIES

In the days following Stilwell's submission of plans for the Burma cam-paign, Chiang's attention shifted from military issues to political and diplomatic ones. He and his top aides now found it imperative to clearly define Chinese territories that had been lost to the Japanese, making geo-strategic concerns dominant in the top Chinese leaders' agenda.[26] Just half a year before the Cairo conference, Chiang had published his book *China's Destiny*, in which he drew an idealized picture of postwar China's territo-rial and defense landscape (see chapter 6). According to Chiang, China's peripheral areas, including Manchuria, Taiwan, the Ryukyu Islands, Mon-golia, Xinjiang, Tibet, and even the remote Pamir and Himalayan regions, were all "strategically essential" for the country's postwar national de-fense.[27] Chiang's grand statements, dealing with such sensitive subjects as China's likely territorial expansion, received mixed reactions and specula-

---

[25] *CKSD*, November 12, 1943, Box 43. In his diary Chiang set the British commitment to launch amphibious and naval operations as his precondition for China's participation in the campaign.

[26] Alan M. Wachman, *Why Taiwan? Geostrategic Rationales for China's Territorial Integ-rity* (Stanford, CA: Stanford University Press, 2007), 69–82.

[27] Chiang Kai-shek, *China's Destiny* (New York: Roy, 1947), 9–11.

tion abroad. Although the British were apprehensive about Chiang's professed ambitions toward Tibet and the adjacent territories under the British Raj, the Americans seemed relieved. Roosevelt, for example, was more than pleased to have the Ryukyu Islands returned to postwar China, an idea he had proposed to T.V. Soong in 1942.[28]

As the summit approached, however, Chiang was perspicacious enough to differentiate idealism from realpolitik in international affairs. To persuade the Allied leaders that it was in their best interest to support China's territorial restoration after V-J Day, Chiang placed pragmatic considerations at the forefront. Legally, the Ryukyu Islands, a quasi-independent kingdom paying tribute to the Qing imperial court, had never been a formal part of China. The Qing lost Taiwan and the Pescadores as a result of its war with Japan in 1894–1995, but it lost its tributary patronage over the Ryukyu Islands through an ambiguous and gradual process. In 1879, Tokyo officially made the islands into its Okinawa Prefecture, marking the end of the kingdom's tributary ties with China. The Qing's defeat by Japan in 1894–1895 dimmed any lingering hope of the islands' return to China's even nominal jurisdiction.[29]

If legality and historical legitimacy may have discouraged Chiang from accepting Roosevelt's goodwill and reclaiming the Ryukyu Islands, pragmatism and realism, especially war-torn China's lack of physical strength in East Asia, were the most decisive in determining the islands' future. As Chiang Kai-shek would argue in Chongqing after he returned from Cairo, China would have difficulty in governing Ryukyu, even were the islands returned to its territorial sway, due to a serious lack of naval capability for decades to come.[30] Considering that both Ryukyu and Korea were once imperial China's tributaries, rather than integrated parts of the

[28] See T.V. Soong's personal memorandum, "Summary of Impressions, 1943," T.V. Soong Papers, Box 32.

[29] George H. Kerr, *Okinawa: The History of an Island People* (North Clarendon, VT: Tuttle, 2000), 342–420. On Qing China's loss of Ryukyu to Japan in the 1870s, see also Michael H. Hunt, *The Making of a Special Relationship: The United States and China to 1914* (New York: Columbia University Press, 1985), 15–142.

[30] See Supreme National Defense Council minute, December 20, 1943, in Qin Xiaoyi, ed., *Guangfu Taiwan zhi chouhua yu shouxiang jieshou* (Taipei: KMT Party Historical Committee, 1990), 36–38.

empire, Chiang decided to remove both territories from the list of areas to be returned to China's orbit, thus leaving Manchuria and Taiwan as his main targets to reclaim, with the Allies' support.[31]

Chiang also contemplated the future status of Hong Kong and Tibet. With little hesitation, he decided to avoid any substantive discussions, not to mention possible quarrels, with the British over the two territories.[32] He again thought about the disposition of Japan and Japan's compensation for China's losses after the war. Ideally, Chiang thought, after Tokyo surrendered Roosevelt would allow China to share an undefined percentage of Japanese naval and commercial ships, as well as its warplanes and ammunition, and to take over Japanese public and private possessions in occupied areas.[33] But judging from his personal diaries, at this point Chiang seemed anguished and anxious, not only undecided about his conference agenda but also troubled about how to present himself in his first meeting with the leaders of the two most powerful Western countries, both of which had been among China's imperialist foes and whose recent friendship with China remained fragile. As a result, while contemplating preserving and reclaiming China's rights and asking for compensation from Japan, Chiang also wrote:

> I will talk with Roosevelt and Churchill in accordance with a spirit of demanding nothing and offering nothing. I should exchange viewpoints frankly with them on military, political, and economic issues, but should not be troubled by any anxiety about gains and losses.[34]

> My orientation for the coming meeting with Roosevelt and Churchill ought to be one of seeking no fame and wealth but self-sufficiency. Not expecting benevolence from the others, I can avoid inviting humiliation. I should also avoid taking the initiative on such issues as the disposal of Japan and Japan's compensation for

---

[31] *CKSD*, November 15, 1943, Box 43.
[32] Ibid.
[33] Ibid., November 14, 1943.
[34] *CKSD*, November 13, 1943, Box 43.

China's losses, and should wait for the Americans and the British to make the first move. Thus, the United States and Britain will appreciate and respect our selfless stance in this world war.[35]

One could argue that, on the eve of Cairo, Chiang agonized over how to achieve China's objectives and how, at the same time, to impress the Western leaders with his sterling motives. He definitely wanted a perfect performance. As it turned out, however, Chiang's comportment in Cairo was a cruel disappointment to his wartime allies, especially President Roosevelt, who had hitherto supported Nationalist China but who afterward became disillusioned and disappointed by Chiang and his government.

CHIANG'S FIRST DAYS AT CAIRO

On the morning of November 18, 1943, just a few hours before his flight was to take off from Chongqing, Chiang Kai-shek and his top aides finalized China's priority list of seven issues to be broached in Cairo: (1) a new international peace organization; (2) the creation of a Far Eastern Commission to cope with postwar Japanese affairs; (3) the CCOS involving China, the United States, and Britain; (4) the regulation of Japanese-occupied territories; (5) the Burma campaign; (6) Korea's independence; and (7) China's recovery of Manchuria and Taiwan.[36] The Chiangs and their entourage then set off for Cairo, with a stopover in Agra, India, where they met with local British officials and toured the Taj Mahal. During Chiang's brief stay in India, many British found him uncompromising and egocentric and felt that his staff were terrified of him.[37] The animosity was mutual; Chiang found the Taj Mahal "a vestige of barbarian past lacking any cultural significance," which "left him with little impression but disdain." He thought that the Taj Mahal was kept intact only by the British colonial authorities and that it could not compare with China's great

---

[35] Ibid., November 17, 1943.
[36] *CKSD*, November 18, 1943, Box 43.
[37] Heiferman, *The Cairo Conference of 1943*, 55–56.

historical sites and legacies.[38] What worried Chiang most was Madame Chiang's serious skin allergy, conjunctivitis, and poisoning from taking the wrong drug; her swollen face would not be relieved until the Chinese party arrived in Cairo on the morning of November 21.[39]

In the afternoon of the twenty-first, Chiang Kai-shek paid a courtesy call on Winston Churchill. Churchill was ill and in a bad mood; most important, however, he had never been enthusiastic about inviting the Chinese to Cairo, noting later that they would "throw the conference out of gear." Churchill was equally upset that he and Roosevelt would have little opportunity to thrash out a united front that they could present to Stalin in Tehran because of the presence of the Chinese and Roosevelt's preoccupation with placating the Chiangs.[40] Chiang's diary, on the other hand, indicates that his first encounter with Churchill left him with a far better impression of the British prime minister than he had expected.[41] But that view would change in a few days.

At 11:00 a.m. on November 22, Churchill made a return visit to the Chiangs at their villa. The prime minister's first impression was that Chiang Kai-shek was "calm, reserved, and efficient," at the "apex of his power." Churchill described Madame Chiang as "a most remarkable and charming personality."[42] In the afternoon, Roosevelt, who had arrived that morning, hosted a tea party in the Chiangs' honor. While Allied leaders were busy socializing, top American and British military officials were planning their first CCOS meeting. When the U.S. military leaders met with their British counterparts at 3:00 p.m., General George Marshall raised the idea of the Chinese participating in CCOS meetings on a regular basis, as proposed by Chiang Kai-shek, when matters relating to the CBI theater were to be discussed. Marshall also suggested that the same invitation be extended to the Soviets when matters of concern to them were brought up.

---

[38] *CKSD*, November 19, 1943, Box 43.

[39] *CKSD*, November 19, 20, and 21, 1943, Box 43.

[40] Heiferman, *The Cairo Conference of 1943*, 61–63.

[41] *CKSD*, November 21, 1943, Box 43.

[42] Winston S. Churchill, *The Second World War*. Vol. 5, *Closing the Ring* (New York: Houghton Mifflin, 1986), 329.

But Marshall's proposal to expand the CCOS to a four-power body did not sit well with the British; even some of his U.S. colleagues, including Admiral Ernst King, objected. After additional discussion, it was agreed that the Chinese be invited to send representatives to CCOS meetings when matters of immediate concern to China were to be discussed, but that they not be granted a permanent place on the CCOS, either before or after the war.[43] One of Chiang's original conference priorities was thus compromised before the formal proceedings had begun.

The first CCOS gathering, on November 22, also concerned the schedule of events and the agenda for the following day, most notably the Burma campaign. Chiang's aides, shocked to discover that they had been excluded from the gathering, sought admission, in vain, with Stilwell's assistance.[44] Later that evening, Chiang was surprised to learn from Stilwell that the agenda for the formal proceedings the next morning had been decided by the Americans and the British at the meeting, with the Chinese proposals largely ignored.[45] According to Stilwell, who was not aware of the true conference agenda until the last minute, Chiang's aides were worried about what would lie in store for the Chinese at the formal proceedings the following day.[46] Chiang's reliance on Stilwell to handle the Burma counteroffensive and the lack of preparation on the part of the Chinese delegation over the issue would exact a heavy price in the days to come.

THE SHOW BEGINS

The first plenary session began at 11:00 a.m. on November 23. As the presiding officer, Roosevelt welcomed Chiang Kai-shek and Madame

[43] U.S. Department of State, *Foreign Relations of the United States Diplomatic Papers: The Conferences at Cairo and Tehran, 1943* (Washington, DC: U.S. Government Printing Office, 1961), 304–6 (hereafter cited as *FRUS 1943*).

[44] *ZMZSC*, vol. 3, no. 3, 514–15.

[45] *CKSD*, November 22, 1943, Box 43; *SLGB* 55:456.

[46] Joseph Stilwell's diary entry for November 22, 1943, Joseph Stilwell Papers, Box 44, Hoover Institution Archives, Stanford, California (hereafter cited as *JSD*).

Chiang to the council of the Allies and said he hoped the Cairo summit would bear fruit for many years to come. Roosevelt then invited Lord Mountbatten, supreme commander of SEAC, to present a survey of the proposed activities in Southeast Asia. Mountbatten outlined his goals for 1944, including a tripartite offensive in Burma that was more restricted in scope than the one discussed in Chongqing; he now called for launching a campaign in northern Burma only, in January 1944, at which time British units based in India would move east toward Burma and seize key positions in that part of the country. According to Mountbatten's plan, as British forces moved east into Burma, a Chinese army, trained by Stilwell in India (the X Force), would join them; a second Chinese army (the Y Force) would move west into Burma from China's Yunnan Province. The hope was that the boldness of the advance, through what was assumed to be impassable jungle, and the novel methods of supply supporting the venture, namely parachute drops, would take the Japanese by surprise.[47]

Chiang, astonished by this unexpected change in the geographic scope of the offensive, asked questions about the logistics of supply and naval and air cover, including whether the Allies could increase monthly tonnage over the Hump, how many additional aircraft the Allies could make available for the offensive, and how large a naval task force the Allies would assemble in the Bay of Bengal. Churchill promised that the "formidable" British Royal Navy would send two large battleships, four large carriers, and ten small carriers to ensure command of the Bay of Bengal. Chiang, although pleased, emphasized again that a major amphibious operation and naval supremacy were essential. Mandalay in central Burma, not Myitkyina in the far north of the country, should be the target, and the Hump air transport should deliver 10,000 tons a month to China.[48] Churchill responded by claiming that British naval operations could not be coordinated with Chinese land operations in Burma because the main British fleet base was almost 3,000 miles from Burma. In Churchill's view, the success of land operations in Burma did not hinge entirely on a simultaneous land and sea action. Because the Royal Navy would not be able to

---

[47] *FRUS 1943*, 311–12; *ZMZSC*, vol. 3, no. 3, 535–36.
[48] *FRUS 1943*, 313–14; *ZMZSC*, vol. 3, no. 3, 536–37.

send a full-strength task force into the Bay of Bengal until the late spring or early summer of 1944, Churchill urged Chiang and Roosevelt to pursue the campaign originally conceived by Mountbatten and Stilwell.[49]

Chiang, although dissatisfied with Churchill's opinions, was, as his diary reveals, not too worried at that moment. Although Churchill disagreed that naval and land operations be coordinated and launched simultaneously, Chiang felt that the other participants had "tacitly consented to [his] opinion." He therefore thought the overall outcome of the first formal session was "not bad" but regretted not having learned his English well, thus preventing him from communicating directly with the Allied leaders.[50]

Mountbatten, concerned about Chiang's reluctance to commit to the Burma offensive, called on the Generalissimo in the afternoon to try to convince him that SEAC's proposed goals were reasonable. According to Mountbatten's recollection, Chiang "approved of" the idea of an offensive in Burma but felt that the current plan was too modest. Chiang wanted a bolder venture that would include the capture of Rangoon and Lashio and the reopening of the land route from Burma to China. Mountbatten explained that such a plan was impossible and could not succeed. But Chiang, unmoved, allegedly told the British lord, "Never mind, we will carry it out [retake Burma] all the same."[51] Curiously, Chinese historical documents only record Mountbatten's verbal explanation to Chiang, but no mention is made of Chiang's response or "approval."[52] Given the subsequent huge controversy surrounding China's participation in recovering Burma, if Mountbatten's recollection was authentic, Chiang's verbal promise might have been one of the crucial factors in the intra-Allied conflict over the Burma campaign the following year.

While Mountbatten was meeting with Chiang, U.S. military chiefs were meeting with their Chinese counterparts to solicit comments and recommendations regarding the Burma campaign. The Chinese, according to General Henry Arnold and Admiral William Leahy, disappointingly

[49] *FRUS 1943*, 314–15; Heiferman, *The Cairo Conference of 1943*, 73–74.
[50] *CKSD*, November 23, 1943, Box 43.
[51] Philip Ziegler, *Mountbatten* (New York: Smithmark, 1986), 262.
[52] *SLGB* 55:466–70.

had little to say other than being willing to commit to an offensive proposed by SEAC.[53] An hour later, that same group of Chinese generals was invited to attend its first CCOS meeting with the Americans and the British, with the focus, again, on Mountbatten's plans for the Burma campaign. The CCOS hoped that the Chinese would clarify Chiang's position, comment on Mountbatten's proposals, raise questions, and put forward suggestions. General Shang Zhen, head of the Chinese delegation, however, stated that he had not had time to study the plans and would prefer to discuss them the next day. The CCOS then suggested that the Chinese discuss their contingency plans for deploying the Yunnan Force in the opening phases of Operation Buccaneer. Once again, there was silence.[54] The Chinese generals' poor performance and lack of preparation alarmed their Allied counterparts, who were disturbed by China's behavior and upset about a "ghastly waste of time."[55] This meeting virtually doomed any hope of Chinese participation in future CCOS meetings.

Chiang Kai-shek had planned to attend the CCOS session and to comment on Mountbatten's plans; for reasons still unclear, however, he canceled at the last minute.[56] We should note that since he began planning for Cairo, Chiang's mind had never been on the Burma campaign. To him, the dinner meeting with Roosevelt that same evening was of paramount importance. To Chiang's delight, the dinner went most satisfactorily. In their three-hour discussion, the two men seemed to agree on virtually all matters. Chiang concurred with Roosevelt's view that Japan's future politics should be up to the Japanese people and proposed that reparations be paid to China in Japanese industrial and war machinery, merchant ships, and other material goods. Chiang listened to Roosevelt's analysis of Communism, and emphasized that Moscow could not be trusted. Roosevelt endorsed the return of Manchuria and Taiwan to China, and both agreed on a vision of the postwar world, especially ending colonialism and independence for Korea and Indochina. In addition, Chiang mentioned, without giving details, that the two leaders discussed China's possible inclusion

---

[53] Heiferman, *The Cairo Conference of 1943*, 75–76.
[54] *FRUS 1943*, 314–15; *ZMZSC*, vol. 3, no. 3, 538–39.
[55] Heiferman, *The Cairo Conference of 1943*, 77–78.
[56] *JSD*, November 23, 1943, Box 44.

in the CCOS, Soviet participation in the Pacific War, the Chinese Communists, and the situation in Xinjiang. The Burma campaign was not mentioned.[57]

In his diary, Chiang summed up the talk as "exceedingly satisfactory," for he finally had the opportunity to present Roosevelt with his ideas, culled from the list of conference priorities that he and his top aides had laboriously compiled before coming to Cairo. Whether Roosevelt was equally sanguine is less certain, and whether Roosevelt was just showing his usual charm and feeling out the Chiangs deserves our further scrutiny. According to Elliott Roosevelt, the president's son, after the meeting his father said he was convinced that many of Chiang's best forces were not being committed to the war against Japan but were being deployed against the Chinese Communists in northwestern China. "Why [aren't] Chiang's troops fighting at all?" Roosevelt asked, suggesting that this might account for Chiang's efforts to obstruct Stilwell's training Chinese troops in India because Stilwell would not tolerate hoarding those troops and their supplies for a postwar civil war.[58] A better grasp of China's situation and a close assessment of the Chiangs during the dinner led Roosevelt to decide to broach the complicated Chinese Communist issue a few days later.

THE BREACH WIDENS

General George Marshall visited Chiang Kai-shek on the afternoon of November 24 to hear Chiang's opinions about Mountbatten's proposals and to persuade Chiang to give them a green light. Chiang remained skeptical, saying that unless the British agreed to increase their commitment substantially to the proposed Burma offensive, he would not commit his India (X) and Yunnan (Y) forces to the fray.[59] According to Chiang, Marshall said he understood China's position and was "deeply moved" by his elaboration and explanation of the situation.[60] Marshall then invited

---

[57] *CKSD*, November 23, 1943, Box 43; *FRUS 1943*, 322–25.
[58] Elliott Roosevelt, *As He Saw It* (New York: Duell, Sloan, and Pearce, 1946), 142.
[59] *FRUS 1943*, 334–35; *SLGB* 55:475.
[60] *CKSD*, November 24, 1943, Box 43.

Chiang to participate in the second CCOS session that afternoon. Chiang agreed, but later decided not to attend. This indecision was repeated and surely frustrated the Allies. When the session began, Marshall was grilled by his British colleagues about Chiang Kai-shek's current view of Operation Buccaneer. Marshall reported that Chiang disapproved of it because the burden of responsibility and losses lay on the Chinese, with no guarantee of victory. Marshall went on to say that Chiang would approve the campaign only under the following conditions: First, the British must commit to launching an amphibious operation, preferably in the Andaman Islands, simultaneously with the Chinese land campaign in Burma. Second, British forces must agree to the occupation of Mandalay in central Burma and, later, of Rangoon, a substantive increase to the scope of Mountbatten's plan but much closer to what had been discussed in October in Chongqing.[61]

The British were shocked and angry. Field Marshal Alan Brooke noted that Chiang had suddenly decided that, unless several "impossible" conditions were fulfilled, he refused to play his part in the Allied operations.[62] When the Chinese generals arrived at the session, they reiterated Chiang's opposition to the Burma campaign, posed a series of trivial technical questions, and even questioned the capability of the British forces, all of which only served to increase the British military chiefs' fury and contempt. As General Shang Zhen reminded his peers that the airlift to China should not drop below 10,000 tons per month, regardless of the needs of the land operation that might be approved by the CCOS, even the patient Mountbatten could not conceal his anger, arguing that it was "illogical" to call for a more extensive land operation in Burma yet no reduction in the 10,000 tons for China. He asked the Chinese to choose between the supplies to China or the land operation in Burma. General Marshall seconded Mountbatten's statement, telling General Shang that, if the Chinese wanted to open a new road from Burma to China, they must fight to do so.[63] Marshall's words added to the already tense atmosphere of the conference. When Chiang Kai-shek learned of the rancorous discussions at

---

[61] *FRUS 1943*, 335–38; *ZMZSC*, vol. 3, no. 3, 541.

[62] Heiferman, *The Cairo Conference of 1943*, 86.

[63] *FRUS 1943*, 343–45; *ZMZSC*, vol. 3, no. 3, 542–44.

the CCOS, he privately complained that Marshall had not defended China's stance strongly enough.[64]

That evening, Churchill hosted a dinner for Chiang Kai-shek and Madame Chiang. According to Chiang's diary, the two leaders discussed Mountbatten's planned offensive in Burma at length. Before dinner, Churchill led Chiang to the map room to show him the details of the proposed deployments of units of the Royal Navy in the Bay of Bengal, including a timetable for completing the buildup. Churchill then assured Chiang that all British forces would be in place by May 1944, which greatly disappointed Chiang, who had wished the deployment to take place in early 1944. According to Chiang, after dinner, Churchill again led Chiang to the map room to lecture him on the current state of affairs of the British military forces in each theater. He continued talking with great enthusiasm for about an hour, while Chiang tired of listening to him. In his diary, Chiang wrote that he regarded Churchill as a "typical figure of the Anglo-Saxon nation ... narrow-minded, slippery, selfish, and stubborn."[65]

Although Churchill's willingness to provide details on the deployment of British forces was a step in the right direction for the Chinese, they still had reservations about the operation in Burma and wanted more information before deciding to join the Allies in a new Burma campaign.[66] Chiang perhaps did not care about, or doubted, whether the campaign could be successful. It was therefore no surprise that, in the third session of the CCOS (convened just after the famous "Big Three" picture-taking session on the afternoon of November 25), the impasse between Chiang and his allies could not be resolved. With no Chinese generals attending the session, Mountbatten, having met with Chiang earlier in the morning, shared more unpleasant news with his American and British peers. Chiang was not only adamant that the Burma campaign was too modest and timid but also vetoed any diversion of Hump supplies from China to support operations in Burma. The Generalissimo intimated that if the CCOS could not

---

[64] *CKSD*, November 24, 1943, Box 43.
[65] Ibid., November 25, 1943, Box 43.
[66] Louis Allen, *Burma: The Longest War, 1941–1945* (London: Cassell, 2000), 157–70.

make such a guarantee, he would take up the matter with Roosevelt.[67] Key CCOS members were angry; Alan Brooke complained bitterly that Chiang was busy bargaining to obtain the maximum possible from the Allies, an impression that Chiang had wanted to avoid before attending the conference.[68] Mountbatten allegedly accused Chiang of playing the Anglo-American Allies against one another at the summit and worried this would sabotage any progress in 1944.[69]

What Chiang really cared about was not Burma but China's relations with the United States. When Roosevelt hosted a tea party for the Chiangs on the evening of November 25, the Generalissimo took the opportunity to discuss a wide variety of issues with the president. Chiang lobbied for Roosevelt's support in organizing a new Sino-American Joint Chiefs of Staff if China's participation in the existing CCOS was unfeasible. He also urged Roosevelt to set up a new Sino-American political council to strengthen bilateral relations and provide military supplies with which to equip Chiang's thirty divisions.[70] Also discussed was the political situation in China, with Chiang indicating he would attempt to improve relations with the Chinese Communists on his return from Cairo, as he had promised in his dinner meeting with the president on November 23.[71]

No source materials have been found to indicate that any serious discussion of the gridlock over plans for the campaign in Burma took place during the tea party. It thus does not appear that Chiang sought the president's support on this issue or that Roosevelt tried to persuade the Generalissimo to give a green light to Mountbatten's more conservative plan to recover only the northern part of Burma. Ronald Heiferman argues that that was because Roosevelt had decided to avoid confronting the Chinese, being more concerned with boosting their morale than forcing them to confront reality.[72] It is equally likely that Chiang had never prioritized the Burma campaign as an agenda issue at the summit; after the

---

[67] *FRUS 1943*, 346–47.
[68] Heiferman, *The Cairo Conference of 1943*, 97.
[69] Ibid.
[70] *CKSD*, November 26, 1943, Box 43.
[71] Roosevelt, *As He Saw It*, 158.
[72] Heiferman, *The Cairo Conference of 1943*, 100.

tea party with Roosevelt, Chiang's mind went back to November 2, when he had begun working on China's conference agendas, including items such as U.S. economic assistance and possible foreign investments. He asked himself if it was possible to gain Roosevelt's support for another loan to China. Having thought about those issues, Chiang decided to send his wife to meet with the president and try her luck the next morning, thinking that it would do no harm to try and that there was nothing to lose.[73]

THE CRUEL REALITY CHECK

In his diary entry for November 26, Chiang noted that, while conversing with Roosevelt at the tea party, the president's attitude toward him was more amicable than in their previous dinner meeting.[74] On an even happier note, when Madame Chiang visited Roosevelt the next morning to discuss the dangerous economic and financial problems faced by the Chinese Nationalist government, the president agreed to provide economic assistance to China, including working out a new loan to Chongqing.[75] Excited at this unbelievable achievement, Chiang gave all the credit to his wife; he later awarded her the Order of the Flying Cloud, the highest-ranking award she could possibly get, on their return to China.[76]

If Chiang believed in Roosevelt's "positive" attitude toward him, he could have been wrong. After a few days of close contact, Roosevelt's opinion of Chiang and the situation in China gradually changed, and he began developing new ideas on how to implement his China policy. Late at night on November 25, a few hours after his tea party with the Chiangs, Roosevelt held a long talk with Stilwell, during which they discussed the many problems the U.S. general faced in the CBI theater, including his difficulties with the Generalissimo. The president, sympathetic to Stilwell's problems, tried to comfort the general by sharing his own frustra-

---

[73] *CKSD*, November 26, 1943, Box 43.
[74] Ibid.
[75] *CKSD*, November 27, 1943, Box 43; *SLGB* 55:495.
[76] Sterling Seagrave, *The Soong Dynasty* (New York: Harper Perennial, 1986), 350.

tion with Chiang. According to Frank Dorn, one of Stilwell's subordinates, Roosevelt, "fed up with" the Generalissimo, advised the general that night to "get rid of him [Chiang] once and for all" if Stilwell could not get along with him and could not replace him with someone else.[77]

It is unlikely that Roosevelt would make a public statement on this matter, and whether Dorn's hostile account is credible remains open to question. More significantly, that night the president told his son Elliott that, in response to U.S. pressure, Chiang had agreed to suspend hostilities against the Chinese Communist Party and to form a democratic government after the war. Roosevelt also mentioned that Chiang had agreed, in principle, to include the Chinese Communists in his postwar government as long as the British were not allowed to return to their privileged positions in Shanghai, Canton, and other former treaty ports.[78] Chiang might have only been paying lip service to Roosevelt's questions regarding the Chinese Communists, but apparently the president took his words seriously. Beginning in 1944, the way in which the Nationalist government handled the Chinese Communist issue would create a large rift between Chongqing and Washington.

On the afternoon of November 26, the American and British military leaders met for their last CCOS session, during which the British raised issues regarding Operation Overlord, the proposed Allied invasion of German-occupied France, and associated activities in the Mediterranean. The British then suggested that, if they received the go-ahead to invade and capture the Greek island of Rhodes in the Mediterranean, Operation Buccaneer might have to be delayed or scrapped because the Allies did not have the resources to carry out operations in Western Europe, Burma, and the Mediterranean simultaneously. The British suggestion shocked and angered the Americans, who argued that the Burma campaign was vital to the Pacific War and that its cancellation would have grave political consequences. The British, who were more interested in defeating Germany than in fighting Japan, pushed back, stating that the Soviets would press Churchill and Roosevelt for an early date for the launch of Operation

[77] Frank Dorn, *Walkout with Stilwell in Burma* (New York: Crowell, 1971), 76.
[78] Roosevelt, *As He Saw It*, 163–64.

Overlord when they met later at Tehran. If this happened, the British claimed, they would have to defer amphibious operations in the Bay of Bengal to ensure enough landing craft in Europe. No agreement had been reached when the session closed.[79]

While the CCOS was debating operations Overlord and Buccaneer, Chiang Kai-shek held his last personal meeting with Roosevelt, during which, for the first time, Chiang broached the impasse over plans for 1944, blaming British unwillingness to commit to the Burma campaign, without which, Chiang told the president, he would have no choice but to withhold Chinese forces from further engagement in Southeast Asia.[80] Unaware of the ongoing CCOS discussion about the possible cancellation of Operation Buccaneer, Roosevelt assured Chiang that, before the conference ended, he would get Churchill's consent to the Burma campaign and to an expanded naval presence in the Bay of Bengal, meaning that there would be simultaneous operations in northern and southern Burma in the spring of 1944, as Chiang had wished.[81] A few days later, before returning to China, Chiang wrote in his personal diary that he was unconvinced that Roosevelt's assurances would hold true; nor did he believe that the British amphibious operations in Burma would happen before the fall of 1944. As the Burma campaign was never Chiang's priority, however, he saw "no harm in hearing what Roosevelt said."[82]

The last act began at 5:00 p.m., November 26, when high officials from the three parties gathered to hammer out a final communiqué to distribute to the press. Because little progress had been made in resolving differences between the Allies and laying plans for 1944, not much could be publicly stated. In the end, the three Allied leaders and their entourages worked to make the communiqué as innocuous and general as possible. The first paragraph stated that the Allies had "agreed upon future military

[79] *FRUS 1943*, 358–65; Keith Sainsbury, *The Turning Point: Roosevelt, Stalin, Churchill, and Chiang Kai-shek, 1943: The Moscow, Cairo, and Teheran Conferences* (Oxford: Oxford University Press, 1985), 119–23.

[80] *SLGB* 55:495; Liang Jingchun, *General Stilwell in China, 1942–1944: The Full Story* (New York: St. John's University Press, 1972), 150–51.

[81] *CKSD*, November 30, 1943, Box 43; *SLGB* 55:495–96; Liang, *General Stilwell in China*, 151.

[82] *CKSD*, November 30, 1943, Box 43; *SLGB* 55:512–13.

operations against Japan" and expressed their resolve to "bring unrelenting pressure against their brutal enemies by sea, land, and air." The second paragraph, which pleased the Chinese, specified, "all the territories Japan has stolen from the Chinese, such as Manchuria, Formosa, and the Pescadores, shall be restored to the Republic of China." It also stated, "in due course, Korea shall be free and independent." At the end, the communiqué expressed the three Allies' intentions that their war with Japan would "continue to persevere in the serious and prolonged operations necessary to procure the unconditional surrender of Japan."[83] With the communiqué finalized, the summit ended.

FINALE

Before Chiang Kai-shek left Cairo for China, he issued two crucial instructions that shed light on his thoughts about the Cairo summit. First, he instructed Wang Chonghui, his national security adviser, to use the Cairo communiqué to advance China's domestic political propaganda. In addition to highlighting the Allied commitments to Japan's unconditional surrender and to restoration of China's lost territories, Chiang especially wanted the Chinese people to recognize his and his wife's achievements in making the summit (1) a significant step in fulfilling Roosevelt's policy of sustaining the freedom and independence of all of the nations; and (2) a turning point in transforming Britain's policy in the Far East. Chiang also dictated that the propaganda emphasize Madame Chiang's contributions to the success of the conference, as well as the Allied leaders' recognition of her performance.[84] Chiang thus used the summit and the resultant communiqué to boost Chinese morale and to further elevate his and his wife's power and prestige at home.

The other instruction Chiang gave was trickier. He told his staff and General Stilwell that he had received verbal assurances from Roosevelt that the British would ultimately agree to the Burma campaign but that a

---

[83] *FRUS 1943*, 366–67, 448–49; *ZMZSC*, vol. 3, no. 3, 530–33.
[84] *ZMZSC*, vol. 3, no. 3, 548.

formal commitment had not yet been made to Operation Buccaneer. Chiang therefore ordered Stilwell to remain in Cairo until Roosevelt and Churchill, who were leaving for Tehran to meet with Joseph Stalin on the morning of November 27, returned to Cairo so that Stilwell could again press the president and the prime minister to give final approval to the amphibious operation in the Andamans.[85] At this point, Chiang felt sure that Churchill, unwilling to devote more resources to SEAC at the expense of the war in Europe, would not make the slightest concession to U.S. opinion regarding Operation Buccaneer. Moreover, he predicted there would be no British amphibious operation against Burma in the spring of 1944.[86] Chiang's decision to ask Stilwell to stay therefore served dual purposes: the American general would be the scapegoat if the plans for the Burma campaign eventually came to naught, which Chiang believed to be the likely scenario, and by keeping Stilwell in Cairo, Chiang wanted to show the Allied leaders that he was enthusiastic about the campaign. Chiang felt that, if China were not to send forces to Burma, lacking a commitment by the British, he would not take the blame.

Stilwell was unhappy to be left behind to clean up the Generalissimo's mess. But perhaps what stunned the American general, a keen supporter of the Burma campaign, was the plan's inevitable outcome. While at Tehran, Stalin insisted that Operation Overlord, plus a coordinated landing in southern France, be undertaken as soon as possible, reiterating that Soviet Russia would join the war against Japan once Germany had been defeated. Although Churchill fought hard for the operations in the Mediterranean, Roosevelt and Stalin's support of Overlord prevailed, promptly supplying the British with an excuse to cancel Buccaneer and use its landing craft for southern France.[87] When the Americans and British returned to Cairo on December 2, Operation Buccaneer became the crux of an intense struggle between them. The Americans vehemently opposed abandoning Bucca-

---

[85] *JSD*, November 27, 1943, Box 44; Liang, *General Stilwell in China*, 161.

[86] *CKSD*, November 28 and 30, 1943, Box 43.

[87] Paul D. Mayle, *Eureka Summit: Agreement in Principle and the Big Three at Tehran, 1943* (Cranbury, NJ: Associated University Presses, 1987), 102–3; Keith Eubank, *Summit at Teheran: The Untold Story* (New York: William Morrow, 1985), 251–54; Sainsbury, *The Turning Point*, 249–55.

neer, for that would mean Chiang's withholding his forces, thus causing the entire Burma campaign to fail. Without that campaign, the Americans feared that the Japanese would be better able to resist the Allied Pacific advance and that the cancellation would damage Chinese morale. The British remained unmoved, continuing to bombard their American counterparts with arguments that recovering Western Europe was far more urgent than recapturing Burma and that Stalin's commitment to fight Japan had greatly reduced the strategic importance of SEAC. On December 5, a fatigued Roosevelt yielded; in a laconic three-word message to Churchill, he wrote, "Buccaneer is off," thus concluding the two weeks of Cairo-Tehran.[88]

Having made his decision, Roosevelt cabled Chiang in Chongqing with the following message: "Conference with Stalin involves us in combined grand operations on European continent in late spring [of 1944]. … These operations impose so large a requirement of heavy landing craft as to make it impracticable to devote a sufficient number to the amphibious operation in the Bay of Bengal simultaneously with launching of Tarzan [the opening of a new land route to China through northern Burma] to insure success of operation." Roosevelt then asked if Chiang were prepared to go ahead with Tarzan, or preferred to delay until November 1944, when heavy amphibious operation in the Bay of Bengal might be possible.[89]

Before leaving Cairo for the United States on December 7, Roosevelt worried how Sino-American relations might be affected when Chiang received word that Operation Buccaneer had been canceled, feeling that the Generalissimo would not react kindly to his cable.[90] Indeed, although Chiang should have been angry about the news from Cairo, he was not. When Roosevelt's cable reached Chongqing on the evening of December 7, Chiang was having dinner with his son Ching-kuo, and the two were discussing the importance of family genealogy. Chiang, as it turned out, was not surprised and also knew that it would be impossible to change the

---

[88] Mayle, *Eureka Summit*, 157–59; Eubank, *Summit at Teheran*, 389–94; Sainsbury, *The Turning Point*, 285–87.

[89] *FRUS 1943*, 803–4; *ZMZSC*, vol. 3, no. 3, 286.

[90] Roosevelt, *As He Saw It*, 213.

decision made in Cairo. Chiang thus accepted the reality of the decision but also decided to exploit Roosevelt's guilt over canceling Operation Buccaneer and capitulating to the British and thus extract as much as possible from the United States. Thus at peace with the "bad news," Chiang went to sleep earlier than usual, at around 10:00 p.m.[91]

Three days later, Chiang sent a guilt-inducing cable to Roosevelt: "If it should now be known to the Chinese army and people that a radical change of policy is being contemplated, the repercussions would be so disheartening that I fear the consequences of China's ability to hold out much longer." Chiang then argued in the cable that the only remedy was to assure the Chinese people and army of America's concern by "assisting China to hold on with a billion-dollar gold loan to strengthen its economic front and relieve its dire economic needs." In that message to Washington, Chiang also requested that the supplies flown into China over the Hump be doubled and that the warplanes be supplied to be stationed and used in China.[92]

Having obtained a clearer picture of the Chiangs and China's domestic situation, Roosevelt decided to abandon his earlier attitude toward the Chinese Nationalists and Sino-American relations. Thus he reacted to the cable politely but firmly, saying that doubling the Hump supplies to China was impossible. He also made no promises about a new loan except to suggest that he would take the matter up with the Treasury Department. Further, instead of taking a sympathetic view on the Burma campaign issue, as he had during the summit, Roosevelt now urged Chiang not to withdraw his forces from Operation Tarzan, intimating that doing so would weaken China's support in the United States.[93] In the meantime, although both Mountbatten and Stilwell were pushing Chiang to give a green light to Operation Tarzan, Chiang's opposition remained steadfast. The Burma campaign had never been Chiang's priority, and he was now further convinced that, without the simultaneous Allied amphibious operation, the Chinese would repeat their disastrous spring 1942 defeat in

[91] *CKSD*, December 7, 1943, Box 43; *ZMZSC*, vol. 3, no. 3, 578.
[92] *ZMZSC*, vol. 3, no. 3, 287–88; *SLGB* 55:595–600.
[93] *ZMZSC*, vol. 3, no. 3, 289–90; *SLGB* 55:643–46.

Burma.[94] During the last weeks of 1943, although most of the Chinese were still exhilarated by the glory their country and top leader had enjoyed at the Cairo summit, the battle between Chiang and his allies had just begun.

AFTERWORD

As 1943 neared its end, China's relationship with its war allies was becoming worse. In March 1944, under heavy pressure from the Allies, Chiang cabled Roosevelt, saying he refused to deploy his Yunnan force into northern Burma, as he now faced a strong Japanese offensive in China.[95] An unsympathetic Roosevelt responded in early April that American aid would be "unjustified" if the Yunnan force did not cross the Salween River into Burma.[96] Meanwhile, Stilwell suggested to Marshall that Washington stop its Lend-Lease aid to Nationalist China unless Chiang's Yunnan force immediately began operations. Thus, on April 13, Marshall instructed Stilwell to stop supplies to the Chinese force in Yunnan and instead allocate them to the U.S. Air Force in China. A furious and frustrated Chiang ordered his troops to move.[97] By the summer of 1944, as a result of Japan's Operation Ichigo in China, Allied strategy in East Asia lay in ruins, further straining the relationship between Chongqing and Washington. The deteriorating situation in China and Burma forced Marshall to warn Roosevelt that all the military power and resources in China must now be entrusted to "one individual capable of directing that effort in a fruitful way against the Japanese." Therefore, on July 6, Roosevelt wrote Chiang suggesting that Stilwell be appointed commander of all Chinese forces. The ensuing well-known dispute over Stilwell's recall further damaged the already strained bilateral relations.[98]

---

[94] *CKSD*, December 15, 16, and 17, 1943, Box 43; *SLGB* 55:637–47; *ZMZSC*, vol. 3, no. 3, 291–92.

[95] *ZMZSC*, vol. 3, no. 3, 297–98.

[96] Ibid., 299.

[97] Tuchman, *Stilwell and the American Experience in China*, 566–67.

[98] Hans van de Ven, *War and Nationalism in China, 1925–1945* (London: Routledge, 2003), 54–58; Thorne, *Allies of a Kind*, 401–16.

Fueling the worsening relations between Chiang and Roosevelt was America's intention, around mid-1944, to urge the Nationalists to reconcile with the Chinese Communists, an idea also stemming from the two leaders' meeting in Cairo. The extremely dire war conditions in the CBI theater, in addition to the increasingly corrupt and inefficient Nationalist government, had convinced the Americans that Chiang must mend his rift with the Communists so as to direct his available military strength against Japan and not to launching a civil war.[99]

To Roosevelt, the original purpose of the Cairo summit was to give Chiang Kai-shek the public recognition he desired and needed and thus boost Chinese morale. The purpose of summit, as perceived by Chiang, was to lobby the Americans for more aid and full recognition of China's status as a world power. As the aforementioned analysis has suggested, however, the issues surrounding the Burma campaign, which Chiang had never prioritized and never perceived as imperative, dominated much of the energy and time of the three Allies during the summit. Worse still, perhaps from Chiang's point of view, the supposedly marginal issue of recapturing Burma gradually evolved into a huge controversy among the Allied leaders in 1944, leading to the reemergence of the Stilwell issue, U.S. pressure on Chiang to reconcile with the Communists, the threat to stop U.S. aid to China, and the rapidly waning Sino-American alliance.

In retrospect, although the Cairo summit marked the zenith of Chiang Kai-shek's prestige as a world leader, it also triggered his subsequent downhill slide and that of his regime. It might have been rather difficult for the Chiangs to balance between the public triumph and celebrations that met them upon their return, and the still-secret failures and frustrations. In reconsidering the Cairo legacy and the wartime Sino-U.S. relationship, we are led to the following thesis: Roosevelt's invitation to Chiang to participate in the Cairo summit, which began as an attempt to bolster the Nationalists in their fight against Japan, resulted in a tangle of conflicting personalities among the Allies, unclear and undetermined mil-

---

[99] Schaller, *The US Crusade in China*, 181–188; Warren I. Cohen, *America's Response to China: A History of Sino-American Relations*, 5th ed. (New York: Columbia University Press, 2010), 155–58.

itary strategies, and needed reality checks. In hindsight, whether the Cairo summit was an asset to Chiang and his government remains open to question. Whether what Roosevelt discovered about Chiang and China in Cairo forced the United States into intervening in China's domestic quagmire and a battle for the control of Asia—a battle that continued from the Chinese civil war into the Cold War era—deserves further scrutiny.

Glossary

Ai Siqi (1910–1966)	艾思奇
Anpu	安浦
Anyang	安陽
Ba Jin (Li Yaotang, 1904–2005)	巴金
Ban Chao (32–102 CE)	班超
bao	保
baohu renquan	保護人權
Baoji	宝鸡
baojia	保甲
baomin dahui	保民大會
baoshouxing	保守性
baozhang	保長
baozhang renmin shenti ziyou banfa	保障人民身體自由辦法
Beihai	北海
Beijing-Hankou Railway (Ping-Han)	京漢鐵路
bu e'si yige ren	不餓死一個人
Bu Lu	布魯
bucheng wuwu	不誠無物
buxin pai	不信派
caipin	才品
Changjiang (Yangzi River)	長江
Chen Boda (1904–1989)	陳伯達
Chen Bulei (1890–1948)	陳佈雷
Chen Lifu (1900–2001)	陳立夫
Chen Long	陳龍

Chen Qitian (1893–1984)   陳啟天
Chen Xuetan (1882–1966)   陳學談
Chen Yinque (1890–1969)   陳寅恪
Chen Zhongjing (1916–2014   陳忠經
cheng   誠
Cheng Muyi   程慕頤
Chenliu   陳留
Chiang Kai-shek (Jiang Jieshi, 1887–1975)   蔣介石
Chikan   赤坎
Chu Fucheng (1873–1948)   褚輔成
Cixian   磁縣

Dagongbao   大公報
Daguangbao (south Guangdong edition)   大光報（粵南版）
Dahoufang   大后方
Dai Chao'en   戴朝恩
Dai Li (1897–1946)   戴笠
daishipin   代食品
dapo mixin, renli shengtian   打破迷信，人力勝天
Deng Benyin (1879–?)   鄧本殷
Di erci xianzheng yundong   第二次憲政運動
Di sanci fangong gaochao   第三次反共高潮
difang zizhi jiguan   地方自治機關
Dihua   迪化
Dong Biwu (1886–1975)   董必武
Dong Zhongshu (179–104 BCE)   董仲舒
Donghai   東海島
duban   督办
dulixing   獨立性
Dushanzi   独山子

Enping   恩平

faguan xunlian suo   法官訓練所
Fan Wenlan (1893–1969)   範文瀾

Fang Zhongying 方仲穎
fanxing 反省
fazhi 法治
Feng Lingyun (1875–1954) 馮淩雲
Feng Yuxiang (1882–1948) 馮玉祥
fenju bao'an xi 分局保安系
Funiu Mountains 伏牛山

gonggong shitang 公共食堂
gongliang 公糧
gongli zhuyi 功利主義
Gu Jiegang (1893–1980) 顾颉刚
Gu Weijun (Wellington Koo, 1887–1985) 顧維鈞
Guangzhouwan 廣州灣
Guofu 國父
Guojia shehuidang 國家社會黨
Guoli xi'nan lianhe daxue 國立西南聯合大學
Guomin canzhenghui 國民參政會
Guomin dahui 國民大會
Guomin zhengfu 國民政府
Guomindang/Kuomintang 國民黨
Guoxun 國訊
guyou 固有
guyou dexing 固有德性

Hami 哈密
Hanjian 漢奸
He Fang (1922–) 何方
He Xiang 何湘
He Yingqin (1890–1987) 何應欽
Heiyanyuan 黑眼元
Henan Minguo ribao 河南民國日報
hepingxing 和平性
Heshun 和順
Hexi 河西

hezuoshe	合作社
Hou Sheng	候聲
Hu Gongmian (1888–1979)	胡公冕
Hu Lancheng (1906–1981)	胡蘭成
Hu Zongnan (1896–1962)	胡宗南
Huabei	華北
Huabei Jidujiao lianhehui cujinhui	華北基督教聯合會促進會
Huabei Zhonghua Jidujiaotuan	華北中華基督教團
Huai River	淮河
Huanghe (Yellow River)	黃河
Huang Jiqing (1904–1995)	黄汲清
Huang Manli (1913–1998)	黄曼梨
Huang Yanpei (1878–1965)	黄炎培
Huang Yao (1917–1987)	黄堯
Huanglongshan	黄龍山
jia	甲
Jialing River	嘉陵江
Jialu River	賈魯河
Jiang Nanxiang (1913–1988)	蔣南翔
jianrenxing	堅韌性
Jiaotong yinhang	交通银行
jiaotuan	教團
jiazhang	甲長
Jidutu huitang	基督徒會堂
Jiefang ribao	解放日報
Ji-Lu-Yu	冀魯豫
jin (1.102 pounds)	斤
jingji minzhu	經濟民主
Jin-Ji-Lu-Yu Border Region	晉冀魯豫邊區
jinshi	進士
Ju Zheng (1876–1951)	居正
Kai Feng (1906–1955)	凱豐
Kaiping	開平

Kan Chongqing, nian Zhongyuan	看重慶，念中原
Kang Sheng (1896–1975)	康生
Kong Xiangxi (H.H. Kung, 1881–1967)	孔祥熙
Lao She (Shu Qingchun1899–1966)	老舍
Lei Haizong (1902–1962)	雷海宗
Lei Zhen (1897–1979)	雷震
Li Bo'ao	李伯敖
Li Choh-Ming (1912–1991)	李卓敏
Li Gongpu (1900–1946)	李公朴
Li Hanhun (1894–1987)	李漢魂
Li Peiji (1886–1969)	李培基
Li Weihan (1896–1984)	李維漢
Li Yimin (1904–1982)	李逸民
Li Zhenni	李珍妮
Lianda	聯大
Liang Hancao (1899–1975)	梁寒操
Liang Shuming (1893–1988)	梁漱溟
lianghao zaimin	良好災民
lianhe zhengfu	聯合政府
Lianjiang County	廉江縣
Liao Xiahuai (1903–1952)	廖俠懷
lieshen	劣紳
Lifayuan	立法院
Lin Biao (1907–1971)	林彪
Lin Boqu (1886–1960)	林伯渠
Lin Sen (1868–1943)	林森
Lin Yutang (1895–1976)	林語堂
Ling Shuhua (1900–1990)	凌叔華
Lingshi jikan	《靈食季刊》
Linshi yuefa	臨時約法
Linxian	林縣
Liu Baiyu (1916–2005)	劉白羽
Liu Shaoqi (1898–1969)	劉少奇
Liu Zhenyun (1958–)	劉震雲

Longhai Railway   隴海鐵路
Long Jiguang (1868–1925)   龍濟光
Lu Dun (1911–2000)   盧敦
Lun minzhu   論民主
Luo Longji (1896–1965)   羅隆基
Luoyang   洛陽
Lushan   魯山

Mao Zedong (1893–1976)   毛澤東
Mazhang   麻章
Mei Qi (1922–1966)   梅綺
meiyou Gongchandang, jiu meiyou Zhongguo   沒有共產黨，就沒有中國
meiyou Zhongguo Guomindang …
  meiyoule Zhongguo   沒有中國國民黨 … 沒有了中國
mi   米
minsheng zhuyi   民生主義
minxian   民憲
minzhi   民治
minzhong   民衆
Minzhu tongmeng   民主同盟
Minzhu xianzheng cujinhui   民主憲政促進會
minzu   民族
mu   畝

Nanyang   南陽
Naozhou   硇洲島
Neiwu zongshu   內務總署

Pan Guangdan (1899–1967)   潘光旦
Peng Dehuai (1898–1974)   彭德懷
Peng Zhen (1902–1997)   彭真
pingdengxing   平等性
pingtiao   平糶

Qianfeng bao   前鋒報
qiangliang   搶糧

Qingnianhui	青年會
qinxin	親信
Qi Sanyi	祁三益
Qixian	杞縣
quzhang	區長
ren	仁
Ren Bishi (1904–1950)	任弼時
renzhi	人治
Sanmin zhuyi	三民主義
Sanmin zhuyi zhi fazhi guo	三民主義之法治國
San-zi aiguo yundong	三自爱国运动
Shao Lizi (1882–1967)	邵力子
Shaping	沙坪
Shen Junru (1875–1963)	沈鈞儒
Shen Zhiyuan (1902–1965)	沈志遠
Sheng Shicai (1897–1970)	盛世才
sheng canyihui	省參議會
shengchan zijiu	生產自救
shenti ziyou	身體自由
Shexian	涉縣
shi canyihui	市參議會
shidou	市斗
Shilüe gaoben	事略稿本
shiqian jiancha	事前檢查
Shi Tianmin	石天民
Shi Zhe (1905–1998)	師哲
Shuidong	水東
si	私
sifa danghua	司法黨化
sifa jiangxi suo	司法講習所
Sifa nianjian	司法年鑑
Sifa renyuan xunlian dagang	司法人員訓練大綱
Sifa xingzheng gongbao	司法行政公報
Sifa xunlian banfa	司法訓練辦法

Siyi	四邑
Song Ailing (1889–1973)	宋靄齡
Song Meiling/Soong Mayling/	
Mme. Chiang Kai-shek (1893–2008)	宋美齡
Song Ziwen (T.V. Soong, 1891–1971)	宋子文
Star Theater Troupe	明星劇團
Suixian	睢縣
Suixi County	遂溪縣
Sun Ke (Sun Fo, 1895–1973)	孫科
Sun Yat-sen (Sun Zhongshan, 1866–1925)	孫中山

Tacheng	塔城
Taihang	太行
Taikang	太康
Taishan	臺山
Taiyue	太岳
Tan Lanqing (1908–1981)	譚蘭卿
Tang Enbo (1898–1954)	湯恩伯
Tang Zong (1905–1981)	唐縱
Tao Xisheng (1899–1988)	陶希聖
Tewu ke	特務科
tianming	天命
Tianshan	天山
Tianshui	天水
tianzai	天災
tiaohexing	調和性
Tiedan	鉄膽
Tongmenghui	同盟會
Tongxu	通許
tongyixing	統一性
tuanjiexing	團結性

Wang Chonghui (1881–1958)	王寵惠
Wang Jingwei (1883–1944)	汪精衛
Wang Keyi	汪克毅

Wang Ming (1904–1974)	王明
Wang Mingdao (1900–1991)	王明道
Wang Shijie (1891–1981)	王世杰
Wang Shiwei (1906–1947)	王實味
Wang Yangming (1472–1529)	王陽明
Wang Yunsheng (1901–1980)	王蕓生
Weishu zongsilingbu	衛戍總司令部
Wen Yiduo (1899–1946)	聞一多
Weng Wenhao (1893–1971)	翁文灝
Wu Aichen (1891–1965)	吳藹宸
Wu Chufan (1910–1993)	吳楚帆
Wu Guozhen (K.C. Wu, 1903–1984)	吳國楨
Wu Nanshan	吳南山
Wu Tiecheng (1888–1953)	吳鐵城
Wu Wenzao (1901–1985)	吳文藻
Wu Yuheng	吳昱恒
Wu Zexiang (1897–1973)	吳泽湘
Wu Zhichun (1894–1971)	吳之椿
Wuchuan	吳川
wuhe zhi zhong	烏合之眾
wuwu bucheng	無物不誠
wuzu yijia	五族一家
Xia Yan (1900–1995)	夏衍
xian	縣
Xianbing dui	憲兵隊
xian canyihui	縣參議會
Xiancao	憲草
xiangzhang	鄉長
xiangzhenmin daibiaohui	鄉鎮民代表會
xianren zhengzhi	賢人政治
xian yihui	縣議會
Xianzheng qichenghui	憲政期成會
Xianzheng shishi xiejinhui	憲政實施協進會
Xianzheng yuekan	憲政月刊

xiao	孝
Xiao Gongquan (1897–1981)	蕭公權
Xiao Jun (1907–1988)	蕭軍
xiaomi	小米
Xie Juezai (1884–1971)	謝覺哉
Xihua	西華
Xinan lianda	西南聯大
Xingzheng yuan	行政院
Xinhua ribao	新華日報
Xinhui	新會
Xining	西宁
Xinminbao	新民報
Xiong Shihui (1893–1974)	熊式輝
Xiong Xianghui (1919–2005)	熊向輝
xishouxing	吸收性
Xiying	西營
Xu Hongdao	徐弘道
Xue Juexian (1904–1956)	薛覺先
Yang Guifei (719–756)	楊貴妃
Yang Xiufeng (1897–1983)	楊秀峰
Yang Zengxin (1867–1928)	杨增新
yangmin	養民
Yantao xiancao yundong	研討憲草運動
Yi jiu si er	一九四二
Yili	伊犁
yong	勇
Yu Jiaju (1898–1976)	余家菊
yuan	元
Yuan Shikai (1859–1916)	袁世凱
Yulin	鬱林
yumin tong ganku	與民同甘苦
Yuzai shilu	豫災實錄
zaimin	災民

Zhu De (1886–1976)	朱德
Zhu Shaoliang (1891–1963)	朱绍良
zongzu	宗族
Zuoquan	左權
Zuo Shunsheng (1893–1969)	左舜生

Contributor Biographies

Xiao Chen graduated from Peking University in China and earned his master's degree in history at the University of California, San Diego. He is now a graduate student in the Department of History at University of Illinois Urbana Champaign. His research focuses on the social and legal history of Qing and Republican China.

Matthew T. Combs is a doctoral candidate in the Department of History at the University of California, Irvine, where he also serves as the Book Review Coordinator and Digital Editor of the *Journal of Asian Studies*. He is preparing a dissertation exploring how the intersection of imperialism, "free trade," and technology in nineteenth-century East Asia led to the invention of plastic, and advances in photographic film and gunpowder. He received his MA from San Diego State University in 2011.

Kathryn Edgerton-Tarpley is associate professor of history at San Diego State University. Her research focuses on changing responses to disaster in late imperial and modern China. Recent publications include *Tears from Iron: Cultural Responses to Famine in Nineteenth-Century China* and disaster-related articles in the *Journal of Asian Studies* and the *Journal of World History*.

Joseph W. Esherick is professor emeritus of the University of California, San Diego, and holds a PhD in history from the University of California, Berkeley. His research focuses on the intersection of social and political history of modern China, and major publications include *Reform and Revolution in China: The 1911 Revolution in Hunan and Hubei*, *The Origins* *of the Boxer Uprising,* and *Ancestral Leaves: A Family Journey through Chinese History.*

Grace C. Huang is associate professor of government and chair of the department at St. Lawrence University and holds a PhD in political science from the University of Chicago. Her research interests include political leadership, the political uses of shame in Chinese leadership, and rural to urban migration in China. Her publications can be found in *Modern China, Twentieth Century China,* and the *International Journal for Asian Studies.*

Jianfei Jia holds a PhD in history from the Chinese Academy of Social Sciences (CASS). He is now in the Central Eurasian Studies Department at Indiana University, Bloomington. His research field is Xinjiang history during the Qing dynasty and the Republic of China (focusing on legal history, immigration history, and environmental history), and the historiography of Qing-era Xinjiang.

Judd C. Kinzley is assistant professor of modern Chinese history at the University of Wisconsin–Madison. He is currently completing a book manuscript that focuses on the connections between natural resources and state power in China's west over the course of the twentieth century.

Daniel D. Knorr is a doctoral candidate in Chinese history at the University of Chicago. His research examines the relationship between elite institutions and identities and the imperial state in mid- to late Qing-era Jinan, Shandong. He received his MA from the University of California, Irvine, in 2013.

Hsiao-ting Lin is research fellow and curator of the East Asian Collection at the Hoover Institution at Stanford University. His academic interests include ethnopolitics and minority issues in greater China, political institutions and bureaucratic systems of the Chinese Nationalist Party, and U.S.-Taiwan relations during the Cold War. He has published extensively on modern Chinese politics, history, and ethnic minorities.

Nobchulee (Dawn) Maleenont received her MA in history from the University of California, San Diego. Her master's thesis focused on family order and intrafamilial crime in the Qing dynasty. She now resides and works in Thailand.

Amy O'Keefe is a doctoral candidate in the Department of History at the University of California, San Diego. She is working on a dissertation that uses the Christianize the Family movements in twentieth-century China to analyze the role of Christian voices in discussions of the family's needs and functions in Chinese society.

Thomas R. Worger received his JD and an MA in history from the University of California, Irvine. His research focuses on court formation and practice in twentieth-century China as viewed through changing attitudes toward legal professionalization and state policies governing judicial and procuratorial practice.

Yidi Wu is a doctoral candidate in the Department of History at the University of California, Irvine. Drawing upon archival documents and oral histories, her dissertation investigates Chinese college students from the Hundred Flowers to the Anti-Rightist Campaigns in 1956-57, and ultimately contributes to a better understanding of student activism beyond activist narratives and social movements in illiberal political settings. She received her B.A. from Oberlin College.

Chuning Xie is a graduate student at the State University of New York, Binghamton. She previously completed an MA in history at the University of California, Irvine, and another at the University of Victoria (British Columbia). She strives to understand people's complicated motivations and actions through microhistory in places of cultural diversity and in times of turmoil.

This page is intentionally left blank.

Index

Academia Sinica, 88
Ai Siqi, 179, 193
Anti-Comintern Pact, 15, 29
Army, Chinese. *See* Chinese Communist Party, Nationalist Army
Asia First Strategy, 46
Assam, 18
assassins, 209
atom bomb, 21
Australia, 20

B-29 bomber, 20, 21
Ba Jin, 304, 305, 310, 318–20
Baldwin, Hanson, 23
bandits, 156, 160, 228, 417–23
Beijing, 4; occupation government in, 383–86
black markets, 293–94. *See also* inflation
blockade: of China by Japan, 26, 320, 349, 400; of border regions by Nationalists, 16, 158, 204
bombing, 4, 5, 415; of Chongqing, 7, 283, 286–87, 304; of Guangzhouwan, 415, 425. *See also* B-29 bomber
Boxer Protocol, 125
Brooke, Alan, 446, 448
Bu Lu, 212
Buck, Pearl, 23, 57–58; on Song Meiling, 70
Burma, 147–78, 162, 401; 1943–1945 campaign 22, 38–39, 162; Japanese

conquest of 5–6, 18–19, 87, 138, 162; Operation Buccaneer, 434, 446, 450–51, 453–55. *See also* Cairo Conference

cadre screening: by CCP, 205, 206, 208, 213, 219, 222, 231, 240
Cairo Conference, xiii, xvii, 37–40, 72–73, 165, 426–58
cannibalism, 156, 337–38
censorship, 27, 177, 268–71, 335–37, 346, 374. *See also* press
C.C. Clique, 31
Central Politics School, 128–30
charity. *See* philanthropy
Chen Boda, 178–79, 184–85, 189, 192–95
Chen Bulei, 31, 172
Chen Jiadong, 420–22
Chen Lifu, 31
Chen Long, 215, 220
Chen Qitian, 248–49, 255
Chen Xuetan, 396, 403–7, 412, 420
Chennault, Claire Lee, 18–19, 40
Chiang Kai-shek: at the Cairo Conference, 37–40, 426–58; *China's Destiny*, xiii, xv, 3, 16, 127, 150, 152, 168–202, 232, 436; and Christianity, 8, 10; and Communists, 13–16, 21, 22, 30, 31, 39, 197, 224–26, 251, 448; on democracy and constitutionalism, 191, 249, 278; on eco-

CORNELL EAST ASIA SERIES

100 Yasushi Yamanouchi, J. Victor Koschmann & Ryūichi Narita, eds., *Total War and 'Modernization'*

101 Yi Ch'ŏng-jun, *The Prophet and Other Stories*, tr. Julie Pickering

102 S.A. Thornton, *Charisma and Community Formation in Medieval Japan: The Case of the Yugyō-ha (1300–1700)*

103 Sherman Cochran, ed., *Inventing Nanjing Road: Commercial Culture in Shanghai, 1900–1945*

104 Harold M. Tanner, *Strike Hard! Anti-Crime Campaigns and Chinese Criminal Justice, 1979–1985*

105 Brother Anthony of Taizé & Young-Moo Kim, trs., *Farmers' Dance: Poems by Shin Kyŏng-nim*

106 Susan Orpett Long, ed., *Lives in Motion: Composing Circles of Self and Community in Japan*

107 Peter J. Katzenstein, Natasha Hamilton-Hart, Kozo Kato, & Ming Yue, *Asian Regionalism*

108 Kenneth Alan Grossberg, *Japan's Renaissance: The Politics of the Muromachi Bakufu*

109 John W. Hall & Toyoda Takeshi, eds., *Japan in the Muromachi Age*

110 Kim Su-Young, Shin Kyong-Nim, & Lee Si-Young, *Variations: Three Korean Poets*, trs. Brother Anthony of Taizé & Young-Moo Kim

111 Samuel Leiter, *Frozen Moments: Writings on Kabuki, 1966–2001*

112 Pilwun Shih Wang & Sarah Wang, *Early One Spring: A Learning Guide to Accompany the Film Video* February

113 Thomas Conlan, *In Little Need of Divine Intervention: Scrolls of the Mongol Invasions of Japan*

114 Jane Kate Leonard & Robert Antony, eds., *Dragons, Tigers, and Dogs: Qing Crisis Management and the Boundaries of State Power in Late Imperial China*

115 Shu-ning Sciban & Fred Edwards, eds., *Dragonflies: Fiction by Chinese Women in the Twentieth Century*

116 David G. Goodman, ed., *The Return of the Gods: Japanese Drama and Culture in the 1960s*

117 Yang Hi Choe-Wall, *Vision of a Phoenix: The Poems of Hŏ Nansŏrhŏn*

118 Mae J. Smethurst & Christina Laffin, eds., *The Noh* Ominameshi: *A Flower Viewed from Many Directions*

119 Joseph A. Murphy, *Metaphorical Circuit: Negotiations Between Literature and Science in Twentieth-Century Japan*

120 Richard F. Calichman, *Takeuchi Yoshimi: Displacing the West*

121 Fan Pen Li Chen, *Visions for the Masses: Chinese Shadow Plays from Shaanxi and Shanxi*

122 S. Yumiko Hulvey, *Sacred Rites in Moonlight: Ben no Naishi Nikki*

123 Tetsuo Najita & J. Victor Koschmann, *Conflict in Modern Japanese History: The Neglected Tradition*

124 Naoki Sakai, Brett de Bary, & Iyotani Toshio, eds., *Deconstructing Nationality*

125 Judith N. Rabinovitch & Timothy R. Bradstock, *Dance of the Butterflies: Chinese Poetry from the Japanese Court Tradition*

126 Yang Gui-ja, *Contradictions*, trs. Stephen Epstein & Kim Mi-Young

127 Ann Sung-hi Lee, *Yi Kwang-su and Modern Korean Literature: Mujŏng*

128 Pang Kie-chung & Michael D. Shin, eds., *Landlords, Peasants, & Intellectuals in Modern Korea*

129 Joan R. Piggott, ed., *Capital and Countryside in Japan, 300–1180: Japanese Historians Interpreted in English*

CORNELL
East Asia Series
eap.einaudi.cornell.edu/publications

This page is intentionally left blank.

CPSIA information can be obtained
at www.ICGtesting.com
Printed in the USA
LVHW090846121119
637017LV00007BA/23/P

9 781939 161802